Lecture Notes in Computer Science 3831

Commenced Publication in 1973
Founding and Former Series Editors:
Gerhard Goos, Juris Hartmanis, and Jan van Leeuwen

T0224966

Jiří Wiedermann   Gerard Tel
Jaroslav Pokorný   Mária Bieliková
Július Štuller (Eds.)

SOFSEM 2006: Theory and Practice of Computer Science

32nd Conference on Current Trends
in Theory and Practice of Computer Science
Měřín, Czech Republic, January 21-27, 2006
Proceedings

 Springer

Volume Editors

Jiří Wiedermann
Július Štuller
Academy of Sciences of the Czech Republic
Institute of Computer Science
Pod Vodárenskou věží 2, 182 07 Prague 8, Czech Republic
E-mail: {jiri.wiedermann,stuller}@cs.cas.cz

Gerard Tel
Universiteit Utrecht
Department of Information and Computing Sciences
Centrumgebouw Noord, office A308, Padualaan 14, De Uithof
3584CH Utrecht, The Netherlands
E-mail: gerard@cs.uu.nl

Jaroslav Pokorný
Charles University, Faculty of Mathematics and Physics
Malostranské nám. 25, 118 00 Prague 1, Czech Republic
E-mail: pokorny@ksi.ms.mff.cuni.cz

Mária Bieliková
Slovak University of Technology in Bratislava
Institute of Informatics and Software Engineering
Faculty of Informatics and Information Technologies
Ilkovičova 3, 842 16 Bratislava 4, Slovak Republic
E-mail: bielik@elf.stuba.sk

Library of Congress Control Number: Applied for

CR Subject Classification (1998): F.2, F.1, D.2, H.3, H.2.8, H.4, F.3-4

LNCS Sublibrary: SL 1 – Theoretical Computer Science and General Issues

ISSN	0302-9743
ISBN-10	3-540-31198-X Springer Berlin Heidelberg New York
ISBN-13	978-3-540-31198-0 Springer Berlin Heidelberg New York

Springer is a part of Springer Science+Business Media

springer.com

© Springer-Verlag Berlin Heidelberg 2006
Printed in Germany

Typesetting: Camera-ready by author, data conversion by Scientific Publishing Services, Chennai, India
Printed on acid-free paper   SPIN: 11611257   06/3142   5 4 3 2 1 0

Preface

This volume contains the invited and the contributed papers selected for presentation at the 32nd Annual Conference on Current Trends in Theory and Practice of Computer Science **SOFSEM 2006**, held January 21–27, 2006, in the Hotel VZ MĚŘÍN, located about 60 km south of Prague on the right shore of Slapská přehrada ("Slapy Dam") in the Czech Republic.

Transformed over the years from a local event to a fully international conference, contemporary SOFSEM keeps the best of its original winter school aspects – high number of invited talks (10) and the multidisciplinary trends in computer science – illustrated this year by the selection of the following four tracks:

- *Computer Science Foundations* (Track Chair: Gerard Tel)
- *Wireless, Mobile, Ad Hoc and Sensor Networks* (Track Chair: Jiří Wiedermann)
- *Database Technologies* (Track Chair: Jaroslav Pokorný)
- *Semantic Web Technologies* (Track Chair: Július Štuller)

An integral part of SOFSEM 2006 was the Student Research Forum (Chair: Mária Bieliková) organized with the aim to discuss students' projects in the theory and practice of computer science and to publish them in a separate local proceedings.

The aim of SOFSEM 2006 was, as always, to promote co-operation among professionals from academia and industry working in various areas of computer science.

The SOFSEM 2006 Program Committee, consisting of 50 members coming from 19 countries, obtained a record number of 157 submissions. After a careful reviewing process (at least three reviewers per paper), followed by a detailed discussion at the PC meeting held on October 3, 2005, in the Institute of Computer Science of the Academy of Sciences of the Czech Republic in Prague, 55 papers were selected for presentation at SOFSEM 2006:

- 45 Contributed Talks papers selected by the SOFSEM 2006 PC for publication in the Springer LNCS series (acceptance rate 28.7 %), including the *Best Paper of the SOFSEM 2006 Student Research Forum*
- 10 Posters to be presented at the SOFSEM 2006 Poster Session and to appear in a separate volume of SOFSEM 2006 proceedings published by MatFyzPres, Charles University, Prague (acceptance rate 6.4 %)

The Springer proceedings comprise the ten Invited Talks papers.

As editors of these proceedings, we are much indebted to all the contributors to the scientific program of the conference, especially to the authors of the papers. Special thanks go to those authors who prepared their manuscripts according to the instructions and made life easier for us. We would also like to thank those who responded promptly to our requests for minor modifications and corrections in their manuscripts.

SOFSEM 2006 is the result of a considerable effort by a number of people. It is a great pleasure to express our thanks to the:

- SOFSEM Steering Committee for its general guidance,
- SOFSEM 2006 Program Committee and additional referees who made an extraordinary effort in reviewing a high number of assigned papers (in average about 10 papers per PC member),
- Springer LNCS series editor, Alfred Hofmann, for his continuing trust in SOFSEM,
- Springer for publishing the proceedings,
- SOFSEM 2006 Organizing Committee for a smooth preparation of the conference.

Our special thanks go to:

- Hana Bílková from the Institute of Computer Science (ICS), Prague, who did an excellent job in the completion of the proceedings,
- Martin Řimnáč from ICS for realizing SOFSEM 2006 web pages,
- Roman Špánek from ICS for running the SOFSEM 2006 submission and review system, which helped to prepare a smooth PC session in Prague.

Finally we highly appreciate the financial support of our sponsors (ERCIM and others) which assisted with the invited speakers and helped the organizers to offer lower student fees.

November 2005

Jiří Wiedermann
Gerard Tel
Jaroslav Pokorný
Mária Bieliková
Július Štuller

Organization

32nd SOFSEM 2006 was organized by:

Institute of Computer Science, Academy of Sciences of the Czech Republic, Prague
Charles University, Faculty of Mathematics and Physics, Prague
Czech Society for Computer Science
Slovak Society for Computer Science
Action M Agency, Prague

⦂▬ Organizing Committee

Július Štuller, *Chair* Institute of Computer Science, Prague, Czech Republic
Hana Bílková   Institute of Computer Science, Prague, Czech Republic
Martin Řimnáč   Institute of Computer Science, Prague, Czech Republic
Roman Špánek   Institute of Computer Science, Prague, Czech Republic
Milena Zeithamlová Action M Agency, Prague, Czech Republic

⦂▬ Sponsoring Institution

ERCIM

⦂▬ Supporting Projects

32nd SOFSEM 2006 was partly supported by the following projects:

Project 1ET100300419 of the Program Information Society (of the Thematic Program II of the National Research Program of the Czech Republic) *"Intelligent Models, Algorithms, Methods and Tools for the Semantic Web Realisation."* Institutional Research Plan AV0Z10300504 *"Computer Science for the Information Society: Models, Algorithms, Appplications."*

⦂▬ Steering Committee

Július Štuller, *Chair*   Institute of Computer Science, Prague, Czech Republic
Mária Bieliková   Slovak University of Technology in Bratislava, Slovakia
Bernadette Charron-Bost   Ecole Polytechnique, France
Keith G. Jeffery   CLRC RAL, Chilton, Didcot, Oxon, UK
Antonín Kučera   Masaryk University, Brno, Czech Republic
Branislav Rovan   Comenius University, Bratislava, Slovakia
Petr Tůma   Charles University in Prague, Czech Republic

:= Program Committee

Jiří Wiedermann, *Chair*	Institute of Computer Science, Prague, Czech Republic
Jaroslav Pokorný, *Co-chair*	Charles University, Prague, Czech Republic
Július Štuller, *Co-chair*	Institute of Computer Science, Prague, Czech Republic
Gerard Tel, *Co-chair*	University of Amsterdam, The Netherlands
Bernd Amann	CEDRIC, France
Grigoris Antoniou	University of Crete, Greece
Zohra Bellahsene	LIRMM, France
Mária Bieliková	Slovak University of Technology in Bratislava, Slovakia
Rob Bisseling	University of Utrecht, The Netherlands
François Bry	University of Munich, Germany
Barbara Catania	Universita'di Genova, Italy
Witold Charatonik	Wroclaw University, Poland
Edgar Chávez	Universidad Michoacana, Mexico
Stefan Dobrev	University of Ottawa, Canada
Jean-Dominique Decotignie	EPFL Lausanne, Switzerland
Patrik Floréen	University of Helsinki, Finland
Nissim Francez	The Technion Haifa, Israel
Rusins Freivalds	University of Latvia, Latvia
Johann Ch. Freytag	Humboldt-Universität zu Berlin, Germany
Henning Fernau	University of Hertfordshire, UK
Juraj Hromkovič	ETH Zurich, Switzerland
Jan Janeček	Czech Technical University, Czech Republic
Rastislav Královič	Comenius University, Slovakia
Ivan Kramosil	Institute of Computer Science, Prague, Czech Republic
Evangelos Kranakis	Carleton University, Canada
Jan Kratochvíl	Charles University, Czech Republic
Lenka Motyčková	Lulea University of Technology, Switzerland
Roman Neruda	Institute of Computer Science, Prague, Czech Republic
Una-May O'Reilly	Computer Science & Artificial Inteligence Lab, USA
Tadeusz Pankowski	University in Poznan, Poland
Dana Pardubská	University of Komensky, Slovakia
Lukáš Petrů	Charles University, Czech Republic
Dimitris Plexousakis	University of Crete, Greece
Klaus Reinhardt	Universität Tubingen, Germany
Karel Richta	Czech Technical University, Czech Republic
Mark Roantree	Dublin City University, Ireland
Peter Rossmanith	Aachen University, Germany
Václav Snášel	TU Ostrava, Czech Republic
Christian Scheideler	Johns Hopkins University, USA
Hans-Joerg Schek	ETH Zurich, Switzerland
Paul Spirakis	Research Academic Computer Technology Institute, Greece

Michael Schröder	TU Dresden, Germany
Vojtěch Svátek	University of Economics, Czech Republic
Václav Šebesta	Institute of Computer Science, Prague, Czech Republic
Jiří Šíma	Institute of Computer Science, Prague, Czech Republic
Rainer Unland	University of Duisburg-Essen, Germany
Athena Vakali	Aristotle University of Thessaloniki, Greece
Peter Vojtáš	Košice University, Slovakia
Marc van Kreveld	University of Utrecht, The Netherlands
Aaron Zollinger	ETH Zurich, Switzerland

⦂☰ Additional Referees

Fuat Akal
Vasiliki Alevizou
Sören Balko
Fredrik Bengtsson
Robbert-Jan Beun
Hans L. Bodlaender
Hans-Joachim Boeckenhauer
Martin Bosman
Stefan Brass
Sergio Bravo
Tomáš Brázdil
Gert Brettlecker
Felix Calderon
David Carr
Ioannis Chatzigiannakis
Jingsen Chen
Jana Chlebíková
Petr Cintula
Ivana Černá
Aspassia Daskalopoulou
Giuseppe Di Battista
Guido Diepen
Virginia Dignum
Pavol Ďuriš
Rogier van Eijk
Jiří Fiala
Michal Foríšek
Leo Galamboš
Holger Gast
Peter Gurský
Jozef Gruska

Dieter Kratsch
Peter M. Lennartz
Andreas Malcher
Daniel Moelle
Yvonne Moh
František Mráz
Daniel Mölle
Marc Müller
Gonzalo Navarro
Rolf Niedermeier
Sotiris Nikoletseas
Pascal Ochem
M. Ojeda-Aciego
Piet van Oostrum
Richard Ostertág
Marion Oswald
George Pallis
Eelko Penninkx
Pino Persiano
Hans Philippi
Tomáš Plachetka
Paola Podestà
Pierre Pompidor
Michael Przybilski
Silja Renooij
Ralf Reussner
Stefan Richter
Antonín Říha
Petr Savický
Satu Elisa Schaeffer
Eike Schallehn

Jurriaan Hage
Herman Haverkort
Petr Hnětynka
Tomáš Horváth
Ela Hunt
Tomas Johansson
Gabriel Juhas
Arno Kamphuis
Ivan Kapustík
Martin Kavalec
Jan Kára
Athanassios Kinalis
Joachim Kneis
Jukka Kohonen
Vassiliki Koutsonikola
Stanislav Krajči
Joachim Kupke
Richard Královič
Bettina Krammer

Michael Ignaz Schumacher
Gabriel Semanišin
Jiří Sgall
Ivo Shterev
Klaas Silkkel
Tomáš Skopal
Michael Springmann
Theodosios Theodosiou
Dirk Thierens
Kamil Toman
Rainer Typke
Walter Unger
Miroslav Vacura
Michal Valenta
Manos Varvarigos
Marinus Veldhorst
Imrich Vrt'o
Stanislav Žák

Table of Contents

The Best Student Paper

How Can Nature Help Us Compute?

S. Barry Cooper

School of Mathematics, University of Leeds,
Leeds LS2 9JT, UK
pmt6sbc@leeds.ac.uk
http://www.maths.leeds.ac.uk/~pmt6sbc

Abstract. Ever since Alan Turing gave us a machine model of algorithmic computation, there have been questions about how widely it is
applicable (some asked by Turing himself). Although the computer on
our desk can be viewed in isolation as a Universal Turing Machine, there
are many examples in nature of what looks like computation, but for
which there is no well-understood model. In many areas, we have to
come to terms with emergence not being clearly algorithmic. The positive side of this is the growth of new computational paradigms based on
metaphors for natural phenomena, and the devising of very informative
computer simulations got from copying nature. This talk is concerned
with general questions such as:

- Can natural computation, in its various forms, provide us with
  genuinely new ways of computing?
- To what extent can natural processes be captured computationally?
- Is there a universal model underlying these new paradigms?

1   Introduction

Freeman Dyson, in his introduction to George Odifreddi's [27] *The Mathematical
Century : The 30 Greatest Problems of the Last 100 Years*, divides scientists into
Cartesians and Baconians:

> "According to Bacon, scientists should travel over the earth collecting
> facts, until the accumulated facts reveal how Nature works. The scientists
> will then induce from the facts the laws that Nature obeys. According to
> Descartes, scientists should stay at home and deduce the laws of Nature
> by pure thought. ... Faraday and Darwin and Rutherford were Baconians:
> Pascal and Laplace and Poincaré were Cartesians. Science was greatly
> enriched by the cross-fertilization of the two contrasting ... cultures."

When it comes to computability, an important role of Cartesians has been to
theoretically map out the boundaries of what is practically computable, while
Baconians may point to new computational paradigms in the real world, so challenging theoretical barriers. Here too there is a synergistic relationship between
these two approaches, and many researchers (Alan Turing is an obvious example
of a Baconian delimiter cum Cartesian practioner) move between them, with
varying degrees of ease and success.

J. Wiedermann et al. (Eds.): SOFSEM 2006, LNCS 3831, pp. 1–13, 2006.

In this short article we make some observations on the extent to which this is important for current attempts to take computing to radically new levels, and to try to give a modest but much needed Cartesian shove to the search for new ways of computing. And far from being put off by the difficulties hypercomputationalists (like Hava Siegelman, Jack Copeland, and Tien Kieu) have run into — with Martin Davis [13], like Tom Sawyer's Aunt Polly, admonishing their foolishness and metaphorically packing them off to bed with no supper — we will argue for a positive role for the black box model of computation, despite its being wielded by Davis with such destructive effect.

Of course, whenever one attempts to characterise some process, one is imposing some kind of inductive structure on nature, often of a particularly simple kind. The argument here is that new computational paradigms are in evidence when nature goes beyond that induction. That homogeneity of information is unknown in nature with its variable divide between matter (information) and energy (algorithmic content). And that on this, and the breakdown of inductive structure, rests a powerful mechanism for elevating information content — one which may well be modelled in new kinds of computers.

2   Natural Phenomena as Discipline Problem — or How We Found Out That Nature Computes Differently to Us

The relationship between nature and computation has always involved a two-way process comprised of observation, prediction and theory. For the scientist, caught by the dream of Laplace's [23] predictive 'demon', the special contribution of nature to the way we think has not been an explicit one. Nature more discipline problem than role model. Implicit in the search for a theory of everything is the assumption that it is a short step from understanding to prediction:

> "Given for one instant an intelligence which could comprehend all the forces by which nature is animated and the respective situations of the beings who compose it — an intelligence sufficiently vast to submit these data to analysis — it would embrace in the same formula the movements of the greatest bodies and those of the lightest atom; for it, nothing would be uncertain and the future, as the past, would be present to its eyes."

But when Albert Einstein [14] wrote in 1950 (p.54 of *Out of My Later Years*):

> "When we say that we understand a group of natural phenomena, we mean that we have found a constructive theory which embraces them."

he opens the door to a world in which a mainstream scientific theory may struggle for predictive consequences, and in which nature may determine observable phenomena, based on well-understood local mechanisms, which are not globally predictable. At the same time we have van Leeuwen and Wiedermann's [39] observation that "the classical Turing paradigm may no longer be fully appropriate to capture all features of present-day computing."

At the mathematical level, the 1930s had already seen the discovery of a whole range of observable, but not predictable, phenomena. As we all know, Turing [36] showed we cannot predict in general whether a given computation of a computer will ever terminate. And (along with Church [6]) that recognising the non-validity of an argument may completely elude us, even though Gödel had given us a computable procedure for listing all valid mathematical arguments. But, as described in [9], the more natural the examples of incomputable sets in mathematics became, the more inured became the working scientist to their irrelevance to the real world. It is not so much that the thickening mathematical smoke (too much for even Martin Davis to explain away) has obscured the flames of real world incomputability — more that the anomalies, decoherence, and lack of persuasiveness at the margins of a number of the most basic of standard scientific models are very hard to characterise in a precise enough way. It is the nature of the connection which is incomplete. And this is often reflected in a parallel dichotomy between Baconians (including many computer scientists) and Cartesians (most mathematicians and logicians). Paradoxically, some of the most determined guardians of this situation are mathematicians, particularly those whose careers have been built on the study of incomputability. But a wide spectrum of scientists know something is wrong, if only they could explain what.

There are some obvious examples of Baconian confrontation with incomputability (or at least something which looks very like it), and Cartesian interpretations of them. For instance, as we commented in [8]:

> "To find a single body of *empirical* evidence which is clearly inconsistent with a narrowly mechanistic Laplacian determinism, one must first look to the quantum level."

While noting that quantum computation, as currently conceived, "appears to hold few surprises for the classical recursion theorist", we went on to mention the problem of explaining why the so-called 'collapse of the wave function', with its associated probabilities, takes the particular form it does. This predictive incompleteness of quantum theory gives rise to different 'interpretations' which leave us a long way from characterising the algorithmic content of the events it seeks to describe. This is how Andrew Hodges sums up the situation (in his article *What would Alan Turing have done after 1954?*, from Teuscher [35]):

> "Von Neumann's axioms distinguished the **U** (unitary evolution) and **R** (reduction) rules of quantum mechanics. Now, quantum computing so far (in the work of Feynman, Deutsch, Shor, etc) is based on the **U** process and so computable. It has not made serious use of the **R** process: the unpredictable element that comes in with reduction, measurement, or collapse of the wave function."

Above the quantum level, Etesi and Nemeti [15] describe how relativistic considerations (involving the actuality of such things as large rotating black holes in galactic nuclei) may lead to effectively computable functions which are not Turing computable. They have since set out to explain more thoroughly how and why such general relativistic computers work.

At all levels between these physical extremes we find chaotic phenomena and turbulence — difficult to handle computationally, but are superficially less threatening to standard *models* of computation. One is reassured by the extent to which one understands the underlying local behaviour, and by the overall patterns emerging to constrain what appears to be merely *practical* unpredictability. If one was just a little cleverer at solving differential equations, one assumes, or had a large enough computer, one could get much closer to predicting the details of chaotic contexts.

Kreisel [21] was one of the first to separate *cooperative phenomena* (not known to have Turing computable behaviour), from classical systems and and proposed [22–p. 143, Note 2] a collision problem related to the 3-body problem as a possible source of incomputability, suggesting that this might result in "an analog computation of a non-recursive function (by repeating collision experiments sufficiently often)". This was before the huge growth in the attention given to chaos theory, with its multitude of different examples of the generation of informational complexity via very simple rules, accompanied by the emergence of new regularities (see for example the two classic papers of Robert Shaw [33], [32]). We now have a much better understanding of the relationship between emergence and chaos, but this still does not provide the basis for a practically computable relationship. As described in Cooper and Odifreddi [11]:

> "As one observes a rushing stream, one is aware that the dynamics of the individual units of flow are well understood. But the relationship between this and the continually evolving forms manifest in the stream's surface is not just too *complex* to analyse — it seems to depend on globally emerging relationships not derivable from the local analysis. The form of the changing surface of the stream appears to constrain the movements of the molecules of water, while at the same time being traceable back to those same movements."

Relevant here is the widely recognised link between structures in nature, and mathematical objects, such as the Mandelbrot and Julia sets, which provide a metaphor for the way real-world complexity is generated by the iteration of simple algorithmic rules. Recently, high-profile names (such as Roger Penrose, Steve Smale) have been associated with investigations of the computability of such objects. Penrose (p. 124) points to the apparent unpredictability of structure in computer generated approximations to the Mandelbrot set as indications of an underlying incomputability:

> "Now we witnessed ... a certain extraordinarily complicated looking set, namely the Mandelbrot set. Although the rules which provide its definition are surprisingly simple, the set itself exhibits an endless variety of highly elaborate structures."

So the extraordinary richness of structure we observe in nature is matched by the as yet unsolved problems of showing that aspects of structures such as the Mandelbrot and certain Julia sets are computable (for recent progress see [20], [31], [1] and [30]).

Of course, just as a turbulent stream is constrained within emergent flow patterns, different scientific disciplines are often associated with successive levels of emergent physical reality, hierarchically resting one on the other. Again, the relationship can be described, but but there is no correspondingly reductive framework to capture it computationally. Just as one cannot develop the theory of fluid dynamics on the basis of quantum mechanics, the life sciences extend over entirely new levels, each with their own distinctive parameters. As we shall see below, the different levels give rise to their own algorithmic content, from which computational paradigms can be extracted. But the higher one goes up the hierarchy, the more controversy there is about exactly how it has developed, and the less clear is the computational content of the links between local mechanisms and emergent global relations. This is Gregory Chaitin's [5] try at extracting incomputability from the complexities of biological evolution (while taking Ω to be the halting probability for a suitably chosen universal computer U):

> "We have seen that Ω is about as random, patternless, unpredictable and incomprehensible as possible; the pattern of its bit sequence defies understanding. However with computations in the limit, which is equivalent to having an oracle for the halting problem, Ω seems quite understandable: it becomes a computable sequence. Biological evolution is the nearest thing to an infinite computation in the limit that we will ever see: it is a computation with molecular components that has proceeded for 10^9 years in parallel over the entire surface of the earth. That amount of computing could easily produce a good approximation to Ω, except that that is not the goal of biological evolution. The goal of evolution is survival, for example, keeping viruses such as those that cause AIDS from subverting one's molecular mechanisms for their own purposes.
>
> This suggests to me a very crude evolutionary model based on the game of matching pennies, in which players use computable strategies for predicting their opponent's next play from the previous ones. I don't think it would be too difficult to formulate this more precisely and to show that prediction strategies will tend to increase in program-size complexity with time.
>
> *Perhaps biological structures are simple and easy to understand only if one has an oracle for the halting problem.*" (italics added)

But the part of nature we are least able to make behave properly, and the part we are most familiar with (but understand least), is the human brain. Baconian experience of it comes first through our everyday experience of solving problems, while feeling nothing like a Turing machine. Such subjective impressions may not be scientific, but they can force themselves on us in a dramatic fashion. And can be the intuitive basis for the most informative of scientific work.

Jacques Hadamard [19] derived seminal observations on the role of intuition in mathematical thinking from this account of how Poincaré struggled unsuccessfully, and then successfully, to solve a problem:

> "At first Poincaré attacked [a problem] vainly for a fortnight, attempting to prove there could not be any such function ... [quoting Poincaré:]

Having reached Coutances, we entered an omnibus to go some place or other. At the moment when I put my foot on the step, the idea came to me, without anything in my former thoughts seeming to have paved the way for it ...I did not verify the idea ...I went on with a conversation already commenced, but I felt a perfect certainty. On my return to Caen, for conscience sake, I verified the result at my leisure."

A few years earlier, Turing envisaged his technically complex 1939 paper [37] as an attempt to pin down the computable content of such creativity. He claimed to clarify there the relationship between 'ingenuity' (subsumed within his ordinal logics) and 'intuition' (needed to identify good ordinal notations for levels of the resulting hierarchy). Turing clearly regarded ingenuity as being what a clever Turing program is capable of, and intuition as something else. There was a clear implication that intuition is a feature of human mental processes, and to that extent Turing is certainly saying that his hierarchies have something to say about how the mathematician's mind transcends his own model of machine computability – even if the results can be subsequently translated into proofs implementable by a Turing machine. This is what Turing [37–pp. 134–5], actually says about the underlying meaning of his paper:

"Mathematical reasoning may be regarded ...as the exercise of a combination of ...*intuition* and *ingenuity*. ...In pre-Gödel times it was thought by some that all the intuitive judgements of mathematics could be replaced by a finite number of ...rules. The necessity for intuition would then be entirely eliminated. In our discussions, however, we have gone to the opposite extreme and eliminated not intuition but ingenuity, and this *in spite of the fact that our aim has been in much the same direction.*"

My emphasis is to highlight the extent to which Turing was striving to bring mental processes within something approaching the standard model of computability, and failing.

An important role of such observation and analysis of mental higher functionality is to bring out, by contrast, differences with more obviously mechanical processes. The main problem with this approach is that because it does not really get us to grips with what underlies this higher functionality — that is, the particularities of the process of emergence — it is hard to fit the real world persuasively within any model derived from it. The temptation is to over-speculate and fudge the details, which is what some logicians think Roger Penrose [28] has succumbed to.

At the other end of the spectrum, bottom-up approaches involving trying to build intelligent machines, or developing models based on what we actually do understand about the physical workings of the brain, struggle to reproduce any recognisable or useful higher functionality. As Rodney Brooks [4] puts it "neither AI nor Alife has produced artifacts that could be confused with a living organism for more than an instant."

But this does not mean that paradigm-stretching features are not strongly in evidence. For instance Smolensky [34–p. 3], in his influential *Behavioral and Brain Sciences* paper, goes so far as to say:

"There is a reasonable chance that connectionist models will lead to the development of new somewhat-general-purpose self-programming, massively parallel analog computers, and a new theory of analog parallel computation: they may possibly even challenge the strong construal of Church's Thesis as the claim that the class of well-defined computations is exhausted by those of Turing machines."

We may be a long way from artificially performing the sort of mental marvels we observe, but there is plenty of evidence that the new ingredients on which to base a workable new computational discipline are already present.

3 Swimming with the Tide

As Boris Kogan, a pioneer developer of the Soviet Union's first analog and hybrid computers, comments (in an interview with Daniel Abramovitch, on pages 52–62 of the June 2005 issue of the IEEE Control Systems Magazine):

"Some of the great physical systems to be studied as objects of control are the dynamic processes in the living organisms, especially under pathological conditions."

In the face of the sheer complexity of natural computational processes, one can take the Baconian outlook one step further, and allow Nature to take over the driving seat. This kind of abrogation of executive control can be quite fruitful. In April, 2001, Daniel Hillis, Chief Technology Officer of Applied Minds, Inc. (and ex-Vice President, Research and Development at Walt Disney Imagineering), was quoted as saying this about his experiences trying to make intelligent machines:

"I used to think we'd do it by engineering. Now I believe we'll evolve them. We're likely to make thinking machines before we understand how the mind works, which is kind of backwards."

It is certainly true that the closest anyone has got so far to actual computers with recognisably hypercomputational ingredients is by surfing physical reality in some way. This is consistent with our Baconian suspicion that the world cannot be satisfactorily located within the standard computational model. Of course, it is not necessary for one to have any interest in hypercomputation for one to have an interest in new computational paradigms based on nature. As in the case of quantum computation, there may be very important operational benefits, even though there is an underlying classical model. But the above suspicion does get stronger the more difficult it is to divorce ones computational approach from its real-world origins.

The way forward adopted very widely now (as remarked in [10]), is to utilise the physical world's rich potential for computation, without worrying too much about understanding the underlying rules of the game. The likely success of this approach may be limited — it takes ingenuity to get a natural process to compute more than itself — but may bring practically useful results and be the best we can do in the short to medium term. Here is the analogy suggested in [10]:

"The domestication of horses around five or six thousand years ago brought a revolution in transportation, only achieved through a creative interaction between humans and the natural world. At that time, trying to understand the principles underlying the equine organism in order to synthesise an artificial horse was unthinkable. But a few thousand years later there was enough understanding of scientific basics to underpin the invention of the 'iron horse', leading, amongst other things, to the opening up of many previously isolated parts of the world to people with no riding skills whatsoever."

While Cartesian theorising may deliver computation with consciousness, wonderful things can still be achieved without consciousness. We would probably still have had present day computers even if Turing had not invented the universal Turing machine when he did. In our introduction to the CiE 2005 LNCS Proceedings volume, we referred to how Bert Hölldobler and Edward O. Wilson's book on *The Ants* runs to over eight-hundred pages, and mentioned how ants and similar biological examples have inspired new problem-solving strategies based on 'swarm intelligence'. But how the limits to what a real-life ant colony can achieve are very apparent, more so than those of recognisably conscious beings. For instance, as the constructors move in and tarmac over our richly structured ant colony, the ants have no hope of expanding their expertise to deal with such eventualities. In contrast, for us algorithmic content gives rise to new emergent forms, which themselves become victim to our algorithmic appetites, and even the inevitable limits on this inductive process we hope to decode. There is an important role for conscious and interventionist observation of our more ant-like everyday computational activities. It may well be that particular computational models expressing metaphors for natural processes, such as quantum and molecular computing, membrane computing, neural networks, evolutionary computation, relativistic computing, or evolving real-world models like grids and the internet, are currently the most exciting and practical examples of new computational paradigms. But we have to keep in mind the Holy Grail of synthesising and controlling in a conscious way that higher functionality which we observe in Nature but not in computers based on the standard Turing model. Conversely, we will never achieve this without engaging with the real world. To quote Rodney Brooks [2–p. 139] again:

"I, and others, believe that human level intelligence is too complex and little understood to be correctly decomposed into the right subpieces at the moment and that even if we knew the subpieces we still wouldn't know the right interfaces between them. Furthermore, we will never understand how to decompose human level intelligence until we've had a lot of practice with simpler level intelligences."

In regard to connectionist models of computation based on the workings of the human brain — these have come a long way since Turing's [38] discussion of 'unorganised machines', and McCulloch and Pitts' early paper [24] on neural nets. But (quoting from [10]) "despite the growth of computational neuroscience as an active research area, putting together ingredients from both artificial neural networks and neurophysiology, something does seem to be missing". For Steven Pinker "...neural networks alone cannot do the job". And focussing again on that elusive higher functionality, he describes [29–p. 124] "a kind of mental fecundity called recursion":

> "We humans can take an entire proposition and give it a role in some larger proposition. Then we can take the larger proposition and embed it in a still-larger one. Not only did the baby eat the slug, but the father saw the baby eat the slug, and I wonder whether the father saw the baby eat the slug, the father knows that I wonder whether he saw the baby eat the slug, and I can guess that the father knows that I wonder whether he saw the baby eat the slug, and so on."

So while there does seem to be a great deal to be got from an ad hoc computational relationship with the real world, we should not be daunted by the sheer wonder natural structures inspire in us. It may be that the human brain, as an emergent phenomenon, has an intimate relationship with processes which are not easily simulable over significantly shorter time-scales than those to which natural evolution is subject. Maybe we will never build an artificial brain, anymore than we can make an artificial horse. But this does not mean we may not one day have a good enough understanding of basic hypercomputational principles to build computers — or firstly non-classical mathematical models of computation — which do things undreamt of today.

4 The Constructive Approach to Computational Barriers: In Defense of the Black-Box Model of Computation

As Robin Gandy [16] points out in his article The confluence of ideas in 1936, Alan Turing did not set out in his 1936 paper to give a mathematical model of machine computation. That is not even a well-defined objective — machines as a part of nature require much more radical analysis. Odifreddi [26] (reporting on his discussions with Georg Kreisel, see pp. 101–123) sets out some of the underlying difficulties. What Turing had in mind was a model of how *humans* compute in a very specific manner:

> 'The real question at issue is "What are the possible processes which can be carried out in computing a [real] number?" '

What is different, and theoretically liberating, about Turing's approach to characterising what a computable function is is his avoidance of the teleological constraints on how computation is viewed. Ultimate aims are put to one side in the interests of seeing and modelling atomic detail. Applying this approach to modelling how Nature computes is much more difficult, and certainly more Cartesian.

The first thing that strikes one about physical processes is their basis in the often illusive dichotomy between matter and energy. This has a parallel in various mathematical frameworks in which data and process are put on an equal footing, with the distinction only re-emerging at the semantical level. To an extent, it is the way the universe is observed which leads to the observer seeing process or information. What science tells us is that energy in nature tends to express algorithmic content, implementable over a wide range of appropriate physical contexts which we seek to encapsulate in corresponding informational content. In fact, it appears that nothing interesting exists without this dichotomy, and this is bad news for those looking for the most reductive of foundational explanatory frameworks. At the same time, this observation gives an important role, corresponding to what we experience in the physical context, for algorithmic content — it provides the glue whereby local information content comes together to form a global entity which is more than the sum of its parts, and which is the source of information content qualitatively different from that of its origins. The classical counterpart of this picture is the so-called Turing universe, giving a framework based on oracle computation for mathematically analysing the computationally complex in terms of its algorithmic content. An important aspect of this way of structuring the Universe in accordance with the observed energy-matter dichotomy is the way in which simple global concepts (like definability and invariance) lead to explicit and structurally integrated counterparts to natural laws and large-scale formations whose origins were previously quite mysterious. As we argued in [7]:

> "If one abstracts from the Universe its information content, structured via the basic ...fundamental laws of nature, one obtains a particular ... manifestation of the Turing universe ..., within which vague questions attain a precise analogue of quite plausible validity."

This is useful not just in an explanatory role, but as a pointer to how we might achieve that control of higher-order computational structure that we observe in human thinking. The key ingredient here is just that local to global transfer and and elevation of information content, based on quite elementary local interactive infrastructure. Here is how Antonio Damasio [12–p. 169] describes the hierarchical development of a particular instance of consciousness within the brain (or, rather, 'organism'), interacting with some external object:

> "...both organism and object are mapped as neural patterns, in first-order maps; all of these neural patterns can become images. ... The sensorimotor maps pertaining to the object cause changes in the maps pertaining to the organism. ... [These] changes ...can be re-represented in yet other maps (second-order maps) which thus represent the relationship of object and organism. ... The neural patterns transiently formed in second-order maps can become mental images, no less so than the neural patterns in first-order maps."

As we commented in [10]:

> "Notice that what is envisaged is the re-representation of neural patterns formed across some region of the brain, in such a way that they can have a computational relevance in forming new patterns. This is where the clear demarcation between computation and computational effect becomes

blurred. The key conception is of computational loops incorporating these 'second-order' aspects of the computation itself. Building on this one can derive a plausible schematic picture of of the global workings of the brain."

How one synthesises in practice the sort of representational mechanisms integral to intelligent thought is a problem which goes far beyond any schematic picture of the underlying structures, but these structures give a reassuring solidity to our attempts. The sort of current developments which are brought to mind are the sort of large interactive structures such as the internet and large computing grids. One already observes global phenomena emerging in such contexts, initially as problems, such as those which threaten economic planning, but potentially with computational outcomes which are more 'new paradigm' than generally expected. Robin Milner commented in his 1991 Turing Award lecture [25–p. 80] that:

"Through the seventies, I became convinced that a theory of concurrency and interaction requires a new conceptual framework, not just a refinement of what we find natural for sequential computing."

Such observations have been taken up by Goldin and Wegner [18] in support of new thinking concerning models of today's highly interactive non-linear computation. This takes us beyond thinking of intelligence as something that resides purely within the autonomous brain. As Brooks [3] points out:

"Real computational systems are not rational agents that take inputs, compute logically, and produce outputs ... It is hard to draw the line at what is intelligence and what is environmental interaction. In a sense, it does not really matter which is which, as all intelligent systems must be situated in some world or other if they are to be useful entities."

Particularly relevant to future computing capabilities is Brooks' [2–p. 139] argument that there is a realistic approach to AI involving no internally generated representations, but rather using "the world as its own model". Which brings us back to Danny Hillis' idea that "we'll evolve" intelligent machines rather than "do it by engineering". A Baconian enterprise, no doubt, but one in which we should be prepared for Cartesian surprises.

References

1. Braverman, M.: Hyperbolic Julia Sets are Poly-Time Computable. In Proceedings of the 6th Workshop on Computability and Complexity in Analysis, Wittenberg, Germany, August 16–20, 2004, Brattka, V., Staiger, L. and Weihrauch, K. (eds), ENTCS **120**, Elsevier, Amsterdam (2005) 17–30
2. Brooks, R.A.: Intelligence without Representations. Artificial Intelligence **47** (1987) 139–159
3. Brooks, R.A.: Intelligence without Reason. A.I. Memo No. 1293, The A.I. Laboratory, M.I.T., Cambridge, MA, April 1991
4. Brooks, R.A.: The Relationship between Matter and Life. Nature **409** (2001) 409–411

5. Chaitin, G.J.: Algorithmic Information Theory. Cambridge University Press, Cambridge, New York (1987)
6. Church, A.: A Note on the Entscheidungsproblem. J. Symbolic Logic **1** (1936) 40–41 and 101–102
7. Cooper, S.B.: Beyond Gödel's Theorem: Turing Nonrigidity Revisited. In Logic Colloquium '95, Makowsky, J.A. and Ravve, E.V. (eds), Proceedings of the Annual European Summer Meeting of the Association of Symbolic Logic, Haifa, Israel, August 9–18, 1995, Lecture Notes in Logic, vol. 11, Springer, Berlin, New York, Tokyo (1998) 44–50
8. Cooper, S.B.: Clockwork or Turing U/universe? – Remarks on Causal Determinism and Computability. In Models and Computability, S.B. Cooper and J.K. Truss (eds), London Mathematical Society Lecture Note Series **259**, Cambridge University Press, Cambridge (1999) 63–116
9. Cooper, S.B.: The Incomputable Alan Turing. In Turing 2004: A Celebration of His Life and Achievements, electronically published by the British Computer Society (2005)
10. Cooper, S.B.: Definability as Hypercomputational Effect. Applied Mathematics and Computation, to appear.
11. Cooper, S.B., and Odifreddi, P.: Incomputability in Nature. In Computability and Models: Perspectives East and West, S.B. Cooper and S.S. Goncharov (eds), Kluwer Academic/ Plenum Publishers, New York, Boston, Dordrecht, London, Moscow (2003) 137–160
12. Damasio, A.: The Feeling Of What Happens. Harcourt, Orlando, FL (1999)
13. Davis, M.: The Myth of Hypercomputation. In Teuscher (2004) 195–211
14. Einstein, A.: Out of My Later Years. Philosophical Library, New York (1950)
15. Etesi, G., and Németi, I.: Non-Turing Computations via Malament-Hogarth Space-Times. Int. J. Theoretical Phys. **41** (2002) 341–370
16. Gandy, R.O.: The Confluence of Ideas in 1936. In The Universal Turing Machine: A Half-Century Survey, Herken R. (ed.), Oxford University Press, New York (1988) 51–102
17. Gandy, R.O., and Yates, C.E.M. (eds): Collected Works of A.M. Turing: Mathematical Logic. North-Holland, Amsterdam, New York, Oxford (2001)
18. Goldin, D., and Wegner, P.: Computation Beyond Turing Machines: Seeking Appropriate Methods to Model Computing and Human Thought. Communications of the ACM **46** (2003) 100–102
19. Hadamard, J.: The Psychology of Invention in the Mathematical Field. Princeton Univ. Press, Princeton (1945)
20. Hertling, P.: Is the Mandelbrot Set Computable? Math. Logic Quarterly **51** (2005) 5–18
21. Kreisel, G.: Mathematical Logic: What Has It Done for the Philosophy of Mathematics? In Bertrand Russell, Philosopher of the Century, R. Schoenman (ed.), Allen and Unwin, London (1967) 201–272
22. Kreisel, G.: Church's Thesis: a Kind of Reducibility Axiom for Constructive Mathematics. In Intuitionism and Proof Theory: Proceedings of the Summer Conference at Buffalo N.Y. 1968, A. Kino, J. Myhill and R.E. Vesley (eds) North-Holland, Amsterdam, London (1970) 121–150
23. de Laplace, P.S.: Essai philosophique sur les probabilités (1819). English trans. by F.W. Truscott and F.L. Emory, Dover, New York (1951)
24. McCulloch, W., and Pitts, W.: A Logical Calculus of the Ideas Immanent in Nervous Activity. Bull. Math. Biophys. **5** 115–133

25. Milner, R.: Elements of Interaction: Turing Award Lecture. Communications of the ACM **36** (1993) 78–89

26. Odifreddi, P.: Classical Recursion Theory. North-Holland, Amsterdam, New York, Oxford, Tokyo (1989)

27. Odifreddi, P.: The Mathematical Century: The 30 Greatest Problems of the Last 100 Years, (trans. A. Sangalli), Princeton University Press, Princeton (2004)

28. Penrose, R.: Shadows of the Mind: A Search for the Missing Science of Consciousness. Oxford University Press, Oxford (1994)

29. Pinker, S.: How the Mind Works. W.W. Norton, New York (1997)

30. Rettinger, R.: A Fast Algorithm for Julia Sets of Hyperbolic Rational Functions. In Proceedings of the 6th Workshop on Computability and Complexity in Analysis, Wittenberg, Germany, August 16–20, 2004, Brattka V., Staiger L. and Weihrauch K. (eds), ENTCS **120**, Elsevier, Amsterdam (2005) 145–157

31. Rettinger, R., and Weihrauch, K.: The Computational Complexity of Some Julia Sets. In Proceedings of the 35th Annual ACM Symposium on Theory of Computing, San Diego, California, USA, June 9–11, 2003, Goemans M.X. (ed.), ACM Press, New York (2003) 177–185

32. Shaw, R.: Strange Attractors, Chaotic Behaviour, and Information Flow. Z. Naturforsch. **36A** (1981) 80–112

33. Shaw, R.: The Dripping Faucet as a Model Chaotic System. The Science Frontier Express Series, Aerial Press, Santa Cruz, CA (1984)

34. Smolensky, P.: On the Proper Treatment of Connectionism. Behavioral and Brain Sciences **11** (1988) 1–74

35. Teuscher, C. (ed.): Alan Turing: Life and Legacy of a Great Thinker. Springer-Verlag, Berlin, Heidelberg (2004)

36. Turing, A.M.: On Computable Numbers, with an Application to the Entscheidungsproblem. Proc. London Math. Soc. **42** 2 (1936–7) 230–265. Reprinted in Turing, A.M.: Collected Works: Mathematical Logic 18–53

37. Turing, A.M.: Systems of Logic Based on Ordinals. Proc. London Math. Soc. **45** 2 (1939) 161–228. Reprinted in Turing, A.M.: Collected Works: Mathematical Logic 81–148

38. Turing, A.M.: Intelligent Machinery. National Physical Laboratory Report (1948). In Machine Intelligence 5, B. Meltzer and D. Michie (eds), Edinburgh University Press, Edinburgh (1969) 3–23. Reprinted in Turing, A.M.: Collected Works: Mechanical Intelligence, D.C. Ince (ed.), North-Holland, Amsterdam, New York, Oxford, Tokyo (1992)

39. van Leeuwen, J. and Wiedermann, J.: The Turing Machine Paradigm in Contemporary Computing. In Mathematics Unlimited — 2001 and Beyond, Enquist B. and Schmidt W. (eds), Lecture Notes in Computer Science, Springer-Verlag (2000)

Evolving Ontology Evolution

Giorgos Flouris, Dimitris Plexousakis, and Grigoris Antoniou

Department of Computer Science, University of Crete,
P.O. Box 2208, GR 71409, Heraklion, Greece
Institute of Computer Science, FO.R.T.H.,
P.O. Box 1385, GR 71110, Heraklion, Greece
{fgeo, dp, antoniou}@ics.forth.gr

Abstract. One of the crucial tasks towards the realization of the Semantic Web vision is the efficient encoding of human knowledge in ontologies. Thus, the proper maintenance of these, usually large, structures and, in particular, their adaptation to new knowledge (ontology evolution) is one of the most challenging problems in the current Semantic Web research. In this paper, we uncover a certain gap in the current research area of ontology evolution and propose a research direction based on belief revision. We present some results in this direction and argue that our approach introduces an interesting new dimension to the problem that is likely to find important applications in the future.

1 Introduction

Originally introduced by Aristotle, *ontologies* are often viewed as the key means through which the vision of the Semantic Web can be realized [4]. The importance of ontologies in current research is emphasized by the interest shown by both the research and the enterprise community to various ontology-related problems [27].

Ontologies are often large and complex structures, whose development and maintenance give rise to certain sturdy and interesting research problems. One of the most important such problems is *ontology evolution*, which is the problem of modifying an ontology in response to a certain change in the domain or its conceptualization.

There are several cases where ontology evolution is applicable. An ontology, just like any structure holding information, may need to change simply because the world has changed [31]; in other cases, we may need to change the perspective under which the domain is viewed [29], or we may discover a problem in the original conceptualization of the domain; we might also wish to incorporate additional functionality, according to a change in users' needs [13]; furthermore, new information, which was previously unknown, classified or otherwise unavailable may become accessible or different features of the domain may become important [18].

In this paper, we argue that the currently used ontology evolution model has several weaknesses. We present an abstract proposition for a future research direction that will hopefully resolve these weaknesses, based on the related field of *belief change* [11]. Finally, we present an application of our research model in which the AGM theory [1] is generalized so as to be applicable to ontology evolution.

J. Wiedermann et al. (Eds.): SOFSEM 2006, LNCS 3831, pp. 14–29, 2006.

2 Ontology Evolution

An ontology can be defined as a specification of a conceptualization of a domain [23]. Thus, ontology evolution may be caused by either a change in the domain, a change in the conceptualization or a change in the specification [23]. Our understanding of the term ontology evolution covers the first two types of change (changes in the domain and changes in the conceptualization). The third type of change (change in the specification) refers to a change in the way the conceptualization is formally recorded, i.e., a change in the representation language; this is dealt with in the field of *ontology translation* [7], [20]. Unlike [30], we don't consider the (important) issue of propagating the changes to dependent elements, as this part of ontology change is handled by the related field of *ontology versioning* [23].

In order to tame the complexity of the problem, six phases of ontology evolution have been identified, occurring in a cyclic loop [30]. Initially, we have the *change capturing* phase, where the changes to be performed are identified; these changes are represented in a suitable format during the *change representation* phase. There are two major types of changes, namely elementary and composite changes [30]. Elementary changes represent simple, fine-grained changes; composite changes represent more coarse-grained changes and can be replaced by a series of elementary changes. However, it is not generally appropriate to use a series of elementary changes to replace a composite change, as this might cause undesirable side-effects [30]. The proper level of granularity should be identified at each case. Examples of elementary changes are the addition and deletion of elements (concepts, properties etc) from the ontology. There is no general consensus on the type and number of composite changes that are necessary. In [30], 12 different composite changes are identified; in [29], 22 such operations are listed; in [32] however, the authors mention that they have identified 120 different interesting composite operations and that the list is still growing! In fact, the number of definable composite operations can only be limited by setting a granularity threshold on the operations considered; if we allow unlimited granularity, we will be able to define more and more operations of coarser and coarser granularity, limited only by our imagination [24].

The third phase of ontology evolution is the *semantics of change* phase, in which possible problems that might be caused in the ontology by the identified changes are determined and resolved; for example, if a concept is removed, we should decide what to do with its instances. The role of the *implementation* phase is to implement the changes identified in the two previous phases, to present the changes to the ontology engineer for final verification and to keep a log of the implemented changes [14]. The *change propagation* phase should ensure that all induced changes will be propagated to the interested parties (agents, ontologies etc). Finally, the *change validation* phase allows the ontology engineer to review the changes and possibly undo them, if desired. This phase may uncover further problems with the ontology, thus initiating new changes that need to be performed to improve the conceptualization; in this case, we need to start over by applying the change capturing phase of a new evolution process, closing the cyclic loop.

3   Discussion on Current Research Directions

Current ontology evolution tools have reached a high level of sophistication; the current state of the art can be found in [14]. While some of these tools are simple ontology editors, others provide more specialized features to the user, like the support for evolution strategies, collaborative edits, change propagation, transactional properties, intuitive graphical interfaces, undo/redo operations etc.

Despite these nice features, the field of ontology evolution is characterized by the lack of adequate formalizations for the various processes involved [7]. Most of the available tools attempt to emulate human behavior, using certain heuristics which are heavily based on the expertise of their developers. They are not theoretically founded and their formal properties remain unspecified. Moreover, they require varying levels of human intervention to work, a rather unrealistic assumption ([7], [20]). In short, current work on ontology evolution resorts to ontology editors or other, more specialized tools whose aim is to *help* users perform the change(s) manually rather than *performing* the change(s) automatically.

We believe that this is not a practical approach to be taken. First of all, the human user that intervenes in the process should be an ontology engineer and have certain knowledge on the domain. Very few people can be both domain and ontology experts. But even for these specialized experts, it is very hard to perform ontology evolution manually [13], [30]. So, it is simply not practical to rely on humans in domains where changes occur often, or where it is difficult, impossible or undesirable for ontology engineers to handle the change themselves (autonomous robots or software agents, time-critical applications etc).

Moreover, different ontology engineers may have different views on how a certain change should be implemented [30]. These views are affected by commonsense knowledge, personal preferences or ideas, subjective opinions on the domain etc. This means that there is no single "correct" way of changing an ontology. Computer-based evolution could (at least) guarantee determinism, objectivity and reproducibility of the results, even though some people may disagree on how a change was implemented. But then, is there a consensus on the effects of a given change even among humans?

Another source of problems for manual ontology evolution is the complexity of modern day ontologies. Complex ontologies are usually developed by several engineers. A change in one part of the ontology might have unintended effects in other parts of the ontology [31]. The person who made the change may be unaware of the full extent of the change's effects, as he doesn't know all the parts of the ontology.

These points uncover the need for automatic ontology evolution; computer-based ontology evolution is not only necessary for many applications, it is also desirable in certain contexts. Human supervision by specialized experts should be highly welcome and encouraged whenever possible; however, the system should be able to work even without it. Human intervention should constitute an optional feature guaranteeing the quality of the evolution process, but should not be a necessary one.

Another problem with current research directions is related to the representation of changes. In tools that are simple ontology editors, there is usually little or no support for any kind of composite changes to the ontology [14]. In more specialized tools for ontology evolution, there is a pre-defined set of elementary and/or composite operations that are supported, providing a greater flexibility to the user. For each such operation, there is an associated procedure that handles the change as well as the effects of the change (semantics of change phase); this procedure can, in some cases, be parameterized to cover different needs. Unfortunately, there is no guarantee that the provided parameterization is enough to cover any possible need of the knowledge engineer. Unforeseeable needs may require unforeseeable reactions to a given change. Furthermore, there is no limit on the number of composite operations that can be considered and, even if we restrict ourselves to the most common types, there is a large number of them [32]; this makes the process non-scalable. A unifying approach is necessary to cover all cases.

The problem becomes even more complicated due to the fact that not all different types of change are readily available at design-time. New needs may require new operations. For operations that are not in the supported list, the ontology engineer should choose a sequence of two or more simpler (more elementary) operations of different granularity. Unfortunately, such a choice will undoubtedly affect the quality of the change, leading to unforeseeable problems [30]. In addition, it cannot be performed without human participation.

In current approaches, a change request is an explicit statement of the modifications to be performed upon the ontology; however, this request must be determined by the knowledge engineer in response to a more abstract need (e.g., an observation). Thus, current systems do not determine the actual changes to be made upon the ontology when faced with a need for a change; the user should determine them and feed them to the system for implementation. This way, whenever the ontology engineer is faced with a new fact (observation), he decides on his alternatives and selects the "best" one for implementation by the system. This decision is based on his expertise on the subject, not on a formal, step-by-step, exhaustive method of evaluation.

However, to develop a fully automatic ontology evolution algorithm, several issues need to be resolved in a definite, formal manner. For example, how could one track down all the alternative ways to address a given change, using a formal and exhaustive process? How can a computer system decide on the "best" of the different alternatives? Most importantly, what is the definition of "best" in this context? Are there any properties that should be satisfied by a "good" ontology evolution algorithm?

Unfortunately, resolving the above issues in a general manner is not easy using the current research direction because each type of change is treated differently, using a stand-alone, specialized process. Unless a more formal path is taken, the ontology evolution research is doomed to never find answers to these questions.

4 Belief Change and Ontology Evolution

4.1 General Idea, Problems and Opportunities

Our key idea towards resolving the aforementioned deficiencies of current research on ontology evolution is to exploit the extensive research that has been performed in the field of belief change. Belief change deals with the adaptation of a Knowledge

Base (KB) to new information [11]; this fact allows us to view ontology evolution as a special case of the more general problem of belief change. Therefore, it makes sense to apply techniques, methods, tools, ideas and intuitions developed by the belief change community to ontology evolution. Recently, the idea of using results from the belief change literature as an inspiration for ontology evolution research has been independently considered in [21], [25], [28], giving interesting preliminary results.

We believe that our approach allows us to kill several birds with one stone. The mature field of belief change will provide the necessary formalizations that can be used by the immature ontology evolution field. Belief change has always dealt with the automatic adaptation of a KB to new knowledge, without human participation; the ideas and algorithms developed towards this aim will prove helpful in our effort to loosen up the dependency of the ontology evolution process on the knowledge engineer. Finally, previous work on belief change can protect us from potential pitfalls and prevent reinventing the wheel for problems whose counterparts have already been studied in the rich belief change literature, while belief change intuitions that are not directly applicable to ontology evolution may serve as an inspiration for developing solutions to similar problems faced by ontology evolution researchers.

Unfortunately, a direct application of belief change theories to ontology evolution is generally not possible, because most such approaches focus on classical logic, using assumptions that fail for most ontology representation languages like Description Logics (DLs) [2] and OWL [6]; despite that, the intuitions behind the theories are usually independent of the underlying language. In the sequel, we revisit some of the most important concepts that have been considered in the belief change literature under the prism of ontology evolution in order to demonstrate the main tradeoffs and intuitions involved in their migration to the ontology evolution context.

4.2 Belief Change Issues in the Context of Ontology Evolution

One of the major issues involved in belief change is a fundamental philosophical choice regarding the representation of the knowledge, i.e., whether the explicitly represented knowledge serves as a justification for our beliefs (a *belief base* under the *foundational* semantics) or whether it simply forms a manageable representation of an infinite structure (a *belief set* under the *coherence* semantics) [12]. Under the foundational model, there is a clear distinction between knowledge stored explicitly (which can be changed directly) and implicit knowledge (which cannot be changed, but is indirectly affected by changes in the explicit knowledge). Under the coherence model, both explicit and implicit knowledge may be directly modified by the ontology evolution (or belief change) algorithm in an unambiguous manner.

The choice of the viewpoint to employ is very important, greatly affecting the ontology evolution (and belief change) algorithms considered. This choice depends on philosophical intuition, personal preference and on the intended use (application) of the KB (ontology in our context). Therefore, all the arguments, ideas and results discussed in the belief change literature ([12], [16]) are equally applicable here.

As already mentioned, standard ontology evolution approaches are "modification-centered": the fact (observation, experiment etc) that initiated the change is not important and is not known by the system; the system is fed with the actual modifications that should be physically performed upon the ontology in response to this fact.

On the other hand, the belief change approaches are "fact-centered": a new fact reflects a certain need for change. This fact is directly fed into the system, which is responsible for identifying the actual modifications to perform upon the KB to address the change (new fact) and for performing these modifications automatically.

We propose the use of the latter model for ontology evolution. Of course, the issue of determining the modifications to perform upon the ontology in the face of some abstract new fact is far from trivial, but there are several belief change techniques that could be of use here. This way, we add an extra layer of abstraction to ontology evolution: the changes to be performed upon the ontology are decided by the system, not by the ontology engineer. This allows the ontology engineer to deal with high-level facts only, leaving the low-level modifications that should be performed upon the ontology in response to these facts to be determined by the system.

There are two general scientific approaches towards the determination of these low-level modifications: *postulation* or *explicit construction* [26]. Under the postulation approach one seeks to formulate a number of formal conditions (postulates) that a belief change (or ontology evolution) algorithm should satisfy in the given context. Under the explicit construction approach, one seeks certain explicit algorithms or constructions leading to algorithms. The two approaches are not rivalrous but complementary [26]. Both methods have been used in belief change with very interesting results. On the other hand, current research on ontology evolution uses only the explicit construction method; one interesting side-effect of our approach is that it provides the necessary formalisms for the development of a postulation method.

Another issue is related to the acceptance of the new information. It is usually assumed that the new information is accepted unconditionally, implying a complete reliance to the incoming data, according to the *Principle of Primacy of New Information* [5]. This principle coincides with common intuition, because the new information generally reflects a newer and more accurate view of the domain. In the ontology evolution context however, the distributed and chaotic nature of the Semantic Web implies that data may be obtained by unreliable or untrustworthy sources; thus, it makes sense to apply techniques from *non-prioritized belief change* [15], where the new data may be partially or totally rejected.

Some researchers argue that semantical (rather than syntactical) considerations should be the driving force behind belief change, so the result of a change should be independent of the syntactical representation of the KB or the change (*Principle of Irrelevance of Syntax* [5]). This principle generally fails for foundational belief bases, because logically equivalent bases may be formed using completely different sets of axioms, implying different justifications [17]. In current works of ontology evolution, this principle is usually ignored, as the explicit part (syntax) of the ontology has a major impact on the result.

Inconsistent KBs (under classical logic) exhibit explosive behavior: anything is implied from them. This is clearly an undesirable behavior, so the result of a change should be a consistent KB, according to the *Principle of Consistency Maintenance* [5]. The only thing that remains to be settled is the exact meaning of the term "consistency"; in the belief change literature, the meaning of the word is clear:

a KB is inconsistent iff it implies a proposition that is tautologically false. For ontology change however, the term "consistency" has been used (others would say abused) to denote several different things.

In [7], several uses of the term were presented and a certain terminology was fixed. More specifically, an ontology was termed *inconsistent* iff it exhibits the explosive behavior of classical logic, implying falsehood; it was termed *incoherent* iff it does not satisfy certain pre-defined conditions related to the quality of the conceptualization. Such conditions include the use of unsatisfiable concepts, properties with no predefined range and/or domain and others. We also argued that ontology evolution needs to be concerned only with consistency (just like belief change); coherency is a very important issue, but is more related to the area of ontology design. We also showed, by means of intuitive examples, that attempting to resolve incoherencies during ontology evolution could lead to unnecessary loss of information (see [7]).

Undoubtedly, the most important issue in belief change is the *Principle of Minimal Change*, which states that the new KB should be as "close" as possible to the original KB, being subject to minimal "loss of information". The terms "closeness" and "loss of information" have no single interpretation in the literature. There have been several proposals on metrics that count information loss in different ways, being used in different algorithms or representation results, as well as postulations that capture this principle in different ways. The formal realization of this principle is in the core of each belief change algorithm, determining its properties to a large extent.

The same considerations are true in the ontology evolution context. In this context, the loss of information could be counted in terms of the number and importance of the modifications that need to be performed upon the ontology during the change. Alternatively, the loss of information could be counted in model-theoretic terms (via some kind of distance metric between the models satisfying the original and the modified ontology), through some specially designed distance metric between ontologies or via certain conditions (postulates) that identify acceptable and non-acceptable transitions. The counterparts of each of these approaches have been considered and evaluated in the belief change literature, greatly simplifying our task.

The above considerations form only a partial list of the issues that have been discussed in the belief change literature. This analysis shows that the determination of the change(s) to be made in response to some new data is a complex and multifaceted issue and that several considerations need to be taken into account before choosing the modifications to be made upon a KB. The same considerations hold for any type of knowledge change, including ontology evolution. Unfortunately, in the ontology evolution literature, most of these issues are dealt with implicitly, if at all, with no formal (or informal) justification of the various choices and without exhaustively considering the different alternatives.

Furthermore, it is interesting to note that, in the belief change literature, there is no human involved in the process of change; all related approaches deal with the problem in a fully automatic manner. In fact, to the authors' knowledge, the option of using a human in the loop of belief change was never even considered as an option, despite the complexity of the problem. This fact forms an additional argument in favor of the use of belief change techniques for automatic ontology evolution.

5   Reformulating the Problem of Ontology Evolution

Notice that the above discussion was made without any explicit mentioning of the underlying knowledge representation formalism; this supports our belief that most of the intuitions involved in belief change are transferable to other contexts as well (including ontology evolution). However, the migration of belief change techniques to ontology evolution will ultimately require some formal setting to be based upon. In this section we will provide some definitions that set the formal foundations upon which future research in this direction could be based.

5.1   Description Logics (DLs) and Web Ontology Language (OWL)

Before going into the details of our formalization, we will make a brief introduction to two important families of logics that will be useful for our purposes, namely DLs and OWL. *Description Logics* [2] form a family of knowledge representation languages, heavily used in the Semantic Web [3]. In DLs, *classes* are used to represent basic concepts, *roles* to represent basic binary relations between objects and *individuals* to represent objects. Those primitive notions can be combined using certain *operators* (such as $\neg$, $\sqcap$, $\exists$ etc) to produce more complex *terms*. Finally, *connectives* are used to represent relationships between terms, such as inclusion ($\sqsubseteq$), disjointness (disj) and others. Each such relationship is called an *axiom*. Axioms dealing with classes and roles form the *Tbox*, while axioms dealing with individuals form the *Abox*. The operators and connectives that a certain DL admits determine the type and complexity of the available axioms, which, in turn, determine the expressive power and the reasoning complexity of the DL. Reasoning in DLs is based on standard model-theoretic semantics. For more details on DLs and their semantics, see [2]. In this paper, the term *DL Knowledge Base* (*DL KB*) will refer to a set of general Tbox and/or Abox axioms representing knowledge regarding a domain of interest.

The *Web Ontology Language* [6], known as OWL, is a knowledge representation language that is expected to play an important role in the future of the Semantic Web, as it has become a W3C Recommendation. OWL comes in three flavors (or species), namely OWL Full, OWL DL and OWL Lite, with varying degree of expressive power and reasoning complexity. In OWL, knowledge is represented using an RDF-like syntax. OWL contains several features allowing the representation of complex relationships between classes, roles and objects in a pattern very similar to the one used in DLs; this close relationship was verified in [19], where OWL DL and OWL Lite (with their secondary annotation features removed) were shown equivalent to the DLs $SHOIN^+(D)$ and $SHIF^+(D)$ respectively. On the other hand, OWL Full provides a more complete integration with RDF, containing features not normally allowed in DLs; furthermore, its inference problem is undecidable [19]. For more details on OWL and the differences between its flavors, refer to [6].

5.2   Representation of Ontologies

Most current ontology evolution algorithms use a graphical representation to visualize the knowledge that is stored in an ontology. This graph-based representation is pervasive in such algorithms, as it affects the decisions on how each change should be implemented. Graphical representations are extremely useful for visualizing the way that the domain conceptualization was implemented in an ontology. They also help novice users and domain experts get acquainted with the field and understand the conceptualization, by hiding much of the semantic and syntactic complexity of the ontology behind intuitive interfaces and simple visual metaphors.

However, such representations are often not expressive enough for certain applications, because some complex facts expressible using DL axioms cannot be easily expressed using a graph [7]. More importantly, they have led ontology evolution research towards a more informal direction, by shifting the relevant research to concepts, roles, individuals and how they are structured in the ontology graph. As a result, most existing work on ontology evolution builds on frame-like or object models [13] and arbitrary axioms are often not considered part of an ontology (little or no attention is paid to them), leading to unnecessary loss of expressive power.

For knowledge engineers and ontology experts, an algebraic representation provides a more concise and formal representation of the conceptualization, has a cleaner semantics and allows easier formal manipulation than the graph-based approach. In fact, a combination of the two approaches usually works best, as it allows us to use the best of both worlds.

Under the algebraic approach, the knowledge of the ontology is stored as a pair <S,A>, where S is the *vocabulary* (or *signature*) containing information on the elements appearing in the ontology (concepts, roles, individuals) and A is a *set of ontological axioms* [20]. The vocabulary may be a single unstructured set containing all the concepts, roles and individuals relevant to the ontology, or it may have some structure denoting, for example, the concept hierarchy; the set of ontological axioms contains an arbitrary number of axioms representing certain facts on these elements.

In this work, we will use a simplification of the algebraic approach, by dropping the signature structure and *representing an ontology as a set of DL axioms* (i.e., a DL KB), under a given, predefined DL. This way, our approach focuses on axioms, following the axiom-centered ontology model [13], ignoring the signature of the ontology. The graphical structure of the ontology can be completely determined by a set of axioms, so our approach provides a more general representation method.

This viewpoint of ontologies facilitates the definition of a common formalism in terms of which both classical logic and ontologies can be described, thus expediting the task of migrating belief change methods (mostly based on classical logic) to ontologies. It is also simpler and more straightforward than the algebraic approach.

The main disadvantage of this model is that we lose the information normally stored in the signature of the ontology. This is not as major a problem as it seems, because most of the information in S can be represented using axioms as well. For example, if S is a poset representing a certain hierarchy between concepts, then the hierarchy information can be expressed in the form of axioms using the subconcept connective of DLs ($\sqsubseteq$). Things become more complicated when one tries to describe the elements relevant to the ontology, because, in current DLs, there is no way to express the information that a certain element (concept, role or individual) is relevant to the ontology (i.e., it exists in the signature of the ontology). To deal with this problem, we have introduced the *Existence Assertion Operator*, the *Closed Vocabulary Assumption* (CVA) and the *Open Vocabulary Assumption* (OVA) [7], [8].

The existence assertion operator enhances the expressiveness of any given DL by allowing the formation of axioms that express the fact that a certain element is relevant to the conceptualization of the ontology; the formal semantics of this operator are described in detail in [8]. CVA asserts that no element is relevant to the ontology unless its relevance can be deduced by the ontology through the semantics of the existence assertion operator; CVA and the existence assertion operator can be used to express the knowledge originally in the signature structure using axioms. On the other hand, under OVA, all elements are assumed relevant to the ontology and the existence assertion operator is not used. For a detailed account on the existence assertion operator and the differences between CVA and OVA see [7], [8].

5.3   Tarski's Logical Model: The Common Ground

The proposed representation for ontologies was chosen because it allows them to be placed under a very general logical framework in a clean and smooth manner; this framework was introduced by Tarski and defines a logic as a pair <L,Cn>, where L is *a set of propositions* of the underlying language and Cn is a function mapping sets of propositions to sets of propositions (*consequence operation*). The intuitive meaning of Cn is that a set $X \subseteq L$ implies exactly the propositions contained in Cn(X). It is assumed that Cn satisfies three intuitive properties (iteration, inclusion, monotony) that allow it to behave in a rational manner. For details see [7], [26].

It can be easily shown that the above framework engulfs most logics used for knowledge representation. In particular, all monotonic DLs and all the formalisms that have been used for belief change are expressible through some <L,Cn> pair. This way, a KB (ontology) is a set $K \subseteq L$ of an underlying logic (DL) <L,Cn>. This viewpoint provides the necessary connection between ontologies and belief change.

5.4   Ontology Evolution Operations

As already mentioned, our approach is "fact-centered": each new fact leads to one operation upon the ontology, which is implemented through an automatically generated sequence of modifications. However, not all types of facts have the same semantics. In this respect, the belief change literature shows the way once again: four types of changes have been identified, each having different semantics and being addressed by a different operation (see [7], [22]). More specifically, a fact may denote that something should be added or retracted from the KB; it may also enhance our knowledge regarding a static world, or denote the way in which the real world has changed (dynamic world). Each of these combinations is handled by a different operation, namely *revision, contraction, update* and *erasure*, as table 1 shows:

Table 1. Operations for Belief Change and Ontology Evolution

Operation	Type of Change (Addition/Retraction)	State of the World (Static/Dynamic)
Revision	Addition	Static
Contraction	Retraction	Static
Update	Addition	Dynamic
Erasure	Retraction	Dynamic

In the same sense, we could define four different operations for ontology evolution. This approach has the advantage of dealing with four operations only (covering all types of changes), thus resolving the scalability problems discussed in section 3. Under this viewpoint, a change involves the identification of the operation (out of the four operations above) as well as the operand of the change (new fact), which are then fed into the system for implementation. But what should be the operand of such an operation? In other words, what constitutes a "change request" in our framework?

In belief change, the change is usually represented using a single proposition; we will slightly generalize this viewpoint by assuming that a change request can be any *set of propositions* (i.e., axioms) of the underlying DL. Our approach is, of course, more general than the standard belief change option; the question is, is this generalization appropriate or necessary for ontology evolution? We argue that the properties of the representation languages commonly used in ontologies (such as DLs) make such an option necessary.

Most belief change approaches assume that the underlying logic contains the usual operators of classical logic (like $\land$, $\lor$ etc) and includes classical tautological implication. Moreover, sets of expressions have conjunctive semantics, so any finite set can be equivalently represented as the conjunction of the set's propositions (i.e., a singular set). The above assumptions fail for DLs and OWL [9], because, in many DLs, the conjunction of axioms is not possible (among other things); thus, in such DLs, there are facts which are expressible by a set of axioms, yet non-expressible by any single axiom. For this reason, we believe it would be unnecessarily restrictive to constraint the change to be a single axiom only, as this does not take full advantage of the expressive power of the underlying DL.

6   An Application: The AGM Theory in Ontologies

The AGM theory of contraction [1] is undoubtedly the most influential work in belief change. For this reason, we chose to apply our ideas to this theory first, and determine whether this particular theory can be applied to ontology evolution. In this section, we provide a short introduction on the generalization of the AGM theory, as well as the main results regarding its applicability in the ontological context. For more details on this work, refer to [8], [9], [10].

6.1 The AGM Theory and Its Generalization

Alchourron, Gärdenfors and Makinson (AGM for short), in their seminal paper [1], dealt with revision and contraction, as well as with a trivial operation, *expansion*. The main contribution of their work was the introduction of a set of rationality postulates that should apply to each of revision and contraction. These postulates provided a solid theoretical foundation upon which most subsequent research on the subject was based. Our work has focused on the operation of contraction which, according to AGM, is the most fundamental among the operators considered [1], [11].

AGM used certain assumptions when formulating their theory. One such assumption is that the underlying logic follows Tarski's model; this was the only assumption that was kept during our generalization of the AGM theory [8], [9]. AGM additionally assumed that the logic is closed under the usual operators ($\neg$, $\wedge$ etc) and that the consequence operator includes classical tautological implication, is compact and satisfies the rule of introduction of disjunctions in the premises. Unfortunately, these additional assumptions fail for DLs and OWL [8]. On the other hand, Tarski's more general framework engulfs DLs, as explained above.

Regarding the operation of contraction, AGM assumed that a KB is a set of propositions of the underlying logic (say $K \subseteq L$) which is closed under logical consequence (i.e., $K=Cn(K)$), also called a *theory*. Any single expression $x \in L$ of the logic can be contracted from the KB. The operation of contraction can be formalized as a function mapping the pair (K, x) to a new KB K' (denoted by $K'=K-x$).

As explained above, these restrictions may cause problems in the ontological context; for this reason, we generalized the AGM model by including cases where both operands are sets of expressions of the underlying logic (i.e., $K'=K-X$, for K, $X \subseteq L$). This is in accordance to the framework we described in section 5.

The above assumptions allow any binary operator to be a "contraction" operator, which, of course, should not be the case; for this reason, AGM introduced several restrictions on the result of a contraction operation. First, the result should be a theory itself. As already stated, contraction is an operation that is used to remove knowledge from the KB; thus the result should not contain any previously unknown information. Moreover, contraction is supposed to return a KB such that the contracted expression is no longer believed or implied. Finally, the result should be syntax-independent and should remove as little information from the KB as possible. The above intuitions were formalized in a set of six postulates, the *basic AGM postulates for contraction*; these are omitted due to lack of space, but can be found in [1].

As shown by the above analysis, the intuitions that led to the development of the AGM postulates are independent of the underlying knowledge representation language. On the other hand, the formulation of the AGM postulates themselves depends on the AGM assumptions (see [1]). This problem is typical of the problems encountered during the migration of belief change techniques to the ontology evolution context: the differences on the underlying intuitions are minimal, but the representation languages and formalisms used are quite different. In such cases, it makes sense to recast the theory under question (in this case the AGM theory) in a setting general enough to contain ontology representation languages (like DLs and OWL).

Towards this aim, each AGM postulate was reformulated so as to be applicable to all logics under our framework, while preserving the intuition that led to its definition. The resulting postulates can be found below, where the naming and numbering of each postulate corresponds to the original AGM naming and numbering [9]:

(K−1) Closure:	$Cn(K−X)=K−X$
(K−2) Inclusion:	$K−X \subseteq Cn(K)$
(K−3) Vacuity:	If $X \nsubseteq Cn(K)$, then $K−X=Cn(K)$
(K−4) Success:	If $X \nsubseteq Cn(\emptyset)$, then $X \nsubseteq Cn(K−X)$
(K−5) Preservation:	If $Cn(X)=Cn(Y)$, then $K−X=K−Y$
(K−6) Recovery:	$K \subseteq Cn((K−X) \cup X)$

It can be easily shown that these postulates are equivalent to the original ones in the presence of the AGM assumptions. Unfortunately, it soon became clear that not all logics in our wide framework can admit a contraction operator that satisfies the (generalized) AGM postulates, unlike the logics satisfying the AGM assumptions.

6.2 AGM-Compliance and Related Results

Following this observation, we defined a logic to be *AGM-compliant* iff a contraction operator that satisfies the generalized AGM postulates can be defined in the given logic. This class of logics was characterized using three different necessary and sufficient conditions based on the notions of *decomposability*, *cuts* and *max-cuts* [9]. These results allow one to determine whether any given logic (in the wide sense of Tarski's model) is AGM-compliant or not; notice that this is true even for logics that are not interesting for the purposes of the Semantic Web or ontology representation.

The above research had several interesting side-effects. Firstly, a certain connection between the AGM theory and the foundational model was uncovered. The AGM theory follows the coherence model and there is a known result from the literature stating that the AGM theory is not suitable for a foundational KB [17]; our results verified that this holds even for the generalized AGM theory. More specifically, the dual notions of *base decomposability* and *base cuts* for the foundational case under a belief base were defined; it was shown that these notions form the basis for two necessary and sufficient conditions under which the AGM theory can be applied in the foundational model. Unfortunately, these conditions are very powerful, being satisfied by only few uninteresting logics (which don't satisfy the AGM assumptions) [9].

Another result follows from the definition of a certain equivalence relation which was shown to preserve AGM-compliance [8]. This relation uncovered a certain connection between the AGM theory and the lattice theory: the class of logics modulo this equivalence relation is isomorphic to the class of complete lattices modulo the standard equivalence relation of lattices. These results combined show that AGM-compliance is a feature that can be solely determined by the structure of the complete lattice that is used to represent the logic under question, allowing us to use the richness of results related to lattice theory in the context of AGM-compliance [8].

Given the theoretical foundations set by this work, we were able to determine the AGM-compliance of many DLs (and OWL), as well as to provide specialized conditions and heuristics allowing one to determine the AGM-compliance of any given DL, including those not covered by our work [10]. These results determine, to a large extent, the applicability of the AGM theory to languages used for ontology representation. In addition, a preliminary study on revision was performed [10].

6.3 Evaluation of AGM-Compliance

There is still a long way to go before fully determining the connection between the AGM theory and ontologies. It should be emphasized that AGM-compliance is a property that simply guarantees the existence of a contraction operator satisfying the (generalized) AGM postulates in the DL under question. The extent to which the richness of results related to the AGM theory [11] can be applied to AGM-compliant DLs still remains undetermined. Also, the connection of AGM-compliance with the operation of revision and the related representation results [11] is still unexplored.

On the other hand, this work indicates that important theories from the belief change literature can be migrated, at least partially, to the world of ontologies. Thus, not only the intuitions of the belief change research can be used in our quest for ontology evolution algorithms; certain theories themselves could also prove helpful. Moreover, the application of the AGM theory in this context showed that our ontological framework is suitable not only for capturing the peculiarities of the ontology representation languages and the needs of the related applications, but also for allowing the application of belief change theories to the problem of ontology evolution.

7 Conclusion and Future Work

This paper introduced a formal, logic-based approach to ontology evolution, which will hopefully provide the necessary formalization to this yet immature [29] field. This approach was based on a reformulation of the problem which allows us to view it as a special case of the more general, and extensively studied, problem of belief change. This way, most of the techniques, ideas, algorithms and intuitions expressed in the belief change field can be migrated to the ontology evolution context.

We argued that our approach will lead to several formal results related to ontology evolution and resolve several weaknesses of the currently used model. Our study did not provide any concrete solutions to the problem; our goal was to provide solid theoretical foundations upon which deeper results can be based, thus paving the road for the development of effective solutions to the problem of ontology evolution.

As an application of the proposed research direction, we evaluated the feasibility of applying the AGM theory of contraction [1], one of the most important belief change theories, to the ontological context. The difficulties encountered during this migration attempt are probably typical of the difficulties that will be encountered during the application of other belief change ideas to ontology evolution.

Our approach uncovered a different viewpoint on the problem of ontology evolution. We have scratched the surface of the relation between this problem and belief change; much more work needs to be done on this issue, both in theoretical and in practical grounds. The application of specific belief change algorithms or postulations in the context of ontology evolution could prove interesting and uncover useful approaches to this problem. The proposed migration of the AGM theory to the ontology evolution context is not complete either, as only the contraction operator was considered; future work should address the problem of revision as well.

References

1. Alchourron, C., Gärdenfors, P., Makinson, D.: On the Logic of Theory Change: Partial Meet Contraction and Revision Functions. Journal of Symbolic Logic 50 (1985) 510-530
2. Baader, F., Calvanese, D., McGuinness, D., Nardi, D., Patel-Schneider, P. (eds): The Description Logic Handbook: Theory, Implementation and Applications. Cambridge University Press (2002)
3. Baader, F., Horrocks, I., Sattler, U.: Description Logics as Ontology Languages for the Semantic Web. In: Hutter, D., Stephan, W. (eds): Festschrift in honor of Jörg Siekmann. Lecture Notes in Artificial Intelligence, Springer-Verlag, (2003)
4. Berners-Lee, T., Hendler, J., Lassila, O.: The Semantic Web. Scientific American **284** 5 (2001) 34-43
5. Dalal, M.: Investigations Into a Theory of Knowledge Base Revision: Preliminary Report. In Proceedings of the 7th National Conference on Artificial Intelligence (1988) 475-479
6. Dean, D., Schreiber, G., Bechhofer, S., van Harmelen, F., Hendler, J., Horrocks, I., McGuiness, D., Patel-Schneider, P., Stein, L.A.: OWL Web Ontology Language Reference. W3C Recommendation (2005) web page: http://www.w3.org/TR/owl-ref/
7. Flouris, G., Plexousakis, D.: Handling Ontology Change: Survey and Proposal for a Future Research Direction. Technical Report FORTH-ICS/TR-362 (2005)
8. Flouris, G., Plexousakis, D., Antoniou, G.: AGM Postulates in Arbitrary Logics: Initial Results and Applications. Technical Report FORTH-ICS/TR-336 (2004)
9. Flouris, G., Plexousakis, D., Antoniou, G.: Generalizing the AGM Postulates: Preliminary Results and Applications. In Proceedings of the 10th International Workshop on Non-Monotonic Reasoning (2004)
10. Flouris, G., Plexousakis, D., Antoniou, G.: On Applying the AGM Theory to DLs and OWL. In Proceedings of the 4th International Semantic Web Conference (2005)
11. Gärdenfors, P.: Belief Revision: An Introduction. In: Gärdenfors, P. (ed): Belief Revision. Cambridge University Press (1992) 1-20
12. Gärdenfors, P.: The Dynamics of Belief Systems: Foundations Versus Coherence Theories. Revue Internationale de Philosophie 44 (1992) 24-46
13. Haase, P., Stojanovic, L.: Consistent Evolution of OWL Ontologies. In Proceedings of the 2nd European Semantic Web Conference (2005)
14. Haase, P., Sure, Y.: D3.1.1.b State of the Art on Ontology Evolution (2004) web page: http://www.aifb.uni-karlsruhe.de/WBS/ysu/publications/SEKT-D3.1.1.b.pdf
15. Hansson, S.O.: A Survey of Non-prioritized Belief Revision. Erkenntnis **50** (1999)
16. Hansson, S.O.: In Defense of Base Contraction. Synthese 91 (1992) 239-245
17. Hansson, S.O.: Knowledge-level Analysis of Belief Base Operations. Artificial Intelligence 82 (1996) 215-235

18. Heflin, J., Hendler, J., Luke, S.: Coping with Changing Ontologies in a Distributed Environment. In Proceedings of the Workshop on Ontology Management of the 16th National Conference on Artificial Intelligence (1999) 74-79

19. Horrocks, I., Patel-Schneider, P.: Reducing OWL Entailment to Description Logic Satisfiability. Journal of Web Semantics 1 4 (2004) 345-357

20. Kalfoglou, Y., Schorlemmer, M.: Ontology Mapping: the State of the Art. Knowledge Engineering Review 18 1 (2003) 1-31

21. Kang, S.H., Lau, S.K.: Ontology Revision Using the Concept of Belief Revision. In Proceedings of the 8th International Conference on Knowledge-Based Intelligent Information and Engineering Systems, part III (2004) 8-15

22. Katsuno, H., Mendelzon, A.O.: On the Difference Between Updating a Knowledge Base and Revising It. Technical Report on Knowledge Representation and Reasoning, University of Toronto, Canada, KRR-TR-90-6 (1990)

23. Klein, M., Fensel, D.: Ontology Versioning on the Semantic Web. In Proceedings of the International Semantic Web Working Symposium (2001) 75-91

24. Klein, M., Noy, N.F.: A Component-Based Framework for Ontology Evolution. In Proceedings of the IJCAI-03 Workshop on Ontologies and Distributed Systems, CEUR-WS, 71 (2003)

25. Lee, K., Meyer, T.: A Classification of Ontology Modification. In Proceedings of the 17th Australian Joint Conference on Artificial Intelligence (2004) 248-258

26. Makinson, D.: How to Give It Up: A Survey of Some Formal Aspects of the Logic of Theory Change. Synthese 62 (1985) 347-363

27. McGuiness, D., Fikes, R., Rice, J., Wilder, S.: An Environment for Merging and Testing Large Ontologies. In Proceedings of the 7th International Conference on Principles of Knowledge Representation and Reasoning (2000)

28. Meyer, T., Lee, K., Booth, R.: Knowledge Integration for Description Logics. In Proceedings of the 7th International Symposium on Logical Formalizations of Commonsense Reasoning (2005)

29. Noy, N.F., Klein, M.: Ontology Evolution: Not the Same as Schema Evolution. Knowledge and Information Systems 6 4 (2004) 428-440

30. Stojanovic, L., Maedche, A., Motik, B., Stojanovic, N.: User-driven Ontology Evolution Management. In Proceedings of the 13th International Conference on Knowledge Engineering and Knowledge Management (2002)

31. Stojanovic, L., Maedche, A., Stojanovic, N., Studer, R.: Ontology Evolution as Reconfiguration-Design Problem Solving. In Proceedings of the 2nd International Conference on Knowledge Capture (2003) 162-171

32. Stuckenschmidt, H., Klein, M.: Integrity and Change in Modular Ontologies. In Proceedings of the 18th International Joint Conference on Artificial Intelligence (2003)

A Formal Comparison
of Visual Web Wrapper Generators*

Georg Gottlob[1] and Christoph Koch[2]

[1] Database and Artificial Intelligence Group,
Technische Universität Wien,
A-1040 Vienna, Austria
gottlob@dbai.tuwien.ac.at
[2] Lehrstuhl für Informationssysteme,
Universität des Saarlandes,
D-66123 Saarbrücken, Germany
koch@infosys.uni-sb.de

Abstract. We study the core fragment of the Elog wrapping language used in the Lixto system (a visual wrapper generator) and formally compare Elog to other wrapping languages proposed in the literature.

1 Introduction

Querying semi-structured data is relevant in two important contexts – first, where information is to be retrieved from XML databases and documents, and second, where information is to be extracted from Web documents formatted in HTML or in similar display-oriented languages. At TU Wien, much work has been dedicated to both aspects of querying semi-structured data in the recent years. We have recognized that many query and extraction tasks are inherently monadic [17] and have, in particular, studied monadic datalog over trees [18], proving among other things that this language has the same expressive power as monadic second order logic, while its combined complexity is much lower (size of the query times size of the database). It was shown that Core XPath, the "clean logical kernel" of the well-known XPath language has the same low complexity as monadic datalog by translating Core XPath in linear time into a version of monadic datalog [17], and fast evaluation algorithms were developed both for Core XPath and for the full XPath 1.0 language [19]. An in-depth study

---

* This is the second part of the long version of work first presented in the extended abstract [16], which appeared in *Proc. 21st ACM SIGMOD-SIGACT-SIGART Symposium on Principles of Database Systems (PODSSemi-structured data 2002)*, Madison, Wisconsin, ACM Press, New York, USA, pp. 17 – 28. The first part [18] studies the expressive power of monadic datalog over trees and establishes the connection to the monadic fragment of the visual wrapper language Elog. The topic of the present second part – this paper – is to study and compare Elog to other practical visual wrapper languages. This research was supported by the Austrian Science Fund (FWF) under project No. I47-N04 Query Induction for Visual Web Data Extraction.

of the complexity of XPath showed that while Core XPath is PTIME-complete (combined complexity), and thus inherently sequential, very large fragments of XPath can actually be evaluated in parallel and reside in the low complexity class LOGCFL [20]. In [18], which is the basis for the present paper, it was shown that monadic datalog appears to be the right formalism for capturing the essence of Web information extraction (web wrapping) with dedicated tools such as the Lixto visual wrapper generator [8]. The present paper continues and refines this work.

The problem of extracting structured information from HTML documents, i.e. the *Web wrapping problem*, and has been intensely studied over the past years due to its significant practical relevance. This research including theoretical research (e.g., [5]) as well as systems. Previous work can be classified into two categories, depending on whether the HTML input is regarded as a sequential character string (e.g., TSIMMIS [28], Editor [5], FLORID [25], and DE-ByE [21]) or a pre-parsed document tree (for instance, W4F [29], XWrap [23], and Lixto [8], [7], [24], [18]).

The practical perspective of tree-based wrapping must be emphasized [18]. Robust wrappers are *easier to program* using a wrapper programming language that models documents as pre-parsed document trees rather than as text strings. A second candidate for a substantial productivity leap, which in practice requires the first (tree-based representation of the source documents) as a prerequisite, is the *visual specification* of wrappers. By visual wrapper specification, we ideally mean the process of interactively defining a wrapper from one (or few) example document(s) using mainly "mouse clicks", supported by a strong and intuitive design metaphor. During this visual process, the wrapper program should be automatically generated and should not actually require the human designer to use or even know the wrapper programming language. Visual wrapping is now a reality supported by several implemented systems [23], [29], [7], however with varying thoroughness.

One may thus want to look for a wrapping language over document trees that (i) has a solid and well understood theoretical foundation, (ii) provides a good trade-off between complexity and the number of practical wrappers that can be expressed, (iii) is easy to use as a wrapper programming language, and (iv) is suitable for being incorporated into visual tools, since ideally all constructs of a wrapping language can be realized through corresponding visual primitives.

The core notion that we base our wrapping approach on is that of an *information extraction function*, which takes a labeled unranked tree (representing a Web document) and returns a subset of its nodes. In the context of the present paper, a wrapper is a program which implements one or several such functions, and thereby assigns unary predicates to document tree nodes. Based on these predicate assignments and the structure of the input tree, a new tree can be computed as the result of the information extraction process in a natural way, along the lines of the input tree but using the new labels and omitting nodes that have not been relabeled.

That way, we can take a tree, re-label its nodes, and declare some of them as irrelevant, but we cannot significantly transform its original structure. This coincides with the intuition that a wrapper may change the presentation of relevant information, its packaging or data model (which does not apply in the case of *Web wrapping*), but does not handle substantial data transformation tasks. We believe that this captures exactly the essence of wrapping.

In [18], we proposed unary queries in monadic second-order logic (MSO) over unranked trees as an expressiveness yardstick for information extraction functions. MSO over trees is well-understood theory-wise [30], [13], [12], [15] (see also [31], [32]) and quite expressive.

We studied monadic datalog and showed that it is equivalent to MSO in its ability to express unary queries for tree nodes (in ranked as well as unranked trees). We also characterized the evaluation complexity of our language. We showed that monadic datalog can be evaluated in linear time both in the size of the data and the query, given that tree structures are appropriately represented. Interestingly, judging from our experience with the Lixto system, real-world wrappers written in monadic datalog are small. Thus, in practice, we do not trade the lowered query complexity compared to MSO for considerably expanded program sizes.

Monadic datalog over labeled trees is a very simple programming language and much better suited as a wrapping language than MSO. Consequently, monadic datalog satisfies the first three of our requirements.

Moreover, in [18] we presented a simple but practical Web wrapping language equivalent to MSO, which we call Elog$^-$. Elog$^-$ is a simplified version of the core wrapping language of the Lixto system, Elog ("**E**xtraction by data**log**"), and can be obtained by slightly restricting the syntax of monadic datalog. Programs of this language (even *recursive* ones) can be completely visually specified, without requiring the wrapper implementor to deal with Elog$^-$ programs directly or to know datalog. We also give a brief overview of this visual specification process. Thus, Elog$^-$ satisfies all of our four desiderata for tree-based wrapping languages.

The work [18] was – to the best of our knowledge – the first to provide a theoretical study of an advanced tree-based wrapping tool and language used in an implemented system.

The present paper extends the results of [18] by the following contributions.

- The capability of producing a hierarchically structured result is essential to tree wrapping. We define the language Elog$_2^*$ in order to be able to make the creation of complex nested structures explicit. Elog$_2^*$ is basically obtained by enhancing Elog$^-$ with binary predicates in a restricted form, which allow to represent hierarchical dependencies between selected nodes in the fixpoint computation of an Elog$^-$ program. Elog$_2^*$ is an actual fragment of the wrapping language Elog used internally in the Lixto system [7], a commercial visual wrapper generator.
- We take a closer look at two other tree-based approaches to wrapping HTML documents. The first is the language of regular path queries (e.g., [1], [2]) with nesting. Regular path queries are considered essential to Web query

languages [1], and by extending the language of regular path queries by capabilities for producing nested output (and for restricting queries by additional conditions), one obtains a useful wrapping language. We show that this formalism is strictly less expressive than Elog_2^*.

- The second formalism that we compare to Elog_2^* is HEL [29], the wrapping language of the commercially available W4F framework, which is the only tree-based wrapping formalism besides Elog of which a formal specification has been published. Again, we are able to show that HEL is strictly less expressive than Elog_2^*.

The structure of the paper follows this list of contributions.

2 Preliminaries

We give a brief background and language definitions and refer to [18] for further material and examples.

2.1 Trees and Regular Languages

Throughout this paper, only *finite* trees will be considered. Trees are defined in the normal way and have at least one node. We assume that the children of each node are in some fixed order. Each node has a label taken from a finite nonempty set of symbols Σ, the alphabet. We consider both ranked and unranked trees. Ranked trees have a ranked alphabet, i.e., each symbol in Σ has some fixed arity or rank $k \leq K$ (and K is the maximum rank in Σ, i.e. a constant integer). We may partition Σ into sets $\Sigma_0, \ldots, \Sigma_K$ of symbols of equal rank. A node with a label $a \in \Sigma_k$ (i.e., of rank k) has exactly k children. Nodes with labels of rank 0 are called leaves. Each ranked tree can be considered as a relational structure

$$t_{rk} = \langle \text{dom, root, leaf, } (\text{child}_k)_{k \leq K}, (\text{label}_a)_{a \in \Sigma} \rangle.$$

In an unranked tree, each node may have an arbitrary number of children. An unranked ordered tree can be considered as a structure

$$t_{ur} = \langle \text{dom, root, leaf, } (\text{label}_a)_{a \in \Sigma}, \text{ firstchild, nextsibling, lastsibling} \rangle$$

where "dom" is the set of nodes in the tree, "root", "leaf", "lastsibling", and the "label$_a$" relations are unary, and "firstchild", "nextsibling", and the "child$_k$" relations are binary. All relations are defined according to their intuitive meanings. "root" contains exactly one node, the root node. "leaf" consists of the set of all leaves. child$_k$ denotes the k-th direct child relation in a ranked tree. In unranked trees, "firstchild(n_1, n_2)" is true iff n_2 is the leftmost child of n_1; "nextsibling(n_1, n_2)" is true iff, for some i, n_1 and n_2 are the i-th and $(i+1)$-th children of a common parent node, respectively, counting from the left. label$_a(n)$ is true iff n is labeled a in the tree. Finally, "lastsibling" contains the set of rightmost children of nodes. (The root node is not a last sibling, as it has no parent.)

Whenever the structure t may not be clear from the context, we state it as a subscript of the relation names (as e.g. in dom_t, root_t, ...).

By default, we will always assume ranked and unranked trees to be represented using the schemata outlined above, and will refer to them as τ_{rk} (for ranked trees) and τ_{ur} (for unranked trees), respectively.

The *regular tree languages* (for ranked as well as for unranked alphabets) are precisely those tree languages recognizable by a number of natural forms of finite automata [9]. A tree language is regular iff it is definable in MSO [30], [13], [27].

A *regular path expression* (cf. [2]) over a set of binary relations Γ is a regular expression (using concatenation ".", the Kleene star "*", and disjunction "|") over alphabet Γ. *Caterpillar expressions* (cf. [10]) furthermore support inversion (i.e. expressions of the form E^{-1}, where E is a caterpillar expression)[1] and unary relations in Γ (cf. [18]).

2.2   Monadic Datalog and Elog⁻

We assume the syntax and semantics of datalog known (cf. [33, 11]). *Monadic datalog* is obtained from full datalog by requiring all intensional predicates to be unary. By unary query, for monadic datalog as for MSO, we denote a function that assigns a predicate to some elements of dom (or, in other words, selects a subset of dom). For monadic datalog, one obtains a unary query by distinguishing one intensional predicate as the *query predicate*. In the remainder of this paper, when talking about a monadic datalog query, we will always refer to a unary query specified as a monadic datalog program with a distinguished query predicate.

Theorem 1 ([18]). *Over τ_{rk} as well as τ_{ur}, monadic datalog has $O(|\mathcal{P}| * |dom|)$ combined complexity (where $|\mathcal{P}|$ is the size of the program and $|dom|$ the size of the tree). A query is definable in unary MSO over τ_{rk} (resp., τ_{ur}) if and only if it is definable in monadic datalog over τ_{rk} (resp., τ_{ur}).*

Definition 1. Let Σ be an alphabet not containing "_". For strings $\pi \in (\Sigma \cup \_)^*$, the predicate subelem_π is defined inductively as follows:

$$\text{subelem}_\epsilon(x, y) := x = y.$$
$$\text{subelem}_{\_.\pi}(x, y) := \text{child}(x, z),\ \text{subelem}_\pi(z, y).$$
$$\text{subelem}_{a.\pi}(x, y) := \text{child}(x, z),\ \text{label}_a(z),\ \text{subelem}_\pi(z, y). \qquad \square$$

Subsequently, we refer to monadic intensional predicates as *pattern predicates* or just *patterns*. Patterns are a useful metaphor for the building blocks of wrappers.

Definition 2. Let $\Pi = (\Sigma \cup \{\_\})^*$ denote our language of fixed paths. The language Elog⁻ is a fragment of monadic datalog over

⟨root, leaf, firstsibling, nextsibling, lastsibling, $(\text{subelem}_\pi)_{\pi \in \Pi}$, $(\text{contains}_\pi)_{\pi \in \Pi}$⟩

---

[1] In [10] the inverse is only supported on atomic expressions, i.e. relations from Γ. We do not assume this restriction, but this is an inessential difference.

where "root", "leaf", "nextsibling", and "lastsibling" are as in τ_{ur}, "firstsibling" has the intuitive meaning symmetric to "lastsibling", "subelem$_\pi$" was defined in Definition 1, "contains$_\pi$" is equivalent to "subelem$_\pi$", except that ϵ-paths must not be used, "leaf", "firstsibling", "nextsibling", "lastsibling", and "contains" are called *condition predicates*, and rules are restricted to the form

$$p(x) \leftarrow p_0(x_0), \text{ subelem}_\pi(x_0, x), \ C, \ R.$$

such that p is a pattern predicate, p_0 – the so-called *parent pattern* – is either a pattern predicate or "root", R (*pattern references*) is a possibly empty set of atoms over pattern predicates, and C is a possibly empty set of atoms over condition predicates. Moreover, the query graph of each rule must be connected.

We may write rules of the form $p(x) \leftarrow p_0(x_0), \text{ subelem}_\epsilon(x_0, x), \ C, \ R.$ equivalently as $p(x) \leftarrow p_0(x), \ C, \ R.$ and call such rules *specialization rules*. $\square$

Proposition 1 ([18]). *An Elog$^-$ program $\mathcal{P}$ can be evaluated on a tree t in time $O(|\mathcal{P}| * |dom_t|)$. A set of information extraction functions is definable in monadic datalog over τ_{ur} iff it is definable in Elog$^-$.*

3   Binary Pattern Predicates and Paths with the Kleene Star and Ranges: Elog$_2^*$

In this section, we step out of our framework of unary information extraction functions. We enhance Elog$^-$ by a *limited* form of binary pattern predicates, which allow to explicitly represent the parent-child relationship of the tree computed as a result of the wrapping process, but not more than that. This approach to wrapping is basically a mild generalization of our wrapping framework based on unary information extraction functions. The syntax of the full Elog language employs binary pattern predicates in precisely the same way as shown below. The subtle increase in expressive power will be needed in Section 4 when we compare Elog with other practical wrapping languages. A further feature that we will need in Section 4 will be a way of specifying a path using a regular expression with the Kleene star and a "range". We will call the new language obtained Elog$_2^*$.

We mildly generalize the predicate subelem$_\pi$ of Definition def:subelem to support arbitrary regular expressions π over Σ (notably, including the Kleene star). Again, subelem$_\pi(v_0, v)$ is true if node v is reachable from v_0 through a downward path labeled with a word of the regular language defined by π.

A range ρ defines, given an integer k, a function that maps each $1 \le i \le k$ to either 0 or 1. Given a word $w = w_1 \cdots w_k$, ρ selects those w_i that are mapped to 1. A range applies to a set of nodes S (written as $S[\rho]$) as follows. Let $v_1 \cdots v_k$ be the sequence of nodes in S arranged in document order. Then, $S[\rho]$ is the set of precisely those nodes v_i for which i is mapped to 1.

Definition 3. Let π be a regular expression over Σ and let ρ be a regular expression in the normal form of Proposition 4.13 in [18] which defines a regular word language of density one over the alphabet $\{0, 1\}$. The binary relation $\text{subelem}_{\pi,\rho}$ is defined as the set of all pairs of nodes $\langle v, v' \rangle$ such that $v' \in S[\rho]$, where S is the set of all nodes v_0 with $\text{subelem}_\pi(v, v_0)$. $\qquad\square$

The normal form of Proposition 4.13 in [18] is a convenient syntax for specifying regular word languages of density one, which in turn allow to elegantly assign a unique word over alphabet $\{0, 1\}$ to a sequence of known length. Note, however, that throughout the remainder of the paper, in all languages that we will discuss, only much weaker forms of ranges will be required that can always be easily encoded as regular expressions of this normal form. For example, a range of the form "i-th to j-th node" (where i and j are constant) can be specified by a regular expression

$$0^{j-1}.1^{j-i+1}.0^*.$$

Lemma 1. *The predicate $\text{subelem}_{\pi,\rho}$ is definable in MSO over τ_{ur}.*

Proof. From the proof of Lemma 5.9 in [18], it is obvious how to define a monadic datalog program $\mathcal{P}_\pi$ which defines a predicate S for the set of all nodes reachable from a node x distinguished by a special predicate. From this we obtain an MSO formula $\varphi_\pi(x, S)$ with the obvious meaning using Proposition 3.3 in [18].

Let ρ be the range definition, as a regular expression over the alphabet $\{0, 1\}$ in the normal form of Proposition 4.13 in [18]. We define an MSO formula $\varphi_\rho(S, Y)$ which is true if there is a word w of length $|S|$ in the language $L(\rho)$ and Y is the set of nodes in S that, when traversed in document order, are at a position which is occupied by a "1" in w.

Let $\mathcal{P}_\rho$ be the program shown in the construction for down transitions of the proof of Theorem 4.14 in [18], with a few modifications. Rather than on a list of siblings, we try to match ρ with the set S put into document order. Thus, we have to replace occurrences of "firstchild" and "nextsibling" with analogous relations for navigating the document order $\prec$. For example, an atom $\text{nextsibling}(x, y)$ is replaced by $\psi_\prec(x, y)$ (using an input relation S), where $\psi_\prec$ is defined in MSO as

$$\psi_\prec(x, y, S) := S(x) \wedge S(y) \wedge x \prec y \wedge (\nexists z)\, S(z) \wedge x \prec z \wedge z \prec y.$$

That the document-order relation $\prec$ itself is MSO-definable is clear from its definition as a caterpillar expression in Example 2.5 in [18], from Lemma 5.9 in [18], and Proposition 3.3 in [18].

In the down-transition construction from the proof of Theorem 4.14 in [18], the goal is to assign (state assignment) predicates that are actually the symbols of the regular language to be matched. In the same way, the unary query that we are interested in is the predicate "1" defined by program $\mathcal{P}_\rho$. The formula φ_ρ such that, given set S, $\varphi_\rho(S, Y)$ is true iff Y is the set of all nodes assigned "1" by $\mathcal{P}_\rho$ is obtained from $\mathcal{P}_\rho$ as described in the proof of Proposition 3.3 in [18].

Now, it is easy to see that

$$\text{subelem}_{\pi,\rho}(x, y) := (\forall S)(\forall Y)\, \big(\varphi_\pi(x, S) \wedge \varphi_\rho(S, Y)\big) \to y \in Y$$

indeed defines the desired relation. $\qquad\square$

Remark 1. The previous proof makes it easy to extend the formalism to support also the matching of the range backward (using the reverse document order relation $\succ$ rather than $\prec$), and in particular selecting only the last element matching path π (using the range 1.0^* and reverse document order).   □

Now we are in the position to define the language Elog_2^*.

Definition 4. Let Elog_2^* be obtained by changing the Elog^- language as follows. All pattern predicates are now binary and all rules are of the form

$$p(x_0, x) \leftarrow p_0(\_, x_0), \text{subelem}_{\pi,\rho}(x_0, x), C, R.$$

where $\text{subelem}_{\pi,\rho}$ is the predicate of Definition 3, C is again a set of condition atoms as for Elog^- but "contains" is now equivalent to $\text{subelem}_{\pi,\rho}$ (permitting ranges and paths defined by arbitrary regular expressions), and R is a set of pattern atoms of the form $p_i(\_, x_i)$. The underscore is a way of writing a variable not referred to elsewhere in the rule. The predicate "root" is also pro-forma binary and can be substituted as a pattern predicate.[2]   □

The meaning of a binary pattern atom $p(v_0, v)$ is that node v is assigned predicate p and the inference was started from a parent pattern at node v_0. We define *unary queries* in Elog_2^* in the natural way, by projecting away the first argument positions of our binary pattern predicates. For instance, a program $\mathcal{P}$ (containing a head predicate p) defines the unary query $Q_p := \{x \mid (\exists x_0)\ p(x_0, x) \in T_{\mathcal{P}}^\omega\}$ based on p.

Theorem 2. *A unary query is definable in Elog_2^* iff it is definable in MSO.*

Proof. Let $\mathcal{P}$ be an Elog_2^* program and let $\mathcal{P}'$ be the program obtained from $\mathcal{P}$ by adding a rule

$$p'(x) \leftarrow p(x_0, x).$$

for each pattern predicate appearing in $\mathcal{P}$. It is easy to show by induction on the computation of $T_{\mathcal{P}'}^\omega$ that replacing each rule

$$p(x_0, x) \leftarrow p_0(\_, x_0), \text{subelem}_\pi(x_0, x), C, p_1(\_, x_1), \ldots, p_n(\_, x_n).$$

of $\mathcal{P}'$ (where C is a set of condition atoms) by

$$p(x_0, x) \leftarrow p_0'(x_0), \text{subelem}_\pi(x_0, x), C, p_1'(x_1), \ldots, p_n'(x_n).$$

does not change the meaning of the program. But then, if we only want to compute the unary versions of the pattern predicates, we can just as well replace the heads $p(x_0, x)$ by $p'(x)$ as well. This leads to a monadic datalog program over $\tau_{ur} \cup \{\text{subelem}_{\pi,\rho}\}$. The theorem now follows immediately from Lemma 1 and Proposition 3.3 in [18].   □

The rationale of supporting binary pattern predicates in Elog is to explicitly build the edge relation of an output graph during the wrapping process. The obvious unfolding of this directed graph into a tree is what we consider the result of a wrapper run.

---

[2] As in Elog^-, we need "root" as a parent pattern "to start with".

Definition 5. The output language of Elog_2^* is defined as follows. An Elog_2^* program $\mathcal{P}$ defines a function mapping each document t to a node-labeled directed graph

$$G = \langle V = \text{dom}_t, \; E = \{\langle v_1, v_2 \rangle \mid p_i(v_1, v_2) \in \mathcal{T}_{\mathcal{P}}^\omega\}, \; (Q_p)_{p \in P} \rangle$$

where $Q_p = \{v \mid (\exists v') \, p(v', v) \in \mathcal{T}_{\mathcal{P}}^\omega\}$ and P is the set of pattern predicate names occurring in $\mathcal{P}$. □

The edge relation E constitutes a partial order of the nodes. The graph is acyclic except for loops of the form $\langle v, v \rangle \in E$, which are due to specialization rules that produce such loops. In all other rules with a head $p(x, y)$, y matches only nodes strictly below the nodes matched by x in the tree.

Lemma 2. *Each Elog_2^* binary pattern predicate is definable in MSO.*

Proof. Let $\mathcal{P}$ be an Elog_2^* program and r be a rule of $\mathcal{P}$ with head $P(x_0, x)$, undistinguished variables $x_{j_1}, \ldots, x_{j_l}$ (i.e., x_0 and x are precisely the variables of rule r not contained in this list), and a body that consists of the pattern atoms $P_{i_1}(\_, x_{i_1}), \ldots, P_{i_m}(\_, x_{i_m})$ and the set B of remaining atoms.

We use the representation of $\mathcal{P}$ as a monadic program $\mathcal{P}'$ as described in the proof of Theorem 2 to define a formula φ such that $\varphi(w_1, \ldots, w_m)$ is true iff there exist nodes $v_1, \ldots, v_m$ such that the atoms $P_{i_1}(v_1, w_1), \ldots, P_{i_m}(v_m, w_m)$ evaluate to true on the input tree. Let

$$\varphi(x_{i_1}, \ldots, x_{i_m}) := (\forall P_1) \cdots (\forall P_n) \, SAT(P_1, \ldots, P_n) \rightarrow \big(P_{i_1}(x_{i_1}) \wedge \cdots \wedge P_{i_m}(x_{i_m})\big)$$

where SAT is obtained from $\mathcal{P}'$ as shown in the proof of Proposition 3.3 in [18]. Clearly,

$$P_r(x_0, x) := (\exists x_{j_1}) \cdots (\exists x_{j_l}) \, \varphi(x_{i_1}, \ldots, x_{i_m}) \wedge B$$

is equivalent to the relation defined by the single rule r in $\mathcal{P}$.

Now let $\mathcal{P}_P \subseteq \mathcal{P}$ be the set of rules in the input program whose head predicate is P. The formula

$$P(x_0, x) := \bigvee_{r \in \mathcal{P}_P} P_r(x_0, x)$$

defines the desired relation of pattern predicate P. □

Theorem 3. *The relations of G are MSO-definable.*

Proof. Let $\mathcal{P}$ be an Elog_2^* program. The edge relation E is simply the union of the relations defined by each of the pattern predicates in $\mathcal{P}$, i.e. a disjunction of their MSO formulae that we have constructed in the proof of Lemma 2. The MSO-definability of the Q_p relations was shown in Theorem 2. □

We have seen that Elog^- has linear-time data complexity (see Theorem 4.1). The fixpoint of an Elog_2^* program (or an Elog program) and equally the edge relation of the output graph, however, can be of quadratic size.

Example 1. Let t be a tree where all leaves are labeled "l", while all other nodes are labeled "b". The single-rule program

$$p(x_0, x) \leftarrow \mathrm{dom}(\_, x_0), \mathrm{subelem}_{\pi = \bar{l}^* l, \rho = *}(x_0, x).$$

evaluates to a fixpoint of quadratic size at worst. For instance, consider a tree with branch nodes $b_1, \ldots, b_m$ and leaf nodes $l_1, \ldots, l_n$ such that b_i is the parent of b_{i+1} (for $1 \leq i < m$) and b_m is the parent of $l_1, \ldots, l_n$. Here, the binary relation defined by p is $\{\langle b_i, l_j \rangle \mid 1 \leq i \leq m, \ 1 \leq j \leq n\}$.   □

Remark 2. Note that in full Elog as currently implemented, a range $[\rho]$ can be put at the end of each rule, such that a rule

$$p(x_0, x) \leftarrow p_0(\_, x_0), \mathrm{subelem}_\pi(x_0, x), C, R \ [\rho].$$

has the meaning that $p(v_0, v)$ is inferred from this rule if $v \in S[\rho]$, where $v' \in S$ iff there is an assignment of the variables in the body of the rule to nodes that renders the body true and x_0 is assigned to v_0 and x to v'.   □

4   Other Wrapping Languages

In this section, we compare the expressiveness of two further wrapping languages, namely regular path queries with nesting and HEL, the wrapping language of the W4F framework [29], to Elog_2^*.

Other previously proposed wrapping languages were evaluated as well. The majority of previous work is string-based (e.g., TSIMMIS [28], EDITOR [5], FLORID [25], DEByE [21], and Stalker [26]) and artificially restricting these languages in some way to work on trees would not be true to their motivation. Thus, we decided not to include them in this discussion. For some other systems (such as XWrap [23], which is essentially tree-based like W4F or Lixto), no formal specifications have been published which can be made subject to expressiveness evaluations.

Web query languages were also evaluated, but some (e.g., WebSQL [4], We-bLOG [22]) are unsuitable for wrapping because they cannot access the structure of Web documents, and others[3] (e.g., WebOQL [3]) are highly expressive query languages that permit data transformations not in the spirit of wrapping.

4.1   Regular Path Queries with Nesting (RPN)

The first language we compare to Elog_2^* is obtained by combining regular path queries [2] with nesting to create complex structures. This new language – which we will call RPN (**R**egular **P**ath queries with **N**esting) – on one hand is simple yet appropriate for defining practical wrappers, and on the other hand serves to prepare some machinery for comparing further wrapping languages later on.

---

[3] For a survey of further Web query languages see [14].

Definition 6. The syntax of *RPN* is defined by the grammar

$$
\begin{array}{ll}
rpn: & patom \text{ '.' } rpn \mid \text{'txt'} \mid \text{'('} \; rpn \text{ '\#'} \cdots \text{'\#'} \; rpn \text{ ')'} \\
patom: & patom_0 \mid patom_0 \; conds \\
patom_0: & path \mid path \text{ '['} \; range \text{ ']'} \\
range: & range_0 \text{ ';'} \cdots \text{';'} \; range_0 \\
conds: & \text{'\{'} \; cond \text{ 'and'} \cdots \text{'and'} \; cond \text{ '\}'} \\
cond: & patom \text{ '.' } cond \mid \text{'txt'} \text{ '='} \; string
\end{array}
$$

where *rpn* is the start production, a "$range_0$" is either '*', i, or $i - j$ (where i and j are integers), "path" denotes the regular expressions over HTML tag names, and "string" the set of strings.   □

Example 2 below shows an RPN wrapper in this syntax.

Definition 7 ((Denotational semantics of RPN)). Let π denote a path, ρ a range, s a string, and v, v' tree nodes. Without loss of generality, we assume that every *patom* has a range[4]. The semantics function $\mathbb{E}$ maps, given a tree, each pair of an RPN statement W and a node to a complex object as follows:

$$
\mathbb{E}[\![\pi[\rho]\{Y_1 \text{ and } \ldots \text{ and } Y_n\}.X]\!]v := \bigcup \{\mathbb{E}[\![X]\!]v' \mid \mathrm{subelem}_{\pi,\rho}(v, v') \text{ is true} \wedge
$$
$$
\mathbb{C}[\![Y_1]\!]v' \wedge \cdots \wedge \mathbb{C}[\![Y_n]\!]v'\}
$$
$$
\mathbb{E}[\![X_1\# \ldots \#X_n]\!]v := \{\langle \mathbb{E}[\![X_1]\!]v, \; \ldots, \; \mathbb{E}[\![X_n]\!]v \rangle\}
$$
$$
\mathbb{E}[\![\mathrm{txt}]\!]v := \{v.\mathrm{txt}\}
$$

Here, $v.\mathrm{txt}$ denotes the string value of a node, the concatenation of all text below node v in the input document. Above we assume that both a range description ρ and n conditions are present in a *patom*, but it is clear how to handle the cases where either one or both are missing.

This definition makes use of the semantics function

$$
\mathbb{C} : L(cond) \to \mathrm{dom} \to Boolean
$$

for RPN conditions, which we define as follows.

$$
\mathbb{C}[\![\pi[\rho]\{Y_1 \text{ and } \ldots \text{ and } Y_n\}.X]\!]v := (\exists v') \, \mathrm{subelem}_{\pi,\rho}(v, v') \text{ is true} \wedge
$$
$$
\mathbb{C}[\![Y_1]\!] \wedge \cdots \wedge \mathbb{C}[\![Y_n]\!] \wedge \mathbb{C}[\![X]\!]
$$
$$
\mathbb{C}[\![\mathrm{txt} = s]\!]v := \textbf{if } v.\mathrm{txt} = s \textbf{ then } true \textbf{ else } false
$$

Given a tree t, an RPN statement X evaluates to $\mathbb{E}[\![X]\!]root_t$.   □

RPN statements can be strongly typed. It is easy the verify that an RPN statement W evaluates to a complex object of type $\mathbb{T}[\![W]\!]$ on all trees, where

$$
\mathbb{T}[\![patom \; X]\!] := \mathbb{T}[\![X]\!]
$$
$$
\mathbb{T}[\![(X_1\# \ldots \#X_n)]\!] := \{\langle \mathbb{T}[\![X_1]\!], \ldots, \mathbb{T}[\![X_n]\!] \rangle\}
$$
$$
\mathbb{T}[\![.\mathrm{txt}]\!] := \{String\}
$$

for *rpn* statements $X, X_1, \ldots, X_n$.

---

[4] We can always add a range [*] to a *patom* without a range without changing the semantics.

Example 2. The RPN statement

$$\text{html.body.table.tr}\{\text{td}[0].\text{txt} = \text{``item''}\}.\text{td}[1].\text{txt}$$

selects the second entries ("td[1]") of table rows ("table.tr") whose first entries have text value "item". The type of this statement is

$$\mathbb{T}[\![\text{html.body.table.tr}\{\text{td}[0].\text{txt} = \text{``item''}\}.\text{td}[1].\text{txt}]\!] = \{String\}$$

Note in particular that the type is not $\{\{String\}\}$, even though there are two patoms not counting the condition! □

Remark 3. Note that the semantics of paths and conditions in RPN is similar to the semantics of a fragment obtained from XPath [34] by prohibiting most of its function library (and therefore its arithmetic and string manipulation features). The simple RPN wrapper of Example 2 is basically equivalent to the XPath query

$$/\text{html}/\text{body}/\text{table}/\text{tr}[\text{td}[1] = \text{''item''}]/\text{td}[2].$$

A path of the form $\cdots //a/ \cdots$ in XPath corresponds to $\cdots \_{}^{*}.a.\cdots$ in RPN.

The main difference is that while XPath selects nodes of the input tree, RPN extracts text below nodes rather than selecting the nodes themselves. Another significant difference between XPath and RPN is that RPN statements may create complex objects (using the nesting construct) that cannot be built in XPath. □

Next, we will show that each wrapper expressible in RPN is also expressible in Elog_2^*. Clearly, there is a mismatch between the forms of output Elog_2^* and RPN produce which needs to be discussed first. The former language produces trees while the latter produces complex objects containing records.

In the following, we will require Elog_2^* programs to be of a special form that allows for a canonical mapping from the binary atoms computed by an Elog_2^* program to a complex object.

Given an RPN statement W, each predicate must be uniquely associated to one set or record entry subterm of the type term $\mathbb{T}[\![W]\!]$.

- For a predicate p that is associated to a distinguished set of $\mathbb{T}[\![W]\!]$, an atom $p(v, w)$ asserts that node w is in a set of the output object uniquely identified by p and v.
- For a predicate p that is associated to a distinguished (set-typed) record entry of $\mathbb{T}[\![W]\!]$, an atom $p(v, w)$ asserts that w is an element of a record entry in the output object uniquely identified by p and v.

By ordering predicates[5] defining the entries of an RPN record appropriately and mapping two nodes w_1, w_2 such that there is a node v and two edges

---

[5] Note that in the reference implementation of Elog (the Lixto system [7], [8]), an ordering of pattern predicates can be defined such that edges of the tree unfolding of the output graph with a common parent node are ordered by their predicate (rather than by document order).

$\langle v, w_1 \rangle, \langle v, w_2 \rangle$ labeled with the same predicate into a common set, we obtain the desired mapping to the complex object model of RPN.

It can be easily argued that the distinction between the complex object model of RPN and the output of an Elog_2^* program that satisfies the above-designed semantics is only cosmetical, indeed that what we produce is a canonical representation of a complex object data model by binary atoms.

RPN also produces string values, while we have not discussed the form in which a tree node is output in Elog so far. We assume that the output of Elog for a node is the concatenation of all text below the node in the document tree. We also assume that text strings are accessible in the document tree (say, string "text" is represented as path-shaped subtree $t \to e \to x \to t \to \perp$) and can be checked using the predicate $\mathrm{contains}_{\pi,\rho}$. (For instance, we can check whether a node x has string value "text" using $\mathrm{contains}_{t.e.x.t.\perp,1^*}(x, y)$, where y is a dummy variable.)

Theorem 4. *For each wrapper expressible in RPN, there is an equivalent wrapper in Elog_2^*.*

Proof. Ranges in RPN are regular and can be encoded using the $\mathrm{subelem}_{\pi,\rho}$ and $\mathrm{contains}_{\pi,\rho}$ predicates. Clearly, each RPN range can be easily encoded as an Elog_2^* range. Without loss of generality, let W be an RPN statement in which every *patom* has a range. We create the Elog_2^* program $\mathcal{P} := \mathcal{P}_{\mathbb{E}}[\![W]\!](\mathrm{root})$ using the function $\mathcal{P}_{\mathbb{E}}$ which maps each pair of an RPN statement and a "context" predicate to an Elog_2^* program, and which is defined as follows.

$$\mathcal{P}_{\mathbb{E}}[\![\pi[\rho]\{X_1 \text{ and } \ldots \text{ and } X_n\}.Y]\!](p_0) :=$$
$$\{ \, p'(x_0, x) \leftarrow p(\_, x_0), \mathrm{subelem}_{\pi,\rho}(x_0, x), r_1(\_, x), \ldots, r_n(\_, x). \, \} \cup$$
$$\mathcal{P}_{\mathbb{C}}[\![X_1]\!](r_1) \cup \cdots \cup \mathcal{P}_{\mathbb{C}}[\![X_n]\!](r_n) \cup \mathcal{P}_{\mathbb{E}}[\![Y]\!](p'),$$

$$\mathcal{P}_{\mathbb{E}}[\![(X_1 \# \ldots \# X_n)]\!](p) := \mathcal{P}_{\mathbb{E}}[\![X_1]\!](p) \cup \cdots \cup \mathcal{P}_{\mathbb{E}}[\![X_n]\!](p),$$
$$\mathcal{P}_{\mathbb{E}}[\![\mathrm{txt}]\!](p) := \emptyset,$$

where $X_1, \ldots, X_n, Y$ are RPN statements, $n \geq 0$, π is a path, ρ is a range, and $p', r_1, \ldots, r_n$ are new predicates.

As an auxiliary function for conditions, we have $\mathcal{P}_{\mathbb{C}}$, defined as

$$\mathcal{P}_{\mathbb{C}}[\![\pi[\rho]\{X_1 \text{ and } \ldots \text{ and } X_n\}.Y]\!](p) :=$$
$$\{ \, p(x_0, x) \leftarrow \mathrm{dom}(x_0, x), \mathrm{contains}_{\pi,\rho}(x, y), r_1(\_, y), \ldots, r_n(\_, y), s(\_, y). \, \} \cup$$
$$\mathcal{P}_{\mathbb{C}}[\![X_1]\!](r_1) \cup \cdots \cup \mathcal{P}_{\mathbb{C}}[\![X_n]\!](r_n) \cup \mathcal{P}_{\mathbb{C}}[\![Y]\!](s)$$

$$\mathcal{P}_{\mathbb{C}}[\![\mathrm{txt} = s]\!](p) := \{ \, p(x_0, x) \leftarrow \mathrm{dom}(x_0, x), \mathrm{contains}_s(x, y). \, \}$$

where s is a string.

A number of predicates generated in this way may correspond to patoms that are followed by further patoms in the RPN statement W and for which no corresponding set exists in $\mathcal{T}[\![W]\!]$ (see Example 2).

The reference implementation of Elog, Lixto, allows to define pattern predicates of a given Elog program as auxiliary. Atoms $p(v_0, v)$ of such predicates are then removed from the result of a wrapper run such that if atom $p'(v, w)$ has also been inferred, we add $p'(v_0, w)$ (closing the "gap" produced by dropping the auxiliary predicate).

It is easy to see that the described mapping produces an Elog_2^* program that, when auxiliary predicates are eliminated in this way, maps to canonically to RPN complex objects.   □

Theorem 5. *There is an Elog_2^* wrapper for which no equivalent RPN wrapper exists.*

Proof. For trees of depth one, all RPN queries are first-order. We therefore cannot check whether, say, the root node has an even number of children, which we can do in MSO and thus, by Theorem 2, in Elog_2^*.   □

4.2   HTML Extraction Language (HEL)

In this section, we compare the expressive power of the HTML Extraction Language (HEL) of the World Wide Web Wrapper Factory (W4F) with the expressiveness of Elog_2^*. For an introduction to and a formal specification of HEL see [29].

Defining the semantics of HEL is a tedious task. (The denotational semantics provided in [29] takes nearly nine pages and does not yet cover all features!) Here, we proceed in three stages to cover HEL reasonably well. We will define a fragment of HEL called HEL$^-$ which drops a number of marginal features and introduce a slightly simplified version of it, HEL_{vf}^-, which does not use HEL's *index variables*. HEL_{vf}^- has the desirable property that the semantics of HEL$^-$ and HEL_{vf}^- entail a one-to-one relationship between wrappers in the two languages [6]. This variable-free syntax is possible because of the very special and restricted way in which index variables may be used in HEL. For simplicity, we first introduce HEL_{vf}^- and subsequently HEL$^-$. Finally, we discuss the remaining features of HEL.

Let RPN$^-$ be the fragment of RPN obtained by requiring that all *patoms* are restricted to the form t or $\_^*.t$ (we will write the latter as $\rightarrow t$), where t is a tag, and conditions may not be nested inside conditions.

The language HEL_{vf}^- (that is, variable-free HEL$^-$) differs from RPN$^-$ semantically in that ranges apply only to those nodes for which all given conditions hold (i.e., intuitively, conditions are evaluated "first").

Let π be either $.t$ or $\rightarrow t$ (where t is a tag), and let $\pi_1 \ldots \pi_m$ be paths without conditions. We denote the HEL_{vf}^- semantics function $\mathbb{H}$ (with ranges) by

$$\mathbb{H}[\![\pi[\rho]\{\pi_1.txt = s_1 \wedge \cdots \wedge \pi_m.txt = s_m\}.X]\!]v :=$$
$$\{\mathbb{H}[\![X]\!]w \mid w \in R_\rho(\mathbb{E}[\![\pi\{\pi_1.txt = s_1 \wedge \cdots \wedge \pi_m.txt = s_m\}]\!]v)\}$$

where $\mathbb{E}$ is the RPN semantics function and $R_\rho(V)$ denotes the set of nodes of V matching the range w.r.t. document order, e.g. for range i

$$R_i(V) := \{y_i \mid (\exists y_0)\cdots(\exists y_{i-1})\ \ y_0,\ldots,y_i \in V \wedge \neg\exists y_{-1} \in V : y_{-1} \prec y_0 \wedge$$
$$\bigwedge_{0 \le k < i}(y_k \prec y_{k+1} \wedge \neg\exists y' \in V : y_k \prec y' \prec y_{k+1})\}.$$

This selects the $i+1$-th node of V. (In HEL, the index of the first node is 0.)

On the remaining forms of HEL^-_{vf} statements $(X_1 \# \ldots \# X_n)$ and txt, $\mathbb{H}$ is defined analogously to $\mathbb{E}$.

Theorem 6. *(1) For each wrapper expressible in the HEL^-_{vf} language, there is an equivalent wrapper in Elog. (2) There is an Elog^*_2 wrapper for which no equivalent HEL^-_{vf} wrapper exists.*

Proof. (1) can be shown using essentially the same proof as that of Theorem 4, with the difference that we use a feature of Elog (see e.g. [8]) that allows to put ranges on the nodes over which the variable x ranges (relative to x_0) and replace rules

$$p'(x_0,x) \leftarrow p(\_,x_0),\ \text{subelem}_{\pi,\rho}(x_0,x),\ r_1(\_,x),\ \ldots,\ r_n(\_,x).$$

by

$$p'(x_0,x) \leftarrow p(\_,x_0),\ \text{subelem}_\pi(x_0,x),\ r_1(\_,x),\ \ldots,\ r_n(\_,x)\ [\rho].$$

(2) can be justified by the same argument used previously for showing Theorem 5.
□

Next we discuss the HEL^- language, a proper fragment of HEL. The syntax of HEL^- is considerably different from that of HEL^-_{vf}, using a form of index variables in ranges and a special "where" block at the end of a wrapper statement that collects all of the conditions, similar to database query languages such as SQL. To give a better overview of the language, we provide its full syntax.

Definition 8. The syntax of the language HEL^- is defined by the following grammar.

HEL^-:	cc | cc 'where' $conds$
cc:	$pseq$.txt | $pseq$ '(' cc '#' $\cdots$ '#' cc ')'
$pseq$:	$patom$ (('.'|'$\rightarrow$') $patom$)*
$patom$:	tag | tag '[' $vrange$ ']'
$vrange$:	$range$ | var ':' $range$ | var
$conds$:	$cond$ 'and' $\cdots$ 'and' $cond$
$cond$:	$pseq$.'txt' = $string$

where "var" is a set of index variable names, "int" is the set of integers, "tag" the set of HTML tag names, "string" the set of strings, and *range* is defined as in RPN (see Definition 6).
□

There are a number of further syntactical conditions that restrict the way in which variables can be used in a wrapper. Each index variable used in a HEL^- statement occurs *exactly once* in its cc construct. Moreover, let P the set of paths that can be constructed by concatenating paths in the cc construct starting from the left and always choosing one element of a record while going to the right. Each cond construct c in the where clause of a wrapper is constrained in that the smallest prefix of c that contains all ranges with index variables has to match a prefix of a path (in terms of both tags and index variables appearing in ranges) in P.

For example,

html.body.table(tr[0].td[0].txt # tr[i:*].td[1].txt)
where html.body.table.tr[i].td[0].txt = "item";

is correct HEL, because we can construct the path html.body.table.tr[i:*].td[1].txt while reading the cc construct from left to right, and this path and its index variables math the condition. (There is a single index variable i occurring in both paths at the same position, and the prefix html.body.table.tr is the same.)

The semantics of HEL$^-$ will not be introduced in detail but index variables are simply a tool to relate paths in the first "construction" part of the wrapper (everything up to the where clause) with conditions in the second part.

A HEL$^-$ wrapper can be easily transformed into HEL$^-_{vf}$ by simply removing its conditions one by one and merging them into the construction part of the wrapper. Starting from the left, each condition is deleted up to the rightmost of its variables, and the remaining condition is nested into the construction part of the wrapper at the position of that variable. For example, the HEL wrapper shown above can be written as

html.body.table(tr[0].td[0].txt # tr[*]{td[0].txt = "item"}.td[1].txt);

in HEL$^-_{vf}$.

Proposition 2 ([6]). *A wrapper is expressible in HEL$^-$ iff it is expressible in HEL$^-_{vf}$.*

Therefore, HEL$^-$ inherits the expressiveness results of Theorem 6.

HEL$^-$ is the fragment of HEL obtained by taking HEL without string extraction using *match* and *split* expressions (although we support strings in conditions as essential to the philosophy of HEL) and without the getNumberOf and getAttr functions. Note that this is done to compare HEL in our framework based on the language Elog$_2^*$. Full Elog again supports string extraction in the way HEL does. Using the getNumberOf function of HEL, one may require that the number of nodes (in the document tree) reachable through a given path starting from some node is equal to some constant number, which is easy to define in MSO. The getAttr function of HEL extracts HTML attributes, which we manage as tree nodes. In our framework, the function is redundant with those for accessing nodes.

Some HEL statements can be required to be single-valued (i.e., for a statement W relative to node v, $\mathbb{E}[\![W]\!]v$ must contain exactly one node). This is in particular true for condition paths, which must always be single-valued. These issues are best handled at runtime (during complex object creation) using an exception handling mechanism as in W4F.

Remark 4. HEL also supports some form of Prolog-like cut "!" with which some conditions can be marked. The cut causes the evaluation of a path to stop if a condition marked with the cut is false. The HEL cut, however, has not been covered in the formal semantics definition of [29] or unambiguously explained elsewhere. Several different meanings are imaginable.

Let us consider one meaning of the cut, where, given a node v, we first evaluate the path π, and then remove all nodes w that either violate a condition or for which there is a different node w_0 such that w_0 is reachable from v through π and $w_0 \prec w$.

We can formally denote the changed semantics of paths with conditions and the cut (but without ranges) by a semantics function $\mathbb{H}_0$ such that

$$\mathbb{H}_0[\![\pi\{\pi_1.txt = s_1 \wedge \cdots \wedge \pi_m.txt = s_m\}]\!]v :=$$
$$\{z \mid \text{subelem}_\pi(v, z) \wedge C(z) \wedge (\forall x)\,(x \preceq z \wedge \text{subelem}_\pi(v, x)) \rightarrow C^!(x)\}$$

where $C(v) := \bigwedge_{1 \le k \le m} \mathbb{C}[\![\pi_k.txt = s_k]\!]v$ and $C^!(z)$ if for all conditions $\pi_k.txt = s_k$ with the cut, $\mathbb{C}[\![\pi_k.txt = s_k]\!]v$ is true.[6] This semantics function $\mathbb{H}_0$ can easily be integrated into the above-described function $\mathbb{H}$ to cover ranges as well.

This essentially provides us with a definition of the edge relation that determines the complex objects computed by full HEL wrappers in MSO (see the previous section where we have discussed the relationship between such a binary relation and complex objects). It follows that all unary HEL queries (for any reasonable definition of such queries) are definable in Elog$^-$.   □

Acknowledgments

We thank Fabien Azavant for insightful discussions.

References

1. Abiteboul, S., Buneman, P., and Suciu, D.: Data on the Web. Morgan Kaufmann Publishers (2000)
2. Abiteboul, S., and Vianu, V.: Regular Path Queries with Constraints. Journal of Computer and System Sciences **58** 3 (1999) 428–452
3. Arocena, G., and Mendelzon, A.: WebOQL: Restructuring Documents, Databases, and Webs. In Proceedings of the 14th IEEE International Conference on Data Engineering (ICDE), Orlando, Florida, USA, Feb. 1998
4. Arocena, G., Mendelzon, A., and Mihaila, G.: Applications of a Web Query Language. In Proceedings of the 6th International WWW Conference, Santa Clara, California, USA, Apr. 1997
5. Atzeni, P., and Mecca, G.: Cut and Paste. In Proceedings of the 16th ACM SIGACT-SIGMOD-SIGART Symposium on Principles of Database Systems (PODS'97), Tucson, AZ USA (1997)

---

[6] Here we assume that conditions c marked with the cut can fail independently of the order in which the conditions appear in the HEL statement. Alternatively, one could e.g. assume that the cut in c applies only if no condition not marked with a cut that appears left of c in the HEL statement fails on a given node.

6. Azavant, F.: Personal communication, Oct. 2001

7. Baumgartner, R., Flesca, S., and Gottlob, G.: Declarative Information Extraction, Web Crawling, and Recursive Wrapping with Lixto. In Proc. LPNMR'01, Vienna, Austria (2001)

8. Baumgartner, R., Flesca, S., and Gottlob, G.: Visual Web Information Extraction with Lixto. In Proceedings of the 27th International Conference on Very Large Data Bases (VLDB'01) (2001)

9. Brüggemann-Klein, A., Murata, M., and Wood, D.: Regular Tree and Regular Hedge Languages over Non-Ranked Alphabets: Version 1, April 3, 2001. Technical Report HKUST-TCSC-2001-05, Hong Kong University of Science and Technology, Hong Kong SAR, China (2001)

10. Brüggemann-Klein, A., and Wood, D.: Caterpillars: A Context Specification Technique. Markup Languages **2** 1 (2000) 81–106

11. Ceri, S., Gottlob, G., and Tanca, L.: Logic Programming and Databases. Springer-Verlag, Berlin (1990)

12. Courcelle, B.: Graph Rewriting: An Algebraic and Logic Approach. In J. van Leeuwen, (ed.), Handbook of Theoretical Computer Science, Elsevier Science Publishers B.V. **2**, chapter 5 (1999) 193–242

13. Doner, J.: Tree Acceptors and some of their Applications. Journal of Computer and System Sciences **4** (1970) 406–451

14. Fernandez, M., Siméon, J., Wadler, P., Cluet, S., Deutsch, A., Levy, D.F.A., Maier, D., Robie, J.M.J., Suciu, D., and Widom, J.: XML Query Languages: Experiences and Exemplars (1999)
http://www-db.research.bell-labs.com/user/simeon/xquery.html.

15. Flum, J., Frick, M., and Grohe, M.: Query Evaluation via Tree-Decompositions. In J. Van den Bussche and V. Vianu (eds), Proc. of the 8th International Conference on Database Theory (ICDT'01), Lecture Notes in Computer Science, Springer, London, UK **1973** (Jan. 2001) 22–38

16. Gottlob, G., and Koch, C.: Monadic Datalog and the Expressive Power of Web Information Extraction Languages. In Proceedings of the 21st ACM SIGACT-SIGMOD-SIGART Symposium on Principles of Database Systems (PODS'02), Madison, Wisconsin, (2002) 17–28

17. Gottlob, G., and Koch, C.: Monadic Queries over Tree-Structured Data. In Proceedings of the 17th Annual IEEE Symposium on Logic in Computer Science (LICS), Copenhagen, Denmark, July 2002, 189–202

18. Gottlob, G. and Koch, C.: Monadic Datalog and the Expressive Power of Web Information Extraction Languages. Journal of the ACM **51** 1 (2003) 74–113

19. Gottlob, G., Koch, C., and Pichler, R.: Efficient Algorithms for Processing xpath Queries. ACM Trans. Database Syst. **30** 2 (2005) 444–491

20. Gottlob, G., Koch, C., Pichler, R., and Segoufin, L.: The Complexity of xpath Query Evaluation and XML Typing. J. ACM **52** 2 (2005) 284–335

21. Laender, A.H.F., Ribeiro-Neto, B., and da Silva, A.S.: DEByE – Data Extraction By Example. Data and Knowledge Engineering **40** 2 (Feb. 2002) 121–154

22. Lakshmanan, L.V., Sadri, F., and Subramanian, I.N: A Declarative Language for Querying and Restructuring the World-Wide-Web. In Workshop on Research Issues in Data Engineering (RIDE-NDS'96), New Orleans, USA, Feb. 1996

23. Liu, L., Pu, C., and Han, W.: XWRAP: An XML-Enabled Wrapper Construction System for Web Information Sources. In Proceedings of the 16th IEEE International Conference on Data Engineering (ICDE), San Diego, USA (2000) 611–621

24. http://www.lixto.com.

25. Ludäscher, B., Himmeröder, R., Lausen, G., May, W., and Schlepphorst, C.: Managing Semistructured Data with Florid: A Deductive Object-oriented Perspective. Information Systems, **23** 8 (1998) 1–25
26. Muslea, I., Minton, S., and Knoblock, C.: STALKER: Learning Extraction Rules for Semistructured, Web-based Information Sources. In Proceedings of the AAAI-98 Workshop on AI and Information Integration. AAAI Press, Menlo Park, CA (1998)
27. Neven, F., and Schwentick, T.: Query Automata on Finite Trees. Theoretical Computer Science **275** (2002) 633–674
28. Papakonstantinou, Y., Gupta, A., Garcia-Molina, H., and Ullman, J.: A Query Translation Scheme for Rapid Implementation of Wrappers. In Proc. 4th International Conference on Deductive and Object-oriented Databases (DOOD'95), Singapore, Springer (1995) 161–186
29. Sahuguet, A., and Azavant, F.: Building Intelligent Web Applications Using Lightweight Wrappers. Data and Knowledge Engineering **36** 3 (2001) 283–316
30. Thatcher, J., and Wright, J.: Generalized Finite Automata Theory with an Application to a Decision Problem of Second-Order Logic. Mathematical Systems Theory **2** 1 (1968) 57–81
31. Thomas, W.: Automata on Infinite Objects. In J. van Leeuwen (ed.), Handbook of Theoretical Computer Science, Elsevier Science Publishers B.V., **2**, chapter 4 (1990) 133–192
32. Thomas, W.: Languages, Automata, and Logic. In G. Rozenberg and A. Salomaa (eds), Handbook of Formal Languages, Springer Verlag **3**, chapter 7 (1997) 389–455
33. Ullman, J.D.: Principles of Database & Knowledge-Base Systems Vol. 1. Computer Science Press, 1988
34. World Wide Web Consortium. XML Path Language (XPath) Recommendation. http://www.w3c.org/TR/xpath/, Nov. 1999

Beyond the Horizon:
Planning Future European ICT R&D

Keith G. Jeffery

Director, IT and Head, Information Technology Department,
CCLRC Rutherford Appleton Laboratory,
Chilton, Didcot, OXON OX11 0QX, UK
k.g.jeffery@rl.ac.uk
http://www.itd.clrc.ac.uk/Person/K.G.Jeffery

Abstract. ERCIM (European Research Consortium for Informatics and Mathematics) has produced over the years, at the request of the EC (European Commission), strategic documents on future ICT research based on work by its technical working groups representing the knowledge and vision of > 12000 ICT researchers in 18 countries. The EC suggested that ERCIM submit a proposal for a coordinated action to produce a focused view for EC DG INFSO Unit F1: Future and Emerging Technologies. The proposal was successful and the BEYOND-THE-HORIZON (BTH) project is underway. The major objectives are: to identify advanced strategic areas and challenging long-term goals; to analyse their scientific, societal, and industrial impact and to deliver roadmaps for paving advances in these areas within a timeframe of fifteen years; and to investigate new frontiers for ICT research, to identify the boundaries with other disciplines, as well as interrelationships among them and opportunities for cross-fertilization. The chosen topics are: Pervasive Computing and Communications; Nanoelectronics and nanotechnology; Security, dependability and trust; Bio-ICT synergies; Intelligent and Cognitive Systems; Software Intensive Systems. This is clearly an important discussion in Europe about future R&D and providing input to the EC for FP7 (Framework Programme 7). The method of the project and the current state of the work are presented and the objective of the presentation is to engage actively the SOFSEM community in the discussion.

1 Introduction

The EC (European Commission) has for many years supported R&D (Research and Development) through various initiatives now brought together under Framework Programmes. The programmes cover all areas of R&D and include as a large component ICT (Information and Communication Technologies). However, the EC R&D funding accounts for < 5% of total European R&D funding. National government R&D funding sources are now being encouraged to cooperate with the EC such that EC–funded R&D can leverage the national R&D funding and results to continental scale. This requires agreement from national representatives and will lead to ERA, the European Research Area.

The EC manages a long-term process for each framework programme starting with indicative budgets and topics, going through various rounds of consultation and

J. Wiedermann et al. (Eds.): SOFSEM 2006, LNCS 3831, pp. 49 – 60, 2006.
© Springer-Verlag Berlin Heidelberg 2006

ending with a published budget and a workprogramme including detailed topic descriptions and milestones for calls for proposals and submission dates for proposals. It is in this process that national governments, individuals and pan-European groupings are invited to contribute to the consultation.

ERCIM has been asked to contribute because it provides wide representation of the academic and industrial communities of 18 countries via national nodes which are the ERCIM member institutions. These node institutes each have a constituency of academic and commercial/industrial organisations with which they interwork. In addition many of the ERCIM institutions host the national or regional W3C office, providing many opportunities for interaction with the community. However, there are many other bodies such as ERCIM including trade groupings.

In addition the EC sets up committees of groups of experts to advise it in the ICT area: the best-known and highest-level committee is ISTAG (Information Systems Technology Advisory Group). This included members from ERCIM institutions, notably José Encarnaçao from Fraunhofer Institute, Germany and Michael Wilson from CCLRC, UK. Recently a particularly effective group of experts has been the NGG (Next Generation GRIDs) expert group. This has also had significant participation by individual experts from ERCIM institutions and was initiated by Thiérry Priol from INRIA, France, Domenico Laforenza from CNR, Italy and the author. Locally to the geographical area of this conference, Ludek Matyska has participated. The first and second NGG expert groups have produced reports [2]; the third NGG started in September 2005.

During May 2004 discussions between the late ERCIM president, Stelios Orphanoudakis, and staff from EC DG INFSO F1: FET (Directorate General, Information Society, Unit F1: Future and Emerging Technologies) led by Thiérry van der Pyl, led to the idea that ERCIM should propose a CA (Coordination Action) to gather and provide advice for FET on the content of their component of FP7 (Framework Programme 7). The proposal was made, accepted and the 'Beyond-the-Horizon' (BTH) Project started in January 2005 with an 18 month timeframe.

2 Beyond-the-Horizon (BTH) Project

2.1 DG INFSO F1: FET

DG INFSO Unit F1 (Future and Emerging Technologies) has a defined remit. Sister Units cover topics such as e-infrastructure, including networks and such services and SGSD (Software, GRIDs, Security, Dependability). These ICT topics are thus not considered directly in F1. As part of IST, the Future and Emerging Technologies (FET) Programme has the role of stimulating the emergence and development of new IST-related disciplines and technologies, which promise to have significant scientific, industrial, and societal impact. In this perspective, FET is supporting long-term, visionary, high-risk research in advanced strategic areas. FET has to address two major challenges. First, information technology is developing at a very high pace, so the horizon comes closer much faster than in many other disciplines. And second, information technologies have become a foundational science for many other disciplines ranging from engineering (nanotechnology, robotics) and life sciences (bioinformatics) to social sciences (economics, sociology, management) and arts and humanities (museums, computer-generated art). As a consequence of this multidisciplinary environment, the full scope of investigation has broadened substantially, making the identification and fostering of emerging research challenges more complex.

2.2 Proposal

Aims. In the light of the above, it is critically important for FET's visionary ambition to regularly receive from the IST-related European research community focused and structured input, based on shared understanding, about emerging trends and strategic areas that require support, in order to build up European excellence, develop a scientific critical mass and keep European research a step ahead. The purpose of the BTH initiative is to provide such input through a well-organised, extensive and systematic consultation of the relevant research community throughout Europe, involving the main actors and experts in the related fields. The main aims of BTH are to:

– identify advanced strategic areas and grand science and technology challenges related to ICT;
– discuss the scientific, commercial and social importance of these challenges;
– draw basic research directions in ICT and related disciplines for addressing the above challenges;
– design roadmaps for making advances in these areas with a timeframe of fifteen years;
– identify new frontiers for ICT basic research, and boundaries between "pure ICT" research and other disciplines;
– identify the potential for cross-fertilization of research in disciplines involved in these areas;
– establish communication and cooperation mechanisms within and beyond Europe in order to facilitate and support the formation and functioning of a related scientific community during the project lifecycle in a field characterised by rapid and continuous evolution.

A secondary objective of BTH is to make a contribution towards raising awareness of IST-related basic research in the European industry and society at large.

The Method. The project follows an open method of consultation and coordination that utilises a continuous working group on methodology, combined with major brainstorming workshops, in the form of a foresight exercise. A scientific coordinator holds the work together advised by a Scientific Steering Committee. The project is managed by the ERCIM Office.

Approach Outline. The project will last 18 months and will be based on a number of Thematic Groups (expert panels) working in a parallel, yet coordinated fashion.
    The thematic groups cover the following topics:

– Pervasive Computing and Communications;
– Nanoelectronics and nanotechnology;

- Security, dependability and trust;
- Bio-ICT synergies;
- Intelligent and Cognitive Systems;
- Software Intensive Systems.

Each Thematic Group will focus on a particular research area, and will deliver a staged roadmap for the particular area, depicting the research paths that are believed to be most promising for achieving substantial progress in the particular area. Each Thematic Group will also analyse the potential scientific, industrial and societal impact of advances in its designated area.

The Thematic Groups were established at Opening Workshops to be held during early months of the project. The intermediate findings of the Thematic Groups will be discussed at a Consolidation Workshop to be held at Month 12. Subsequently, the Thematic Groups will finalise their work, and the outcomes of the individual Thematic Groups' reports will be integrated into a final project report.

Initiating a Successful Exercise. The first significant milestone of the project is the preparation of a Background Document by the Scientific Steering Committee. The aims of this document were to suggest an initial, non-binding list of Grand Challenges, to be taken into consideration during the Opening Workshops. The document takes into account already identified proactive FET initiatives under FP6, as well as related initiatives in the USA and Japan. In practice – and as a result of the shortened timescale required by the EC - the recently-prepared ERCIM Research Strategy Document (November 2004) [1] was taken as the background.

Bringing the Scientific Community Together. Given the complexity of the tasks to be carried out, the selection of the participants in this exercise is a critical issue. The invited participants were carefully selected by the Scientific Steering Committee to include expertise across all IST-related science and technology fields, high quality researchers, research managers, representatives of other stakeholders (scientific disciplines and sectors of society) of IT, and industry representatives. In addition, the contribution of other relevant foresight activities in Europe is assured.

Many Grand Challenges, related to IST, have an interdisciplinary nature, thus it is critical to mobilise communities other than ICT, so as to ensure the formation of interdisciplinary teams. This mobilization is expected to be successful for two reasons. First, the key role of ICT in other areas is widely recognised, therefore, other scientific communities will appreciate the opportunity of shaping the future of ICT research towards taking into account the needs of their specific domains. And second, there is already a number of interdisciplinary research teams working on current research challenges, e.g. in the context of the FET Proactive initiatives; the interdisciplinary nature of areas, such as robotics, complex systems, nanotechnology, etc., is self-evident. BTH intends to capitalise on such existing interactions between IST and other disciplines.

BTH involves industry representatives in all its activities. In fact, a secondary objective of the project is to raise awareness of IST-related basic research in industry, thus promoting industrial participation in "curiosity-driven" (or basic/-foundational) research as a mechanism for ensuring its long-term competitiveness.

Advanced Collaboration Support. Beyond the Opening Workshops, the operation of the Thematic Groups is based on teleconferencing and on advanced on-line communication facilities rather than on physical meetings, to increase cost efficiency and to minimize time and place constraints imposed on their members. An *online community* dedicated to each one of the Thematic Groups is established, based on the deployment of an information portal and a collaborative work system. Technological support for BTH online communities is provided through a suite of web-based tools that facilitate the sharing of information among a group of people, and collaboration towards the achievement of shared goals. The technological infrastructure is designed to support authorization, virtual networking facilities, task allocation and monitoring, voting and survey tools, and navigation and query facilities in an easy-to-use environment. Online communities are not restricted to the core Thematic Group members. They are open to any interested party to comment on preliminary findings, ensuring that the Thematic Groups do not work in a closed environment, but are able to receive critical feedback, especially during the early stages of their work.

In addition to the use of the online community infrastructure, physical meetings take place, as necessary. In fact, each Thematic Group plans its own operation making use of the available tools (workshops, online community, other communication means, physical meetings).

Delivering an Integrated View on FET. The Consolidation Workshop, that will take place during Month 12 (December 2005) of the project, together with the integration of the Thematic Groups' outcomes, will deliver a shared vision of future directions, which will be analysed for scientific and technological validity, industrial and societal impact, and level of payoff compared to risks. The project outcomes will, therefore, have the potential to contribute to the structuring and the shaping of the content of RTD and Innovation schemes within the Seventh Framework Programme (FP7) and the European Research Area (ERA) through comprising a guide for the IST/FET policy-making authorities in Europe.

Disseminating the Objectives and Results. The BTH project plans an intense dissemination strategy to publicise broadly its objectives and results in order to: (a) mobilise the European IST-related research potential in individuals and institutions, so as to maximise their participation in the project; (b) increase awareness of key stake holders in the so-called horizontal themes (application domains); (c) influence future ERA policies towards materialising the forecast future; and (d) foster bottom-up research activities in the recommended emerging areas. This strategy is being implemented through an integrated marketing plan for the project and its results (through the use of WWW, CORDIS, affiliated institutes, European Research Consortium for Informatics and Mathematics - ERCIM, ERCIM News, conferences, etc.). As part of this strategy, a number of reports targeting different audiences, such as the research community, industry, policy makers and the general public, will be produced.

2.3 Project

The topics were chosen by ERCIM bearing in mind the area of responsibility of FET and the topics arising through analysis by ERCIM. This analysis covered technology foresight and business foresight – but with a long-term perspective of future requirements and opportunities in a timeframe greater than 15 years – in ICT this is truly beyond the horizon. As an example, fifteen years ago the Web was a prototype on a desktop computer in a workshop at CERN and had not yet reached any kind of acceptance.

Each topic was addressed by a task group with a nominated leader. The aim was to provide, based on foresight and analysis, a roadmap for the particular theme or area of technology.

The project objectives included consensus-building in the community on how to address 'grand challenges'; the building of networks of excellence for European research and the stimulation of interdisciplinary research where it is widely predicted much wealth creation and quality of life advances will be made in the future. The project is intended to stimulate both the R&D community and to engage industry. Furthermore it is intended to engage in a public debate on the challenges facing Europe. Finally, the project intends to provide for the EC appropriate text for use in the construction of FP7, the seventh framework programme.

All areas identified as Grand Challenges fulfill certain criteria:

- They pose unsolved challenges and require significant, long-term basic research to address these challenges;
- They will have possible significant impact on industry in the future;
- They will potentially improve in a significant way the quality of life of citizens in the European Information Society.

There is a considerable risk that some of the visions may not necessarily materialise to their full extent, even in a timeframe of fifteen years. However, based on today's facts, all Grand Research Challenges appear to be scientifically and technologically feasible if significant investment (intellectual and financial) is made in them.

2.4 Project Schedule

The project was planned to run from January 2005 to end-June 2006 in order to coincide with the schedule for creating the FP7 workprogramme. In fact the formation of the workprogramme has been brought forward, and the key components will need to be in place in December 2005 although they are subject to refinement in the succeeding months. This has put considerable pressure on the project to provide deliverables earlier than previously envisaged.

2.5 Synergy and Emergent Themes

One expectation of the project was that the task groups, in mapping the 15-year future for each topic, would come across emergent sub-topics or themes that would have implications on the work and planning of other task groups and which may open up new interdisciplinary areas of R&D leading to novel products and services for wealth creation and improvement of the quality of life.

3 Results to Date

This paper is written at the half-way point of the project and so only interim results are presented. By the time of the SOFSEM conference (January 2006) more up-to-date results will be available, particularly from the major project workshop in December 2005.

3.1 Pervasive Computing and Communications

Ambient systems refer to ICT systems for the user-centric provision of services aiming at enhancing the quality of life by seamlessly offering relevant information and services to the individual, anywhere and at any time. This is realised by a synergistic combination of intelligent-aware interfaces, and ubiquitous computing and networking.

Intelligence and context awareness of interfaces enables: the support of natural ways of interaction; automatic adaptation to users' personal preferences; proactive interactive behaviour, based on users' location, history and activities.

The ubiquitous (pervasive) and global properties imply a useful, pleasant, flexible, dependable, secure and efficient presence of a system everywhere in the physical environment, e.g. at home, en route, in public spaces, at work, etc. The computing and networking facilities are distributed and accessible through a variety of devices, as needed.

Progress on these problems will have a clear impact on procurement, brokerage and financial transactions, and will affect industry developing large scale information systems for national security, control of safety-critical systems, and services to the citizen.

The realization of this vision requires massive foundational research to determine how to design such systems, how to analyse them and reason about their behaviour, how to control systems and their environments, and an in-depth understanding of their potential and limits. Also how to model and understand their behaviour, since the global, ubiquitous and ambient systems are arguably the largest engineered artefact in human history. Advances are needed in various areas of ICT, including mobile technology, hardware systems, sensors, low-cost broadband communications, mobile communications, software architectures, context management, adaptive services, models of computation, programming languages, system development methodologies, theories of modelling large-scale, distributed and dynamic systems.

3.2 Nanoelectronics and Nanotechnology

With nanoscale devices reaching characteristic dimensions of 10 nanometres (nm) in 2015-2020, new opportunities will emerge to combine ultimate "top-down" semiconductor platforms with "bottom-up" developments in materials, physics, chemistry and biology. A number of Grand Challenges were identified that summarise the multidisciplinary research themes where research is required for bringing these visions into tomorrow's innovations.

Advances in nano-scale materials science will provide the basis for adding significant extra functionality and performance to devices and systems on mainstream silicon platforms. These in turn will require new system architectures that will underpin new applications in ICTs and life sciences. Two main issues demand particular attention, namely heat generation and dissipation, and architectures. Inorganic nanowires and nanotubes will likely have a prominent position in these developments. The second Grand Challenge is to enable the combination and interfacing of a growing diversity of materials, functions, devices and information carriers. These "information carriers" could be electrons, photons, spins, ions, etc.

New materials, devices and circuits will require cost-effective fabrication techniques for complex systems integrating deep nanometre scale devices. Nanoscale components must be grown and patterned at scales around and below 10 nm, going far beyond the current limitations of lithography. Self-assembly of nano-objects mediated by (bio)chemical interactions appears as one of the promising routes for a sustainable manufacturing of downscaled nano-components.

Pushing the limits of miniaturisation to the nanometre scale requires new methods and tools to accurately model, manipulate, fabricate and characterise nano-objects down to the atomic scale. It also requires new paradigms to exchange information with single atoms or molecules. Denser integration and combination of top-down, bottom up and self-organised devices will vastly increase the complexity of ICT components and architectures. These require methods and tools to master the giga-complexity of future ICT architectures, integrating billions of devices with nano-scale dimensions and coping with variability, defects and energy-dissipation issues. Inspiration from biosystems is likely to lead to innovative and lower cost solutions.

A number of new physical phenomena or properties of matter at the meso-scale have recently been discovered or demonstrated. These should be further investigated and, as appropriate, developed into new functions or technological developments for the ICT. Research for the discovery and further investigation of such new phenomena also needs to be supported.

The increasingly fading boundaries between ICT and other related fields such as materials sciences, physics, chemistry, biochemistry and life sciences, were stressed all long the discussions in this session. Future research is hence expected to become more multidisciplinary and to be based on strong and effective integration of excellent researchers from all these disciplines.

Breakthroughs towards achieving these goals are anticipated to have great impact. Application scenarios include health and environment, engineering, consumer electronics, efficient scientific computations etc.

3.3 Security, Dependability and Trust

As human dependence on technical infrastructure and systems grows, the threats of major failures grow accordingly. This fact calls for a concentrated effort to improve the quality of ICT-based systems along the following axes:

- Security: Factors that contribute to increased risks include: growing autonomy and mobility of technologies and systems; increasing size and complexity; increased heterogeneity; inherent interdependencies resulting from the pervasiveness of technologies and systems. These challenges call for novel, advanced methods to address the involved problems, such as real-time detection and response to threats, and proactive measures. Additionally, in the new technological environment threats may be caused not only by system failures, but also through active human involvement. Interesting social and ethical questions will be raised in this process, for example concerning the acceptable trade-off between level of risk and privacy.
- Dependability: There are many application areas where system failure may lead to loss of financial resources, and even loss of human lives (e.g., control of aircraft and nuclear plants). In such cases, scientifically rigorous evidence is needed in advance to back up promises about a product's future service. The problem is complicated by the need for practical ICT systems to evolve in response to changes in their requirements, technology and environments, without compromising their dependability. This is even stronger in applications where system boundaries are not fixed and are subject to constant urgent change (e.g. in e-business). Scientific and technological advances are required to (a) demonstrate that commercial and industrial-scale software can be developed to be truly dependable, and with less development risk than today; and (b) dependable systems can be evolved dependably including, for a class of applications, just-in-time creation of required services.
- Trust: Even if a technological infrastructure is secure and dependable, users will not necessarily trust it. For example, lack of trust is considered to be a major inhibiting factor for a much stronger and faster development of B2C e-commerce. Additionally, privacy concerns may in the future inhibit the take up of location-based services. To overcome these problems it is necessary to develop novel methods for trust creation and management, possibly inspired by social human behaviour.

While these objectives mostly call for ICT basic research (e.g. in cryptography), interaction with other disciplines will be useful. For example, social sciences and ethics may give useful input regarding the trade-off between security and privacy, and the emergence of trust; and input from mathematics will be essential for the development of novel cryptography techniques.

3.4 Bio-ICT Synergies

The convergence of ICT with bio and life sciences, but also with cognitive science and nanotechnology promises to initiate a new technological revolution, with implications ranging from medicine to education and response to natural and man-made threats. Particular objectives in this direction include:

- Large-scale functional genomics and proteomics: The availability of (nearly) complete genome sequences of a growing number of model organisms, offers scientists a unique opportunity to study global biomolecular changes in cellular compartments, cells, tissues and organisms. As for studying proteins, the genome should be regarded as a sort of blueprint since the gene products (proteins) are the key players in all aspects of cell structure and function. Proteomics enables researchers to study the overall protein content of a subcellular compartment, cell, tissue or organism at a particular moment in time and under certain environmental conditions.

- Modelling the development of behaviour in plants and animals: model development from fertilised cells to full organisms, model cell function and interaction, capture interactions between organisms and the surrounding environment.
- Modelling of the function of organs and their simulation: Theoretical modelling of the brain and mind (Human Cognome Project): chart the structure and functions of the human mind; create a computational architecture of the brain and mind which is inspired both by the neural architecture of the brain and high level cognitive functioning of humans; capture information processing principles present in the brain, leading to bio-inspired computational paradigms; explain how low-level neuronal processes are linked to high-level cognitive capabilities, such as self awareness and creativity.
- Enhancing and/or substituting human performances: once progress on the previous points is made, we can come up with a host of devices that enhance human sensory capabilities, extent or substitute deficient human senses, organs and physical capabilities (e.g. motor skills) through intimate sensory, cognitive and neural bi-directional connections (for example using a nano-bio processor for programming complex biological pathways on a chip that mimic responses of a human body).

The above problems demonstrate the great impact ICT will have in biology and medicine. However, this field poses also challenges to IT. Here we mention a few:

- Develop methods for maintenance and interoperability of biological data, and for the semantic organisation of biological knowledge;
- Develop methods for visualising biological data;
- Increase the reliability of bioinformatics predictions.
- In addition, if we manage to capture the information processing principles present in organisms and the human brain, we will be able to develop advanced bio-inspired computational paradigms.

From a scientific perspective, research in these directions is most promising and fulfilling. And the potential impact on health, engineering, education, etc. are obvious. These challenges call for interdisciplinary research including ICT, cognitive science, biology and biotechnology.

3.5 Intelligent and Cognitive Systems

With virtually limitless computing power available for the first time, it is possible to build truly intelligent systems that perceive, reason, understand and learn. Such systems will be useful for extracting meaning from huge data flows, thus addressing one of the key emerging problems of human participation in an Information Society, namely the information overflow. Truly intelligent systems will be able to operate in an autonomous way, naturally interact with the world and with human users, and be (self-)adaptive to changing situations and contexts, including users' preferences and needs. Long-term objectives included in this Grand Research Challenge include:

- Complex adaptive systems consisting of collections of simple, often heterogeneous, entities exhibiting collective behaviour and functionality through high connectivity. This idea is based on studies of complex systems that occur in nature and society, such as living organisms, animal societies, ecosystems, markets and cultural groupings.
- Introspective reasoning: self-awareness, knowledge of internal state and capacity; intensional query answering; knowledge communication among introspective systems; multi-modal reasoning.
- Emotional and affective computing: develop systems that can make hypotheses on a user's likely affective state and produce believable, affective behaviour, where necessary.
- Mixed realities: This includes pulling ICT systems out of the digital and into our physical world. This includes handling massive sensory input, as a tool for establishing more genuine communication between humans and machines. Also projecting a human's mind through media to other places and designed environments.

The research challenges outlined above call for interdisciplinary research effort from disciplines such as: AI, engineering (robotics and control), cognitive science and philosophy.

3.6 Software Intensive Systems

Society's dependence on software-intensive systems is increasing, to the point where a growing range of products and services from all sectors of economic activity, but also our daily lives, depend on software-intensive systems, e.g. banking, communications, transportation, entertainment and health. While a large number of methods and tools for engineering software-intensive systems has been developed, they suffer from some severe quality and methodological deficiencies: pragmatic modelling languages and techniques lack a formal foundation, thus inhibiting the development of powerful analysis and development tools, while formal approaches are not well-integrated with pragmatic methods, do not scale easily to complex software- intensive systems and are often too difficult to use.

The increasing complexity of software systems, e.g. in the area of pervasive computing, poses new engineering challenges for modelling data and processes; building adequate system architectures; ensuring reliability, dependability and compliance; supporting interoperability; managing change and enhancing usability. The Grand Challenge is to develop practically useful and theoretically well-founded methods and tools for engineering complex software-intensive systems, supporting the entire life cycle.

An interesting line for future research lies with Service-Oriented Computing, a computing paradigm that utilizes services as fundamental elements for developing distributed applications/solutions. Services are self-describing, platform-agnostic computational elements that support rapid, low-cost and easy composition of loosely coupled distributed applications; moreover formal methods may be used to verify/ensure the correctness and dependability of service-oriented software systems. The service-oriented computing paradigm promises to revolutionise the process of developing and deploying distributed software applications. Benefits of applying the service-oriented computing paradigm include reduced complexity and costs, exposing and reusing core business functionality, increased flexibility, resilience to technology shifts and improving operational efficiency.

3.7 Synergy and Emergent Themes

At the time of writing, some synergies are starting to emerge. It is expected that these will be clearer at the Month 12 consolidation workshop.

4 Conclusion

The BTH project is providing DG INFSO F1: Future and Emerging Technologies with appropriate input for a future research programme drawing on widespread representative community input coordinated by ERCIM. It has also made many people aware of the process of producing a workprogramme. It has clearly established ERCIM as an authoritative and representative organisation for this strategic work. The project encourages participation from all researchers. This is best achieved by contacting the thematic leaders or the project leader (details on the website http://www.beyond-the-horizon.net/).

Acknowledgements. The Beyond the Horizon project arose out of discussions between the late ERCIM President, Stelios Orphanoudakis, and staff of DG INFSO F1 particularly Thierry van der Pyl. The project proposal and project initiation were handled by Grigoris Antoniou of FORTH. The project was subsequently led by Dimitris Plexousakis of the University of Crete with management support from Jessica Michel of the ERCIM Office. The project has benefited greatly from the wisdom of the Scientific Steering Committee and could not have been executed without the dedication of the thematic leaders and their task groups. This paper is but a presentational summary of their work.

References

[1] [ERCIMStrat] http://www.ercim.org/publication/policy/ERCIM_IT_Strategy_2004.pdf
[2] [NGG] www.cordis.lu/ist/grids/index.htm

Selfish Routing in Networks[*]

Burkhard Monien

Department of Computer Science, Electrical Engineering and Mathematics,
University of Paderborn, Fürstenallee 11, 33102 Paderborn, Germany
bm@uni-paderborn.de

Abstract. One of the most widely used solution concepts for strategic games is the concept of Nash equilibrium. A Nash equilibrium is a state in which no player can improve its objective by unilaterally changing its strategy. A Nash equilibrium is called pure if all players choose a pure strategy, and mixed if players choose probability distributions over strategies. Of special interest are fully mixed Nash equilibria where each player chooses each strategy with non-zero probability.

Rosenthal [12] introduced a special class of strategic games, now widely known as congestion games. Here, the strategy set of each player is a subset of the power set of given resources. The players share a private objective function, defined as the sum (over their chosen resources) of functions in the number of players sharing this resource. In his seminal work, Rosenthal showed with help of a potential function that congestion games (in sharp contrast to general strategic games) always admit at least one pure Nash equilibrium. An extension to congestion games are weighted congestion games, in which the players have weights and thus different influence on the congestion of the resources. In (weighted) network congestion games the strategy sets of the players correspond to paths in a network.

In order to measure the degradation of social welfare due to the selfish behavior of the players, Koutsoupias and Papadimitriou [8] introduced a global objective function, usually coined as social cost. They defined the price of anarchy, also called coordination ratio, as the worst-case ratio between the value of social cost in a Nash equilibrium and that of some social optimum. Thus the coordination ratio measures the extent to which non-cooperation approximates cooperation. As a starting point for studying the coordination ratio, Koutsoupias and Papadimitriou considered a very simple weighted network congestion game, now known as KP-model. Here, the network consists of a single source and a single destination which are connected by parallel links. The load on a link is the total weight of players assigned to this link. Associated with each link is a capacity representing the rate at which the link processes load. Each of the players selfishly routes from the source to the destination by choosing a probability distribution over the links. The private objective function of a player is defined as its expected latency. In the KP-model the social cost is defined as the expected maximum latency on a link, where the expectation is taken over all random choices of the players.

[*] This work has been partially supported by the DFG-SFB 376 and by the European Union within the 6th Framework Programme under contract 001907 (DELIS).

J. Wiedermann et al. (Eds.): SOFSEM 2006, LNCS 3831, pp. 61–62, 2006.

In this paper, we give a thorough survey on the most exciting results on finite (weighted) congestion games and on special classes which are related to the KP-model. In particular, we review the findings on the existence and computational complexity of pure Nash equilibria. Furthermore, we discuss results on the price of anarchy. Last but not least, we survey known facts on fully mixed Nash equilibria.

References

1. Awerbuch, B., Azar, Y., and Epstein, A.: The Price of Routing Unsplittable Flow. In Proceedings of the 37th Annual ACM Symposium on Theory of Computing (STOC'05) (2005)
2. Christodoulou, G., and Koutsoupias, E.: The Price of Anarchy of Finite Congestion Games. In Proceedings of the 37th Annual ACM Symposium on Theory of Computing (STOC'05) (2005)
3. Czumaj, A., and Vöcking, B.: Tight Bounds for Worst-Case Equilibria. In Proceedings of the 13th Annual ACM-SIAM Symposium on Discrete Algorithms (SODA'02) (2002) 413–420
4. Fabrikant, A., Papadimitriou, C.H., and Talwar, K.: The Complexity of Pure Nash Equilibria. In Proceedings of the 36th Annual ACM Symposium on Theory of Computing (STOC'04) (2004) 604–612
5. Feldmann, R., Gairing, M., Lücking, T., Monien, B., and Rode, M.: Nashification and the Coordination Ratio for a Selfish Routing Game. In Proceedings of the 30th International Colloquium on Automata, Languages, and Programming (ICALP'03), LNCS **2719** (2003) 514–526
6. Fotakis, D., Kontogiannis, S., Koutsoupias, E., Mavronicolas, M., and Spirakis, P.: The Structure and Complexity of Nash Equilibria for a Selfish Routing Game. In Proceedings of the 29th International Colloquium on Automata, Languages, and Programming (ICALP'02), LNCS **2380** (2002) 123–134
7. Gairing, M., Lücking, T., Mavronicolas, M., and Monien, B.: Computing Nash Equilibria for Scheduling on Restricted Parallel Links. In Proceedings of the 36th Annual ACM Symposium on Theory of Computing (STOC'04) (2004) 613–622
8. Koutsoupias, E., and Papadimitriou, C.H.: Worst-Case Equilibria. In Proceedings of the 16th International Symposium on Theoretical Aspects of Computer Science (STACS'99), LNCS **1563** (1999) 404–413
9. Lücking, T., Mavronicolas, M., Monien, B., Rode, M., Spirakis, P., and Vrto, I.: Which is the Worst-Case Nash Equilibrium? In Proceedings of the 28th International Symposium on Mathematical Foundations of Computer Science (MFCS'03), LNCS **2747** (2003) 551–561
10. Mavronicolas, M., and Spirakis, P.: The Price of Selfish Routing. In Proceedings of the 33rd Annual ACM Symposium on Theory of Computing (STOC'01) (2001) 510–519
11. Nash, J.F.: Non-Cooperative Games. Annals of Mathematics 54 2 (1951) 286–295
12. Rosenthal, R.W.: A Class of Games Possessing Pure-Strategy Nash Equilibria. International Journal of Game Theory **2** (1973) 65–67
13. Roughgarden, T., and Tardos, É.: How Bad Is Selfish Routing? Journal of the ACM **49** 2 (2002) 236–259
14. Wardrop, J.G.: Some Theoretical Aspects of Road Traffic Research. In Proceedings of the Institute of Civil Engineers, Pt. II, **1**, (1956) 325–378

New Physics and Hypercomputation

Istvan Németi and Hajnal Andreka

Alfred Renyi Institute of Mathematics, Hungary
{nemeti, andreka}@math-inst.hu

Abstract. Does new physics give us a chance for designing computers, at least in principle, which could compute beyond the Turing barrier? By the latter we mean computers which could compute some functions which are not Turing computable. Part of what we call "new physics" is the surge of results in black hole physics in the last 15 years, which certainly changed our perspective on certain things [3], [9], [1]. The two main directions in this line seem to be quantum computers and relativistic, i.e. spacetime-theory-based, ones. We will concentrate on the relativistic case, e.g. [1], [2], [4], [6]. Is there a remote possibility that relativity can give some feedback to its "founding grandmother", namely, to logic?

References

1. Németi, I., and Dávid, Gy.: Relativistic Computers and the Turing Barrier. Journal of Applied Mathematics and Computation, to appear.
   http://ftp.math-inst.hu/pub/algebraic-logic/beyondturing.pdf
2. Etesi, G., and Németi, I.: Non-Turing Computations via Malament-Hogarth Space-Times. International Journal of Theoretical Physics **41** 2 (2002) 341–370.
   http://arxiv.org/abs/gr-qc/0104023
3. Reynolds, C.S., Brenneman, L.W., and Garofalo, D.: Black Hole Spin in AGN and GBHCs. ArXiv: astro-ph/0410116v1, Oct 5, 2004.
   http://arxiv.org/abs/astro-ph/0410116 (This reference is about observational evidence for spinning black holes.)
4. Hogarth, M.L.: Predictability, Computability, and Spacetime. PhD Dissertation, University of Cambridge, UK, 2000.
   http://ftp.math-inst.hu/pub/algebraic-logic/Hogarththesis.ps.gz
5. Hogarth, M.L.: Deciding Arithmetic Using SAD Computers. Brit. J. Phil. Sci. **55** (2004) 681–691
6. Earman, J., and Norton, J.: Forever Is a Day: Supertasks in Pitowsky and Malament-Hogarth Spacetimes. Philosophy of Science **60** 1993 22–42
7. Wiedermann, J., and van Leeuwen, J.: Relativistic Computers and Non-Uniform Complexity Theory. In: Calude et al, (eds.) UMC 2002, Lecture Notes in Computer Science **2509**, Springer-Verlag, Berlin (2002) 287–299
8. Cooper, S.B.: Computability and Emergence. In: Mathematical Problems from Applied Logics. New Logics for the XXIst Century II, D.M. Gabbay et al (eds), International Mathematical Series, Kluwer/Springer (2005)
9. Wüthrich, C.: On Time Machines in Kerr-Newman Spacetime. Master Theses, University of Berne (1999).
   http://www.itp.unibe.ch/diploma_thesis/wuthrich/wuthrichLiz.pdf

J. Wiedermann et al. (Eds.): SOFSEM 2006, LNCS 3831, p. 63, 2006.
© Springer-Verlag Berlin Heidelberg 2006

Models and Algorithms
for Wireless Sensor Networks (Smart Dust)

Sotiris Nikoletseas

Department of Computer Engineering and Informatics,
University of Patras, and Computer Technology Institute (CTI), Greece
nikole@cti.gr

Abstract. Recent rapid developments in micro-electro-mechanical systems (MEMS), wireless communications and digital electronics have already led to the development of tiny, low-power, low-cost sensor devices. Such devices integrate sensing, limited data processing and restricted communication capabilities.

Each sensor device individually might have small utility, however the effective distributed co-ordination of large numbers of such devices can lead to the efficient accomplishment of large sensing tasks. Large numbers of sensors can be deployed in areas of interest (such as inaccessible terrains or disaster places) and use self-organization and collaborative methods to form an ad-hoc network.

We note however that the efficient and robust realization of such large, highly-dynamic, complex, non-conventional networking environments is a challenging technological and algorithmic task, because of the unique characteristics and severe limitations of these devices.

This talk will present and discuss several important aspects of the design, deployment and operation of sensor networks. In particular, we provide a brief description of the technical specifications of state-of-the-art sensor, a discussion of possible models used to abstract such networks, a discussion of some key algorithmic design techniques (like randomization, adaptation and hybrid schemes), a presentation of representative protocols for sensor networks, for important problems including data propagation, collision avoidance and energy balance and an evaluation of crucial performance properties (correctness, efficiency, fault-tolerance) of these protocols, both with analytic and simulation means.

1 Introduction

1.1 A Short Description of Wireless Sensors

Recent dramatic developments in micro-electro-mechanical (MEMS) systems, wireless communications and digital electronics have already led to the development of small in size, low-power, low-cost sensor devices. Such extremely small devices integrate sensing, data processing and wireless communication capabilities. Current devices have a size at the cubic centimeter scale, a CPU running at 4 MHz, some memory and a wireless communication capability at a 4Kbps

J. Wiedermann et al. (Eds.): SOFSEM 2006, LNCS 3831, pp. 64–83, 2006.

rate. Also, they are equipped with a small but effective operating system and are able to switch between "sleeping" and "awake" modes to save energy. Pioneering groups (like the "Smart Dust" Project at Berkeley, the "Wireless Integrated Network Sensors" Project at UCLA and the "Ultra low Wireless Sensor" Project at MIT) pursue further important goals, like a total volume of a few cubic millimeters and extremely low energy consumption, by using alternative technologies, based on radio frequency (RF) or optical (laser) transmission.

Their wide range of applications is based on the possible use of various sensor types (i.e. thermal, visual, seismic, acoustic, radar, magnetic, etc.) in order to monitor a wide variety of conditions (e.g. temperature, object presence and movement, humidity, pressure, noise levels etc.). Thus, sensor networks can be used for continuous sensing, event detection, location sensing as well as microsensing. Hence, sensor networks have important applications, including (a) military (like forces and equipment monitoring, battlefield surveillance, targeting, nuclear, biological and chemical attack detection), (b) environmental applications (such as fire detection, flood detection, precision agriculture), (c) health applications (like telemonitoring of human physiological data) and (d) home applications (e.g. smart environments and home automation). For an excellent survey of wireless sensor networks see [1] and also [7], [13].

1.2   Critical Challenges

Features including the huge number of sensor devices involved, the severe power, computational and memory limitations, their dense deployment and frequent failures, pose *new design, analysis and implementation aspects* which are essentially different not only with respect to distributed computing and systems approaches but also to ad-hoc networking techniques. We emphasize the following characteristic differences between sensor networks and ad-hoc networks:

- The number of sensor particles in a sensor network is extremely large compared to that in a typical ad-hoc network.
- Sensor networks are typically prone to faults.
- Because of faults as well as energy limitations, sensor nodes may (permanently or temporarily) join or leave the network. This leads to highly dynamic network topology changes.
- The density of deployed devices in sensor networks is much higher than in ad-hoc networks.
- The limitations in energy, computational power and memory are much more severe in sensor networks.

Because of the above rather unique characteristics of sensor networks, efficient and robust distributed protocols and algorithms should exhibit the following critical properties:

Scalability. Distributed protocols for sensor networks should be highly scalable, in the sense that they should operate efficiently in extremely large networks composed of huge numbers of nodes. This feature calls for an urgent need to prove by analytical means and also validate (by large scale simulations) certain efficiency and robustness (and their trade-offs) guarantees for asymptotic network sizes.

Efficiency. Because of the severe energy limitations of sensor networks and also because of their time-critical application scenaria, protocols for sensor networks should be efficient, with respect to both energy and time.

Fault-Tolerance. Sensor particles are prone to several types of faults and unavailabilities, and may become inoperative (permanently or temporarily). Various reasons for such faults include physical damage during either the deployment or the operation phase, permanent (or temporary) cease of operation in the case of power exhaustion (or energy saving schemes, respectively). The sensor network should be able to continue its proper operation for as long as possible despite the fact that certain nodes in it may fail.

1.3   Trade-Offs, Algorithmic Design and Modeling

Since one of the most severe limitations of sensor devices is their limited energy supply, one of the most crucial goals in designing efficient protocols for wireless sensor networks is minimizing the energy consumption in the network. This goal has various aspects, including: (a) minimizing the total energy spent in the network (b) minimizing the number (or the range) of data transmissions (c) combining energy efficiency and fault-tolerance, by allowing redundant data transmissions which however should be optimized to not spend too much energy (d) maximizing the number of "alive" particles over time, thus prolonging the system's lifetime and (e) balancing the energy dissipation among the sensors in the network, in order to avoid the early depletion of certain sensors and thus the breakdown of the network.

We note that it is very difficult to achieve all the above goals at the same time. There even exist trade-offs between some of the goals above. Furthermore, the importance and priority of each of these goals may depend on the particular application. Thus, it is important to have a variety of protocols (and hybrid combinations of protocols), each of which may possibly focus at some of the energy efficiency goals above (while still performing well with respect to the rest goals). Furthermore, there exist fundamental, inherent trade-offs between important performance measures, most notably between energy dissipation and latency (i.e. time for information to get to the control center). Also, the performance of protocols in such networks depends highly on a diverse variety of parameters and each protocol seems to best fit a certain network type. Finally, such networks are highly changing (sensors come and go, sleep and awake, the network connectivity changes) or even heterogeneous (i.e. composed of sensors of various types and capabilities) thus adaptive distributed algorithms that locally (and implicitly) sense network changes and appropriately adapt (possibly performing random choices) are very useful.

In this chapter, we present three energy efficient protocols:

- *The Local Target Protocol (LTP)*, that performs a local optimization trying to minimize the number of data transmissions.

- *The Probabilistic Forwarding Protocol (PFR)*, that creates redundant data transmissions that are probabilistically optimized, to trade-off energy efficiency with fault-tolerance.
- *The Energy Balanced Protocol (EBP)*, that focuses on guaranteeing the same per sensor energy dissipation, in order to prolong the lifetime of the network.

We believe that a complementary use of rigorous analysis and large scale simulations is needed to fully investigate the performance of data propagation protocols in wireless sensor networks. In particular, asymptotic analysis may lead to provable efficiency and robustness guarantees towards the desired scalability of protocols for sensor networks that have extremely large size. On the other hand, simulation allows to investigate the detailed effect of a great number of technical specifications of real devices, a task that is difficult (if possible at all) for analytic techniques which, by their nature, use abstraction and model simplicity.

The definition of abstract (yet realistic) models for wireless sensor networks is very important, since it enables rigorous mathematical analysis of protocol performance. Such models include: a) random geometric graphs [9], [18], where a random plane network is constructed by picking points (that abstract sensors) in the plane by a Poisson process, with density d points per unit area, and then joining each pair of points by a line if they are at distance less than r (this captures transmission range). Interesting properties under this model are investigated in [5]. b) Another interesting model is that of random sector graphs, where each randomly chosen point (sensor) in the plane chooses an angle and a euclidean distance (that together define a cyclic sector corresponding to the sensor's transmission area [6]). Interesting properties (connectivity, chromatic number) are investigated in [20]. A new relevant model is that of random intersection graphs, where each vertex randomly picks elements from a universe, and two vertices are adjacent when they pick at least one element in common ([14]). Independence properties and algorithms are proposed in [16].

2   LTP: A Hop-by-Hop Data Propagation Protocol

2.1   The Model

The LTP Protocol was introduced by Chatzigiannakis, Nikoletseas and Spirakis in [2]. The authors adopt a two-dimensional (plane) framework: A *smart dust cloud* (a set of particles) is spread in an area (for a graphical presentation, see Fig. 1).

Let d (usually measured in numbers of *particles/m^2*) be the *density* of particles in the area. Let $\mathcal{R}$ be the maximum (radio/laser) transmission range of each grain particle.

A *receiving wall* $\mathcal{W}$ is defined to be an infinite line in the smart-dust plane. Any particle transmission within range $\mathcal{R}$ from the wall $\mathcal{W}$ is received by $\mathcal{W}$. The wall represents in fact the authorities (the fixed control center) who the realization of a crucial event should be reported to. The wall notion generalizes that of the sink and may correspond to multiple (and/or moving) sinks. Note that a wall of appropriately big (finite) length suffices.

The notion of multiple sinks which may be static or moving has also been studied in [21], where Triantafilloy, Ntarmos, Nikoletseas and Spirakis introduce "NanoPeer Words", merging notions from Peer-to-Peer Computing and Smart Dust.

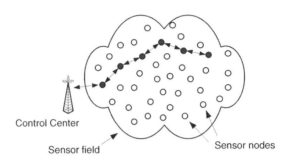

Fig. 1. A Smart Dust Cloud

Furthermore, there is a set-up phase of the smart dust network, during which the smart cloud is dropped in the terrain of interest, when using special control messages (which are very short, cheap and transmitted only once) each smart dust particle is provided with the direction of $\mathcal{W}$. By assuming that each smart-dust particle has individually *a sense of direction*, and using these control messages, each particle is aware of the general location of $\mathcal{W}$.

2.2   The Protocol

Let $d(p_i, p_j)$ the distance (along the corresponding vertical lines towards $\mathcal{W}$) of particles p_i, p_j and $d(p_i, \mathcal{W})$ the (vertical) distance of p_i from $\mathcal{W}$. Let $info(\mathcal{E})$ the information about the realization of the crucial event $\mathcal{E}$ to be propagated. Let p the particle sensing the event and starting the execution of the protocol. In this protocol, each particle p' that has received $info(\mathcal{E})$, does the following:

- *Search Phase*: It uses a periodic low energy directional broadcast in order to discover a particle nearer to $\mathcal{W}$ than itself. (i.e. a particle p'' where $d(p'', \mathcal{W}) < d(p', \mathcal{W})$).
- *Direct Transmission Phase*: Then, p' sends $info(\mathcal{E})$ to p''.
- *Backtrack Phase*: If consecutive repetitions of the *search phase* fail to discover a particle nearer to $\mathcal{W}$, then p' sends $info(\mathcal{E})$ to the particle that it originally received the information from.

For a graphical representation see figures 2, 3. [2] first provides some basic definitions.

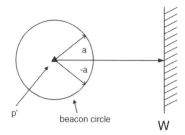

Fig. 2. Example of the Search Phase

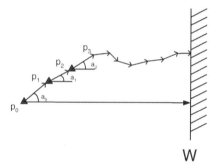

Fig. 3. Example of a Transmission

Definition 1. Let $h_{opt}(p, \mathcal{W})$ be the (optimal) number of "hops" (direct, vertical to $\mathcal{W}$ transmissions) needed to reach the wall, in the *ideal* case in which particles always exist in pair-wise distances $\mathcal{R}$ on the vertical line from p to $\mathcal{W}$. Let Π be *a smart-dust propagation protocol*, using *a transmission path* of length $L(\Pi, p, \mathcal{W})$ to send info about event $\mathcal{E}$ to wall $\mathcal{W}$. Let $h(\Pi, p, \mathcal{W})$ be the actual number of hops (transmissions) taken to reach $\mathcal{W}$. The *"hops" efficiency* of protocol Π is the ratio

$$C_h = \frac{h(\Pi, p, \mathcal{W})}{h_{opt}(p, \mathcal{W})}$$

Clearly, the number of hops (transmissions) needed characterizes the energy consumption and the time needed to propagate the information $\mathcal{E}$ to the wall. Remark that $h_{opt} = \left\lceil \frac{d(p, \mathcal{W})}{\mathcal{R}} \right\rceil$, where $d(p, \mathcal{W})$ is the (vertical) distance of p from the wall $\mathcal{W}$.

In the case where the protocol Π is randomized, or in the case where the distribution of the particles in the cloud is a random distribution, the number of hops h and the efficiency ratio C_h are random variables and one wishes to study their expected values.

The reason behind these definitions is that when p (or any intermediate particle in the information propagation to $\mathcal{W}$) "looks around" for a particle as near to $\mathcal{W}$ as possible to pass its information about $\mathcal{E}$, it may not get, for a variety of reasons, any particle in the perfect direction of the line vertical to $\mathcal{W}$.

Note that any given distribution of particles in the smart dust cloud may not allow the ideal optimal number of hops to be achieved at all. In fact, the least possible number of hops depends on the input (the positions of the grain particles). [2] however, compares the efficiency of protocols to the ideal case. A comparison with the best achievable number of hops in each input case will of course give better efficiency ratios for protocols.

To enable a first step towards a rigorous analysis of smart dust protocols, [2] makes the following simplifying assumption: *The search phase always finds a p'' (of sufficiently high battery) in the semicircle of center the particle p' currently possessing the information about the event and radius R, in the direction towards $\mathcal{W}$.* Note that this assumption on always finding a particle can be relaxed in many ways.

[2] also assumes that the position of p'' is uniform in the arc of angle $2a$ around the direct line from p' vertical to $\mathcal{W}$. Each data transmission (one hop) takes constant time t (so the "hops" and time efficiency of our protocols coincide in this case). It is also assumed that each target selection is stochastically *independent* of the others, in the sense that it is always drawn uniformly randomly in the arc $(-\alpha, \alpha)$.

Lemma 1 ([2]). *The expected "hops efficiency" of the local target protocol in the a-uniform case is*

$$E(C_h) \simeq \frac{\alpha}{\sin \alpha}$$

for large h_{opt}. Also

$$1 \le E(C_h) \le \frac{\pi}{2} \simeq 1.57$$

for $0 \le \alpha \le \frac{\pi}{2}$.

Proof. A sequence of points is generated, $p_0 = p, p_1, p_2, \ldots, p_{h-1}, p_h$ where p_{h-1} is a particle within $\mathcal{W}$'s range and p_h is part of the wall. Let α_i be the (positive or negative) angle of p_i with respect to p_{i-1}'s vertical line to $\mathcal{W}$. It is:

$$\sum_{i=1}^{h-1} d(p_{i-1}, p_i) \le d(p, \mathcal{W}) \le \sum_{i=1}^{h} d(p_{i-1}, p_i)$$

Since the (vertical) progress towards $\mathcal{W}$ is then $\Delta_i = d(p_{i-1}, p_i) = \mathcal{R} \cos \alpha_i$, we get:

$$\sum_{i=1}^{h-1} \cos \alpha_i \le h_{opt} \le \sum_{i=1}^{h} \cos \alpha_i$$

From Wald's equation for the expectation of a sum of a random number of independent random variables (see [19]), then

$$E(h-1) \cdot E(\cos \alpha_i) \leq E(h_{opt}) = h_{opt} \leq E(h) \cdot E(\cos \alpha_i)$$

Now, $\forall i$, $E(\cos \alpha_i) = \int_{-\alpha}^{\alpha} \cos x \frac{1}{2\alpha} dx = \frac{\sin \alpha}{\alpha}$. Thus

$$\frac{\alpha}{\sin \alpha} \leq \frac{E(h)}{h_{opt}} = E(C_h) \leq \frac{\alpha}{\sin \alpha} + \frac{1}{h_{opt}}$$

Assuming large values for h_{opt} (i.e. events happening far away from the wall, which is the most interesting case in practice since the detection and propagation difficulty increases with distance) we have (since for $0 \leq \alpha \leq \frac{\pi}{2}$ it is $1 \leq \frac{\alpha}{\sin \alpha} \leq \frac{\pi}{2}$) and the result follows.

2.3 Local Optimization: The Min-Two Uniform Targets Protocol (M2TP)

[2] further assumes that the search phase always returns *two points* p'', p''' each uniform in $(-\alpha, \alpha)$ and that a modified protocol M2TP selects the best of the two points, with respect to the local (vertical) progress. This is in fact an optimized version of the Local Target Protocol.

In a similar way as in the proof of the previous lemma, the authors prove the following result:

Lemma 2 ([2]). *The expected "hops" efficiency of the min-two uniform targets protocol is*

$$1 \leq E(C_h) \leq \frac{\pi^2}{8} \simeq 1.24$$

for large h and for $0 \leq \alpha \leq \frac{\pi}{2}$.

Remark that, with respect to the expected hops efficiency of the local target protocol, the min-two uniform targets protocol achieves, because of the one additional search, a relative gain which is $(\pi/2 - \pi^2/8)/(\pi/2) \simeq 21.5\%$. [2] also experimentally investigates the further gain of additional (i.e. $m > 2$) searches.

3 PFR – A Probabilistic Forwarding Protocol

The LTP protocol, as shown in the previous section manages to be very efficient by always selecting exactly one next-hop particle, with respect to some optimization criterion. Thus, it tries to minimize the number of data transmissions. LTP is indeed very successful in the case of dense and robust networks, since in such networks a next hop particle is very likely to be discovered. In sparse or faulty networks however, the LTP protocol may behave poorly, because of many backtracks due to frequent failure to find a next hop particle. To combine energy efficiency and fault-tolerance, the Probabilistic Forwarding Protocol (PFR) has been introduced. The trade-offs in the performance of the two protocols implied above are shown and discussed in great detail in [4].

3.1   The Model

The PFR protocol was introduced by Chatzigiannakis, Dimitriou, Nikoletseas and Spirakis in [3]. They assume the case where particles are *randomly deployed* in a given area of interest. Such a placement may occur e.g. when throwing sensors from an airplane over an area.

As a *special case*, they consider the network being a lattice (or grid) deployment of sensors. This grid placement of grain particles is motivated by certain applications, where it is possible to have a pre-deployed sensor network, where sensors are put (possibly by a human or a robot) in a way that they form a *2-dimensional lattice*.

Let N be the number of deployed grain particles. There is a single point in the network area, which we call the sink S, and represents a control center where data should be propagated to.

We assume that each grain particle has the following abilities:

(i)   It can estimate the direction of a received transmission (e.g. via the technology of direction-sensing antennae).

(ii) It can estimate the distance from a nearby particle that did the transmission (e.g. via estimation of the attenuation of the received signal).

(iii) It knows the direction towards the sink S. This can be implemented during a set-up phase, where the (very powerful in energy) sink broadcasts the information about itself to all particles.

(iv) All particles have a common co-ordinates system.

Notice that GPS information is not needed for this protocol. Also, there is no need to know the global structure of the network.

3.2   The Protocol

The PFR protocol is inspired by the probabilistic multi-path design choice for the Directed Diffusion paradigm mentioned in [11]. Its basic idea of the protocol (introduced in [3]) lies in probabilistically favoring transmissions towards the sink within a *thin zone* of particles around the line connecting the particle sensing the event $\mathcal{E}$ and the sink (see Fig. 4). Note that transmission along this line is energy optimal due to a variety of reasons.

The protocol evolves in two phases:

Phase 1: The "Front" Creation Phase. Initially the protocol builds (by using a limited, in terms of rounds, flooding) a sufficiently large "front" of particles, in order to guarantee the survivability of the data propagation process. During this phase, each particle having received the data to be propagated, deterministically forwards them towards the sink. In particular, and for a sufficiently large number of steps $s = 180\sqrt{2}$, each particle broadcasts the information to all its neighbors, towards the sink. Remark that to implement this phase, and in particular to count the number of steps, we use a counter in each message. This counter needs at most $\lceil \log 180\sqrt{2} \rceil$ bits.

Phase 2: The Probabilistic Forwarding Phase. During this phase, each particle P possessing the information under propagation, calculates an angle ϕ by calling the subprotocol "ϕ-calculation" (see description below) and broadcasts $info(\mathcal{E})$ to all its neighbors with probability $\mathbb{P}_{fwd}$ (or it does not propagate any data with probability $1 - \mathbb{P}_{fwd}$) defined as follows:

$$\mathbb{P}_{fwd} = \begin{cases} 1 & \text{if } \phi \geq \phi_{threshold} \\ \frac{\phi}{\pi} & \text{otherwise} \end{cases}$$

where ϕ is the angle defined by the line EP and the line PS and $\phi_{threshold} = 134^{o}$ (the selection reasons of this $\phi_{threshold}$ will become evident in Section 3.4).

In both phases, if a particle has already broadcast $info(\mathcal{E})$ and receives it again, it ignores it. Also the PFR protocol is presented for a single event tracing. Thus no multiple paths arise and packet sizes do not increase with time.

Remark that when $\phi = \pi$ then P lies on the line ES and vice-versa (and always transmits).

If the density of particles is appropriately large, then for a line ES there is (with high probability) a sequence of points "closely surrounding ES" whose angles ϕ are larger than $\phi_{threshold}$ and so that successive points are within transmission range. All such points broadcast and thus essentially they follow the line ES (see Fig. 4).

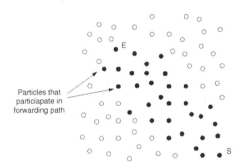

Particles that particiapate in forwarding path

Fig. 4. Thin Zone of particles

3.3 Properties of PFR

Consider a partition of the network area into small squares of a fictitious grid G (see Fig. 5). Let the length of the side of each square be l. Let the number of squares be q. The area covered is bounded by ql^2. Assuming that we randomly throw in the area at least $\alpha q \log q = N$ particles (where $\alpha > 0$ a suitable constant), then the probability that a particular square is avoided tends to 0. So with very high probability (tending to 1) all squares get particles. [3] conditions all the analysis on this event, call it F, of at least one particle in each square.

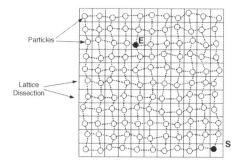

Fig. 5. A Lattice Dissection G

3.4   The Correctness of PFR

Without loss of generality, we assume each square of the fictitious lattice G to have side length 1.

In [3] the authors prove the correctness of the PFR protocol, by using a geometric analysis. We below sketch their proof. Consider any square Σ intersecting the ES line. By the occupancy argument above, there is with high probability a particle in this square. Clearly, the worst case is when the particle is located in one of the corners of Σ (since the two corners located most far away from the ES line have the smallest ϕ-angle among all positions in Σ). By some geometric calculations, [3] finally proves that the angle ϕ of this particle is $\phi > 134^{\circ}$. But the initial square (i.e. that containing E) always broadcasts and any intermediate intersecting square will be notified (by induction) and thus broadcast because of the argument above. Thus the sink will be reached if the whole network is operational.

Lemma 3 ([3]). PFR *succeeds with probability 1* in sending the information from E to S given the event F.

3.5   The Energy Efficiency of PFR

[3] considers the fictitious lattice G of the network area and let the event F hold. There is (at least) one particle inside each square. Now join all nearby particles of each particle to it, thus by forming a new graph G' which is "lattice-shaped" but its elementary "boxes" may not be orthogonal and may have varied length. When G's squares become smaller and smaller, then G' will look like G. Thus, for reasons of analytic tractability, in [3] the authors assume that particles form a lattice. They also assume length $l = 1$ in each square, for normalization purposes. Notice however that when $l \rightarrow 0$ then "$G' \rightarrow G$" and thus all results in this Section hold for any random deployment "in the limit".

The analysis of the energy efficiency considers particles that are active but are as far as possible from ES. Thus the approximation is suitable for remote particles.

[3] estimates an upper bound on the number of particles in an $n \times n$ (i.e. $N = n \times n$) lattice. If k is this number then $r = \frac{k}{n^2}$ ($0 < r \leq 1$) is the "energy efficiency ratio" of PFR.

More specifically, in [3] the authors prove the (very satisfactory) result below. They consider the area around the ES line, whose particles participate in the propagation process. The number of active particles is thus, roughly speaking, captured by the size of this area, which in turn is equal to $|ES|$ times the maximum distance from $|ES|$ (where maximum is over all active particles).

This maximum distance is clearly a random variable. To calculate the expectation and variance of this variable, the authors in [3] basically "upper bound" the stochastic process of the distance from ES by a random walk on the line, and subsequently "upper bound" this random walk by a well-known stochastic process (i.e. the "discouraged arrivals" birth and death Markovian process, see e.g. [15]). Thus they prove the following:

Theorem 1 ([3]). The energy efficiency of the PFR protocol is $\Theta\left(\left(\frac{n_0}{n}\right)^2\right)$ where $n_0 = |ES|$ and $n = \sqrt{N}$, where N is the number of particles in the network. For $n_0 = |ES| = o(n)$, this is $o(1)$.

3.6   The Robustness of PFR

To prove the following robustness result, the authors in [3] consider particles "very near" to the ES line. Clearly, such particles have large ϕ-angles (i.e. $\phi > 134^\circ$). Thus, even in the case that some of these particles are not operating, the probability that none of those operating transmits (during the probabilistic phase 2) is very small. Thus, [3] proves the following.

Lemma 4 ([3]). PFR manages to propagate the crucial data across lines parallel to ES, and of constant distance, with *fixed* nonzero probability (not depending on n, $|ES|$).

4   The Energy Balance Problem

Most data propagation techniques do not *explicitly* take care of the possible overuse of certain sensors in the network. As an example, remark that in hop-by-hop transmissions towards the sink, the sensors lying closer to the sink tend to be utilized exhaustively (since all data passes through them). Thus, these sensors may die out very early, thus resulting to network collapse although there may be still significant amounts of energy in the other sensors of the network. Similarly, in clustering techniques the cluster-heads that are located far away with respect to the sink, tend to spend a lot of energy.

In this section, we present a protocol trying to balance energy dissipation among the sensors in the network: the EBP (Energy Balance) protocol, introduced in [8] by Euthimiou, Nikoletseas and Rolim, that probabilistically chooses between either propagating data one hop towards the sink or sending directly to the sink. The first choice is more energy efficient, while the latter bypasses the critical (close to the sink) sectors. The appropriate probability for each choice in order to achieve energy balance is calculated in [8].

4.1   The Model and the Problem

We assume that crucial events, that should be reported to a control center, occur in the network area. Furthermore, we assume that these events are happening at random uniform positions. Let N be their total number in a certain period (i.e. during the execution of the protocol).

The sensors are spread in the network area randomly uniformly so their number in a certain area is proportional to the area's size. Sensors can be aware of the direction (and position) of the sink, as well as of their distance to the sink. We assume the transmission range of sensors can vary with time (in fact, for each sensor our protocol may use only two different ranges: R and $i \cdot R$, where i is a measure of the sensor's distance to the sink). The sensors do not move.

We virtually "cover" the network area by a cycle sector of angle ϕ (see Fig. 6). The cycle sector is divided into n ring sectors or "slices". The first slice has radius R (i.e. the sensors' transmission range). Slice i ($2 \le i \le n$) is defined by two cycles sectors, one of radius $i \cdot R$ and the other of radius $(i-1) \cdot R$. Taking a sufficiently large angle ϕ and/or by taking multiple sectors, we can cover the whole area.

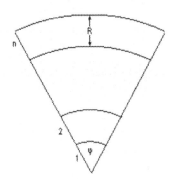

Fig. 6. Sensor Network with n ring sectors, angle ϕ and ring "width" R

As far as energy dissipation is concerned, we assume that the energy spent at a sensor when transmitting data is proportional to the square of the transmitting distance. Our protocol's performance analysis can be however extended to any energy cost model. Note that the energy dissipation for receiving is not always negligible with respect to the energy when sending such as in case when transmissions are too short and/or radio electronics energy is high (see [10]).

Definition 2. The area between two consecutive cycle sectors is called a *ring sector* (or "slice"). Let T_i ($1 \leq i \leq n$) be the i-th ring sector of the network.

T_1 stands for the ring sector with center the sink and radius equal to R.

Definition 3. Let S_i be the area size of the ring sector T_i of the network ($1 \leq i \leq n$).

We wish to solve the *"energy balanced data propagation problem"*, i.e. to propagate data to the sink in such a way that the "average" energy dissipation in each sensor is at each time the same. The average energy dissipation per sensor is taken to be the fraction of the total energy spent by sensors in a ring sector over the number of sensors in that sector. Because of our assumption that the number of sensors in an area is proportional to the area size, the average energy dissipation per sensor is calculated by dividing the total energy spent in a sector by the sector size.

4.2   The Protocol

A sensor sensing an event generates then a data message which should be eventually delivered to the sink. On each ring sector, T_i, a number of events occur and a corresponding number of messages (one for each event) is generated.

Randomization is used to achieve some "load balancing" by evenly spreading the "load" (energy dissipation). In particular, on ring sector T_i each event is propagated to T_{i-1} (i.e. the *"next"* sector towards the sink) with probability p_i, while with probability $1 - p_i$ it is propagated directly to the sink S. Each message in T_i is handled stochastically independently of the other events' messages.

The choice of probability p_i for T_i is made so as the average energy consumption per area unit (and thus per sensor) is the same for the whole network. There is a trade-off from choosing p_i: if p_i increases then transmissions tend to happen locally, thus energy consumption is low, however sensors closer to the sink tend to be overused since all data passes through them. On the other hand, if p_i decreases, there are distant transmissions (thus a lot of energy is consumed) however closer to sink particles are bypassed. Calculating the appropriate probability p_i for each T_i and solving the problem of energy balance is very important since it combines efficient data propagation with increased network's lifetime.

By using an underlying subprotocol ([2], [11]) we can guarantee that only one "next hop" sensor receives the transmitted message. Note also that data messages are of fixed size i.e. no further info is added to a message on its route towards the sink.

4.3   Basic Definitions – Preliminaries

We aim at calculating probability p_i for each i in order to ensure the energy balance property. Using simple geometry, one can easily prove the following Lemmas.

Lemma 5. The area size, S_1, of the ring sector T_1 is $S_1 = \frac{\phi}{2} \cdot R^2$

Lemma 6. The relation between the area size of the ring sector T_i and that of T_1 is $S_i = (2i - 1) \cdot S_1$

Definition 4. Let λ_i the probability that an event will occur on the ring sector T_i.

There are n ring sectors in the network.

Lemma 7. Assuming a random uniform generation of events in the network area, the probability λ_i of an event occurring on the ring sector T_i $(1 \le i \le n)$, is:

$$\lambda_i = \frac{(2i - 1)}{n^2}$$

Let us now consider sector T_i.

Definition 5. An area T_i "handles" an event generated in ring sector j if either the message was generated in the area T_i (i.e. $j = i$) or the message was propagated to T_i from the ring sector T_{i+1}.

Definition 6. Let h_i be the number of the messages that are "handled" by the area T_i.

We now define energy ϵ_{ij} spent for message j when sector i handles it.

Definition 7. Let ϵ_{ij} a random variable which measures the energy that dissipates the sector T_i so as to handle the message j. For ϵ_{ij} we have that:

$$\epsilon_{ij} = \begin{cases} cR^2 & \text{with probability } p_i \\ c(iR)^2 & \text{with probability } 1 - p_i \end{cases}$$

where cR^2 is the energy dissipation for sending a message j from T_i to its adjacent ring sector T_{i-1} and c is a constant.

Thus, the expected energy dissipation in sector i for handling a message is

$$E[\epsilon_{i,j}] = cR^2 \cdot [i^2 - p_i(i^2 - 1)] \tag{1}$$

Note: The expected energy above is the same for all messages; we use j just for counting purposes.

Definition 8. Let $\mathcal{E}_i$ the *total energy* spent by sensors in T_i. Clearly:

$$\mathcal{E}_i = \sum_{j=1}^{h_i} \epsilon_{ij} \tag{2}$$

Energy balance is defined as follows:

Definition 9. The network is energy balanced if the average per sensor energy dissipation is the same for all sectors, i.e. when

$$\frac{E[\mathcal{E}_i]}{S_i} = \frac{E[\mathcal{E}_j]}{S_j} \quad i, j = 1, \ldots, n \tag{3}$$

4.4   The General Solution

We next provide a lemma useful in the estimation of the total energy dissipation in a sector.

Lemma 8. The expected total energy dissipation in sector i is:

$$E[\mathcal{E}_i] = E[h_i] \cdot E[\epsilon_{ik}]$$

Definition 10. Let g_i be the number of the messages that are *generated* in the area T_i.

Note that messages are generated in an area only when events occur in this area.

Definition 11. Let f_i be the number of the messages that are *forwarded to* the area T_i.

We note that messages are forwarded to a ring sector (say i) only because of an event generation at a sector $j > i$ and successive one-hop propagations from sector j to sector i.

We notice the following important relation:

$$h_i = g_i + f_i \tag{4}$$

which means that the number of messages that area T_i handles equals the number of the messages that are generated in T_i, plus the number of messages that are forwarded to it. By linearity of expectation, we get:

Lemma 9. $E[h_i] = E[g_i] + E[f_i]$

We establish a relationship between $E[f_i]$ and $E[h_{i+1}]$.

Lemma 10. $E[f_i] = p_{i+1} \cdot E[h_{i+1}]$

Recall that, according to Definition 9, to achieve the same on the average energy dissipation *per area unit* (and thus per sensor) in the network area, the following equality should hold:

$$E\left[\frac{\sum_{k=1}^{h_i} \epsilon_{ik}}{S_i}\right] = E\left[\frac{\sum_{k=1}^{h_j} \epsilon_{jk}}{S_j}\right] \quad \forall i, j \in \{1, \ldots n\} \tag{5}$$

i.e. the average energy consumption per sensor should be equal in any two ring sectors. By induction, it suffices to guarantee this for any two adjacent sectors. In what follows, we guarantee the above balance property, requiring a certain recurrence relation to hold. This recurrence basically relates 3 successive terms of the $E[f_i]$ sequence (the $E[g_i]$ terms depend only on i and on input parameters).

Theorem 2. To achieve energy balance in the network, the following recurrence equation should hold:

$$a_{i+1}E[f_{i+1}] - (d_i + a_i)E[f_i] + d_{i-1}E[f_{i-1}] = a_i E[g_i] - a_{i+1}E[g_{i+1}]$$

where

$$a_i = \frac{i^2}{2i-1} \qquad d_i = \frac{(i+1)^2-1}{2i+1}$$

To solve the above recurrence we must compute $E[g_i]$.

Lemma 11. If N is the total number of events that are generated in the network, the mean value of g_i is given by the following relationship:

$$E[g_i] = N \cdot \lambda_i$$

In order to have a simpler recurrence involving only two (successive in fact) terms of the $E[f_i]$ sequence, we will transform the recurrence relation of Theorem 2 into the following (easier to solve) relation:

Lemma 12. The recurrence relation:

$$t_i - t_{i-1} = a_i \cdot E[f_i] - a_{i+1} \cdot E[f_{i+1}]$$
$$\text{for} \quad i = 1, \dots n-1$$
$$\text{and} \quad t_0 = a_1 \cdot E[f_1]$$

has as a solution the function

$$t_i = \sum_{j=1}^{i} (a_j E[g_j] - a_{j+1} E[g_{j+1}]) + a_1 \cdot E[f_1]$$

Now the recurrence relation of Thrm 2 is simplified:

$$a_{i+1} \cdot E[f_{i+1}] - d_i \cdot E[f_i] = t_i \quad i = 1, \dots, n-1$$

Thus, we get a recurrence for sequence $E[f_i]$ involving only two successive terms of the sequence:

Theorem 3. The recurrence relation

$$a_{i+1} E[f_{i+1}] - d_i E[f_i] = t_i \quad i = 1, \dots n-1$$

where t_i is defined in lemma 12, has the following solution

$$E[f_{n-i}] = - \sum_{k=1}^{i} \frac{\prod_{j=k}^{i-1} a_{n-j}}{\prod_{j=k}^{i} d_{n-j}} \cdot t_{n-k}$$

The full expression for $E[f_i]$ can be expressed by substituting i with $n-i$, thus

$$E[f_i] = - \sum_{k=1}^{n-i} \frac{\prod_{j=k}^{n-i+1} a_{n-j}}{\prod_{j=k}^{n-i} d_{n-j}} \cdot \left(\sum_{j=1}^{n-k} (a_j E[g_j] - a_{j+1} E[g_{j+1}]) + a_1 \cdot E[f_1] \right)$$

where $\prod_i^{i-1} a_i = 1$.

We note that all the parameters of the recurrence solution above are expressed as a function of $E[f_1]$ and i. So as to compute them, we firstly compute the value of $E[f_1]$. Then we can compute all the other parameters by replacing the already computed $E[f_1]$.

Now, the calculation of the probabilities p_i is quite easy.

Theorem 4. The energy balance property is achieved if any ring sector (say T_i) propagates each message it handles with probability p_i to the next ring sector, T_{i-1}, and with probability $1 - p_i$ it propagates the message directly to the sink. The value of each p_i is given by the following relation

$$p_i = \frac{E[f_{i-1}]}{E[g_i] + E[f_i]}$$

where the values of $E[f_i]$ and $E[g_i]$ are obtained from lemma 3 and lemma 11, respectively.

We note that the analysis above allows the exact derivation of probabilities p_i's as a function of i and n which (although complicated and not obviously leading to a closed form) can be easily calculated by the sensors in the network by carrying out very simple calculations.

4.5 A Closed Form

Under specific assumptions (that we discuss and motivate in [8]) we can make the calculation of probabilities p_i simpler. Combining lemma 9 and lemma 11 we have that:

Theorem 5. If $E[f_i] \simeq E[f_{i-1}]$, $3 \le i \le n$, then the one-hop forwarding probability, guaranteeing energy balance, is

$$p_i = 1 - \frac{3x}{(i+1)(i-1)}$$

where $p_2 = x \in (0,1)$ a free parameter and $p_1 = 0$.

5 Future Directions

Wireless sensor networks constitute a new fascinating field, where complementary approaches (algorithms, systems, applications and technology) are needed. From an algorithmic perspective, new abstract models and model extensions are needed (hiding details but still being realistic) to enable the necessary performance analysis – occasionally evel asymptotic analysis. The interplay of geometry, graph theory and randomness create many challenging problems for rigorous treatment ([17]). Inherent trade-offs, lower bounds and impossibility results should be further investigated towards properly guiding technological efforts by pointing out inherent limitations. New efficient but simple algorithms should be designed and analysed and paradigms should be established. At the system level, versatile network stacks and lightweighted operating systems and middleware are needed.

References

1. Akyildiz, I.F., Su, W., Sankarasubramaniam, Y., and Cayirci, E.: Wireless Sensor Networks: a Survey. In the Journal of Computer Networks **38** (2002) 393-422
2. Chatzigiannakis, I., Nikoletseas, S., Spirakis, P.: Smart Dust Protocols for Local Detection and Propagation. Distinguished Paper. In Proc. 2nd ACM Workshop on Principles of Mobile Computing – POMC'2002, 9-16. Also, accepted in the ACM Mobile Networks (MONET) Journal, Special Issue on Algorithmic Solutions for Wireless, Mobile, Adhoc and Sensor Networks **10** 1 (February 2005)
3. Chatzigiannakis, I., Dimitriou, T., Nikoletseas, S., and Spirakis, P.: A Probabilistic Algorithm for Efficient and Robust Data Propagation in Smart Dust Networks. In the Proceedings of the 5th European Wireless Conference on Mobile and Wireless Systems beyond 3G (EW 2004), 2004. Also, accepted in the Journal of Ad-Hoc Networks, to appear in 2005
4. Chatzigiannakis, I., Dimitriou, T., Mavronicolas, M., Nikoletseas, S., and Spirakis, P.: A Comparative Study of Protocols for Efficient Data Propagation in Smart Dust Networks. In Proc. International Conference on Parallel and Distributed Computing – EUPOPAR 2003. Also accepted in the Parallel Processing Letters (PPL) Journal, to appear in 2004
5. Diaz, J., Penrose, M., Petit, J., and Serna, M.: Approximation Layout Problems on Random Geometric Graphs. J. of Algorithms **39** (2001) 78-116
6. Diaz, J., Petit, J., and Serna, M.: A Random Graph Model for Optical Networks of Sensors. In J. of IEEE Transactions on Mobile Computing **2** 3 (2003)
7. Estrin, D., Govindan, R., Heidemann, J., and Kumar, S.: Next Century Challenges: Scalable Coordination in Sensor Networks. In Proc. 5th ACM/IEEE International Conference on Mobile Computing – MOBICOM'1999
8. Euthimiou, H., Nikoletseas, S., and Rolim, J.: Energy Balanced Data Propagation in Wireless Sensor Networks. In Proc. 4th International Workshop on Algorithms for Wireless, Mobile, Ad-Hoc and Sensor Networks (WMAN '04), IPDPS 2004, 2004. Also, in the Journal of Wireless Networks (WINET), Special Issue on best papers of WMAN 04, 2005
9. Gilbert, E.N.: Random Plane Networks. J. Soc. Ind. Appl. Math **9** 4 (1961) 533-543
10. Heinzelman, W.R., Chandrakasan, A., and Balakrishnan, H.: Energy-Efficient Communication Protocol for Wireless Microsensor Networks. In Proc. 33rd Hawaii International Conference on System Sciences – HICSS'2000
11. Intanagonwiwat, C., Govindan, R., and Estrin, D.: Directed Diffusion: A Scalable and Robust Communication Paradigm for Sensor Networks. In Proc. 6th ACM/IEEE International Conference on Mobile Computing – MOBICOM'2000
12. Intanagonwiwat, C., Govindan, R., Estrin, D., Heidemann, J., and Silva, F.: Directed Diffusion for Wireless Sensor Networking. Extended version of [11].
13. Kahn, J.M., Katz, R.H., and Pister, K.S.J.: Next Century Challenges: Mobile Networking for Smart Dust. In Proc. 5th ACM/IEEE International Conference on Mobile Computing (September 1999) 271-278
14. Karoński, M., Scheinerman, E.R., and Singer-Cohen, K.B.: On Random Intersection Graphs: The Subgraph Problem. Combinatorics, Probability and Computing Journal **8** (1999) 131-159
15. Kleinrock, L.: Queueing Systems, Theory. John Wiley & Sons, **I** (1975) pp. 100

16. Nikoletseas, S., Raptopoulos, C., and Spirakis, P.: The Existence and Efficient Construction of Large Independent Sets in General Random Intersection Graphs. In the Proceedings of the 31st International Colloquium on Automata, Languages and Programming (ICALP), Lecture Notes in Computer Science (Springer Verlag), 2004. Also, invited paper in the Theoretical Computer Science (TCS) Journal, Special Issue on Global Computing, under review, to appear in 2005
17. Papadimitriou, C.: Algorithmic Problems in Ad Hoc Networks. In IEEE International Conference on Distributed Computing in Sensor Systems (DCOSS 05), Springer/LNCS 3560 (2005)
18. Penrose, M.: Random Geometric Graphs. Oxford University Press (2003)
19. Ross, S.M.: Stochastic Processes, 2nd Edition. John Wiley and Sons, Inc. (1995)
20. Sanwalani, V., Serna, M., and Spirakis, P.: Chromatic Number of Random Scaled Sector Graphs. In the Theoretical Computer Science (TCS) Journal, to appear in 2006
21. Triantafilloy, P., Ntarmos, N., Nikoletseas, S., and Spirakis, P.: NanoPeer Networks and P2P Worlds. In Proc. 3rd IEEE International Conference on Peer-to-Peer Computing (2003)

SomeWhere in the Semantic Web

M.-C. Rousset, P. Adjiman, P. Chatalic, F. Goasdoué, and L. Simon

LSR-IMAG, BP 72 38402 St Martin D'Heres, Cedex, France
PCRI: Université Paris-Sud XI & CNRS (LRI), INRIA (UR Futurs),
Bâtiment 490, Université Paris-Sud XI 91405 Orsay, Cedex, France
Marie-Christine.Rousset@imag.fr

Abstract. In this paper, we describe the SomeWhere semantic peer-to-peer data management system that promotes a "small is beautiful" vision of the Semantic Web based on simple personalized ontologies (e.g., taxonomies of classes) but which are distributed at a large scale. In this vision of the Semantic Web, no user imposes to others his own ontology. Logical mappings between ontologies make possible the creation of a web of people in which personalized semantic marking up of data cohabits nicely with a collaborative exchange of data. In this view, the Web is a huge peer-to-peer data management system based on simple distributed ontologies and mappings.

1   Introduction

The Semantic Web [1] envisions a world wide distributed architecture where data and computational resources will easily inter-operate based on semantic marking up of web resources using *ontologies*. Ontologies are a formalization of the semantics of application domains (e.g., tourism, biology, medicine) through the definition of classes and relations modeling the domain objects and properties that are considered as meaningful for the application. Most of the concepts, tools and techniques deployed so far by the Semantic Web community correspond to the "big is beautiful" idea that high expressivity is needed for describing domain ontologies. As a result, when they are applied, the current Semantic Web technologies are mostly used for building thematic portals but do not scale up to the web. In contrast, SomeWhere promotes a "small is beautiful" vision of the Semantic Web [2] based on simple personalized ontologies (e.g., taxonomies of atomic classes) but which are distributed at a large scale. In this vision of the Semantic Web introduced in [3], no user imposes to others his own ontology but logical mappings between ontologies make possible the creation of a web of people in which personalized semantic marking up of data cohabits nicely with a collaborative exchange of data. In this view, the web is a huge peer-to-peer data management system based on simple distributed ontologies and mappings.

Peer-to-peer data management systems have been proposed recently [4]-[7] to generalize the centralized approach of information integration systems based on single mediators. In a peer-to-peer data management system, there is no central mediator: each peer has its own ontology and data or services, and can

J. Wiedermann et al. (Eds.): SOFSEM 2006, LNCS 3831, pp. 84–99, 2006.

mediate with some other peers to ask and answer queries. The existing systems vary according to (a) the expressive power of their underlying data model and (b) the way the different peers are semantically connected. Both characteristics have impact on the allowed queries and their distributed processing.

In Edutella [8], each peer stores locally data (educational resources) that are described in RDF relatively to some reference ontologies (e.g., http://dmoz.org). For instance, a peer can declare that it has data related to the concept of the dmoz taxonomy corresponding to the path *Computers/Programming/ Languages/Java*, and that for such data it can export the *author* and the *date* properties. The overlay network underlying Edutella is a hypercube of super-peers to which peers are directly connected. Each super-peer is a mediator over the data of the peers connected to it. When it is queried, its first task is to check if the query matches with its schema: if that is the case, it transmits the query to the peers connected to it, which are likely to store the data answering the query; otherwise, it routes the query to some of its neighbour super-peers according to a strategy exploiting the hypercube topology for guaranteeing a worst-case logarithmic time for reaching the relevant super-peer.

In contrast with Edutella, Piazza [4], [9] does not consider that the data distributed over the different peers must be described relatively to some existing reference schemas. Each peer has its own data and schema and can mediate with some other peers by declaring *mappings* between its schema and the schemas of those peers. The topology of the network is not fixed (as in Edutella) but accounts for the existence of mappings between peers: two peers are logically connected if there exists a mapping between their two schemas. The underlying data model of the first version of Piazza [4] is relational and the mappings between relational peer schemas are inclusion or equivalence statements between conjunctive queries. Such a mapping formalism encompasses the *Local-as-View* and the *Global-as-View* [10] formalisms used in information integration systems based on single mediators. The price to pay is that query answering is undecidable except if some restrictions are imposed on the mappings or on the topology of the network [4]. The currently implemented version of Piazza [9] relies on a tree-based data model: the data is in XML and the mappings are equivalence and inclusion statements between XML queries. Query answering is implemented based on practical (but not complete) algorithms for XML query containment and rewriting. The scalability of Piazza so far does not go up to more than about 80 peers in the published experiments and relies on a wide range of optimizations (mappings composition [11], paths pruning [12]), made possible by the centralized storage of all the schemas and mappings in a global server.

In SomeWhere, we have made the choice of being fully distributed: there are neither super-peers nor a central server having the global view of the overlay network. In addition, we aim at scaling up to thousands of peers. To make it possible, we have chosen a simple class-based data model in which the data is a set of resource identifiers (e.g., URIs), the schemas are (simple) definitions of classes possibly constrained by inclusion, disjunction or equivalence statements, and mappings are inclusion, disjunction or equivalence statements between classes of different peer schemas. That data model is in accordance with the W3C recommendations since it is captured by the propositional fragment of the OWL ontology language (http://www.w3.org/TR/owl-semantics).

The paper is organized as follows. Section 2 defines the SomeWhere data model. In Section 3, we show how the corresponding query rewriting problem can be reduced by a propositional encoding to distributed reasoning in propositional logic. In Section 4, we describe the properties of the message based distributed reasoning algorithm that is implemented in SomeWhere, and we report experiments on networks of 1000 peers. Section 5 surveys some recent related work on peer-to-peer data management systems. We conclude and present our forthcoming work in Section 6.

2   SomeWhere Data Model

In SomeWhere a new peer joins the network through some peers that it knows (its acquaintances) by declaring mappings between its own ontology and the ontologies of its acquaintances. Queries are posed to a given peer using its local ontology. The answers that are expected are not only instances of local classes but possibly instances of classes of peers distant from the queried peer if it can be inferred from the peer ontologies and the mappings that those instances are answers of the query. Local ontologies, storage descriptions and mappings are defined using a fragment of OWL DL which is the description logic fragment of the Ontology Web Language recommended by W3C. We call OWL PL the fragment of OWL DL that we consider in SomeWhere, where PL stands for propositional logic. OWL PL is the fragment of OWL DL reduced to the disjunction, conjunction and negation constructors for building class descriptions.

2.1   Peer Ontologies

Each peer ontology is made of a set of class definitions and possibly a set of equivalence, inclusion or disjointness axioms between class descriptions. A class description is either the universal class ($\top$), the empty class ($\bot$), an atomic class or the union ($\sqcup$), intersection ($\sqcap$) or complement ($\neg$) of class descriptions.

The name of atomic classes are unique to each peer: we use the notation $P{:}A$ for identifying an atomic class A of the ontology of a peer P. The *vocabulary* of a peer P is the set of names of its atomic classes.

Class descriptions

	Logical notation	OWL notation
universal class	$\top$	*Thing*
empty class	$\bot$	*Nothing*
atomic class	$P{:}A$	*classID*
conjunction	$D1 \sqcap D2$	*intersectionOf(D1 D2)*
disjunction	$D1 \sqcup D2$	*unionOf(D1 D2)*
negation	$\neg D$	*complementOf(D)*

Axioms of class definitions

	Logical notation	OWL notation
Complete	$P{:}A \equiv D$	$Class(P{:}A \ complete \ D)$
Partial	$P{:}A \sqsubseteq D$	$Class(P{:}A \ partial \ D)$

Axioms on class descriptions

	Logical notation	OWL notation
equivalence	$D1 \equiv D2$	$EquivalentClasses(D1 \ D2)$
inclusion	$D1 \sqsubseteq D2$	$SubClassOf(D1 \ D2)$
disjointness	$D1 \sqcap D2 \equiv \bot$	$DisjointClasses(D1 \ D2)$

2.2 Peer Storage Descriptions

The specification of the data that is stored locally in a peer P is done through the declaration of atomic *extensional classes* defined in terms of atomic classes of the peer ontology, and assertional statements relating data identifiers (e.g., URIs) to those extensional classes. We restrict the axioms defining the extensional classes to be inclusion statements between an atomic extensional class and a description combining atomic classes of the ontology. We impose that restriction in order to fit with a *Local-as-View* approach and an open-world assumption within the information integration setting [10]. We will use the notation $P{:}ViewA$ to denote an extensional class $ViewA$ of the peer P.

Storage description
declaration of extensional classes:

Logical notation	OWL notation
$P{:}ViewA \sqsubseteq C$	$SubClassOf(P{:}ViewA \ \ C)$

assertional statements:

Logical notation	OWL notation
$P{:}ViewA(a)$	$individual(a \ type(P{:}ViewA))$

2.3 Mappings

Mappings are disjointness, equivalence or inclusion statements involving atomic classes of different peers. They express the semantic correspondence that may exist between the ontologies of different peers.

The *acquaintance graph* accounts for the connection induced by the mappings between the different peers within a given SomeWhere peer-to-peer network.

Definition 1 (Acquaintance graph). *Let* $\mathcal{P} = \{P_i\}_{i \in [1..n]}$ *a collection of peers with their respective vocabularies* Voc_{P_i}. *Let* $Voc = \bigcup_{i=1}^{n} Voc_{P_i}$ *be the vocabulary of* $\mathcal{P}$. *Its* acquaintance graph *is a graph* $\Gamma = (\mathcal{P}, \text{ACQ})$ *where* $\mathcal{P}$ *is the set of vertices and* $\text{ACQ} \subseteq Voc \times \mathcal{P} \times \mathcal{P}$ *is a set of labelled edges such that for every* $(c, P_i, P_j) \in \text{ACQ}$, $i \neq j$ *and* $c \in Voc_{P_i} \cap Voc_{P_j}$.

A labelled edge (c, P_i, P_j) expresses that peers P_i and P_j know each other to be sharing the class c. This means that c belongs to the intentional classes of P_i (or P_j) and is involved in a mapping with intentional classes of P_j (or P_i).

2.4   Schema of a SomeWhere Network

In a SomeWhere network, the schema is not centralized but distributed through the union of the different peer ontologies and the mappings. The important point is that each peer has a partial knowledge of the schema: it just knows its own local ontology and the mappings with its acquaintances.

Let $\mathcal{P}$ be a SomeWhere peer-to-peer network made of a collection of peers $\{P_i\}_{i \in [1..n]}$. For each peer P_i, let O_i, V_i and M_i be the sets of axioms defining respectively the local ontology of P_i, the declaration of its extensional classes and the set of mappings stated at P_i between classes of O_i and classes of the ontologies of the acquaintances of P_i. The schema $\mathcal{S}$ of $\mathcal{P}$ is the union $\bigcup_{i \in [1..n]} O_i \cup V_i \cup M_i$ of the ontologies, the declaration on extensional classes and of the sets of mappings of all the peers of $\mathcal{P}$.

2.5   Semantics

The semantics is a standard logical formal semantics defined in terms of *interpretations*. An interpretation I is a pair $(\Delta^I, .^I)$ where Δ is a non-empty set, called the domain of interpretation, and $.^I$ is an interpretation function which assigns a subset of Δ^I to every class identifier and an element of Δ^I to every data identifier.

An interpretation I is a *model* of the distributed schema of a SomeWhere peer-to-peer network $\mathcal{P} = \{P_i\}_{i \in [1..n]}$ iff each axiom in $\bigcup_{i \in [1..n]} O_i \cup V_i \cup M_i$ is satisfied by I.

Interpretations of axioms rely on interpretations of class descriptions which are inductively defined as follows:

- $\top^I = \Delta^I$, $\perp^I = \emptyset$
- $(\neg C)^I = \Delta^I \backslash C^I$
- $(C_1 \sqcup C_2)^I = C_1^I \cup C_2^I$, $(C_1 \sqcap C_2)^I = C_1^I \cap C_2^I$

Axioms are satisfied if the following holds:

- $C \sqsubseteq D$ is satisfied in I iff $C^I \subseteq D^I$
- $C \equiv D$ is satisfied in I iff $C^I = D^I$
- $C \sqcap D \equiv \perp$ is satisfied in I iff $C^I \cap D^I = \emptyset$

A SomeWhere peer-to-peer network is *satisfiable* iff its schema has a model.

Given a SomeWhere peer-to-peer network $\mathcal{P} = \{P_i\}_{i \in [1..n]}$, a class description C *subsumes* a class description D iff in each model I of the schema of $\mathcal{P}$, $D^I \subseteq C^I$.

2.6   Illustrative Example

We illustrate the SomeWhere data model on a small example of four peers modeling four persons Ann, Bob, Chris and Dora, each of them bookmarking URLs about restaurants they know or like, according to their own taxonomy for categorizing restaurants.

Ann, who is working as a restaurant critics, organizes its restaurant URLs according to the following classes:

- the class $Ann{:}G$ of restaurants considered as offering a "good" cooking, among which she distinguishes the subclass $Ann{:}R$ of those which are rated: $Ann{:}R \sqsubseteq Ann{:}G$
- the class $Ann{:}R$ is the union of three disjoint classes $Ann{:}S1$, $Ann{:}S2$, $Ann{:}S3$ corresponding respectively to the restaurants rated with $1, 2$ or 3 stars:
$$Ann{:}R \equiv Ann{:}S1 \sqcup Ann{:}S2 \sqcup Ann{:}S3$$
$$Ann{:}S1 \sqcap Ann{:}S2 \equiv \bot \quad Ann{:}S1 \sqcap Ann{:}S3 \equiv \bot$$
$$Ann{:}S2 \sqcap Ann{:}S3 \equiv \bot$$
- the classes $Ann{:}I$ and $Ann{:}O$, respectively corresponding to Indian and Oriental restaurants
- the classes $Ann{:}C$, $Ann{:}T$ and $Ann{:}V$ which are subclasses of $Ann{:}O$ denoting Chinese, Taï and Vietnamese restaurants respectively: $Ann{:}C \sqsubseteq Ann{:}O$, $Ann{:}T \sqsubseteq Ann{:}O$, $Ann{:}V \sqsubseteq Ann{:}O$

Suppose that the data stored by Ann that she accepts to make available deals with restaurants of various specialties, and only with those rated with 2 stars among the rated restaurants. The extensional classes declared by Ann are then:
$Ann{:}ViewS2 \sqsubseteq Ann{:}S2$, $Ann{:}ViewC \sqsubseteq Ann{:}C$,
$Ann{:}ViewV \sqsubseteq Ann{:}V$, $Ann{:}ViewT \sqsubseteq Ann{:}T$,
$Ann{:}ViewI \sqsubseteq Ann{:}I$

Bob, who is found of Asian cooking and likes high quality, organizes his restaurant URLs according to the following classes:

- the class $Bob{:}A$ of Asian restaurants
- the class $Bob{:}Q$ of high quality restaurants that he knows

Suppose that he wants to make available every data that he has stored. The extensional classes that he declares are $Bob{:}ViewA$ and $Bob{:}ViewQ$ (as subclasses of $Bob{:}A$ and $Bob{:}Q$): $Bob{:}ViewA \sqsubseteq Bob{:}A$, $Bob{:}ViewQ \sqsubseteq Bob{:}Q$

Chris is more found of fish restaurants but recently discovered some places serving a very nice cantonese cuisine. He organizes its data with respect to the following classes:

- the class $Chris{:}F$ of fish restaurants,
- the class $Chris{:}CA$ of Cantonese restaurants

Suppose the extensional classes $Chris{:}ViewF$ and $Chris{:}ViewCA$ as subclasses of $Chris{:}F$ and $Chris{:}CA$ class respectively: $Chris{:}ViewF \sqsubseteq Chris{:}F$, and $Chris{:}ViewCA \sqsubseteq Chris{:}CA$

Dora organizes her restaurants URLs around the class $Dora{:}DP$ of her preferred restaurants, among which she distinguishes the subclass $Dora{:}P$ of pizzerias and the subclass $Dora{:}SF$ of seafood restaurants.

Suppose that the only URLs that she stores concerns pizzerias: the only extensional class that she has to declare is $Dora{:}ViewP$ as a subclass of $Dora{:}P$: $Dora{:}ViewP \sqsubseteq Dora{:}P$

Ann, **Bob**, **Chris** and **Dora** express what they know about each other using mappings stating properties of class inclusion or equivalence.

Ann is very confident in Bob's taste and agrees to include Bob' selection as good restaurants by stating $Bob{:}Q \sqsubseteq Ann{:}G$. Finally, she thinks that Bob's Asian restaurants encompass her Oriental restaurant concept: $Ann{:}O \sqsubseteq Bob{:}A$

Bob knows that what he calls Asian cooking corresponds exactly to what Ann classifies as Oriental cooking. This may be expressed using the equivalence statement : $Bob{:}A \equiv Ann{:}O$ (note the difference of perception of Bob and Ann regarding the mappings between $Bob{:}A$ and $Ann{:}O$)

Chris considers that what he calls fish specialties is a particular case of Dora seafood specialties: $Chris{:}F \sqsubseteq Dora{:}SF$

Dora counts on both Ann and Bob to obtain good Asian restaurants : $Bob{:}A \sqcap Ann{:}G \sqsubseteq Dora{:}DP$

Figure 1 describes the resulting acquaintance graph. In order to alleviate the notations, we omit the local peer name prefix except for the mappings. Edges are labeled with the class identifiers that are shared through the mappings.

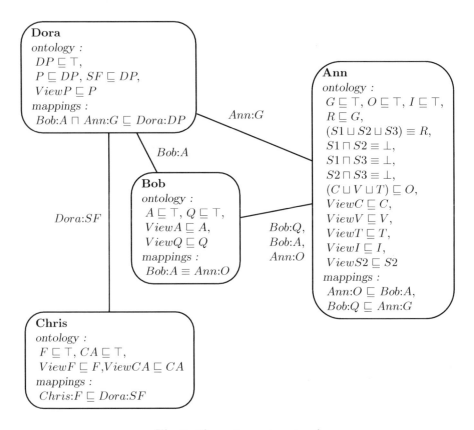

Fig. 1. The restaurants network

3   Query Rewriting

In SomeWhere, each user interrogates the peer-to-peer network through one peer of his choice, and uses the vocabulary of this peer to express his query. Therefore, queries are logical combinations of classes of a given peer ontology.

The corresponding answer sets are expressed in intention in terms of the combinations of extensional classes that are *rewritings* of the query. The point is that extensional classes of several distant peers can participate to the rewritings, and thus to the answer of a query posed to a given peer.

Given a SomeWhere peer-to-peer network $\mathcal{P} = \{P_i\}_{i \in [1..n]}$, a logical combination Q_e of extensional classes is a *rewriting* of a query Q iff Q subsumes Q_e. Q_e is a *maximal rewriting* if there does not exist another rewriting Q'_e of Q (strictly) subsuming Q_e.

In the SomeWhere setting, query rewriting can be equivalently reduced to distributed reasoning over logical propositional theories by a straightforward propositional encoding of the distributed schema of a SomeWhere network.

Before presenting the propositional encoding in Section 3.2 and the distributed consequence finding algorithm in Section 4, we illustrate the corresponding query processing on the example of Section 2.6.

3.1   Illustrative Example (Continued)

Consider that a user queries the restaurants network through the **Dora** peer by asking the query *Dora:DP*, meaning that he is interested in getting as answers the set of favorite restaurants of Dora:

- Using $Dora{:}P \sqsubseteq Dora{:}DP$ and $Dora{:}ViewP \sqsubseteq Dora{:}P$, we obtain *Dora: ViewP* as a local rewriting corresponding to the extensional class of pizzeria URLs stored by Dora.

- Using $Dora{:}SF \sqsubseteq Dora{:}DP$, the fact that *Dora:SF* is shared with *Chris* by the mapping $Chris{:}F \sqsubseteq Dora{:}SF$, and $Chris{:}ViewF \sqsubseteq Chris{:}F$, we obtain *Chris:ViewF* as a new rewriting meaning that another way to get restaurants liked by Dora is to obtain the Fish restaurants stored by Chris.

- Finally, using the mapping $Bob{:}A \sqcap Ann{:}G \sqsubseteq Dora{:}DP$, the query leads to look for rewritings of $Bob{:}A \sqcap Ann{:}G$, where both *Bob:A* and *Ann:G* are shared with neighbor peers. In such cases our algorithm uses a split/recombination approach. Each shared component (here *Bob:A* and *Ann:G*) is then processed independently as a subquery, transmitted to its appropriate neighbors and associated with some queue data structure, where its returned rewritings are accumulated. As soon as at least one rewriting has been obtained for each component, the respective queued rewritings of each component are recombined to produce rewritings of the initial query. This recombination process continues incrementally, as new rewritings for a component are produced. Note that since each subcomponent is processed asynchronously, the order in which recombined rewritings are produced is unpredictable. For the sake of simplicity, in the following we consider sequentially the results obtained for the two subqueries *Bob:A* and *Ann:G*:

– On the Bob peer, because of $Bob{:}ViewA{\sqsubseteq}Bob{:}A$, $Bob{:}ViewA$ is a local rewriting of $Bob{:}A$, which is transmitted back to the Dora peer, where it is queued for a future combination with rewritings of the other subquery $Ann{:}G$.

In addition, guided by the mapping $Ann{:}O{\equiv}Bob{:}A$, the Bob peer transmits to the Ann peer the query $Ann{:}O$. The Ann peer processes that query locally and transmits back to the Bob peer the rewriting $Ann{:}ViewC \sqcup Ann{:}ViewT \sqcup Ann{:}ViewV$, which in turn is transmitted back to the Dora peer as an additional rewriting for the subquery $Bob{:}A$ and queued there.

– On the Ann peer, using $Ann{:}R{\sqsubseteq}Ann{:}G$, $(Ann{:}S1{\sqcup}Ann{:}S2 {\sqcup}Ann{:}S3){\equiv}Ann{:}R$ and $Ann{:}ViewS2{\sqsubseteq}Ann{:}S2$, $Ann{:}ViewS2$ is obtained as a local rewriting of $Ann{:}G$. It is transmitted back to the Dora peer where it is queued for recombination. Let us suppose that the two rewritings of $Bob{:}A$ ($Bob{:}ViewA$ and $Ann{:}ViewC{\sqcup}Ann{:}ViewT{\sqcup}Ann{:}ViewV$) have already been produced at that time. Their combination with $Ann{:}ViewS2$ gives two rewritings which are sent back to the user:

* $Ann{:}ViewS2{\sqcap}Bob{:}ViewA$, meaning that a way to obtain restaurants liked by Dora is to find restaurants that are both stored by Ann as rated with 2 stars and by Bob as Asian restaurants,

* $Ann{:}ViewS2{\sqcap}(Ann{:}ViewC{\sqcup}Ann{:}ViewT{\sqcup}Ann{:}ViewV)$ meaning that another way to obtain restaurants liked by Dora is to find restautants stored by Ann as restaurants rated with 2 stars and also as Chinese, Thai or Vietnamese restaurants. Note that this rewriting, although obtained via different peers after splitting/recombination, turns out to be composed only of extensional classes of the same peer: Ann.

Still on the Ann peer, because of the mapping $Bob{:}Q \sqsubseteq Ann{:}G$, Ann transmits the query $Bob{:}Q$ to Bob, which transmits back to Ann $Bob{:}ViewQ$ as a rewriting of $Bob{:}Q$ (and thus of $Ann{:}G$). Ann then transmits $Bob{:}ViewQ$ back to Dora as a rewriting of $Ann{:}G$, where it is queued for combination. On Dora's side, $Bob{:}ViewQ$ is now combined with the queued rewritings of $Bob{:}A$ ($Bob{:}ViewA$ and $Ann{:}ViewC \sqcup Ann{:}ViewT{\sqcup}Ann{:}ViewV$). As a result, two new rewritings are sent back to the user:

* $Bob{:}ViewQ{\sqcap}Bob{:}ViewA$ meaning that to obtain restaurants liked by Dora one can take the restaurants that Bob stores as high quality restaurants and as Asian restaurants,

* $Bob{:}ViewQ{\sqcap}(Ann{:}ViewC{\sqcup}Ann{:}ViewT{\sqcup}Ann{:}ViewV)$ providing a new way of getting restaurants liked by Dora: those that are both stored as high quality restaurants by Bob and as Chinese, Thai or Vietnamese restaurants by Ann.

3.2   Propositional Encoding of Query Rewriting in SomeWhere

The propositional encoding concerns the schema of a SomeWhere network and the queries. It consists in transforming each query and schema statement into a propositional formula using class identifiers as propositional variables.

The propositional encoding of a class description D, and thus of a query, is the propositional formula $Prop(D)$ obtained inductively as follows:

- $Prop(\top) = true$, $Prop(\bot) = false$
- $Prop(A) = A$, if A is an atomic class
- $Prop(D_1 \sqcap D_2) = Prop(D_1) \wedge Prop(D_2)$
- $Prop(D_1 \sqcup D_2) = Prop(D_1) \vee Prop(D_2)$
- $Prop(\neg D) = \neg(Prop(D))$

The propositional encoding of the schema $\mathcal{S}$ of a SomeWhere peer-to-peer network $\mathcal{P}$ is the distributed propositional theory $Prop(\mathcal{S})$ made of the formulas obtained inductively from the axioms in $\mathcal{S}$ as follows:

- $Prop(C \sqsubseteq D) = Prop(C) \Rightarrow Prop(D)$
- $Prop(C \equiv D) = Prop(C) \Leftrightarrow Prop(D)$
- $Prop(C \sqcap D \equiv \bot) = \neg Prop(C) \vee \neg Prop(D)$

From now on, for simplicity purpose, we use the propositional clausal form notation for the queries and SomeWhere peer-to-peer network schemas.

As an illustration, let us consider the propositional encoding of the example presented in Section 2.6. Once in clausal form and after the removal of tautologies, we obtain (Figure 2) the acquaintance graph where each peer schema is described as a propositional theory.

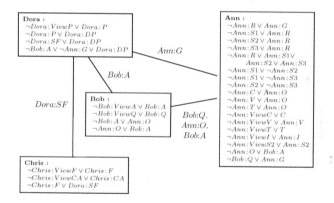

Fig. 2. Propositional encoding for the restaurant network

Proposition 1 states that the propositional encoding transfers satisfiability and establishes the connection between (maximal) conjunctive rewritings and clausal proper (prime) implicates.

Definition 2 (Proper prime implicate wrt a theory). *Let T be a clausal theory and q be a clause. A clause m is said to be:*

- *a prime implicate of q wrt T iff $T \cup \{q\} \models m$ and for any other clause m', if $T \cup \{q\} \models m'$ and $m' \models m$ then $m' \equiv m$.*
- *a proper prime implicate of q wrt T iff it is a prime implicate of q wrt T and $T \not\models m$.*

Proposition 1 (Propositional transfer). *Let $\mathcal{P}$ be a SomeWhere peer-to-peer network and let $Prop(S(\mathcal{P}))$ be the propositional encoding of its schema. Let V_e be the set of all the extensional classes.*

- *$S(\mathcal{P})$ is satisfiable iff $Prop(S(\mathcal{P}))$ is satisfiable.*
- *q_e is a maximal conjunctive rewriting of a query q iff $\neg Prop(q_e)$ is a proper prime implicate of $\neg Prop(q)$ wrt $Prop(S(\mathcal{P}))$ such that all its variables are extensional classes.*

Proposition 1 gives us a way to compute *all* the answers of a query. The maximal conjunctive rewritings of a query q within a peer-to-peer network $\mathcal{P}$ correspond to the negation of the proper prime implicates of $\neg q$ wrt the propositional encoding of the schema of $S(\mathcal{P})$. Since the number of proper prime implicates of a clause wrt a clausal theory is finite, every query in SomeWhere has a finite number of maximal conjunctive rewritings. Therefore, according to [13], the set of *all* of its answers is exactly the union of the answer sets of its rewritings and is obtained in PTIME data complexity.

In the following section, we present a distributed consequence finding algorithm which computes the set of proper prime implicates of a literal wrt a distributed propositional clausal theory. According to Proposition 1, if this algorithm is applied to a distributed theory resulting from the propositional encoding of the schema of a SomeWhere network, with the extensional classes symbols as *target variables*, and triggered with a literal $\neg q$, it computes in fact the negation of the maximal conjunctive rewritings of the *atomic* query q. Since in our setting the maximal rewritings of an arbitrary query can be obtained by combining the maximal rewritings of its atomic components, we focus on the computation of the rewritings of atomic queries.

4   Algorithmic Machinery

The SomeWhere peer-to-peer data management system relies on a distributed algorithm presented in [14]. For this paper to be self-contained, we describe the three message passing procedures of the algorithm which are implemented locally at each peer. They are triggered by the reception of a *query* (resp. *answer*, *final*) message, sent by a Sender peer to a receiver peer, denoted by Self, which executes the procedure. Procedures handle an history initialized to the empty sequence. An history *hist* is a sequence of triples (l, P, c) (where l is a literal, P a peer, and c a clause). An history $[(l_n, P_n, c_n), \ldots, (l_1, P_1, c_1), (l_0, P_0, c_0)]$ represents a branch of reasoning initiated by the propagation of the literal l_0 within the peer P_0, and the splitting of the clause c_0: for every $i \in [0..n-1]$, c_i is a consequence of l_i and P_i, and l_{i+1} is a literal of c_i, which is propagated in P_{i+1}.

RECEIVEQUERYMESSAGE is triggered by the reception of a *query* message $m(Sender, Receiver, query, hist, l)$ sent by the peer $Sender$ to the peer $Receiver$ which executes the procedure: on the demand of $Sender$, with which it shares the variable of l, it processes the literal l.

RECEIVEANSWERMESSAGE is triggered by the reception of an *answer* message $m(Sender, Receiver, answer, hist, r)$ sent by the peer *Sender* to the peer *Receiver* which executes the procedure: it processes the answer r (which is a clause the variables of which are target variables) sent back by *Sender* for the literal l (last added in the history) ; it may have to combine it with other answers for literals being in the same clause as l.

RECEIVEFINALMESSAGE is triggered by the reception of a *final* message $m(Sender, Receiver, final, hist, true)$: the peer *Sender* notifies the peer *Receiver* that computation for the literal l (last added in the history) is completed.

Those procedures handle two local data structures:

ANSWER$(l, hist)$ caches answers resulting from the propagation of l within the reasoning branch corresponding to $hist$;

FINAL$(q, hist)$ is set to true when the propagation of q within the reasoning branch of the history $hist$ is completed. The reasoning is initiated by the user (denoted by a particular peer $User$) sending to a given peer P a message $m(User, P, query, \emptyset, q)$, which triggers the procedure RECEIVEQUERYMESSAGE$(m(User, P, query, \emptyset, q))$ that is locally executed by P.

In the following procedures, since they are locally executed by the peer which receives the message, we denote by $Self$ the receiver peer. We also assume that:

- for a literal q, $Resolvent(q, P)$ denotes the set of clauses obtained by resolution between q and a clause of P,
- for a literal q, $\bar{q}$ denotes its complementary literal,
- for a clause c of a peer P, $S(c)$ (resp. $L(c)$) denotes the disjunction of literals of c whose variables are shared (resp. not shared) with any acquaintance of P. $S(c) = \square$ thus expresses that c does not contain any shared variable,
- $Target(P)$ is the language of clauses (including $\square$) involving only variables that are extensional classes of P.
- $\oslash$ is the distribution operator on sets of clauses: $S_1 \oslash \cdots \oslash S_n = \{c_1 \vee \cdots \vee c_n | c_1 \in S_1, \ldots, c_n \in S_n\}$. If $L = \{l_1, \ldots, l_p\}$, $\oslash_{l \in L} S_l$ denotes $S_{l_1} \oslash \cdots \oslash S_{l_p}$.

The following theorems summarize the main properties of this distributed message passing algorithm and thus of the SomeWhere peer-to-peer data management system. Theorem 1 states the termination and the soundness of the algorithm. Theorem 2 states its completeness under the condition that each peer theory is saturated by resolution. Theorem 3 states that the user is notified of the termination when it occurs, which is crucial for an anytime algorithm. Full proofs are given in [15]. In the following theorems, let $\mathcal{T}$ be the propositional encoding of the schema $S(\mathcal{P})$ of a peer-to-peer SomeWhere network, let $\neg q$ the negation of an atomic query q, let T be the propositional encoding of the local schema and mappings of the asked peer.

Theorem 1 (Soundness). *If T receives from the user the message $m(User, T, query, \emptyset, \neg q)$, then:*

- *a finite number of answer messages will be produced ;*
- *each produced answer message $m(T, User, answer, [(\neg q, T, \_)], r)$ is such that r is an implicate of $\neg q$ wrt $S(\mathcal{P})$ which belong to $Target(\mathcal{P})$.*

Algorithm 1. Message passing procedure for processing queries

RECEIVEQUERYMESSAGE($m(Sender, Self, query, hist, q)$)
(1) **if** $(\bar{q}, \_, \_) \in hist$
(2)   **send** $m(Self, Sender, answer, [(q, Self, \Box)|hist], \Box)$
(3)   **send** $m(Self, Sender, final, [(q, Self, true)|hist], true)$
(4) **else if** $q \in Self$ or $(q, Self, \_) \in hist$
(5)   **send** $m(Self, Sender, final, [(q, Self, true)|hist], true)$
(6) **else**
(7)   LOCAL($Self$) $\leftarrow \{q\} \cup Resolvent(q, Self)$
(8)   **if** $\Box \in$ LOCAL($Self$)
(9)   **send** $m(Self, Sender, answer, [(q, Self, \Box)|hist], \Box)$
(10)   **send** $m(Self, Sender, final, [(q, Self, true)|hist], true)$
(11)   **else**
(12)   LOCAL($Self$) $\leftarrow \{c \in$ LOCAL($Self$)$|\ L(c) \in \mathcal{T}arget(Self)\}$
(13)   **if** for every $c \in$ LOCAL($Self$)$, S(c) = \Box$
(14)   **foreach** $c \in$ LOCAL($Self$)
(15)   **send** $m(Self, Sender, answer, [(q, Self, c)|hist], c)$
(16)   **send** $m(Self, Sender, final, [(q, Self, true)|hist], true)$
(17)   **else**
(18)   **foreach** $c \in$ LOCAL($Self$)
(19)   **if** $S(c) = \Box$
(20)   **send** $m(Self, Sender, answer, [(q, Self, c)|hist], c)$
(21)   **else**
(22)   **foreach** literal $l \in S(c)$
(23)   **if** $l \in \mathcal{T}arget(Self)$
(24)   ANSWER($l, [(q, Self, c)|hist]$) $\leftarrow \{l\}$
(25)   **else**
(26)   ANSWER($l, [(q, Self, c)|hist]$) $\leftarrow \emptyset$
(27)   FINAL($l, [(q, Self, c)|hist]$) $\leftarrow false$
(28)   **foreach** $RP \in$ ACQ($l, Self$)
(29)   **send** $m(Self, RP, query, [(q, Self, c)|hist], l)$

Algorithm 2. Message passing procedure for processing answers

RECEIVEANSWERMESSAGE($m(Sender, Self, answer, hist, r)$)
(1) $hist$ is of the form $[(l', Sender, c'), (q, Self, c)|hist']$
(2) ANSWER($l', hist$) $\leftarrow$ ANSWER $(l', hist) \cup \{r\}$
(3) RESULT $\leftarrow \otimes_{l \in S(c) \setminus \{l'\}}$ ANSWER($l, hist$) $\otimes \{L(c) \vee r\}$
(4) **if** $hist' = \emptyset$, $U \leftarrow User$ **else** $U \leftarrow$ the first peer P' of $hist'$
(5) **foreach** $cs \in$ RESULT
(6)   **send** $m(Self, U, answer, [(q, Self, c)|hist'], cs)$

Theorem 2 (Completeness). *If each local theory is saturated by resolution and if T receives from the user the message $m(User, T, query, \emptyset, \neg q)$, then for each proper prime implicate r of $\neg q$ wrt $S(\mathcal{P})$ belonging to $\mathcal{T}arget(\mathcal{P})$, an answer message $m(T, User, answer, [(\neg q, T, \_)], r)$ will be produced.*

Theorem 3 (Termination notification). *If r is the last result returned in an answer message $m(T, User, answer, [(\neg q, T, \_)], r)$ then the user will be notified of the termination by a message $m(T, User, final, [(\neg q, T, true)], true)$.*

Algorithm 3. Message passing procedure for notifying termination

RECEIVEFINALMESSAGE($m(Sender, Self, final, hist, true)$)

(1) $hist$ is of the form $[(l', Sender, true), (q, Self, c)|hist']$
(2) FINAL($l', hist$) $\leftarrow true$
(3) **if** for every $l \in S(c)$, FINAL($l, hist$) $= true$
(4)   **if** $hist' = \emptyset$ $U \leftarrow User$ **else** $U \leftarrow$ the first peer P' of $hist'$
(5)   **send** $m(Self, U, final, [(q, Self, true)|hist'], true)$
(6)   **foreach** $l \in S(c)$
(7)   ANSWER($l, [(l, Sender, \_), (q, Self, c)|hist']$) $\leftarrow \emptyset$

It is important to notice that $\Box$ can be returned by our algorithm as a proper prime implicate because of the lines (1) to (3) and (8) to (10) in RECEIVE-QUERYMESSAGE. In that case, as a corollary of the above theorems, the union the propositional encoding of the schema of the SomeWhere network and the query is detected unsatisfiable. Therefore, our algorithm can be exploited for checking the satisfiability of the global schema at each join of a new peer.

5   Related Work

As we have pointed it out in the introduction, the SomeWhere peer data management system distinguishes from Edutella [8] by the fact that there is no need of super-peers. It does not require either a central server having the global view of the overlay network, as in Piazza [4], [9] or in [16].

The recent work around the coDB peer data management system [17] supports dynamic networks but the first step of the distributed algorithm is to let each node know the network topology. In contrast, in SomeWhere no node does not have to know the topology of the network.

The Kadop system [18] is an infrastructure based on distributed hash tables for constructing and querying peer-to-peer warehouses of XML resources semantically enriched by taxonomies and mappings. The mappings that are considered are simple inclusion statement between atomic classes. Compared to KadoP (and also to DRAGO [19]), the mapping language that is dealt with in SomeWhere is more expressive than simple inclusion statements between atomic classes. It is an important difference which makes SomeWhere able to *combine* elements of answers coming from different sources for answering a query, which KadoP or DRAGO cannot do.

SomeWhere implements in a simpler setting the vision of peer-to-peer data management systems proposed in [20] for relational databases.

6   Conclusion and Future Work

We have presented the SomeWhere semantic peer-to-peer data management system. Its data model is based on the propositional fragment of the Ontology Web Language recommended by W3C. SomeWhere implements a fully peer-to-peer approach. We have conducted a significant experimentation on networks of

1000 peers. It is presented in [21]. To the best of our knowledge, this is the first experimental study on such large peer-to-peer data management systems. The motivations of this experimentation was twofold. First, to study how deep and how wide reasoning spreads on the network. Second, to evaluate the time needed to obtain answers and to check to what extent SomeWhere is able to support the traffic load.

SomeWhere is the basis of the MediaD project with France Télécom, which aims at enriching peer-to-peer web applications (e.g., Someone [3]) with reasoning services.

We plan to extend SomeWhere in three directions.

We first plan to tackle the problem of possible inconsistency of the distributed schema which can occur because of the mappings, even if the local theories are all consistent. In principle, our algorithm is able to check whether adding a new theory and set of mappings to a consistent SomeWhere network of theories leads to an inconsistency. Therefore, we could forbid a new peer to join the network if it makes the global schema inconsistent, and thus guarantee by construction that query processing applies on consistent SomeWhere networks. However, this solution is probably too rigid and restrictive to be accepted in practice by users who want to join a SomeWhere network. At least, a new peer whose join leads to an inconsistency would like to know with which other peer(s) its ontology is inconsistent. The problem of detecting the causes of an inconsistency is not trivial and has been extensively studied for centralized theories or knowledge bases. We need to investigate that issue in the SomeWhere distributed setting. We could also decide not to correct the inconsistency but to confine it and answer queries within consistent sub-networks.

Second, we want to extend the SomeWhere data model with binary relations. We are currently exhibiting another propositional transfer for peers relying on the RDF/RDFS data model and accepting conjunctive queries.

Finally, we plan to plug SomeWhere onto a Chord infrastructure [22] in order to make SomeWhere more robust to frequent changes in the network due to peers joins and leaves. In addition, the look-up service offered by Chord could be exploited for optimization purposes of the current SomeWhere query processing.

References

1. Berners-Lee, T., Hendler, J., Lassila, O.: The Semantic Web. Scientific American **284** (2001) 35–43 Essay about the possibilities of the semantic web.
2. Rousset, M.C.: Small Can Be Beautiful in the Semantic Web. In: ISWC 2004, International Semantic Web Conference (2004)
3. Plu, M., Bellec, P., Agosto, L., van de Velde, W.: The Web of People: A Dual View on the WWW. In: Int. World Wide Web Conf. (2003)
4. Halevy, A., Ives, Z., Suciu, D., Tatarinov, I.: Schema Mediation in Peer Data Management Systems. In: ICDE'03. (2003)
5. Ooi, B., Shu, Y., Tan, K.L.: Relational Data Sharing in Peer Data Management Systems. **23** (2003)

6. Arenas, M., Kantere, V., Kementsietsidis, A., Kiringa, I., Miller, R., Mylopoulos, J.: In: The Hyperion Project: From Data Integration to Data Coordination. (2003)
7. Bernstein, P., Giunchiglia, F., Kementsietsidis, A., Mylopoulos, J., Serafini, L., Zaihraheu, I.: Data Management for p2p Computing: A Vision. In: WebDB. (2002)
8. Nedjl, W., Wolf, B., Qu, C., Decker, S., Sintek, M., al.: Edutella: a p2p Networking Infrastructure Based on rdf. In: WWW'02 (2002)
9. Halevy, A., Ives, Z., Tatarinov, I., Mork, P.: Piazza: Data Management Infrastructure for Semantic Web Applications. In: WWW'03 (2003)
10. Halevy, A.Y.: In: Logic-Based Techniques in Data Integration. Kluwer Academic Publishers (2000) 575–595
11. Madhavan, J., Halevy, A.: Composing Mappings among Data Sources. In: VLDB 03 (2003)
12. Tatarinov, I., Halevy, A.: Efficient Query Reformulation in Peer Data Management Systems. In: SIGMOD 04 (2004)
13. Goasdoué, F., Rousset, M.C.: Answering Queries Using Views. ACM Journal - Transactions on Internet Technology (TOIT) **4** (2004)
14. Adjiman, P., Chatalic, P., Goasdoué, F., Rousset, M.C., Simon, L.: Distributed Reasoning in a p2p Setting, short paper. In: ECAI. (2004) 945–946
15. Adjiman, P., Chatalic, P., Goasdoué, F., Rousset, M.C., Simon, L.: Distributed Reasoning in a p2p Setting. Technical report,
http://www.lri.fr/~goasdoue/bib/ACGRS-TR-1385.pdf (2004)
16. Calvanese, D., Giacomo, G.D., Lenzerini, M., Rosati, R.: Logical Foundation of p2p Data Integration. In: PODS, Paris, France (2004)
17. Franconi, E., Kuper, G., Lopatenko, A., Zaihrayeu, I.: Queries and Updates in the codb p2p Database System. In: VLDB 2004. (2004)
18. Abiteboul, S., Manolescu, I., Preda, N.: Constructing and Querying p2p Warehouses of xml Resources. In: Workshop on Semantic Web and Databases (2004)
19. Serafini, L., Tamilin, A.: Drago: Distributed Reasoning Architecture for the Semantic Web. Technical report, ITC-IRST (2004)
20. Bernstein, P., Giunchiglia, F., Kementsietsidis, A., Mylopoulos, J., Serafini, L., Zaihrayeu, I.: Data Management for p2p Computing: a Vision. In: Proceedings of WebDB 2002 (2002)
21. Adjiman, P., Chatalic, P., Goasdoué, F., Rousset, M.C., Simon, L.: Scalability Study of p2p Consequence Finding. In: IJCAI, IJCAI (2005)
22. Stoica, I., Morris, R., Karger, D., Kaasshoek, M., Balakrishnan, H.: Chord: a Scalable p2p Lookup Service for Internet Applications. In: Conference on Applications, Technologies, Architecture and Protocols for Computer Communications (2001)

Mobility in Wireless Networks

Christian Schindelhauer*

Heinz Nixdorf Institute, University of Paderborn, Germany
schindel@uni-paderborn.de

Abstract. This article surveys mobility patterns and mobility models for wirelss networks. Mobility patterns are classified into the following types: pedestrians, vehicles, aerial, dynamic medium, robot, and outer space motion. We present the characteristics of each and shortly mention the specific problems.

We shortly present the specifics of cellular networks, mobile ad hoc networks, and sensor networks regarding mobility. Then, we present the most important mobility models from the literature. At last we give a brief discussion about the state of research regarding mobility in wireless networks.

1 Introduction

Today, it is hard to imagine the difficulties to send information over large distances before the invention of radio communication. First, such devices were so large and heavy that they could not be carried around but had to be carried by vehicles. So, the history of mobile communication starts with radio devices on boats which emerged in the 1890s and helped ocean vessels to overcome insulation for navigation and emergency situations. It took some time until mobile radio transceiver could be used on non-marine vehicles. Such technology was available in the 1930s when a radio transceiver could be operated on a bicycle and a radio sender could be operated on an airplane. Both as show cases and not really for practical use. At the end of the 30s portable solutions were available in form of the famous "walky-talky", which could be carried by a single person. In the beginning of the 1940s a radio transceiver was available which could be held in a single hand: "The Handy-Talky", see Fig. 1. Needless to say that these communication devices played an important role in the second world war. With the upcoming of transistors, large scale integrated chip layout, and new battery technology allowed the size of radio devices to shrink unbelievably small. Today, one can buy fully equipped sensor nodes with radio transceiver and micro-controller in the size of a small coin (and within reasonable price), see Fig. 2. Furthermore, there is the vision of communication devices being so small called "smart dust".

---

* Supported by the DFG Sonderforschungsbereich 376: "Massive Parallelität: Algorithmen, Entwurfsmethoden, Anwendungen." and by the EU within the 6th Framework Programme under contract 001907 "Dynamically Evolving, Large Scale Information Systems" (DELIS).

J. Wiedermann et al. (Eds.): SOFSEM 2006, LNCS 3831, pp. 100–116, 2006.

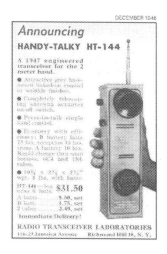

Fig. 1. The Handy-Talky   **Fig. 2.** The Mica2Dot from Crossbow

Also the underlying radio communication technology has changed much from the analogous broadcast signal (still surprisingly widely distributed) to digital multi-hop networks with time, frequency and code division multiplexing for the parallel use of the medium. Such packet oriented radio devices have been developed in the 1970s and filled the interior of a van, i.e. Vint Cerf's Stanford Research Institute (SRI) van. Then, the packet radio underwent a miniaturization process and packet radio has become the dominating radio technology, so far.

For two-way radio communication central radio stations are used which serve as relay station for transmitting the radio signals. Many of these central relay stations partition the radio landscape into cells. In such cellular networks the mobility of users (more or less) reduces to problems of handover from one radio station to a neighbored station. Networks without such centralized infrastructure are called mobile ad hoc networks. There, the impact of mobility is much higher, since everything is moving. One can easily imagine the possible negative impact of mobility on wireless networking. Recent results point out that mobility has also a positive impact.

This article surveys mobility and radio networks from a wide perspective. We refrain from going into the very details of mobility aspects and head for giving a broader picture. The goal of this survey is to endorse new approaches to mobility in wireless networks based on the current situation. For this, we discuss on mobility patterns, mobility models, algorithmic aspects and on mobile ad hoc networks. Very often the mobility models and mobility patterns are mixed up. However, one must carefully distinguish between them. Real mobility pattern can be obtained by tracking moving objects of reality, while mobility models try to generalize such patterns by forming a mathematical model.

We begin with a very short introduction of cellular networks, ad hoc networks, and wireless sensor networks. Then, we continue with an overview how and where mobility occurs and how it might affect wireless networks. After that we elaborate mobility models from literature. In the last section we present positive aspects of mobility on the wireless networks, research perspectives, and open research problems.

This is not the first survey on mobility of wireless networks. There is an excellent survey paper of Camp, Boleng and Davies [12] which presents and discusses mobility models for ad hoc networks. It is based on the more detailed PhD thesis of Vannessa A. Davies [17]. A survey of random direction based models can be found in [41].

2   Wireless Networks in a Nutshell

The radio frequency spectrum is divided into several bands, starting as low as 30 kHz for maritime communication and ranging up to 300 GHz. Low frequency radio waves easily pass through human bodies, walls, water, etc. Higher frequencies are absorbed and reflected by obstacles. There are numerous other facts to be told from physics. For some frequency bands the ionosphere reflects signals. The background noise level differs in various bands. Signal strength is influenced by obstruction, diffusion, reflection, multi-path fading, and the Doppler effect. A man-made problem is the interference of radio signals of multiple senders.

Furthermore, in theory the signal strength is fading with a power of two with respect to the distance, which is only true in empty space. In other environments the exponent is larger and can have values from 3-5. This implies that if one tries to send over a distance of d transmission power has to chosen $\sim d^2$ in empty space. Many transmission models assume that the covered area by a radio signal can be modeled by a disc. However, practical measurements show that this is not at all the case.

2.1   Cellular Networks

Cellular networks are defined by static base stations which divide the fields into cells. All radio communication is between these base stations and the clients. Usually, each static base station forwards and receives packets to other base stations by another (hard-wired) network. Regarding movement of clients one is only interested in whether the node enters or leaves a cell. It is not interesting where the node is exactly located within a cell. In some cellular networks (like UMTS) the size of the cell changes with the number of nodes. Usually network cells overlap and so, there are areas where a client can choose among several base stations.

The main mobility problems and applications for cellular networks are *Cellular Handoff:* Provide a robust protocol that allows to move between cells without interrupting and disturbing communication; *Location Service:* Use the cell information and the power strength to locate a client within the network.

2.2   Mobile Ad Hoc Networks

A Mobile Ad Hoc Wireless Network (MANET) is a self-configuring network of mobile nodes. Nodes serve as routers and may move arbitrarily. There is no static infrastructure and the communication network must be able to adapt to changes because of movement and other dynamics. Most of the MANET protocols do not assume that position data is available. However, if such position data is available then efficient location based communication protocols are applicable (for a survey on such routing algorithms see [39]). The main problem in MANET is to find a multi-hop route between the source and the target of information. It is clear that if all the intermediate router nodes are moving that this type of network is very much affected by mobility. Especially if one takes into account that the transmitting range is rather restricted to a limited supply of energy (e.g. batteries). See [44] as an introduction to ad hoc networks.

The main mobility problems for a MANET are routing a message, multicasting a message, and upholding the network routing tables for these issues.

2.3   Sensor Networks

A sensor network is a wireless network connecting many, specially distributed sensor devices. These devices are equipped with sensors, such as for temperature, vibration, pressure, sound, or motion. Like in a mobile ad hoc network this information has to be communicated without a special infrastructure over a multi-hop path. Similar as for cellular networks there are specially equipped base stations (sometimes connected over an ad hoc network) to collect this information and control the network.

The main difference between a sensor network and a mobile ad hoc network is that a sensor network is data-driven. It is important to receive the temperature reading of an area not from a specific device. So, some of the sensors may be switched off for most of the time. Furthermore, these cheap and massively deployed sensors are equipped with the bare minimum of computing resources. Sometimes they have to work for some 10 years being solely powered by small coin cell batteries.

The main application of a sensor network is to read out the sensor reading of a particular area. At the moment mobile sensor networks are the exception (which we will discuss here). For surveys on sensor networks, see [14], [30], [46], [57].

3   Mobility Patterns: How People and Things Move

We now give a overview over realistic mobility patterns and classify them as follows: pedestrians, vehicles, aerial, dynamic medium, robot, and outer space motion. We present their characteristics and mention the specific radio problems.

3.1   Pedestrians

The oldest and most common way of mobility is to walk. Pedestrian mobility has the slowest velocity compared to other modern mobility patterns. Although low in speed, even in cellular networks walking patterns cause sincere trouble since typically people walk through places where obstacles obstruct the signal. It is often a matter of meters whether or not the access point is to be reached by a client (fast signal fading). In such a case clients need to be handed over rapidly to the next available access point.

So, pedestrian mobility describes the walking patterns of people or animals. Its main characteristics are the full use of the two-dimensional plane with occasional obstacles and its chaotic nature. Group behavior may occur, but has not necessarily to be. Such pedestrian mobility is always limited in speed because the legs act like inverted pendula.

Typical examples of pedestrian mobility in wireless networks are people in the street or mall using cellular phones or PDAs (personal digital assistants), and animals in herds with sensor nodes being observed by biologists, e.g zebras [56]. Upcoming examples of wireless mobility patterns are mobile devices attached to any moving object (parasitic mobility) [31], or even radio devices for pets. A side effect is that pedestrian clients have limited energy-resources. So they need to carry their batteries around to communicate, by that imposing further restraints to the communication network.

3.2   Marine and Submarine Mobility

Like pedestrians boats and vessels are limited by an intrinsic maximum speed, resulting from the friction in the water and the available motor power. Unlike in vehicular (earth bound) mobility the motion is truly two-dimensional, and in the case of submarine mobility even three-dimensional, whereas for most cases no group mobility is involved (except regattas, fleet operation and fish swarms). The communication upon the water service is very good and only the globe's curvature may become a problem.

Water absorbs radio signals with high frequencies. Submarine boats circumvent this problem by using very low frequencies ranging form 15 kHz to 33 kHz with an antenna length of 10 to 20 meters. A solution to this problem is acoustic communication, since sound travels very well underwater [2]. Also under water speed is the decisive limitation to mobility. Unlike in aerial mobility ascent and descent is easily possible (if the devices are equipped to withstand to the enormous changes of water pressure), so truly three-dimensional movement is realistic.

3.3   Earth Bound Vehicles

Such as pedestrian mobility is connected to the pendulum, the *vehicular mobility* is connected to the wheel. By this term we describe the mobility patterns of cars, railways, bicycles, motor bikes, etc. The wheel based movement reduces friction and allows high speed. So, the danger of collision increases dramatically, and this is the reason why (nearly) all vehicles are bound to one-dimensional movement on streets, paths, or tracks. This reduces the problem of preventing collisions to certain places like crossings.

For railway traffic there is fixed predictable train schedule and only delays cause aberrations. However, even in the seemingly well-planned world of the railway companies, freight wagons do disappear. This happens very often in the large wide-spread network of railway system spanning over different countries and railway network providers. Therefore, some companies start to use GPS-based wireless tracking devices to locate the wagons.

Another feature of railway traffic is an extreme group mobility pattern. When the passengers are inside a train, then their relative speed reduces to nearly zero, while the whole train can move up to some 300 km/h. The high relative speed between trains makes direct communication very challenging, especially since they move through a landscape with obstacles, or even tunnels. At these speeds the Doppler-effect starts to kick in. Further the noise of reflections of the scenery decreases the quality of the connection.

A very interesting study of this effect in practice can be seen in [38]. It shows the difficulty that already arises if cars traveling on the same road in the same direction communicate with each other over W-LAN, both in simulation and in practice. Even a street sign impacts the quality of communication by its reflection of radio signals.

3.4 Aerial Mobility

In this context monitoring flying patterns of migratory birds is a challenging task for biologists. In former times, marking caught exemplars was the only reliable source of information. Nowadays, some birds are equipped with radio tracking devices and can be publicly monitored over the Internet, likewise the monitoring of the black storks by the WWF[1].

Flying objects reach high speeds and travel over long distances. Actually birds and airplanes behave quite similar, here. As a communication medium open air is nearly optimal. Still, the signal fades quadratically with the distance, such that multihop communications may reduce the energy consumption of the radio transceiver.

The aerial mobility pattern can be best described as a two and a half dimensional individual movement with limited (yet high) speed. The motion is not completely three-dimensional since each ascent is very costly to the flying object. So, flying objects usually preserve their flight heights. One exception may be air fights between a raptor and his prey, or flight combats between warplanes. Another exception is the group mobility of bird swarms which perfectly coordinate their flight behavior.

The main applications of radio communication in aerial mobility are anti-collision systems, message passing, position tracking, and of course flight control.

3.5 Medium Based Mobility

One method to explore the interior of hurricanes are dropwindsondes [18]. These are sensor devices dropped from an airplane equipped with a parachute, sensors,

---

[1] See http://www.flyingover.net/

GPS-system, and a radio unit. Besides the constant drop speed the main movement comes from the interior winds of the hurricanes. Other wireless devices with medium based mobility are weather balloons and drifting buoys in the oceans. The main application of all these devices is to measure the currents of the medium. Dropwindsondes communicate directly to the aircraft releasing them. Also for other such sensor nodes cellular networks is the prevalent technique to collect the tracking information. A different approach has been used for measuring the currents at the British coast. In [47] a mobile ad hoc network has been used to collect the information of the sensor network over a multihop path (with hardware equipped as few as 384 Bytes of RAM). Using flying sensor devices for the exploration of mars was recently suggested by [3].

To understand the mobility of the sensor devices in the medium one has to study the medium itself. This can be done by numerical solution of the underlying Navier-Stokes-equations. Medium based mobility can be one-, two- or three-dimensional depending on the medium and the circumstances (piped gas, surface of fluids, open air). Group behavior can occur and is usually unwanted since grouping sensors deliver less information than individual moving sensors.

3.6   Mobility in Outer Space

For radio communication outer space is the perfect environment. Energy for communication is usually no tight resource since space vehicles are equipped with solar paddles. Mobility is, however, restricted since common space ships use rockets for acceleration and fuel supply is limited. Hence, space vehicles drift through space most of the time to save on this resource. At the moment numerous satellites surround the earth forming a mobility pattern of a giant chaotic carrousel, see Fig. 3. But space explorations may produces even more complicated mobility patterns.

Space ships closely fly by planets to increase speed, e.g. Voyager 2 used Saturn's strong gravity to change its course and gather speed (to continue its mission to Uranus and Neptune). Herds of space vehicles may be used for a coordinated view into deep space. These herds will be placed in non-circular orbits between earth and sun. Note that there exist five further stable positions, called Lagrange or libration points (see Fig. 4), between every pair of massive bodies such the sun and its planets, the planets and their moons, and so on. And around these Lagrange points non-circular orbits exist, see Fig 5. These herds of space vehicles have to change formation from time to time forming complicated mobility patterns. Ad hoc networks will coordinate this movement, prevent collisions and recalibrate the relative positions [29].

3.7   Robot Motion

Any of the above mobility scenarios can occur in robot motion. The main difference is the mobility pattern given by the designer of the robots. For some application this pattern is easy to predict, likewise other robots seem to move completely erratic and unpredictable. Clearly, the robot motion is driven by the

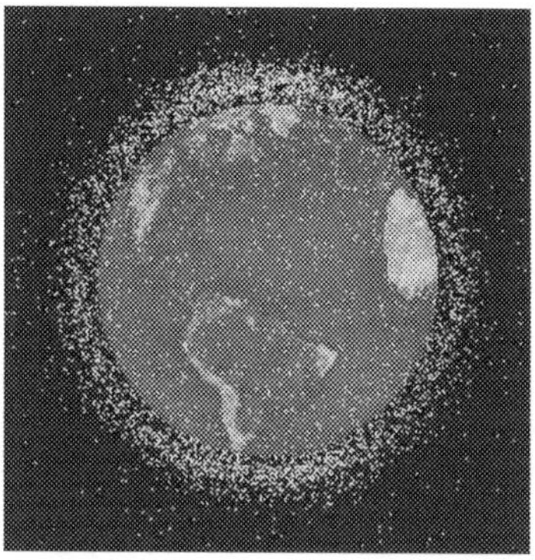

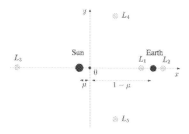

Fig. 4. The five Langrange points [28]

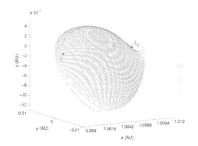

Fig. 3. Space vehicles and debris in low orbit (from NASA Orbital Debris Program Office)

Fig. 5. Family of Halo orbits in the vicinity of the Lagrange point [28]

robot's task and usually little attention is given to the impact of the robot's behavior on the communication network.

Currently, in Paderborn the project "Smart Team"[2] has been launched to make a difference. The goal of this project is to coordinate the robots' task with the necessities of a radio communication network.

3.8   Characterization of Mobility Patterns

We have seen that in our modern world mobility is manifold and ubiquitous. Radio communication networks are strongly affected by the different types of mobility and the understanding of each observed mobility pattern can help to improve the network behavior. Throughout this section the following properties played a role.

- *Group behavior*: Is there a set of nodes staying together for a considerably long time? Clearly, exploiting group behavior improves the performance of radio communication by clustering.
- *Limitations*: What are the speed and/or acceleration bounds in the mobility pattern?
- *Dimensions*: Do the nodes move in three-dimensions or only planar or linear?

---

[2] Funded by the DFG SPP 1183 Organic computing.

– *Predictability*: How well can the behavior of the nodes be predicted, e.g. by a simulation model? Is the behavior completely erratic? Or can it be described by a random process or even by deterministic selfish behavior?

Also hybrid models might appear. In this context we would like to mention the *parasitic mobility* pattern [31]. They present a sensor network where the nodes harvest the mobility from people, animals, vehicles, fluids, cellular organisms, and nature. Furthermore, the nodes can change hosts. Depending on the type of host, parasitic mobility can reproduce nearly all of the above mobility patterns. Such parasitic mobility pattern does not constitute a mobility pattern of its own.

3.9   Measuring Mobility Patterns by Localization

To measure a mobility pattern one needs to track a large number of nodes for a long period of time. In fact this is the perfect application area for wireless sensor networks specialized in localization. Localization can be solved by measuring ranging information from signal strength [5], time of arrival [53], or the time difference of arrival [50], or angle of arrival [42]. Other localization schemes make use of the quantities of base stations seeding sensors. Some hopcount based techniques avoid this large number of seeding base stations, [43], [45] by relying on a uniform node distribution. In [26] a different approach is presented. They exploit the mobility of the sensor networks to improve the accuracy and reliability of the sensor node localization even if the sensors are seeded by mobile base stations. This is only one of many examples where mobility helps to improve the network behavior.

4   Models of Mobility

We classify the mobility models as cellular mobility models, random trip models, group mobility models, particle based models, non-recurrent models, and worst case mobility models.

4.1   Cellular Mobility Model

Since for cellular networks the main aspect of mobility is the handoff between cells, one is not particularly interested in every detail of the movement of a mobile node. For a survey for cellular models see [32].

1. The Random Walk Model
   In this model, a node stays in a cell or moves to a neighbored cell according to some given transition probabilities. These probabilities are often adjusted to practical observations of client behavior in cells. The Random Walk Mobility Model is one of the most widely used mobility models because it describes individual movements relative to cells [7, 49, 58]. Since this model is memoryless, there is no such concept as a path or consecutive movement. Therefore, nodes stay in a vicinity of the starting cell for a rather long time.

2. Trace based Models

Cellular phone companies have large records of mobility patterns of their users. These traces are a valuable source for the evaluation and improvement of handoff protocols. The only drawback is that usually such data is not publicly available and therefore cannot serve as benchmarks for the scientific community.

3. Fluid Flow Mobility Model

In this model the individual nodes are modeled on a macroscopic level [32], [54], [36], [52]. The behavior of the generated traffic is similar to a fluid flowing through a pipe. As a result, the Fluid-Flow Mobility Model represents traffic on highways very well (for cellular networks). In [33] this model is used to represent the behavioral characteristics of traffic on a highway. [34] shows that the Fluid-Flow Mobility Model is insufficient for individual movements including stopping and starting.

4.2 Random Trip Mobility

These mobility models are the prevalent mobility model for MANETs. There are numerous variants of this model. In [12] these models are presented as follows.

1. Random Walk Mobility Model

Each node moves from its current location to a new location by randomly choosing an arbitrary direction and speed from a given range. Such a move is performed either for a constant time for a constant distance traveled. Then new speed and direction are chosen. At the boundaries nodes bounce off like billiard balls on a pool table.

In [34] the Random Walk Mobility Model is described as a memory-less mobility pattern because it retains no knowledge concerning its past locations and speed values. This characteristic inhibits the practicality of the Random Walk Mobility Model because mobile nodes typically have a pre-defined destination and speed in mind, which in turn affects future destinations and speeds.

One observation is that the stationary probability distribution can be described depending on the probabilites. But, the convergence against this stable distribution can be slow, if the points are not randomly chosen [55]. So, there is some danger that the simulation result highly depends on the start position, if the simulation time is not long enough.

In the Smooth Random Mobility Model [9] an extension of the simpler random walk model is given. Here, two independent stochastic processes choose direction and speed changes. The new speeds (or directions) are chosen from a weighted distribution of preferred speeds. Upon a trigger, the speed (resp. direction) changes as determined by a Poisson process.

2. Random Waypoint Mobility Model

The model is equivalent to the Random Walk model except that before any change of speed and direction a predetermined pause time is performed [11]. This model is widely used for evaluating ad hoc network routing protocols.

3. Random Direction Mobility Model

   Here, the node must travel to the edge of the simulation area (or some other condition is met) at a constant speed and direction. Then, the nodes pause and a new direction and velocity is chosen randomly [48]. Then, the process repeats.

4. A Boundless Simulation Area Mobility Model: The model exchanges the planar rectangular simulation field by a boundless torus.

5. Gauss-Markov Mobility Model: A model that uses one tuning parameter to vary the degree of randomness in the mobility pattern.

   The Random Gauss-Markov Mobility Model is introduced as an improvement over the Smooth Random mobility model [34]. A node's next location is generated by its past location and velocity. Depending upon parameters set, this allows modeling along a spectrum from Random Walk to Fluid-Flow.

6. A Probabilistic Version of the Random Walk Mobility Model [15]

   In this model the last step made by the random walk influences the next one. Under the condition that a node has moved to the right the probability that it continues to move in this direction is then higher than to stop movement. This leads to a walk that leaves the starting point much faster than the original random walk model.

7. City Section Mobility Model [17]

   Here the random waypoint movement is combined with a street map of a virtual city. The paths of the mobile nodes are limited to these streets in the field. In a related model, the streets are replaced by Voronoi graphs [27]. Furthermore, obstacle are used which obstruct also radio signals.

For some models there is a slow convergence towards the stationary distribution [40]. This influences simulation results, since in previous work simulation usually starts with the uniform distribution which is not necessarily the stationary distribution of the mobility model. Some random waypoint models do not provide a stationary distribution at all. These problems are mentioned in [55] for many random waypoint mobility models.

In [10] the Random Trip model has ben defined. This model describes a wide class of mobility models, contain most of the mobility models in this section. Therefore we use this name for this class of mobility models. Examples include random waypoint on general connected domain, restricted random waypoint, random walk models with either wrap-around or reflection, and the city street model. In [10] it is shown how a simulation algorithm can start from unique steady-state distribution. So, no time must be spent for waiting until the random process stabilizes in the simulator.

4.3   Group-Mobility Models

The group-mobility models are usually an extension of the above models, where either a function describes the group behavior or the nodes are somehow associated with a group leader or a target. For a more extensive description of these models we refer to [12] and [25].

1. Exponential Correlated Random Mobility Model: Here a motion function creates a group behavior.
2. Column Mobility Model: The set of mobile nodes form a line and move forward in a particular direction.
3. Nomadic Community Mobility Model: A group mobility model where a set of MNs move together from one location to another.
4. Pursue Mobility Model: For each group the group members follow a target node moving over the simulation area.
5. Reference Point Group Mobility Model: The group movement is based upon the path traveled by a logical center. Again the logical center moves according to an individual mobility model.

4.4   Particle Based Mobility

There has been a lot of research in predicting pedestrian behavior. One of the main motivations is to understand erratic mass panic caused by many pedestrians causing the death and injuries of hundreds of people in a single event [24]. The best model to describe the individual behavior of each person in such occasions is a *particle based model* [23]. Each person is characterized by a sum of forces, describing his desire to move in a direction, keeping a distance to others and the result of contact and frictions with other persons. The simplicity and the accuracy of this model is surprising. It allows even to simulate typical behavior in crowded streets where strangers form queue patterns.

4.5   Combined Mobility Models

Many the above mobility models have been combined in a number of theoretical frameworks, simulation environments and analysis toolboxes [6], [9], [22].

4.6   Non-recurrent Models

In the context of computational geometry Basch et al. introduced the concept of *kinetic data structures* (KDS) [8] which describes a framework for analyzing algorithms on mobile objects. In this model the mobility of objects is described by pseudo-algebraic functions of time. These functions are fully or partially predictable. The analysis of a KDS is done by counting the combinatorial changes of the geometric structure that is maintained by the KDS. The worst case mobility depends, therefore, on the specific application for which the KDS is designed. Another approach capturing unpredictable mobility is the concept of *soft kinetic data structures* (SKDS) [16].

Usually the underlying trajectories of the points are described by polynomials. Then, the corresponding Davenport-Schinzel-sequences [1] can be used to receive an overall bound on the number of events. Because of the polynomials these trajectory eventually move to infinity, which is somehow the worst case for a wireless network.

The idea of kinetic data structures is also used in [19] to maintain a clustering of moving objects. This approach is used in [20] to determine the head of each cluster in a mobile network. In each cluster the nodes are directly connected to the head. To react on mobility the clustering is updated by an event-based kinetic data structure.

Another non-recurrent approach has been proposed in [37]. They investigate a contraction mobility model, an expansion mobility model, and a circling mobility model (which is the only recurrent model). In the contraction model the nodes move toward a center on a straight line. Within some time interval a new speed will be chose from time interval and in addition the nodes may pause. The expansion model is the same model, but now the nodes move from the center on some beams. In the circling model the nodes move on concentric circles around a center. These mobility models can be combined with a street network.

4.7   Worst-Case Mobility Models

A worst case model is introduced in [51]. Here, any movement is allowed as long as it is bounded by a velocity or an acceleration bound. The authors call the first model the *pedestrian mobility* model. Here all mobile nodes obey a system-wide speed limit. The other model, where all mobile nodes can move arbitrarily fast, yet obey the same acceleration bound, is called *vehicular mobility*. Based on this worst case assumption the authors try to maintain a network for some constant amount of time and then allow to completely rebuild the infrastructure. For this the location (and speed vector) at the beginning of a round is known, yet further movement is completely unpredictable (within the limits). So, the transmission length needs to be adjusted appropriately. In this model the authors investigate the quality of the topology control similar to the models presented in [4].

In this worst-case approach scenarios may appear where all networks have bad performance. These scenarios are caused by large crowds of mobile nodes. They introduce a location dependent measure, called crowdedness, and can prove for restricted crowdedness that the optimal network topology can be approximated in both mobility models by the so-called Hierarchical Grid topology.

5   Discussion

5.1   Mobility Is Helpful

One might think that mobility has only a negative impact on the behavior of wireless networks. But recent work has shown that this is not the case. Mobility improves the coverage of wireless sensor networks [35]. It helps security in ad hoc networks [13]. Furthermore it can help with network congestion as shown in [21]. This approach overcomes the natural lower bound for throughput of $\Omega(\sqrt{n})$ by instrumenting the random movement of nodes. They design a protocol where mobile nodes relay packets and literally transport them towards the destination node.

5.2   Mobility Models and Reality

There is an obvious discrepancy between the manifold mobility pattern observable in reality and the mobility models used as benchmark tools and as theoretical models for wireless networks. The prevalent mobility are the random trip models. It relies on the assumption that individuals move more or less erratically. Some of the random trip models have been adapted with realistic assumptions like street maps, velocity bounds, etc. Yet, on the one hand it is still unproven whether these modifications describe realistic mobility patterns. And even if this is the case they describe only the earthbound pedestrian or vehicular mobility patterns.

In the case of group mobility, little information is available on how real group mobility patterns look like. Sometimes group mobility patterns are not caused by social interaction but by a physical process. As an example, pedestrians in crowded pathways form queues merely to avoid the approaching pedestrians [23]. At the moment little is known whether the group mobility models actually describe the reality.

The worst-case mobility approach seems to be a step towards a more general understanding of mobility. Some drawbacks need to be mentioned. First, it relies on homogeneous velocity or acceleration bounds, which is not at all realistic. Second, the implications for wireless networks are rather weak. For that, the performance of the network depends very much of the crowdedness of the underlying mobility pattern.

In principle, is possible to formulate the missing mobility models for marine, aerial, medium based, and outer space mobility patterns. Also for the pedestrian and vehicular models we expect even more realistic mobility models to be considered as benchmarks for wireless networks. The research of mobility models is quite vivid. Nevertheless, some challenges remain:

– Find mobility models for specific mobility patterns and prove their validity by comparing them with reality.
– Prove the efficiency and reliability of a real network protocols with respect to a given mobility model.

References

1. Agarwal, P.K., and Sharir, M.: Davenport–Schinzel Sequences and Their Geometric Applications. Cambridge, New York, Cambridge University Press (1995)
2. Akyildiz, I.F., Pompili, D., and Melodia, T.: Underwater Acoustic Sensor Networks: Research Challenges. Ad Hoc Networks (Elsevier) **3** 3 (May 2005) 257–279
3. Antol, J., Calhoun, P., Flick, J., Hajos, G.A., Kolacinski, R., Minton, D., Owens, R., and Parker, J.: Low Cost Mars Surface Exploration: The Mars Tumbleweed. Technical Report, NASA Langley Research Center. NASA/TM 2003 212411 (August 2003)
4. Meyer auf der Heide, F., Schindelhauer, C., Volbert, K., and Grünewald, M.: Energy, Congestion, and Dilation in Radio Networks. In Proceedings of the 14th Annual ACM Symposium on Parallel ALgorithms and Architectures (SPAA-02), New York, ACM Press, August 10–13 2002, 230–237

5. Bahl, P., and Padmanabhan, V.N.: RADAR: An in-Building RF-Based User Location and Tracking System. In INFOCOM **2** (2000) 775–784
6. Bai, F., Sadagopan, N., and Helmy, A.: Important: a Framework to Systematically Analyze the Impact of Mobility on Performance of Routing Protocols for Adhoc Networks. In Proceedings of INFOCOM 2003, San Francisco, CA. (2003)
7. Bar-Noy, A., Kessler, I., and Sidi, M.: Mobile Users: To Update or Not to Update. In IEEE Conference on Computer Communications (INFOCOM 94) (1994) 570–576
8. Basch, J., Guibas, L.J., and Hershberger, J.: Data Structures for Mobile Data. Journal of Algorithms **31** 1 (1999) 1–28
9. Bettstetter, C.: Smooth is Better than Sharp: a Random Mobility Model for Simulation of Wireless Networks. In MSWIM '01: Proceedings of the 4th ACM International Workshop on Modeling, Analysis and Simulation of Wireless and Mobile Systems, ACM Press (2001) 19–27
10. Le Boudec, J., and Vojnovic, M.: Perfect Simulation and Stationarity of a Class of Mobility Models. In Proceedings of IEEE INFOCOM '05 (2005), to appear in
11. Broch, J., Maltz, D.A., Johnson, D.B., Hu, Y.-C., and Jetcheva, J.: A Performance Comparison of Multi-Hop Wireless ad Hoc Network Routing Protocols. In Mobile Computing and Networking (1998) 85–97
12. Camp, T., Boleng, J., and Davies, V.: A Survey of Mobility Models for Ad Hoc Network Research. Wireless Communications & Mobile Computing (WCMC): Special issue on Mobile Ad Hoc Networking: Research, Trends and Applications, **2** 5 (2002) 483–502
13. Capkun, S., Hubaux, J.-P., and Buttyán, L.: Mobility Helps Security in Ad Hoc Networks. In MobiHoc '03: Proceedings of the 4th ACM International Symposium on Mobile Ad Hoc Networking & Computing, ACM Press, (2003) 46–56
14. Chatzigiannakis, I., Dimitriou, T., Mavronicolas, M., Nikoletseas, S., and Spirakis, P.: A Comparative Study of Protocols for Efficient Data Propagation in Smart Dust Networks. In Lecture Notes in Computer Science **2790** (2003) 1003–1016
15. Chiang, C.: Wireless Network Multicasting. PhD thesis, University of California, Los Angeles (1998)
16. Czumaj, A., and Sohler, C.: Soft Kinetic Data Structures. In Symposium on Discrete Algorithms (SODA'01) (2001) 865–872
17. Davies, V.: Evaluating Mobility Models within an Ad Hoc Network. Master's Thesis, Colorado School of Mines (2000)
18. Franklin, J.L., Black, M.L., and Valde, K.: Eyewall Wind Profiles in Hurricanes Determined by gps Dropwindsondes. Technical Report, NOAA/ National Weather Service National Centers for Environmental Prediction National Hurricane Center (2000)
19. Gao, J., Guibas, L.J., Hershberger, J., Zhang, L., and Zhu, A.: Discrete Mobile Centers. In Proc. of the 17th Symposium on Computational Geometry (SOCG'01) (2001) 188–196
20. Gao, J., Guibas, L.J., Hershberger, J., Zhang, L., and Zhu A.: Geometric Spanner for Routing in Mobile Networks. In ACM Symposium on Mobile Ad Hoc Networking and Computing (MOBICOM'01) (2001) 45–55
21. Grossglauser, M., and Tse, D.N.C.: Mobility Increases the Capacity of Ad Hoc Wireless Networks. IEEE/ACM Trans. Netw. **10** 4 (2002) 477–486
22. Haerri, J., Filali, F., and Bonnet, C.: A Framework for Mobility Models Generation and Its Application to Inter-Vehicular Networks. In MobiWac 2005, The 3rd IEEE International Workshop on Mobility Management and Wireless Access, June 13-16, 2005, Maui, Hawaii, U.S.A. (2005)

23. Helbing, D., Farkas, I., Molnar, P., and Vicsek, T.: Simulation of Pedestrian Crowds in Normal and Evacuation Situations. In M. Schreckenberg and S.D. Sharma (eds.) Pedestrian and Evacuation Dynamics (Springer, Berlin) (2002) 21–58

24. Helbing, D., Farkas, I., and Vicsek, T.: Simulating Dynamical Features of Escape Panic. Nature **407** (2000) 487–490

25. Hong, X., Gerla, M., Pei, G., and Chiang, C.-C.: A Group Mobility Model for Ad Hoc Wireless Networks. In Proc. of the 2nd ACM int. workshop on Modeling, Analysis and Simulation of Wireless and Mobile Systems (1999) 53–60

26. Hu, L., and Evans, D.: Localization for Mobile Sensor Networks. In MobiCom '04: Proceedings of the 10th Annual International Conference on Mobile Computing and Networking, ACM Press, (2004) 45–57

27. Jardosh, A., Belding-Royer, E.M., Almeroth, K.C., and Suri, S.: Towards Realistic Mobility Models for Mobile Ad Hoc Networks. In MobiCom '03: Proceedings of the 9th Annual International Conference on Mobile Computing and Networking, ACM Press (2003) 217–229

28. Junge, O., Levenhagen, J., Seifried, A., and Dellnitz, M.: Identification of Halo Orbits for Energy Efficient Formation Flying. In Proceedings of the International Symposium Formation Flying, Toulouse (2002)

29. Junge, O., and Ober-Blöbaum, S.: Optimal Reconfiguration of Formation Flying Satellites. In Accepted for IEEE Conference on Decision and Control and European Control Conference ECC 2005, Seville, Spain (2005)

30. Karl, H., and Willig, A.: Protocols and Architectures for Wireless Sensor Networks. John Wiley & Sons (2005)

31. Laibowitz, M., and Paradiso, J.A.: Parasitic Mobility for Pervasive Sensor Networks. In H.W. Gellersen, R. Want and A. Schmidt (eds), Pervasive Computing, Third International Conference, PERVASIVE 2005, Munich, Germany, May 2005, Proceedings. Springer-Verlag, Berlin (2005)s 255–278

32. Lam, D., Cox, D., and Widom, J.: Teletraffic Modeling for Personal Communications Services. IEEE Communications Magazine Special Issue on Teletraffic Modeling, Engineering and Management in Wireless and Broadband Networks **35** 2 (February 1997) 79–87

33. Leung, K.K., Massey, W.A., and Whitt, W.: Traffic Models for Wireless Communication Networks. In INFOCOM **3** (1994) 1029–1037

34. Liang, B., and Haas, Z.J.: Predictive Distance-Based Mobility Management for PCS Networks. In Proceedings of IEEE INFOCOM'99 (1999) 1377–1384

35. Liu, B., Brass, P., Dousse, O., Nain, P., and Towsley, D.: Mobility Improves Coverage of Sensor Networks. In MobiHoc '05: Proceedings of the 6th ACM International Symposium on Mobile Ad Hoc Networking and Computing, New York, NY, USA, ACM Press (2005) 300–308

36. Lo, C.N., Wolff, R.S., and Bernhardt, R.C.: An Estimate of Network Database Transaction Volume to Support Universal Personal Communication Services. In 1st Int. Conf. Universal Personal Communications (1992) 09.03/16

37. Lu, Y., Lin, H., Gu, Y., and Helmy, A.: Towards Mobility-Rich Performance Analysis of Routing Protocols in Ad Hoc Networks: Using Contraction, Expansion and Hybrid Models. In IEEE International Conference on Communications (ICC) (June 2004)

38. Maurer,J.: Strahlenoptisches Kanalmodell für die Fahrzeug-Fahrzeug-Funkkommunikation. PhD Thesis, Universität Fridericiana Karlsruhe (2005)

39. Mauve, M., Widmer, J., and Hartenstein, H.: A Survey on Position-Based Routing in Mobile Ad Hoc Networks. IEEE Network Magazine **15** 6 (November 2001) 30–39

40. McGuire, M.: Stationary Distributions of Random Walk Mobility Models for Wireless Ad Hoc Networks. In MobiHoc '05: Proceedings of the 6th ACM International Symposium on Mobile Ad Hoc Networking and Computing, ACM Press (2005) 90–98
41. Nain, P., Towsley, D., Liu, B., and Liu, Z.: Properties of Random Direction Models. Technical Report, INRIA Technical Report RR-5284 (July 1994)
42. Niculescu, D., and Nath, B.: Ad Hoc Positioning System (APS) Using AoA. In Proceedings of INFOCOM 2003, San Francisco, CA. (2003)
43. Niculescu, D., and Nath, B.: Position and Orientation in Ad Hoc Networks. Ad Hoc Networks **2** (2004) 133–151
44. Perkins, C.E.: Ad Hoc Networking. Addision-Wesley (2001)
45. Nagpal, J.B.R., and Shrobe, H.: Organizing a Global Coordinate System from Local Information on an Ad Hoc Sensor Network. Lecture Notes in Computer Science **2634** (January 2003) 333–348
46. Raghavendra, C.S., Sivalingam, K.M., and Znati, T., (eds): Wireless Sensor Networks. Springer (2005)
47. Roadknight, C., Gonzalez, A., Parrot, L., Boult, S., and Marshall, I.: An Intelligent Sensor Network for Oceanographic Data Acquisition. In AD HOC NOW 2005 4th International Conference on Ad Hoc Networks and Wireless Cancun (October 6-8, 2005)
48. Royer, E.M., Melliar-Smith, P.M., and Moser, L.E.: An Analysis of the Optimum Node Density for Ad Hoc Mobile Networks. ICC 2001 - IEEE International Conference on Communications (June 2001) 857–861
49. Rubin, I., and Choi, C.: Impact of the Location Area Structure on the Performance of Signaling Channels in Wireless Cellular Networks. IEEE Communications Magazine (February 1997) 108–115
50. Savvides, A., Han, C.-C., and Strivastava, M.B.: Dynamic Fine-Grained Localization in Ad-Hoc Networks of Sensors. In Mobile Computing and Networking (2001) 166–179
51. Schindelhauer, C., Lukovszki, T., Rührup, S., and Volbert, K.: Worst Case Mobility in Ad Hoc Networks. In Proceedings of the 15th Annual ACM Symposium on Parallelism in Algorithms and Architectures (SPAA-03), New York, ACM Press (June 7–9 2003) 230–239
52. Frost, B.M.V.: Traffic Modeling for Telecommunications Networks. IEEE Communications Magazine **32** 3 (March 1994) 70–81
53. Wellenhoff, B.H., Lichtenegger, H., and Collins, J.: Global Positioning System: Theory and Practice. Springer Verlag (1997)
54. Xie, H., Tabbane, S., and Goodman, D.: Dynamic Location Area Management and Performance Analysis. In IEEE VTC'93 (1993) 536–539
55. Yoon, J., Liu, M., and Noble, B.: Random Waypoint Considered Harmful. In Proceedings of INFOCOM. IEEE (2003)
56. Zhang, P., Sadler, C.M., Lyon, S.A., and Martonosi, M.: Hardware Design Experiences in Zebranet. In SenSys '04: Proceedings of the 2nd International Conference on Embedded Networked Sensor Systems, ACM Press (2004) 227–238
57. Zhao, F., and Guibas, L.: Wireless Sensor Networks: An Information Processing Approach. Morgan Kaufmann (2004)
58. Zonoozi, M., and Dassanayake, P.: User Mobility Modeling and Characterization of Mobility Pattern. IEEE Journal on Selected Areas in Communications **15** 1 (September 1997) 1239–1252

Group Communication:
From Practice to Theory [*]

André Schiper

Ecole Polytechnique Fédérale de Lausanne (EPFL),
1015 Lausanne, Switzerland

Abstract. Improving the dependability of computer systems is a critical and essential task. In this context, the paper surveys techniques that allow to achieve fault tolerance in distributed systems by *replication*. The main replication techniques are first explained. Then *group communication* is introduced as the communication infrastructure that allows the implementation of the different replication techniques. Finally the difficulty of implementing group communication is discussed, and the most important algorithms are presented.

1 Introduction

Computer systems become every day more and more complex. As a consequence the probability of problems in these systems increases over the years. To avoid this from becoming a major issue, researchers have since many years worked on improving the dependability of these systems. The methods involved are traditionally classified as *fault prevention, fault tolerance, fault removal* and *fault forecasting* [22]. *Fault prevention* refers to methods for preventing the occurrence or the introduction of faults in the system. *Fault tolerance* refers to methods allowing the system to provide a service complying with the specification in spite of faults. *Fault removal* refers to methods for reducing the number and the severity of faults. *Fault forecasting* refers to methods for estimating the presence of faults (with the goal to locate and remove them). We concentrate here on fault tolerance.

Several techniques to achieve fault tolerance have been developed over the years. The different techniques are related to the specificity of applications. For example, a centralized application differs from a distributed application involving several computing systems. We consider here distributed applications. Fault tolerance for distributed applications can be achieved with different techniques: *transactions, checkpointing* and *replication*.

Transactions have been introduced many years ago in the context of database systems [3]. A transaction allows us to group a sequence of operations while

---

[*] The same paper will appear under the title *Dependable Systems* in *Dependable Information and Communication Systems*, to be published in the Springer LNCS series, 2006. Research supported by the Hasler Stiftung under grant number DICS-1825.

J. Wiedermann et al. (Eds.): SOFSEM 2006, LNCS 3831, pp. 117–136, 2006.

ensuring some properties on these operations, called *ACID* properties [3]: *Atomicity, Consistency, Isolation* and *Durability*. *Atomicity* requires that either all operations of the transaction are preformed, or none of them. *Consistency* is a requirement on the set of operations, namely that the sequence of operations brings the database from a consistent state to another consistent state. Transactions can be executed concurrently. The *isolation* property requires that the effect of transactions executed concurrently is the same as if the transactions where executed in some sequential order (in *isolation* from each other). *Durability* requires that the effect of the operations of the transaction are permanent, i.e., survive crashes. Durability is achieved by storing data on stable storage, e.g., on disk. Atomicity and durability are the two properties specifically related to fault tolerance. A single protocol is used to ensure these two properties, the so called *atomic commitment* protocol executed at the end of the transaction. If all the data accessed by a transaction is located on the same machine, the transaction is a *centralized* transaction. If the data is located on different machines, the transaction is a *distributed* transaction. Distributed transactions are more difficult to implement then centralized transactions. The main technical difficulty lies in the atomic commitment protocol. Except for this problem, the implementation of distributed transactions derives more or less easily from the implementation of centralized transactions. We discuss atomic commitment in Section 4.5.

Checkpointing is another technique for achieving fault tolerance. It consists of periodically saving the state of the computation on stable storage; in case of a crash, the computation is restarted from the most recently saved state. The technique has been developed for long running computations, e.g., simulations that last for days or weeks, and run on multiple machines. These computations are modelled as a set of processes communicating by exchanging messages. The main problem is to ensure that, after crash and recovery, the computation is restarted in a consistent state. We do not discuss checkpointing techniques here. A good survey can be found in [12].

Replication is the technique that allows the progress of the computation during failures (which is called failure *masking*). In a system composed of several components, without replication, if one single component fails the system is no more operational. Replicating a component C, and ensuring that the replicas of C fail independently, allows the system to be tolerant to the failure of one or several replicas of C. Replicating a component is very easy if the component is stateless or if its state does not change during the computation. If the state of the component changes during the computation, then maintaining the consistency among the replicas is a difficult problem. Surprisingly, it is one of the most difficult problems in distributed computing. We concentrate here on the problems related to replication.

While replication allows us to mask failures, this is not the case of transactions or checkpointing. However, the different techniques mentioned above can be combined, e.g., transactions can be run on replicated data. Implementing such a technique requires to combine transaction techniques and replication techniques. This will not be discussed here.

The rest of the paper is structured as follows. Section 2 introduces issues related to replication, and presents the two main replication techniques. Section 3 defines group communication as the middleware layer providing the tools for implementing the different replication techniques. The implementation of these tools is discussed in Section 4. Finally, Section 5 concludes this survey.

2   Replication

In this section we first introduce a model for discussing replication. Then we define what it means for replicas to be consistent. Finally we introduce the two main replication techniques.

2.1   Model for Replication

Consider a system composed of a set of components. A component can be a *process*, an *object*, or any other system structuring unit. Whatever the component is, we can model the interaction between components in terms of inputs and outputs. A component CO receives inputs and generates outputs. The inputs are received from another component CO_{in}, and the outputs are sent to some component CO_{out}. Whether CO_{in} is equal or not to CO_{out} does not make any difference for CO. In the case $CO_{in} = CO_{out}$, the component CO is called a *server*, and the component $CO_{in} = CO_{out}$ is called a *client*. In this case we will denote the server component by S and the client component by C. The input sent by the client C to the server S is called a *request*, and the output sent by the server S to the client C is called a *response*. From the point of view of the client, the pair *request/response* is sometimes called an *operation*: for a client C, an operation consists of a request sent to a server and the corresponding response. We assume here that the client is blocked while waiting for the response.

2.2   Consistency Criteria

A server S can have many clients C, C', C'', etc. For a non-replicated server S, the simplest implementation is to handle client requests sequentially, one at a time. A more efficient implementation could consist for the server to spawn a new thread for each new incoming request. However, in this case the result that the client obtains must be the same as if the operations were executed sequentially, one after the other. The same holds if the server S is replicated, with replicas $S_1, \ldots, S_n$: the result that the clients obtain must be the same as if the operations were executed sequentially by one single server. This can be defined more precisely, by the consistency criterion called *linearizability* [16] (also called *atomic consistency* [24]). A weaker consistency criterion is called *sequential consistency* [19]. We discuss only linearizability, which is the consistency criterion that is usually implemented.

Linearizability. An execution σ is linearizable if it is equivalent to a sequential execution such that *(a)* the request and the response of each operation occur both at some time t, and *(b)* t is in the interval $[t_{req}, t_{res}]$, where t_{req} is the time when the request is issued in σ, t_{res} is the time when the response is received in σ. We explain this definition on two examples. A formal definition can be found in [16].

Consider a server S that implements a *register* with the two operations *read* and *write*:

- $S.write(v)$ denotes the request to write value v in the register managed by server S. The operation returns an empty response, denoted by *ok*.
- $S.read(\,)$ denotes the request to read the register managed by server S. The operation returns the value read.

Figure 1 shows an execution σ that is linearizable:

- Client C issues the request $write(0)$ at time t_1, and receives the empty response *ok* at time t_3.
- Client C' issues the request $write(1)$ at time t_2, and receives the empty response *ok* at time t_5.
- Client C issues the request $read(\,)$ at time t_4, and receives the response 0 at time t_7.
- Client C' issues the request $read(\,)$ at time t_6, and receives the response 1 at time t_8.

The bottom time-line in Figure 1 shows a sequential execution equivalent to σ that satisfies the two requirements *(a)* and *(b)* above (t_a is in the interval $[t_1, t_3]$, t_b is in the interval $[t_4, t_7]$, etc.).

Figure 2 shows an execution that is not linearizable. In an equivalent sequential execution $write(1)$ issued by C' must precede $read(\,)$ issued by C. So there is no way to construct a sequential execution in which $read(\,)$ returns 0 to C.

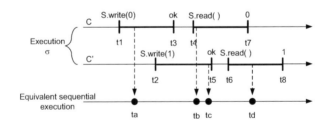

Fig. 1. A linearizable execution

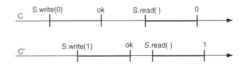

Fig. 2. A non linearizable execution

2.3   Linearizability *vs.* Isolation

Linearizability differs from the isolation property of transactions. There are two main differences. First, linearizability is defined on the *whole sequence of operations* issued by a client process in the system, while isolation is defined on a *subset of the operations* of a client process. Consider for example that process p issues operations op_1 and op_2 within transaction T_1, and later operations op_3 and op_4 within transaction T_2. Isolation does not require that the operations of T_1 are ordered before the operations of T_2 (they can be ordered after those of T_2). However, if op_i precedes op_j on process p, then linearizability requires op_i to be ordered before op_j.

The second difference is that linearizability does not ensure isolated execution of a sequence of operations. If process p issues operation $op_p^1 = S.read(\ )$ that returns v and later $op_p^2 = S.write(v{+}1)$, and process q issues operation $op_q^1 = S.read(\ )$ that returns v' and later $op_q^2 = S.write(v'{+}1)$, linearizability does not prevent the operation op_q^1 of q to be executed between the two operations op_p^1 and op_p^2 of p. There are basically two ways to prevent this from occurring. The first solution is for p and q to explicitly use locks or semaphores. The second solution is to add a new operation to the server S, e.g., *increment*, and to invoke this single operation instead of *read* followed by *write*. The second solution is better than the first one (locks and semaphores lead to problems in the presence of failures).

2.4   Replication Techniques

In the previous section, linearizability defined the desired semantics for operations issued by clients on servers. In the definition of linearizability, servers are black boxes. This means that the definition applies to non-replicated single-threaded servers, to non-replicated multi-threaded servers, to replicated single-threaded servers and to replicated multi-threaded servers. In this section we address the question of implementing a replicated server while ensuring linearizability. We discuss only the single-threaded case. The two main replication techniques are called *active replication* and *passive replication*. Other replication techniques can be seen as variants or combinations of these two basic techniques.

Active Replication. Active replication is also called *state-machine replication* [18], [28]. The principle is illustrated on Figure 3, which shows a replicated server S with three replicas S_1, S_2 and S_3. The client sends its request to all the replicas, each replica processes the request and sends back the response to the client. The client waits for the first response and ignores the others. This client's behavior is correct if we assume that the servers do not behave maliciously, and the servers are deterministic[1]: in this case all the responses are identical.

In Figure 3 there is only one client. The problem becomes more difficult with multiple clients that concurrently send their requests. In this case it is sufficient

---

[1] A server is deterministic if its new state and the response depend only on the request and on the state before processing the request.

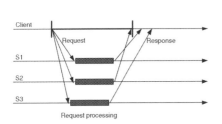

Fig. 3. Active replication

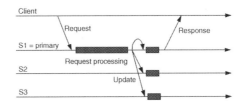

Fig. 4. Active replication: requests received in the same order

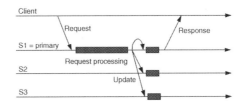

Fig. 5. Passive replication

that all replicas S_i receive the clients' requests in the *same order*, as shown in Figure 4. This allow the replicas to process the clients' requests in the same order. In Section 3 we introduce a group communication primitive that ensures such an ordering of client requests.

Passive Replication. The principle of passive replication is illustrated on Figure 5, which shows the same replicated server S with its three replicas S_1, S_2 and S_3. One of the replicas, here S_1, is the *primary* replica; the other replicas, S_2 and S_3 are called *backups*. The client sends its request only to the primary, and waits for the response. Only the primary processes the request. Once this is done, the primary sends an *update* message to the backups, to bring them to a state that reflects the processing of the client request. In Figure 5 the update message is also sent to the primary. The reason is that, if we include failures, it is simpler to assume that the modification of the state of the primary occurs only upon handling of the update message, and not upon processing of the request.

If several clients sent their requests at the same time, the primary processes them sequentially, one after the other. Since the primary sends an update message to the backups, the processing can be non-deterministic, contrary to active replication. Note that this superficial presentation hides most of the problems related to the implementation of passive replication. We mention them in the next paragraph. With active replication, the implementation problems are hidden in the implementation of the group communication primitive that orders the clients' requests.

Problems Implementing Passive Replication. When the primary crashes, a new primary must be selected. However, requiring the failure detection of the primary to be reliable (i.e. never making mistakes) is a very constraining assumption. For this reason, solutions to passive replication that do no require a reliable failure detection mechanism for the primary have been developed. The three main problems to address are the following: (a) prevention of multiple primaries being able to process requests, *(b)* prevention of multiple executions of a request, and *(c)* reception of the update message by all replicas. Problem *(a)* is related to the unreliable failure detection mechanism. Problem *(b)* arises when the current primary is falsely suspected to have crashed. Consider a client C sending its request to the primary S_1. Assume that S_1 is incorrectly suspected to have crashed, and S_2 becomes the new primary. If this happens, and C did not receive any response, it will resend its request to S_2. This may lead to execute the client request twice. Multiple execution of a request can be prevented by attaching a unique identifier to each request (this request identifier being piggybacked on the update message). Problem *(c)* arises when the primary crashes while multicasting the update message. In this case, we must prevent the undesirable situation where the update message is received by some replicas, but not by all of them. In Section 3 we present the group communication primitive that allows us to solve the problems *(a)* and *(c)*.

3   Group Communication

In the previous section we have introduced the two basic replication techniques, namely active replication and passive replication. We have also pointed out the need for communication primitives with well defined ordering properties to implement these techniques. *Group communication* is the infrastructure that provides these primitives. A group is simply a set of processes with an identifier. Messages can be multicast to the members of some group g simply by referring to the identifier of group g: the sender of the message does not need to know what processes are members of g. For example, if we consider a replicated server S with three replicas S_1, S_2 and S_3, we can refer to these replicas as the group $g_S = \{S_1, S_2, S_3\}$. As illustrated by Figure 6, group communication is a middleware layer between the transport layer and the layer that implements replication. In this section we define the two main group communication prim-

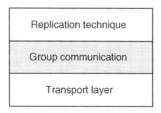

Fig. 6. Group communication

itives for replication, namely *atomic broadcast* and *generic broadcast*. Before doing so, we introduce some concepts needed to understand the various aspects of group communication.

3.1   Various Group Models

Static Group *vs.* Dynamic Group. A *static* group is a group whose membership is constant over time: a static group is initialized with a given membership, and this membership never changes. This is the simplest type of group. However, static groups are often too restrictive. For example consider the replicated server S implemented by the group $g_S = \{S_1, S_2, S_3\}$. If one of the replicas S_i crashes, it might be desirable to replace S_i with a new replica, in order to maintain the same degree of replication. A group whose membership changes over time is called a *dynamic* group. Dynamic groups require to manage the addition and the removal of members to/from the group. This problem is called the *group membership* problem: it is discussed in Section 3.4.

Benign *vs.* Malicious Faults. The group (or system) model encompasses also the type of faults that are considered. The distinction is made between *benign* faults and *malicious* faults (also called *Byzantine* faults). With benign faults, a process or a channel does its job correctly, or does not do its job. A process crash, or a channel that looses a message, are benign faults. With malicious faults, a process or a channel can behave arbitrarily.

Crash-Stop *vs.* Crash-Recovery. In the context of benign faults, the distinction is made between the crash-stop and the crash-recovery process model. In the *crash-stop* model processes do not have access to stable storage. In this case, a process that crashes looses its state: upon recovery, the process is indistinguishable from a newly started process. In the *crash-recovery* model processes have access to stable storage, allowing them to periodically save their state. In this case, a process that crashes can recover its most recently saved state.

Combining these Models. Combining these three dimensions lead to different models for group communication. The simplest model is the benign static crash-stop model. Other models have been considered in the literature, but they lead to more complexity in the specification of group communication and in the algorithms. There are some subtle differences between the different models, as we explain now.

Figure 7 shows the difference between active replication with dynamic crash-stop groups (left) and active replication with static crash-recovery groups (right). In the crash-stop model, to keep the same replication degree, a crashed process (here replica S_3) must be replaced with a new process (here S_4). The initial membership of the group g_S is denoted by $v_0(g_S) = \{S_1, S_2, S_3\}$ (v stands for *view*, see Section 3.4). When S_3 crashes, the membership becomes $v_1(g_S) = \{S_1, S_2\}$. Once S_4 is added, we have the membership $v_2(g_S) = \{S_1, S_2, S_4\}$. Note that the state of p_4 must be initialized. This is done by an operation called *state transfer*: when S_4 joins the group, the state of one of its members

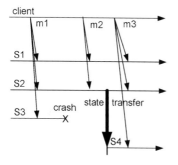 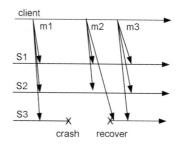

Fig. 7. Active replication with a dynamic crash-stop group (left), or a static crash-recovery group (right)

(here S_2) is used to initialize the state of S_4. In the static crash-recovery model (Figure 7, right), the same degree of replication is kept by assuming that crashed replicas recover (here S_3). However in this context, since S_3 remains all the time a member of g_S, a message broadcast to the group while S_3 is down *must be delivered to S_3* (here m_2). As a result, no state transfer is needed. The static crash-recovery model is preferable to the dynamic crash-stop model whenever the state of the replicas is large.

In the following we consider mainly the static crash-stop model, which is the most widely model considered in the literature, and the simplest. Dynamic groups are briefly mentioned in Section 3.4.

3.2 Atomic Broadcast for Active Replication

One of the most important group communication primitives is *atomic broadcast* [8]. Atomic broadcast is also sometimes called *total order broadcast*, or simply *abcast*. The primitive ensures that messages are delivered ordered. To give a more formal specification of the properties of abcast, we need to introduce the following notation:

- The atomic broadcast of message m to the members of some group g is denoted by $abcast(g, m)^2$.
- The delivery of message m is denoted by $adeliver(m)$.

It is important to make the distinction between *abcast/adeliver*, and the *send/receive* primitives at the transport layer (see Figure 8). The semantics of *send/receive* is defined by the transport layer. The semantics of *abcast/adeliver* is defined by atomic broadcast. An atomic broadcast protocol uses the semantics of *send/receive* to provide the semantics of *abcast/adeliver*.

The definition of atomic broadcast in the static crash-stop model relies on the definition of a *correct* process: a process is correct if it does not crash. Otherwise it is *faulty*. Note that even though these definitions are simple, they are

---

^{2} The primitive should be called atomic *multicast*. For simplicity, we keep the term *broadcast* here.

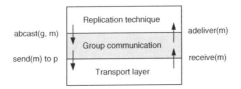

Fig. 8. *Send/receive* vs. *abcast/adeliver*

easily wrongly understood. Correct/faulty are predicates that characterize the *whole lifetime* of a process. This means that if some process p crashes at time $t = 10$, then p is faulty (even at time $t = 9$). With this definition, atomic broadcast in the static/crash-stop model is specified by the following four properties [15], [2][3]:

- *Validity:* If a correct process executes *abcast(g,m)*, then some correct process in g eventually adelivers m or no process in g is correct.
- *Uniform agreement:* If a process in g adelivers a message m, then all correct processes in g eventually adeliver m.
- *Uniform integrity:* For any message m, every process p adelivers m at most once, and only if p is in g and m was previously abcast to g.
- *Uniform total order:* If process p in g adelivers message m before message m', then no process in g adelivers m' before having previously adelivered m.

Validity, uniform agreement and uniform integrity define the primitive called *reliable broadcast*[4]. Atomic broadcast is defined as reliable broadcast with the uniform total order property.

It is easy to see that active replication is easily implemented using atomic broadcast. If g_S is the group of replicas that provide some service S, clients C send requests using the primitive *abcast(g_S, req)*. The validity property ensures that if C does not crash, its request is received by at least one member of g_S (unless all members of g_S crash). Combining this guarantee with uniform agreement ensures that all correct processes in g_S eventually adeliver m. The uniform total order property ensures that all replicas adeliver the clients' requests in the same order.

The response from a replica in g_S to a client is sent using a unicast message, i.e., a point-to-point message. The transport layer must ensure the following *quasi-reliable channel* property [1]: if a correct process p sends message m to a correct process q, then q eventually receives m. This property is stronger than the property provided by TCP (if a TCP connection breaks, reliability is no more guaranteed).

---

[3] More precisely, the specification corresponds to the primitive called *uniform atomic broadcast*. We will call it here simply *atomic broadcast*.

[4] More precisely, *uniform* reliable broadcast.

3.3   Generic Broadcast for Passive Replication

Atomic broadcast can also be used to implement passive replication, but this is not necessarily the best solution in terms of cost. Atomic broadcast can be used as follows. Consider a replicated server S defined by the (static) group g_S, and assume that the members of g_S are ordered in a list. Initially, the member at the head of the membership list is the primary. The primary sends the update message to g_S using abcast. Whenever some member of g_S suspects the current primary to have crashed, it abcasts the message $\langle primary\ change \rangle$. Upon adelivery of this message every process moves the process at the head of the list to the tail. The new primary is the new process at the head of the list.

Passive replication can also be implemented using the group communication primitive called *generic broadcast* [25], [2], which can be cheaper to implement than atomic broadcast. While atomic broadcast orders *all* messages, generic broadcast orders only messages that *conflict*. Conflicts are defined by a relation on the set of messages. This conflict relation is part of the specification of the primitive, and makes the primitive *generic*. The generic broadcast of message m to the group g is denoted by $gbcast(g, m)$; the delivery of message m is denoted by $gdeliver(m)$. Formally, generic broadcast is defined by the same properties that define atomic broadcast, except that the uniform total order property is replaced with the following weaker property:

– *Generic total order:* If process p in g gdelivers message m before message m', and m, m' conflict, then no process in g gdelivers m' before having previously gdelivered m.

We have seen that passive replication can be implemented with atomic broadcast for the *update* messages and the *primary-change* messages. Consider the following conflict relation between these two types of messages:

– Messages of type *primary-change* do not conflict with messages of the same type, but conflict with messages of type *update*.
– Messages of type *update* conflict with messages of the same type, and also with messages of type *primary-change*.

This ensures enough ordering to implement generic broadcast correctly. Note that most of the time one single process considers itself to be the primary, and during this period no concurrent update messages are issued. So most of the time no concurrent conflicting messages are issued.

The implementation of generic broadcast (and atomic broadcast) is discussed in Section 4.

3.4   About Group Membership

With dynamic groups, the successive membership of a group is called a *view*. Consider for example a group g, with initially three processes p, q, r. This initial membership is called the *initial view* of g, and is denoted by $v_0(g)$. Assume that later r is removed from g. The new membership is denoted by $v_1(g) = \{p, q\}$. If s is added later to the group the resulting membership is denoted by $v_2(g) = \{p, q, s\}$. So the history of a dynamic group is represented as a sequence of views, and all group members must see the sequence of views in the same order. The problem of maintaining the membership of a dynamic group is called the *group membership problem* [27].

3.5   About View Synchronous Broadcast

View synchronous broadcast or *vscast* (sometimes also called *view synchrony*), is another group communication primitive, defined in a dynamic group model [4],[7]. However, the importance of vscast has been overestimated, and stems from a time where the difference between static groups and dynamic groups was not completely understood.

Consider some message m vscast by process p in view $v_i(g)$: vscast orders m with respect to view changes. In other words, vscast ensures that m is delivered by all processes in the same view v_j. The property is also called *same view delivery* [7]. A stronger property, called *sending view delivery*, requires $i = j$: the view in which the message is delivered is the view in which the message was sent [7].

The overestimated importance given to view synchronous broadcast has led to several misunderstandings. The first is that dynamic groups are needed to implement passive replication: Section 3.3 has sketched an implementation of passive replication with a static group. The second misunderstanding is that the specification of group communication with dynamic groups is inherently different from the specification of group communication with static groups. This is not the case, as shown in [26].

3.6   Group Communication *vs.* Quorum Systems

In the previous sections we have shown the use of group communication for implementing replication. *Quorum systems* is another technique for replication, anterior to group communication and also more widely known. In this section we explain the advantage of group communication over quorum systems in the context of replication [11].

Definition of Quorum Systems. Consider a set $\Pi = \{p_1, \ldots, p_n\}$ of processes. The set of all subsets of Π is called the *powerset* of Π, and is denoted by 2^Π. We have for example:

$$\{p_1\}, \{p_2\}, \{p_1, p_2\}, \{p_2, p_3, p_4\}, \ldots, \{p_1, \ldots, p_n\} \in 2^\Pi.$$

A *quorum system* of Π is defined as any set $Q \subset 2^\Pi$ such that any two $Q_i \in Q$ have a non empty intersection:

$$\forall Q_1, Q_2 \in Q, \text{ we have } Q_1 \cap Q_2 \neq \emptyset.$$

Each $Q_i \in Q$ is called a *quorum*. For example, if $\Pi = \{p_1, p_2, p_3\}$, then the set $Q = \{\{p_1, p_2\}, \{p_1, p_3\}, \{p_2, p_3\}\}$ is a quorum system of Π; $\{p_1, p_2\}$, $\{p_1, p_3\}$, $\{p_2, p_3\}$ are quorums.

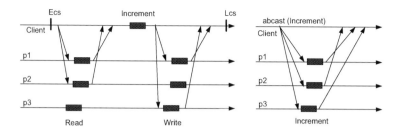

Fig. 9. Replication: quorum systems (left) *vs.* group communication (right)

Quorum Systems for Implementing a Fault Tolerant Register. The use of quorums systems for fault tolerance can be illustrated on a very simple example: a server that implements a *register*. A register is an object with two operations *read* and *write*: *read* returns the value of the register, i.e., the most recent value written; *write* overwrites the value of the register.

The register can be made fault tolerant by replication on three replicas e.g., $\Pi = \{p_1, p_2, p_3\}$ with the quorum system $Q = \{\{p_1, p_2\}, \{p_1, p_3\}, \{p_2, p_3\}\}$. Each operation needs only to be executed on one quorum of Q, i.e., on $\{p_1, p_2\}$, on $\{p_1, p_3\}$, or on $\{p_2, p_3\}$. In other words, the quorum system Q tolerates the crash of one out of the three replicas. Using the quorum system Q, linearizability of the read and write operations is easy to implement [11].

Requiring Isolation. A fault tolerant register is easy to implement using quorum systems. However, clients usually want to perform more complex operations. Consider for example the operations *(a) increment* a register and *(b) decrement* a register. These two operations can be implemented as follows: (1) read the register, then (2) update the value read, and finally (3) write back the new value. However, one client C may increment the register, while at the same time another client C' decrements the register. To ensure a correct execution, the two operations must be executed in mutual exclusion. With group communication, no mutual exclusion is needed: atomic broadcast can be used to send the corresponding operation to the replicated servers.

This difference between quorum systems and group communication is illustrated in Figure 9. The left part illustrates the quorum solution, and the right part the group communication solution. In the quorum solution, the increment operation is performed by the client, after reading the register and before writing the new value. The implementation requires mutual exclusion, represented by E_{CS} (enter critical section) and L_{CS} (leave critical section). In the group communication solution, the increment operation is sent to the replicas using atomic broadcast; no mutual exclusion is required[5]. Implementing atomic broadcast requires weaker assumptions about the crash detection mechanism than implementing mutual exclusion [11].

---

[5] The reader may wonder why no *increment* operation can be sent with quorum systems. Sending the *increment* operation requires atomic broadcast!

4   Implementation of Group Communication

In the previous section we have seen the role of group communication for replication. We discuss now the implementation of the two group communication primitives that we have introduced, namely atomic broadcast and generic broadcast. We consider only static groups, non Byzantine processes and the crash-stop model.

4.1   Impossibility Results

Consider a static group g, and processes in g communicating by message exchange. The most general assumption is to consider that the time between the sending of a message m and the reception of m by its destination is not bounded, i.e., the transmission delay can be arbitrarily long. Similarly, if we model the execution of a process as a sequence of steps, the most general assumption is to consider that while the slowest process performs one step, the fastest process can perform an unbounded number of steps. These two assumptions define the *asynchronous system model*. The absence of bounds for the message transmission delay models an open network in which the load of the links are unknown. The absence of bounds on the relative speed of processes models processes running on CPUs with an unknown load. The asynchronous system model is the most general model, but it has a major drawback: several problems are impossible to solve in that model when one single process may crash.

One of these problems is *consensus*. The problem is defined on a set of processes, e.g., on some group g. Every process p in g starts with an initial value v_p, and all correct processes in g have to decide on some common value v that is the initial value of one of the processes. Formally, the consensus problem is defined by the following properties [6]:

- *Validity:* If a process decides v, then v is the initial value of some process.
- *Agreement:* No two correct processes decide differently.
- *Termination:* Every correct process eventually decides some value.

An explanation of *problem solvability* is needed here. Consider a distributed algorithm A_P that is supposed to solve problem P. Algorithm A_P can be launched many times. Due to the variability of the transmission delay of messages, each execution of A_P can go through a different sequence of states. However, in all of these executions, A_P must solve P. If there is one single execution in which this is not the case, then we say that algorithm A_P does not solve P. This clarification is important in the context of the consensus problem: it has been shown that consensus is not solvable by a deterministic algorithm in an asynchronous system with reliable links if one single process may crash. This result is known as the *FLP impossibility result* [13].

The FLP impossibility result is easy to extend to atomic broadcast by the following argument [9]. Assume for a contradiction that atomic broadcast can be implemented in an asynchronous system with process crashes. Then consensus can be solved as follows (in the context of some group g):

- Each process p in g executes $abcast(v_p)$, where v_p is p's initial value.
- Let v be the first message adelivered by p.
- Process p decides v.

If there is a least one correct process, then at least one message is adelivered. By the property of atomic broadcast, every correct process adelivers the same first message, and so decides on the same value. Consensus is solved, which shows the contradiction.

4.2   Models for Solving Consensus

Consensus and atomic broadcast are not solvable in an asynchronous system when processes may crash. We thus need to find a system model in which consensus is solvable (whenever consensus is solvable, atomic broadcast is also solvable, see Section 4.3). One such system is the *synchronous* system model, defined by the following two properties:

- There is a known bound on the transmission delay of messages.
- There is a known bound on the relative speed of processes.

Consensus is solvable in a synchronous system [23], but the synchronous system model has drawbacks from a practical point of view. The model requires to consider the *worst case*: the worst case for the transmission delay of messages, the worst case for the relative speed of processes. These bounds have a direct impact on the time it takes to detect the crash of a process: the higher these bounds are, the higher the time it takes to detect a process crash, i.e., the longer it takes to react to a crash. In a replicated service a long reaction to a crash leads to a long delay before clients get the replies.

The drawback of the synchronous model has led to look for system models weaker than the synchronous model, but strong enough to solve consensus (and so atomic broadcast). The first of these models is called the *partially synchronous* model [10]. The model considers bounds on the message transmission delay and on the relative speed of processes. There are two variants of the model:

1. There is a bound on the relative speed of processes and a bound on the message transmission delay, but these bounds are *not known*.
2. There is a *known* bound on the relative speed of processes and on the message transmission delay, but these bounds hold only from some unknown point on.

The two definitions are equivalent, but the first variant seems more appealing from a practical point of view.

A different approach was proposed later in [6]. It consists in *augmenting* the asynchronous model with an *oracle* that satisfies some well defined properties. In other words, the system is assumed to be asynchronous, but the processes can query an oracle about the status *crashed/not crashed* of processes. For this reason the oracle is called *failure detector oracle*, or simply *failure detector*. If the failure detector returns the reply *crashed* q to process p, we say p *suspects* q. Note that this information may be incorrect: failure detectors can make mistakes. The legal replies to a query of the failure detector are defined by two properties called *completeness* and *accuracy*. For example, the replies of the failure detector called $\Diamond \mathcal{S}$ must satisfy the following completeness and accuracy properties [6]:

- *Strong completeness:* Eventually every process that crashes is permanently suspected to have crashed by every correct process.
- *Eventual weak accuracy:* There is a time after which some correct process is never suspected by any correct process.

Consensus is solvable in the asynchronous system augmented with the failure detector $\Diamond \mathcal{S}$ and a majority of correct processes [6]. Moreover, it has been shown that $\Diamond \mathcal{S}$ is the weakest failure detector that allows us to solve consensus in an asynchronous system [5]. This result shows the power of the failure detector approach and explains its popularity.

4.3   Solving Consensus

The first algorithm to solve consensus in a model weaker than the synchronous model is the consensus algorithm by Dwork, Lynch and Stockmeyer for the partially synchronous model [10]. The algorithm – called here *DLS* – requires a majority of correct processes, and is based on the *rotating coordinator* paradigm. In this paradigm, the computation is decomposed into rounds $r = 0, 1, 2, \ldots$, and in each round another process, in some predetermined order, is the coordinator. Typically, with n processes $p_0, \ldots, p_{n-1}$, the coordinator of round r is process $p_{r \bmod n}$. In each round the coordinator leads the computation in order to try to decide on a value. The algorithm is based on the notions of *locked* value and *acceptable* value. The coordinator of round r tries to lock a value, say v, and if it learns that a majority of processes have locked v in round r, it can decide v. If the coordinator of round r is suspected to have crashed, then the computation proceeds to the next round $r + 1$ with a new coordinator. Note that a process can become coordinator more than once, e.g., in rounds k, $n + k$, $2n + k$, etc. The key property of the *DLS* algorithm is that the safety properties of consensus (validity and agreeement) hold even if the properties of the partially synchronous model do not hold. In other words, these properties are only needed for liveness, i.e., to ensure the termination property of consensus.

Two other consensus algorithms had a major impact and led to the development of variations of these algorithms. The first one is the *Paxos* algorithm proposed by Lamport [20], [21]. The second one is the Chandra-Toueg consensus algorithm (denoted *CT* hereafter) based on the failure detector $\Diamond \mathcal{S}$ [6]. *Paxos* and *CT*, similarly to *DLS*, require a majority of correct processes. *CT*, similarly to *DLS*, is based on the rotating coordinator paradigm. *Paxos* is also based on a coordinator, but the coordinator role is not predetermined as in the rotating coordinator paradigm, but determined during the computation (the algorithm tolerates multiple coordinators for the same round). *Paxos* and *CT* are also based on the notion of *locked* value (but there is no notion of *acceptable* value): each coordinator, one after the other, tries to lock a value v, and if it learns that a majority of processes have locked v, it can decide v. In this sense *Paxos* and *CT* are very similar. The two algorithms also share the key property of *DLS*, namely that no matter how asynchronous the system behaves, the safety properties of consensus are never violated. However, *Paxos* and *CT* differ on the following issues:

- *CT* requires reliable channels, while *Paxos* tolerates message loss (similarly to *DLS*).
- The condition for termination is rigorously defined for *CT*, namely the *eventual weak accuracy* property of $\Diamond S$. No such condition that ensure termination exists for *Paxos*.

Note that after the publication of *Paxos*, the failure detector Ω – which eventually outputs at each process the identity of the same correct process [5] – has been mentioned as ensuring the termination of *Paxos*. However, this makes sense only if we consider *Paxos* with reliable channels.

4.4   Implementing Atomic Broadcast and Generic Broadcast

A large number of atomic broadcast algorithms have been proposed in the last 20 years. These algorithms can be classified according to several criteria. One of those criteria is the mechanisms used for message ordering [8]: *fixed sequencer, moving sequencer, privilege-based, communication history, destinations agreement*. For example in a *fixed sequencer* algorithm, one process is elected as the sequencer and is responsible for ordering messages. Obviously this solution is not tolerant to the crash of the sequencer. The solution must be completed by a mechanism for electing a new sequencer in case the current sequencer crashes. This is usually done using a group membership service (see Section 3.4) to remove the current sequencer from the group. Once this is done, a new sequencer can be elected. Thus the solution implements atomic broadcast in the context of dynamic groups (see Section 3.1). The same comment applies to most of the implementations of atomic broadcast described in the literature. These implementations *require order to provide order*: the group membership service orders views, and this order is used to implement the ordering required by atomic broadcast.

Atomic broadcast can also be solved in the context of static groups. The solutions rely on consensus (which explains the fundamental role of the consensus problem in the context of fault tolerance computing). The consensus problem allows processes to agree on a value. This value can be of any type. Atomic broadcast can be implemented by solving a sequence of consensus problems, where each instance of consensus agrees on a *set of messages*. The idea is the following [6]. Consider a static group g and $abcast(g, m)$. Each process p in g has a variable k_p used to number the various instances of consensus. Whenever p has received messages that need to be ordered, p starts a new instance of consensus, uniquely identified by k_p, with the set of messages to be ordered as its initial value. By the properties of consensus, all processes agree on the same set of messages for consensus $\#k_p$, say $msg(k_p)$. Then the messages in the set $msg(k_p)$ are adelivered in some deterministic order (e.g., according to their IDs), and before the messages in the set $msg(k_p + 1)$. This solution for static groups can be extended to dynamic groups [26].

The implementation of generic broadcast is more difficult to sketch. The basic idea of the implementation is to control whether conflicting messages have been gbcast. As long as only non conflicting messages are gbcast, these messages can be gdelivered without invoking consensus, i.e., without the cost of consensus. However, as soon as conflicting messages are detected, the gdelivery of messages require to execute an instance of the consensus problem. More details can be found in [25], [2].

4.5   Solving the Atomic Commitment Problem

In Section 1 we have mentioned the *atomic commitment* problem as the main problem related to the implementation of distributed transactions. The problem has similarities with the consensus problem, but also has significant differences.

In the atomic commitment problem, each process involved in the transaction votes at the end of the transaction. The vote can be *yes* or *no*. A *yes* vote indicates that the process is ready to commit the transaction; a *no* vote indicates that the process cannot commit the transaction. As in the consensus problem, all processes must decide on the same outcome: *commit* or *abort*. The conditions under which commit and abort can be decided make the difference between consensus and atomic commitment. If one single process votes *no*, the decision must be *abort*; if no failure occurs and all processes vote *yes*, then the decision must be *commit*; if there are failures, the decision can be *abort*. So "failures" can influence the decision of atomic commitment, which is not the case for consensus.

Another important difference is that, for practical reasons, the atomic commitment problem needs to be solved in the crash-recovery model (in the context of transactions, processes have access to stable storage). A third difference is related the notion of *blocking* vs. *non-blocking* solution, a difference that has not been made for consensus (the distinction between a blocking and a non-blocking solution exists only in the crash-recovery model). In the crash-recovery model, a protocol is *blocking* if a single crash during the execution of the protocol prevents the termination of the protocol until the crashed process recovers. In contrast, a non-blocking protocol can terminate despite one single process crash (or even despite more than one crash).

The most popular atomic commitment protocol is the blocking *2PC* (2 Phase Commit) protocol [3]. The first non-blocking atomic commitment protocol was proposed by Skeen [29]. At that time the consensus problem was not yet identified as the key problem in distributed fault tolerant computing. This explains that the protocol proposed in [29] does not solve atomic commitment by reduction to consensus. Today such a reduction is considered to be the best way to solve the non-blocking atomic commitment problem (see for example [14], for a solution in the crash-stop model).

5 Conclusion

More than twenty years of research have contributed to a very good understanding of many issues related to fault tolerance, replication and group communication. However, the understanding of theoretical issues is not the same in all models. For example, while static group communication in the crash-stop model has reached maturity, the same level of maturity has not yet been reached for dynamic group communication or for group communication in the crash-recovery model. More work needs also to be done to quantitatively compare different algorithms in the context of replication. Typically, while a lot of atomic broadcast algorithms have been published, little has been done to compare these algorithms from a quantitative point of view. Specifically, more work needs to be done to compare these algorithms under different fault-loads, as done for example in [30]. Addressing real-time constraints, e.g., [17], needs also to get more attention.

Acknowledgments. I would like to thank Sergio Mena and Olivier Rütti for their comments on an earlier version of the paper.

References

1. Aguilera, M.K., Chen, W. and Toueg, S.: Heartbeat: a Timeout-Free Failure Detector for Quiescent Reliable Communication. In Proceedings of the 11th International Workshop on Distributed Algorithms (WDAG'97), Saarbrücken, Germany (September 1997) 126–140
2. Aguilera, M.K., Delporte-Gallet, C., Fauconnier, H., and Toueg, S.: Thrifty Generic Broadcast. In Proceedings of the 14th International Symposium on Distributed Computing (DISC'2000) (October 2000)
3. Bernstein, P.A., Hadzilacos, V., and Goodman, N.: Concurrency Control and Recovery in Distributed Database Systems. Addison-Wesley (1987)
4. Birman, K., and Joseph, T.: Reliable Communication in the Presence of Failures. ACM Trans. on Computer Systems **5** 1 (February 1987) 47–76
5. Chandra, T.D., Hadzilacos, V., and Toueg, S.: The Weakest Failure Detector for Solving Consensus. Journal of ACM, **43** 4 (1996) 685–722
6. Chandra, T.D., and Toueg, S.: Unreliable Failure Detectors for Reliable Distributed Systems. Journal of ACM **43** 2 (1996) 225–267
7. Chockler, G.V., Keidar, I., and Vitenberg, R.: Group Communication Specifications: A Comprehensive Study. ACM Computing Surveys **4** 33 (December 2001) 1–43
8. Défago, X., Schiper, A., and Urban, P.: Totally Ordered Broadcast and Multicast Algorithms: Taxonomy and Survey. ACM Computing Surveys, **4** 36 (December 2004) 1–50
9. Dolev, D., Dwork, C., and Stockmeyer, L.: On the Minimal Synchrony Needed for Distributed Consensus. Journal of ACM **34** 1 (January 1987) 77–97
10. Dwork, C., Lynch, N., and Stockmeyer, L.: Consensus in the Presence of Partial Synchrony. Journal of ACM, **35** 2 (April 1988) 288–323
11. Ekwall, R., and Schiper, A.: Replication: Understanding the Advantage of Atomic Broadcast over Quorum Systems. Journal of Universal Computer Science **11** 5 (May 2005) 703–711

12. Elnozahy, E.N., Alvisi, L., Wang, Y.-M., and Johnson, D.B.: A Survey of Rollback-Recovery Protocols in Message-Passing Systems. ACM Computing Surveys **34** 3 (September 2002) 375–408

13. Fischer, M., Lynch, N., and Paterson, M.: Impossibility of Distributed Consensus with One Faulty Process. Journal of ACM **32** (April 1985) 374–382

14. Guerraoui, R., Larrea, M., and Schiper, A.: Reducing the Cost for Non-Blocking in Atomic Commitment. In IEEE 16th Intl. Conf. Distributed Computing Systems (May 1996) 692–697

15. Hadzilacos, V., and Toueg, S.: Fault-Tolerant Broadcasts and Related Problems. Technical Report 94-1425, Department of Computer Science, Cornell University (May 1994)

16. Herlihy, M., and Wing, J.: Linearizability: a Correctness Condition for Concurrent Objects. ACM Trans. on Progr. Languages and Syst. **12** 3 (1990) 463–492

17. Hermant, J.-F., Le Lann, G.: Fast Asynchronous Uniform Consensus in Real-Time Distributed Systems. IEEE Transactions on Computers **51** 8 (August 2002) 931–944

18. Lamport, L.: Time, Clocks, and the Ordering of Events in a Distributed System. Comm. ACM **21** 7 (July 1978) 558–565

19. Lamport, L.: How to Make a Multiprocessor Computer that Correctly Executes Multiprocess Programs. IEEE Trans. on Computers **C28** 9 (1979) 690–691

20. Lamport, L.: The Part-Time Parliament. TR 49, Digital SRC (September 1989)

21. Lamport, L.: The Part-Time Parliament. ACM Trans. on Computer Systems **16** 2 (May 1998) 133–169

22. Laprie, J.C. (ed.): Dependability: Basic Concepts and Terminology. Springer-Verlag (1992)

23. Lynch, N.A.: Distributed Algorithms. Morgan Kaufmann (1996)

24. Misra, J.: Axioms for Memory Access in Asynchronous Hardware Systems. ACM Trans. on Progr. Languages and Syst. **8** 1 (1986) 142–153

25. Pedone, F., and Schiper, A.: Handling Message Semanticas with Generic Broadcast Protocols. Distributed Computing **15** 2 (April 2002) 97–107

26. Schiper, A.: Dynamic Group Communication. TR IC/2003/27, EPFL (April 2003). To appear in ACM Distributed Computing.

27. Schiper, A., and Toueg, S.: From Set Membership to Group Membership: A Separation of Concerns. TR IC/2003/56, EPFL - IC (September 2003)

28. Schneider, F.B.: Implementing Fault Tolerant Services Using the State Machine Approach: A Tutorial. Computing Surveys **22** 4 (December 1990)

29. Skeen, D.: Nonblocking Commit Protocols. In ACM SIGMOD Intl. Conf. on Management of Data (1981) 133–142

30. Urbán, P., Shnayderman, I., and Schiper, A.: Comparison of Failure Detectors and Group Membership: Performance Study of Two Atomic Broadcast Algorithms. In Proc. Int'l Conf. on Dependable Systems and Networks, San Francisco, CA, USA (June 2003) 645–654

A General Data Reduction Scheme for Domination in Graphs[*]

Jochen Alber[1], Britta Dorn[2], and Rolf Niedermeier[3]

[1] DIgSILENT GmbH, Power System Applications & Consulting,
Heinrich-Hertz-Str. 9, D-72810 Gomaringen, Germany
j.alber@digsilent.de
[2] Mathematisches Institut, Universität Tübingen,
Auf der Morgenstelle 10, D-72076 Tübingen, Germany
brdo@fa.uni-tuebingen.de
[3] Institut für Informatik, Friedrich-Schiller-Universität Jena,
Ernst-Abbe-Platz 2, D-07743 Jena, Germany
niedermr@minet.uni-jena.de

Abstract. Data reduction by polynomial-time preprocessing is a core concept of (parameterized) complexity analysis in solving NP-hard problems. Its practical usefulness is confirmed by experimental work. Here, generalizing and extending previous work, we present a set of data reduction preprocessing rules on the way to compute optimal dominating sets in graphs. In this way, we arrive at the novel notion of "data reduction schemes." In addition, we obtain data reduction results for domination in directed graphs that allow to prove a linear-size problem kernel for DIRECTED DOMINATING SET in planar graphs.

1 Introduction

Data reduction and kernelization rules are one of the primary outcomes of research on parameterized complexity: Attacking computationally hard problems, it always makes sense to simplify and reduce the input instance by efficient preprocessing. In this work, considering the graph problem DOMINATING SET, we introduce and study the notion of a data reduction *schemes*.

Our work is based on two lines of research both concerned with solving NP-hard problems. On the one hand, there is the concept of polynomial-time approximation algorithms and, in particular, the concept of polynomial-time approximation schemes (PTAS) where one gets a better approximation guarantee at the cost of higher running times (see [4] for details). On the other hand, there is the paradigm of local search (see [1] for details). In this paper, we combine ideas from both research areas. More specifically, based on DOMINATING SET, generalizing and extending previous work [3], we develop a whole scheme of data

[*] Supported by the Deutsche Forschungsgemeinschaft (DFG), project PEAL (parameterized complexity and exact algorithms), NI 369/1, and Emmy Noether research group PIAF (fixed-parameter algorithms), NI 369/4.

J. Wiedemann et al. (Eds.): SOFSEM 2006, LNCS 3831, pp. 137–147, 2006.

reduction rules. The central goal is to gain a stronger data reduction at the cost of increased preprocessing time (thus relating to the PTAS paradigm) through an approach that searches through "increasing neighborhoods" of graph vertices (thus relating to local search).

The DOMINATING SET problem is: given a graph $G = (V, E)$ and a positive integer k, find a dominating set of size at most k, i.e., a set $V' \subseteq V$, $|V'| \leq k$, and every vertex in $V \setminus V'$ is adjacent to at least one vertex in V'. When dealing with the corresponding optimization problem, we will use $\mathrm{ds}(G)$ to denote the size of an optimal dominating set in G.

The idea of data reduction is to efficiently "cut away easy parts" of the given problem instance and to produce a new and size-reduced instance where then exhaustive search methods etc. can be applied. In [3] it is shown that, for planar graphs, with two easy to implement polynomial-time data reduction rules one can transform an instance (G, k) of DOMINATING SET into a new instance (G', k') with $k' \leq k$ and the number of vertices of G' bounded by $O(k)$ such that (G, k) is a yes-instance iff (G', k') is a yes-instance. Thus, by means of these rules in polynomial time one can usually find several vertices that are part of an optimal dominating set, whilst reducing the size of the input graph considerably.

In this work, we provide a whole scheme of data reduction for minimum domination in graphs. We develop a general framework of data reduction rules from which the two data reduction rules given in [3] can be obtained as easy special cases. In fact, the more complex one of these two rules is even improved. Moreover, we demonstrate that this extension makes it possible to handle graphs that are not amenable to the previous rules. Exploring the joint neighborhood of ℓ vertices for fixed $\ell \geq 1$, our data reduction rules run in $n^{O(\ell)}$ worst-case-time[1]. Besides introducing and analyzing the concept of a general data reduction scheme for domination in undirected graphs, we additionally demonstrate how to transfer data reduction for undirected graphs to directed graphs. Despite its practical significance (e.g., in biological and social network analysis [2]), domination in directed graphs so far has been neglected in parameterized algorithmics. First, we show a direct translation of undirected into directed reduction rules. Second, we present new reduction rules that make it possible to prove a linear-size problem kernel for DOMINATING SET on directed planar graphs.

Due to the lack of space, some details and proofs had to be omitted. Significant parts of this work are based on [6].

2   Preliminaries and Previous Work

A *data reduction rule* for, e.g., DOMINATING SET replaces, in polynomial time, a given instance (G, k) by a "simpler" instance (G', k') such that (G, k) is a yes-instance iff (G', k') is a yes-instance. A parameterized problem (the parameter is k) is said to have a *problem kernel* if, after the application of the reduction rules, the resulting reduced instance has size $g(k)$ for a function g depending only

---

[1] Based on our experiences [2] with implementing the two reduction rules from [3], we would expect to get faster running times in practice.

on k. For instance, DOMINATING SET restricted to planar graphs has a problem kernel consisting of at most $335 \cdot k$ vertices [3], recently improved to the upper bound $67 \cdot k$ [5]. Extensions to graphs of bounded genus appear in [7].

All our data reduction rules have in common that they explore local structures of a given graph. Depending on these structures the application of a reduction rule may have the following two effects:

1. Determine vertices that can be chosen for an optimal dominating set.
2. Reduce/shrink the graph by removing edges and vertices.

We revisit two polynomial-time reduction rules which were introduced in [3].

Neighborhood of a single vertex. Consider a vertex $v \in V$ of a given graph $G = (V, E)$. Partition the vertices of the *open neighborhood* $N(v) := \{ u \in V \mid \{u, v\} \in E \}$ of v into three different sets:

- the *exit vertices* $N_{\text{exit}}(v)$, through which we can "leave" the *closed neighborhood* $N[v] := N(v) \cup \{v\}$,
- the *guard vertices* $N_{\text{guard}}(v)$, which are neighbors of exit vertices, and
- the *prisoner vertices* $N_{\text{prison}}(v)$, which have no neighboring exit vertex:

$$N_{\text{exit}}(v) := \{ u \in N(v) \mid N(u) \setminus N[v] \neq \emptyset \},$$
$$N_{\text{guard}}(v) := \{ u \in N(v) \setminus N_{\text{exit}}(v) \mid N(u) \cap N_{\text{exit}}(v) \neq \emptyset \},$$
$$N_{\text{prison}}(v) := N(v) \setminus (N_{\text{exit}}(v) \cup N_{\text{guard}}(v)).$$

A vertex in $N_{\text{prison}}(v)$ can only be dominated by vertices from $\{v\} \cup N_{\text{guard}}(v) \cup N_{\text{prison}}(v)$. Since v will dominate at least as many vertices as any other vertex from $N_{\text{guard}}(v) \cup N_{\text{prison}}(v)$, it is safe to place v into an optimal dominating set we seek for, which we simulate by adding a suitable *gadget* to G.

Old-1-Rule. *Consider a vertex v of the graph. If $N_{prison}(v) \neq \emptyset$ then choose v to belong to the dominating set: add a "gadget vertex" v' and an edge $\{v, v'\}$ to G and remove $N_{guard}(v)$ and $N_{prison}(v)$ from G.*[2]

Neighborhood of a pair of vertices. Similar to Old-1-Rule, explore the union of the joint neighborhood $N(v_1, v_2) := (N(v_1) \cup N(v_2)) \setminus \{v_1, v_2\}$ of two vertices $v_1, v_2 \in V$. Setting $N[v_1, v_2] := N[v_1] \cup N[v_2]$, define

$$N_{\text{exit}}(v_1, v_2) := \{ u \in N(v_1, v_2) \mid N(u) \setminus N[v_1, v_2] \neq \emptyset \},$$
$$N_{\text{guard}}(v_1, v_2) := \{ u \in (N(v_1, v_2) \setminus N_{\text{exit}}(v_1, v_2)) \mid N(u) \cap N_{\text{exit}}(v_1, v_2) \neq \emptyset \},$$
$$N_{\text{prison}}(v_1, v_2) := N(v_1, v_2) \setminus (N_{\text{exit}}(v_1, v_2) \cup N_{\text{guard}}(v_1, v_2)).$$

Here, we try to detect an optimal domination of the vertices $N_{\text{prison}}(v_1, v_2)$ in our local structure $N(v_1, v_2)$. A vertex in $N_{\text{prison}}(v_1, v_2)$ can only be dominated by vertices from $\{v_1, v_2\} \cup N_{\text{guard}}(v_1, v_2) \cup N_{\text{prison}}(v_1, v_2)$. The following rule determines cases in which it is "safe" to choose one of the vertices v_1 or v_2 (or both) to belong to an optimal dominating set we seek for.

---

[2] Of course, in practical implementations (as in [2]) one would directly put v into the dominating set. Similar observations hold for the other data reduction rules.

Old-2-Rule. *Consider a pair of vertices* $v_1 \neq v_2 \in V$ *with* $|N_{prison}(v_1, v_2)| > 1$ *and suppose that* $N_{prison}(v_1, v_2)$ *cannot be dominated by a single vertex from* $N_{guard}(v_1, v_2) \cup N_{prison}(v_1, v_2)$.

Case 1. *If* $N_{prison}(v_1, v_2)$ *can be dominated by a single vertex from* $\{v_1, v_2\}$:

  (1.1) *If* $N_{prison}(v_1, v_2) \subseteq N(v_1)$ *as well as* $N_{prison}(v_1, v_2) \subseteq N(v_2)$, *then*
  - *as a gadget add two new vertices* w_1, w_2 *and edges* $\{v_1, w_1\}$, $\{v_2, w_1\}$, $\{v_1, w_2\}$, $\{v_2, w_2\}$ *to* G *and*
  - *remove* $N_{prison}(v_1, v_2)$ *and* $N_{guard}(v_1, v_2) \cap N(v_1) \cap N(v_2)$ *from* G.

  (1.2) *If* $N_{prison}(v_1, v_2) \subseteq N(v_1)$, *but not* $N_{prison}(v_1, v_2) \subseteq N(v_2)$, *then*
  - *add a gadget vertex* v_1' *and an edge* $\{v_1, v_1'\}$ *to* G *and*
  - *remove* $N_{prison}(v_1, v_2)$ *and* $N_{guard}(v_1, v_2) \cap N(v_1)$ *from* G.

  (1.3) *If* $N_{prison}(v_1, v_2) \subseteq N(v_2)$, *but not* $N_{prison}(v_1, v_2) \subseteq N(v_1)$, *then choose* v_2: *proceed as in (1.2) with roles of* v_1 *and* v_2 *interchanged.*

Case 2. *If* $N_{prison}(v_1, v_2)$ *cannot be dominated by a single vertex from* $\{v_1, v_2\}$,
  - *add two gadget vertices* v_1', v_2' *and edges* $\{v_1, v_1'\}$, $\{v_2, v_2'\}$ *to* G *and*
  - *remove* $N_{prison}(v_1, v_2)$ *and* $N_{guard}(v_1, v_2)$ *from* G.

The practical usefulness of these two rules on real-world graphs (e.g., Internet graphs) has been demonstrated in [2].

3   A Data Reduction Scheme for Domination

In this section we establish the "mother rule" from which Old-1-Rule and Old-2-Rule can be derived as easy special cases. The idea is to explore the joint neighborhood of ℓ distinct vertices for a given constant ℓ. To cope with this more complex setting we will introduce a new *gadget* which generalizes the easy gadget vertices as they were used in the above two basic reduction rules.

A General Gadget. Our general reduction rule will – on the fly – generate a boolean "constraint formula" for an optimal dominating set D of the given graph: We identify the vertices V of a graph $G = (V, E)$ with 0/1-variables, where the meaning of a 1(0)-assignment is that the corresponding vertex will (not) belong to D. A boolean formula over the variables V then can be thought of as a constraint on the choice of vertices for an optimal dominating set.

Definition 1. *Let* $\mathcal{W} \subseteq 2^V$ *be a collection of subsets of* V. *The constraint associated with* $\mathcal{W}$ *is a boolean formula* $F_{\mathcal{W}}$ *in disjunctive normal form:*

$$F_{\mathcal{W}} := \bigvee_{W \in \mathcal{W}} \bigwedge_{w \in W} w.$$

A set $D \subseteq V$ *fulfills constraint* $F_{\mathcal{W}}$ *if the assignment where each vertex in* D *is set to 1 and each vertex in* $V \setminus D$ *is set to 0 satisfies* $F_{\mathcal{W}}$.

A constraint that was generated by a reduction rule will be encoded by a corresponding gadget in our graph which "implements" the formula as a subgraph. To keep the gadget as small as possible, it is desirable that the constraint itself is as compact as possible. We use the following notion of "compactification." A set system $\mathcal{W} \subseteq 2^V$ is said to be *compact* if no two elements in $\mathcal{W}$ are subsets of each other, i.e., if for all $W, W' \in \mathcal{W}$ we have: $W \subseteq W' \Rightarrow W = W'$.

Lemma 1. *Let $\mathcal{W} \subseteq 2^V$. There exists a minimal compact subset $\widehat{\mathcal{W}} \subseteq \mathcal{W}$ such that $F_{\mathcal{W}}$ is logically equivalent to $F_{\widehat{\mathcal{W}}}$ and $\widehat{\mathcal{W}}$ can be found in polynomial time.*

In the remainder, we call $\widehat{\mathcal{W}}$ the *compactification* of $\mathcal{W}$.

The above mentioned gadgets will be of the following form.

Definition 2. *Let $G = (V, E)$ and let $F_{\mathcal{W}}$ be a constraint associated with some set system $\mathcal{W} = \{W_1, \ldots, W_s\} \subseteq 2^V$ of $\ell := |\bigcup_{i=1}^{s} W_i|$ vertices. An $F_{\mathcal{W}}$-gadget is a set of $p := \prod_{i=1}^{s} |W_i|$ new selector vertices*

$$S := \{ u_{(x_1, \ldots, x_s)} \mid x_i \in \{1, \ldots, |W_i|\} \}$$

and if $p < \ell$ another $(\ell - p)$ blocker vertices B which are connected to G by the following additional edges: For each $1 \leq i \leq s$ with $W_i = \{w_{i1}, \ldots, w_{i|W_i|}\}$ and each $1 \leq j \leq |W_i|$, we add edges between w_{ij} and all selector vertices in $\{u_{(x_1, \ldots, x_s)} \in S \mid x_i = j\}$ and between w_{ij} and all blocker vertices in B. We denote the resulting graph by $G \oplus F_{\mathcal{W}}$.

The idea is, firstly, that a set of vertices $V' \subseteq V$ fulfills the constraint $F_{\mathcal{W}}$ iff V' dominates all selector vertices in the $F_{\mathcal{W}}$-gadget. And, secondly, the blocker vertices are used to enforce that we can always find an optimal dominating set of $G \oplus F_{\mathcal{W}}$ without using any selector or blocker vertex at all. Encoding a constraint $F_{\mathcal{W}}$ by an $F_{\mathcal{W}}$-gadget, indeed, has the desired effect:

Proposition 1. *Let $G = (V, E)$ and let $F_{\mathcal{W}}$ be a constraint associated with some set system $\mathcal{W} \subseteq 2^V$. Then the size of an optimal dominating set of G which fulfills $F_{\mathcal{W}}$ is equal to the size of an optimal dominating set of $G \oplus F_{\mathcal{W}}$. Moreover, there exists an optimal dominating set of $G \oplus F_{\mathcal{W}}$ which contains only vertices in V, i.e., it contains no selector or blocker vertex.*

A Reduction Rule for the Joint Neighborhood of ℓ Vertices. In analogy to Old-1-Rule and Old-2-Rule, we explore the union of the neighborhoods of ℓ vertices. As a convention, we let, for $V' \subseteq V$, $N(V') := (\bigcup_{v \in V'} N(v)) \setminus V'$ and $N[V'] := \bigcup_{v \in V'} N[v]$. Consider a fixed set of ℓ vertices $V_\ell := \{v_1, \ldots, v_\ell\} \subseteq V$ and set

$$N_{\text{exit}}(V_\ell) := \{ u \in N(V_\ell) \mid N(u) \setminus N[V_\ell] \neq \emptyset \},$$
$$N_{\text{guard}}(V_\ell) := \{ u \in N(V_\ell) \setminus N_{\text{exit}}(V_\ell) \mid N(u) \cap N_{\text{exit}}(V_\ell) \neq \emptyset \},$$
$$N_{\text{prison}}(V_\ell) := N(V_\ell) \setminus (N_{\text{exit}}(V_\ell) \cup N_{\text{guard}}(V_\ell)).$$

The left-hand side of Figure 1 shows an example for these three sets for $\ell = 3$.

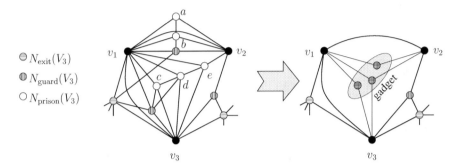

Fig. 1. Example for 3-Rule. The left-hand side shows the partitioning of $N(V_3)$ for $V_3 := \{v_1, v_2, v_3\}$ into the sets $N_{\text{exit}}(V_3)$, $N_{\text{guard}}(V_3)$, and $N_{\text{prison}}(V_3)$. The compactification of $\mathcal{W}$ (all subsets of vertices in V_3 that dominate $N_{\text{prison}}(V_\ell)$) is $\widehat{\mathcal{W}} = \{\{v_1\}, \{v_2, v_3\}\}$. The compactification of all alternative dominations of $N_{\text{prison}}(V_\ell)$ is $\widehat{\mathcal{W}}_{\text{altern}} = \{\{v_1\}, \{v_2, v_3\}, \{v_2, c\}, \{v_2, d\}, \{v_3, a\}, \{v_3, b\}, \{a, d\}, \{b, d\}\}$. Since, for each element in $\widehat{\mathcal{W}}_{\text{altern}}$, we find a better element in $\widehat{\mathcal{W}}$, 3-Rule applies. The compactified formula generated by 3-Rule is $F_{\widehat{\mathcal{W}}} = v_1 \vee (v_2 \wedge v_3)$. The right-hand side shows $N(V_3)$ after the application of 3-Rule. The $F_{\widehat{\mathcal{W}}}$-gadget is constructed according to Definition 2 using two selector vertices of degree 2 and one blocker vertex of degree 3.

Definition 3. *For two sets $\emptyset \neq W, W' \subseteq V$, we say that W is* better *than W' if $|W| \leq |W'|$ and $N[W] \supseteq N[W']$. If W is better than W', we write $W \leq W'$. If $W' = \emptyset$ and $W \neq \emptyset$, then always $W \leq W'$.*

Checking whether $W \leq W'$ can be done in $O((|W| + |W'|) \cdot n)$ time if we use the adjacency matrix of the given graph.

Using this notation, for each $\ell \geq 1$, we obtain the following generalization of the first two reduction rules, yielding a whole scheme of reduction rules. The idea of the reduction scheme below is to deduce a constraint based on the question which vertices from a given set V_ℓ dominate $N_{\text{prison}}(V_\ell)$.

ℓ-Rule. *Consider ℓ pairwise distinct vertices $V_\ell := \{v_1, \ldots, v_\ell\} \subseteq V$ and suppose $N_{prison}(V_\ell) \neq \emptyset$.*

- *Compute the set*

$$\mathcal{W} := \left\{ W \subseteq V_\ell \mid N_{prison}(V_\ell) \subseteq N[W] \right\}$$

  of all vertex subsets of V_ℓ that dominate all prisoner vertices $N_{prison}(V_\ell)$, and the set of all alternatives to dominate $N_{prison}(V_\ell)$ with less than ℓ vertices:

$$\mathcal{W}_{altern} := \left\{ W \subseteq N[N_{prison}(V_\ell)] \mid N_{prison}(V_\ell) \subseteq N[W] \text{ and } |W| < \ell \right\}.$$

- *Compute the compactifications $\widehat{\mathcal{W}}$ of $\mathcal{W}$ and $\widehat{\mathcal{W}}_{altern}$ of $\mathcal{W}_{altern}$.*

- *If ($\forall W \in \widehat{\mathcal{W}}_{altern} \exists W' \in \widehat{\mathcal{W}} : W' \leq W$), then*

- remove $\mathcal{R} := \left\{ v \in N_{guard}(V_\ell) \cup N_{prison}(V_\ell) \mid N[v] \subseteq \bigcap_{W \in \widehat{\mathcal{W}}} N[W] \right\}$, and
- put an $F_{\widehat{\mathcal{W}}}$-gadget to G for the constraint associated with $\widehat{\mathcal{W}}$.

An example for $\ell = 3$ is given in Figure 1. If V_ℓ forms a size-ℓ dominating set, then ℓ-Rule actually solves the domination problem. Moreover, ℓ-Rule provides a mathematically more elegant formalism than for instance Old-2-Rule does. In addition, it generalizes Old-2-Rule:

Theorem 1. *For each* ℓ, ℓ-*Rule is correct, i.e., for every graph* G, *we have* $\mathrm{ds}(G) = \mathrm{ds}(G')$, *where* G' *denotes the graph obtained from* G *by applying the rule to* ℓ *distinct vertices. Moreover, 1-Rule is identical to Old-1-Rule and 2-Rule applies to even more cases than Old-2-Rule.*

Proof (Sketch). Observe that ℓ-Rule only applies if for all $W \in \widehat{\mathcal{W}}_{\mathrm{altern}}$ we find a $W' \in \widehat{\mathcal{W}}$ such that $W' \leq W$ (∗). Let $G'' := G \oplus F_{\widehat{\mathcal{W}}}$. We first of all argue that $\mathrm{ds}(G'') = \mathrm{ds}(G)$. It is clear that $\mathrm{ds}(G'') \geq \mathrm{ds}(G)$. Conversely, suppose that D is an optimal dominating set for G. We distinguish two cases. First, suppose that $N_{\mathrm{prison}}(V_\ell)$ needs less than ℓ vertices to be dominated. Then, by definition of $\mathcal{W}_{\mathrm{altern}}$, D has to fulfill $F_{\mathcal{W}_{\mathrm{altern}}}$. Hence, by the definition of compactification, we know that D also fulfills $F_{\widehat{\mathcal{W}}_{\mathrm{altern}}}$. In other words, this means that there has to be a $W \in \widehat{\mathcal{W}}_{\mathrm{altern}}$ with $W \subseteq D$. But then, by assumption (∗), we have a $W' \in \widehat{\mathcal{W}}$ with $W' \leq W$. Since W' is better than W, this implies that $D' := (D \setminus W) \cup W'$ is a dominating set for G which fulfills $F_{\widehat{\mathcal{W}}}$ and, hence, it is a dominating set for G'' (by Proposition 1) with $|D'| \leq |D|$. Second, suppose that $N_{\mathrm{prison}}(V_\ell)$ needs exactly ℓ vertices $D' \subseteq D$ to be dominated. Then, it is clear that $D'' := (D \setminus D') \cup V_\ell$ also forms a dominating set for G. But then, by construction, D'' dominates all $F_{\widehat{\mathcal{W}}}$-gadget vertices, and, thus, D'' is a dominating set for G'' with $|D''| = |D|$.

It remains to show $\mathrm{ds}(G'') = \mathrm{ds}(G')$. Observe that $G' = G'' \setminus \mathcal{R} = (G \oplus F_{\widehat{\mathcal{W}}}) \setminus \mathcal{R} = (G \setminus \mathcal{R}) \oplus F_{\widehat{\mathcal{W}}}$ with $\mathcal{R}$ as defined in ℓ-Rule. First of all, we show that $\mathrm{ds}(G'') \leq \mathrm{ds}(G')$. To see this, let D be an optimal dominating set for G'. Then, by Proposition 1, there exists a dominating set $D' \subseteq V(G)$ of equal size for $G \setminus \mathcal{R}$ which fulfills $F_{\widehat{\mathcal{W}}}$. This means that there exists a $W \in \widehat{\mathcal{W}}$ with $W \subseteq D'$. By definition of $\mathcal{R}$, this implies that $\mathcal{R} \subseteq N[\mathcal{R}] \subseteq N[\bigcap_{X \in \widehat{\mathcal{W}}} X] \subseteq N[W] \subseteq N_{G'=G'' \setminus \mathcal{R}}[D'] \subseteq N_{G''}[D']$, which shows that D' is a dominating set for $G'' = G \oplus F_{\widehat{\mathcal{W}}}$ with $|D'| = |D|$. Similarly, one shows that $\mathrm{ds}(G') \leq \mathrm{ds}(G'')$.

It is not hard to see that 1-Rule is identical to Old-1-Rule and that 2-Rule applies whenever Old-2-Rule applies. In addition, there are examples where Old-2-Rule does not apply and where 2-Rule does apply. For instance, we can construct a graph where a single vertex v from $N_{\mathrm{prison}}(V_2)$ dominates $N_{\mathrm{prison}}(V_2)$. (i.e., Old-2-Rule does not apply) and 2-Rule still applies, since, e.g., $\{v\} \leq \{w\}$ where $w \in V_2$.   □

The following proposition gives a simple worst-case estimate on the time needed to apply ℓ-Rule, and, together with the subsequent Theorem 2, shows that we have a relationship between "quality" of data reduction and running time as mentioned in the introductory section.

Proposition 2. *Let $G = (V, E)$. Applying ℓ-Rule for all size-ℓ vertex sets $V_\ell :=$ $\{v_1, \ldots, v_\ell\} \subseteq V$ takes $O(n^{2\ell})$ time for $\ell > 1$ and $O(n^3)$ time for $\ell = 1$.*

A graph $G = (V, E)$ is said to be *reduced with respect to ℓ-Rule* if there is no set of distinct vertices $v_1, \ldots, v_\ell$ for which ℓ-Rule can be applied. In a sense, the data reduction scheme given by ℓ-Rule builds a "strict hierarchy" of rules:

Theorem 2. *Let $\mathcal{H}_\ell := \{1\text{-Rule}, \ldots, \ell\text{-Rule}\}$, $\ell \geq 1$. Then, for each $\ell > 1$, $\mathcal{H}_\ell$ is strictly more powerful than $\mathcal{H}_{\ell-1}$.*

Proof (Sketch). For each level $\ell > 1$ of this hierarchy, we can construct a graph which is reduced with respect to all rules in $\mathcal{H}_{\ell-1}$ but which is still reducible with respect to ℓ-Rule. For example, let $G_\ell = \mathcal{P}_2 \times \mathcal{P}_{2\ell-1}$ be the complete grid graph of width 2 and length $2\ell - 1$. Then, it can be verified by induction on ℓ that G_ℓ has the above mentioned property. $\qquad\square$

4   Directed Dominating Set

In several applications we have to deal with directed graphs $\overrightarrow{G} = (V, A)$. Here, a vertex $v \in V$ is *dominated* iff it is in the dominating set or if there is an arc $(u, v) \in A$ (i.e., v is an outgoing neighbor of u) and u is in the dominating set.

Transforming Directed Graphs into Undirected Graphs. Let $\overrightarrow{G} = (V, A)$ be a directed graph. Construct an undirected graph $G' = (V', E)$, where $V' := \{u', u'' \mid u \in V\}$, and $E := \{\{u', u''\} \mid u \in V\} \cup \{\{u'', v'\}, \{u'', v''\} \mid (u, v) \in A\}$.

Proposition 3. *Using the notation above, $\mathrm{ds}(\overrightarrow{G}) = \mathrm{ds}(G')$.*

Clearly, in order to find an optimal dominating set for a directed graph $\overrightarrow{G}$, we can use the above transformation and then apply our undirected reduction rules (see Section 3) to the transformed instance G'. The drawback of this process is that the transformed graph G' contains twice as many vertices as $\overrightarrow{G}$. Moreover, the transformation in general does not preserve planarity. Hence, we subsequently modify the data reduction scheme for the undirected case to obtain a "directed data reduction scheme" for domination.

A Reduction Scheme for Directed Dominating Set. Let $\overrightarrow{G} = (V, A)$ be a directed graph. Define $N(v) := \{w \in V \mid (v, w) \in A\}$. For an ℓ-vertex set $V_\ell := \{v_1, \ldots, v_\ell\}$, explore $N(V_\ell) := \bigcup_{v \in V_\ell} N(v) \setminus V_\ell$.

   Suppose we defined the partitioning $N_{\mathrm{exit}}(V_\ell)$, $N_{\mathrm{guard}}(V_\ell)$, and $N_{\mathrm{prison}}(V_\ell)$ and the reduction scheme in complete analogy to the undirected case, then we would run into the following problem: The vertices in $N_{\mathrm{prison}}(V_\ell)$ (if this set is non-empty) may also be dominated by vertices outside $N[V_\ell]$.[3] This difficulty

---

[3] For example, there might be a single vertex v (with in-degree 0) which dominates $N(V_\ell)$, but which is not contained in $N(V_\ell)$. Then, clearly, it would be optimal to choose v. Deducing a constraint—based on the question which vertices from V_ℓ dominate $N_{\mathrm{prison}}(V_\ell)$ as done in the undirected case—would lead to a wrong result.

is circumvented by slightly modifying the definition of the sets $N_{\text{guard}}(V_\ell)$ and $N_{\text{prison}}(V_\ell)$. More precisely, we additionally define the set

$$N_{\text{enter}}(V_\ell) := \{\, u \in (N(V_\ell) \setminus N_{\text{exit}}(V_\ell)) \mid \exists w \in (V \setminus N[V_\ell]) : (w, u) \in A \,\}.$$

Herein, we used

$$N_{\text{exit}}(V_\ell) := \{\, u \in N(V_\ell) \mid \exists w \in (V \setminus N[V_\ell]) : (u, w) \in A \,\}.$$

The modified versions of $N_{\text{guard}}(V_\ell)$ and $N_{\text{prison}}(V_\ell)$ are defined as follows:

$$N_{\text{guard}}(V_\ell) := \{\, u \in (N(V_\ell) \setminus (N_{\text{exit}}(V_\ell) \cup N_{\text{enter}}(V_\ell))) \mid (N(u) \cap N_{\text{exit}}(V_\ell)) \neq \emptyset \,\},$$
$$N_{\text{prison}}(V_\ell) := N(V_\ell) \setminus (N_{\text{exit}}(V_\ell) \cup N_{\text{enter}}(V_\ell) \cup N_{\text{guard}}(V_\ell)).$$

In this way, we can build a data reduction scheme for DIRECTED DOMINATING SET as a slight modification of ℓ-Rule in the undirected case.

Directed ℓ-Rule. *Consider ℓ pairwise distinct vertices $V_\ell := \{v_1, \ldots, v_\ell\} \subseteq V$ and suppose $N_{prison}(V_\ell) \neq \emptyset$. Compute the sets*

$$\mathcal{W} := \{\, W \subseteq V_\ell \mid N_{prison}(V_\ell) \subseteq N[W] \,\},$$
$$\mathcal{W}_{altern} := \{\, W \subseteq N[N_{prison}(V_\ell)] \mid N_{prison}(V_\ell) \subseteq N[W] \text{ and } |W| < \ell \,\},$$

and the compactifications $\widehat{\mathcal{W}}$ of $\mathcal{W}$ and $\widehat{\mathcal{W}}_{altern}$ of $\mathcal{W}_{altern}$.
If ($\forall W \in \widehat{\mathcal{W}}_{altern} \exists W' \in \widehat{\mathcal{W}} : W' \leq W$), then remove

- $\mathcal{R} := \{\, v \in N_{enter}(V_\ell) \cup N_{guard}(V_\ell) \cup N_{prison}(V_\ell) \mid N[v] \subseteq \bigcap_{W \in \widehat{\mathcal{W}}} N[W] \,\}$ *and*
- *put an $F_{\widehat{\mathcal{W}}}$-gadget[4]*

Directed Dominating Set on Planar Graphs. Here, we provide a linear-size problem kernel for domination on directed planar graphs. To show this, we cannot make use of the transformation from directed to undirected graphs as described at the beginning of the section because the construction there does not preserve planarity. Hence, we use the Directed ℓ-Rules ($\ell = 1$ and $\ell = 2$ suffice and preserve planarity), yielding:

Theorem 3. DIRECTED DOMINATING SET *on planar graphs has a linear-size problem kernel which can be found in $O(n^4)$ time. This implies that* DIRECTED DOMINATING SET *on planar graphs is fixed-parameter tractable.*

We again omit the proof and just remark on the pitfalls behind: An ad-hoc idea to prove this result might be to take a reduced directed graph and to replace each arc by an undirected edge. If the directed graph was reduced, then one might hope that the corresponding undirected one is, too. But this is generally wrong. Moreover, even if the corresponding undirected graph was reduced,

---

[4] In contrast to the gadget with undirected edges as introduced in Definition 2, the newly introduced arcs now point *from* vertices in $W \in \widehat{\mathcal{W}}$ to selector vertices.

then still it is a problem that, as a rule, the undirected graph would have a usually smaller dominating set than the original directed one; however, there is no general relationship between these two set sizes. Hence one has to turn back to a direct analysis of the Directed ℓ-Rules. Fortunately, much of the proof work can be carried out by similar constructions as in the undirected case dealt with in [3].

5 Outlook

We showed (Theorem 2) that the presented reduction rules form a strict hierarchy when considering larger and larger joint neighborhoods. It would be of hight interest to strengthen this result in the sense that one can mathematically relate the degree of increased reduction (e.g., by proving smaller problem kernel sizes) and the running time to be spent. Note that this would parallel relations that hold in the case of approximation schemes, and it would tie the notions of data reduction scheme and PTAS closer.

Presenting our reduction rules, for theoretical reasons we expressed boolean constraints as graph gadgets. From a practical point of view, in implementations it might make more sense not to use the graph gadgets (as has also been done when (successfully) experimentally testing the two reduction rules from [3] in [2]) but to use the boolean constraint formulas in a direct combination with the reduced graph instance. So far, this issue is completely unexplored.

From a parameterized complexity point of view, it would be interesting to gain further "tractability results" for W[1]-hard problems with respect to data reduction. More specifically, consider DOMINATING SET: Since DOMINATING SET is W[2]-complete, unless an unlikely collapse in parameterized complexity theory occurs, our data reduction scheme *cannot* serve for showing that using 1-Rule, 2-Rule, ..., c-Rule, for some constant c, generates a problem kernel in general graphs. A more realistic and nevertheless interesting kind of investigation would be to see what happens when c becomes dependent on the dominating set size k, e.g., $c = k/4$ or $c = \sqrt{k}$. If then the generated problem kernel consisted of $g(k)$ vertices, this would imply an algorithm with $O(2^{g(k)} + n^{2c})$ running time for DOMINATING SET, which might be considered as a significant (theoretical) improvement over the trivial exact algorithm running in $O(n^{k+2})$ time.

References

1. Aarts, E., and Lenstra, J.K., (eds): Local Search in Combinatorial Optimization. Wiley-Interscience Series in Discrete Mathematics and Optimization (1997)
2. Alber, J., Betzler, N., and Niedermeier, R.: Experiments on Data Reduction for Optimal Domination in Networks. To appear, Annals of Operations Research (2005)
3. Alber, J., Fellows, M.R., and Niedermeier, R.: Polynomial Time Data Reduction for Dominating Set. Journal of the ACM **51** 3 (2004) 363–384
4. Ausiello, G., Crescenzi, P., Gambosi, G., Kann, V. Marchetti-Spaccamela, A., and Protasi, M.: Complexity and Approximation. Springer-Verlag (1999)

5. Chen, J., Fernau, H., Kanj, I.A., and Xia, G.: Parametric Duality and Kernelization: Lower Bounds and Upper Bounds on Kernel Size. In Proc. 22d STACS, LNCS, Springer **3404** (2005) 269–280
6. Dorn, B.: Extended Data Reduction Rules for Domination in Graphs (in German). Student Project, WSI für Informatik, Universität Tübingen, Germany (2004)
7. Fomin, F.V., and Thilikos, D.M: Fast Parameterized Algorithms for Graphs on Surfaces: Linear Kernel and Exponential Speed-up. In Proc. 31st ICALP, LNCS, Springer, **3142** (2004) 581–592

Incremental Method for XML View Maintenance in Case of Non Monitored Data Sources

Xavier Baril and Zohra Bellahsène

LIRMM - UMR 5506 CNRS / Université Montpellier 2,
161 Rue Ada - F-34392 Montpellier Cedex 5
{baril, bella}@lirmm.fr

Abstract. In this paper, we are dealing with the topic of view maintenance which consists of maintaining materialized views in response to data modifications on the data sources. We propose an incremental method to maintain XML views. This is achieved by defining first how to store XML views, which may be obtained over different data sources, in a relational DBMS. The identifiers used to store the view definition (in particular mapping patterns, unions and joins) allow the definition of the incremental method in the sense that the materialization of the view does not require re-computing all stored data to maintain XML views.

1 Introduction

To provide data access in large scale and/or dynamic environments with autonomous data sources, pertinent data are often collected and stored in a redundant way using a data warehouse. At abstract level, a data warehouse can be defined as set of materialized views. An important feature in a data warehouse is taking changes arising on the data sources into account. In this paper, we are dealing with the topic of view maintenance which consists of maintaining the materialized views in response to data modifications on the data sources. More precisely, we are interested in maintaining XML views that are stored in relational DBMS.

The main contribution of this paper is how to specify source patterns, and how to maintain materialized views of such source patterns. This is achieved by defining first how to store XML views (which may be obtained over different data sources) in a relational DBMS. We have designed a method using a relational DBMS for storing XML views. The originality of this method lies in the use of multi view graph, which allows representing common sub expressions between different views in order to reduce the cost of the view maintenance. This means that each view is not materialized as a whole part but as a set of fragments. Work that we present in this article was implemented like a functionality of the prototype DAWAX [2].

This paper is organized as follows. In Section 2, we present our view model for integrating XML data. The related view specification language is described in Section 3. Our storage method is presented in Section 4. The algorithms of view maintenance are presented in Section 5. Section 6 presents an overview of related work and Section 7 contains the conclusion and future work.

J. Wiedermann et al. (Eds.): SOFSEM 2006, LNCS 3831, pp. 148–157, 2006.

2   The View Model VIMIX

We have designed the VIMIX (VIew Model for Integration of XML sources) to integrate XML data sources. Due to the lack of space, we will not present the whole view model [2]. XML data are represented by a graph having three types of nodes (element, attribute and text). Moreover, operations were defined to handle the nodes of the graph (navigation and treatment of strings). The integration process consists in: (i) specifying the data to be extracted from the sources by defining patterns on them (source-pattern), (ii) reorganizing the views data by using relational like operations: union and join and (iii) specifying the result form of the XML views.

Our view specification language is based on pattern-matching: the data of the sources are related to variables which are declared in a pattern describing the source. The definition of the variables is done using a mechanism of research axes like in XPath for location steps in an XML document.

```
<<source-pattern name="sp_authors_biblio" source="biblio">>
<search-axis function="children">
    <source-node reg-expression="author" type="element">
        <search-axis function="children">
            <source-node reg-expression="firstname"
                    type="element"
                    bindto="fname">
            </source-node>
            <source-node reg-expression="lastname"
                    type="element"
                    bindto="lname">
            </source-node>
        </search-axis>
    </source-node>
</search-axis>
</source-pattern>
```

Fig. 1. VIMIX Source Pattern

Figure 1 gives an example of a VIMIX source pattern, which retrieves first and lastname of authors. This pattern is named sp_authors_biblio and is defined over the data source biblio. The first element search-axis is the principal research axis of the pattern, meaning that one applies the function children starting from the root of the document. This function returns a set of nodes, which will be filtered starting from the contents of this axis: the element source-node specifies that the nodes must match the regular expression author and be of type element. The specification of this source node is supplemented by a research axis specifying that the nodes must have two subelements firstname and lastname. These subelements are bound to variables (attribute bindto).

In our approach, the data extracted by patterns are stored in relational tables. Therefore, this allows makes it possible to restructuring the data by using relational algebra. We namely adapted two operations of them which are relevant for data integration: union and join. The operation of union that we defined takes as input several operands, which result from patterns, either union or join. The result is stored in a relational table whose attributes are computed as the union of the attributes of the operand tables. This table values is built as the union of the tuples of the sources and by assigning NULL value to the attributes which do not exist at a source. Unlike the relational union ours may be applied when the sources have different schemas. Moreover, our operation of union allows to filter the data and to solve conflicts of identity by eliminating the duplicates coming from different sources. To solve the conflicts we use a mechanism specifying a priority source.

The join operation allows to "cross" information coming from two sources, patterns, union or other join. Its result is stored in a relational table, whose columns are computed as the union of the attributes of the sources. The join predicate is evaluated by applying a function which returns the textual representation of the nodes.

3 Specification of the Views

A VIMIX view is defined as a tuple including the following properties: (i) its name, (ii) a source pattern, union or join which contains the data to populate the view (iii) a pattern which describes the result structure using a tree. This tree has three types of nodes: element, attribute and expression. The expression nodes allow to populate the view result. We have defined conversion functions of types to facilitate this task. Finally, *aggregation* functions and *group by* expressions may be also used in the view result specification.

Figure 2 describes the view computing for each author: its name, the number of books which he wrote, the average price and titles of these books.

The name view is v_books is defined over the data source j_books_lirmm. The tree specifying the result of the view is the element source-node and is structured as follows: each element author will have three attributes: name, number of books and their average price. The titles of the books of an author are sub-elements.

```
<view name="v_books"
      source="j_ books "
      order-by="author"
      group-by="author">
<result-node type="element" value="author">
  <result-node type="attribute" value="name">
    <result-node type="expression" value="text(author)" />
  </result-node>
  <result-node type="attribute" value="nb- books">
    <result-node type="expression" value="count()" />
  </result-node>
  <result-node type="attribute" value="Avrage-price">
    <result-node type="expression" value="avg(float(price))" />
  </result-node>
  <result-node type="element" value="book">
    <result-node type="expression" value="text(title)" />
  </result-node>
</result-node>
 </view>
```

Fig. 2. Integrated view of the books for each author

4 Storage of VIMIX Views

Our storage architecture avoids redundancy of XML data in the warehouse since we separate the data storage of that of the metadata (i.e. the mappings).

4.1 Generic Schema of XML Data Storage

The generic schema which we utilize to store the XML data is described in Figure 3. The generic schema is designed to store nodes coming from the sources, without storing all the data of these sources. For each source (or document) one needs simply to know his identifier and his URL, without being concerned with root of the document which is not necessarily stored in the data warehouse. The table Document contains the urls of the data sources.

The tables Element and Attribute are dictionaries of the elements and attributes. They contain a code identifying the element or the attribute like its name. The dictionaries accelerate the queries involving an element name or attribute.

The table XmlNode stores the data nodes. Each node has an identifier: nodeID. Our data model considers three types of nodes: Element, Attribute and Text which respectively represents elements, attributes and text in a XML document. The columns elemID and attID provide the type of a node of the table. If elemID is not NULL, the node is of type element and elemID indicates its name. If attID is not NULL, the node is of type attribute and attID indicates its name. The value of the attribute is stored in the column value. Lastly, if elemID and attID have both NULL value, the node is of type text and value contains the string.

The table Children contains the composition links between the nodes of the stored documents and has as attributes:

− parentID contains the identifier of the parent node,
− childID contains the identifier of the child node,
− rank contains the row of the son.

Table	Column	Role
Document	docID, url	Dict. of sources
Element	elemID, name	Dict. of elements
Attribute	**attID**, name	Dict. of attributes
XmlNode	nodeID, *elemID*, *attID*, value, *docID*	XML Nodes
Children	*ParentID*, *childID*, rank	Links
Descendants	*ParentId*, *childId*, rank	Links

Fig. 3. The generic schema for storing the XML data

The table Descendants contains the descendance links between the nodes. These links can be computed from the children table, using the fact that descendants are children and children of children and so on. However, SQL doesn't offer a way to compute children at any level; it's why we prefer storing them in the Descendants table, which is made up of the following columns:

- parentID contains the identifier of the parent node,
- childID contains the identifier of the children node,
- rank initially contains the rank of the children by considering an in-depth traversal. The identifiers parentID and childID are foreign keys of the column nodeID in the table XmlNode.

The tables Element and Attribute contain the metadata of the elements and the attributes. The table XmlNode contains all the nodes of the source which are stored in the warehouse. The table Children contains the composition links between the nodes of XML documents in the warehouse. It involves the following columns:

- parentID contains the identifier of the parent node,
- childID contains the identifier of the child node,
- rank contains the rank of the child node.

4.2 Storage of the Mappings

The key idea of our approach is: rather than materializing complete views, it is better to materialize portions (fragments) of views, to allow reuse and improved incremental maintenance. Obviously, it allows reducing space storage. Figure 4 describes the graph of mapping between the data sources and the views. The nodes of this graph are tables names storing the data specified by patterns on the sources, union or join.

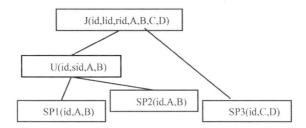

Fig. 4. The Graph of Mappings

The table schema of the pattern *SP*: *SP(id, variables$_{sp}$)* where *SP* is the name of the pattern, *id* is a numerical identifier of integer type. This identifier value corresponds to the order in the table defined by the extraction of the data. Finally, *variables$_{sp}$* describe the pattern variables.

The schema of the union table is: *U(id; sid; variables$_u$)* where *U* is the name of the union and *id* is numerical identifier of real type, whose semantics of the integer and decimal parts is defined as follows. The integer part contains the sequence number of the source whose the tuple comes from data of the union. This sequence number is obtained by the position of the source in the list of the sources of the union.

The decimal part contains the identifier of the source whose data come from. If this identifier is a real number, it is transformed into an integer number by concatenating the integer and decimal parts. For example, if the identifier of a tuple of the source to be inserted in the union is 2123, the transformation will give the result 2123. Moreover, the decimal part of the source at the position i is preceded by n-k zeros, with n and k are defined as follows. 10^n is the minimal upper limit of the number of sources of the union and 10^k is the minimal upper limit of i. For example, if a union is defined over a list of 11 sources, the minimal upper limit of the number of sources of the form 10^n is 10^2, therefore one has n = 2. The decimal part of the identifiers of the tuples coming from the sources at the position i, for $i \in [1..9]$ will be preceded by one zero, because the minimal upper limit of i, is 10^1, say k = 1, one thus has n - k = 1. The decimal part of the identifiers of the tuples coming from the sources at the position i, for $i \in [10..11]$ will be preceded by no zero, because the minimal upper limit of i is 10^2, say k = 2, one thus has n- k = 0. This method allows to preserve the order between the tuples of the tables containing the sources of the union. In this way, this identifier preserves the order defined during the retrieval of the data.

The column *sid* is the identifier of the inserted tuple, in the source from which it comes. This column is of real type, because it must contain the identifiers of the data sources of the union, which can be of type integer or real. Finally, $variables_u$ is the set of the variables specified by the union U. Each variable references a data node stored in the generic schema.

The schema of the join mapping table is: $J(id; lid; rid; variable_j)$ where J is the name of the join; $id\ i$ is a numerical identifier of real type, whose semantics of the integer and decimal parts is defined as follows. The integer part contains the identifier of the data coming from the left part of the join. If this identifier is a real number, it is transformed into an integer number. The decimal part contains the identifier of the data coming from the right part of the join. If this identifier is a real number, it is transformed into an integer number. *lid* is an identifier of real type, which references the identifier of the tuple used to calculate the left part of the join. This column is of real type, because it must contain the identifiers of the two sources of the join which can be of type integer or real. *rid* is also identifier of real type, which references the identifier of the tuple used to calculate the right part of the join. This identifier is of real type, because it must contain the identifiers of the two sources of the join which can be of type integer or real. *variables_j* are the variables specified by the join. Each variable references a data node stored in the generic schema.

5   Maintenance of VIMIX Views

5.1   Refreshing a *Pattern* XML View from a Data Source

Data sources available on the Web or produced by various applications cannot easily be monitored. Therefore, the smallest operation of refreshing the data stored in the warehouse is thus the one of pattern matching expression defined over one source. Our method is incremental because it does not require to re-compute the entire view but only the view fragment defined over the source that has been updated.

The algorithm1 runs as follows. For each pattern *sp* defined over this source, the content of the table `Tsp` is copied into table `Tdeletes` then the table `Tsp` is cleared. This process of data extraction is repeated to populate again the table `Tsp`. At this stage, the data of a pattern on the source are updated. It is then necessary to propagate the update to the related mappings: union and join. For that, the function refresh-mappings is executed for all the tables which are parents nodes of in the graph of mappings. Lastly, one removes the XML data coming from the source, which are stored in the tables of the generic schema. The deletion cannot be made earlier, because the data of the old mappings could be necessary for the maintenance.

Algorithm 1. Refresh-Pattern *(s)*
Result : refreshing data from a source *s*

> **foreach** *pattern sp related to the source s* **do**
>> copy the table *Tsp* in *Tdeletes*;
>> clear the table *Tsp*;
>> extract the data from the source *s* to populate *Tsp*;
>> **foreach** *Tparent parent of Tsp in the graph of mappings* **do**
>> refresh-mappings(*Tparent*, *sp*, *Tdeletes*, *Tsp*) ;
>> **end**
> **end**

delete the data coming from the source *s*;

5.2   Refreshing the Union and the Join Views

The algorithm 2 presents the strategy of updating a table representing a union or a join in the graph of mappings. The function *refresh-mappings* has four parameters: (i) the table containing the data of a union or a join which must be updated, (ii) the *child* source representing the pattern, the union or the join which were updated and (iii) the table *Tdelete* containing the deleted tuples and the table *Tinsert* containing the added tuples.. This Algorithm is incremental, because it uses the data removed and added to the updated source to carry out only the necessary modifications. The updates are propagated to the parent tables of the graph of mappings. This propagation is carried out by a recursive call of the function. The condition is carried out by the tables which do not have a parent, which is ensured by the fact that the graph of mappings is acyclic.

Algorithm 2. refresh-mappings(*Ts*, *child*, *Tdeleteschild*, *Tinsertchild*)

> **Result :** Refreshing the mappings of an union or a join *Ts*
>> computes in *Tdeletes* the tuples to be deleted in *Ts* (by using *Tdeleteschild*) ;
>> compute in *Tinserts* the tuples to be added in *Ts* (by using *Tinsertchild*) ;
>> delete in *Ts* the tuples of *Tdeletes*;
>> add in *Ts* the tuples of *Tinserts*;
>> **foreach** *Tparent parent of Ts in the graph of mappings* **do**
>>> refresh-mappings(*Tparent*, *s*, *Tdeletes*, *Tinserts*);
>> **end**

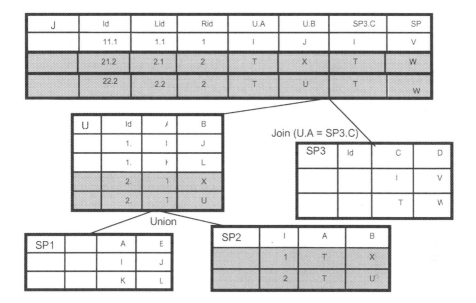

Fig. 5. Illustration of the update propagation

Figure 5 illustrates the update propagation. The graph of mappings used on this example consists of three patterns on three sources, noted SP1, SP2 and SP3. The variable u contains the union of the data of the patterns of SP1 and SP2. Finally, j contains the join of the data of u and SP3. To facilitate the legibility of the example, the patterns store the values of the elements XML corresponding to the instantiation of the variables rather than the references to these elements (which should be stored by using the generic schema). This example illustrates the propagation of updates when the source of the pattern SP2 is modified. The dashed tuples of the mappings corresponds to those which have been updated. As it is shown in this figure, the maintenance is incremental.

6 Related Work

There are mainly two approaches for storing XML data: the *flat storage* and the *meta-modelling*. In Flat storage approach, XML data are stored by using their textual form. It is the simplest method to implement, because it is sufficient to use a files system, or the type BLOB of a DBMS to store the documents in a database. This method is very efficient when one tries to find the whole document or large contiguous parts of an XML document. The main disadvantage of this method is the need for parsing the document to discover its structure: that results into slow down the query processing.

In meta-modelling approach XML data are stored in the target DBMS by using *transformation rules* [3, 6]. This method is very efficient when queries are based on the structure of the stored data. Indeed, the data were already analyzed at the time of their transformation to be stored in the target DBMS. The principal disadvantage of this method lies in the transformations which are necessary to store and rebuild the data of the XML documents. When the XML documents to be stored are bulky, this phase of transformation is costly.

Inside the meta-modelling, there is two approaches:.(i) *generic* schema which can be used for any XML data instance and (ii) The schemas *depending of the data* which must be generated for each data instance to store. Intuitively, the use of a generic schema can be simpler when the data to be stored come from heterogeneous documents. Indeed, if one uses a schema depending of the data, it would be necessary to generate a schema of storage for each document.

There is also a third family of solutions which combines the two previous approaches: the hybrid approaches. There are two ways of doing it.

The first one is redundant; it consists in storing the data by using the two methods. That allows a fast querying of the documents thus stored, but naturally the updates are slowed down and storage spaces it is far from being optimal because all the data are duplicated. The second method consists in using a mixed approach: starting from a certain level of granularity called threshold, the data are stored as flat whereas with the top of this level they are stored in a DBMS by using the meta-modelling [7], [8].

The maintenance of XML views is a recent problem which is currently studied. Early work was on semi-structured views had been considered for OEM data [1]: proposed an algorithm which calculates a set of queries used to propagate a source modification on a view. An index for accelerating the update of XML data was proposed in [4]: APIX. This work has been done in the case of monitored data sources. Another algorithm was proposed to calculate the changes between two XML documents [5]. XML views can be used like interfaces to update relational sources [3], [9].

The major differences between the related work and our approach are the following. Related work is based on the full materialization of the view therefore view maintenance is performed view per view. Our contribution is the first one dealing with the XML view maintenance for fragment-based approach. In our approach, view maintenance is performed regarding all the materialized views therefore it encourages the reuse of materialized fragments.

7 Conclusion and Future Work

In this paper, we present a storage method and algorithms for the maintenance of XML views stored in a relational DBMS. We have designed a storage method which separates the storage of XML data from that of the metadata describing the mappings. The identifiers used to store the view definition (in particular mapping patterns, unions and joins) allow incremental maintenance in the sense that the materialization of the view does not require re-computing all stored data to maintain XML views. The other originality of this method lies in the use of multi view graph, which allows representing common sub expressions between different views. Consequently, this allows reducing the storage space and the view maintenance time. Querying XML views stored in a relational DBMS requires a phase of rebuilding them. As future work, we are planning to develop a cache strategy to store the XML data which are frequently rebuilt.

References

1. Abiteboul, S., Hugh, J.M., Rys, M., Vassalos, V., Wiener, J.: Incremental Maintenance for Materialized Views over Semistructured Data. Intern. Conf. on Very Large Databases (1998)
2. Baril, X.: Un modèle de vues pour l'intégration de sources de données XML : VIMIX. PhD thesis, Université Montpellier II, December (2003)
3. Braganholo, V., Davidson, S., Heuser, C.: On the Updatability of XML Views over Relational databases. WebDB'2003, San Diego, California (2003)
4. Chen, L., Rundensteiner, E.A.: APIX: An Efficient Approach to Maintain Web Views. Technical Report WPI-CS-TR-00-08, Worcester Polytechnic Institute, Dept. of Computer Science (2000)
5. Cobena, G., Abiteboul, S., Marian, A.: Detecting Changes in XML Documents. In: Proceedings of the 18th International Conference on Data Engineering, ICDE'2002, San José, California, IEEE Computer Society (2002)
6. Florescu, D., Kossmann, D.: Storing and Querying XML Data using an RDMBS. IEEE Data Engineering Bulletin 22 (1999) 27–34
7. Kanne, C., Moerkotte, G.: Efficient Storage of XML data. Technical Report 899, Mannheim University (1999)
8. Kanne, C.C., Moerkotte, G.: Efficient Storage of XML Data. In: Proceedings of the 16th International Conference on Data Engineering, ICDE'2000, San Diego, California, IEEE Computer Society (2000)
9. Katica D., El-Sayed, M., Rundensteiner, E.A.: Order-Sensitive View Maintenance of Materialized XQuery Views. ER 2003: 144-157

Non-intersecting Complexity

Aleksandrs Belovs

Department of Computer Science, University of Latvia,
Raiņa bulvāris 29, LV-1459, Rīga, Latvia
stiboh@inbox.lv

Abstract. A new complexity measure for Boolean functions is introduced in this article. It has a link to the query algorithms: it stands between both polynomial degree and non-deterministic complexity on one hand and still is a lower bound for deterministic complexity. Some inequalities and counterexamples are presented and usage in symmetrisation polynomials is considered.

1 Introduction

This paper deals with the approach of *query algorithm* in the theory of computational complexity. It is, perhaps, the simplest approach when we narrow down to the calculation of one fixed Boolean function and do not care about resources needed to get values of the variables. We act as if they are already given in one of the forms (depending on the type of algorithm) and the only we deal with is the number of *queries* about their values we must ask to get known the value of the function.

The theory of computation studies various models of computation: deterministic, non-deterministic, probabilistic and quantum (see [7] on traditional models of computation and [3] on quantum computation). Similarly, there are query algorithms of all those types [2].

Although we consider only traditional models in this paper, in fact all these models have a lot of connections. For example, we forward our attention for polynomial degree that is of a great importance in *quantum exact computation*. Respectively, holds [2] inequality $Q_E \geq deg/2$. And still we need a better understanding of traditional models, because it is the only we can compare the power of quantum or other non-traditional computation with.

The concept of non-intersecting complexity has arisen from the study of functions with a low polynomial degree. Kushilevitz function described further is the best known example in this field. It has $D = 6$ and $deg = 3$. It is the case when sensitivity is a lower bound for the deterministic complexity, respectively, this function has $s = bs = 6$. But nobody knows whether this approach cannot fail constructing better examples. As it is proved in [2] $bs \leq 2 \cdot deg^2$, but simultaneously the best known estimation on the deterministic complexity [4] is $D = O(deg^3)$. So, a need for other lower bounds for the deterministic complexity arises.

J. Wiedermann et al. (Eds.): SOFSEM 2006, LNCS 3831, pp. 158–165, 2006.

Moreover, the approach of non-intersecting complexity comparing to the other complexities such as deterministic complexity or polynomial degree has a simple geometric interpretation and it is similar with a number of well-known combinatorial quizzes.

2 Preliminaries

For more information about mentioned definitions and results see [2]. Let $F : \{0,1\}^n \to \{0,1\}$ be a Boolean function throughout all this section.

Deterministic complexity. A decision tree is a rooted binary tree each internal node of which is marked with a variable x_i and each leaf contains a value 0 or 1. Decision tree computes in a following way. It starts with the root and depending on the value of the variable it is marked with continues with the computing of the left or right subtree. When it reaches a leaf it outputs a value it contains.

A decision tree is said to compute a Boolean function F, if its output is equal with the value of F for all possible variable values. A complexity of the decision tree is its depth (the longest path from the root to a leaf). A deterministic complexity of a function F notated as $D(F)$ is a minimal complexity of a decision tree that computes this function.

Non-deterministic complexity. This complexity is mentioned under the name of certificate complexity in [2]. We slightly changed the definition in order to show a similarity with the non-intersecting complexity presented later.

In this case we represent a function using a ND table. Its columns correspond to the variables. Each cell contains one of symbols '0', '1' (fixed elements) or '-' (arbitrary element). Each row describes a set of input vectors where each variable is fixed to a value of 0, 1 or can be arbitrary.

Table consists of two parts, describing input vectors with function value equal to 0 and 1. The table fully describes function, i.e. each input vector must be in at least one row. Note that no vector can appear in both 0- and 1-parts of a table.

A complexity of the table is a maximal number of fixed elements in a row. Non-deterministic complexity of a function $(ND(F))$ is equal with a minimal complexity of a table representing this function. Complexity of the 0-part (1-part) of the best ND table we will notate as $ND_0(F)$ $(ND_1(F))$.

Sensitivity and block sensitivity. Let x be an input vector. A block sensitivity of the function F on this vector $bs_x(F)$ is a maximal number of disjoint blocks $B_1, \ldots, B_k \subset \{1, \ldots, n\}$ $(i \neq j \Rightarrow B_i \cap B_j = \emptyset)$ such that $\forall i F(x) \neq F(x^{B_i})$. Here variables from B_i in x^{B_i} are flipped $((x_k^{B_i} = x_k) \Leftrightarrow (k \notin B_i))$.

A *block sensitivity* of a function is defined with $bs(F) = \max_x bs_x(F)$. We will use also notations $bs_i(F) = \max_{x \in F^{-1}(i)} bs_x(F)$ where $i = 0, 1$. Notation $F^{-1}(i)$ stands for a full preimage.

Sensitivity of a function is block sensitivity with sizes of all blocks restricted to 1. In other words, sensitivity $s_x(F)$ of the function F on a vector x is equal with the number of indexes i such that

$$F(x_1, \ldots, x_{i-1}, x_i, x_{i+1}, \ldots, x_n) \neq F(x_1, \ldots, x_{i-1}, 1 - x_i, x_{i+1}, \ldots, x_n).$$

Complexities $s_0(F), s_1(F)$ and $s(F)$ are defined in a same way as in the case of block sensitivity. Obviously, $s_i(F) \leq bs_i(F)$. It is proved also that $s(F) \leq bs(F) \leq ND(F) \leq D(F)$.

Representing polynomial. For any Boolean function F there exists a unique multilinear polynomial $P(x_1, \ldots, x_n)$ that is representing F. This means that equality

$$P(x_1, \ldots, x_n) = F(x_1, \ldots, x_n)$$

holds for all possible x values. The degree of the representing polynomial notated as $deg(F)$ is a significant property of a Boolean function.

3 Definition of the NI Complexity

Let F be a Boolean function. As it has been done in a non-deterministic case we will construct a table describing the function. The only difference: we demand that any two rows must be *non-intersecting*, i.e. no input vector can satisfy two different rows. In other words, for any two rows there exists a column which is intersecting with these rows on cells containing '0' and '1'. We say these two cells *ensures* a non-intersection of this pair of rows.

A table describing input vectors for a function value of 0 we will call a *NI 0-table*. In a same way we define a *NI 1-table*. A table containing both parts is a *full NI table*. An example of a full NI table (with 0 part on the left, and 1 part on the right) follows:

$$S: \quad \begin{array}{|cccc|}
\hline
x_1 & x_2 & x_3 & x_4 \\
0 & 1 & - & 1 \\
- & 0 & 1 & 1 \\
1 & - & 0 & 1 \\
0 & 0 & 0 & - \\
\hline
\end{array} \quad \begin{array}{|cccc|}
\hline
x_1 & x_2 & x_3 & x_4 \\
1 & 1 & 1 & - \\
0 & 1 & - & 0 \\
- & 0 & 1 & 0 \\
1 & - & 0 & 0 \\
\hline
\end{array} \tag{1}$$

A maximal number of fixed elements in a row for the best NI 0-table we will notate as NI_0. NI_1 complexity is defined in a same way. Also we will use notations $NI_{\min} = \min\{NI_0, NI_1\}$ and $NI_{\max} = \max\{NI_0, NI_1\}$.

4 Some Inequalities on the NI Complexity

Given a new characteristic of an object, one of the first questions to appear is the way it goes on with other characteristics. In this section we will show some main inequalities containing NI complexity.

4.1 Main Inequalities

The four main inequalities that rise the interest to this complexity are following:

$$NI_{\max}(F) \leq D(F) \tag{2}$$

Proof. This one is a key inequality. For each leaf we write down a row that describes all input vectors when this leaf is reached. It is obvious that number of fixed elements in every row is equal with a depth of a leaf and rows are non-intersecting. □

$$ND(F) \leq NI_{\max}(F) \tag{3}$$

Every full NI table is also a full ND table.

$$NI_{\min}(F) \leq NI_{\max}(F) \tag{4}$$

Trivial.

$$deg(F) \leq NI_{\min}(F) \tag{5}$$

Proof. We can suppose that $NI_{\min}(F) = NI_1(F)$, in the opposite case we consider a function $1 - F(x)$ instead. Each row of the NI 1-table can be represented by a polynomial $\prod_{i=1}^{n} p_i$, where

$$p_i = \begin{cases} 1, & x_i \text{ is a free variable} \\ x_i, & x_i \text{ is fixed to } 1 \\ 1 - x_i, & x_i \text{ is fixed to } 0 \end{cases}$$

Obviously, the degree of this product is equal with the number of fixed elements. Entire function is given as a disjunction of all row-functions that can be replaced by a sum because rows are non-intersecting. □

4.2   Other Inequalities

Sometimes the following result can be useful

Lemma 1. $bs_i(F) \leq ND_i(F) \leq NI_i(F)$ *for* $i = 0, 1$.

The first inequality is well-known [2]. Every row in the ND-table, containing the input vector with the maximal bs, must contain at least one fixed variable from any of the blocks. The proof of the second inequality is the same as for (3). The following result is not so trivial.

Theorem 1. *For any non-constant Boolean function* F:

$$bs(F) \leq 2 \cdot NI_{\min}(F) - 1.$$

Proof. If the maximal block sensitivity is reached on an input vector x such that $NI_{F(x)}(F) = NI_{\min}(F)$ then $bs(F) \leq NI_{\min}(F)$ (lemma 1). The function is non-constant, hence $NI_{\min}(F) \geq 1$ and $NI_{\min}(F) \leq 2NI_{\min}(F) - 1$.

Let us focuss on another case. At first, we can suppose that bs is maximal on the input vector 0 consisting of all zeros. Otherwise we can replace some variables with their negations. Let us consider a NI table for a function value that is opposite to the function value on this input. It will be table for $NI_{\min}$. Let $\{B_k\}$ be the blocks from the definition of block sensitivity.

Vectors 0^{B_k} must be in this table. As $B_i \cap B_j = \emptyset$ for $i \neq j$ and vector 0 should not be in this table then there can be extracted such $bs(F)$ rows that

- each of them suits for exactly one of the vectors 0^{B_k},
- at least one variable is fixed to 1 in each of them,
- no variable is fixed to 1 in more than 2 rows (there is at most one '1' in any column).

Hence each zero on the selected rows ensures a non-intersection of at most one pair of these rows. There are $\frac{1}{2}bs(F)(bs(F) - 1)$ pairs, so there are at least the same number of zeroes. Using the pigeonhole principle there is a row with at least $\frac{1}{2}bs(F) - 1)$ zeroes and remembering variables fixed to 1: $NI_{\min}(F) \geq \frac{1}{2}(bs(F) - 1) + 1$. Or $bs(F) \leq 2NI_{\min}(F) - 1$.   □

As a special case we have $s(F) \leq 2 \cdot NI_{\min}(F) - 1$. This inequality is tight as it can be considered from the following example [1] of a function with such a NI 1-table:

x_1	x_2	x_3	x_4	x_5
0	0	1	-	-
-	0	0	1	-
-	-	0	0	1
1	-	-	0	0
0	1	-	-	0

In a same way for any natural k a function with $NI_{\min} = k$ and $s = 2k - 1$ can be constructed.

5   Some Other Results

5.1   A Case When NI Complexity Is Equal with the Number of Variables

It seems natural to study a case when $NI_{\max}$ is maximal possible to guarantee that deterministic complexity also is maximal. It can be taken into attention then that a system of all possible input vectors can be treated as a graph G in which two vectors are connected with an edge if and only if they differ in exactly one variable. This graph is bichromatic. Following obvious result holds:

Lemma 2. $NI_i \leq n - 1$ if and only if the graph $G \cap F^{-1}(i)$ has a maximal matching.

Maximal matching here means that all vertices of this graph are divided into disjoint pairs and two vertices in any of these pairs are connected with an edge. This result makes it possible to use classical theorems (such as Hall theorem) and algorithms to check whether non-intersecting complexity is a maximal possible.

5.2   Iterations

One way of getting new functions from existing ones is to iterate them. Given a Boolean function $F(x_1, \ldots, x_n)$ and n functions $G_i : \{0,1\}^{k_i} \to \{0,1\}$ the iteration is a function of $s = \sum k_i$ variables of a form:

$$F(G_1(x_1, x_2, \ldots, x_{k_1}), G_2(x_{k_1+1}, \ldots, x_{k_1+k_2}), \ldots, G_n(x_{s-k_n+1}, \ldots, x_s)).$$

As a special case the second iteration of a function F is

$$F^2 = F(F(x_1, \ldots, x_n), F(x_{n+1}, \ldots, x_{2n}), \ldots, F(x_{n^2-n+1}, \ldots, x_{n^2})).$$

Next iterations are defined in a similar way:

$$F^{i+1} = F(F^i, F^i, \ldots, F^i).$$

It is known that $D(G^k) = D(G)^k$, $deg(G^k) = deg(G)^k$ and $ND(G^k) \leq ND(G)^k$. The NI complexity also can be estimated from the top having NI complexities of iterated functions. In fact it is rather tricky operation because using NI tables (not essentially the best ones for NI complexity) bounds can be improved.

Let us consider a case of a function $H = F(G_1, G_2, \ldots, G_m)$. Having the NI table for the function F we can put 0-table of $G_1, \ldots, G_m$ in the place of 0, 1-tables in the place of 1 and take all possible combinations of rows. It is the way NI table of iteration function can be constructed. So the bound can be: $NI_{\max}(H)$ is not larger than the sum of $NI_{\max}(F)$ maximal numbers from the set $\{NI_{\max}(G_1), NI_{\max}(G_2), \ldots, NI_{\max}(G_m)\}$. As a special case it can be got that $NI_{\max}(G^k) \leq NI_{\max}(G)^k$.

6   Counterexamples

Considering the section 4.1 three questions can appear. We answer negative on all these three questions constructing corresponding counterexamples.

6.1 $NI_{\max} \overset{?}{=} D$

We will use a function S from the example (1). As it can be seen $NI_{\max}(S) = 3$. But still $D(S) = 4$. Following algorithm of answering guarantees such complexity:

> While the value of the last variable from the set $\{x_1, x_2, x_3\}$ is not asked, answer '0', otherwise answer '1'.

Using results from the section 5.2 we have $NI_{\max}(S^k) \leq 3^k$ and $D(S^k) = 4^k$.

6.2 $NI_{\min} \overset{?}{=} deg$

A good example here is Kushilevitz function (quoted in [6]). It is a function $F(x_1, \ldots, x_6)$ defined with

- $F = 0$ if $x_1 + \ldots + x_6$ is equals with 0,4 or 5.
- $F = 1$ if $x_1 + \ldots + x_6$ is equals with 1,2 or 6.
- If $x_1 + \ldots + x_6 = 3$ then $F = 0$ only in this 10 cases: $x_1 = x_2 = x_3 = 1, x_2 = x_3 = x_4 = 1, x_3 = x_4 = x_5 = 1, x_4 = x_5 = x_1 = 1, x_5 = x_1 = x_2 = 1, x_1 = x_3 = x_6 = 1, x_1 = x_4 = x_6 = 1, x_2 = x_4 = x_6 = 1, x_2 = x_5 = x_6 = 1, x_3 = x_5 = x_6 = 1$.

It is known that $deg(F) = 3$ and $NI_{min}(F) = 6$ because of sensitivity 6 on input vectors of all ones and of all zeros due to what $s_0(F) = s_1(F) = 6$. In a similar way we have $deg(F^k) = 3^k$ and $NI_{min}(F^k) = 6^k$.

6.3 $NI_{max} \overset{?}{=} \max\{NI_{min}, ND\}$

In this case a counterexample can be constructed. Consider a function T with following NI 0-table and ND 1-table.

x_1	x_2	x_3	x_4
1	-	-	0
0	0	-	1
0	1	1	-
-	1	0	1

x_1	x_2	x_3	x_4
0	-	0	0
0	0	-	0
1	0	-	1
1	-	1	1

But this function does not have a NI 1-table with a complexity 3 (see section 5.1). So we have: $ND(T) = 3$, $NI_{min}(T) = 3$, but $NI_{max}(T) = 4$.

7   Usage in Symmetrisation Polynomials

7.1   Symmetrisation

In a study of function degree a subject of symmetrisation polynomial presented in [5] is used. Symmetrisation polynomial of a Boolean function F is such a one-variable polynomial $F^{sym}(x)$ that

$$F^{sym}(x) = \frac{1}{\binom{n}{x}} \sum_{x_1+x_2+\cdots+x_n=x} F(x_1, x_2, \ldots, x_n).$$

for $x \in \{0, 1, \ldots, n\}$. It always exists due to the Lagrange interpolation polynomial method.

It is proved that $deg(F) \geq deg(F^{sym})$. For the last expression $deg(F^{sym})$ we will use a notation $deg^{sym}(F)$.

7.2   Usage of the NI Complexity

Non-intersecting complexity goes well into symmetrisation. Given a symmetrisation polynomial F^{sym} it is possible to lower bound NI_i with a NI_i^{sym} constructed in way described further($i = 0, 1$).

Let us assume that there exists NI i-table for initial Boolean function. We can consider a case when all rows in this NI table is of equal number of fixed elements. Otherwise we can divide a row having smaller number of fixed elements into several rows fixating arbitrary variable. Each row geometrically describes a hypercube of a known dimension. We known number of elements on all levels of $x_1 + x_2 + \cdots + x_n$ in this hypercube, the only it can be shifted as a whole. Because hypercubes are non-intersecting knowing the total number of elements on each level (and we know it because we know symmetrisation polynomial) we can make the following consideration:

We know the number of input vectors from the preimage $F^{-1}(i)$ with $x_1 + x_2 + \cdots + x_n = 0$. It is equal with the number of rows in NI i-table that has no elements fixed to '1'. Substract number of elements these rows use on each level from the total number of elements on it. Then consider the number of remaining vectors from $F^{-1}(i)$ with $x_1 + x_2 + \cdots + x_n = 1$. It is equal with number of rows with exactly one element fixed to 1. And so on.

The minimal number of fixed elements in a row when this process goes through we will notate with NI_i^{sym}. So $NI_i(F) \geq NI_i^{\mathrm{sym}}(F^{\mathrm{sym}})$.

8   Future Work

We have already described one of the possible usage of this complexity in the preface. It was the usage for functions with a low polynomial degree, of course any other usage in order to show that deterministic complexity is high enough could be very nice. But the situation can be watched in another direction. Non-intersecting complexity is higher than a couple of other complexities and the study of functions with a large gap between non-intersecting and deterministic complexity can success in some problems because it is still possible that there exists some unnoticed links between these majored complexities and some other investigated complexity. For example we are mostly interested in the usage for quantum exact computing. Developing of some methods to link NI_{max} and Q_{E} complexities seems to be of great importance.

Of course some questions can appear not only in the usage. One possible direction is to try to enlarge gaps in the mentioned counterexamples especially between NI complexity and the deterministic one. Also it is interesting to get some results like the theorem 1 but for non-deterministic or NI_{max} complexities. And finally it can be possible to find some other lower bounds for the deterministic complexity.

References

1. Belovs, A.: A Way of constructing Functions with a Low Polynomial Degree. Scientific papers University of Latvia. **673** (2004) 13–17
2. Burhman, H., de Wolf, R.: Complexity Measures and Decision Tree Complexity: a Survey. Theoretical Computer Science **288** (2001) 21–43
3. Gruska, J.: Quantum Computing. McGraw Hill, London (1999) 439 pp
4. Midrijānis, G.: On Randomized and Quantum Query Complexities. Unpublished http://arxiv.org/abs/quant-ph/0501142
5. Minsky, M., Papert, S.: Perceptrons. MIT Press, Cambridge, MA (1988)
6. Nisan, N., Wigderson, A.: On Rank vs. Communication Complexity. Combinatorica **15** (1995) 557–565
7. Papadimitriou, C.: Computational Complexity. Addison-Wesley, Reading (1994) 500 pp.

Constructing Interference-Minimal Networks

Marc Benkert[1,*], Joachim Gudmundsson[2],
Herman Haverkort[3,**], and Alexander Wolff[1,*]

[1] Department of Computer Science, Karlsruhe University,
P.O. Box 6980, D-76128 Karlsruhe, Germany
http://i11www.ilkd.uka.de/algo/group
[2] NICTA[***], Sydney, Australia
joachim.gudmundsson@nicta.com.au
[3] Department of Computer Science, TU Eindhoven,
The Netherlands
cs.herman@haverkort.net

Abstract. A wireless ad-hoc network can be represented as a graph in which the nodes represent wireless devices, and the links represent pairs of nodes that communicate directly by means of radio signals. The *interference* caused by a link between two nodes u and v can be defined as the number of other nodes that may be disturbed by the signals exchanged by u and v. Given the position of the nodes in the plane, links are to be chosen such that the maximum interference caused by any link is limited and the network fulfills desirable properties such as connectivity, bounded dilation or bounded link diameter. We give efficient algorithms to find the links in two models. In the first model, the signal sent by u to v reaches exactly the nodes that are not farther from u than v is. In the second model, we assume that the boundary of a signal's reach is not known precisely and that our algorithms should therefore be based on acceptable estimations. The latter model yields faster algorithms.

1 Introduction

Wireless ad-hoc networks consist of a number of wireless devices spread across a geographical area. Each device has wireless communication capability, some level of intelligence for signal processing and networking of the data, and a typically limited power source such as a small battery.

This paper studies networks that do not depend on dedicated base stations: in theory, all nodes may communicate directly with each other. In practice however, this is often a bad idea: if nodes that are far from each other would exchange signals directly, their signals may interfere with the communication between

* Supported by grant WO 758/4-2 of the German Science Foundation (DFG).
** Part of this research was done while HH was working at Karlsruhe University, supported by the European Commission, FET open project DELIS (IST-001907).
*** Funded by the Australian Government's Backing Australia's Ability initiative, in part through the Australian Research Council.

J. Wiedermann et al. (Eds.): SOFSEM 2006, LNCS 3831, pp. 166–176, 2006.
© Springer-Verlag Berlin Heidelberg 2006

other nodes within reach. This may cause errors, so that messages have to be sent again. Communicating directly over large distances would also require sending very strong signals, since the necessary strength depends at least quadratically on the distance (in practice the dependency tends to be cubic or worse). Both issues could lead to rapid depletion of the devices' limited power sources.

Therefore it is advisable to organize communication between nodes such that direct communication is restricted to pairs of nodes that can reach each other with relatively weak signals that will not disturb many other nodes. We model such a network as a graph $G = (V, E)$, in which the vertices V represent the positions of the mobile devices in the plane, and the links (or: edges) E represent the pairs of nodes that exchange signals directly. Communication between nodes that do not exchange signals directly should be routed over other nodes on a path through that network. According to Prakash [13], the basic communication between direct neighbours becomes unacceptably problematic if the acknowledgement of a message is not sent on the same link in opposite direction. Hence, we will assume that the links are undirected.[1] Our problem is therefore to find an undirected graph on a given set of nodes in the plane, such that all nodes are connected with each other through the network (preferably over a short path), interference problems are minimized, and direct neighbours in the network can reach each other with signals of bounded transmission radius. In this paper we focus on guaranteeing connectivity and minimizing interference; bounding the transmission radius is an easy extension, which we discuss in the full paper. Since wireless devices tend to move frequently, we need to be able to construct networks with the desired properties fast.

The optimal network structure depends ultimately on the actual communication that takes place. This is generally not known a priori. Therefore we strive to optimize a property of nodes or links in the network that is expected to be a good indicator of the likelihood that interference problems will in fact occur. Assuming that each node can adjust the strength of each signal so that it can just reach the intended receiver, such indicators may be:

sending-link-based interference of a link $\{u, v\}$**:** the number of third nodes that are within reach of the signals from the communication over a particular link $\{u, v\}$ in the network (proposed by Burkhart et al. [2], also studied by Moaveni-Nejad and Li [9])—in other words: the number of nodes that are hindered when the link $\{u, v\}$ is active. This is the definition of interference we focus on in this paper.

sending-node-based interference of a node u**:** the number of nodes that receive signals transmitted by u (proposed by Moaveni-Nejad and Li [9])—in other words: the number of nodes that are hindered when u is active.

receiving-node-based interference of a node u**:** the number of nodes transmitting signals that reach u (proposed by Rickenbach et al. [16])—that is: the number of nodes that may prevent u from communicating effectively.

---

[1] Nevertheless, most of the algorithms presented in this paper can be extended to work in the directed model, as will be discussed in the full version of the paper.

Previous results. To construct a network that connects all nodes and minimizes the maximum and total sending-link-based interference, we could run Prim's minimum-spanning-tree algorithm [14] with a Fibonacci heap. Assuming that the interference for each feasible link is given in advance, this takes $\mathcal{O}(m + n \log n) = \mathcal{O}(n^2)$ time, where n is the number of nodes and m is the number of eligible links. If all $\binom{n}{2}$ possible links are considered, we can compute their interference values in $\mathcal{O}(n^{9/4} \operatorname{polylog} n)$ time (see the proof of Lemma 3). This will then dominate the total running time.

To make sure that nodes are connected by a relatively short path in the network, one could construct a t-spanner on the given set of nodes. A network G is said to be a t-spanner if, for every pair of vertices u and v, the length of the shortest path in the network is at most a chosen constant t times the Euclidean distance between u and v. The *dilation* of a graph G is the smallest t such that G is a t-spanner. Burkhart et al. [2] presented a first algorithm to construct a t-spanner for given $t > 1$. It was later improved by Moaveni-Nejad and Li in [9]. Assuming that the interference for each possible link is again given in advance, the running time of their algorithm is $\mathcal{O}(n \log n(m + n \log n))$. If all $\binom{n}{2}$ possible links are considered, the running time is $\mathcal{O}(n^3 \log n)$.

The approach for sending-linked-based interference also works for sending-node-based interference, by defining the interference of a link (u, v) to be the maximum of the sending-node-based interferences of u and v. Unfortunately the same approach does not work for receiving-node-based interference. With sending-link-based interference we can decide whether a link causes too much interference independently of the other links that may be active. With receiving-node-based interference this is not possible, so that completely different algorithms would be needed. Rickenbach et al. [16] only give an approximation algorithm for the case where all nodes are on a single line (the *highway model*).

Our results. We improve and extend the results of Burkhart et al. and Moaveni-Nejad and Li in two ways.

First, apart from considering networks that are simply connected (spanning trees) and networks with bounded dilation (t-spanners), we also consider networks with bounded link diameter, that is: networks such that for every pair of nodes $\{u, v\}$, there is a path from u to v that consists of at most d links (or: 'hops'), where d is a parameter given as input to the algorithm. Such d-hop networks for small d are useful since much of the delay while sending signals through a network is typically time spent by signals being processed in the nodes rather than time spent by signals actually travelling.

Second, we remove the assumption that the interference of each possible link is given in advance. For each of the three properties (connectivity, bounded dilation or bounded link diameter), we present algorithms that decide whether the graph G_k with all links of interference at most k has the desired property. The main idea is that we significantly restrict the set of possible links for which we have to determine the interference, in such a way that we can still decide correctly whether G_k has the desired property. To find the smallest k such that there is a network with interference k and the desired property, we do a combined

Table 1. Running times of our algorithms to find a minimum-interference network with the required property. The running times are given in $\mathcal{O}$-notation, n is the number of nodes, k is the maximum interference of any link in the resulting network, and ε specifies the relative inaccuracy with which a signal's reach and the dilation of a spanner is known. Worst-case running times for deterministic algorithms for the exact model are slightly worse than the expected running times of the randomized algorithms listed in the table. The listed running times for the estimation model are worst-case.

	exact model (expected)	estimation model (determ.)
spanning tree	$\min\{n^{9/4}\operatorname{polylog} n, nk^2 + n\log n\}$	$n\log n/\varepsilon^2 + n/\varepsilon^3$
t-spanner	$n^2 k\log k + n^2\log n\log k$	$n^2\log n\log k/\varepsilon^4$
d-hop network	$\min\{n^{9/4}\operatorname{polylog} n, nk^2\} + n^2\log n\log k$	$n^2\log k/\varepsilon^2 + n/\varepsilon^3$

exponential and binary search that calls the decision algorithm $\mathcal{O}(\log k)$ times. The resulting algorithms are output-sensitive: their running times depend on k, the interference of the resulting network.

Our algorithms work for sending-link-based and sending-node-based interference. We present algorithms that optimize these interference measures for two models of the area that is reached by a sender. In the *exact* model, we assume that the signal sent by a node u to a node v reaches exactly the nodes that are not farther from u than v is. Our algorithms for this model are faster than the algorithm by Moaveni-Nejad and Li [9] for $k \in o(n)$. In the *estimation* model, we assume that it is not realistic that the boundary of a signal's reach is known precisely: for points w that are slightly farther from u than v is, counting w as being disturbed by the signal sent from u to v is as good a guess as not counting w as disturbed. It turns out that with this model, the number of links for which we actually have to compute the interference can be reduced much further, so that we get faster algorithms, especially for spanning trees with larger values of k. Our results are listed in Table 1.

Most of the techniques discussed in this paper generalize to three (or more) dimensions. Details are in the full paper.

This paper is organized as follows. In Section 2 we propose our output-sensitive algorithms for the case of exact interference values, and examine their running times. In Section 3 we introduce our model for reasonable estimations of link interference and describe one algorithm for each of the network properties (connectivity, bounded dilation, and bounded link diameter). All proofs are omitted from this extended abstract but can be found in the full paper.

2   Computing Exact-Interference Graphs

We are given a set V of n points in the plane in general position. Our aim is to establish a wireless network that minimizes interference. First, we define interference. Let u, v be any two points in V. If the edge (link) $\{u, v\}$ is contained in a communication network, the range of u must be at least $|uv|$. Hence, if u sends a signal to v this causes interferences within the closed disk $D(u, |uv|)$ that has center u and radius $|uv|$. The same holds for v. This leads to the following definition that was first given by Burkhart et al. [2]. See also Figure 1.

Definition 1 ([2]). *The* sphere *of an edge* $e = \{u, v\}$ *is defined as* $S(e) := D(u, |uv|) \cup D(v, |uv|)$. *For any edge* $e = \{u, v\}$ *in* $V \times V$ *we define the* interference *of* e *by* $\text{Int}(e) := |V \cap S(e) \setminus \{u, v\}|$. *The* interference $\text{Int}(G)$ *of a graph* $G = (V, E)$ *is defined by* $\text{Int}(G) := \max_{e \in E} \text{Int}(e)$.

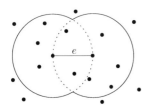

Fig. 1. The sphere of e. Here $\text{Int}(e) = 9$.

In this section, we will give algorithms to compute interference-minimal networks of three types. The first type is a spanning tree $\mathcal{T}$. The algorithm that we use to compute $\mathcal{T}$ can simply be extended such that the resulting tree $\mathcal{T}$ not only minimizes $\text{Int}(\mathcal{T})$ but also $\sum_{e \in \mathcal{T}} \text{Int}(e)$. The second type of network is, for an additionally given $t \geq 1$, a t-spanner. And the third type is a d-hop network, for a given integer $d > 1$.

The main idea of the algorithms is the same. For given $j \geq 0$ let, in the following, $G_j = (V, E_j)$ denote the graph where E_j includes all edges e with $\text{Int}(e)$ *leq* j. Exponential and binary search are used to determine the minimum value of k for which G_k has the desired property $\mathcal{P}$, see Algorithm 1. We first try $k = \lfloor upper \rfloor = 0$, and compute all edges of G_0. If G_0 does not have the desired property, we continue with $upper = 1$ and then keep doubling $upper$ until G_{upper} has the desired property. We compute the interference values for each of its edges, and continue with a binary search between $lower = upper/2$ and $upper$. In each step we construct G_{middle}, the graph to be tested, by selecting the edges with interference at most $middle$ from G_{upper}, which had already been computed.

To get a spanning tree, we test with the property $\mathcal{P} = $ connectivity. After running Algorithm MININTERFERENCENETWORK that finds the minimum k for which G_k is connected, we run a standard minimum spanning tree algorithm on G_k. The result is a tree $\mathcal{T}$ that minimizes both $\max_{e \in \mathcal{T}} \text{Int}(e)$ and $\sum_{e \in \mathcal{T}} \text{Int}(e)$ among all spanning trees. For the t-spanner and the d-hop network, the test consists of determining the dilation or the link diameter of the network. We do this with an all-pairs-shortest-paths computation.

Note that the only non-trivial steps in algorithm MININTERFERENCENETWORK are the subroutines *FulfillsProperty* and *ComputeEdgeSet*. We first give details on how to implement *ComputeEdgeSet*, that is: how to compute E_j and the interference values of the edges in E_j efficiently for any j.

2.1   Computing Edge Interferences

An edge $\{u, v\}$ is an *order-j Delaunay edge* if there exists a circle through u and v that has at most j points of V inside [5].

Algorithm 1. MININTERFERENCENETWORK$(V, \mathcal{P})$

// exponential search
$upper \leftarrow \frac{1}{4}$, **repeat**
  $lower \leftarrow upper, \; upper \leftarrow 2 \cdot upper$
  $E_{upper} \leftarrow ComputeEdgeSet(V, \lfloor upper \rfloor), \; G_{upper} \leftarrow (V, E_{upper})$
until $FulfillsProperty(G_{upper}, \mathcal{P})$
// binary search
while $upper > lower + 1$ **do**
  $middle \leftarrow \frac{1}{2}(lower + upper)$
  $G_{middle} \leftarrow (V, \quad$ all edges in E_{upper} with interference at most $middle)$
  if $FulfillsProperty(G_{middle}, \mathcal{P})$ **then** $upper \leftarrow middle$ **else** $lower \leftarrow middle$
return G_{upper}

Lemma 1. *All edges in E_j are order-j Delaunay edges.*

There is a close connection between order-j Delaunay edges and higher-order Voronoi diagrams that we will use.

Lemma 2. *(Lemma 2 in [5])*
Let V be a set of n points in the plane, let $j \leq n/2 - 2$, and let $u, v \in V$. The edge $\{u, v\}$ is an order-j Delaunay edge if and only if there are two incident faces, F_1 and F_2, in the order-$(j + 1)$ Voronoi diagram such that u is among the $j + 1$ points closest to F_1 but not among the $j + 1$ points closest to F_2, while v is among the $j + 1$ points closest to F_2 but not among those closest to F_1.

Since the worst-case complexity of the order-$(j + 1)$ Voronoi diagram is $\mathcal{O}((j + 1)(n - j - 1))$ [8], it follows that $\mathcal{O}(nj)$ pairs of points give rise to all order-j Delaunay edges. This is because any two incident faces induce exactly one point pair that corresponds to a Delaunay edge. These pairs can be computed in $\mathcal{O}(nj2^{c \log^* j} + n \log n)$ expected time [15] (the best-known deterministic algorithm has a worst-case running time that is only slightly worse [4]). Note that this also implies that the number of edges in E_j is bounded by $\mathcal{O}(nj)$.

Lemma 3. *Given n points in the plane, (i) any edge set E_j with $j \leq n/2 - 2$ can be computed in $\mathcal{O}(nj^2 + n \log n)$ expected time; (ii) after $\mathcal{O}(n^{9/4} \operatorname{polylog} n)$ preprocessing time, any edge set E_j can be computed in $\mathcal{O}(nj)$ worst-case time.*

Proof. (i) Computing the order-$(j + 1)$ Voronoi diagram and thus all $\mathcal{O}(nj)$ order-j Delaunay edges takes $\mathcal{O}(nj2^{c \log^* j} + n \log n)$ expected time. In the full version we explain how to compute the interference of an order-j Delaunay edge, and thus, whether or not it is in E_j, in $\mathcal{O}(j)$ time. Thus, computing E_j takes $\mathcal{O}(nj^2 + n \log n)$ expected time in total.

(ii) We use results by Matoušek [10] to preprocess the set of points in $\mathcal{O}(n^{9/4} \operatorname{polylog} n)$ time, so that we can answer range queries with disks and intersections of two disks in $\mathcal{O}(n^{1/4} \operatorname{polylog} n)$ time. We query this data structure for all $\mathcal{O}(n^2)$ possible edges, which takes $\mathcal{O}(n^{9/4} \operatorname{polylog} n)$ time, sort the results for all edges by interference value, and store them. After that, any edge set E_j can be computed by selecting only those with interference at most j.   □

2.2   The Total Running Time

Theorem 1. *Algorithm* MININTERFERENCENETWORK *can run in* $O(\min\{nk^2 + n\log n, n^{9/4}\text{ polylog } n\} + P(n, nk)\log k)$ *expected time, where* n *is the number of nodes,* k *is the interference of the network output, and* $P(n, m)$ *is the running time of FulfillsProperty on a graph with* n *nodes and* m *edges.*

Proof. During the exponential-search phase, *ComputeEdgeSet* is called $\mathcal{O}(\log k)$ times to compute an edge set $E_{\lfloor upper \rfloor}$, for geometrically increasing values of *upper*. Thus, the last call to *ComputeEdgeSet* dominates and the total expected time spent by *ComputeEdgeSet* is $\mathcal{O}(nk^2 + n\log n)$ (by Lemma 3). Once the total time spent by *ComputeEdgeSet* has accumulated to $\Omega(n^{9/4}\text{ polylog } n)$, we compute the interference values for all possible edges at once in $\mathcal{O}(n^{9/4}\text{ polylog } n)$ time, after which we can identify all sets $E_{\lfloor upper \rfloor}$ easily in $\mathcal{O}(nk)$ time. In the binary-search phase, selecting edges of E_{middle} from E_{upper} takes $\mathcal{O}(nk)$ time, which is done $\mathcal{O}(\log k)$ times for a total of $\mathcal{O}(nk\log k)$. A total of $\mathcal{O}(\log k)$ tests for the property $\mathcal{P}$ on graphs with $\mathcal{O}(nk)$ edges takes $\mathcal{O}(P(n, nk)\log k)$ time.   □

For a graph with n nodes and m edges, connectivity can be tested in $\mathcal{O}(n + m)$ worst-case time by breadth-first search. The dilation can be computed in $\mathcal{O}(nm + n^2\log n)$ time by computing all pairs' shortest paths, where the length of an edge $\{u, v\}$ is the Euclidean distance between u and v. The link diameter can be computed in the same time (defining the length of every edge to be 1), or in $\mathcal{O}(n^2\log n)$ expected time with the all-pairs-shortest-paths algorithm by Moffat and Takaoka [11]. By filling in $P(n, m)$ in Theorem 1 we get the following:

Corollary 1. *We can compute a minimum-interference...*
(i) ...spanning tree in $\mathcal{O}(\min\{nk^2 + n\log n, n^{9/4}\text{ polylog } n\})$ *expected time.*
(ii) ...t-spanner in $\mathcal{O}(n^2 k\log k + n^2\log n\log k)$ *expected time.*
(iii) ...d-hop network in $\mathcal{O}(\min\{nk^2, n^{9/4}\text{ polylog } n\} + n^2\log n\log k)$ *expected time.*

3   Estimating Interference

In this section we show how to compute interference-minimal networks if nodes w just outside the intended transmission radius of a node u may or may not be counted as being disturbed by u—it may not be realistic anyway to assume that we could predict correctly whether w will actually be disturbed. We define estimated interference as follows:

Definition 2. *Let* $D(u, r)$ *be the closed disk centered at* u *with radius* r. *The* $(1+\varepsilon)$-*sphere* $S_{1+\varepsilon}(e)$ *of an edge* $e = \{u, v\}$ *is defined as* $S_{1+\varepsilon}(e) := D(u, (1 + \varepsilon) \cdot |uv|) \cup D(v, (1 + \varepsilon) \cdot |uv|)$. *For* $0 \le \varepsilon' \le \varepsilon$ *we say that an integer* I *is an* $(\varepsilon', \varepsilon)$-*valid estimation of the interference of* e *if and only if* $\left|V \cap S_{1+\varepsilon'}(e) \setminus \{u, v\}\right| \le I \le \left|V \cap S_{1+\varepsilon}(e) \setminus \{u, v\}\right|$.

We will use ε-*valid estimation* as a shorthand for $(0,\varepsilon)$-*valid estimation*. Our aim is to compute interference-minimal networks based on ε-valid estimations of interference. We will do so for a particular assignment $\mathrm{Int}_\varepsilon : V \times V \to \mathbb{N}$ of estimations for all edges, which will be explained below. This assignment Int_ε has the following properties that allow for efficient algorithms:

sparseness. It comes with a set of $\mathcal{O}(n/\varepsilon^2)$ representative edges $E'_{n,\varepsilon} \subseteq V \times V$.

representing interference. Each edge $e \in V \times V$ is represented by an edge $e' \in E'_{n,\varepsilon}$ s.t. $\mathrm{Int}_\varepsilon(e) = \mathrm{Int}_\varepsilon(e')$ and $\mathrm{Int}_\varepsilon(e)$ is an ε-valid estimation of $\mathrm{Int}(e)$.

representing properties. We can test whether the graph $G_{j,\varepsilon} = (V, E_{j,\varepsilon})$, with $E_{j,\varepsilon} = \{e \mid e \in E \wedge \mathrm{Int}_\varepsilon(e) \le j\}$, has the desired property $\mathcal{P}$, by testing the graph $G'_{j,\varepsilon} = (V, E'_{n,\varepsilon} \cap E_{j,\varepsilon})$.

For larger values of j and ε, we have better bounds on the size of $G'_{j,\varepsilon}$ than for $G_{j,\varepsilon}$ or G_j and we get better bounds on the running times of the algorithms to construct and test $G'_{j,\varepsilon}$ than for the graphs G_j used in the exact model.

Below we define the edge set $E'_{n,\varepsilon}$ and the assignment Int_ε. Its sparseness follows from the method of construction. In the full paper we prove that Int_ε correctly represents interference. We describe how to determine the connectivity, dilation, and link diameter of $G_{j,\varepsilon}$ efficiently by running a test on $G'_{j,\varepsilon}$. Our construction uses the well-separated pair decomposition by Callahan and Kosaraju [3], which we briefly review before we define $E'_{n,\varepsilon}$ and Int_ε.

Definition 3 ([3]). *Let $s > 0$ be a real number, and let A and B be two finite sets of points in $\mathbb{R}^2$. We say that A and B are* well-separated *with respect to s, if there are two disjoint disks D_A and D_B of same radius r, such that (i) D_A contains A, (ii) D_B contains B, and (iii) the minimum distance between D_A and D_B is at least $s \cdot r$.*

Definition 4 ([3]). *Let V be a set of n points in $\mathbb{R}^2$, and let $s > 0$ be a real number. A* well-separated pair decomposition *(WSPD) for V with respect to s is a sequence of pairs of non-empty subsets of V, $\{A_1, B_1\}, \{A_2, B_2\}, \ldots, \{A_m, B_m\}$, such that (i) A_i and B_i are well-separated w.r.t. s, for $i = 1, \ldots, m$, and for any two distinct points u and v of V, there is exactly one pair $\{A_i, B_i\}$ in the sequence, such that (a) $u \in A_i$ and $v \in B_i$, or (b) $v \in A_i$ and $u \in B_i$. The integer m is called the* size *of the WSPD.*

Callahan and Kosaraju [3] showed that a WSPD of size $\mathcal{O}(s^2 n)$ can be computed in $\mathcal{O}(s^2 n + n \log n)$ time.

We now define the assignment Int_ε and the set $E'_{n,\varepsilon}$. For a well-separated pair $\{A_i, B_i\}$, let $\mathcal{E}_i$ be the set $\{\{u, v\} \mid u \in A_i, v \in B_i\}$. To obtain Int_ε we compute an $(\frac{1}{3}\varepsilon, \frac{2}{3}\varepsilon)$-valid interference estimation of one exemplary edge $e_i \in \mathcal{E}_i$ for each pair $\{A_i, B_i\}$. We then assign that interference estimation $\mathrm{Int}_\varepsilon(e_i)$ to all edges in $\mathcal{E}_i$, that is, $\mathrm{Int}_\varepsilon(e) := \mathrm{Int}_\varepsilon(e_i)$ for all edges $e \in E_i$. The set $E'_{n,\varepsilon}$ consists of the exemplary edges $e_1, \ldots, e_m$ for all well-separated pairs.

Algorithm 2. MinEstimatedInterferenceNetwork$(V, \mathcal{P})$

$E'_{n,\varepsilon} \leftarrow \emptyset, \quad s \leftarrow 4 + 16/\varepsilon$
$W \leftarrow \text{ComputeWSPD}(V, s)$
$B \leftarrow \text{ComputeBBDTree}(V)$
for each $\{A_i, B_i\} \in W$ **do**
    choose an arbitrary edge $e \in \mathcal{E}_i$
    query B to determine a $(\frac{1}{3}\varepsilon, \frac{2}{3}\varepsilon)$-valid estimation $\text{Int}_\varepsilon(e)$ of $\text{Int}(e)$
    add e to $E'_{n,\varepsilon}$
// exponential search
$upper \leftarrow \frac{1}{4}$
repeat
    $lower \leftarrow upper, \quad upper \leftarrow 2 \cdot upper$
    $E'_{upper,\varepsilon} \leftarrow$ all edges in $E'_{n,\varepsilon}$ with estimated interference at most $upper$
    $G'_{upper,\varepsilon} \leftarrow (V, E'_{upper,\varepsilon})$
until *FulfillsProperty*$(G'_{upper,\varepsilon}, \mathcal{P})$
// binary search
while $upper > lower + 1$ **do**
    $middle \leftarrow \frac{1}{2}(lower + upper)$
    $E'_{middle,\varepsilon} \leftarrow$ all edges in $E'_{n,\varepsilon}$ with interference at most $middle$
    $G'_{middle,\varepsilon} \leftarrow (V, E'_{middle,\varepsilon})$
    if *FulfillsProperty*$(G'_{middle,\varepsilon}, \mathcal{P})$ **then** $upper \leftarrow middle$ **else** $lower \leftarrow middle$
return $G_{upper,\varepsilon}$

In the full paper we show that if we choose the separation constant of the well-separated pair decomposition to be at least $4 + 16/\varepsilon$, the estimated interference $\text{Int}_\varepsilon(e)$ of any edge e is indeed an ε-valid estimation of $\text{Int}(e)$. The general algorithm for finding a minimum-interference network based on estimated interferences is given in Algorithm 2.

3.1   The Total Running Time

Theorem 2. *Algorithm* MinEstimatedInterferenceNetwork *can run in* $O(n/\varepsilon^3 + n \log n/\varepsilon^2 + P(n, n/\varepsilon^2) \log k)$ *time, where n is the number of nodes, k is the maximum ε-valid estimated interference of any edge in the network output, and $P(n, m)$ is the running time of FulfillsProperty on a graph $G'_{j,\varepsilon}$ with n nodes and m edges.*

Proof. We first construct a well-separated pair decomposition in $\mathcal{O}(n/\varepsilon^2 + n \log n)$ time, and choose, for each of its $\mathcal{O}(n/\varepsilon^2)$ pairs, a representative edge. We construct a BBD-tree [1] on the points in $O(n \log n)$ time, and do a range query in the BBD-tree for each representative edge to determine its estimated interference in $\mathcal{O}(1/\varepsilon + \log n)$ time per edge (following the analysis by Haverkort et al. [7]). In total this amounts to $\mathcal{O}(n/\varepsilon^3 + n \log n/\varepsilon^2)$ time. We then do exponential and binary search in $\mathcal{O}(\log k)$ steps, each of which takes $\mathcal{O}(n/\varepsilon^2)$ time to select edges from $E'_{n,\varepsilon}$ and $\mathcal{O}(P(n, n/\varepsilon^2))$ time to test the graph, for a total of $\mathcal{O}(n \log k/\varepsilon^2 + P(n, n/\varepsilon^2) \log k)$ time. $\qquad\square$

In the full paper we prove that we can test if $G_{j,\varepsilon}$ is connected by testing if $G'_{j,\varepsilon}$ is connected in time $O(n+m)$. Furthermore, we prove that any minimum spanning tree of $G'_{j,\varepsilon}$ is a minimum spanning tree of $G_{j,\varepsilon}$.

When the dilation of $G_{j,\varepsilon}$ is t, an approximate dilation t' such that $t/\sqrt{1+\varepsilon} \leq t' \leq t\sqrt{1+\varepsilon}$ can be computed in $\mathcal{O}(n^2 \log n/\varepsilon^2 + mn/\varepsilon^2)$ time with the algorithm by Narasimhan and Smid [12].

The link diameter of $G_{j,\varepsilon}$ can be computed in $\mathcal{O}(mn)$ time by doing an implicit breadth-first search from each node. The algorithm is essentially the same as the one in [6] but slightly modified to fit our setting. The search traverses the edges of $G'_{j,\varepsilon}$ and the split tree used to construct the well-separated pair decomposition, rather than following the edges of $G_{j,\varepsilon}$ itself.

By filling in $P(n,m)$ in Theorem 2 we get the following:

Corollary 2. *We can compute a:*
(i) minimum-estimated-interference spanning tree in $\mathcal{O}(n \log n/\varepsilon^2 + n/\varepsilon^3)$ *time.*
(ii) $(1+\varepsilon)t$*-spanner with estimated interference at most* $\min\{k \mid G_{k,\varepsilon} \text{ is a } t\text{-spanner }\}$ *in* $\mathcal{O}(n^2 \log n \log k/\varepsilon^4)$ *time.*
(iii) minimum-estimated-interference d-hop network in $\mathcal{O}(n^2 \log k/\varepsilon^2 + n/\varepsilon^3)$ *time.*

References

1. Arya, S., and Mount, D.: Approximate Range Searching. Compututational Geometry: Theory & Applications **17** 3–4 (2000) 135–152
2. Burkhart, M., von Rickenbach, P., Wattenhofer, R., and Zollinger, A.: Does Topology Control Reduce Interference? In Proc. 5th ACM Int. Symp. Mobile Ad Hoc Networking and Computing (MobiHoc) (2004) 9–19
3. Callahan, P.B., and Kosaraju, S.R.: A Decomposition of Multidimensional Point Sets with Applications to k-Nearest-Neighbors and n-Body Potential Fields. Journal of the ACM **42** (1995) 67–90
4. Chan, T.M.: Random Sampling, Halfspace Range Reporting, and Construction of ($\leq$k)-Levels in Three Dimensions. SIAM J. on Computing **30** 2 (2000) 561–575
5. Gudmundsson, J., Hammar, M., and van Kreveld, M.: Higher Order Delaunay Triangulations. Computational Geometry: Theory & Appl. **23** 1 (2002) 85–98
6. Gudmundsson, J., Narasimhan, G., and Smid, M.: Distance-Preserving Approximations of Polygonal Paths. FST & TCS (2003) 217–228
7. Haverkort, H.J., de Berg, M., and Gudmundsson, J.: Box-Trees for Collision Checking in Industrial Installations. Computational Geometry: Theory & Applications **28** 2-3 (2004) 113–135
8. Lee, D.T.: On k-Nearest Neighbor Voronoi Diagrams in the Plane. IEEE Transactions on Computing **31** (1982) 478–487
9. Moaveni-Nejad, K., and Li, X.-Y.: Low-Interference Topology Control for Wireless Ad Hoc Networks. Ad Hoc & Sensor Wireless Networks. Accepted for publ. (2004)
10. Matoušek, J.: Range Searching with Efficient Hierarchical Cuttings. Discrete Computational Geometry **10** (1993) 157–182
11. Moffat, A., and Takaoka, T.: An All Pairs Shortest Path Algorithm with Expected Time O($n^2 \log n$). SIAM Journal on Computing **16** 6 (1987) 1023–1031

12. Narasimhan, G., and Smid, M.: Approximating the Stretch Factor of Euclidean Graphs. SIAM Journal of Computing **30** 3 (2000) 978–989
13. Prakash, R.: Unidirectional Links Prove Costly in Wireless Ad-Hoc Networks. In Proc. 3rd Int. Workshop on Discrete Algorithms and Methods for Mobile Computing and Communications (DIAL-M) (1999) 15–22
14. Prim, R.C.: Shortest Connection Networks and Some Generalisations. Bell Systems Technical Journal (1957) 1389–1410
15. Ramos, E.A.: On Range Reporting, Ray Shooting and k-Level Construction. In Proc. 15th Symp. on Computational Geometry (1999) 390–399
16. von Rickenbach, P., Schmid, S., Wattenhofer, R., and Zollinger, A.: A Robust Interference Model for Wireless Ad-Hoc Networks. In Proc. 5th Int. Worksh. Alg. for Wireless, Mobile, Ad Hoc and Sensor Networks (WMAN), CD ROM (2005)

Matching Points with Rectangles and Squares[⋆]

Sergey Bereg[1], Nikolaus Mutsanas[2], and Alexander Wolff[2]

[1] Department of Computer Science,
University of Texas at Dallas, U.S.A
besp@utdallas.edu

[2] Fakultät für Informatik, Universität Karlsruhe,
P.O. Box 6980, D-76128 Karlsruhe, Germany
Nikolaus.Mutsanas@stud.uni-karlsruhe.de
http://i11www.ira.uka.de/people/awolff

Abstract. In this paper we deal with the following natural family of geometric matching problems. Given a class $\mathcal{C}$ of geometric objects and a point set P, a $\mathcal{C}$-matching is a set $M \subseteq \mathcal{C}$ such that every $C \in M$ contains exactly two elements of P. The matching is *perfect* if it covers every point, and *strong* if the objects do not intersect. We concentrate on matching points using axis-aligned squares and rectangles. We give algorithms for these classes and show that it is NP-hard to decide whether a point set has a perfect strong square matching. We show that one of our matching algorithms solves a family of map-labeling problems.

1 Introduction

The problem of matching points with geometric objects is an attempt to generalize the notion of a graph-theoretical matching to geometric environments. Regarding edges of a geometric graph as line segments is a first step towards matching with geometric objects. Instead of using segments to match points, a matching can be defined to consist of axis-aligned rectangles that contain exactly two points. Analogously, a matching can be defined to consist of elements of any family of convex geometric objects, like squares and disks. This class of geometric matching problems has been introduced by Ábrego et al. [1].

In this paper we deal with the problem of matching points with axis-aligned rectangles and squares. Given a set of points in the plane, a rectangle matching is a set of axis-aligned closed rectangles such that each rectangle contains exactly two points of the point set. A square matching is defined analogously for axis-aligned squares. A geometric matching of either type is called *strong*, if the geometric objects do not intersect. Otherwise the matching is called *weak*. Similar to matchings in graphs, we call a geometric matching *perfect*, if it covers every point of the point set. We describe the general problem and give a summary of previous results in Section 2.

Whereas a strong perfect rectangle matching always exists if the point set is in general position, we show in Section 3 that there are point sets which only

---

[⋆] Work supported by grant WO 758/4-2 of the German Science Foundation (DFG).

J. Wiedermann et al. (Eds.): SOFSEM 2006, LNCS 3831, pp. 177–186, 2006.

allow strong rectangle matchings that cover less than a fraction of 2/3 of the points. We also give an algorithm that always matches $4n/7 - 5$ out of n points.

For the problem of matching points with axis-aligned squares, we give in Section 4 efficient algorithms that decide the following problems: given a point set and a combinatorial matching of the points, can the matching be realized by a weak or by a strong square matching? In Section 5 we show that our algorithm for strong square matching can also be used to solve a family of point-labeling problems. Finally, in Section 6 we show that it is NP-hard to decide whether a given point set admits a perfect strong square matching.

2   The General Problem

Following Ábrego et al. [1] we define the problem formally as follows:

Definition 1. *Let $\mathcal{C}$ be a family of geometric objects and P a point set with an even number of points. A $\mathcal{C}$-matching for P is a set $M \subseteq \mathcal{C}$, such that every $C \in M$ contains exactly two points of P. A $\mathcal{C}$-matching M is called* strong *if no two elements of M intersect, and it is called* perfect *if every $p \in P$ is contained in some $C \in M$.*

The link between a matching with geometric objects and a graph-theoretical matching is established by the following definition:

Definition 2. *Let $\mathcal{C}$ be a family of geometric objects and P a point set in the plane. The matching graph for $\mathcal{C}, P$ is the graph $G_{\mathcal{C}}(P, E_{\mathcal{C}})$, where two nodes $p \neq q$ are adjacent if and only if there is an object $C \in \mathcal{C}$ that contains exactly those two points, i.e. $C \cap P = \{p, q\}$. We regard a geometric matching as a* realization *of the underlying combinatorial matching.*

The problem of matching points with geometric objects was introduced by Ábrego et al. [1]. Their results base on the assumption that the points are in general position, i.e. if there are no two points with the same x- or y-coordinate. Ábrego et al. showed that for a point set in general position a matching with axis-aligned squares always exists. They also showed that for every point set P with n points, there is always a strong square matching that covers at least $2\lceil n/5 \rceil$ points. If the point set is additionally in convex position, a perfect strong square matching always exists, provided that n is even. On the other hand, they give point sets with $13m$ points such that any strong matching covers at most $6m$ of the points.

For the family $\mathcal{D}$ of disks, Ábrego et al. also showed that a disk matching always exists, provided that n is even. They prove this assumption by using the matching graph for $\mathcal{D}$. By definition, two points $p, q \in P$ are adjacent in $G_{\mathcal{D}}$ if and only if there is a disk that contains exactly those two points. This is equivalent to p and q being neighbors in the Delaunay triangulation of P. Dillencourt [2] proved that for n even the Delaunay triangulation always contains a perfect matching. Ábrego et al. also showed that for any point set there is always a strong disk matching covering at least $2\lceil (n - 1)/8\rceil$ points. On the other hand, there are arbitrarily large point sets with n points, such that any strong disk matching covers at most $72n/73$ points.

3 Rectangle Matching

If points are in general position, the problem of matching points with axis-aligned rectangles is trivial. An obvious algorithm that yields a perfect strong rectangle matching is the following: Sort the points lexicographically and connect every point with odd index to its successor. Since the order of the x-coordinates is strictly monotonous, two consecutive rectangles cannot overlap.

However, if we drop the condition of general position, the problem becomes interesting. Consider the point set $P_n = \{(i, i), (i - 1, i), (i, i - 1) \mid 1 \leq i \leq n\}$ $\cup \{(n, n + 1), (n + 1, n)\}$ and its matching graph G_n, which has $3n + 2$ vertices and $4n$ edges. Each of the *central* nodes $(1, 1), \ldots, (n, n)$ has degree 4 in G_n, and each edge is incident to a central node. Clearly, only one of the edges incident to a central node can be in a matching. Thus a maximum rectangle matching of P_n has cardinality n; it covers $2n$ out of $3n + 2$ points. This shows that $2/3$ is an upper bound for the ratio of points that can always be covered by a rectangle matching.

We now present a simple and efficient algorithm that always yields a strong rectangle matching that covers at least $4n/7 - c$ points in an n-element point set, where c is a small constant. The algorithm has been implemented and is accessible via a Java applet at the URL `http://i11www.ira.uka.de/matching`. The idea of our algorithm is the following. We partition the given point set P into *vertical subsets* V_i, maximum chains of points with equal x-coordinate (allowing $|V_i| = 1$). Let v_i be the cardinality of V_i. We process these subsets from left to right, making a cut as soon as a matching for the current point set has been found that matches at least a fraction of $4/7$ of the points since the last cut. After making a cut, we disregard the points already processed and start over again. If each of the subsets – except possibly the last – has a matching that covers at least a fraction of $4/7$ of the points, the overall matching will cover at least $4n/7 - c$ of the points in P if c is the size of the last subset.

If v_1 is even or if $v_1 \geq 3$ is odd, we can match at least a fraction of $2/3 > 4/7$ of the points and make a cut after V_1. Thus we assume $v_1 = 1$ and consider $V_1 \cup V_2$. Again, if v_2 is even or if $v_2 \neq 3$ is odd, we can match enough points to make a cut after V_2. However, if $v_2 = 3$, the middle point in V_2 may have the same y-coordinate as the point in V_1, see Figure 1(a). This is the only configuration with cardinalities $v_1 = 1$ and $v_2 = 3$ (for short $[1, 3]$) that we cannot match perfectly. In this case consider the point set $V_1 \cup V_2 \cup V_3$. If v_3 is even or if $v_3 \geq 5$ is odd, we can match enough points to make a cut after V_3. The cases $[1, 3, 1]$ and $[1, 3, 3]$ need to be considered separately.

In case $v_3 = 1$, the points may only allow two out of five points to be matched, as shown in Figure 1 (b) (in every other configuration we can match four out of five points and make a cut). In this case, consider $V_1 \cup V_2 \cup V_3 \cup V_4$. It can be

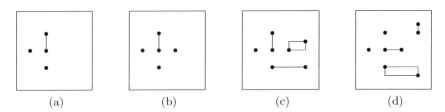

Fig. 1. Some special cases for the 4/7-approximation: a) only 2 out of 4 points can be matched, b) only 2 out of 5 points can be matched. Matching that covers at least 2/3 of the points c) for v_4 even and d) for v_4 odd.

shown that we can always match at least 2/3 of these points, regardless of the cardinality of V_4 (see Figures 1 (c) and (d)).

In case $v_3 = 3$, we can always match four points within their respective vertical sets. This covers four out of seven points, and allows us to make a cut after V_3.

Note that there might be some points left after the last cut, that cannot be processed. The number of left-over points is at most 5, since we can always cut after $[1, 3, 1, *]$ and after $[1, 3, \geq 2]$. This means that our algorithm in fact always matches at least $4n/7 - 5$ out of n points. We assume that a similar technique may be used to find an approximation algorithm that covers at least 2/3 of the points minus some constant, which would reach the highest fixed ratio that can be guaranteed. The time complexity of our algorithm is $O(n \log n)$ due to the lexicographical sorting. We summarize:

Theorem 1. *There are point sets of arbitrary size where any strong rectangle matching covers at most 2/3 of the points. There is an algorithm that computes in $O(n \log n)$ time a strong rectangle matching that covers at least $4n/7 - 5$ points in an n-element point set.*

4   Square Matching

Note that, contrary to rectangle matchings, a square matching is not uniquely defined by a given combinatorial matching. In this section we present efficient algorithms that decide whether a given combinatorial matching $M \subseteq \binom{P}{2}$ of a point set P has a weak or a strong square realization, where $\binom{P}{2} = \{\{p, q\} \mid p, q \in P, p \neq q\}$ is the set of all unordered pairs of points in P.

Consider a square matching for a given point set P. Let the squares of this matching shrink as much as possible while still covering the points. The resulting squares are of minimum size among all squares that contain the two points, and the points now lie on the square boundary. This new matching consists of squares that are contained in the squares of the initial matching. This means that when deciding whether a given matching can be realized as a square matching, it suffices to examine square matchings where all the squares are of minimum size.

How many ways are there to place a minimum-size square Q_i that contains two given points p_i and q_i? It is easy to see that the edge length α_i of a minimal square is the distance of the two points in the maximum (or L_∞-) metric (see

Figure 2). If the two coordinate differences are not equal, the square can be slid – to some extend – in the direction of the smaller coordinate difference β_i. This leads to the model of the sliding squares illustrated in Figure 2.

The *kernel* K_i of a point pair $\{p_i, q_i\}$ is their bounding box, i.e. the smallest axis-aligned rectangle that contains the two points. The kernel consists of the part of the plane that is contained in *every* (minimal) square that contains the two points. In other words, the kernel is the intersection of these squares. We define the *sliding space* S_i of $\{p_i, q_i\}$ to be the union of those squares minus the kernel, see Figure 2. Note that the kernel degenerates to an axis-parallel line segment if the two points share a coordinate, and that the sliding space vanishes if the two points lie on a line of slope $+1$ or -1. Then the minimal square that contains the two points is uniquely defined. In spite of this we will consider such squares to be vertically sliding. In what follows, the *position* of a vertically sliding square Q_i always corresponds to the y-coordinate of its bottom edge and the position of a horizontally sliding square correspond to the x-coordinate of its left edge. Let Q be a minimal square that contains p and q. If at least one of the two points lies in a corner of Q, we say that Q is in *extremal position*.

Now it is easy to give an algorithm that checks whether a given matching M of a point set P has a weak square realization: for each point pair $\{p, q\}$ in M we compute kernel and sliding space. If the kernel contains input points other than p or q, then M does not have a square realization. Otherwise we check whether there are input points in both connected components of the sliding space. If not we can place a square matching p and q into the union of the kernel and the empty component. If both components contain input points, we compute in each component the point closest to the kernel. We call the resulting points a and b. If the L_∞-distance a and b is larger than the L_∞-distance of p and q, then we can place a square that contains the kernel and matches p and q anywhere between a and b. Otherwise, if the L_∞-distance of a and b is at most that of p and q, M does not have a square realization. Using priority search trees [6], this algorithm can be implemented to run in $O(n \log n)$ time.

Theorem 2. *Given a set P of n points and a combinatorial matching $M \subseteq \binom{P}{2}$, it can be decided in $O(n \log n)$ time whether M has a weak square realization.*

Now we turn to the problem of finding a strong square realization for a given combinatorial matching. Due to the above observations, this problem simplifies to examining combinations of placements of squares of *fixed size*. The idea behind our algorithm for solving the strong realization problem is that instead of considering a combination among all possible positions of the squares, we need only check combinations among a few relevant positions for each square. The correctness of the algorithm follows if we prove that the existence of a strong realization implies the existence of a strong realization among the combinations we considered.

It turns out that a problem in map labeling is related to our problem, namely the problem of labeling a rectilinear map with sliding labels. That problem is defined as follows: Given a set of axis-aligned segments that do not intersect and a positive real h, is there a labeling with axis-aligned rectangles with width

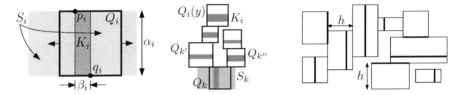

Fig. 2. Notation for sliding squares

Fig. 3. (k, k') causes $Q_i(y)$; (k, k'') doesn't

Fig. 4. Set of line segments (bold) with height-h rectangle labeling

the same as the segment and height h? Each label must contain the segment it labels. See Figure 4 for an example.

The link between the two problems is obvious: in both cases the solution consists of positioning axis-aligned objects of fixed size that can slide in one axis direction. In both problems the sliding objects must contain some other given geometric object (a segment or a kernel). Contrary to the map-labeling problem, in our case the kernels expand in both dimensions and the sliding objects are not of fixed height h, which makes the problem harder. Kim et al. [3] showed that the map-labeling problem can be solved in $O(n \log^2 n)$ time. In this paper we adapt their algorithm to solve the matching problem within the same time.

Note that there is no strong matching if two kernels intersect. This can be checked in $O(n \log n)$ time by a simple plane sweep [9]. Furthermore, if the sliding space of a square and a kernel intersect, the sliding space can be truncated. This can be done via a trapezoidal (i.e. vertical) decomposition in $O(n \log n)$ time.

We define the *interaction graph* $G(\{1, \ldots, n\}, E)$ in which $\{i, j\} \in E$ if and only if the truncated sliding spaces S_i and S_j *interact*, i.e. $S_i \cap S_j \neq \emptyset$. Recall that α_i is the edge length of Q_i. It is easy to see that S_i intersects only a constant number of truncated sliding spaces S_j with $\alpha_j \geq \alpha_i$. Thus $|E| \in O(n)$. Let (x_i, y_i) be the lower left corner of kernel K_i. Define $K_i < K_j$ to hold if $y_i < y_j$ or if $y_i = y_j$ and $x_i < x_j$. In the sequel we assume that $K_1 < \cdots < K_n$. Now we direct the edges of the interaction graph G, namely from small to large index (according to the new order). For ease of disposition we add a dummy node 0 and dummy edges $(1, 0), \ldots, (n, 0)$ to G.

Now we discretize the problem. For each point pair $\{p_i, q_i\}$ in M we compute $O(n)$ positions of the minimal square Q_i that contains $\{p_i, q_i\}$. We only detail how to do this for vertically sliding squares, the algorithm for horizontally sliding squares is analogous. We denote the square Q_i in position y by $Q_i(y)$. We say that an edge $(k, k') \in E$ *causes* $Q_i(y)$ if (a) there is a directed path $k = v_1, v_2, \ldots, v_m = i$ in G, (b) the squares $Q_{v_2}, \ldots, Q_{v_m}$ are vertically sliding, (c) Q_k is vertically sliding if $k' = 0$, else Q_k is horizontally sliding and $v_2 = k'$, and (d) $\overline{y_k} + \alpha_{v_2} + \cdots + \alpha_{v_{m-1}} = y$, where $\overline{y_k}$ is the y-coordinate of the top edge of K_k. See Figure 3 for illustration.

For $i \in \{1, \ldots, n\}$ our algorithm computes a set Π_i of pairs of the form (y, e), where $y \in \mathbb{R}$ is the y-coordinate of some position of Q_i and $e \in E$ causes $Q_i(y)$.

for $i \leftarrow 1$ to n do

  1. if Q_i is vertically sliding then

        $\Pi_i \leftarrow \Pi_i \cup \{(y_i - \alpha_i + \beta_i,\ (i, 0))\}$ {lower extremal position}

  2. for each $e \in E$ do $t_e \leftarrow -\infty$ {initialize auxiliary variables}

  3. for each $(j, i) \in E$ do

    (a) if Q_j is horizontally sliding then

        $\Pi_i \leftarrow \Pi_i \cup \{(y_j + \alpha_j, (j, i))\}$ {y-coordinate of top edge}

    (b) else   {Q_j vertically sliding}

       for each $(y, e) \in \Pi_j$ with $Q_j(y) \cap S_i \neq \emptyset$ do

          $t_e \leftarrow \max\{t_e, y + \alpha_j\}$ {update position of Q_i caused by e}

  4. for each $e \in E$ do

    if $t_e > -\infty$ then $\Pi_i \leftarrow \Pi_i \cup \{(t_e, e)\}$

The asymptotic running time of the above algorithm is dominated by the total time spent in step 3(b), which sums up to $O(\sum_{(i,j) \in E} |\Pi_j|)$. Note that for every edge in E there is at most one element in Π_j. Thus $|\Pi_j| \leq |E|$, and the algorithm runs in $O(|E|^2) = O(n^2)$ time.

Now assume that there is a strong realization R of the given matching M. We show that we can transform it into a strong realization R' in *canonical form* such that for each square $Q_i(y)$ there is a pair $(y, e) \in \Pi_i$. We go through the squares in order $Q_1, \ldots, Q_n$. Let Q_i be a vertically sliding square. The proof for horizontally sliding squares is analogous. Move Q_i downwards until Q_i reaches its lower extremal position, or the top edge of the sliding space of a horizontally sliding square, or the top edge of some other vertically sliding square (that has already been moved). Let $Q_i(y)$ be the resulting position of Q_i. If $Q_i(y)$ is the lower extremal position of Q_i, we are done due to step 1 of our algorithm. If $Q_i(y)$ touches the top edge of a sliding space of a horizontally sliding square, we are done due to step 3(a). Finally, if $Q_i(y)$ touches the top edge of a vertically sliding square $Q_j(z)$ with $z = y - \alpha_j$, then we know (by induction over i) that there is an edge $e \in E$ that has caused $Q_j(z)$ and that $(z, e) \in \Pi_j$. Now due to step 3(b) of the algorithm it is clear that the top edge y of $Q_j(z)$ was considered in the computation of t_e and that $Q_j(y)$ is also caused by $e = (k, k')$. This in turn yields that $(y, e) \in \Pi_i$, since there cannot be another path from k, the origin of e, to i in G that uses only vertically sliding squares and ends in a higher y-coordinate than y. Otherwise Q_i would have stopped there.

After we have computed the sets of type Π_i, it remains to check whether the square positions stored in these sets can be combined such that no two squares overlap. Poon et al. [7] showed that this can be solved by examining the satisfiability of a 2-SAT formula in $O(k_{\max} n^2)$ time, where $k_{\max} = \max_i |\Pi_i|$. Strijk and van Kreveld [10] improved the running time to $O(k_{\max} n \log n)$. Since $k_{\max} \in O(n)$, the resulting time complexity of our algorithm is $O(n^2 \log n)$.

Since every strong square matching can be mapped to one in canonical form as described above, the non-satisfiability of the 2-SAT formula implies the non-existence of a strong square matching. On the other hand, if the 2-SAT formula is satisfiable, a witness of its satisfiability translates into a strong square matching (in canonical form). We conclude with the following theorem.

Theorem 3. *Given a set P of n points and a combinatorial matching $M \subseteq \binom{P}{2}$, it can be decided in $O(n^2 \log n)$ time whether M has a strong square realization.*

5   Application to Point Labeling

In this section we show that the algorithm for strong square matching described in Section 4 can be applied to solve a family of point-labeling problems.

Poon et al. [8] describe the problem of labeling points with sliding labels as follows: The labels are fixed-size rectangles that touch the point they label with their boundary. Every label may slide along a fixed direction (horizontally or vertically) and may not occlude other points.

The transformation of an instance of the point-labeling problem to an instance of the square-matching problem is obvious, provided that labels are squares. The algorithm of Section 4 can solve a more general problem though. Varying the position of the auxiliary point, one can vary the size of the quadratic label. The space within which the label may slide can be shortened too, by forming a kernel of the respective thickness with the use of a different auxiliary point. Note that the sliding space may even be shortened asymmetrically. Shortening the sliding space of some labels can be of practical interest, e.g. when there are physical landmarks on the map—like rivers—that must not be occluded.

Note that, even though labeling points with rectangles cannot be reduced to examining the realizability of a square matching, the same techniques used for the square-matching algorithm can be applied to sliding rectangles, too. This generalizes the family of solvable point-labeling problems even further.

6   NP-Completeness

In this section we investigate the complexity of square matching.

Theorem 4. *It is NP-hard to decide whether a given point set admits a perfect strong square matching.*

Proof. Our proof is by reduction from PLANAR 3-SAT, which is NP-hard [5]. Note that the variables and clauses of ϕ can be embedded in the plane such that all variables lie on a horizontal line and all clauses are represented by *non-intersecting* three-legged combs [4]. Let ϕ be a planar 3-SAT formula. We construct a finite point set S such that S has a perfect square matching if and only if ϕ is satisfiable.

For the general layout of our variable and clause gadgets, see Figure 5. Each variable of ϕ is represented by a *box*, i.e. an axis-parallel rectangle (dark shaded in Figure 5). The points on the boundary of these rectangles can only be matched among each other and only in two different ways. This is true for two reasons: neighboring points on the boundary are closer to each other than to any other point, and between any two corner points there is an odd number of other points.

If the center point of the left edge of the rectangle is matched to its neighbor above, the corresponding variable is true, otherwise it is false. The point pairs in the matching are connected by thick solid line segments in Figure 5, respectively.

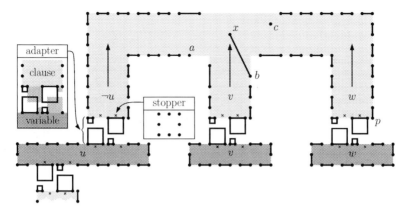

(a) Non-perfect matching corresponding to $u = true$, $v = false$, $w = false$

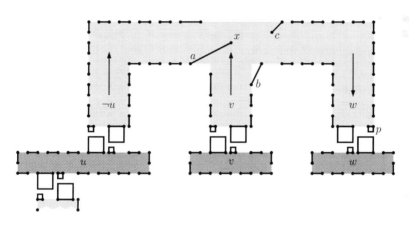

(b) Perfect matching corresponding to $u = true$, $v = false$, $w = true$

Fig. 5. A gadget for the clause $\neg u \vee v \vee w$

The variable boxes are connected via *adapters* to vertical *pipes*, the legs of our clause gadgets. We say that a pipe *transmits pressure* if the lowest point on its right side is matched upwards. This is the case e.g. for the point p in Figure 5 (a), but not in Figure 5 (b). Generally the long vertical arrows in the pipes in Figure 5 indicate that (no) pressure is transmitted if they point upwards (downwards). Note that our description assumes that the clause gadget lies above the variable boxes; the reverse case is symmetric.

The adapters between the variable boxes and the pipes make sure that pressure is transmitted if and only if the variable (such as v or w in Figure 5 (a)) is set to false and occurs as a positive literal in the clause or the variable (such as u in Figure 5 (a)) is set to true, but occurs as a negated literal. For the adapters we need a special construct, so-called *stoppers*, i.e. configurations of eight points arranged in a 3×3 grid without the center point. A stopper is designed such that its points can only be matched to neighboring points on its boundary, but not to any other points –

just like a variable box. The stoppers make sure that the large squares stick out sufficiently far from the variable box and the clause legs to synchronize each other.

Our clause gadget (light shaded in Figure 5) with the special points a, b, c, and x is built such that two points cannot be matched if all three pipes transmit pressure, see e.g. the points a and c in Figure 5 (a). This corresponds to the situation where all three literals of a clause are false. Note that no point of a clause gadget can be matched to any point of another clause gadget if the clauses are nested. In the case of neighboring clause gadgets this can simply be avoided by making sure that they have sufficient distance and different height (or by placing stoppers next to the corner vertices).

On the other hand we claim that all points in a clause gadget can be matched if at most two pipes transmit pressure. To prove the claim it is enough to check all seven cases of at most two pipes transmitting pressure. Figure 5 (b) depicts one of these cases. We conclude that the point set S has a perfect square matching if and only if ϕ is satisfiable. Our reduction is polynomial.   □

Corollary 1. *Perfect strong square matching is NP-complete.*

Proof. Theorem 4 yields the NP-hardness. To show that the problem actually lies in $\mathcal{NP}$, we non-deterministically guess a combinatorial matching. Then we have to decide deterministically and in polynomial time whether this matching has a strong square realization. For this we use the algorithm of Theorem 3.   □

Acknowledgments. We thank one of the anonymous referees for valuable comments and Marc van Kreveld for information on [10].

References

1. Ábrego, B.M., Arkin, E.M., Fernández-Merchant, S., Hurtado, F., Kano, M., Mitchell, J.S.B., and Urrutia, J.: Matching Points with Geometric Objects: Combinatorial Results. In J. Akiyama et al. (eds), Proc. 8th Jap. Conf. Discrete Comput. Geometry (JCDCG'04), LNCS, Springer-Verlag **3742** (2005). To appear.
2. Dillencourt, M.B.: Toughness and Delaunay Triangulations. Discrete Comput. Geom. **5** (1990) 575–601
3. Kim, S.K., Shin, C.-S., and Yang, T.-C.: Labeling a Rectilinear Map with Sliding Labels. Int. J. Comput. Geom. Appl. **11** 2 (2001) 167–179
4. Knuth, D.E., and Raghunathan, A.: The Problem of Compatible Representatives. SIAM J. Discr. Math. **5** 3 (1992) 422–427
5. Lichtenstein, D.: Planar Formulae and Their Uses. SIAM J. Comput. **11** 2 (1982) 329–343
6. McCreight, E.M.: Priority Search Trees. SIAM J. Comput. **14** 2 (1985) 257–276
7. Poon, C.K., Zhu, B., and Chin, F.: A Polynomial Time Solution for Labeling a Rectilinear Map. Information Processing Letters **65** 4 (1998) 201–207
8. Poon, S.-H., Shin, C.-S., Strijk, T., Uno, T., and Wolff, A.: Labeling Points with Weights. Algorithmica **38** 2 (2003) 341–362
9. Preparata, F.P., and Shamos, M.I.: Computational Geometry: An Introduction. Springer-Verlag, 3rd edition (1990)
10. Strijk, T., and van Kreveld, M.: Labeling a Rectilinear Map More Efficiently. Information Processing Letters **69** 1 (1999) 25–30

Searching Paths of Constant Bandwidth

Bernd Borchert and Klaus Reinhardt

Universität Tübingen, Sand 13, 72076 Tübingen, Germany
{borchert, reinhard}@informatik.uni-tuebingen.de

Abstract. As a generalization of paths, the notion of paths of bandwidth w is introduced. We show that, for constant $w \geq 1$, the corresponding search problem for such a path of length k in a given graph is NP-complete and fixed-parameter tractable (FPT) in the parameter k, like this is known for the special case $w = 1$, the LONGEST PATH problem. We state the FPT algorithm in terms of a guess and check protocol which uses witnesses of size polynomial in the parameter.

1 Introduction

A *path* within a graph is one of the most elementary notions of graph theory and its applications. The LONGEST PATH is the computational problem which asks for a given graph G and an integer k whether there is a path of length k in G which is simple, i.e. all vertices are different from each other. The LONGEST PATH is NP-complete [4]. Moreover, the LONGEST PATH problem is fixed-parameter tractable (FPT) in the parameter k. This was shown by Monien [5] and improved with respect to running time by Alon, Yuster, Zwick [1], using randomization techniques.

In this paper we generalize the notion of a path: a path of bandwidth w, or for short w-path, in a graph G is a sequence $(v_1, \ldots, v_n)$ of vertices such that for all v_i, v_j with $1 \leq j - i \leq w$ the pair (v_i, v_j) is an edge in G, see Fig. 1 for an example of a 2-path. 1-paths are paths in the usual sense. It will be easy to show that for every $w \geq 1$ the corresponding computational problem BANDWIDTH-w-PATH, which asks for a given graph G and an integer k whether there exists a simple w-path of length k in G, is NP-complete.

The BANDWIDTH-w-PATH problem for every w is fixed-parameter tractable in the parameter k, this will be shown according to the characterization of FPT ∩ NP by Cai, Chen, Downey & Fellows [2] via an "FPT guess and check protocol" using witnesses of size only dependent on the parameter. The runtime obtained for our guess and check protocol, for the case $w = 1$, which is the LONGEST PATH problem, and seen as a deterministic exhaustive search algorithm, is worse than the algorithms of Monien [5] and Alon, Yuster, Zwick [1]. On the other hand, our algorithm is more easily stated and can immediately be applied to the BANDWIDTH-w-PATH problem. Moreover, the algorithms of [5], [1] do not seem to give better FPT guess and check protocols.

J. Wiedermann et al. (Eds.): SOFSEM 2006, LNCS 3831, pp. 187–196, 2006.
© Springer-Verlag Berlin Heidelberg 2006

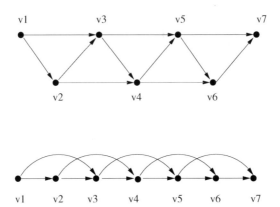

Fig. 1. Two drawings of the same 2-path of length 5, vertex-disjoint and deterministic

2   Paths of Constant Bandwidth

Let G be a digraph and let $w, k \geq 1$. A *path of bandwidth w and length k* in G is a sequence of $k + w$ vertices $(v_1, \ldots, v_{k+w})$ such that the pair (v_i, v_{i+j}) is an edge of G for every i with $1 \leq i \leq k$ and every j with $1 \leq j \leq w$. A path of bandwidth w and length k will also be called *w-path of length k* or, even shorter, *(w, k)-path*. A 1-path of length k is a path of length k in the usual sense. (For a path of length k some authors count the number of vertices while others count the number of edges – which is one less. In this paper we count the number of edges.) In Figures 2 and 3 some 2-paths and 3-paths are shown. Note that a $(w, 1)$-path is a $(w + 1)$-clique: every two nodes are connected by an edge. A (w, k)-path can actually be seen as a sequence of k $(w + 1)$-cliques with two subsequent cliques "glued" together by their common w elements.

A (w, k)-path $(v_1, \ldots, v_{k+w})$ is *vertex-disjoint* if all v_i are different from each other, it is *simple* if all k w-tuples $(v_1, \ldots, v_w), (v_2, \ldots, v_{w+1}), \ldots, (v_k, \ldots, v_{k+w})$ are different from each other. A vertex-disjoint (w, k)-path is simple, but not vice versa for $w \geq 2$, see Figure 3. A vertex-disjoint (w, k)-path, as a graph on its own, is the graph with $k + w$ vertices having bandwidth w and a maximal set of edges, that is why we choose the name "bandwidth" for the number w (see [6], [4] for the definition of bandwidth of a graph).

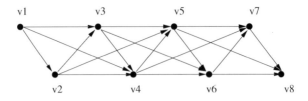

Fig. 2. A 3-path of length 5, vertex-disjoint and deterministic

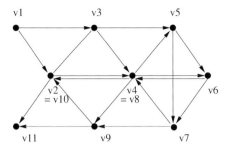

Fig. 3. A 2-path of length 10, deterministic and simple but not vertex-disjoint

Though the notion of w-paths within a graph G is a rather natural generalization of paths the authors could not find references for it in the literature. The closest concept found is the w-*ray* from Proskurowski & Telle [6], corresponding to a vertex-disjoint w-path (as a graph on its own).

A (w, k)-path $(v_1, \ldots, v_{k+w})$ is *deterministic in* G if for every $1 \leq i \leq k$ v_{i+w} is the only vertex in the graph G having the property that all edges $(v_i, v_{i+w}), \ldots, (v_{i+w-1}, v_{i+w})$ are edges of the graph. For example, a deterministic 1-path has the property that every vertex of it – besides the last one – has exactly one outgoing edge in G.

For $w < k$, a (w, k)-path $(v_1, \ldots, v_{k+w})$ is a *cycle of bandwidth w and length k*, for short w-cycle of length k or (w, k)-*cycle*, if $(v_{k+1}, \ldots, v_{k+w}) = (v_1, \ldots, v_w)$. The cycle is *vertex-disjoint* if $v_1, \ldots, v_k$ are different from each other, it is *simple* if $(v_1, \ldots, v_{k+w-1})$ is a simple w-path, see Fig. 4 for an example. For undirected graphs the definitions can be transfered literally. For a fixed w let BANDWIDTH-w-PATH be the set of pairs $\langle G, k \rangle$ such that the digraph G contains a simple (w, k)-path. BANDWIDTH-1-PATH = LONGEST-PATH. Let BANDWIDTH-PATH be the double-parameterized problem consisting of the triples $\langle G, w, k \rangle$ such that the digraph G contains a simple (w, k)-path.

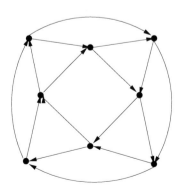

Fig. 4. A 2-cycle of length 8, deterministic and vertex-disjoint

Some variations of these problems: Let the prefixes UNDIRECTED- and DISJOINT- in front of these problem names indicate that the input graph is undirected, or, independently, that the path to be found has to be not only simple but vertex-disjoint, respectively. Let CYCLE instead of PATH in a problem name denote that the path to be found has to be a cycle. Call these further 7 problems the *variations* of the BANDWIDTH-w-PATH problem, resp. BANDWIDTH-PATH.

Proposition 1. *For every $w \geq 1$ the problem* BANDWIDTH-w-PATH *is NP-complete, likewise its variations.*

Proof. Obviously all problems are in NP. In order to show NP-completeness of BANDWIDTH-w-PATH we reduce LONGEST PATH to it. Let some directed graph $G = (V, E)$ be given. Let the vertices V' of the graph $\phi(G) = (V', E')$ consist of $3w$ copies v_i with $1 \leq i \leq 3w$ for each $v \in V$ and w copies $(u, v)_i$ with $1 \leq i \leq w$ for each $(u, v) \in E$ and let the edges be $E' = \{(u_i, u_j) \mid i < j, u \in V\} \cup \{(u_{i+w}, (u, v)_j), ((u, v)_i, v_{j+w}) \mid 1 \leq j \leq i \leq w, (u, v) \in E\} \cup \{((u, v)_i, (u, v)_j) \mid i < j, (u, v) \in E\}$.

It holds: G has a simple path of length k iff $\phi(G)$ has a simple w-path of length $(2k + 3)w$ iff $\phi(G)$ has a vertex-disjoint w-path of length $(2k + 3)w$. Observe that a w-path $(\ldots u_{w+1}, \ldots, u_{2w}, (u, v)_1)$ in $\phi(G)$ can only be continued by $((u, v)_2, \ldots, (u, v)_w, v_{w+1}, \ldots, v_{2w}, \ldots)$ which forces a simple w-path to be vertex-disjoint and to correspond with a path in G. Starting with $(v_1, \ldots, v_w, \ldots)$ or ending with $(\ldots v_{2w+1}, \ldots, v_{3w})$ allows to have the same length as starting in vertices corresponding to possibly unused edges in G.   **q.e.d.**

DISJOINT-BANDWIDTH-PATH is NP-complete because LONGEST PATH is a subproblem and the length of a path is still at most linear. On the other hand, a simple path may have a length of $\binom{n}{w}$ and we conjecture PSPACE-completeness for BANDWIDTH-PATH.

We mention that for fixed w the problem of searching for a *deterministic* simple w-path of a given length k can be done in PTIME by a straightforward marking algorithm.

3   Fixed-Parameter Tractability

The following notion is from Downey & Fellows [3] though it can already be found – without giving it a name – in Monien [5–p. 240, the two paragraphs before and after Th. 1, resp.].

Definition 1 (fixed-parameter tractability [5], [3]). *A computational problem consisting of pairs $\langle x, k \rangle$ is fixed-parameter tractable in the parameter k if there is a deciding algorithm for it having run-time $f(k) \cdot |x|^c$ for some recursive function f and some constant c.*

We use the following characterization of FPT $\cap$ NP by Cai, Chen, Downey & Fellows [2]:

Theorem 1 (Cai et al. [2]). *A language $L \in \mathrm{NP}$ consisting of pairs $\langle x, k \rangle$ is fixed-parameter tractable in the parameter k iff there exists a recursive function $s(k)$ and a PTIME computable language C such that $\langle x, k \rangle \in L \iff \exists y \leq s(k)$: $\langle x, k, y \rangle \in C$.*

We call the function s the *witness size function*, and the language C the *witness checker*, and we say that these two together form an FPT *guess and check protocol* for L.

Theorem 2. *For every $w \geq 1$ the problem* BANDWIDTH-w-PATH *is fixed parameter tractable in the parameter k, likewise its variations. More specifically, there exists an* FPT *guess and check protocol for it with a witness size function $s(k) = \binom{k}{2} \cdot \log k$ and a witness checker having running time $O(w \cdot k^2 \cdot |E|^w \cdot |V|^w)$.*

Proof. We first consider the case $w = 1$, i.e. the LONGEST PATH problem. Afterwards we will see that the algorithm is generalizable to the BANDWIDTH-w-PATH problem for $w > 1$. We state an FPT guess and check protocol for LONGEST PATH with the witness size function $s(k) = \binom{k}{2} \cdot \log k$ and a witness checker with runtime $O(k^2 \cdot |E| \cdot |V|)$.

$a_{2,1}$	$a_{2,2}$	$a_{2,3}$	$a_{2,4}$	$= a_2 =$	1	1	0	0
$a_{3,1}$	$a_{3,2}$	$a_{2,3}$		$= a_3 =$	1	2	0	
$a_{4,1}$	$a_{4,2}$			$= a_4 =$	2	0		
$a_{5,1}$				$= a_5 =$	0			

Fig. 5. Witness table for a simple path of length 4

Let a digraph G with n vertices be given. We want to find out whether the graph contains a simple path $p = (v_1, \ldots, v_{k+1})$ of length k. We will work with *witnesses*. The intention of a witness is to tell the algorithm in the moment when it is trying to build an initial segment $(v_1, \ldots, v_i)$ of the simple path of length k which are the future vertices $v_{i+1}, \ldots, v_{k+1}$ of the simple path – so that the algorithm does not pick one of these future vertices as a part of the initial segment. Unfortunately, we cannot use the tuple $(v_1, \ldots, v_{k+1})$ as a witness, because that way we would have n^{k+1} potential witnesses, so we would need at least $(k+1) \log(n)$ bits to encode them, a number growing in n. But for the FPT guess and check protocol we need some witness size function $s(k)$ only dependent on k.

We choose the following kind of witnesses. A *witness* for such a simple path of length k consists of $k(k+1)/2 = \binom{k+1}{2}$ numbers $a_{i,j} \in \{0, 1, \ldots, k\}$, for $2 \leq i \leq k+1$ and $j \in \{1, \ldots, k-i+2\}$. The witness can be visualized as a half-matrix a, see Figure 5. Let a_i for $2 \leq i \leq k+1$ be the tuple $(a_{i,1}, \ldots, a_{i,k-i+2})$.

We can restrict the witnesses to have these properties: a_i contains only numbers $\leq i - 1$ and at least one 0. There is some redundancy, for example $a_{k+1,1}$ will always be 0. Nevertheless, the order of magnitude of the witness size function s(k) does not seem to be improvable by these "little savings".

For every witness a the main algorithm C does the following: In each of the k steps $i = 2, 3, \ldots, k + 1$ it uses a_i to compute for every vertex v a value $f_{a,i}(v)$, defined further below, which is either a vertex or has the value **nil** (standing for "not existing"), and stores this function for use in the following steps. The following pseudo code shows the main structure of the algorithm.

Main algorithm C

  Input: graph G, number $k \leq |G|$, and a witness a

  for every vertex v set $f_{a,1}(v) := v$;

  for $i = 2, \ldots, k + 1$ do

      for every vertex v in G do

         compute $f_{a,i}(v)$ and store it;

         if $i = k + 1$ and $f_{a,i}(v) \neq$ **nil** ACCEPT and STOP;

    REJECT and STOP;

The computation of the value $f_{a,i}(v)$ – which is either **nil** or a vertex – is described in the pseudo code below. Assume w.l.o.g. that for each vertex there is a list of incoming edges (ending with the **nil** list element) in which the edges appear according to the order on the vertices. As a useful abbreviation let $f_{a,i}^d(v)$ for a vertex v and d with $1 \leq d \leq i + 1$ be defined via

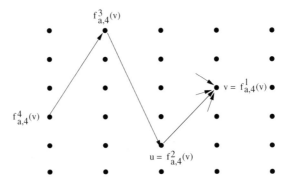

Fig. 6. A "backward path", starting in v

$f_{a,i}^1(v) := v$, $f_{a,i}^2(v) := f_{a,i}(v)$, and $f_{a,i}^{d+1}(v) := f_{a,i-1}^d(f_{a,i}(v))$ with this value being **nil** in case $f_{a,i}(v)$ or $f_{a,i-1}^d(f_{a,i}(v))$ equals **nil**. Intuitively, $f_{a,i}^d(v)$ follows – starting in v – for growing $d = 1, \ldots, i+1$ the "backward path" given by the $f_{a,i-d}$-functions, see Figure 6. The upper index d numbers the vertices of this path, and the witness elements $a_{i,j} \geq 0$ will refer to this numbering. The information provided by $a_{i,j} \geq 0$ means that the $a_{i,j}$-th vertex in the "backward path" starting with a vertex u is the "reason" to dismiss the j-th attempt to assign a possible predecessor u of v to $f_{a,i}(v)$. (The set F in the following pseudo code collects such "reasons".)

By easy induction on i, the following invariant will be guaranteed for every witness a, every i with $2 \leq i \leq k+1$, and every vertex v:

(Inv1) If $f_{a,i}(v) \neq$ **nil** then the "backward path" $(f_{a,i}^i(v), \ldots, f_{a,i}^2(v), f_{a,i}^1(v))$ is a simple path of length $i-1$.

Computing $f_{a,i}(v)$

Input: i, a, and v. Already computed: $f_{a,1}, \ldots, f_{a,i-1}$.

set $F := \{v\}$;

set $j := 1$;

if there are no incoming edges for v set $f_{a,i}(v) :=$ **nil** and STOP;

set $e = (u, v)$ to be the first edge incoming to v;

while $e \neq$ **nil** do

    if $f_{a,i-1}(u) \neq$ **nil** and

        none of the vertices $f_{a,i-1}^1(u), f_{a,i-1}^2(u), \ldots, f_{a,i-1}^i(u)$ is in F do

        set $c := a_{i,j}$;

        if $c = 0$

            set $f_{a,i}(v) := u$ and STOP;

        otherwise

            set $F := F \cup \{f_{a,i-1}^c(u)\}$;

            set $j := j + 1$;

    set $e = (u, v) :=$ next edge going into v;

set $f_{a,i}(v) :=$ **nil** and STOP;

Verification of the main algorithm C: If the algorithm accepts, then it has found for this witness a a vertex v such that $f_{a,k+1}(v) \neq$ **nil**. By invariant (Inv1), case $i = k + 1$, the backward path starting in v is a simple path of length k.

On the other hand assume that there is a simple path of length k in G. Let $s = (s_1, \ldots, s_{k+1})$ be the lexicographically smallest among them (largest weight on s_{k+1}, unlike, for example, with decimal numbers). With the knowledge of this path and its vertices we will construct a witness b such that the main algorithm will accept for witness b.

Constructing b

Input: $s_1, \ldots, s_{k+1}$.

for every vertex v set $f_{b_1,1}(v) = v$;

for $i = 2$ to $k + 1$ do

    set $e = (u, s_i) :=$ first edge going into s_i;

    set $F = \{s_i\}$;

    set $j := 1$;

    repeat

        while $f_{b_{i-1},i-1}(u) = \textbf{nil}$

        or some of the vertices $f^1_{b_{i-1},i-1}(u), \ldots, f^i_{b_{i-1},i-1}(u)$ is in F

            set $e = (u, s_i) :=$ next edge going into s_i;

        if there is a $c \in \{1, \ldots, i\}$ such that $f^c_{b_{i-1},i-1}(u) \in \{s_{i+2}, \ldots, s_{k+1}\}$

            set $b_{i,j} := c$ for the smallest such c;

            set $F := F \cup \{f^c_{b_{i-1},i-1}(u)\}$;

            set $j := j + 1$;

    until there is no such c;

    $b_{i,j} := 0$

    compute $f_{b_{,},i}(v)$ for all vertices v;

The crucial invariant kept by this construction is the following:

(Inv2) For every i with $2 \leq i \leq k + 1$ it holds: $f_{b,i}(s_i) = s_{i-1}$.

The invariant holds via induction on i: the construction of b_i prevents $f_{b,i}(s_i)$ from choosing one of the vertices $s_{i+1}, \ldots, s_{k+1}$ which will be needed in the future but which would be – without the witness – unknown at step i. Because there are at most $k-i+1$ such vertices the repeat loop will always terminate and, moreover, the part b_i of the witness has sufficient size. For every $2 \leq i \leq k+1$ it is guaranteed that the computation of $f_{b,i}(s_i)$ will terminate, i.e. will be not-**nil**, because at least (s_{i-1}, s_i) is a suitable edge, and this will be the first suitable edge which $f_{b,i}(s_i)$ will find, i.e. $f_{b,i}(s_i) = s_{i-1}$, because otherwise $s = (s_1, \ldots, s_{k+1})$ would not be lexicographically minimal. Invariant (Inv2) implies for $i = k+1$ that the backward path $(f_{b,k+1}^{k+1}(s_{k+1}), \ldots, f_{b,k+1}^2(s_{k+1}), f_{b,k+1}^1(s_{k+1}))$ at s_{k+1} equals $s = (s_1, \ldots, s_{k+1})$, i.e. the main algorithm C will accept the input graph for this witness b via a non-**nil** value of $f_{b,k+1}$ at vertex s_{k+1}. This finishes the correctness proof for the FPT guess and check protocol.

The running time of all $f_{a_i}(v)$ for a fixed i is $O(k \cdot |E|)$ as it is dominated by checking the backward path of length $\leq k$ for each edge incoming to v (we ignore some $\log(k)$ factors for the comparison algorithms). Therefore, the main algorithm C has runtime $O(k^2 \cdot |V| \cdot |E|)$. Representing all witnesses can be done with $\binom{k}{2} \cdot \log k$ bits, i.e. the witness size function can be chosen this way (note that the diagonal of the half matrix does not need to be stored – it can be assumed to consist of 0's). This finishes the proof that an FPT guess and check protocol exists for LONGEST PATH.

Cases $w > 1$. We first do a graph transformation. From the given graph G construct the following graph G': Consider all w-tuples $(v_1, \ldots, v_w)$ of vertices of G. Make such a tuple a vertex of G' if the tuple represents a directed w-clique in G, i.e. (v_i, v_j) is an edge in G for $1 \leq i < j \leq w$. The edges in G' are defined to consist of the pairs of such w-cliques of the special form $((v_1, \ldots, v_w), (v_2, \ldots, v_w, v_{w+1}))$ such that also (v_1, v_{w+1}) is an edge in G. We have the property: G contains a simple w-path of length k iff G' contains a 1-path of length k. The witness checker consists therefore of this graph transformation and subsequently the checking algorithm C for $w = 1$ running on G'. In total the checking takes $O(w \cdot |V|^w \cdot |E|^w)$ time, the first w stems from a slightly higher comparison time for tuples. The witnesses size function does not change.

Variants: For the vertex disjoint case with $w > 1$ it is not enough to do the graph transformation, one has to go inside the checking algorithm C and maintain the vertex lists appropriately. **q.e.d.**

4   Conclusions and Open Questions

We introduced for every $w \geq 1$ the NP-complete problem BANDWIDTH-w-PATH and showed that it is fixed-parameter tractable in the length parameter k by presenting an FPT guess and check protocol for it, according to the characterization of Cai et al. [2].

As an open problem we suggest to study whether the witness size function, especially for the case LONGEST PATH, can be improved from the quasi-quadratic function $\binom{k}{2} \log k$ to some quasi-linear function, for example by the methods of Monien [5] or Alon, Yuster & Zwick [1].

References

1. Alon, N., Yuster, R., Zwick, U.: Color-Coding. J. ACM **42** 4 (1995) 844–856
2. Cai, L., Chen, J., Downey, R.G., Fellows, M.R.: On the Structure of Parameterized Problems in NP. Inf. Comput. **123** 1 (1995) 38–49

3. Downey, R.G., Fellows, M.R.: Fixed-Parameter Intractability. Structure in Complexity Theory Conference (1992) 36–49
4. Garey, M.R., Johnson, D.S.: Computers and Intractability. Freeman, Ney York (1979)
5. Monien, B.: How to Find Long Paths Efficiently. Annals of Discrete Mathematics **25** (1985) 239–254
6. Proskurowski, A., Telle, J.A.: Classes of Graphs with Restricted Interval Models. Discrete Mathematics & Theoretical Computer Science **3** 4 (1999) 167–176

Graph Searching and Search Time

Franz J. Brandenburg and Stephanie Herrmann

Lehrstuhl für Informatik, Universität Passau, 94030 Passau, Germany
brandenb@informatik.uni-passau.de

Abstract. Graph searching is the game of capturing a fugitive by a team of searchers in a network. There are equivalent characterizations in terms of path-width, interval thickness, and vertex separation. So far the interest has mainly focused on the search number of a graph, which is the minimal the number of searchers to win the game, and accordingly on the width and the thickness. These parameters measure the needed resources and correspond to space complexity. As its dual, we introduce the search time, which has not yet been studied in graph searching. We prove that all main results on graph searching can be generalized to include search time, such as monotone or recontamination free graph searching, and the characterizations in terms of path-width, interval graphs, and vertex separation, for which we introduce appropriate length parameters. We establish the NP-completeness of both search-width and search-time. Finally we investigate the speed-up by an extra searcher. There are 'good' classes of graphs where a single extra searcher reduces the search time to one half and 'bad' ones where some extra searchers are no real help.

1 Introduction

Graph searching has been introduced by Parsons [26] as a game on graphs, where an invisible fugitive moving fast along paths shall be captured by a team of searchers. Alternatively, we may think of a network whose edges are contaminated with a gas, and the objective is to clean the network. However, the gas immediately recontaminates cleaned edges, if its expansion is not blocked by valves at the vertices, and the fugitive may re-enter already searched parts of the graph, if there are unguarded paths. Several variants of graph searching have been investigated and equivalent characterization have been elaborated, relating graph searching e.g., to path-width and tree-width, see e.g. [2], [3], [9], [11], [12], [13], [14], [19], [20], [21], [25], [23], [26].

In a move a searcher is placed at a vertex, and searchers are removed from other vertices of the graph. A searcher at a vertex v guards all paths through v and prevents the fugitive or the gas to pass. In *node searching* an edge is cleared if simultaneously both ends are visited by a searcher. In edge searching an edge is cleared by a sweep of a searcher along the edge. Mixed versions allow the clearance of an edge by either mode. These versions are closely related [21]. In other versions of graph searching the fugitive is visible [28] or it is lazy [9]. Then the number of searchers is directly related to the tree-width of the graph. Yet

J. Wiedermann et al. (Eds.): SOFSEM 2006, LNCS 3831, pp. 197–206, 2006.

another variant with mobility restrictions of the fugitive has been studied in [15] to model issues of privacy in distributed systems.

The classical goal of graph searching is a sequence of moves to win the game and definitively capturing the fugitive while minimizing the maximal number of searchers needed at any time. This minimum value is the *search number* of a graph G. The search number aims at minimizing the used resources. As such it corresponds to space complexity. It has been shown that the search number equals the interval thickness of G and is one above than the path-width and the search number of G [11], [19], [21]. Thus graph searching corresponds directly to other important graph parameters. Fomin et al. [13], [14] have introduced the expenditure as another optimality criterion. The expenditure minimizes the total payment for the searchers and equals the sum of the lengths of the intervals in the canonical interval representation of the graph. Finally, Chang [8] has investigated the single step edge search problem. Then node searching and edge searching differ essentially. Every graph with n vertices and m edges can be searched in one step by n node searchers, and m edge searchers are necessary and sometimes not sufficient. Here every odd cycle needs one extra searcher, and it is NP-hard to determine the minimal number of single step edge searchers [8].

In this paper we consider time complexity and introduce the *length* as a new cost measure in graph searching. How fast can a team of k searchers search a graph, and conversely how many searchers are needed to search a graph in time t. This induces parameterized double-complexity and time-space trade-offs, which parallels traditional approaches in computational complexity [30]. And it introduces time as a graph parameter in representations with restricted path-width or interval thickness. In general, if k searchers are sufficient to search a connected graph of size n and $n \geq 2$, then the search time ranges between $\lceil (n - k)/(k - 1) \rceil + 1$ and $n + 1 - k$. Hence, there is at most a factor of $k - 1$ between the fastest and the slowest search strategy, provided k searchers suffice.

The objective of this paper is a generalization of the main results on graph searching to include search time. This can be accomplished completely. First, we prove the monotonicity of graph searching or graph searching without recontamination. As a consequence the graph searching problem is in NP, and optimal graph searching is NP-hard. For the search number this has been shown in [25] and for the search time it is proved in Section 3. However, while search number is fixed parameter tractable, this is yet unknown for search time. Secondly, we establish the equivalence between graph searching and path-width, interval thickness and search number, both for time and space parameters. Finally, we consider the speed-up by an extra searcher. There are classes of graphs where an extra searcher reduces the search time roughly to one half, and there are other classes of graphs where some extra searchers do not really help in saving time.

The paper is organized as follows: In Section 2 we introduce the concepts from graph searching. We establish the monotonicity in Section 3 and prove the NP-hardness. Section 4 shows the equivalence between graph searching, path-width, interval thickness and search number with the generalization to time or length. Finally, in Section 5, we discuss the speed-up by an extra searcher.

2   Preliminaries

We consider node searching on simple, connected, undirected graphs $G = (V, E)$ with a set of vertices V and a set of edges E. For convenience there are no loops and no multiple edges. By n we denote the size of G, and we assume $n \geq 2$, which excludes trivial cases.

The rules for node searching are as follows: Initially, all edges are contaminated and in the end all edges must be cleared. In a move at time $i = 1, 2, \ldots$ searchers are placed on vertices, or searchers are removed from other vertices. In a move many searchers can be placed or removed, but not simultaneously at a single vertex. An edge is *cleared* at time i, if both endnodes are visited by a searcher and both searchers remain at least one unit of time. A contaminated edge is not cleared if a searcher is placed at one endnode and simultaneously the last searcher is removed from the other endnode. A clear edge e is instantaneously *recontaminated*, if there is a path from a contaminated edge to e without a searcher on a vertex of that path. A *search strategy* is a sequence of moves that results in all edges being simultaneously clear. Then the search game is won. A search strategy describes the computation on a graph by the rules of node searching. For linear graph languages, i.e., the sets of graphs generated by linear graph grammars, the search strategy can be represented by a finite state graph automaton, which accepts the linear graph language [7].

Our formal definition generalizes the concepts of Bienstock and Seymour [3] and Fomin et al. [13], [14].

Definition 1. *A search strategy σ on a (connected) graph $G = (V, E)$ is a sequence of pairs $\sigma = ((C_0, B_0), (C_1, B_1), \ldots, (C_t, B_t))$ such that:*

1. *For $i = 0, \ldots, t$, $C_i \subseteq E$ is the set of clear edges and $B_i \subseteq V$ is the set of boundary vertices which are visited by searchers at time i. The edges from $E - C_i$ are contaminated.*
2. *(initial state) $C_0 = \emptyset$ and $B_0 = \emptyset$. All edges are contaminated.*
3. *(final state) $C_t = E$ and $B_t = \emptyset$. All edges are cleared.*
4. *(place and remove searchers and clear edges) For $i = 0, \ldots, t - 1$ there are sets of vertices $P_i \subseteq V - B_i$ and $R_i \subseteq B_i$ such that $B_{i+1} = B_i - R_i \cup P_i$. Then searchers are places at the vertices from P_i and are removed from R_i. The set of cleared edges is $C_{i+1} = C_i \cup \{\{u, v\} \in E \mid u, v \in B_{i+1}\} - \{\{u, v\} \in C_i \mid$ there is a path from a vertex w with an edge $\{w, w'\} \in E - C_i$ to u or v such that no vertex on the path is in $B_{i+1}\}$.*

Let $width(\sigma) = max\{|B_i| \mid i = 0, \ldots, t\}$ and $length(\sigma) = t - 1$ be the maximum number of searchers and the number of moves of σ. Note that we discard the last move, which only removes searchers.

A search strategy σ is *monotone*, if $C_{i-1} \subseteq C_i$ for every $i = 1, \ldots, t$. At other places the term progressive [3], [14], augmenting [13], and recontamination free [21], [23] is used.

Definition 2. *For a connected graph G with at least two vertices and integers k and t let search-width$_G(t)$ be the least width(σ) for all search strategies σ with length$(\sigma) \leq t$ and let search-time$_G(k)$ be the least length(σ) for all search strategies σ with width$(\sigma) \leq k$. Set search-width$_G(t)$ resp. search-time$_G(k)$ to infinity, if there is no such search strategy.*

A search strategy σ is called *time-space optimal*, if width$(\sigma) = $ search-width$_G(t)$ with length$(\sigma) = t$ for a given t, or if length$(\sigma) = $ search-length$_G(k)$ with width$(\sigma) = k$ for a given k.

search-width$_G(t)$ is the least number of searchers that can search G in time at most t (with at most $t+1$ moves), and search-time$_G(k)$ is the shortest time such that at most k searchers can search G. Thus, we can parameterize search-width in terms of search-time, and vice versa. Clearly, search-width$_G(t) = k$ implies search-time$_G(k) \leq t$, and search-time$_G(k) = t$ implies search-width$_G(t) \leq k$.

The commonly known node search number equals search-width$_G(t)$ for all sufficiently large t, and $t \leq n$ by the monotonicity. Search-time has not yet been studied for node search. The single step edge search in [8] is different.

Example 1. Consider an $n \times m$ grid G with $m \leq n$ and $m \geq 2$. Then G can be searched by $m + 1$ searchers, and this is minimal. $m + 1$ searchers search G by a plane-sweep in time $m * (n - 1)$ and with $m * (n - 1) + 1$ moves first placing m searchers at the vertices of the leftmost row and the $m + 1$-st searcher in the second row. In every further move one searcher is *free* and is placed at a new vertex in the next row. In the final move all searchers are removed.

Here $m + 2$ searchers can do much better visiting two new vertices at every move and so reducing the search time to $m(n - 1)/2$, and $2m$ searchers can win the game in time $n - 1$ searching a new row in every move.

3   Monotonicity

Recomputations must be avoided in the design of time efficient algorithms. Classical paradigms are the greedy method and dynamic programming. In graph searching recomputations are necessary after a recontamination of cleared edges. This can be avoided, as was first shown by LaPaugh [23] for edge searching. The existence of monotone or progressive search strategies with the same number of searchers has been proved for several versions of graph searching and cost measures, see [3], [14], [13], [21], [28]. We follow the technique of Bienstock and Seymour [3] and adapt the construction from Fomin and Golovach [13], [14]. This is a key requirement for the characterizations in terms of the graph representations in Section 4.

For a subset of edges $X \subseteq E$ of a graph $G = (V, E)$ let $V(X) \subseteq V$ be the set of endnodes of the edges from X and let $B(X) = V(X) \cap V(E - X)$ denote the *boundary vertices* of X. Every boundary vertex of X is incident to at least one edge in X and an edge not in X. v is an *inner vertex* of X, if all incident edges of v are in X.

We consider clews in graphs of a special structure. Let $G^0 = (V, E^0)$ be obtained by adding a loop $\{v, v\}$ at every vertex of a graph $G = (V, E)$. A *clew* in G^0 is a sequence $\gamma = (X_0, X_1, \ldots, X_t)$ of subsets of E^0 such that the following holds:

1. $X_0 = \emptyset$ and $X_t = E^0$.
2. for $i = 1, \ldots, t$, $|V(X_i) - V(X_{i-1})| \le k$ for some $k \ge 1$.
3. for $i = 1, \ldots, t$, if $v \in V(X_i)$ then the loop at v belongs to X_i.

The *width* of γ is $\max\{|B(X_i)| \,|\, i = 1, \ldots, t\}$, the *length* is $t - 1$ and the *weight* is $\sum_{i=0}^{t} |B(X_i)|$.

A clew is *monotone* if $X_0 \subseteq X_1 \subseteq \ldots \subseteq X_t$ and $|V(X_i) - V(X_{i-1})| \ge 1$ for $i = 1, \ldots, t$.

Our clews are extensions of the ones in [14] with up to k vertices between $V(X_i)$ and $V(X_{i-1})$ and at least one for monotone clews. Fomin and Golovach enforce $k = 1$ which implies long clews of length at least $n - 1$.

Our first theorem establishes the existence of a monotone search strategy with the same width and length as a given strategy.

Theorem 1. *For every (connected, simple) graph G and integers $k, t \ge 1$ the following statements are equivalent:*

1. *there is a search strategy σ with $width(\sigma) \le k$ and $length(\sigma) \le t$*
2. *there is a clew γ on G^0 with width at most k and length at most t*
3. *there is a monotone clew γ on G^0 with width at most k and length at most t*
4. *there is a monotone search strategy σ with $width(\sigma) \le k$ and $length(\sigma) \le t$.*

Proof (Sketch). We argue as in the monotonicity proofs in [3], [13], [14]. The monotone strategy can be obtained from the 'lightest' clew, which is the clew with the least weight and such that the sum of the size of the sets of edges is a secondary criterion.

As a consequence, we can restrict ourselves to monotone graph searching. There are linear bounds on the lengths of optimal search strategies, and graph searching is in NP. Moreover, good and bad searches differ at most by a factor of $(k - 1)$ in time and by a factor of t in width. This comes from the fact that in the first move at most k vertices are visited and in any other move at most $k - 1$ new vertices can be visited, since at least one searcher must remain on an 'old' vertex by the connectivity. The upper bound comes from monotone graph searching.

Theorem 2. *For every connected graph G with $|G| = n$ and integers k and t such that k is at least the search number of G there is a (monotone) search strategy σ such that*

$$\lceil (n - k)/(k - 1) \rceil + 1 \le length(\sigma) \le n + 1 - k \quad \text{and} \tag{1}$$

$$\lceil n - 1/t \rceil + 1 \le width(\sigma) \le n. \tag{2}$$

From the complexity point of view graph searching is NP-hard. It has been shown that whether or not the search number of a graph is less than a given bound k is NP-complete, see [24] and [25]. The computation of the search number remains NP-hard even for chordal graphs [17], star-like graphs [17], bipartite [22] and cobipartite (i.e. complement of bipartite) graphs [1], and for planar graphs of maximum degree three [29], whereas it can be computed in polynomial time, e.g., for cographs [6], permutation graphs [5], split graphs [17], [22], and graphs of bounded treewidth [4]. Hence, it is NP-hard whether or not search-$width_G(t) \leq k$ for $t = n$, or with unbounded time.

Concerning search-time, Chang [8] has considered edge searching in a single step. In unit time a searcher can sweep an edge and search it. Hence, at least m searchers are necessary to search a graph with m edges. This number may not suffice. A fugitive can hide between two edge searchers, if they leave a gap. For example, a path of length l cannot be searched by l searchers, if they move in the same direction. In particular, an odd cycle needs one more searcher than its length. In this model, Chang states that it is NP-hard, whether or not k searchers can search a graph in a single step. This result cannot be transferred to node searching, where n searchers are necessary and sufficient to search a connected graph of size n. Hence, search time leads to a distinction between node and edge searching.

For independent parameters k and t we show the NP-hardness both for search-time and for search-width by a reduction from 3-PARTITION [16]. Given an instance of 3-PARTITION with $3m$ items and a total size of mB, the size $s(a)$ of every item is transformed into a clique of that size, and every vertex is connected to a distinguished center to establish connectivity. Then $B + 1$ searchers can search the graph in time m if and only if there is a solution of the instance of 3-PARTITION.

Theorem 3. *For connected graphs G and integers k and t it is NP-complete whether or not search-time$_G(k) \leq t$ and search-width$_G(t) \leq k$.*

From the equivalence between graphs searching and path-width and interval thickness and 2D layouts established in the next section we can conclude the NP-completeness of the following question:

Corollary 1. *For (connected) graphs and integers k and t it is NP-complete whether or not there is a path-decomposition, an interval representation, or a 2D layout of G of width k and length t.*

The computation of the width is known to be *fixed parameter tractable* FPT [10], and for fixed k there are linear time algorithms to compute the search number, the path-width of the interval thickness of a graph. We don't know of a similar result for search time or the length of the graph representations. It would be interesting to see how far the NP-hardness for the length goes, when the width is chosen freely. In particular, is the width computable in polynomial time for bounded length? Is search-time fixed parameter tractable?

4 Path-Width, Interval Thickness, and Search Number

In this section we generalize well-know characterizations of graph searching in terms of particular graph representations. At the first glance the correspondence between the search number of a graph, its path-width, interval thickness and vertex separation is surprising. First, we recall the necessary definitions, and add the notion of length.

The notions of tree-width and path-width were introduced by Robertson and Seymour [27].

Definition 3. *The path-decomposition of a graph* $G = (V, E)$ *is a sequence* $(X_1, X_2, \ldots, X_r)$ *of subsets of* V *such that*

– $\bigcup_{i=1}^{r} X_i = V$
– *for every edge* $e = \{u, v\}$ *there is an* i *with* $u, v \in X_i$
– *for all* i, j, k *with* $1 \leq i < j < k \leq r$: $X_i \cap X_k \subseteq X_j$.

The *width* of a path-decomposition $(X_1, X_2, \ldots, X_r)$ is $\max_{1 \leq i \leq r} |X_i| - 1$, and the *length* is r. For integers k and t the parameterized path-width and path-length of a graph G are the minimum width over all path-decompositions of length at most t and the minimum length over all path-decompositions of width at most k. The (absolute) path-width of a graph is the minimum path-width over all lengths t. Clearly, $t \leq n$ and in fact $t \leq n - k + 1$, where k is the absolute path-width. The absolute path-length is meaningless, since it is one for $k = n$.

Interval graphs have first been defined by Hajos [18]. The interval representation of a graph G consists of an open interval $I_v = (l_v, r_v)$ on the real line with integer boundaries l_v, r_v for every vertex v and such that for every edge $\{u, v\}$ the intervals I_u and I_v overlap.

The *thickness* (or width) of an interval representation is the maximal number of intervals that overlap at some point. The interval thickness is the smallest thickness over all interval representations. The *length* of an interval representation is the maximal difference between interval boundaries. This is $r_v - l_u$, where r_v is is maximal for all vertices v und l_u is minimal for all vertices u. For integers k and t the *interval-thickness* and the *interval-length* of a graph G are the minimum thickness over all interval representations of length at most t, and the minimum length over all interval representations of thickness at most k. The (absolute) interval thickness of a graph is the minimum interval-thickness over all lengths t, where $t \leq n$ suffices. The absolute interval-length is meaningless, since it is one for $k = n$, where G is seen as a subgraph of the complete graph K_n.

Finally, we consider the vertex separation of a graph and its relation to graph searching as established by Ellis et al. [11]. The vertex separation uses a linear layout of the graph, which is folded into a 2D layout for a more compact representation in X-dimension.

A *linear layout* of a graph G is a one to one mapping L of the vertices into the set $\{1, \ldots, n\}$. Now identify each vertex with its position. For every i consider the set of left endpoints of edges $\{u, v\}$ with $u \leq i$ and with a right endpoint to the right $v > i$. The *vertex separation* of G with respect to L is the maximum size of the above sets of left endpoints over all positions i. Thus at every position p count the number of vertices to the left of and including p which have an edge to a vertex to the right of p.

For a more compact representation we fold the linear layout in two dimensions. Let f be a one to one function with $f(i) = (x, y)$ with integers x and y and $x \geq 1$ and such that $i < i'$ implies $f(i') = (x', y')$ with $x < x'$ or $x = x'$ and $y < y'$. Thus f transforms the linear into a lexicographic order.

The *2D layout* of a graph is obtained by the composition of L and f. The *width* of a 2D layout at some x is the number of vertices (x', y') with $x = x'$ plus the number of vertices (x', y') with $x' < x$ and such that there is an edge of G which is mapped to $((x', y'), (x'', y''))$ and $x'' > x$. In other words, we count the vertices in the x-th column and add the number of vertices to the left of the x-th column with an edge to the right of the x-th column. The *length* of the 2D-layout is the maximal x-coordinate.

For integers k and t the *2D vertex separation width* and the *2D vertex separation length* of a graph G are the minimum width over all 2D layouts of length at most t, and the minimum length over all 2D layouts of width at most k. The vertex separation of a graph is the minimum 2D vertex separation over all lengths t. Here $t = n$ suffices, which is the known linear layout. The absolute vertex separation length is meaningless, since all vertices are mapped to a single column with coordinates $(1, y)$ for the vertices $y = 1, \ldots, n$ of G.

With these extensions of the measures on the path-width, interval thickness, and vertex separation, we obtain the following characterization.

Theorem 4. *For a connected graph G and parameters k and t the following are equivalent:*

1. *search-width$_G(t) = k$ and search-length$_G(k) = t$.*
2. *path-width$_G(t) = k - 1$ and path-length$_G(k) = t$.*
3. *interval thickness$_G(t) = k$ and interval thickness$_G(k) = t$.*
4. *vertex-separation$_G(t) = k - 1$ and vertex-length$_G(k) = t$.*

Proof (Sketch). For the proof we use the monotonicity of graph searching and follow the constructions from [11], [19], [20], [21]. For a path decomposition $(X_1, X_2, \ldots, X_r)$ of G let $(Y_1, Y_2, \ldots, Y_r)$ be a 2D layout with $Y_1 = X_1$ and $Y_i = X_i - \cup_{j<i} X_j$ for $j = 2, \ldots, r$, and construct the interval representation with $I_v = (l_v, r_v)$ for every vertex v, where l_v and r_v are the first resp. last occurrences of v in the sets X_i from the path decomposition, and vice versa. Finally, let $X_0 = \emptyset$ and in the i-th move place searchers on the vertices from $X_i - \cup_{j<i} X_j$ and remove searchers from all vertices in $\cup_{j<i} X_j$ which have no edge to a vertex in $\cup_{q \geq i} X_q$, and vice versa. Then the width and the length are preserved by these constructions.

5   Speed-Up

If k searchers can search a connected graph G of size n in time t, how much faster can $k + 1$ searchers do? From the observation in Section 3 it is known that good and bad search strategies differ at most by a factor of $k - 1$.

Clearly, increasing the path-width by a factor of q reduces the path-length accordingly. Hence, if k searchers can search a (connected) graph G in time t, then for every integer $q \geq 2$, $qk - (q - 1)$ searchers can search G in time $\lceil t/q \rceil$. In particular, $2k - 1$ searchers are twice as fast as k. However, there are classes of graphs where a single extra searcher achieves a twofold speed-up. Conversely, there a classes of graphs where some extra searchers do not help.

Theorem 5. *There are classes of graphs $G_{i,i \in I}$ and $H_{i,i \in I}$ with search-number k_i such that*

1. *G_i is searched by k_i searchers in time $t_i = |G_i| + 1 - k_i$, and $k_i + 1$ searchers can search G_i in time $1 + \lceil t_i/2 \rceil$.*
2. *search-time$_{H_i}(k_i)$ = search-time$_{H_i}(2k_i - 1)$.*

Proof. First consider the set of k-1-paths, which are degenerated k-1-trees, see [1]. These graphs consist of a sequence of cliques of size k-1 and can be searched by k searchers. k is also the lower bound. Then search-time$_G(k) = n - k + 1$ and search-time$_G(k + 1) \leq \lceil (n - k)/2 \rceil$. Observe that $n \times m$ grids have a similar behaviour.

Secondly, consider graphs C_q which are a 'star' of q-cliques. Thus the graphs have $pq + 1$ vertices with a center Z and p disjoint q-*cliques*. Z is connected with every other vertex. Then C_q needs exactly $q + 1$ searchers, which search C_q in p moves. A single or up to q-1 extra searchers do not really help since search-time$_{C_q}(k) = p$ for every k with $q + 1 \leq k \leq 2q$.

6   Conclusion

We have introduced the notion of time or length to graph searching, path-width, interval thickness and search number and have shown that the major results can be generalized to include time.

This introduces a speed-up by extra searchers, which raises the question which classes of graphs have good and which have a bad speed-up. What does this mean for the path-width?

References

1. Arnborg, S., Corneil, D.G., and Proskurowski, A.: Complexity of Finding Embeddings in a k-Tree. SIAM J. Alg. Disc. Meth. **8** (1987) 277–284
2. Bienstock, D.: Graph Searching, Path-Width, Tree-Width and Related Problems (a Survey). DIMACS Series in Discrete Mathematics and Theoretical Computer Science, American Mathematical Society, Providence, RI **5** (1991) 33–49
3. Bienstock, D., and Seymour, P.D.: Monotonicity in Graph Searching. J. Algorithms **12** (1991) 239–245
4. Bodlaender, H.L.: A Linear Time Algorithm for Finding Tree-Decompositions of Small Treewidth. SIAM J. Comput. **25** (1996) 1305–1317
5. Bodlaender, H.L., Kloks, T., and Kratsch, D.: Treewidth and Pathwidth of Permutation Graphs. SIAM J. Discrete Math. **8** (1995) 606–616

6. Bodlaender, H.L., and Möhring, R.: The Pathwidth and Treewidth of Cographs. SIAM J. Discrete Math. **6** (1993) 181–188
7. Brandenburg, F.J., and Skodinis, K.: Finite Graph Automata for Linear and Boundary Graph Languages. Theoret. Computer Sci. **332** (2005) 199–232
8. Chang, R.S.: Single Step Graph Search Problem. Inform. Proc. Letters **40** (1991) 107–111
9. Dendris, N.D., Kirousis, L.M., and Thilikos, D. M.: Fugitive-Search Games on Graphs and Related Parameters. Theoret. Computer Sci. **172** (1997) 233–254
10. Downey, R.G., and Fellows, M.R.: Parametrized Complexity. Springer, Heidelberg (1999)
11. Ellis, J.A., Sudborough, I.H., and Turner, J.: The Vertex Separation and Search Number of a Graph. Inform. and Comput. **113** (1994) 50–79
12. Fomin, F.: Helicopter Search Problems, Bandwidth and Pathwidth. Discrete Appl. Math. **85** (1998) 59–71
13. Fomin, F.V.: Searching Expenditure and Interval Graphs. Discrete Appl. Math. **135** (2004) 97–104
14. Fomin, F.V., and Golovach, P.A.: Graph Searching and Interval Completion. SIAM J. Discrete Math. **13** (2000) 454–464
15. Franklin, M., Galil, Z., and Yung, M.: Eavesdropping Games: a Graph-Theoretic Approach to Privacy in Distributed Systems. J. Assoc. Comput. Mach. **47** (2000) 225–243
16. Garey, M.R., and Johnson, D.S.: Computers and Intractability: A Guide to the Theory of NP-Completeness. Freeman, San Francisco, 1979.
17. Gustedt, J.: On the Pathwidth of Chordal Graphs. Discrete Applied Math. **45** (1993) 223–248
18. Hajos, G.: Über eine Art von Graphen. Mathematische Nachrichten **11** (1957)
19. Kinnersley, N.G.: The Vertex Separation Number of a Graph Equals Its Path-Width. Inform. Proc. Letters **42** (1992) 345–350
20. Kirousis, L.M., and Papadimitriou, C.H.: Interval Graphs and Searching. Discrete Appl. Math. **55** (1985) 181–184
21. Kirousis, L.M., and Papadimitriou, C.H.: Searching and Pebbling. Theoret. Comput. Sci. **47** (1986) 205–218
22. Kloks, T.: Treewidth - Computations and Applications Lecture Notes in Computer Science, Springer, Berlin **842** (1994)
23. LaPaugh, A.S.: Recontamination Does Not Help to Search a Graph. J. Assoc. Comput. Mach. **40** (1993) 224–245
24. Lengauer, T.: Black-White Pebbles and Graph Separation. Acta Inform. **16** (1981) 465–475
25. Megiddo, N., Hakimi, S.L., Garey, M.R., Johnson, D.S., and Papadimitriou, C.H.: The Complexity of Searching a Graph. J. Assoc. Comput. Mach. **35** (1988) 18–44
26. Parsons, T.D.: Pursit-Evasion in Graphs. In Theory and Application in Graphs, Springer, Berlin (1976) (1976) 426–441
27. Robertson, N., and Seymour, P.D.: Graph Minors I. Excluding a Forest. J. Combin. Theory Ser. B **35** (1983) 39–61
28. Seymour, P.D., and Thomas, R.: Graph Searching and a Min-Max Theorem for Tree-Width. Journal of Combinatorial Theory, Series B **58** (1993) 22–33
29. Skodinis, K.: Construction of Linear Tree-Layouts which Are Optimal with Respect to Vertex Vertex Separation in Linear Time. J. Algorithms **47** (2003) 40–59
30. Wagner, K., and Wechsung, G.: Computational Complexity. Reidel, Dordrecht (1986)

Reasoning About Inconsistent Concurrent Systems: A Non-classical Temporal Logic[*]

Donghuo Chen[1] and Jinzhao Wu[1,2]

[1] Chengdu Institute of Computer Applications,
Chinese Academy of Sciences, Chengdu 610041, China
[2] Fakultät für Mathematik und Informatik,
Universität Mannheim, D7, 27, 68131 Mannheim, Germany

Abstract. It has been widely recognized that inconsistencies often appear and are inevitable when specifying large and complex concurrent systems. The logic QCL (quasi-classical logic) has therefore been developed for handling such specifications. But, on the one hand, temporal aspects, significant for ensuring the correct behavior of concurrent systems, cannot be specified by QCL, on the other hand, Classical temporal logics like CTL (computation tree logic) fail for system specifications with inconsistent information due to the trivial inference problem. To bridge this gap, in this paper a non-classical temporal logic QCTL (quasi-classical temporal logic) is introduced, including a novel semantics in term of paraKripke structures and a sound and complete proof system. It is paraconsistent, i.e., it can be used to non-trivially reason about inconsistent system specifications. Furthermore, an example is presented, showing the use of QCTL for reasoning about concurrent systems containing inconsistent information.

1 Introduction

In recent years, researchers and practitioners have to focus their mind on how to properly handle those unavoidable inconsistent information frequently existing in the stage of developing large and complex concurrent systems [1]. In fact, the development of most complex concurrent systems necessarily involves many people with their own perspectives on the systems, therefore, inconsistencies inevitably appear when integrating components developed by these people; Moreover, in some stages like requirements specifications, information is ambiguous and even inconsistent. In a word, inconsistencies are a fact of life, and we must learn to live with them.

Traditionally, inconsistencies are seen as undesirable and something to be avoided if at all possible, therefore tools and techniques are developed to remove

---
[*] Partially supported by a NKBRPC (2004CB318000) and by National Science Foundation of China (60373113).

J. Wiedermann et al. (Eds.): SOFSEM 2006, LNCS 3831, pp. 207–217, 2006.

the inconsistencies as soon as or soon after they are detected. But such an approach is always unrealistic in practice. For example, in a number of case studies it is revealed that some inconsistencies never get fixed in some period. Even if some inconsistencies have been fixed, the decision to repair them is risk-based, which may bring about more other inconsistencies in open distributed processing, or even sometimes a completely consistent stage is unreachable in practice [2]-[4]. Furthermore, checking consistency of specifications from multiple sources is computationally expensive.

From another point of view, existing inconsistencies are not always bad things, which can be used as a tool to improve the developers' shared understanding to targeted systems, guide the future development, and assist with verification and validation.

Thus it is a better choice to manage inconsistencies in a more general fashion [1], [5]. But, to the best of our knowledge, many formal specification languages, like Z, are based on classical logics. When concurrent specifications contain inconsistent information, classical logic is insufficient due to the trivial inference problem. Therefore, it is natural and necessary to employ other logical foundations to handle inconsistent specifications, such as paraconsistent logics, as did Hunter and Nuseibeh in [2].

Paraconsistent logics [6], [7] provide a solution to reasoning under inconsistency, which permit some contradictions to be true, without resulting in trivialization of classical logics. Generally speaking, paraconsistent logics are weaker than classical logics in the sense that not all classically valid inferences are possible. This is achieved by non-standard behavior of logical connectives, by the introduction of new logical connectives, by disallowing established proof rules, or by other means. More details about paraconsistent logics can been found in [8]-[10]. Additionally, Multi-valued logics [11], [12] provide a mean for non-trivially reasoning under inconsistency.

The paraconsistent logic QCL [2], [7] is a suitable replacement for many other logics in the context of inconsistent specifications. In [3], [13], QCL is used to reason about inconsistent Z specifications. However, it cannot be used to specify temporal properties of concurrent systems. Temporal aspects [14] are significant and vital for ensuring the correct behavior of concurrent systems. On the other hand, as we have already mentioned classical temporal logics like CTL cannot effectively handle inconsistent system specifications. Motivated by this, we present in this paper a non-classical temporal logic termed QCTL, which subsumes both QCL and CTL. QCTL is a paraconsistent logic. Within QCTL, properties especially temporal properties of concurrent systems with inconsistent specifications can be handled non-trivially.

The paper is organized as follows: Section 2 defines the syntax and semantics of QCTL. Section 3 proposes a sound and complete proof system for QCTL. Section 4 shows the use of QCTL for reasoning about concurrent systems by a simple phone system. Section 5 summarizes the paper. For lack of space, all involved proofs have been omitted.

2   QCTL

2.1   Syntax

The syntax of QCTL is that of CTL, but they are very different in essence. QCTL is based on the paraconsistent logic methodology, whereas CTL is based on classical propositional logic. This fact leads to great difference in its proof system and semantics.

Temporal operators are introduced as follows: $\bigcirc$ – at the next state, $\Diamond$ – eventually, $\Box$ – always, and U – until. Moreover, the two path quantifiers E and A have the intuitive meaning "there is a path" and "for all paths", respectively. Let $\mathcal{P}$ denote a set of atomic propositions. Formulas of QCTL have the following abstract syntax, where p ranges over $\mathcal{P}$:

$$\alpha := p \mid \neg\alpha \mid \alpha_1 \wedge \alpha_2 \mid \alpha_1 \vee \alpha_2 \mid \mathsf{E(A)} \bigcirc \alpha \mid \mathsf{E(A)}\Diamond\alpha \mid \mathsf{E(A)}\Box\alpha \mid \mathsf{E(A)}(\alpha_1 \ \mathsf{U} \ \alpha_2)$$

Let $\mathcal{L}_t$ denote the set of formulas by the above abstract syntax. Moreover, $\alpha \rightarrow \beta$ is the abbreviation for $\neg\alpha \vee \beta$ as usual. Conventionally for each $p \in \mathcal{P}$, p or $\neg p$ is called a literal. A formula of the form $l_1 \vee \ldots \vee l_n$ for $n \geq 1$ is called a clause, where $l_1, \ldots, l_n$ are literals.

Definition 2.1.1.   Such formula in the form of $\sigma(\alpha \ \mathsf{U} \ \beta)$, $\neg\sigma(\alpha \ \mathsf{U} \ \beta)$, $\sigma\mathsf{x}\alpha$ or $\neg\sigma\mathsf{x}\alpha$ for $\alpha, \beta \in \mathcal{L}$ is called a quasi-literal, where σ represents the path quantifier E or A and x represents one of the temporal operators $\bigcirc, \Box, \Diamond$. $l_1 \vee \ldots \vee l_n \vee ql_1 \vee \ldots \vee ql_m \in \mathcal{L}$ is called a quasi-clause, where $\forall i.1 \leq i \leq n$, l_i is a literal and $\forall i.1 \leq i \leq m$, ql_i is a quasi-literal. Moreover, a clause or quasi-literal is a special quasi-clause (note that σ and x have the above meaning in the context, when they are not explicitly interpreted).

QCTL has the same syntax with the classical temporal logic CTL, but it differs from CTL at the semantic level. This is exactly the point making QCTL a paraconsistent logic.

2.2   Semantics: ParaKripke Structures

QCTL is motivated by the need to reason about concurrent systems with inconsistent specifications. The notion of truth or falsity is thus discarded. We here view each formula as a belief, following the idea in [7]. QCTL achieves the paraconsistent methodology by decoupling the relationship between a formula and its negation at the level of semantics. To reach this aim, a set of positive and negative objects is first constructed from the set $\mathcal{P}$ of atomic propositions. For each $p \in \mathcal{P}$, $+p$ is called a positive object and $-p$ a negative object.

Definition 2.2.1.   The set of positive and negative objects in QCTL is defined as $\mathcal{O}_t = \{+p \mid p \in \mathcal{P}\} \cup \{-p \mid p \in \mathcal{P}\}$.

As well known, Kripke structures are widely used as semantic models of temporal logics such as CTL [15]. We provide QCTL a novel semantics by extending Kripke structures to paraKripke structures.

Definition 2.2.2. A tuple $M = (S, R, L)$ is called a paraKripke structure, where

- S is a non-empty state set.
- $R \subseteq S \times S$ is a total relation, which implies for each $s \in S$ there exists $t \in S$ satisfying $(s, t) \in R$.
- $L : S \mapsto 2^{\mathcal{O}_t}$ is a label function, which labels each state with a set of the positive or negative objects satisfiable in this state.

ParaKripke structures are similar to the general Kripke structures except for the label functions. The label function grasps the essential idea behind the structures. In a paraKripke structure, the states are labelled by positive or negative objects included in $\mathcal{O}_t$. In what follows, we will define the semantic models of QCTL in terms of paraKripke structures.

Definition 2.2.3. Let $M = (S, R, L)$ be a paraKripke structure. A computing path x of M is defined as $x = (s_1, \ldots, s_i, \ldots)$, where for all $i \geq 1$, $s_i \in S$ and $(s_i, s_{i+1}) \in R$. s_1 is called the initial state of x, and $(s_1, s_2, \ldots, s_k)$ for $k \geq 1$ an initial prefix of x.

Before defining the satisfiability relation in QCTL, we first present the satisfiability notion of a literal belief in a state. For a paraKripke structure $M = (S, R, L)$, let $s \in S$, $E_s = L(s)$ and $p \in \mathcal{P}$. Then (1) p is satisfiable in s iff $+p \in E_s$, and (2) $\neg p$ is satisfiable in s iff $-p \in E_s$.

From the above discussion, we see that paraKripke structures incorporate the notion of belief, in which it is possible that both an atomic proposition and its negation are satisfiable in a same state. Therefore, QCTL decouples the link between a formula and its negation at the level of semantics. This makes it a paraconsistent logic.

For achieving the non-trivial inference under inconsistencies, a proof procedure in QCTL is a two-stage affair: decompositional steps followed by compositional steps, as shown in the next section. To capture this idea, we need to establish the semantics for both stages. Here we present the notion of strong satisfaction, which corresponds to the decompositional phase and the notion of weak satisfaction, which corresponds to the compositional phase.

Definition 2.2.4. Let $M = (S, R, L)$ be a paraKripke structure. The strong satisfiability relation $\models_{ts}$ is defined as follows, where $p, q \in \mathcal{L}_t$:

1. For atomic formula p, $(M, s) \models_{ts} p$ iff $+p \in L(s)$.
2. For atomic formula p, $(M, s) \models_{ts} \neg p$ iff $-p \in L(s)$.
3. $(M, s) \models_{ts} \alpha \wedge \beta$ iff $(M, s) \models_{ts} \alpha$ and $(M, s) \models_{ts} \beta$.
4. For a clause $\alpha = l_1 \vee \ldots \vee l_n$, where $l_1, \ldots, l_n$ are literals, $(M, s) \models_{ts} \alpha$ iff $\exists i.1 \leq i \leq n$, $(M, s) \models_{ts} l_i$ and $\forall i.1 \leq i \leq n$, $(M, s) \models_{ts} \neg l_i$ implies $(M, s) \models_{ts} Disj(\alpha, l_i)$, where $Disj(\alpha, l_i)$ is the original formula $l_1 \vee \ldots \vee l_n$ without the disjunct l_i (note that when α is only a literal, $Disj(\alpha, l_i)$ is its own).

5. For a quasi-clause $\alpha = l_1 \vee \ldots \vee l_n \vee ql_1 \vee \ldots \vee ql_m$, $(M, s) \models_{ts} \alpha$ iff $(M, s) \models_{ts}$
   $l_1 \vee \ldots \vee l_m$ or $\exists i.1 \leq i \leq m$, $(M, s) \models_{ts} ql_i$, where $l_1, \ldots, l_n$ are literals, and
   $ql_1, \ldots, ql_m$ are quasi-literals.
6. $(M, s) \models_{ts} E \bigcirc \alpha$ iff there is $t \in S$ satisfying $(s, t) \in R$ and $(M, t) \models_{ts} \alpha$.
7. $(M, s) \models_{ts} A \bigcirc \alpha$ iff for all $t \in S$ with $(s, t) \in R$, $(M, t) \models_{ts} \alpha$.
8. $(M, s) \models_{ts} E \Diamond \alpha$ iff there is a computing path $x = (s_0, \ldots, s_n, \ldots)$ with $s_0 = s$
   and $\exists i.i \geq 1$, $(M, s_i) \models_{ts} \alpha$.
9. $(M, s) \models_{ts} A \Diamond \alpha$ iff for all computing paths $x = (s_0, \ldots, s_n, \ldots)$ with $s_0 = s$,
   $\exists i.i \geq 1$, $(M, s_i) \models_{ts} \alpha$.
10. $(M, s) \models_{ts} E(\alpha \cup \beta)$ iff there is an initial prefix $(s_0, \ldots, s_k)$ of a computing
    path x with the initial state $s_0 = s$, satisfying that $(M, s_k) \models_{ts} \beta$ and
    $(M, s_i) \models_{ts} \alpha$ for all $i < k$.
11. $(M, s) \models_{ts} A(\alpha \cup \beta)$ iff for all computing paths with initial state s, there
    is an initial prefix $(s_0, \ldots, s_k)$ with the initial state $s_0 = s$, satisfying that
    $(M, s_k) \models_{ts} \beta$ and $(M, s_i) \models_{ts} \alpha$ for all $i < k$.
12. $(M, s) \models_{ts} E \Box \alpha$ iff there is a computing path $x = (s_0, \ldots, s_n, \ldots)$ with $s_0 = s$
    and $\forall i.i \geq 0$, $(M, s_i) \models_{ts} \alpha$.
13. $(M, s) \models_{ts} A \Box \alpha$ iff for each computing path $x = (s_0, \ldots, s_n, \ldots)$ with the
    initial state $s_0 = s$, $(M, s_i) \models_{ts} \alpha$, where $i \geq 0$.

Definition 2.2.5. The weak satisfiability relation $\models_{tw}$ is defined as follows:

1. In all the items except for the fourth in Definition 2.2.4, $\models_{ts}$ is replaced
   by $\models_{tw}$.
2. For a clause $\alpha = l_1 \vee \ldots \vee l_n$, $(M, s) \models_{tw} \alpha$ iff $\exists i.1 \leq i \leq n, (M, s) \models_{tw} l_i$.

The strong satisfiability is much more restricted than the weak satisfiability
relation with regard to disjunction, as shown in the fourth and fifth items of
Definition 2.2.4. The reason we need such motivation is that we have decoupled
the link between a formula and its negation. By putting the link between each
disjunct in a quasi-clause and its negation into the definition for disjunction, we,
on the one hand, to some degree provide the meaning of negation operator $\neg$, on
the other hand, provide a semantics account for paraconsistent reasoning using
resolution.

Clearly, the strong and weak satisfiability relations do not cover all formulae
in $\mathcal{L}_t$, For instance, $\alpha \wedge (\beta \vee \gamma)$ and $\neg E \Diamond p$, where $\alpha, \beta, \gamma, p \in \mathcal{L}_t$, therefore we need
extend Definition 2.2.4 and 2.2.5. Before accomplishing this, we define a binary
relation $\approx_t$ on $\mathcal{L}_t$.

Definition 2.2.6. Let $\alpha, \beta \in \mathcal{L}_t$. $\alpha \approx_t \beta$ iff for every paraKripke structure $M = (S, R, L)$ and every $s \in S$, $(M, s) \models_{ts} \alpha$ ($(M, s) \models_{tw} \alpha$) implies $(M, s) \models_{ts} \beta$
(respectively $(M, s) \models_{tw} \beta$), and vice versa.

Proposition 2.2.1. $\approx_t$ is an equivalence relation on $\mathcal{L}_t$.

For defining full semantics of QCTL, we make the strong and weak satisfiability
relations cover all formulae in $\mathcal{L}_t$ by extending Definition 2.2.4 and 2.2.5. The
strong and weak satisfiability models of formulae of the form $\neg \sigma x \alpha$ and $\neg \sigma (\alpha \cup \beta)$

can be indirectly defined as E'1-E'6 by $\approx_t$. In a similar way, we further define the full behavior of $\neg, \vee,$ and $\rightarrow$ as E1-E7 in order that the strong and weak satisfiability relations cover all formulas in $\mathcal{L}_t$.

E1. $\neg\neg\alpha \vee \beta \approx_t \alpha \vee \beta$

E'1. $\neg E \bigcirc \alpha \approx_t A \bigcirc (\neg\alpha)$

E2. $\neg(\alpha \wedge \beta) \vee \gamma \approx_t \neg\alpha \vee \neg\beta \vee \gamma$

E'2. $\neg A \bigcirc \alpha \approx_t E \bigcirc (\neg\alpha)$

E3. $\neg(\alpha \vee \beta) \vee \gamma \approx_t (\neg\alpha \wedge \neg\beta) \vee \gamma$

E'3. $\neg E \Diamond \alpha \approx_t A \Box (\neg\alpha)$

E4. $\alpha \vee (\beta \wedge \gamma) \approx_t (\alpha \vee \beta) \wedge (\alpha \vee \gamma)$

E'4. $\neg A \Diamond \alpha \approx_t E \Box (\neg\alpha)$

E5. $\alpha \wedge (\beta \vee \gamma) \approx_t (\alpha \wedge \beta) \vee (\alpha \wedge \gamma)$

E'5. $\neg E(\alpha\ U\ \beta) \approx_t A\Box(\neg\beta) \vee A((\alpha\wedge$
$\neg\beta)U(\neg\alpha \wedge \neg\beta))$

E6. $(\alpha \rightarrow \beta) \vee \gamma \approx_t \neg\alpha \vee \beta \vee \gamma$

E'6. $\neg A(\alpha\ U\ \beta) \approx_t E\Box(\neg\beta) \vee E((\alpha\wedge$
$\neg\beta)U(\neg\alpha \wedge \neg\beta))$

E7. $\neg(\alpha \rightarrow \beta) \vee \gamma \approx_t (\alpha \wedge \neg\beta) \vee \gamma$

So far, all preparations have been made for defining the entailment relation $\models_t$ of QCTL. Let $2^{\mathcal{L}_t}$ denote the power set of $\mathcal{L}_t$:

Definition 2.2.7. The entailment relation $\models_t$ of QCTL is defined as follows:

- $\models_t \subseteq (2^{\mathcal{L}_t} - \emptyset) \times \mathcal{L}_t$, where $\emptyset$ is the empty set.
- For $\Gamma \in 2^{\mathcal{L}_t} - \emptyset$ and $\beta \in \mathcal{L}_t$, $\Gamma \models_t \beta$ iff for all paraKripke structure $M = (S, R, L)$ and $s \in S$, $(M, s) \models_{ts} \alpha$ for all $\alpha \in \Gamma$ implies $(M, s) \models_{tw} \beta$.

In this section, we have developed a logic QCTL, including its syntax and semantics. In the next section, we propose a sound and complete formal proof system for QCTL, which makes QCTL suited for reasoning under inconsistent system specifications.

3   A Proof System for QCTL

The logic QCTL is used to handle beliefs rather than the truth, and it specifies the change of beliefs with abstract time in concurrent systems. We provide a novel proof theory in this section, which is different from that of classical temporal logics. Like QCL, it is presented as a set of decomposition rules and a set of composition rules, but not as a set of axioms and a set of inference rules. Decomposition rules apply to the assumptions and composition rules apply to the query. In QCTL, we regard a proof procedure as a two-stage affair: decomposing and composing. Moreover, the composing step applying composition rules must follow the decomposing step applying decomposition rules.

Let $R(\mathcal{L}_t) = \{\frac{\alpha}{\beta} \mid \alpha, \beta \in \mathcal{L}_t\}$, where $\frac{\alpha}{\beta}$ reads "β is a consequence of α".

Definition 3.1. $\mathcal{T}: R(\mathcal{L}_t) \rightarrow 2^{R(\mathcal{L}_t)}$ is a function, which satisfies that for $\alpha, \beta \in \mathcal{L}_t$,

$$\mathcal{T}(\tfrac{\alpha}{\beta}) = \{\tfrac{\sigma x \alpha}{\sigma x \beta} \mid \sigma \in \{A, E\}, x \in \{\Box, \Diamond, \bigcirc\}\} \cup \{\tfrac{\sigma(\gamma\ U\ \alpha)}{\sigma(\gamma\ U\ \beta)} \mid \sigma \in \{A, E\}, \gamma \in \mathcal{L}_t\}$$
$$\cup \{\tfrac{\sigma(\alpha\ U\ \gamma)}{\sigma(\beta\ U\ \gamma)} \mid \sigma \in \{A, E\}, \gamma \in \mathcal{L}_t\}.$$

Example 3.1. For $\alpha, \beta \in \mathcal{L}_t, \dfrac{E \bigcirc (\alpha \wedge \beta)}{E \bigcirc \alpha}, \dfrac{A \Diamond (E \bigcirc (\alpha \wedge \beta))}{A \Diamond (E \bigcirc \alpha)} \in \mathcal{T}(\dfrac{\alpha \wedge \beta}{\alpha})$.

The decomposition and composition rules of the proof system of QCTL are given in the following.

Definition 3.2. Let conjunction and disjunction be commutative and associative. Decomposition rules are as follows:

- Conjunction elimination: $\dfrac{\alpha \wedge \beta}{\alpha}$ $\quad \dfrac{\sigma x(\alpha \wedge \beta)}{\sigma x \alpha}$ $\quad \dfrac{\sigma((\alpha \wedge \beta) \, U \, \gamma)}{\sigma(\alpha \, U \, \gamma)}$

- Negation elimination: $\dfrac{\neg\neg\alpha \vee \beta}{\alpha \vee \beta}$ $\quad \dfrac{\neg E \bigcirc \alpha}{A \bigcirc (\neg\alpha)}$ $\quad \dfrac{\neg A \Diamond \alpha}{E \Box (\neg\alpha)}$

  $\dfrac{\neg A \bigcirc \alpha}{E \bigcirc (\neg\alpha)}$ $\quad \dfrac{\neg A(\alpha \, U \, \beta)}{E \Box (\neg\beta) \vee E((\alpha \wedge \neg\beta) U (\neg\alpha \wedge \neg\beta))}$

  $\dfrac{\neg E \Diamond \alpha}{A \Box (\neg\alpha)}$ $\quad \dfrac{\neg E(\alpha \, U \, \beta)}{A \Box (\neg\beta) \vee A((\alpha \wedge \neg\beta) U (\neg\alpha \wedge \neg\beta))}$

- Quasi-resolution: $\dfrac{\neg\alpha \vee \beta_1 \quad \alpha \vee \beta_2}{\beta_1 \vee \beta_2}$ $\quad \dfrac{\neg\alpha \vee \beta_1 \vee \gamma_1 \quad \alpha \vee \beta_2 \vee \gamma_2}{\beta_1 \vee \beta_2 \vee \gamma_1 \vee \gamma_2}$

  Here α, β_1 and β_2 are literals, and γ_1 and γ_2 are formulae in the form of $\sigma x p, \sigma(p \, U \, q)$ or their negation

- Disjunction contraction: $\dfrac{\alpha \vee \alpha \vee \beta}{\alpha \vee \beta}$ $\quad \dfrac{\alpha \vee \alpha}{\alpha}$

- Arrow elimination: $\dfrac{\alpha \vee (\beta \rightarrow \gamma)}{\alpha \vee \neg\beta \vee \gamma}$ $\quad \dfrac{\alpha \vee \neg(\beta \rightarrow \gamma)}{\alpha \vee (\beta \wedge \neg\gamma)}$

- Decompositional distribution: $\dfrac{\alpha \vee (\beta \wedge \gamma)}{(\alpha \vee \beta) \wedge (\alpha \vee \gamma)}$ $\quad \dfrac{(\alpha \wedge \beta) \vee (\alpha \wedge \gamma)}{\alpha \wedge (\beta \vee \gamma)}$

- Decompositional de Morgan laws: $\dfrac{\neg(\alpha \wedge \beta) \vee \gamma}{\neg\alpha \vee \neg\beta \vee \gamma}$ $\quad \dfrac{\neg(\alpha \vee \beta) \vee \gamma}{(\neg\alpha \wedge \beta) \vee \gamma}$

- The increment of temporal operator rule: If $\dfrac{\alpha}{\beta}$ is a decomposition rule, then each $\dfrac{\alpha'}{\beta'} \in \mathcal{T}(\dfrac{\alpha}{\beta})$ is also one.

In the decomposition rules, the quasi-resolution rule plays a similar role as the resolution theory for classical logics [16]. It can be applied to quasi-clauses to generate further quasi-clauses.

Definition 3.3. Let conjunction and disjunction be commutative and associative. Composition rules are as follows:

- Conjunction introduction: $\dfrac{\alpha \quad \beta}{\alpha \wedge \beta}$

- Disjunction introduction: $\dfrac{\alpha}{\alpha \vee \beta}$ $\quad \dfrac{\sigma x \alpha}{\sigma x(\alpha \vee \beta)}$ $\quad \dfrac{\sigma(\alpha \, U \, \gamma)}{\sigma((\alpha \vee \beta) \, U \, \gamma)}$

- Negation introduction: $\dfrac{\alpha \vee \beta}{\neg\neg\alpha \vee \beta}$ $\quad \dfrac{A \bigcirc (\neg\alpha)}{\neg E \bigcirc \alpha}$ $\quad \dfrac{E \Box (\neg\alpha)}{\neg A \Diamond \alpha}$

  $\dfrac{E \bigcirc (\neg\alpha)}{\neg A \bigcirc \alpha}$ $\quad \dfrac{E \Box (\neg\beta) \vee E((\alpha \wedge \neg\beta) U (\neg\alpha \wedge \neg\beta))}{\neg A(\alpha \, U \, \beta)}$

  $\dfrac{A \Box (\neg\alpha)}{\neg E \Diamond \alpha}$ $\quad \dfrac{A \Box (\neg\beta) \vee A((\alpha \wedge \neg\beta) U (\neg\alpha \wedge \neg\beta))}{\neg E(\alpha \, U \, \beta)}$

- Arrow introduction: $\dfrac{\neg\beta \vee \gamma}{\beta \rightarrow \gamma}$ $\quad \dfrac{\beta \wedge \neg\gamma}{\neg(\beta \rightarrow \gamma)}$

- Compositional distribution: $\dfrac{(\alpha \vee \beta) \wedge (\alpha \vee \gamma)}{\alpha \vee (\beta \wedge \gamma)}$ $\quad \dfrac{\alpha \wedge (\beta \vee \gamma)}{(\alpha \wedge \beta) \vee (\alpha \wedge \gamma)}$

- Compositional de Morgan laws: $\dfrac{\neg\alpha \vee \neg\beta \vee \gamma}{\neg(\alpha \wedge \beta) \vee \gamma}$ $\dfrac{\neg(\alpha \wedge \beta) \vee \gamma}{\neg\alpha \vee \neg\beta \vee \gamma}$
- The increment of temporal operator rule: If $\frac{\alpha}{\beta}$ is a composition rule, then each $\frac{\alpha'}{\beta'} \in T(\frac{\alpha}{\beta})$ is also one.

In essence, the strong satisfiability relations and weak satisfiability relation grasp respectively the ideas of the decomposition and composition rules. This fact is easily affirmed from their definitions. The inference relation $\vdash_t$ on $\mathcal{L}_t$ is defined by using the decomposition rules and composition rules.

Definition 3.4. The inference relation $\vdash_t$ of QCTL is defined as follows:

- $\vdash_t \in (2^{\mathcal{L}_t} - \emptyset) \times \mathcal{L}_t$, where $\emptyset$ is the empty set.
- For $\Gamma \in (2^{\mathcal{L}_t} - \emptyset)$ and $\psi \in \mathcal{L}_t$, $\Gamma \vdash_t \psi$ iff there exists $\gamma_1, \ldots, \gamma_n \in \Gamma$ by applying the decomposition rules of Definition 3.2 and ψ is a consequence of $\gamma_1, \ldots, \gamma_n$ by applying the composition rules of Definition 3.3.

According to the principle of paraconsistency [8, 9, 10], the following conclusion can be derived:

Proposition 3.1. QCTL equipped with the inference relation $\vdash_t$ does not lead to trivial reasoning, that is, the principle that anything can be derived from inconsistent assumptions in classical logics does not hold.

Theorem 3.1. The proof system for QCTL is sound and complete.

The next section will demonstrate that QCTL can be used to specify and verify inconsistent concurrent systems by a simple example.

4   Example

To motivate our work, we here present an example of a simplified phone system. In what follows, we first provide the notion of models of specifications of inconsistent concurrent systems using paraKripke structures. Because the entailment relation $\models_t$ of QCTL is defined in a mode very different from that of classical logics, the notion of models based on paraKripke structures differs from that based on standard Kripke structures:

Definition 4.1. Let $\alpha \in \mathcal{L}_t$, and $M = (S, R, L, S_0)$ be a paraKripke structure, where $S_0 \subseteq S$ is a non-empty set of initial states. M is a model of α iff for all $s \in S_0$, there exists a finite set of formulas $\Gamma \subseteq \mathcal{L}_t$, which satisfies that for all $\gamma \in \Gamma$, $(M, s) \models_{ts} \gamma$ and $\Gamma \models_t \alpha$.

We now demonstrate how QCTL can be used to derive fewer and more useful information in a paraKripke model of a phone system containing inconsistent information.

A phone system can be taken into account from different angles of view. Fig.1(a) and (b) show two different visions of viewpoints of callee1 and callee2 on the phone system. The two models are specified using standard Kripke structures based on two-valued logic. Note that in this example, each state has a transition back to itself, which is not explicitly drawn for simplicity, and the meaning expressed by the state names and the propositions in states can be literally understood. We can easily find that the disagreement arises between callee1 and callee2. Callee1 considers that a phone allows one to replace the receiver during an incoming call without getting disconnected, and yet callee2 considers that replacing the receiver always leads to disconnect the call.

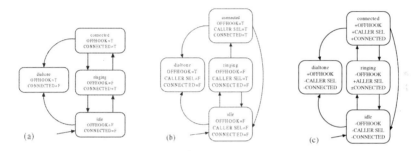

Fig. 1. (a) Viewpoint of Callee1; (b) Viewpoint of Callee2; (c) Merger of Two Viewpoints

Having specified the models of the targeted system, even though partial and inconsistent, we wish to deeply analyze these models. Naturally, we can separately reason about these models, but more interestingly, we can integrate the two models (even if they are inconsistent) to perform reasoning about the merged model containing more comprehensive information on the phone system. Integrating multiple models is complicated when inconsistent information exists among models. We here do this as follows:

- Choose the underlying logic QCTL for the merged model.
- Choose signature maps, which stipulate the relationships of items between the merged model and the corresponding source models, such as states' names and propositional variables in states. We adopt the similar principle in [17].
- Choose the measure of handling the inconsistencies existing among models. Optimistically, we argue that some conflicting viewpoints on the system do not exclude each other, for instance, each model does not deny the existence of transitions that it does not describe. This argument, we think, is appropriate for evolving specifications, especially in the early stage of the development.

Fig.1(c) shows the resulting paraKripke model. Despite conflicting viewpoints on the system, we can verify some temporal properties of the phone system. The representational examples include:

1. A□(CONNECTED → E ◯ (¬OFFHOOK))   "if you are connected, you can hang up."
2. A□(¬CALLER_SEL → ¬CONNECTED)   "if no caller is selected, you cannot be connected."
3. A□(¬OFFHOOK → ¬CONNECTED)   "if you hang up, you are disconnected".

According to Definition 4.1, we can easily derive that the first property is satisfiable in the merged model, that is, Fig.1(c) is a model of the first property. The rest of the three properties is more interesting. The second property is not expressible in callee1, but callee1 can have this property as long as it accepts the definitions in callee2 for CALLER_SEL, which callee1 does not describe. Consider the third, from Fig.1(c), we know the merged model satisfies the property. Just on this property are callee1 and callee2 conflicting. Note that the listed properties are simple, therefore, we do not explicitly explain the details of deriving the three properties from Fig.1(c). In essence, the paraconsistent character of the entailment relation increases the complexity of model checking over QCTL.

Though this example mentioned above is small and rather artificial, it suffices for illustrating the type of reasoning under inconsistency one might wish to perform.

5   Concluding Remarks

In this paper, we presented a non-classical temporal logic QCTL with a novel semantics and proof system. It extends QCL with the ability to specify temporal properties of concurrent systems such as safety and liveness properties, and extends CTL with the ability to reason under inconsistent system specifications.

Just as shown in Section 4, QCTL provides a temporal logic framework for nontrivially reasoning under inconsistent specifications, which provides a formal support for the continually evolving process. But it is inadequate job. We intend to conduct a series of nontrivial case studies, showing that the proposed paraconsistent temporal logic QCTL provides developers with a efficient automated reasoning tool when the developers have to face the unavoidable inconsistencies. Further, it is not accepted to directly transform a model checking to an inference problem according to Definition 4.1, hence the efficient algorithm for model checking over QCTL is absolutely required. Finally, combining the foregone work, et al., we will study the framework of managing inconsistencies integrating automated reasoning tools in the context of inconsistency.

References

1. Schwanke, R.W., Kaiser, G.E.: Living with Inconsistency in Large Systems. Proc. the International Workshop on Software Version and configuration control (1988) 98–118
2. Hunter, A., Nuseibeh, B.: Managing Inconsistent Specification: Reasoning, Analysis and Action. ACM Transaction on Software Engineering and Methodology **7** (1998) 335–367

3. Miarka, R.: Inconsistent and Underdefinedness in Z Specification. Phd thesis, The University of Kent (2002)
4. Valentine, S.H.: Inconsistency and Undefinedness in Z - a Practical Quide. Lecture Notes in Computer Science **1493** (1998) 233–249
5. Mortensen, C.: Inconsistent Mathematics. Kluwer Academic Publishers Group (1995)
6. da Costa, N.C.: On the Theory of Inconsistent Formal System. Notre Dame Journal of Formal Logic **15** (1974) 497–510
7. Hunter, A.: Reasoning with Contradictory Information Using Quasi-Classical Logic. J. of Logic and Computation **10** 5 (2000) 677–703
8. Batens, D., Mortensen, C., Priest, G., and Bendegem, J.P.V.: Frontiers of Paraconsistent Logic. King's College Publications (2000)
9. Ottaviano, I.D.: On the Development of Paraconsistent Logic and da Costa's Work. Journal of Non-Classical Logic **7** (1990) 9–72
10. Hunter, A.: Paraconsistent Logic. Volume II of Handbook of Defeasible Reasoning and Uncertain Information, D. Gabbay, Ph. Smets (eds), Kluwer (1998) 13–44
11. Belnap, N.D.: A Useful Four-Valued Logic. Modern Uses of Multiple-Valued Logic, G. Epstein, J.M. Dunn (eds), Reidel Publishing Company (1977) 7–37
12. Bruns, G., Godefroid, P.: Generalized Model Checking: Reasoning about Partial State Spaces. Proc of International Conference on Concurrency Theory, LNCS **1877** (2000) 168–182
13. Miarka, R., Derrick, J., and Boiten, E.: Handling Inconsistencies in Z Using Quasi-Classical Logic. Lecture Notes in Computer Science **2272** (2002) 204–225
14. Manna, Z., Pnueli, A.: Verification of Concurrent Programs: The Temporal Framework. The Correctness Problem in Computer Science, R.S. Boyer and J.S. Moore (eds), Academic Press, (1981) 215–273
15. Emerson, E.A.: Temporal and Modal Logic. Handbook of Theoretical Computer Science, J.V. Leeuwen (ed.), Elseier Science Publisher B.V. (1990)
16. Chang, C.-L., Lee, R.C.: Symbolic Logic and Mechanical Theorem Proving. Academic Press (1973)
17. Sabetzadeh, M., Easterbrook, S.: An Algebraic Framework for Merging Incomplete and Inconsistent Views. Technical Report CSRG-496, University of Toronto (2004)

Simple Algorithm for Sorting the Fibonacci String Rotations

Manolis Christodoulakis, Costas S. Iliopoulos, and Yoan José Pinzón Ardila

King's College London, Department of Computer Science,
London WC2R 2LS, UK
{manolis, csi}@dcs.kcl.ac.uk, Yoan.Pinzon@kcl.ac.uk

Abstract. In this paper we focus on the combinatorial properties of the Fibonacci strings rotations. We first present a simple formula that, in constant time, determines the rank of any rotation (of a given Fibonacci string) in the lexicographically-sorted list of all rotations. We then use this information to deduce, also in constant time, the character that is stored at any one location of any given Fibonacci string. Finally, we study the output of the Burrows-Wheeler Transform (BWT) on Fibonacci strings to prove that when BWT is applied to Fibonacci strings it always produces a sequence of 'b's' followed by a sequence of 'a's'.

Keywords: Block-sorting, Fibonacci strings, data compression, text compression, BWT Transformation.

1 Introduction

Fibonacci strings[1] have been widely studied and are considered to be a matter of common knowledge, see, for example, [1] for a good reference. Fibonacci strings are important in many contexts, but they are frequently often cited in journal articles and elsewhere as *worst-case scenarios* for string pattern matching algorithms such as KMP[2], Boyer-Moore and Aho-Corasick automaton, and in *string statistics* like for computing all the Abelian squares in a given string [3]. Another domain in which the combinatorial properties of the Fibonacci strings are of great interest is in some aspects of mathematics and physics, such as number theory, fractal geometry, formal language, computational complexity, quasicrystals, etc.

Informally, a Fibonacci string F_n is a string of characters with the property that each successive string of the sequence is obtained as the concatenation of the previous two. For example, the first five Fibonacci strings are: b, a, ab, aba and abaab (*c.f.* also Fig. 1(left)). Here we are concerned with the lexicographic ordering of the rotations of a Fibonacci string, we show that for a given rotation of a particular Fibonacci string, one can identify the order

---

[1] *a.k.a.* Fibonacci words.

[2] Knuth-Morris-Pratt.

J. Wiedermann et al. (Eds.): SOFSEM 2006, LNCS 3831, pp. 218–225, 2006.

of that rotation in the lexicographically-sorted list of all the rotations of F_n, without the need for explicit sorting of the rotations. The inverse problem, consisting of finding the rotation that has a given order in the sorted list, can also be solved without sorting. In addition, we show how the ordering of the rotations can be used to determine the symbols of any Fibonacci string without using the traditional recursive definition of Fibonacci strings or the Golden Ratio ϕ.

Analysing rotations of strings can be useful for algorithms whose operation depends on rotations of strings and their lexicographic ordering. One such algorithm is the block-sorting transformation known as Burrows-Wheeler Transform (BWT) [4] used to bring repeated characters together as a preliminary to compression. When BWT is applied to a string x of length n, it produces the lexicographically-sorted list of all n rotations of x and outputs the last symbol of every rotation of the sorted list together with the rank of the $0th$ rotation. By making best use of the already mentioned rationale, we show how to compute the output of BWT when applied on Fibonacci strings without engaging in any costly sorting operation. In particular, we prove that the output is always the permutation that consists of all the 'b's that are contained in the particular Fibonacci string, followed by all its 'a's. Fibonacci strings are closely related to Sturmian words[3], hence related work can be found in [5], where Mantaci et. al. derived a very similar result using a different approach.

The remainder of this paper is organised as follows. In the next section, we provide some basic definitions and prove some properties of the Fibonacci numbers which will play a key role in proving the main results in the succeeding sections. In Sect. 3 we prove that the rank of any rotation of a Fibonacci string in the sorted list of all rotations of the particular Fibonacci string, can be computed in constant time. Section 4 explains how to use the above results to instantly deduce the symbol stored in any position of a Fibonacci string. Finally, in Sect. 5 we prove why the output of BWT when applied to a Fibonacci string, produces a sequence of 'b's followed by a sequence of 'a's. Concluding remarks follow in the last section.

2   Preliminaries

We define Fibonacci number by $f_0 = 1, f_1 = 1, f_n = f_{n-1} + f_{n-2}$ and Fibonacci strings are defined by $F_0 = \mathsf{b}, F_1 = \mathsf{a}, F_n = F_{n-1}F_{n-2}$, for $n \geq 2$. Obviously, $|F_i| = f_i$. See Fig. 1(a) for some examples.

Definition 1. *The ith rotation of a string $x = x_0 \ldots x_{n-1}$ is defined by the string $\mathcal{R}_i(x) = x_i x_{i+1} \ldots x_{n-1} x_0 x_1 \ldots x_{i-1}$.*

---

[3] Sturmian words are infinite words over a two-letter alphabet of minimal subword complexity which are not eventually periodic, or, in other words, that have exactly $n + 1$ factors of length n for each $n \geq 0$.

n	F_n	f_n
0	b	1
1	a	1
2	ab	2
3	aba	3
4	abaab	5
5	abaababa	8
6	abaababaabaab	13
7	abaababaabaababaababa	21

rank (ρ)	rotation index (i)	rotation
0	7	$\mathcal{R}_7$ = aabaabab
1	2	$\mathcal{R}_2$ = aababaab
2	5	$\mathcal{R}_5$ = abaabaab
3	0	$\mathcal{R}_0$ = abaababa
4	3	$\mathcal{R}_3$ = ababaaba
5	6	$\mathcal{R}_6$ = baabaaba
6	1	$\mathcal{R}_1$ = baababaa
7	4	$\mathcal{R}_4$ = babaabaa

(a) Fibonacci strings and numbers   **(b)** Lexicographically-sorted rotations of F_5

Fig. 1. Fibonacci strings and their rotations

Note that $\mathcal{R}_{i+j}(x) = \mathcal{R}_i(\mathcal{R}_j(x)) = \mathcal{R}_j(\mathcal{R}_i(x))$. Thus the ith rotation[4] can be defined for $0 < i \geq n$ as $\mathcal{R}_i(x) = \mathcal{R}_{i \bmod n}(x)$. For F_5, for example, Fig. 1(b) gives the sorted list of all rotations.

We denote by $rank(i, x)$ the rank of $\mathcal{R}_i(x)$ in the lexicographically-sorted list of all rotations of x. We write $rot(\rho, x)$ to denote the index of the rotation with rank ρ, that is, $rot(\rho, x) = i$ iff $rank(i, x) = \rho$. For instance, in Fig. 1(b) $rank(3, F_5) = 4$, and $rot(5, F_5) = 6$.

Next, we state, without proof, two easily established lemmas that will be required later. The first is an elementary result from number theory, while the second corresponds to Fibonacci number analysis.

Lemma 1 ([7–page 243]). *The congruence* $ax \equiv b \pmod{n}$ *has a unique solution* $x \in [0, n)$ *if* a *is relatively prime to* n.

Lemma 2 ([8–page 151]). f_n *is relatively prime to* f_{n-1}*, for every* $n \geq 2$.

2.1 Some New Properties of Fibonacci Numbers

Here we prove some properties of Fibonacci numbers which will be used in the proofs of subsequent lemmas regarding Fibonacci strings.

Lemma 3. f_n *is relatively prime to* f_{n-2}*, for every* $n \geq 2$.

Proof. Assume f_n is not relatively prime to f_{n-2}; that is, $f_n = mk$ and $f_{n-2} = m\ell$ for some integers m, k, ℓ, where $m \neq 1$ and $k > \ell$. Then

$$f_n = f_{n-1} + f_{n-2} \iff mk = f_{n-1} + m\ell \iff m(k - \ell) = f_{n-1}$$

and thus f_{n-1} is not relatively prime to f_n, since they have a common factor, $m \neq 1$. This contradicts Lemma 2. □

Lemma 4.

$$f_{n-1}^2 \bmod f_n = \begin{cases} -1, & \text{if } n \text{ odd} \\ 1, & \text{if } n \text{ even} \end{cases} \quad \text{for } n \geq 2$$

---

[4] In the sequel, when refering to the ith rotation, we imply the $(i \bmod n)$th rotation.

Proof. By Cassini's identity [2–page 80] $f_{n-1}f_{n+1} - f_n^2 = (-1)^n$.

$$f_{n-1}f_{n+1} - f_n^2 = (-1)^n \implies$$
$$f_{n-1}(f_n + f_{n-1}) - f_n^2 = (-1)^n \implies$$
$$f_{n-1}f_n + f_{n-1}f_{n-1} - f_n^2 = (-1)^n \implies$$
$$(f_{n-1}f_n + f_{n-1}^2 - f_n^2) \bmod f_n = (-1)^n \bmod f_n \implies$$
$$f_{n-1}^2 \bmod f_n = (-1)^n \bmod f_n \implies$$
$$f_{n-1}^2 \bmod f_n = \begin{cases} -1 & \text{if } n \text{ odd} \\ 1 & \text{if } n \text{ even} \end{cases}$$

$\square$

Corollary 1.

$$f_{n-2}^{-1} \bmod f_n = \begin{cases} f_{n-1} & \text{if } n \text{ odd} \\ f_{n-2} & \text{if } n \text{ even} \end{cases}$$

Proof. By Lemma 4, for n odd:

$$f_{n-1}^2 \bmod f_n = -1 \iff$$
$$f_{n-1}(f_n - f_{n-2}) \bmod f_n = -1 \iff$$
$$f_{n-1}f_n - f_{n-1}f_{n-2} \bmod f_n = -1 \iff$$
$$f_{n-1}f_{n-2} \bmod f_n = 1 \iff$$
$$f_{n-2}^{-1} \bmod f_n = f_{n-1}$$

By Lemma 4, for n even:

$$f_{n-1}^2 \bmod f_n = 1 \iff$$
$$(f_n - f_{n-2})^2 \bmod f_n = 1 \iff$$
$$(f_n^2 - 2f_nf_{n-2} + f_{n-2}^2) \bmod f_n = 1 \iff$$
$$f_{n-2}^2 \bmod f_n = 1 \iff$$
$$f_{n-2}^{-1} \bmod f_n = f_{n-2}$$

$\square$

3 Ranking the Rotations of Fibonacci Strings

Lemma 5. *For every integer* $n \geq 2$, $F_n = F_{n-2}F_{n-3} \ldots F_1 u$, *where*

$$u = \begin{cases} \mathsf{ba} & \text{if } n \text{ odd} \\ \mathsf{ab} & \text{if } n \text{ even} \end{cases}$$

Proof. This follows from Lemma 2.8 in [6]. $\square$

Lemma 6. *The* ith *rotation of* F_n $\mathcal{R}_i(F_n)$, *for* $i \in [0, f_n)$, $n \geq 2$, *matches the* $(i + f_{n-2})$th *rotation,* $\mathcal{R}_{i+f_{n-2}}(F_n)$ *in all but two positions. Moreover, if* $i \neq f_{n-1} - 1$ *the two mismatches occur in consecutive positions.*

Proof. Consider $i = 0$, then $\mathcal{R}_0(F_n) = F_n = F_{n-2}F_{n-3} \ldots F_1 u$, by Lemma 5, where $u = \mathsf{ba}$ if n is odd, and $u = \mathsf{ab}$ if even. Then the $(i + f_{n-2})th$ rotation is

$$\mathcal{R}_{f_{n-2}}(F_n) = F_{n-3} \ldots F_1 u F_{n-2} \tag{1}$$

but also

$$\mathcal{R}_0(F_n) = F_n = F_{n-1}F_{n-2} = F_{n-3}\ldots F_1 u' F_{n-2} \tag{2}$$

where F_{n-1} has been written in the form given by Lemma 5, and $u' = $ ab if $n-1$ is even (*i.e* n is odd), $u' = $ ba for $n-1$ odd (*i.e* n is even). So for $i = 0$ the rotations do not match at positions $f_{n-1} - 2$ and $f_{n-1} - 1$ (the positions where the two symbols of u occur; *see* (1) and (2)).

For any $i \in [0, f_n)$ the rotations $\mathcal{R}_i(F_n) = \mathcal{R}_i(\mathcal{R}_0(F_n))$ and $\mathcal{R}_{i+f_{n-2}}(F_n) = \mathcal{R}_i(\mathcal{R}_{f_{n-2}}(F_n))$ do not match in the same two symbols located now at positions $f_{n-1} - 2 - i$ and $f_{n-1} - 1 - i$ (modulo f_n). These two positions are unconsecutive only for rotation $i = f_{n-1} - 1$, because for this rotation, the first symbol of u will be located at position $(f_n - 1)$, and the second symbol of u will be located at position 0. □

Lemma 7. *The ith rotation of F_n ($n \geq 2$), $\mathcal{R}_i(F_n)$, is lexicographically smaller (resp. larger) than the $(i+f_{n-2})$th rotation, $\mathcal{R}_{i+f_{n-2}}(F_n)$, for n odd (resp. even), for all $i \in [0, f_n)$, $i \neq f_{n-1} - 1$. For $i = f_{n-1} - 1$, the ith rotation is lexicographically larger (resp. smaller) for n odd (resp. even).*

Proof. From the proof of Lemma 6 we know that

$$\mathcal{R}_0(F_n) = F_{n-3}\ldots F_1 u' F_{n-2} \quad \text{and} \quad \mathcal{R}_{f_{n-2}}(F_n) = F_{n-3}\ldots F_1 u F_{n-2}$$

where $u' = $ ab and $u = $ ba when n is odd, $u' = $ ba and $u = $ ab when n is even. Thus, the 0th rotation is lexicographically smaller (*resp.* larger) from the f_{n-2}th for n odd (*resp.* even). The same is true for every other rotation $i \neq f_{n-1} - 1$, since the two symbols of u (and u') occupy consecutive positions.

For $i = f_{n-1} - 1$ and n odd

$$\mathcal{R}_{f_{n-1}-1}(F_n) = \mathsf{b}F_{n-2}\ldots F_1\mathsf{a} \ (u' = \mathsf{ab})$$
$$\mathcal{R}_{f_{n-1}-1+f_{n-2}}(F_n) = \mathcal{R}_{f_n-1}(F_n) = \mathsf{a}F_{n-2}\ldots F_1\mathsf{b} \ (u = \mathsf{ba}).$$

Consequently $\mathcal{R}_i$ is lexicographically larger than $\mathcal{R}_{i+f_{n-2}}$. Similarly, for n even $\mathcal{R}_i$ is lexicographically smaller than $\mathcal{R}_{i+f_{n-2}}$. □

Theorem 1. *The rotation of F_n $rot(\rho, F_n)$ with rank ρ in the lexicographically-sorted list of all the rotations of F_n, for $n \geq 2$, $\rho \in [0..f_n)$, is the rotation*

$$rot(\rho, F_n) = \begin{cases} (\rho \cdot f_{n-2} - 1) \bmod f_n & \text{if } n \text{ odd} \\ (-(\rho+1) \cdot f_{n-2} - 1) \bmod f_n & \text{if } n \text{ even} \end{cases}$$

Proof. We will prove the theorem by constructing the list of lexicographically sorted rotations. Consider n odd, intuitively, rotation $\mathcal{R}_i = \mathcal{R}_{f_n-1}$ is the smallest and therefore the first in the sorted list (it is the only rotation not preceded by $\mathcal{R}_{i-f_{n-2}}$, using Lemma 7). We will prove later that no other rotation can be smaller. Now, consider that $\mathcal{R}_i = \mathcal{R}_{f_n-1}$ occupies position 0 in the sorted list. By Lemma 7, underneath (but maybe not immediately below, but at some later point) there will be $\mathcal{R}_{i+f_{n-2}}$. This rotation at the same time will be followed by $\mathcal{R}_{i+2f_{n-2}}$, followed by ..., followed by $\mathcal{R}_{i+kf_{n-2}}$ ($k \geq 2$), for as long as

$$i + kf_{n-2} \neq f_{n-1} - 1 \pmod{f_n}$$

(by Lemma 7). We solve the following equation to find the smallest k for which the above inequality is not true:

$$
\begin{aligned}
i + kf_{n-2} &= f_{n-1} - 1 \pmod{f_n} \\
f_n - 1 + kf_{n-2} &= f_{n-1} - 1 \pmod{f_n} \\
f_n + kf_{n-2} &= f_{n-1} \pmod{f_n} \\
f_n - f_{n-1} + kf_{n-2} &= 0 \pmod{f_n} \\
f_{n-2} + kf_{n-2} &= 0 \pmod{f_n} \\
(k+1)f_{n-2} &= 0 \pmod{f_n}
\end{aligned}
$$

which means that $(k+1)f_{n-2}$ and f_n share a common factor $m \neq 1$. By Lemma 3, f_{n-2} is relatively prime to f_n, thus it must be $k+1 = 0 \pmod{f_n}$, or identically $k = f_n - 1$.[5] Therefore, there are no more rotations left out which could possibly be placed anywhere between the rotations that we have already inserted in the sorted list. Hence the ρth position in the sorted list is occupied by rotation

$$(f_n - 1 + \rho f_{n-2}) \bmod f_n = (\rho f_{n-2} - 1) \bmod f_n.$$

For n even, we construct the sorted list in a similar fashion, only now we start by placing $\mathcal{R}_{f_n-1}$ at the bottom of the list (position $f_n - 1$), and place any $\mathcal{R}_{i+f_{n-2}}$ atop rotation i. Thus now, $\mathcal{R}_{(f_n-1+kf_{n-2}) \bmod f_n} = \mathcal{R}_{(kf_{n-2}-1) \bmod f_n}$ take up position $f_n - k - 1$; that is, the ρth position is occupied by rotation

$$((f_n - \rho - 1)f_{n-2} - 1) \bmod f_n = (-(\rho + 1)f_{n-2} - 1) \bmod f_n. \qquad \square$$

Corollary 2. *The rank of the ith rotation of F_n, $rank(i, F_n)$, in the lexicographically sorted list of all the rotations of F_n, for $i \in [0..f_n)$, $n \geq 2$, is:*

$$rank(i, F_n) = \begin{cases} ((i+1) \cdot f_{n-2}) \bmod f_n & \text{if } n \text{ odd} \\ ((i+1) \cdot f_{n-2} - 1) \bmod f_n & \text{if } n \text{ even.} \end{cases}$$

Proof. For n odd, by Theorem 1, the ith position is occupied by rotation $(i \cdot f_{n-2} - 1) \bmod f_n$, thus the ith rotation is located at position

$$(i+1) \cdot f_{n-2}^{-1} \bmod f_n = (i+1) \cdot f_{n-2} \bmod f_n$$

since, by Lemma 1, $f_{n-2}^{-1} = f_{n-2}$ for n odd.

Similarly, for n even, by Theorem 1, the ith position is occupied by rotation

$$(-(i+1) \cdot f_{n-2} - 1) \bmod f_n = ((i+1) \cdot f_{n-1} - 1) \bmod f_n$$

thus the ith rotation is located at position

$$((i+1) \cdot f_{n-1}^{-1} - 1) \bmod f_n = ((i+1) \cdot f_{n-2} - 1) \bmod f_n$$

since, by Lemma 1, $f_{n-1}^{-1} = f_{n-2}$ for n even. $\qquad \square$

---

[5] Note that, by Lemma 1, this solution is unique in $[0, f_n)$.

4   Predicting the Symbols of Fibonacci Strings

Lemma 8. *The number of* 'a'*s in* F_n *(*$n \geq 2$*) is* f_{n-1}*.*

Proof. By induction.

- [basis] The number of 'a's in $F_2 = \text{ab}$ is $f_{2-1} = f_1 = 1$.
- [hypothesis] Assume that the number of 'a's in F_k is f_{k-1}, for all $k \in [2, n)$.
- [induction proof] The number of 'a's in $F_n = F_{n-1}F_{n-2}$ is the sum of 'a's in F_{n-1} and F_{n-2}, *i.e.* by induction hypothesis $f_{n-2} + f_{n-3} = f_{n-1}$. $\square$

Lemma 9. *The number of* 'b'*s in* F_n *(*$n \geq 2$*) is* f_{n-2}*.*

Theorem 2. *For all* $i \in [0, f_n)$*, the* i*th symbol of* F_n *(*$n \geq 2$*) is*

$$
F_n[i] = \begin{cases} \text{a}, & \text{if } n \text{ odd and } ((i+1) \cdot f_{n-2}) \bmod f_n < f_{n-1}, \\ & \text{or } n \text{ even and } ((i+1) \cdot f_{n-2} - 1) \bmod f_n < f_{n-1} \\ \text{b}, & \text{otherwise} \end{cases}
$$

Proof. Observe that, the ith symbol of F_n is the first symbol of the ith rotation. In the lexicographically-sorted list of rotations, all rotations that start with 'a' appear before all rotations that start with 'b'. Therefore, $F_n[i]$ will be 'a' iff the ith rotation has rank less than f_{n-1}; otherwise it is 'b'. $\square$

5   Burrows-Wheeler Transform on Fibonacci Strings

Lemma 10. *The first* f_{n-2} *rotations in the lexicographically-sorted list of rotations of* F_n *(*$n \geq 2$*) end in* 'b'*.*

Proof. The last symbol of the ith rotation is the $((i + f_n - 1) \bmod f_n)th$ symbol of F_n; that is, the $((i - 1) \bmod f_n)th$ symbol of F_n.

Consider n odd. By Theorem 1, the first f_{n-2} rotations are the rotations $(i \cdot f_{n-2} - 1) \bmod f_n$, $i \in [0, f_{n-2})$. The last symbol of these rotations is then $(i \cdot f_{n-2} - 2) \bmod f_n$, $i \in [0, f_{n-2})$. Whence, by using Theorem 2 we identify the last symbol of the first f_{n-2} rotations:

$$
(i \cdot f_{n-2} - 2 + 1)f_{n-2} \bmod f_n = if_{n-2}^2 - f_{n-2} = i - f_{n-2} = i + f_{n-1}
$$

which is $\geq f_{n-1}$, since $i \in [0, f_{n-2})$. Thus the symbol is 'b'.

Equally for n even, by Theorem 1, the first f_{n-2} rotations are $(-(i + 1) \cdot f_{n-2} - 1) \bmod f_n$, $i \in [0, f_{n-2})$. The last symbol of these rotations is then $(-(i + 1) \cdot f_{n-2} - 2) \bmod f_n$, $i \in [0, f_{n-2})$. Then, by using Theorem 2 we identify the last symbol of the first f_{n-2} rotations:

$$
[(-(i + 1) \cdot f_{n-2} - 2 + 1)f_{n-2} - 1] \bmod f_n = (-(i + 1) \cdot f_{n-2}^2) - f_{n-2} - 1 =
$$
$$
= (i + 1) - f_{n-2} - 1 = i - f_{n-2} = i + f_{n-1} \geq f_{n-1}
$$

since again $i \in [0, f_{n-2})$. Thus the symbol is 'b'. $\square$

Corollary 3. *The last f_{n-1} rotations in the lexicographically-sorted list of rotations of F_n, $n \geq 2$, terminate in an 'a'.*

Theorem 3. *The output of BWT when applied to F_n, $n \geq 2$ is*

$$(\underbrace{\mathtt{bb\ldots ba}}_{f_{n-2}}\underbrace{\mathtt{aa\ldots a}}_{f_{n-1}} , \ k)$$

where k denote the rank of the 0th rotation in the lexicographically-sorted list, which is

$$k = \begin{cases} f_{n-2} + 1 & \text{if } n \text{ odd} \\ f_{n-2} & \text{if } n \text{ even.} \end{cases}$$

Proof. The output string of BWT is the last column of the lexicographically-sorted list of rotations, which by Lemma 10 and Corollary 3 is $\mathtt{bb\ldots baa\ldots a}$.

The index produced by BWT is the rank of the initial string (the 0th rotation), which by Corollary 2 is

$$rank(0, F_n) = \begin{cases} f_{n-2} \bmod f_n & \text{if } n \text{ odd} \\ (f_{n-2} - 1) \bmod f_n & \text{if } n \text{ even.} \end{cases} \qquad \square$$

6   Conclusion

In this paper we focused on the combinatorial properties of the rotations of Fibonacci strings. We first presented a simple formula that determines the rank of any rotation (of a given Fibonacci string) in the lexicographically-sorted list of all rotations and then used this information to deduce, also in constant time, the symbols stored in any position of that Fibonacci string. We also proved that the output of the Burrows-Wheeler Transform (BWT) when applied to a Fibonacci string F_n, is always the permutation of F_n consisting of all the 'b's of F_n followed by all the 'a's.

References

1. Berstel, J.: Fibonacci Words—a Survey. In Rozenberg, G., Salomaa, A. (eds), The Book of L. Springer-Verlag (1986) 13–27
2. Knuth, D.E.: The Art of Computer Programming. 3rd edn. Volume 1. Addison-Wesley, Reading, Massachusetts (1997)
3. Cummings, L.J., Smyth, W.F.: Weak Repetitions in Strings. The Journal of Combinatorial Mathematics and Combinatorial Computing **24** (1997) 33–48
4. Burrows, M., Wheeler, D.: A Block-Sorting Lossless Data Compression Algorithm. Technical Report 124, Digital Equipment Corporation (1994)
5. Mantaci, S., Restivo, A., Sciortino, M.: Burrows–Wheeler Transform and Sturmian Words. Information Processing Letters **86** (2003) 241–246
6. Iliopoulos, C.S., Moore, D., Smyth, W.F.: A Characterization of the Squares in a Fibonacci String. Theoretical Computer Science **172** (1997) 281–291
7. Eccles, P.: An Introduction to Mathematical Reasoning: Numbers, Sets and Functions. Cambridge University Press (1997)
8. Koshy, T.: Elementary Number Theory with Applications. Elsevier (2001)

Oriented Coloring:
Complexity and Approximation

Jean-François Culus[1] and Marc Demange[2]

[1] UTM, équipe Grimm - SMASH, 5 Allée Antonio Machado
31000 Toulouse cedex 9 France
culus@univ-tlse2.fr
[2] ESSEC, département SID Avenue Bernard HIRSH,
BP 105, 95021 Cergy Pontoise cedex France
demange@essec.fr
(Also CERMSEM, Université Paris 1, 106–112 bd de l'Hôpital, F-75013 Paris, France)

Abstract. This paper is devoted to an oriented coloring problem motivated by a task assignment model. A recent result established the NP-completeness of deciding whether a digraph is k-oriented colorable; we extend this result to the classes of bipartite digraphs and circuit-free digraphs. Finally, we investigate the approximation of this problem: both positive and negative results are devised.

1 Introduction

1.1 The Problem

In this paper, $G = (V(G), E(G))$ denotes a simple graph and $\overrightarrow{G} = (V(\overrightarrow{G}), A(\overrightarrow{G}))$ a digraph (i.e. a directed graph). A *mixed graph* $M = (V(M), A(M), E(M))$ contains both arcs $(A(M))$ and edges $(E(M))$. Graphs and digraphs can be seen as mixed graphs. We do not allow loops or parallel arcs or edges, but M may have an edge and an arc with the same end-vertices. If S is a subset of $V(M)$, we denote by $M[S]$ the sub-mixed graph of M induced by S. If $v \in V(M)$, $\Gamma^+(v) = \{w|(v, w) \in A(M)\}$ and $\Gamma^-(v) = \{w|(w, v) \in A(M)\}$. Given $U \subset V(M)$, we denote $\Gamma^+(U) = \bigcup_{v \in U} \Gamma^+(v)$; $\Gamma^-(U) = \bigcup_{v \in U} \Gamma^-(v)$.

Let G, G' be graphs, and $\overrightarrow{G}, \overrightarrow{G'}$ be digraphs. An *homomorphism* of G to G' [resp. of $\overrightarrow{G}$ to $\overrightarrow{G'}$] is a mapping $f : V(G) \to V(G')$ [resp. $f : V(\overrightarrow{G}) \to V(\overrightarrow{G'})$] which preserves the edges [resp. the arcs]: i.e. $\{x, y\} \in E(G)$ [resp. $(x, y) \in A(G)$] implies $\{f(x), f(y)\} \in E(G')$ [resp. $(f(x), f(y)) \in A(G')$]. Homomorphisms of undirected and directed graphs have been studied as a generalization of graph coloring in the literature [8], [9]. A k-*coloring* of a graph G is equivalent to an homomorphism of G to the complete graph K_k. Therefore, the chromatic number $\chi(G)$ of a graph G is equal to the smallest integer k such that there exists an homomorphism of G to K_k and Min Coloring is to find such an homomorphism.

Generalizing previous definition, an *oriented k-coloring* of $\overrightarrow{G}$ is an homomorphism of $\overrightarrow{G}$ to an oriented graph $\overrightarrow{G'}$ on k vertices. The *oriented chromatic number*

J. Wiedermann et al. (Eds.): SOFSEM 2006, LNCS 3831, pp. 226–236, 2006.

of a digraph $\overrightarrow{G}$, denoted by $\chi_o(\overrightarrow{G})$, is the smallest integer k such that there is an oriented k-coloring of $\overrightarrow{G}$. This problem will be called Min Oriented Coloring. Given an homomorphism c of $\overrightarrow{G}$ to $\overrightarrow{G'}$, the *color digraph* of $\overrightarrow{G}$ (for homomorphism c) will refer to digraph $\overrightarrow{G'}$. For $i \in \{1, 2, \ldots, |V(\overrightarrow{G'})|\}$, subsets $c^{-1}(i)$ of $V(\overrightarrow{G})$ are independent set of $V(\overrightarrow{G'})$. We call those sets monochromatic classes (for c) of digraph $\overrightarrow{G}$. If there is no possible confusion, we omit the reference to homomorphism c.

An oriented coloring of $\overrightarrow{G}$ can also be define as follows. Given two independent sets S and S' in a graph G, we say that they don't respect the *unidirection-property* if two arcs (i, i') and (j', j) exist such that $\{i, j\} \subset S$ and $\{i', j'\} \subset S'$ (we may have $i = j$ or $i' = j'$); in the opposite case, the unidirection-property holds (and we note $S \rightarrow S'$). Then, an oriented k-coloring is a partition of the vertex set into k independent sets such that, all pairs of independent sets in this family respect the unidirection-property.

The notion of oriented chromatic number has been first introduced by Nesetril and Sopena [16], [14] and has been also studied in [15], [17], [11], [13]. Most of these works focus on upper and lower bounds of the oriented chromatic number. Recently, Klostermeyer and MacGillivray [12] studied its complexity, but to our knowledge, its approximation behavior has not been studied until now. In [12], it is stated that, deciding if the oriented chromatic number of a given digraph is at most k is **NP**-complete for every $k \geq 4$. In section 2, we extend this result to the case of bipartite digraphs or circuit-free digraphs.

In section 3, we are interested in polynomial time algorithms providing guarantees on the number of colors. Two kinds of approximation ratios are usually used to characterize the performance guarantees of an approximation algorithm $\mathcal{A}$. The most classical one is, for a given instance G, the ratio between the minimum number $\chi_0(\overrightarrow{G})$ of colors required and the number of colors used by the algorithm, denoted by $m_{\mathcal{A}}(\overrightarrow{G})$. Algorithm $\mathcal{A}$ is said to guarantee a ratio of $\rho(G)$ if, for every instance, the related ratio is bounded below by $\rho(G)$. $\mathcal{A}(\overrightarrow{G})$ will denote the solution computed by $\mathcal{A}$ for $\overrightarrow{G}$. The analysis of approximation algorithms for Min Coloring started with Johnson [10] who showed that the greedy algorithm colors k-colorable graphs with $O(n/\log_k n)$ colors, leading to a performance guarantee of $O(n/\log n)$. So far, the best known approximation algorithm achieves a $O(n(\log\log(n)^2/(\log(n))^3$-approximation [5]. Another framework, called differential ratio or also z-approximation, is also widely used [6], [2], [18], particularly for coloring problems [7], [3], [1]; Min Coloring is known to be constant approximable under this ratio although it is hard to approximate in the usual sense. Given an instance G, the differential ratio of an algorithm $\mathcal{A}$ is defined by $[w(G) - m_{\mathcal{A}}(G)]/[w(G) - \beta(G)]$, where $m_{\mathcal{A}}(G), \beta(G)$ and $w(G)$ respectively denote the value of the computed solution, the optimal value of instance G and its worse value. $w(G)$ is obtained by maximizing (minimizing) the same objective under the same constraints for a minimization (maximization) problem. In the frame of Min Oriented Coloring, the worst value of an instance $\overrightarrow{G}$ is the number

n of vertices and the ratio for $\overrightarrow{G}$ is $[n - m_{\mathcal{A}}(\overrightarrow{G})]/[n - \chi_o(\overrightarrow{G})]$. For this problem, we can see the differential framework as maximizing the number of unused colors among n potential colors.

1.2   Motivation

Oriented coloring is a natural extension of Min Coloring arising in scheduling models. Indeed, Min coloring models some simple tasks assignment problems. Let us consider a set $V = \{T_1, T_2, \ldots, T_n\}$ of different tasks to be handled on n identical processors when no preemption is possible. Every processor can perform only one task at a time and every task is supposed to have a unit processing time on any processor. Let $E \subset \{\{t, t'\}/t \in V, t' \in V, t \neq t'\}$ be a set of incompatibilities: two incompatible tasks cannot be performed during the same time by (different) processors. On the other hand, a set of p tasks without incompatibility can be performed at a time by using p processors. Let us consider the incompatibility graph $G = (V, E)$; it is well known that the minimum time required to handle all tasks in V is the chromatic number of G, denoted by $\chi(G)$. Color classes correspond to tasks that are performed simultaneously.

Let us now consider a similar model where incompatibilities are oriented and defined by $\overrightarrow{E} \subset \{(t, t')/t \in V, t' \in V, t \neq t'\}$; an incompatibility $(t, t') \in \overrightarrow{E}$ means that t' cannot be neither performed (on any processor) at the same time as t, nor during the next time unit after t: if t and t' are performed consecutively, then t must be performed after t'. One has to find a feasible scheduling minimizing the total amount of time, that is a proper coloring (in the usual sense) together with the order in which colors have to be performed. If color i is performed just after color j, then only arcs from i to j are allowed. Let us also note that such problem can be defined with a mixed incompatibility graph. Suppose now that such a scheduling is organized in two steps. First, batches of compatible tasks are performed (middle-term decisions) and one wants to minimize their number. During the second step, (short-term step) a subset of p batches with priority is selected and one wants to perform every p selected batches in p time units (without break). The batches defined during the first step correspond to independent sets in the incompatibility graph; a family of p such independent sets corresponds to batches that can be handled in p time units if they can be numbered $S_1, \ldots, S_p$ in such a way there is no arc from S_i to S_{i+1}. It is easily shown that such a numbering exists for every family of p sets if and only if every two independent sets satisfy the unidirection-property. So this scheduling problem can be seen as an oriented coloring problem.

2   The Complexity of Oriented Chromatic Number

The k-chromatic number problem OCN_k is formally defined as follows: *an instance is an oriented graph $\overrightarrow{G}$ and the question is: does $\overrightarrow{G}$ have an oriented k-coloring ?*

Theorem 1. *([12]) Let k be a fixed positive integer. If $k \leq 3$, then OCN_k can be decided in polynomial time. If $k \geq 4$, then OCN_k is **NP**-complete, even if the input is restricted to connected digraphs.*

In what follows, we study the complexity of Min Oriented Coloring for particular classes of digraphs.

Proposition 1. *Let G be a tree (with at least one edge), and let $\overrightarrow{G}$ be an orientation of G. Then, $\overrightarrow{G}$ admits an oriented k-coloring, with $k = 2$ or $k = 3$. Consequently OCN_k is polynomial when the input is restricted to an oriented tree.*

Proof is done by induction on the order n. Bipartite or circuit-free digraph are natural generalization of orientation of tree. In what follows, we show that OCN_k is **NP**-complete even if the input graph is supposed to be bipartite or circuit-free.

A *tournament* is a complete antisymmetric digraph. If $\overrightarrow{G}$ is a tournament of order n, then $\chi_o(\overrightarrow{G}) = n$. We denote by $B(\overrightarrow{G})$ the bipartite representation of $\overrightarrow{G}$ defined by: $V(B(\overrightarrow{G})) = \{x_i, y_i / i \in V(\overrightarrow{G})\}$, $A(B(\overrightarrow{G})) = \{(x_i, y_j), (y_i, x_j)/(i, j) \in A(\overrightarrow{G})\}$. Then, the following lemma can be easily shown:

Lemma 1. *$\chi_o(B(\overrightarrow{G})) = n$. Moreover, $\overrightarrow{G}$ is the color-digraph of $B(\overrightarrow{G})$ and the only optimal oriented coloring of $B(\overrightarrow{G})$ is given by: $c(x_i) = c(y_i) = i, \forall i \in V(\overrightarrow{G})$.*

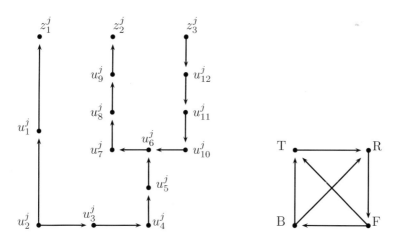

Fig. 1. Digraph $\overrightarrow{L_j}$ and its color digraph T_4^1

Let c be an homomorphism of $\overrightarrow{L_j}$ to the tournament T_4^1 (cf. Fig.1) such that $c(z_1^j), c(z_2^j), c(z_3^j) \in \{T, F\}$, then we have:

Lemma 2. *c exists if and only if $(c(z_1^j), c(z_2^j), c(z_3^j)) \neq (F, F, F)$.*

The main argument of the proof is: if $c(z_3^j) = c(z_2^j) = F$, then $c(u_6^j) = F$.

Theorem 2.

*(i) OCN_4 is **NP**-complete even if the input is restricted to bounded degree bipartite digraphs.*

*(ii) OCN_4 is **NP**-complete even if the input is restricted to bounded degree circuit-free digraphs.*

Proof (Sketch): (i) OCN_4 trivially belongs to **NP**. We then reduce 3-Sat to OCN_4. Let us consider an instance (X, C) of 3-Sat: $X = \{x_1, x_2, \dots, x_n\}$ is a set of boolean variables and $C = \{C_1, \dots, C_m\}$ contains m clauses of 3 literals. The main idea is the following: every clause C_j is associated to the gadget $\overrightarrow{L_j}$ guaranteeing that at least one among z_1^j, z_2^j, z_3^j is associated to color "True" and every variable x_i is associated to the gadget $\overrightarrow{H_i}$ defined below guaranteeing that vertices x_i and $\bar{x}_i$ are assigned to color "True" or "False" and have different colors.

More precisely, the reduction devises the following digraph $\overrightarrow{G}$: $V(\overrightarrow{G}) = \bigcup_{1 \leq j \leq m} U_j \cup \bigcup_{1 \leq i \leq n} V_i$, with $U_j = V(L_j) = \{u_l^j / 1 \leq l \leq 12\}$ and $V_i = \{x_i, \bar{x}_i, e_{x_i}, a_i^l, x_i^F, y_i^F, x_i^T, y_i^T, x_i^R, y_i^R, x_i^B, y_i^B / 1 \leq l \leq 16\}$. The arc set of $\overrightarrow{G}$ is $A(\overrightarrow{G}) = \bigcup_{1 \leq j \leq m} A(\overrightarrow{L_j}) \cup \bigcup_{1 \leq i \leq n} A(\overrightarrow{H_i})$, where $\overrightarrow{H_i} = (V_i, A(\overrightarrow{H_i}))$, $1 \leq i \leq n$, is defined by Fig. 2:

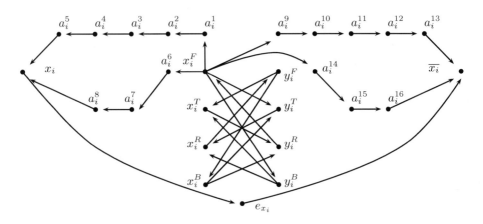

Fig. 2. Digraph $\overrightarrow{H_i}$

For each clause $C_j = z_1^j \vee z_2^j \vee z_3^j$, with $z_k^j \in \{x_i, \bar{x}_i, i \in \{1, 2, \dots, n\}\}$, $k = 1, 2, 3$, ($j \in \{1, 2, \dots, m\}$), we take a copy of $\overrightarrow{L_j}$, identifying vertices z_1^j, z_2^j, z_3^j to the related vertices of $\bigcup_{1 \leq i \leq n} V_i$.

The construction of $\overrightarrow{G}$ can be performed in polynomial time. Digraph $\overrightarrow{G}$ is bipartite and its degree is bounded by $Max(p + 3; 7)$, where p denotes the maximum number of occurrences of a literal in clauses.

If c is an oriented coloring of $\overrightarrow{G}$, as x_i and $\overline{x_i}$ are linked by a 2-path, $c(x_i) \neq c(\overline{x_i})$. The sub-digraph $\overrightarrow{H_i}[\{x_i^F, X_i^T, x_i^R, x_i^B, y_i^F, y_i^T, y_i^R, y_i^B\}]$ is isomorphic to $B(T_4^1)$ for any fixed i in $\{1, 2, \ldots, n\}$. Then, $\chi_o(\overrightarrow{G}) \geq 4$ and if c is an oriented 4-coloring of $\overrightarrow{G}$, its color digraph is tournament T_4^1. Moreover, using lemma 1, x_i^F is necessarily colored by F and the existence of a 4-path and a 6-path from x_i^F to x_i and $\overline{x_i}$ imply that $\{c(x_i), c(\overline{x_i})\} = \{T, F\}$.

Given a truth assignment $t : \{x_i, \overline{x_i}, i \in \{1, 2, 3, \ldots, n\}\} \longrightarrow \{True, False\}$, we associate mapping $c : V(\overrightarrow{G}) \to \{T, F\}$ defined as $c(x_i) = T$ if $t(x_i) = True$, $t(x_i) = F$ otherwise. If t satisfies all clauses $\{C_j\}_{1 \leq j \leq m}$, then applying lemma 2, there exists an homomorphism of $\overrightarrow{G}$ to T_4^1.

Conversely, if such an homomorphism c exists, then we define the truth assignment t by $t(x_i) = True$ if $c(x_i) = T$, $t(x_i) = False$ otherwise. By previous lemma, t satisfies all clauses C_j ($1 \leq j \leq n$).

Consequently, there exists a truth assignment $t : \{x_i, \overline{x_i}, i \in \{1, 2, 3, \ldots, n\}\} \longrightarrow \{True, False\}$ satisfying all clauses $\{C_j\}_{1 \leq j \leq m}$, if and only if $\overrightarrow{G}$ admits an oriented 4-coloring. As $\overrightarrow{G}$ is bipartite, statement (i) of the theorem is proved.

Proof of statement (ii.) is similar by replacing $\overrightarrow{H_i}$ by $\overrightarrow{H_i'}$:

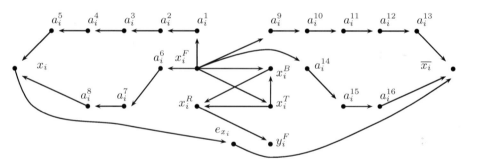

Fig. 3. Digraph $\overrightarrow{H_i'}$

The resulting digraph $\overrightarrow{G}$ is circuit-free and its color digraph is T_4^1.

2.1   Case of Complete Multipartite Digraphs

The bipartite representation of a tournament gives existence of bipartite graphs of order $2n$ with $\chi_o(B) = n$. We focus here on the analysis of general multipartite digraphs. Let $\overrightarrow{G} = (V_1 \cup V_2 \cup \cdots \cup V_l, A(\overrightarrow{G}))$ be a complete multipartite digraph. Given a digraph $\overrightarrow{G}$, we define the mixed graph $M(\overrightarrow{G})$ associated to $\overrightarrow{G}$ by: $V(M(\overrightarrow{G})) = V(\overrightarrow{G})$, $A(M(\overrightarrow{G})) = A(\overrightarrow{G})$ and $E(M(\overrightarrow{G})) = \{\{x, y\} | \exists z \in V(\overrightarrow{G}), (x, z), (z, y) \in A(\overrightarrow{G})$ or $(y, z), (z, x) \in A(\overrightarrow{G})\}$.

Proposition 2.

(i) $\chi_o(\overrightarrow{G}) = \sum_{i=1}^{l} \chi(M(\overrightarrow{G})[V_i])$.

(ii) for $i \in \{1, 2, \ldots, l\}$, if $x, y \in M(\overrightarrow{G})[V_i]$,

$$\{y, x\} \notin E(M(\overrightarrow{G})) \Rightarrow \forall z, \{x, z\} \in E(M(\overrightarrow{G})), \{y, z\} \in E(M(\overrightarrow{G}))$$

(iii) Min Oriented Coloring is polynomial for complete multipartite digraphs.

Proof:(i) Any given optimal oriented coloring of $\overrightarrow{G}$ induces a (usual) coloring of (undirected) graphs $\{M(\overrightarrow{G})[V_i]\}_{1 \leq i \leq l}$. As no oriented color class contains vertices from both V_i and V_j for $1 \leq i \neq j \leq l$, we have: $\chi_o(\overrightarrow{G}) \geq \sum_{i=1}^{l} \chi(M(\overrightarrow{G})[V_i])$. For $i \in \{1, 2, \ldots, l\}$, let c_i be a k_i-coloring of $M(\overrightarrow{G})[V_i]$. Any couple of monochromatic classes in $\{c_i\}_{1 \leq i \leq l}$ satisfies the unidirection property in $\overrightarrow{G}$. Indeed, let $1 \leq i < j \leq l$ and let $\{x, y\} \in M(\overrightarrow{G})[V_i]$ and $\{z, t\} \in M(\overrightarrow{G})[V_j]$. Without lost of generality, we suppose $(x, z) \in A(\overrightarrow{G})$. As $\{x, y\} \notin E(M(\overrightarrow{G})[V_i])$, then $(x, t) \in A(\overrightarrow{G})$. As $\{z, t\} \notin E(M(\overrightarrow{G})[V_j])$, then $(y, t) \in A(\overrightarrow{G})$. Then $\{x, y\} \to \{z, t\}$, and the unidirection property is verified. Mapping $c : V(\overrightarrow{G}) \to \{1, 2, \ldots, k_1 + k_2 + \cdots + k_l\}$ defined by $c(x) = c_i(x) + \sum_{j=1,\ldots,i} k_j$ if $x \in V_i$, is an oriented $(k_1 + k_2 + \cdots + k_l)$-coloring of $\overrightarrow{G}$.

(ii) Let x, y, z be vertices of $M(\overrightarrow{G})[V_i]$ $(1 \leq i \leq l)$, such that $\{y, x\} \notin E(M(\overrightarrow{G}))$ and $\{z, x\} \in E(M(\overrightarrow{G}))$. Without lost of generality, we suppose that the 2-path from x to z (x, α, z) exists. As $\{y, x\} \notin E(M(\overrightarrow{G}))$, $\{y, \alpha\} \in E(\overrightarrow{G})$, then $\{z, y\} \in E(M(\overrightarrow{G}))$.

(iii) Note finally that graphs $\{M(\overrightarrow{G})[V_i]\}_{1 \leq i \leq l}$ are cographs (P_4-free) and consequently their chromatic number can be computed in polynomial time ([4]).

3 Approximation

As OCN_k is $\mathcal{NP}$-complete, for $k \geq 4$ and for various classes of digraphs, we are interested in approximate this problem. The objective of the first subsection is to obtain negative results by the use of a reduction from a well known problem: Maximum Independent Set. In the second subsection, we obtain positive result by the analysis of a greedy algorithm.

3.1 Reduction from Maximum Independent Set

Let $G = (V, E)$ be an instance of the Maximum Independent Set problem with $V = \{1, 2, 3, \ldots, n\}$. Let us define a digraph $\overrightarrow{G'}$ as follows:

$V(\overrightarrow{G'}) = X \cup Y \cup Z$ with: $X = \{x_1, x_2, \ldots, x_n\}$, $Y = \{y_1, y_2, \ldots, y_n\}$ and $Z = \{z_1, z_2, \ldots, z_n\}$. $A(\overrightarrow{G'}) = A_{XY} \cup A_{XZ} \cup A_{YZ}$ with: $A_{XZ} = \{(x_i, z_j), i \leq j\} \cup \{(z_i, x_j), i < j\}$, $A_{YZ} = \{(y_i, z_j), i \leq j\} \cup \{(z_i, y_j), i < j\}$ and $A_{XY} = \{(x_i, y_j), i < j\} \cup \{(x_j, y_i), i < j \text{ and } (j, i) \in E\} \cup \{(y_i, x_j), i < j, (i, j) \notin E\}$.

Let us note that digraphs $\overrightarrow{G'}[X \cup Z]$ and $\overrightarrow{G'}[Y \cup Z]$ are isomorphic, that $\overrightarrow{G'}[X \cup Z]$ and $\overrightarrow{G'}[Y \cup Z]$ are complete bipartite digraphs and that $\overrightarrow{G'}[X \cup Y] \cup \{(x_i, y_i)/1 \leq i \leq n\}$ is a complete bipartite digraph. Moreover, $\chi_o(\overrightarrow{G'}[X \cup Z]) = \chi_o(\overrightarrow{G'}[Y \cup Z]) = 2n$: indeed, as there is always an oriented 2-path from x_i to x_j ($i < j$), and from z_i to z_j, color classes contain only one vertex.

Lemma 3. *Let* $n = |G|$, *then,* $\chi_o(\overrightarrow{G}) = 3n - \alpha(G)$, *where* $\alpha(G)$ *denotes the independent number of* G, *and every* k-*oriented coloring of* $\overrightarrow{G'}$ *allows us to compute in polynomial time an independent set of* G *of size* $3n - k$.

Proof: Any color class of $\overrightarrow{G'}$ is either a single vertex or the pair $\{x_i, y_i\}$ for $i \in \{1, 2, \ldots, n\}$. Consequently $\chi_o(\overrightarrow{G'}) = k$ with $2n \leq k \leq 3n$. Any k-oriented coloring of $\overrightarrow{G'}$ is formed by $(3n - k)$ pairs of vertices and $(2k - 3n)$ single sets. Let S be the set $\{i \in V/\{x_i, y_i\}$ *is a color* $\}$. $\forall (i, j) \in S \times S, i < j$, both definition of A_{XY} and the unidirection property imply that $\{(x_i, y_j), (y_i, x_j)\} \subset A(\overrightarrow{G'})$; consequently $(i, j) \notin E$. Then, S is an independent set of G.

Conversely, let $S \subset V$ be an independent set of G. By definition of $\overrightarrow{G'}$, it is straightforward to verify that we can define an oriented coloring c of $\overrightarrow{G'}$ as follows: color by a same color x_i and y_i, for $i \in S$, and color every other vertex by a new color. Consequently, there is a bijection between the oriented colorings of $\overrightarrow{G'}$ and the independent sets of G, which achieves the lemma.

Theorem 3. *There exists a reduction from Maximum Independent Set to Min Oriented Coloring transforming any differential ratio* $\rho(n)$ *for the Min Oriented Coloring into a* $\rho(3n)$-*standard approximation for the Maximum Independent Set.*

Proof: Let $\mathcal{A}$ be an algorithm guaranteeing a differential ratio of $\rho(n)$ for the Min Oriented Coloring. Let G be a graph. We define $\overrightarrow{G'}$ as previously. We denote by $\chi'_o(\overrightarrow{G'})$ be the number of color classes used by algorithm $\mathcal{A}$ for instance $\overrightarrow{G'}$. By lemma 3, we get an independent set of G of size $\alpha'(G) = 3n - \chi'_o(\overrightarrow{G'})$. So we have: $\alpha'(G)/\alpha(G) = (3n - \chi'_o(\overrightarrow{G'}))/(3n - \chi_o(\overrightarrow{G'})) \geq \rho(3n)$, which concludes the proof.

Corollary 1. *If* **P** $\neq$ **NP**, *then Min Oriented Coloring is not approximable within a constant differential approximation ratio. If* **P** $\neq$ **ZPP**, *then Min Oriented Coloring is not approximable within a differential ratio of* $O(n^{\epsilon - 1})$, $\epsilon > 0$.

3.2   A Greedy Algorithm

In this section, we propose a natural generalization of the usual greedy algorithm consisting in iteratively applying a greedy independent set algorithm [10]. The

main difference for the oriented case arises from the fact that an oriented coloring
of a sub-digraph cannot systematically be completed into an oriented coloring
of the whole digraph (two vertices of the same color in the sub-digraph can
be connected by a 2-path in the whole graph). To overcome this difficulty, the
algorithm is devised in the framework of mixed graphs.

We first introduce a generalization of oriented coloring to mixed graph. A
mixed k-coloring of a mixed graph $M = (V, A, E)$ is a mapping $c : V(M) \rightarrow$
$\{1, 2, \ldots, k\}$ such that, for all $1 \leq i \leq k$, sub-mixed graph $M[c^{-1}(i)]$ of M
contains no arc nor edge, and for all $1 \leq i \leq k$, color classes $c^{-1}(i)$ and $c^{-1}(j)$
are in unidirection in M. Given a mixed graph $M = (V, A, E)$ and a vertex
$v \in V$, we define $B(v, 2)$ as the set of vertices y such that $c(v) \neq c(y)$ for all
mixed coloring c of M: $B(v, 2) = \{y | [\{v, y\} \in E] \vee [(v, y) \in A] \vee [(y, v) \in A] \vee [\exists z \in$
$V, (v, z), (z, y) \in A] \vee [\exists z \in V, (y, z), (z, v) \in A]\}$.

It is obvious that an oriented k-coloring of $\overrightarrow{G}$ is also a mixed k-coloring
of $M(\overrightarrow{G})$, and conversely. Note also that notions of Γ^+ and Γ^- in $\overrightarrow{G}$ and
$M(\overrightarrow{G})$ coincide. It is straightforward to verify that the following proposition
holds for mixed coloring of $M(\overrightarrow{G})$ and does not hold for oriented coloring of $\overrightarrow{G}$.
Nevertheless, every mixed k-coloring of $M(\overrightarrow{G})$ induces an oriented k-coloring
of $\overrightarrow{G}$.

Proposition 3. Let $\overrightarrow{G}$ be a digraph and $z \in V(\overrightarrow{G})$. Every mixed k-coloring c
of $M(\overrightarrow{G})[V(\overrightarrow{G}) \setminus \{z\}]$ can be completed into a mixed $(k + 1)$-coloring of $M(\overrightarrow{G})$.

We then consider Greed-monochromatic (GMC) algorithm which can be seen as
an adaptation of the usual greedy independent set algorithm:

Proposition 4. : Let $\overrightarrow{G}$ be a directed graph and $M(\overrightarrow{G})$ its associated mixed
graph. GMC computes an independent set S of $(M(\overrightarrow{G}))$ (and hence of $\overrightarrow{G}$) such
that $|S| \geq log_{\chi_o(\overrightarrow{G})}(|\overrightarrow{G}|)$ and $\forall z \in V(\overrightarrow{G})$, $\{z\}$ and S verify the unidirection
property implying: $\Gamma^+(S) \cap \Gamma^-(S) = \emptyset$

The proof is a simple adaptation of the usual analysis of greedy independent set
algorithm [10].

GMC
Input: A mixed graph $MG = (V, A, E)$.
Output: GMC(MG) is an independent set S of MG.
(0) $S \leftarrow \emptyset, U \leftarrow V$;
(1) While $U \neq \emptyset$ do:
(2)   Let v minimizing $|B(v, 2)|$ in $MG[U]$;
(3) $S \leftarrow S \cup \{v\}; U \leftarrow U \setminus B(v, 2)$

Let us now consider algorithm Greed-Oriented-Coloring (GOC) that iteratively calls GMC:

GOC

Input A digraph $\overrightarrow{G} = (V, A)$.

Output GOC($\overrightarrow{G}$) is a mixed coloring of $\overrightarrow{G}$.

(0) Construct $M(\overrightarrow{G})$; $U \leftarrow V$, $i \leftarrow 1$.

(a) While $|U| > 0$ do:

(b)   Select at most $\log(|U|)$ vertices in GMC($G[U]$) for color i.

(c)   Let V_{min} be the subset of minimum order between $\Gamma^+($GMC($G[U]$)) and $\Gamma^-($GMC($G[U]$)).

(d)   Every vertex of V_{min} receives a different color in $\{i+1, \ldots, i+|V_{min}|\}$.

(e) $U \leftarrow U \setminus ($GMC($G[U]$) $\cup V_{min})$; $i \leftarrow i + |V_{min}| + 1$.

Let G_i denote the mixed graph $G[U]$ at the ith iteration of inner loop. Let $n_i = |G_i|$ and $\lambda_i = Min\{\log(n_i); |GMC(G_i)|\}$ and let $k = \chi_o(\overrightarrow{G})$. Then we have: $\log_k(n_i) \le |$GMC$(G_i)| \le \log(n_i)$ and $n_{i+1} \ge \frac{n_i - \lambda_i}{2} \ge \frac{n_i - \log(n_i)}{2} \ge \frac{n_i}{3}$ if $n_i \ge 5$.

Thus, with $p = \lfloor \log_3(n) \rfloor$ calls of algorithm GMC, the number of vertices colored by these p colors is at least:

$$\log_k(n) + \log_k(\frac{n}{3}) + \log_k(\frac{n}{3^2}) + \ldots \log_k(\frac{n}{3^{p-1}}) = O(\frac{\log^2(n)}{\log(k)})$$

Then, the number of colors used by the algorithm GOC is at most $\log_3(n) + n - O(\frac{\log^2(n)}{\log(k)})$. We deduce : $(n - \lambda)/(n - k) \ge O[(\log^2(n))/(n \log k)]$. So we have:

Theorem 4. *Min-Oriented-Coloring admits a differential* $O[(\log^2(n))/(n \log (\chi_o(\overrightarrow{G})))]$-*algorithm. In particular, if* $\chi_o(\overrightarrow{G})$ *is bounded, then a differential ratio of* $O[(\log^2(n))/n]$ *is guaranteed.*

Acknowledgement. We are grateful to anonymous referees for their helpful comments.

References

1. Demange, M., Ekim, T., and de Werra, D.: On the Approximation of Min Split-Coloring and Min Cocoloring. Manuscript
2. Demange, M., Grisoni, P., and Paschos, V.Th.: Differential Approximation Algorithms for Some Combinatorial Optimization Problems. Theoretical Computer Science **209** (1998) 107–122
3. Duh, R., and Fürer, M.: Approximation of k-Set Cover by Semi-Local Optimization. In Proc. of the Twenty-Ninth Annual ACM Symposium on Theory of Computing (1997) 256–264
4. Golumbic, M.C.: Algorithmic Graph Theory and Perfect Graphs. Academic Press, New York

5. Halldórsson, M.M.: A Still Better Performance Quarantee for Approximate Graph Coloring. Information Processing Letters **45** (1993) 19–23
6. Hassin, R., and Khuller, S.: z-Approximations. Journal of Algorithms **41** (2001) 429–442
7. Hassin, R., and Lahav, S.: Maximizing the Number of Unused Colors in the Vertex Coloring Problem. Information Processing Letters **52** (1994) 87–90
8. Hell, P., and Nesetril, J.: On the Complexity of h-Coloring. Journal of Combinatorial Theory (B) **18** (1990) 92–110
9. Hell, P. and Nesetril, J.: Graphs and Homomorphisms. Oxford Lecture Series in Mathematics and its Applications (2004)
10. Johnson, D.S.: Approximation Algorithms for Combinatorial Problems. Journal of Computer and System Sciences **9** (1974) 256–278
11. Kierstead, H.A., and Trotter, W.T.: Competitive Colorings of Oriented Graphs. Electronic Journal of Combinatorics **8** (2001)
12. Klostermeyer, W.F., and MacGillivray, G.: Homomorphisms and Oriented Colorings of Equivalence Classes of Oriented Graphs. Discrete Mathematics **274** (2004) 161–172
13. Nesetril, J., and Sopena, E.: On the Oriented Game Chromatic Number. The Electronic Journal of Combinatorics **8** 2 R14 (2001)
14. Nesetril, J., Sopena, E., and Vignal, L.: t-Preserving Homomorphisms of Oriented Graphs. Comment. Math. Univ. Carolinae **38** 1 (1997) 125–136
15. Sopena, E.: Computing Chromatic Polynomials of Oriented Graphs. Proc. Formal power series and Algebraic Combinatorics. DIMACS (1994) 413–422
16. Sopena, E.: Oriented Graph Coloring. Discrete Mathematics **229** (2001)
17. Wood, D.R.: Acyclic, Star and Oriented Colorings of Graph Subdivisions. Submitted (2005)
18. Zemel, E.: Measuring the Quality of Approximate Solutions to Zero-One Programming Problems. Mathematics of Operations Research **6** (1981) 319–332

NONBLOCKER: Parameterized Algorithmics for MINIMUM DOMINATING SET

Frank Dehne[1], Michael Fellows[2], Henning Fernau[2,3,4],
Elena Prieto[2], and Frances Rosamond[2]

[1] School of Computer Science, Carleton University, Canada
[2] School of Electrical Engineering and Computer Science,
The University of Newcastle, Australia
[3] University of Hertfordshire, College Lane, Hatfield, Herts AL10 9AB, UK
[4] Universität Tübingen, WSI für Informatik, Sand 13, 72076 Tübingen, Germany

Abstract. We provide parameterized algorithms for NONBLOCKER, the parametric dual of the well known DOMINATING SET problem. We exemplify three methodologies for deriving parameterized algorithms that can be used in other circumstances as well, including the (*i*) use of extremal combinatorics (known results from graph theory) in order to obtain very small kernels, (*ii*) use of known exact algorithms for the (nonparameterized) MINIMUM DOMINATING SET problem, and (*iii*) use of exponential space. Parameterized by the size k_d of the non-blocking set, we obtain an algorithm that runs in time $\mathcal{O}^*(1.4123^{k_d})$ when allowing exponential space.

1 Introduction

The *minimum dominating set* of a graph $G = (V, E)$ is a subset $V' \subseteq V$ of minimum cardinality such that for all $u \in V - V'$ there exists a $v \in V'$ for which $(u, v) \in E$. The problem of finding a minimum dominating set in a graph is arguably one of the most important combinatorial problems on graphs, having, together with its variants, numerous applications and offering various lines of research [11]. The problem of finding a set of at most k vertices dominating the whole n-vertex graph is not only $\mathcal{N}P$-complete but also hard to approximate [2], [10]. Moreover, this problem is also intractable when viewed as a parameterized problem [5]. The status is different if the problem is to find a set of at most $k = n - k_d$ vertices dominating a given n-vertex graph, where k_d (k−dual) is considered the parameter. Our focus in this paper is to present a new $\mathcal{O}^*(2.0226^{k_d})$-algorithm for this dual problem which we will henceforth call the NONBLOCKER problem. (We will make use of the $\mathcal{O}^*$-notation that has now become standard in exact algorithmics: in contrast to the better known $\mathcal{O}$-notation, it not only suppresses constants but also polynomial-time parts.)

Interesting relationships are known for the optimum value $\mathrm{nb}(G)$ of k_d for a graph G: Nieminen [16] has shown that, for a non-trivial connected graph, $\mathrm{nb}(G)$ equals the maximum number of *pendant edges* among all spanning forests for G (an edge $\{u, v\}$ in a forest F is pendant iff either u or v have degree one

J. Wiedermann et al. (Eds.): SOFSEM 2006, LNCS 3831, pp. 237–245, 2006.

in F), and therefore $\mathrm{nb}(G)$ is again equal to the size of a maximum minimal edge cover of G due to a result of Hedetniemi [12]. How to algorithmically relate minimum dominating sets and maximum minimal edge covers is shown in [14].

On graphs of degree at least one, Ore [17] has shown (using different terminology) that the NONBLOCKER problem admits a kernel of size $2k_d$. Ore's result was improved by McCuaig and Shepherd [15] for graphs with minimum degree two; in fact, their result was a corollary to the classification of graphs that satisfy a certain inequality stated by Ore with equality. Independently, the result had been discovered by the Russian mathematician Blank [3] more than fifteen years ago, as noticed by Reed in [19]. More precisely, they have shown:

Theorem 1. *If a connected graph $G = (V, E)$ has minimum degree two and is not one of seven exceptional graphs (each of them having at most seven vertices), then the size of its minimum dominating set is at most $2/5 \cdot |V|$.*

The algorithms we present are easy to implement, addressing an important need of professional programmers. They essentially consist only of exhaustively applying simple data reduction (preprocessing) rules and then doing some search in the reduced problem space. (The mathematical analysis of our simple algorithm is quite involved and non-trivial, however.)

Our data reduction rules make use of several novel technical features. We introduce a special annotated *catalytic vertex*, a vertex which is forced to be in the dominating set we are going to construct. The catalytic vertex is introduced by a *catalyzation rule* which is applied only once. The graph is reduced and when no further reduction rules are applicable, a special *de-catalyzation rule* is applied. The *de-catalyzation rule* also is applied only once. We believe that the use of (de-)-catalyzation rules that might also *increase* the parameter size (since they are only applied once) is a technique that might find more widespread use when developing kernelization algorithms.

2   Definitions

We first describe the setting in which we will discuss MINIMUM DOMINATING SET in the guise of NONBLOCKER.

A *parameterized problem* $\mathcal{P}$ is a subset of $\Sigma^* \times \mathbb{N}$, where Σ is a fixed alphabet and $\mathbb{N}$ is the set of all non-negative integers. Therefore, each instance of the parameterized problem $\mathcal{P}$ is a pair (I, k), where the second component k is called the *parameter*. The language $L(\mathcal{P})$ is the set of all YES-instances of $\mathcal{P}$. We say that the parameterized problem $\mathcal{P}$ is *fixed-parameter tractable* [5] if there is an algorithm that decides whether an input (I, k) is a member of $L(\mathcal{P})$ in time $f(k)|I|^c$, where c is a fixed constant and $f(k)$ is a recursive function independent of the overall input length $|I|$. The class of all fixed-parameter tractable problems is denoted by $\mathcal{FPT}$.

The problems DOMINATING SET and NONBLOCKER are defined as follows: An instance of DOMINATING SET (DS) is given by a graph $G = (V, E)$, and the parameter, a positive integer k. The question is: Is there a *dominating set*

$D \subseteq V$ with $|D| \leq k$? An instance of NONBLOCKER (NB) is given by a graph $G = (V, E)$, and the parameter, a positive integer k_d. The question is: Is there a *non-blocking set* $N \subseteq V$ with $|N| \geq k_d$?

A subset of vertices V' such that every vertex in V' has a neighbor in $V \setminus V'$ is called a *non-blocking set*. Observe that the complement of a non-blocking set is a dominating set and vice versa. Hence, $G = (V, E)$ has a dominating set of size at most k if and only if G has a non-blocking set of size at least $k_d = n - k$. Hence, DOMINATING SET and NONBLOCKER are called *parametric duals*.

Let $\mathcal{P}$ be a parameterized problem. A *kernelization* is a function K that is computable in polynomial time and maps an instance (I, k) of $\mathcal{P}$ onto an instance (I', k') of $\mathcal{P}$ such that (I, k) is a YES-instance of $\mathcal{P}$ if and only if (I', k') is a YES-instance of $\mathcal{P}$, $|I'| \leq f(k)$, and $k' \leq g(k)$ for arbitrary functions f and g. The instance (I', k') is called the *kernel* (of I). The importance of these notions for parameterized complexity is due to the following characterization.

Theorem 2. *A parameterized problem is in $\mathcal{FPT}$ iff it is kernelizable.*

Hence, in order to develop $\mathcal{FPT}$-algorithms, finding kernelizations can be seen as the basic methodology. The search for a small kernel often begins with finding local reduction rules. The reduction rules reduce the size of the instance to which they are applied; they are exhaustively applied and finally yield the kernelization function. In this paper we introduce a small variation of this method; namely, we introduce a catalyzation and a de-catalyzation rule, both of which are applied only once. Contrary to our usual reduction rules, these two special rules might increase the instance size.

We use this approach to solve the following *Catalytic Conversion* form of the problem. An instance of NONBLOCKER WITH CATALYTIC VERTEX (NBCAT) is given by a graph $G = (V, E)$, a catalytic vertex c, and the parameter, a positive integer k_d. The question is: Is there a *non-blocking set* $N \subseteq V$ with $|N| \geq k_d$ such that $c \notin N$? The special annotated catalytic vertex is assumed to be in the dominating set (not the non-blocking set).

3   Catalytic Conversion: $\mathcal{FPT}$ Agorithm for NONBLOCKER

Our kernelization algorithm for solving NONBLOCKER uses two special rules 1 and 2 to introduce and then finally to delete the catalytic vertex. The actually preprocessing then uses five more rules that work on an instance of NBcat.

Reduction rule 1 (Catalyzation rule). *If (G, k_d) is a NONBLOCKER-instance with $G = (V, E)$, then (G', c, k_d) is an equivalent instance of NONBLOCKER WITH CATALYTIC VERTEX, where $c \notin V$ is a new vertex, and $G' = (V \cup \{c\}, E)$.*

Reduction rule 2 (De-catalyzation rule). *Let (G, c, k_d) be an instance of NONBLOCKER WITH CATALYTIC VERTEX. Then, perform the following surgery to obtain a new instance (G', k_d') of NONBLOCKER (i.e., without a catalytic vertex):*

Add three new vertices u, v, and w and introduce new edges cu, cv, cw, uv and vw. All other vertices and edge relations in G stay the same. This describes the new graph G'. Set $k'_d = k_d + 3$.

Reduction rule 3 (The Isolated Vertex Rule). *Let (G, c, k_d) be an instance of NBCAT. If C is a complete graph component (complete subgraph) of G that does not contain c, then reduce to $(G - C, c, k_d - (|C| - 1))$.*

Observe that Rule 3 applies to isolated vertices. It also applies to instances that do *not* contain a catalytic vertex. A formal proof of the soundness of the rule is contained in [18]. Notice that this rule alone gives a $2k_d$ kernel for general graphs with the mentioned result of Ore (details are shown below). By getting rid of vertices of degree one, we can improve on the kernel size due to Theorem 1.

Reduction rule 4 (The Catalytic Rule). *Let (G, c, k_d) be an instance of* NONBLOCKER WITH CATALYTIC VERTEX. *Let $v \neq c$ be a vertex of degree one in G with $N(v) = u$ (where $N(v)$ refers to the set of neighbor vertices of v). Transform (G, c, k_d) into $(G', c', k_d - 1)$, where:*

- *If $u \neq c$ then $G' = G_{[c \leftrightarrow u]} \setminus v$, i.e., G' is the graph obtained by deleting v and merging u and c into a new catalytic vertex $c' = \langle c \leftrightarrow u \rangle$.*
- *If $u = c$ then $G' = G \setminus v$ and $c' = c$.*

Lemma 1. *Rule 4 is sound.*

Proof. "Only if:" Let (G, c, k_d) be an instance of NBCAT. Let $V' \subset V(G)$ be a non-blocking set in G with $|V'| = k_d$. The vertex v is a vertex of degree one in G. Let u be the neighbor of v in G. Two cases arise:

1. If $v \in V'$ then it must have a neighbor in $V(G) \setminus V'$ and thus $u \in V(G) \setminus V'$. Deleting v will decrease the size of V' by one. If $u = c$, then $(G', c', k_d - 1)$ is a YES-instance of NBCAT. If $u \neq c$, merging u and c will not affect the size of V' as both vertices are now in $V(G') \setminus V'$. Thus, $(G', c', k_d - 1)$ is a YES-instance of NBCAT.
2. If $v \in V(G) \setminus V'$, then two cases arise:
   2.1. If u is also in $V(G) \setminus V'$ then deleting v does not affect the size of V'. Note that this argument is valid whether $u = c$ or $u \neq c$.
   2.2. If $u \in V'$ then $u \neq c$. If we make $v \in V'$ and $u \in V(G) \setminus V'$, the size of V' remains unchanged. Since u did not dominate any vertices in the graph, this change does not affect $N(u) \setminus v$, and Case 1 now applies.

"If:" Conversely, assume that $(G', c', k_d - 1)$ is a YES-instance of NBCAT.

1. If $u = c$, then we can always place v in V' and thus (G, c, k_d) is a YES-instance for NONBLOCKER WITH CATALYTIC VERTEX.
2. If $u \neq c$, getting from G' to G can be seen as (1) splitting the catalytic vertex c' into two vertices c and u, (2) taking c as the new catalytic vertex, and (3) attaching a pendant vertex v to u. As the vertex u is in

$V(G) \setminus V'$, v can always be placed in V', increasing the size of this set by one. Thus (G, c, k_d) is a YES-instance for NBCAT, concluding the proof of Lemma 4. ∎

Reduction Rule 3 can be generalized as follows:

Reduction rule 5 (The Small Degree Rule). *Let (G, c, k_d) be an instance of* NONBLOCKER WITH CATALYTIC VERTEX. *Whenever you have a vertex $x \in V(G)$ whose neighborhood contains a non-empty subset $U \subseteq N(x)$ such that $N(U) \subseteq U \cup \{x\}$ and $c \notin U$ (where $N(U)$ is the set of vertices that are neighbors to at least one vertex in U), then you can merge x with the catalytic vertex c and delete U (and reduce the parameter by $|U|$).*

Without further discussion, we now state those reduction rules that can be used to get rid of all consecutive degree-2-vertices in a graph:

Reduction rule 6 (The Degree Two Rule). *Let (G, c, k_d) be an instance of* NBCAT. *Let u, v be two vertices of degree two in G such that $u \in N(v)$ and $|N(u) \cup N(v)| = 4$, i.e., $N(u) = \{u', v\}$ and $N(v) = \{v', u\}$ for some $u' \neq v'$. If $c \notin \{u, v\}$, then merge u' and v' and delete u and v to get $(G', c', k_d - 2)$. If u' or v' happens to be c, then c' is the merger of u' and v'; otherwise, $c' = c$.*

Reduction rule 7 (The Degree Two, Catalytic Vertex Rule). *Let (G, c, k_d) be an instance of* NBCAT, *where $G = (V, E)$. Assume that c has degree two and a neighboring vertex v of degree two, i.e., $N(v) = \{v', c\}$. Then, delete the edge vv'. Hence, we get the new instance $((V, E \setminus \{vv'\}), c, k_d)$.*

Notice that all cases of two subsequent vertices u, v of degree two are covered in this way: If u or v is the catalytic vertex, then Rule 7 applies. Otherwise, if u and v have a common neighbor x, then Rule 5 is applicable; x will be merged with the catalytic vertex. Otherwise, Rule 6 will apply. This allows us to eliminate all of the exceptional graphs of Theorem 1 (since all of them have two consecutive vertices of degree two).

Algorithm 1. A kernelization algorithm for NONBLOCKER

Input(s): an instance (G, k_d) of NONBLOCKER
Output(s): an equivalent instance (G', k'_d) of NONBLOCKER with $V(G') \subseteq V(G)$, $|V(G')| \leq 5/3 \cdot k'_d$ and $k'_d \leq k_d$ OR YES

    Apply the catalyzation rule.
    Exhaustively apply Rules 3 to 7. In the case of Reduction Rule 5, do so only for neighborhoods U up to size two.
    Apply the de-catalyzation rule.
    {This leaves us with a reduced instance (G', k'_d).}
    if $|V(G')| > 5/3 \cdot k'_d$ **then**
        return YES
    else
        return (G', k'_d)
    end if

Corollary 1. *Alg. 1 provides a kernel of size upperbounded by $5/3 \cdot k_d + 3$ for any* NONBLOCKER-*instance* (G, k_d), *where the problem size is measured in terms of the number of vertices.*

4   Searching the Space

4.1   Brute Force

With a very small kernel, the remaining reduced NONBLOCKER-instance can be solved by brute-force search. Hence, we have to test all subsets of size k_d within the set of vertices of size at most $5/3 \cdot k_d$. Stirling's formula gives:

Lemma 2. *For any $a > 1$,* $\dbinom{ak}{k} \approx a^k \left(\frac{a}{a-1} \right)^{(a-1)k}$.

Corollary 2. *By testing all subsets of size k_d of a reduced instance* (G, k_d) *of* NONBLOCKER, *the* NONBLOCKER *problem can be solved in time $\mathcal{O}^*(3.0701^{k_d})$.*

4.2   Using Nonparameterized Exact Algorithmics

The above corollary can be considerably improved by making use of the following recent result of F. Fomin, F. Grandoni, and D. Kratsch [7] on general graphs:

Theorem 3. MINIMUM DOMINATING SET *can be solved in time $\mathcal{O}^*(1.5260^n)$ with polynomial space on arbitrary n-vertex graphs.*

The corresponding algorithm is quite a simple one for HITTING SET, considering the open neighborhoods of vertices as hyperedges in a hypergraph; the quite astonishing running time is produced by an intricate analysis of that algorithm. Due to the $5/3 \cdot k_d$-kernel for NONBLOCKER, we conclude:

Corollary 3. *By applying the algorithm of Fomin, Grandoni, and Kratsch [7] to solve* MINIMUM DOMINATING SET *on a reduced instance* (G, k_d) *of* NONBLOCKER, *the* NONBLOCKER *problem can be solved in time $\mathcal{O}^*(2.0226^{k_d})$ with polynomial space.*

4.3   Trading Time and Space

Due to the fact that the kernel we obtained for NONBLOCKER is very small, it may be worthwhile looking for an algorithm that uses exponential space. According trade-off computations are contained in [7], so that we may conclude:

Corollary 4. *By using exponential space,* NONBLOCKER *can be solved in time (and space) $\mathcal{O}^*(1.4123^{k_d})$.*

5   Discussion: Further Results and Open Questions

Questions on general graphs. We have presented two efficient parameterized algorithms for the NONBLOCKER problem, the parametric dual of DOMINATING SET. With the help of known (non-trivial) graph-theoretic results and new exact algorithms for MINIMUM DOMINATING SET, we were able to further reduce the involved constants.

It would be possible to use the result of Reed [19] to obtain a smaller kernel for NONBLOCKER if rules could be found to reduce vertices of degree two. Perhaps such rules may be possible only for restricted graph classes, e.g., NONBLOCKER restricted to bipartite graphs.

Finally, notice that our reduction rules get rid of all degree-two vertices that have another degree-two vertex as a neighbor. Is there an "intermediate" kernel size theorem (that somehow interpolates between the result of Blank, McCuaig and Shepherd and that of Reed)? Our use of the additional structural properties of the reduced graphs was to cope with the exceptional graphs from [15].

Planar graphs. Since the rules that merge the catalyst with other vertices may destroy planarity, we may only claim the $2k_d$ kernel in the case of planar graphs.

We now use the following result on planar graphs by Fomin and Thilikos [9]:

Theorem 4. *Every planar n-vertex graph has treewidth at most $9/\sqrt{8} \cdot \sqrt{n}$.*

Together with the treewidth-based algorithm for MINIMUM DOMINATING SET as developed in [1], we can conclude:

Corollary 5. *The* NONBLOCKER *problem, restricted to planar graphs, can be solved in time* $\mathcal{O}^*(2^{9\sqrt{k_d}})$.

Is it possible to find a better kernelization in the planar case? This would be interesting in view of lower bound results of J. Chen, H. Fernau, I. A. Kanj, and G. Xia [4] who have shown there is no kernel smaller than $(67/66 - \epsilon)k_d$. Such a result would immediately entail better running times for algorithms dealing with the planar case. Observe that the kernelization of Ore also applies to planar cubic graphs. Since NONBLOCKER is also $\mathcal{N}P$-complete for that graph class (see [13]) and since DOMINATING SET has a $4k$-kernel in that case, we know that there is no $(4/3 - \epsilon)k_d$-kernel for NONBLOCKER on planar cubic graphs.

Graphs of bounded degree. Interestingly, there are better algorithm for solving MINIMUM DOMINATING SET on cubic graphs (graphs whose degree is bounded by three). More precisely, in [8] it is shown that this restricted problem can be solved in time $\mathcal{O}^*(3^{n/6}) = \mathcal{O}^*(1.2010^n)$ based on pathwidth decomposition techniques. As in the planar case, we cannot make use of the catalyst rule, since its application may increase the degree of a vertex.

Due to the $2k_d$-kernel for NONBLOCKER based on Ore's result [17], we conclude:

Corollary 6. *By applying the algorithm of Fomin, Grandoni, and Kratsch [8] to solve* MINIMUM DOMINATING SET *on a reduced instance* (G, k_d) *of* NON-BLOCKER, *the* NONBLOCKER *problem, restricted to instances of maximum degree three, can be solved in time* $\mathcal{O}^*(3^{k_d/3}) = \mathcal{O}^*(1.4423^{k_d})$ *with polynomial space.*

Notice however that we can even do better in this case. Namely, by applying all of our reduction rules but the decatalyzation rule, at most one vertex (namely the catalyst) will have a degree higher than three, when starting with a graph of maximum degree of three. Now, we can incorporate the information that all neighbors of the catalyst are already dominated in the pathdecomposition based algorithm for MINIMUM DOMINATING SET run on the graph G obtained from the reduced graph by deleting the catalyst. Since G has maximum degree three, the pathwidth bound of Fomin, Grandoni, and Kratsch [8] applies, so that we can conclude:

Corollary 7. *By applying the algorithm of Fomin, Grandoni, and Kratsch [8] to solve* MINIMUM DOMINATING SET *on a reduced instance* (G, k_d) *of* NONBLOCKER *(that is modified as described), the* NONBLOCKER *problem, restricted to instances of maximum degree three, can be solved in time* $\mathcal{O}^*(3^{5k_d/18}) = \mathcal{O}^*(1.3569^{k_d})$ *with polynomial space.*

Moreover, the kernelization primal/dual game can be played, since there is a trivial $4k$ kernel for MINIMUM DOMINATING SET on cubic graphs (each vertex in a dominating set can dominate at most three vertices). The lower bound results of J. Chen, H. Fernau, I. A. Kanj, and G. Xia [4] on kernel sizes yield a $2k$ kernel size lower bound for MINIMUM DOMINATING SET on cubic graphs. So, in that case, upper and lower bound are not far off each other, at least when compared to the planar case.

Related problems. Our approach seem to be transferrable to similar problems, although then several additional technical hurdles appear. For example, for a suitable definition of "parametric dual", we were able to derive similar kernel results as given in this paper for MINIMUM ROMAN DOMINATION, see [6].

In view of the fact that the MINIMUM DOMINATING SET algorithm only makes use of MINIMUM HITTING SET in its analysis, the same time bounds are also valid for the variant of MINIMUM TOTAL DOMINATING SET, where each vertex is required to be dominated by a neighbor (also the ones in the dominating set). However, our catalyzator technique only works for vertices that are in the dominating set and that are already dominated; vertices that are in the dominating set (e.g., since they are neighbors of a vertex of degree one) but not yet dominated themselves cannot be merged (only if their open neighborhoods are comparable with respect to inclusion). There exist results similar to Blank, Mc-Cuaig and Shepard's that might provide kernelizations for TOTAL NONBLOCKER, see [20].

References

1. Alber, J., Bodlaender, H.L., Fernau, H., Kloks, T., and Niedermeier, R.: Fixed Parameter Algorithms for DOMINATING SET and Related Problems on Planar Graphs. Algorithmica **33** (2002) 461–493
2. Ausiello, G., Creczenzi, P., Gambosi, G., Kann, V. Marchetti-Spaccamela, A., and Protasi, M.: Complexity and Approximation; Combinatorial Optimization Problems and Their Approximability Properties. Springer (1999)
3. Blank, M.: An Estimate of the External Stability Number of a Graph without Suspended Vertices (in Russian). Prikl. Math. i Programmirovanie Vyp. **10** (1973) 3–11
4. Chen, J., Fernau, H., Kanj, I.A., and Xia, G.: Parametric Duality and Kernelization: Lower Bounds and Upper Bounds on Kernel Size. In V. Diekert and B. Durand (eds), Symposium on Theoretical Aspects of Computer Science STACS 2005, LNCS, Springer **3404** (2005) 269–280
5. Downey, R.G., and Fellows, M.R.: Parameterized Complexity. Springer (1999)
6. Fernau, H.: ROMAN DOMINATION: a Parameterized Perspective. This volume (2006)
7. Fomin, F.V., Grandoni, F., and Kratsch, D.: Measure and Conquer: Domination – a Case Study. In L. Caires, G. F. Italiano, L. Monteiro, C. Palamidessi, and M. Yung (eds), Automata, Languages and Programming, 32nd International Colloquium, ICALP, LNCS, Springer **3580** (2005) 191–203
8. Fomin, F.V., Grandoni, F., and Kratsch, D.: Some New Techniques in Design and Analysis of Exact (Exponential) Algorithms. Technical Report 307, Department of Informatics, University of Bergen (2005)
9. Fomin, F.V., and Thilikos, D.: A Simple and Fast Approach for Solving Problems on Planar Graphs. In V. Diekert and M. Habib (eds), Symposium on Theoretical Aspects of Computer Science STACS 2004, LNCS, Springer (2004) 56–67
10. Garey, M.R., and Johnson, D.S.: Computers and Intractability. New York: Freeman (1979)
11. Haynes, T.W., Hedetniemi, S.T., and Slater, P.J.: Fundamentals of Domination in Graphs, Monographs and Textbooks in Pure and Applied Mathematics, Marcel Dekker **208** (1998)
12. Hedetniemi, S.T.: A Max-Min Relationship between Matchings and Domination in Graphs. Congressus Numerantium **40** (1983) 23–34
13. Kikuno, T., Yoshida, N., and Kakuda, Y.: The NP-Completeness of the Dominating Set Problem in Cubic Planar Graphs. Transactions of the Institute of Electronics and Communication Engineers of Japan **E63** 6 (1980) 443–444
14. Manlove, D.F.: On the Algorithmic Complexity of Twelve Covering and Independence Parameters of Graphs. Discrete Applied Mathematics **91** (1999) 155–175
15. McCuaig, B., and Shepherd, B.: Domination in Graphs of Minimum Degree Two. Journal of Graph Theory **13** (1989) 749–762
16. Nieminen, J.: Two Bounds for the Domination Number of a Graph. Journal of the Institute of Mathematics and its Applications **14** (1974) 183–187
17. Ore, O.: Theory of Graphs, Colloquium Publications. American Mathematical Society **XXXVIII** (1962)
18. Prieto, E.: Systematic Kernelization in FPT Algorithm Design. PhD thesis, The University of Newcastle, Australia (2005)
19. Reed, B.: Paths, Stars, and the Number Three. Combinatorics, Probability and Computing **5** (1996) 277–295
20. Thomassé, S., and Yeo, Y.: Total Domination of Graphs and Small Transversals of Hypergraphs. To appear in Combinatorica (2005)

Quantum Finite Automata and Logics

Ilze Dzelme

Institute of Mathematics and Computer Science, University of Latvia,
Raiņa bulvāris 29, LV–1459 Riga, Latvia

Abstract. The connection between measure once quantum finite automata (MO-QFA) and logic is studied in this paper. The language class recognized by MO-QFA is compared to languages described by the first order logics and modular logics. And the equivalence between languages accepted by MO-QFA and languages described by formulas using Lindström quantifier is shown.

1 Introduction

The connection between automata and logic goes back to the work of Büchi [10] and Elgot [13]. They showed that finite automata and monadic second-order logic over finite words have the same expressive power, and that the transformation from finite automata to monadic second order formulas and vice versa are effective. Later Büchi [11], McNaughton [21], and Rabin [24] showed equivalence between finite automata and monadic second-order logics over infinite words and trees. In the eighties, temporal logics and fixed-point logics took the role of specification languages and more efficient transformations from logic formulas to automata were found. The research of the equivalence between automata and logic formalism also influenced language theory, the classification theory of formal languages was deepened by including notations and techniques, and the logical approach helped in generalizing language theoretical results from the domain of words to more general structures like trees and partial orders.

The equivalence between logic formulas and automata has also influenced complexity theory. Fagin [14] showed that many complexity classes, such as NP, P, PSPACE, could be characterized by different versions of second-order logic, involving such operators as fixed point operator or transitive closure operator.

A finite automaton is a natural model of classical computing with finite memory, the same is a quantum finite automaton (QFA), it is a natural model of quantum computation. There are known several models of quantum automata. The two most popular quantum finite automata are quantum finite automata introduced by Moore and Crutchfield [22] and quantum finite automata introduced by Kondacs and Watrous [19] and they have a seemingly small difference, the first definition of quantum finite automata allows the measurement only at the end of the computation, but the second definition of quantum automata allows the measurement at every step of the computation. Because of this difference these kinds of quantum automata are usually called measure-once quantum finite automata (MO-QFA) and measure-many quantum finite automata (MM-QFA). MO-QFA

J. Wiedermann et al. (Eds.): SOFSEM 2006, LNCS 3831, pp. 246–253, 2006.

and MM-QFA with isolated cut point recognise only the subset of the regular languages. The notions of quantum finite automata which are strictly more capable than MM-QFA are quantum finite automata with mixed states (introduced by D.Aharonov, A.Kitaev and N.Nisan [1]) and quantum finite automata with quantum and classical states (introduced by A.Ambainis and J.Watrous [5]). If quantum finite automata are compared to their classical counterparts, QFA have their strengths and weaknesses. The strength of quantum automata is in the fact that QFA can be exponentially more effective [3], but the weakness is caused by necessity that a quantum process has to be reversible.

For most of the notations of quantum finite automata the problem to describe the class of the languages recognizable by the quantum automata is till open and as logic has had a large impact on Computer Science, it is interesting to look at the languages recognizable of quantum finite automata in the terms of logic. The connection between measure once quantum finite automata and first order logics and modular first order logics has been studied in this paper. As well as the equivalence between measure once quantum finite automata and formula with Lindström quantifier has been shown.

2   Main Notations

2.1   Quantum Finite Automata

Definition 1. *A measure-once quantum finite automaton is a tuple*

$$A = (Q; \Sigma; \delta; q_0; Q_{acc}; Q_{rej})$$

where Q is a finite set of states, Σ is an input alphabet, $q_0 \in Q$ is a initial state, $Q_{acc} \subseteq Q$ and $Q_{rej} \subseteq Q$ are sets of accepting and rejecting states ($Q_{acc} \cap Q_{rej} = \varnothing$), and δ is the transition function $\delta : Q \times \Gamma \times Q \to C_{[0,1]}$, where $\Gamma = \Sigma \cup \{\,\sharp;\$\,\}$ is working alphabet of A, and $\sharp$ and $\$$ are the left and the right endmarkers.

The computation of A is performed in the inner-product space $l_2(Q)$, i.e., with the basis $\{|\,q\rangle \mid q \in Q\}$, using the linear operators V_σ, $\sigma \in \Gamma$, defined by $V_\sigma(|\,q\rangle) = \sum_{q' \in Q} \delta(q, \sigma, q') \mid q'\rangle$, which are required to be unitary.

A computation of A on input $\sharp \sigma_1 \sigma_2 \ldots \sigma_n \$$ proceeds as follows. It starts in superposition $|\,q_0\rangle$. Then a transformation corresponding to the left end marker $\sharp$, the letters of the input word and the right end marker $\$$ are performed. After reading the right end marker $\$$ the final superposition is observed with respect to E_{acc} and E_{rej} where $E_{acc} = span\{|\,q\rangle : q \in Q_{acc}\}$ and $E_{rej} = span\{|\,q\rangle : q \in Q_{rej}\}$. It means if the final superposition is $\psi = \sum_{q_i \in Q_{acc}} \alpha_i \mid q_i\rangle + \sum_{q_j \in Q_{rej}} \beta_j \mid q_j\rangle$ then the measure once quantum finite automaton A accepts the input word with probability $\sum \alpha_i^2$ and rejects $\sum \beta_j^2$.

2.2   Logics and Classical Automata

Let A a finite alphabet and let $\omega = a_1 a_2 \ldots a_n$ be a word over A. The corresponding *word model* for the word ω is represented by the relational structure

$$\underline{\omega} = (dom(\omega), S, <, (Q_a)_{a \in A})$$

where $dom(\omega) = \{1, 2, \ldots, n\}$ is the set of the letter "positions" of ω (the "domain" of ω), S is the successor relation on $dom(\omega)$ with $(i, i + 1) \in S$ for all $1 \leq i \leq n$, $<$ is the order relation on $dom(\omega)$, and $Q_a = \{i \in dom(\omega) \mid a_i = a\}$ ("position carries letter a").

Consider word models over the finite alphabet A. The corresponding first order language has variables $x, y, \ldots$ ranging over positions in the word models, and is built from atomic formulas of the form

$$x = y, \; S(x, y), \; Q_a(x)$$

by means of the connectivities $\neg, \vee, \wedge, \rightarrow, \leftrightarrow$ and quantifiers $\exists$ and $\forall$. The notation $\varphi(x_1, x_2, \ldots, x_n)$ indicates that in the formula φ at most the variables $x_1, x_2, \ldots, x_n$ are free, i.e. they are not in the scope of some quantifier. A *sentence* is a formula with no free variables. If $p_1, p_2, \ldots, p_n$ are positions from $dom(\omega)$ then $(\underline{\omega}, p_1, p_2, \ldots, p_n) \models \varphi(x_1, x_2, \ldots, x_n)$ means that φ is satisfied in word model $\underline{\omega}$ when $p_1, p_2, \ldots, p_n$ serve as an interpretation of $x_1, x_2, \ldots, x_n$. The language defined by sentence φ is $L(\phi) = \{\omega \in A^* \mid \underline{\omega} \models \varphi\}$. Languages defined by such sentences are first-order languages. For example, the sentence $\forall x(Q_a(x))$ over the alphabet $A = \{a, b\}$ defines the language containing all the words that have only letters a. This language is first-order language. The classical equivalence result of first-order logic is results by Schützenberg[25]:

Theorem 1. *For a language $L \in A^*$ the following are equivalent*

1. *L is star-free (the smallest class that satisfies - all finite languages over A belong to star free languages, if languages L_1, L_2 are star free then so are $L_1 \cdot L_2$, $L_1 \cup L_2$, $L_1 \cap L_2$ and $\bar{L}_1 = A^* \setminus L$).*
2. *L is recognizable by a finite aperiodic monoid - a finite monoid M for which there is and $n \geq 1$ such that $m^{n+1} = m^n$ holds for all $m \in M$.*
3. *L is defined by a first-order formula.*

We will consider a new quantifier $\exists^{m,n} x \varphi(x)$ that means $\varphi(x)$ is true for a number of x equal to n mod m. It is called a *modular quantifier*. Languages defined by first-order atomic formulas by means of the connectivities $\neg, \vee, \wedge, \rightarrow, \leftrightarrow$ and the modular quantifier are modular logic definable. An example of such language is the language containing all words that has even number of letter "a", the corresponding formula for this language is $\exists^{2,0} x Q_a(x)$. Straubing, Therie and Thomas [26] characterized the subclass of regular languages that can be expressed by modular logic, as exactly those regular languages which have solvable syntactic monoids.

The first-order logical formalism can be extended by second-order variables $X, Y, \ldots$ which range over the element's sets of the model, i.e, sets of letter positions, and atomic formulas $X(x), X(y), \ldots$ that means "x belongs to X", "y belongs to X", etc. Since the sets are "monadic second-order objects" the resulting logical system is called *monadic second $-$ order logic* (MSO). The language $(aa)^*$ is defined by the formula

$$\exists X \exists Y (\forall x(first(x) \rightarrow X(x)) \wedge \forall x, y(X(x) \wedge S(x, y) \rightarrow Y(y)) \wedge \forall y(last(y) \rightarrow$$
$$Y(y)) \wedge \forall x Q_a(x))$$

where $first(x) : \neg \exists y(y < x)$ and $last(x) : \forall y(y \leq x)$. The most important result for Monadic second-order logic is Büchi theorem.

Theorem 2. *(Büchi [10], Elgot [13]) A language of finite words is recognizable by a finite automaton iff it is monadic second-order definable, and both conversations, from automata to formulas and vice versa, are effective.*

Logical framework can also be extended with generalized quantifiers; they have been introduced by Mostowski [23]. One of such quantifiers is Lindström quantifier that is studied in this paper.

Definition 2. *Consider a language L over the alphabet $\Sigma = (a_1, a_2, \ldots, a_s)$. Let $\bar{x}$ be a k-tuple of variables (each ranging from 1 to the input length n). In the following, we assume the lexical ordering on $\{1, 2, \ldots, n\}^k$, and we write $X_1, X_2, \ldots, X_{n^k}$ for this sequence of the potential values taken on by $\bar{x}$. Let $\phi_1(\bar{x}), \phi_2(\bar{x}), \ldots, \phi_{s-1}(\bar{x})$ be s-1 Γ-formulas for some alphabet Γ. The*

$$Q_L \bar{x}[\phi_1(\bar{x}), \phi_2(\bar{x}), \ldots, \phi_{s-1}(\bar{x})]$$

holds on string $\omega = \omega_1 \omega_2 \ldots \omega_n$, iff the word of length n^k whose i-th letter ($1 \leq i \leq n^k$) is

$$
\left\{
\begin{array}{l}
a_1 \ if \ \omega \models \phi_1(X_i), \\
a_2 \ if \omega \models \neg\phi_1(X_i) \wedge \phi_2(X_i), \\
a_3 \ if \omega \models \neg\phi_1(X_i) \wedge \neg\phi_2(X_i) \wedge \phi_3(X_i), \\
\ldots \\
a_s \ if \omega \models \neg\phi_1(X_i) \wedge \neg\phi_2(X_i) \wedge \ldots \wedge \neg\phi_{s-1}(X_i),
\end{array}
\right\}
$$

belongs to L.

Consider alphabet $\Sigma = \{0, 1\}$ and a language L which is defined by regular expression $(0, 1)^*0(0, 1)^*$, then formula $Q_L(\phi(x))$ is equal to the classical first-order existential quantifier applied to some quantifier-free formula ϕ with free variable x, i.e. $\exists x \phi(x)$. It is easy to see, that the formula will be true if there is at least one position of x for which $\phi(x)$ will be true.

3   Quantum Finite Automata and Logics

As it is already know the most popular notations of quantum finite automata (measure-once quantum finite automata and measure-many quantum finite automata) recognize only regular languages but not all regular languages. It follows from the theorem of Büchi that the logical description of these language classes should be weaker than monadic second-order logic described by Büchi. The first intention is to study "natural" subclasses of MSO.

Theorem 3. *If a language in alphabet Σ can be recognized by measure-once quantum finite automaton and it is first-order definable, then it is trivial, i.e. an empty language or Σ^*.*

Proof. Suppose that there exists a language L which is not trivial, it can be recognized by MO-QFA, and it is first-order definable. If the language L is recognized by MO-QFA, it can also be recognized by a deterministic finite reversible automaton (RFA). As L is not trivial, the corresponding RFA has accepting and rejecting states. Look at the one of accepting states q_a, it can be reached by a word ω, and there exists a letter δ, such that after reading the word δ^k ($k > 1$) the RFA returns in the state q_a. Consider the monoid which recognizes the language, as it accepts words ω and $\omega\delta^k$, it means that the monoid has subgroup $\{1_M, \delta_\delta, \delta_{\delta^2}, \ldots, \delta_{\delta^{k-1}}\}$, but from this follows that this monoid is not aperiodic, so the language cannot be first-order definable.

Another "natural" attempt could be look at connection between modular logic and measure-once quantum finite automata. If we consider languages in a single letter alphabet, it is easy to see that all such languages accepted by measure-once quantum finite automaton can be defined by modular logic. But it is not true for larger alphabets.

Lemma 1. *There exists a language that can be recognized by measure-once quantum finite automata, but cannot be defined by modular logic.*

Proof. One of such languages is the language accepted by quantum finite automaton $A = (Q, \Sigma, \delta, q_0, Q_a, Q_r)$, where $Q = \{q_0, q_1, q_2, q_3\}$, $\Sigma = \{a, b,\}$, $Q_a = \{q_0\}$, $Q_r = \{q_1, q_2, q_3\}$, for letter a corresponds transformation with matrix

$$\begin{pmatrix} 0 & 1 & 0 & 0 \\ 0 & 0 & 1 & 0 \\ 1 & 0 & 0 & 0 \\ 0 & 0 & 0 & 1 \end{pmatrix}, \text{ and } \begin{pmatrix} 0 & 0 & 0 & 1 \\ 0 & 0 & 1 & 0 \\ 0 & 1 & 0 & 0 \\ 1 & 0 & 0 & 0 \end{pmatrix},$$

for letter b. The monoid which accepts given language is $M = \{1_M, \delta_a, \delta_b, \delta_{aa}\}$ and its binary operation is defined as follows:

$$\begin{aligned} 1_M \cdot 1_M &= 1_M; \\ 1_M \cdot \delta_a &= \delta_a = 1_M \cdot \delta_a; \\ 1_M \cdot \delta_b &= \delta_b = 1_M \cdot \delta_b; \\ 1_M \cdot \delta_{aa} &= \delta_{aa} = 1_M \cdot \delta_{aa}; \\ \delta_a \cdot \delta_a &= \delta_{aa}; \\ \delta_a \cdot \delta_b &= \delta_{ab}; \\ \delta_a \cdot \delta_{aa} &= 1_M; \\ \delta_b \cdot \delta_a &= \delta_b; \\ \delta_b \cdot \delta_b &= 1_M; \\ \delta_b \cdot \delta_{aa} &= \delta_b; \\ \delta_{aa} \cdot \delta_a &= 1_M; \\ \delta_{aa} \cdot \delta_b &= \delta_a; \\ \delta_{aa} \cdot \delta_{aa} &= \delta_a. \end{aligned}$$

This monoid is a group. Next we will find out if this group is solvable. Given a group G and elements $g, h \in G$ we define the *commutator of g and h*, denoted

$[g, h]$, as $[g, h] = g^{-1}h^{-1}gh$, and for any two subgroups $H, K \subseteq G$ we write $[G, K]$ to denote the subgroup of G generated by all commutators $[g, k]$ with $k \in K$ and $g \in G$. The *derived subgroup* of G is $G' = [G, G]$, and in general we write $G^{(0)} = G, G^{(1)} = G', G^{(2)} = (G')', .., G^{(j)} = (G^{(j-1)})'$,etc. A group is said to be *solvable* if $G^{(m)} = 1$ for some value of m.

$G_0 = \{1_M, \delta_a, \delta_b, \delta_{aa}\}$; $G_1 = \{1_M, \delta_a, \delta_{aa}\} = G_2 = G_3 = ...$ The group M is unsolvable, and from this follows that this language cannot be defined by modular logic.

Lemma 2. *There exists a language that cannot be recognized by measure-once quantum finite automata, but is definable by modular logic.*

Proof. Consider language L_1 which have all those words that have odd number of occurrences of the substring "*ab*". The language L_1 can be defined by modular formula $\exists^{(2,1)}xy(Q_a(x) \wedge S(x, y) \wedge Q_b(y))$. The minimal deterministic finite automaton of this language contains "forbidden construction" [4] that means the language L_1 cannot be recognized by a measure-once quantum finite automaton.

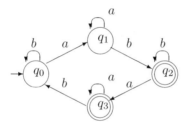

MO-QFA recognizable languages could not be described by these "natural" subclasses of MSO, so less standard logic should be considered, one of extensions could be use of generalized quantifiers.

Theorem 4. *A language can be recognized by a measure-once quantum finite automaton if and only if this language can be described by Lindström quantifier formula corresponding to the group languages (languages recognized by deterministic finite reversible automata) using atomic formulas $Q_a(x)$.*

Proof. As group languages are those languages that are recognized by a deterministic finite reversible automaton, these languages are also recognized by measure-once quantum automata. So for given MO-QFA, that recognizes a language L in alphabet $\Sigma = \{a_1, \ldots, a_k\}$ the corresponding formula with Lindström quantifier the Lindström quantifier is over the language L in the same alphabet and the formula is $Q_L x(Q_{a_1}(x), Q_{a_2}(x), .., Q_{a_{k-1}}(x))$.

For a given formula $Q_{LG}x(Q_{a_1}, Q_{a_2}, .., Q_{a_{s-1}})$ in alphabet $\Sigma_f = \{b_1, \ldots, b_k\}$ and $a_i \in \Sigma_f$ over a group language LG in alphabet $\Sigma_L = \{\delta_1, \delta_2, \ldots, \delta_s\}$ consider the language, that it defines. And look at mapping from Σ_f to Σ_{LG}. If the letter b_i is in the position x, then there are three possibilities:

1. Lindström quantifier has exactly one Q_{b_i} then for the letter b_i the corresponding letter is δ_j, where j is occurrence of Q_{b_i}.

2. Lindström quantifier contain more than one Q_{b_i} then for the letter b_i the corresponding letter is δ_j, where j is first occurrence of Q_{b_i}.
3. Lindström quantifier has none Q_{b_i} then for the letter b_i the corresponding letter is δ_s.

The transformation of MO-QFA that recognizes the given language for a letter b_i corresponds to transformation of MO-QFA that recognizes language LG for b_i mapping.

References

1. Aharonov, D., Kitaev, A., and Nisan, N.: Quantum Circuits with Mixed States. STOC (1998) 20–30
2. Amano, M., and Iwama, K.: Undecidability on Quantum Finite Automata. STOC (1999) 368–375
3. Ambainis, A., and Freivalds, R.: 1-Way Quantum Finite Automata: Strengths, Weaknesses and Generalizations. In: Proc. FOCS (1998) 332–341
4. Ambainis, A., and Kikusts, A.: Exact Results for Accepting Probabilities of Quantum Automata. Theoretical Computer Science **295** 1 (2003) 5–23
5. Ambainis, A., and Watrous, J.: Two-Way Finite Automata with Quantum and Classical States. Theoretical Computer Science **287** 1 (2002) 299–311
6. Baader, F.: Automata and Logic. Technische Universittät Dresden (2003)
7. Barrington, D.A., Compton, K., Straubing, H., and Therien, D.: Regular Languages in NC^1, BCCS-88-02 (1988)
8. Barrington, D.A., Corbett, J.: On the Relative Complexity of Some Languages in NC^1. Inf. Proc. Letters **32** (1989) 251–256
9. Brodsky, A., Pippenger, N.: Characterizations of 1-Way Quantum Finite Automata. SIAM Journal on Computing **31** 5 (2002) 1456–1478
10. Büchi, J.R.: Weak Second-Order Arithmetic and Finite Automata. Z. Math. Logik Grundl. Math **6** (1960) 66–92
11. Büchi, J.R.: On Decision Method in Restricted Second-Order Arithmetic. In: Proc. 1960 Int. Congr. for Logic, Methodology and Philosophy of Science, Stanford Univ. Press, Stanford (1962) 1–11
12. Eilenberg, S.: Automata, Languages, and Machines. Vol. B. New York: Academic Press (1976)
13. Elgot, C.C.: Decision Problems of Finite Automata Design and Related Arithmetics. Trans. Amer. Math Soc. **98** (1961) 21–52
14. Fagin, R.: Generalized First-Order Spectra and Polynomial-Time Recognizable Sets. In: Complexity of Computation, SIAM-AMS Proceedings **7** (1974) 43–73
15. Gruska, J.: Quantum Computing. McGraw-Hill **439** (1999)
16. Immerman, N.: Relational Queries Computable in Polynomial Time. Information and Control **68** (1986) 86–104
17. Immerman, N.: Languages that Capture Complexity Classes. SIAM J. Comput **16** 4 (1987) 760–778
18. Immerman, N.: Nondeterministic Space Is Closed under Complementation. SIAM J. Comput **17** 5 (1988) 953–938
19. Kondacs, A., Watrous, J.: On the Power of Quantum Finite State Automata. In: Proc. FOCS'97 66–75
20. McNaugton, R.: Symbolic Logic and Automata. Technical Note, (1960) 60–244

21. McNaughton, R.: Testing and Generating Infinite Sequences by Finite Automaton. Inform. Contr. **9** (1966) 521–530
22. Moore, C., Crutchfield, J.: Quantum Automata and Quantum Grammars. Theoretical Computer Science **237** (2000) 275–306
23. Mostowski, A.: On a Generalization of Quantifiers. Fundamenta Mathenaticae **44** (1957) 12–36
24. Rabin, M.O.: Decidability of Second-Order Theories and Automata on Infinite Trees. Trans. Amer. Math. Soc. **141** (1969) 1–35
25. Schüzenberg, M.P.: On Finite Monoids Having only Trivial Subgroups. Information and Control **8** (1965) 283–305
26. Straubing, H., Therien, D., and Thomas, W.: Regular Languages Defined with Generalized Quantifiers. In: Proc. 15th ICALP (1988) 561–575

FDSI-Tree: A Fully Distributed Spatial Index Tree for Efficient & Power-Aware Range Queries in Sensor Networks*

Sang Hun Eo[1], Suraj Pandey[1], Myung-Keun Kim[1], Young-Hwan Oh[2], and Hae-Young Bae[3]

[1,3] Department of Computer Science and Information Engineering, Inha University,
Yonghyun-dong, Nam-gu, Incheon, 402-751, Korea
{eosanghun, suraj, kimmkeun}@dblab.inha.ac.kr, hybae@inha.ac.kr
[2] Department of Information Science, Korea Nazarene University, 456 Ssangyong-Dong,
Cheonan, Choongnam 330-718, S. Korea
yhoh@kornu.ac.kr

Abstract. In this paper, a fully distributed spatial index tree (FDSI-tree) is proposed for efficient & power-aware range queries in sensor networks. The proposed technique is a new approach for range queries that uses spatial indexing. Range queries are most often encountered under sensor networks for computing aggregation values. However, previous works just addressed the importance but didn't provide any efficient technique for processing range queries. A FDSI-tree is thus designed for efficiently processing them. Each node in the sensor network has the MBR of the region where its children nodes and the node itself are located. The range query is evaluated over the region which intersects the geographic location of sensors. It ensures the maximum power savings by avoiding the communication of nodes not participating over the evaluation of the query.

1 Introduction

A sensor network consists of many spatially distributed sensors, which are used to monitor or detect phenomena at different locations, such as temperature changes or pollutant level. Sensor nodes, such as the Berkeley MICA Mote [1] which already support temperature sensors, a magnetometer, an accelerometer, a microphone, and also several actuators, are getting smaller, cheaper, and able to perform more complex operations, including having mini embedded operating systems. The applications have gained significant momentum during the past three years with the acceleration in wireless sensor network research. The heterogeneity in the available sensor technologies and applications, hence, requires a common standardization to achieve the practicality of sensor networks applications.

* This research was supported by the MIC (Ministry of Information and Communication), Korea, under the ITRC (Information Technology Research Center) support program supervised by the IITA (Institute of Information Technology Assessment).

J. Wiedermann et al. (Eds.): SOFSEM 2006, LNCS 3831, pp. 254–261, 2006.
© Springer-Verlag Berlin Heidelberg 2006

While these advances are improving the capabilities of sensor nodes, there are still many crucial problems with deploying sensor networks. Limited storage, limited network bandwidth, poor inter-node communication, limited computational ability, and limited power still persist.

The works we describe under have laid out the importance to the need of spatial indexing schemes in sensor networks, and have even proposed [8], [9] a similar structure. Traditionally, the database community has focused mostly on centralized indices [7], [10] and our approach essentially is to embed them into sensor nodes. But, the index structure is decided not just upon the data, but also considering the performance metrics and power measurements of collective sensors. Hence our design is different from the traditional indexing techniques.

The Cougar project at Cornell [12] discusses queries over sensor networks, which has a central administration that is aware of the location of all the sensors. Madden et.al., in [13], Fjord architecture for management of multiple queries is introduced focusing on the query processing in the sensor environment. However the information is available in a catalog. The TinyOS group at UC Berkeley has published a number of papers describing the design of motes, the design of TinyOS, and the implementation of the networking protocols used to conduct ad-hoc sensor networks. TAG [5] was proposed for an aggregation service as a part of TinyDB[1] [14], which is a query processing system for a network of Berkeley motes. They also described a distributed index, called Semantic Routing Trees (SRT). SRTs are based on single attributes, historical sensor reading and fixed node query originations, as contrasting to our design over these aspects. The work on directed diffusion [4], which is a data centric framework, uses flooding to find paths from the query originator node to the data source nodes. The notion is grouping to compute aggregates over partitions of sensor readings. [15] proposes a scheme for imposing names onto related groups of sensors in a network, in much the same way our scheme groups sensor nodes into regions according to their geographic location. Interestingly, [8] has an R-tree based scheme, but no verification and/or evaluation is presented. Moreover, it is more concerned over the text book discussions of spatial queries lacking focus on range queries and their energy requirements. Our work is most closely related to geographic hash-tables (GHTs) [16], DIFS [17] and DIMENSIONS [18]. DIMENSIONS and DIFS can be thought of as using the same set of primitives as GHT (storage using consistent hashing). The scheme for routing followed by the tributaries and delta approach [19] is more efficient. Pre-computed indices are used to facilitate range queries in traditional database systems, and have been adopted by the above mentioned works. Indices trade-off some initial pre-computation cost to achieve a significantly more efficient querying capability. For sensor networks, we emphasize that a centralized index for range queries are not feasible for energy-efficiency as the energy cost of transmitting 1Kb a distance of 100m is approximately the same as that for executing 3 million instructions by a 100 (MIPS)/W processor [2], [3].

In this paper, we propose the design of fully distributed spatial index tree (FDSI-tree), with specifications to work under the constraints of individual sensor node. The concept of traversal and node selection is the derived version of traditional

---

[1] http://telegraph.cs.berkeley.edu/tinydb/

R-tree [7] structure. As R-tree is the primary choice when handling spatial attributes efficiently, almost all index structures are motivated from it.

The remainder of this paper is structured as follows. In section 2, we propose the structure and energy efficient & power-aware query processing of the FDSI-tree, under the assumptions and system model. Section 3 presents the performance evaluation based on emulated environment. Finally, we conclude in Section 4 providing insights into future works.

2 FDSI-Tree

In this section, we propose the Fully Distributed Spatial Index tree (FDSI-tree) used for querying with spatial attributes. All the schemes reviewed earlier are based on grouping of the sensor nodes either by event/attribute, which are data centric demanding communication that is redundant. Our scheme overcomes these inherent deficiencies.

2.1 Assumptions and System Model

Wireless Sensor networks have the following physical resource constraints and unique characteristics:

Communication. The wireless network connecting the sensor nodes is usually limited, with only a very limited quality of service, with high variance in latency, and high packet loss rates.

Power consumption. Sensor nodes have limited supply of energy, most commonly from a battery source.

Computation. Sensor nodes have limited computing power and memory sizes that restrict the types of data processing algorithms that can be used and intermediate results that can be stored on the sensor nodes.

Streaming data. Sensor nodes produce data continuously without being explicitly asked for that data.

Real-time processing. Sensor data usually represent real-time events. Moreover, it is often expensive to save raw sensor streams to disk at the sink. Hence, queries over streams need to be processed in real time.

Uncertainty. The information gathered by the sensors contains noise from environment. Moreover, factors such as sensor malfunction, and sensor placement might bias individual readings.

We consider a static sensor network distributed over a large area. All sensors are aware of their geographical position. Each sensor could be equipped with GPS device or use location estimation techniques. The network structure, which is common to both Cougar and TinyDB, consists of nodes connected as a tree (tree-based routing). As it's evident that nodes within the same level do not communicate with each other, the communication boundary is constrained within children and their respective parent. This communication relationship is viable to changes due to moving nodes, the power shortage of the nodes, or when new nodes appear. TinyDB has a list of parent candidates. The parent changes if link quality degrades sufficiently. The Cougar has a similar mechanism: a parent sensor node will keep a list of all its children, which is called the *waiting list,* and will not report its reading until it hears from all the sensor nodes on its waiting list. We use Cougar's approach in our system under similar semantics.

2.2 The Tree Structure

A FDSI-tree is an index designed to allow each node to efficiently determine if any of the nodes below it will need to participate in a given query over some queried range.

The routing protocol, the tributary-delta approach for example, determines the parent-child relationship and their extent. However, to accommodate the spatial query in the network we need additional parameters to be stored by individual nodes. Each node must store the calculated[2] MBR of its children along with the aggregate values as have already been existing in each node under the in-network query processing paradigm and noted by several literatures, [22,23] in particular. The parent node of each region in the tree has a structure in the form *<child-pointers, child-MBRs, overall-MBR, location-info>*. The *child-pointers* helps traverse the node structure. As we are following the Cougar, the *waiting-list* carries the same semantics as these pointers. In addition, we have added the MBR in each node which confines the children into a box over which a query can be made. The confinement algorithm is responsible to analyze and distribute the sensor nodes into the appropriate MBR. This classification is largely based on their proximity to their respective parent and the contribution factor to the dead space of the resulting MBR. Any other promising factor can be explored and analyzed, which we consider for our future work. However, it is this classification that brings about efficient routing and accuracy to the queried result.

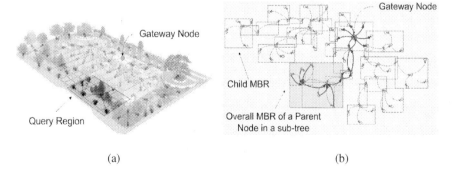

(a)   (b)

Fig. 1. Node positions in one section of our sensor test bed. (a) Simulated Physical Environment showing region of interest. (b) The MBR under each parent node of a sub tree.

---

[2] Each MBR is updated during the ascending of the tree so that the modified MBR is stored in each node.

Figure 1 shows an emulated environment settings consisting of distributed sensor nodes on which we base our experiments. For the construction of FDSI-tree, in the descending stage, a bounded box which overlaps the children and the parent itself should be stored by each parent in that region. Each descent correspondingly stores the MBR of the region where link exists until the leaf node is reached. At the end of the descent, when all the nodes have been traversed, the parent node of each region is notified about their child nodes' MBR. Hence, in the ascending stage the parent of each region gets updated the new MBR of their children which now should include the sub-tree under that node, and a distributed R-tree like structure is formed among the sensor nodes.

2.3   Energy Efficient & Power-Aware Query Processing

One critical operation of FDSI-tree, called *energy efficient forwarding*, is to isolate the regions containing the sensor nodes that can contribute to the range query. Our prime objective is to maintain the minimum count of nodes taking part in the query. As we explained in section 2.2, the construction of the FDSI-tree determines the ease of forwarding the query to pin point the sensor nodes.

Having established the structure and the objectives, we have some routing algorithms handy to our scheme. Using GPRS [16] algorithm the packets are delivered to a node at a specified location. It includes efficient techniques for perimeter traversal that are based on *planarized graphs*. Tributary-delta provides a suitable solution for sensor networks. Unlike TAG and synopsis diffusion [11], it can yield significantly more accurate answers for the same energy cost. The resulting aggregation topology has an analogy to a river flowing to a gulf, where the aggregation initially proceeds along trees and then switches to multi-path when obstacles are encountered.

A range query returns all the relevant data collected/relayed that is associated with regions within a given query window W (e.g., a rectangle in a two-dimensional space). To process a range query with FDSI-tree, at first the root node receives the query; originating at any node. The disseminating of this request to the children node now is based on the calculation of the child node/s whose *overall-MBR* overlaps W. Each parent under that overlapping region receives this query and based on the overlapping regions of its children, the corresponding network (sub-tree) is flooded. It is here that the *child-MBR* is used to decide the particular regions which need precise selection in-order to limit unnecessary node traversal. These *child-MBRs* are comparatively small regions that cover only the perimeter of the children including their parent. So the selection operation needs minimum traversal to include the nodes in the list needed for range query. The optional parameter *location-info* should help to get accurate result for overlapping, independent regions. Its inclusion is based on the type of sensor network and its scalability factor. In addition to the geographic information it may include additional values e.g., time *t*, location attributes etc., that should act as a filter, which again is largely dependent on the computational power of each sensor node. Figure 1 also shows the pictorial representation of node selection. The path for node selection is highlighted. The code isn't provided so as to leverage the robustness in choosing efficient algorithm for independent implementations of our design.

3 Performance Evaluation

To study the performance of the proposed scheme in sensor networks, we created a emulation environment using AVRORA [20]. Following typical sensor network simulation practices, the emulated network of sensors was chosen to be consisting of regular tessellation, in particular like grid squares. Each node could transmit data to sensors that were at most one hop away from it. In a grid this means it could only transmit to at most 8 other nodes.

Our calculations are based on sensor nodes distributed over a large area where scalability factor determines the cost, efficiency and quality of data thus obtained. Another factor to be considered is the delivery cost. The query delivery cost directly depends upon the size of range query. As we base our experiments upon the TinyDB, we assume the same use of motes and sensors for our test bed. Light and humidity values are sensed and transmitted.

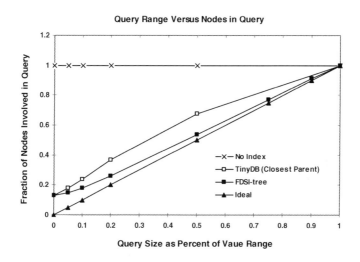

Fig. 2. Number of nodes participating in range queries of different sizes (20 × 20 grid, 400 nodes)

In the emulation we evaluated the performance of our proposed scheme, FDSI-tree, against the *best-case* approach and *closest parent* as used by TinyDB. We used the random distribution to select the query range. As due to the lack of any benchmarks for evaluating query performance in sensor networks, we selected the queries that would be regarded as suitable for range queries, resembling to Sequoia 2000 [2]. Figure 2 shows the number of nodes that participate in queries over variably sized range query. It is drawn over the average values obtained after the emulation. TinyDB concludes that only 1% of the 81% energy spent is on processing. As per the example given in that literature, 41% was spent in communication. That amount of communication can be reduced by 20% if our design is incorporated in the system. But, the processing time is increased due to the addition of extra message bits, approximately 17 bits, and also due to the related algorithms. Nevertheless, this slight increase over shadows the significant decrease in communication. So, the number of nodes that are involved in the query is significantly reduced in comparison to the closest parent approach of TinyDB in its SRT. In order to emphasize the effectiveness of using the partially aggregated value for in-network aggregation and thus to reduce the power utilization, we also simulated the performance following the TiNA [22] scheme and due to space constraints couldn't include. We can readily conclude that our approach is up to 20% more energy efficient than the centralized version as evident from the graph.

There exist rooms for integrating existing as well as new techniques that optimizes the performance of the query processing. *Lifetime* estimation in TinyDB performed periodically in network for better performance. Cross-layer interaction, using network filters as in Cougar, or collapsing the whole network stack as in TinyDB, is indeed the necessity for avoiding unnecessary communication between sensor nodes.

In addition to the choosing of the optimized algorithm for splitting MBR, periodic reorganization of some indexes would largely increase the performance. This mean, for the long running queries, if regions that are most frequently queried be tracked, the MBR associated with those regions can be expanded to include all the relevant sensor nodes. The query would then be accessing only one or a few MBRs.

4   Conclusion and Future Work

In this paper, we contribute a new technique to group the sensors in a region for spatial range queries. We proposed an energy efficient design for range query processing using the FDSI-tree in sensor networks.

FDSI-tree can reduce the number of nodes that disseminate queries by nearly an order of magnitude. Isolating the overlapping regions of sensor nodes with the range query, non-relevant nodes can be avoided in the communication. Only the sensor nodes leading to the path of the requested region are communicated, and hence substantial reduction in power is achieved due to reduced number of sub-trees involved. In addition, the aggregate values for the region of interest is collected, following the in-network aggregation paradigm which has an advantage over the centralized index structure in that it does not require complete topology and sensor value information to be collected at the root of the network. Since data transmission is the biggest energy-consuming activity in sensor nodes, using FDSI-tree results in significant energy savings.

In conclusion, FDSI-tree provides a scalable solution to facilitate range queries adopting similar protocols and query processing used so far, making it highly portable. Currently, we are expanding our scheme to consider moving objects trying to achieve moreover the same throughput as in static networks. Our work on clustering the nodes based on several factors contributing to the performance of the network is still underway. Adoption of distributed redundant architecture for efficient processing of concurrent queries and for supporting join operations, are challenges which are under scrutiny as the capabilities of sensor nodes reaches higher levels.

References

1. Hill, J., and Culler, D.: Mica: A Wireless Platform for Deeply Embedded Networks. IEEE Micro., **22** 6 (2002) 12-24
2. http://s2k-ftp.cs.berkeley.edu:8000/sequoia/schema/.

3. Rappaport, T.: Wireless Communications: Principles and Practice. PH Inc. (1996)
4. Intanagonwiwat, C., Govindan R., and Estrin, D.: Directed Diffusion: A Scalable and Robust Communication Paradigm for Sensor Networks. ACM MobiCom'00.
5. Madden, S.R., Franklin, M.J., Hellerstein, J.M., and Hong, W.: TAG: a Tiny AGgregation Service for Ad-Hoc Sensor Networks. OSDI (2002)
6. Shenker, S., Ratnasamy, S., Karp, B., Govindan, R., and Estrin, D.: Data-Centric Storage in Sensornets. In Proc. ACM SIGCOMM Workshop on Hot Topics In Networks, Princeton, NJ (2002)
7. Guttman, A.: R-Trees: A Dynamic Index Structure for Spatial Searching. In Proc. ACMSIGMOD 1984, Annual Meeting, USA, ACM Press (1984) 47–57
8. Coman, A., et al.: A Framework for Spatio Temporal Query Processing over Wireless Sensor Networks. In Proc. DMSN Workshop (with VLDB), (2004) 104–110
9. Demirbas, M. and Ferhatosmanoglu, H.: Peer-to-Peer Spatial Queries in Sensor Networks. In Proc. International Conference on Peer-to-Peer Computing, (2003) 32-39
10. Comer, D.: The Ubiquitous B-tree. ACM Computing Surveys, 11 2 (1979) 121-137
11. Nath, S., Gibbons, P., Seshan, S.: Synopsis Diffusion for Robust Aggregation in Sensor Networks. In Proc. ACM Symposium on Networked Embedded Systems (2004)
12. Yao, Y., and Gehrke, J.: The Cougar Approach to In-Network Query Processing in Sensor Networks, SIGMOD'02
13. Madden, S., and Franklin, M.J.: Fjording the Stream: An Architecture for Queries over Streaming Sensor Data. In Proc.18th Int. Conference on Data Engineering (2002) 555-566
14. Madden, S.R., Franklin M.J., and Hellerstein, J.M.: TinyDB: An Acquisitional Query Processing System for Sensor Networks. ACM Transactions on Database Systems 30 1 (March 2005) 122-173
15. Heidemann, J., Silva, F., Intanagonwiwat, C., Govindan, R., Estrin, D., and Ganesan, D.: Building Efficient Wireless Sensor Networks with Low-Level Naming. In SOSP (2001)
16. Karp, B., and Kung, H.T.: GPRS: Greedy Perimeter Stateless Routing for Wireless Networks. In Proc. Sixth Annual ACM/IEEE International Conference on Mobile Computing and Networking (Mobicom 2000), Boston, MA (August 2000)
17. Greenstein, B., Estrin, D., Govindan, R., Ratnasamy, S., and Shenker, S.: DIFS: A Distributed Index for Features in Sensor Networks. In Proc.1st IEEE International Workshop on Sensor Network Protocols and Applications, Anchorage, AK (2003)
18. Ganesan, D., Estrin, D., and Heidemann, J.: DIMENSIONS: Why Do We Need a New Data Handling Architecture for Sensor Networks? In Proc. First Workshop on Hot Topics In Networks (HotNes-I), Princeton, NJ (October 2002)
19. Manjhi, A., Nath, S., Gibbons, P.B.: Tributaries and Deltas: Efficient and Robust Aggregation in Sensor Network Streams. In SIGMOD 2005, USA
20. Titzer, B.L., Lee, D.K., and Palsberg, J.: Avrora: Scalable Sensor Network Simulation with Precise Timing. In Proceedings of IPSN, April 2005. A research project of the UCLA Compilers Group, http://compilers.cs.ucla.edu/avrora/index.html
21. Shih, E.et al.: Physical Layer Driven Protocol and Algorithm Design for Energy-Efficient Wireless Sensor Networks. ACM Mobicom'01 (2001) 272-286
22. Sharaf, M.A., Beaver, J., Labrinidis, A., and Chrysanthis, P.: TiNA: A Scheme for Temporal Coherency-Aware in-Network Aggregation. In Proceedings of 2003 International Workshop in Mobile Data Engineering
23. Beaver, J., Sharaf, M.A., Labrinidis, A., and Chrysanthis, P.K.: Power-Aware In-Network Query Processing for Sensor Data. Proc. 3rd ACM MobiDE Workshop (2003)

ROMAN DOMINATION: A Parameterized Perspective

Henning Fernau[1,2,3]

[1] University of Hertfordshire, Hatfield, UK
[2] The University of Newcastle, Australia
[3] Universität Tübingen, WSI für Informatik, Germany
fernau@informatik.uni-tuebingen.de

Abstract. We analyze ROMAN DOMINATION from a parameterized perspective. More specifically, we prove that this problem is W[2]-complete for general graphs. However, parameterized algorithms are presented for graphs of bounded treewidth and for planar graphs. Moreover, it is shown that a parametric dual of ROMAN DOMINATION is in $\mathcal{FPT}$.

1 Introduction

ROMAN DOMINATION is one of the many variants of dominating set problems [7], [11], [15]. It comes with a nice (hi)story: namely, it should reflect the idea of how to secure the Roman Empire by positioning the armies (legions) on the various parts of the Empire in a way that either (1) a specific region r is also the location of at least one army or (2) one region r' neighboring r has two armies, so that r' can afford sending off one army to the region r (in case of an attack) without loosing self-defense capabilities.

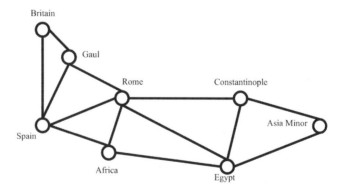

Fig. 1. The Roman Empire in the times of Constantine

More specifically, Emperor Constantine had a look at the map of Fig. 1 or a variant thereof (as discussed in [21]). The historical background is also nicely

J. Wiedermann et al. (Eds.): SOFSEM 2006, LNCS 3831, pp. 262–271, 2006.

described in the online John Hopkins Magazine, more specifically, visit page
http://www.jhu.edu/~jhumag/0497web/locate3.html. This problem is similar to the island hopping strategy pursued by General MacArthur in World War
II in the Pacific theater to gradually increase the US-secured areas.

A good overview on problems related to Roman domination can be found
in [2]. We assume that solving algorithms similar to the ones presented in this
paper can be also found for most of these variants, in particular regarding multi-
attack variants [8], [14], [16], [17]. Efficient algorithms for various graph classes
have been presented in [11], [19]. Relations with the concrete problem under
consideration and (more practical) network problems have been exhibited in [20].

2 Definitions

Let us first formally describe the problem. To this end, notice that we will use
standard notions from graph theory. Throughout the paper, we deal with simple
undirected graphs. $N(v)$ is the open neighborhood of vertex v, and $N[v] = N(v) \uplus \{v\}$ is the closed neighborhood, where $\uplus$ denotes disjoint set union. An
instance of ROMAN DOMINATION (ROMAN) is given by a graph $G = (V, E)$,
and the parameter, a positive integer k. The question is: Is there a *Roman
domination* function R such that $R(V) := \sum_{x \in V} R(x) \leq k$?

Here, a *Roman domination* function of a graph $G = (V, E)$ is a function
$R : V \to \{0, 1, 2\}$ with

$$\forall v \in V : R(v) = 0 \Rightarrow \exists x \in N(v) : R(x) = 2.$$

$D_R = R^{-1}(\{1, 2\})$ is then the *Roman domination set*. The minimum of $R(V)$
over all valid Roman domination functions R is also called the *Roman domination
number* of a given graph.

In the following, we give the necessary background on parameterized com-
plexity: A *parameterized problem* P is a subset of $\Sigma^* \times \mathbb{N}$, where Σ is a fixed
alphabet and $\mathbb{N}$ is the set of all non-negative integers. Therefore, each instance of
the parameterized problem P is a pair (I, k), where the second component k is
called the *parameter*. The language $L(P)$ is the set of all YES-instances of P. We
say that the parameterized problem P is *fixed-parameter tractable* [10] if there is
an algorithm that decides whether an input (I, k) is a member of $L(P)$ in time
$f(k)|I|^c$, where c is a fixed constant and $f(k)$ is a function independent of the
overall input length $|I|$. The class of all fixed-parameter tractable problems is
denoted by $\mathcal{FPT}$.

There is also a hardness theory, most notably, the W[t] hierarchy, that complements fixed-parameter tractability:

$$\mathcal{FPT} = W[0] \subseteq W[1] \subseteq W[2] \subseteq \dots$$

It is commonly believed that this hierarchy is strict. Since only the second level
W[2] will be of interest to us in this paper, we will only define that class below.
We do this in the "Turing way" as (partially) followed in [5], [4], [6], [12].

A *parameterized reduction* is a function r that, for some polynomial p and some function g, is computable in time $\mathcal{O}(g(k)p(|I|))$ and maps an instance (I, k) of $\mathcal{P}$ onto an instance $r(I, k) = (I', k')$ of $\mathcal{P}'$ such that (I, k) is a YES-instance of $\mathcal{P}$ if and only if (I', k') is a YES-instance of $\mathcal{P}'$ and $k' \leq g(k)$. We also say that $\mathcal{P}$ *reduces to* $\mathcal{P}'$.

W[2] can be characterized by the following problem on Turing machines:

An instance of SHORT MULTI-TAPE NONDETERMINISTIC TURING MACHINE COMPUTATION (SMNTMC) is given by a multi-tape nondeterministic Turing machine M (with two-way infinite tapes), an input string x, and the parameter, a positive integer k. The question is: Is there an accepting computation of M on input x that reaches a final accepting state in at most k steps?

More specifically, a parameterized problem is in W[2] iff it can be reduced with a parameterized reduction to SHORT MULTI-TAPE NONDETERMINISTIC TURING MACHINE COMPUTATION, see [4].

3   ROMAN DOMINATION on General Graphs Is Hard

Lemma 1. ROMAN DOMINATION *is in W[2]*.

Proof. Let $G = (V, E)$ be an instance of ROMAN DOMINATION. We have to transform it into an instance of SHORT MULTI-TAPE NONDETERMINISTIC TURING MACHINE COMPUTATION. We also assume that $k > 0$ ($k = 0$ is a trivial instance).

The corresponding Turing machine T has $|V| + 1$ tapes; let they be indexed by $\{0\} \cup V$. As tape symbols, we will use $(V \times \{1, 2\})$ on tape 0 and $\#$ on the other tapes (besides the blank symbol). The edge relation of G is "hard-wired" into the transition function of T as described below. The input string is empty.

In a first phase, T nondeterministically guesses the Roman domination function R and writes it on tape 0 using the letters from $V \times \{1, 2\}$ as follows: T moves the head on tape 0 one step to the right, and writes there a guess $(v, i) \in (V \times \{1, 2\})$. Upon writing (v, i), T also increments an internal-memory counter c by i. As long as $c \leq k$, T can nondeterministically continue in phase one or transition into phase two; if $c > k$, T hangs up.

In a second phase, T has to verify that the previous guesses are correct. To this end, upon reading symbol $(v, 1)$ on tape 0, T writes $\#$ on the tape addressed by v and moves that head one step to the right. Upon reading $(v, 2)$ on tape 0, T writes $\#$ on all tapes addressed by vertices from $N[v]$ and moves the corresponding heads one step to the right. Moreover, after reading symbol (v, i) on tape 0, T moves the head on tape 0 one step to the left. Upon reading the blank symbol on tape 0, T moves all other heads one step to the left; only if then all V-addressed tapes show $\#$ under their respective heads, T accepts. The second phase will take another $k + 1$ steps.

It is now easy to see that (G, k) is a YES-instance to ROMAN DOMINATION iff T has an accepting computation within $2k + 1$ steps, so that we actually described a parameterized reduction.   ∎

We will show W[2]-hardness with the help of the following problem: An instance of RED-BLUE DOMINATING SET (RBDS) is given by a graph $G = (V, E)$ with V partitioned as $V_{\text{red}} \uplus V_{\text{blue}}$, and the parameter, a positive integer k. The question is: Is there a *red-blue dominating set* $D \subseteq V_{\text{red}}$ with $|D| \leq k$, i.e., $V_{\text{blue}} \subseteq N(D)$?

We need the following result, that can be easily distilled from [10]:

Lemma 2. RED-BLUE DOMINATING SET, RESTRICTED TO BIPARTITE GRAPHS *is W[2]-hard.*

To prove the hardness result, we need one fact about the Roman domination of complete graphs that follows from [7–Prop. 9].

Lemma 3. *For the complete graph K_n on n vertices, the Roman domination number is two iff $n \geq 2$.*

Theorem 1. ROMAN DOMINATION *is W[2]-complete.*

Proof. By Lemma 1, we already know that ROMAN DOMINATION lies in W[2].

Assume that $G = (V, E)$ is an instance of RED-BLUE DOMINATING SET, RE-STRICTED TO BIPARTITE GRAPHS (see Lemma 2), i.e., $V = V_{\text{red}} \uplus V_{\text{blue}}$. W.l.o.g., we can assume that $|V_{\text{red}}| > 1$. In the simulating ROMAN DOMINATION instance, we construct a graph $G' = (V', E')$, where

$$V' = (V_{\text{red}} \cup \{1, \ldots, 2k+1\}) \times \{1, \ldots, k\} \cup V_{\text{blue}},$$

and E' contains the following edges (and no others):

1. $G'[V_{\text{red}} \times \{i\}]$ is a complete graph for each $i \in \{1, \ldots, k\}$.
2. For all $i \in \{1, \ldots, k\}$ and $x \in V_{\text{red}}$, $y \in V_{\text{blue}}$, $\{x, y\} \in E$ iff $\{[x, i], y\} \in E'$.
3. For all $i \in \{1, \ldots, k\}$, $j \in \{1, \ldots, 2k+1\}$ and $x \in V_{\text{red}}$: $\{[x, i], [j, i]\} \in E'$.

We are going to show the following <u>claim</u>: G has a red-blue dominating set D of size k iff G' has a Roman domination function R with $\sum_{x \in D_R} R(x) = 2k$.

If G has a red-blue dominating set $D = \{d_1, \ldots, d_k\}$ of size k, then consider the following function $R : V' \to \{0, 1, 2\}$: R assigns zero to all vertices but to $d'_i = [d_i, i]$, to which R assigns two. Since d'_i is connected to all vertices in $(V_{\text{red}} \cup \{1, \ldots, 2k+1\}) \times \{i\}$, the vertices in $V' \setminus V$ are all dominated by this assignment. Moreover, since D is a red-blue dominating set of G, all vertices in V_{blue} are dominated in G', as well.

Now consider a Roman domination function R for G' with $\sum_{x \in D_R} R(x) = 2k$. Due to Lemma 3 and according to the first condition on edges, the Roman domination number of each induced graph $G'[V_{\text{red}} \times \{i\}]$ is two, assuming $|V_{\text{red}}| > 1$. Since $G'[V_{\text{red}} \times \{1, \ldots, k\}]$ can be decomposed into k components, the Roman domination number of $G'[V_{\text{red}} \times \{1, \ldots, k\}]$ is $2k$. More specifically, to achieve that bound, the domination function would have to assign two to one vertex from $V_{\text{red}} \times \{i\}$ for each i and zero to all other vertices. Observe that such an assignment would be also a valid Roman domination function R' for $G'[(V_{\text{red}} \cup \{1, \ldots, 2k+1\}) \times \{1, \ldots, k\}]$ if we assign zero to all vertices from $\{1, \ldots, 2k+1\} \times \{1, \ldots, k\}$.

Since there are "too many" vertices in $\{1, \ldots, 2k+1\} \times \{1, \ldots, k\}$, we cannot simply replace one or more vertices to which R' assigns two by vertices from $\{1, \ldots, 2k+1\} \times \{1, \ldots, k\}$ to which R' (as constructed) had assigned zero.

Observe that we have left over yet some degrees of freedom for finally constructing a valid Roman domination function R from R'; namely, we have not been specific about how to choose a vertex from $V_{\mathrm{red}} \times \{i\}$ (for each i) to which we assign two. However, if we find k assignments of two to vertices from $V_{\mathrm{red}} \times \{1, \ldots, k\}$ such that also all vertices from V_{blue} are dominated, i.e., $D_R = \{[d_1, 1], \ldots, [d_k, k]\} = R^{-1}(\{2\})$, then $D = \{d_1, \ldots, d_k\}$ is a valid dominating set of G.

Since there are no edges between vertices from $\{1, \ldots, 2k+1\} \times \{1, \ldots, k\}$ and V_{blue}, there is no way of replacing some of the vertices selected from $(V_{\mathrm{red}} \cup \{1, \ldots, 2k+1\}) \times \{1, \ldots, k\}$ (by assigning two to them) by vertices from V_{blue}, so that there cannot be a Roman domination function R that assigns one or two to any of the vertices from V_{blue} without violating the condition $\sum_{x \in D_R} R(x) = 2k$. So, the Roman domination function as constructed above is the only possibility; that construction works if and only if G has a dominating set of size k.   ∎

The previous Theorem also sharpens [11–Theorem 2.42].

Let us finally mention one further problem, also taken from [20]; in fact, some more (and similar) problems can be found there and treated alike. An instance of DOMINATING REARRANGEMENT (DR) is given by a graph $G = (V, E)$, a subset $S \subseteq V$, and the parameter, a positive integer $k = |S|$. The question is: Is there a *dominating rearrangement* $r : S \to N[S], s \mapsto r(s) \in N[s]$ such that $r(S) \subseteq V$ is a dominating set?

Again, this problem can be viewed from a military perspective: S is the set of locations where currently armies are placed on, and the question is if by a one-step rearrangement of each army (if necessary) a situation can be created in which each region (modeled by graph vertices) is sheltered by either a defending army in the region itself or in a neighboring region.

This problem is interesting for at least two reasons from a parameterized perspective:

- The parameterization is not arising from an optimization problem.
- The problem can be viewed as a *local search problem*, parameterized by a given "temporary" solution. Such type of problems can show up in many disguises in practice.

Theorem 2. DOMINATING REARRANGEMENT *is W[2]-complete.*

Proof. Membership in W[2] can be seen by a guess-and-verify strategy as seen in the proof of Lemma 1. For the hardness, take again an instance $(G = (V = V_{red} \uplus V_{blue}, E), k)$ of RED-BLUE DOMINATING SET. Let $S = \{1, \ldots, k\}$ be disjoint from V, and consider the graph $G' = (V', E')$ with $V' = V \cup S$ and $E' = E \cup (S \times V_{red})$. Hence, $G'[S \cup V_{red}]$ forms a complete bipartite graph. This gives the instance (G', S) of DOMINATING REARRANGEMENT. Obviously, $D \subseteq V_{red}$ is a dominating set of size (at most) k iff (G', S) can be solved by moving $|D|$ of the armies in S onto the vertices from D.   ∎

4   ROMAN DOMINATION on Planar Graphs

From a historical perspective, this is somehow the "original" problem, indeed: taking a map of the Roman Empire and assuming firstly that different regions are interpreted as vertices of a graph and finally that regions are neighbored if they share a common borderline (as opposed to having boundaries meeting in a single point), then this neighborhood (multi-)graph is (as the geometric dual of the map) planar.

We will first sketch a search tree algorithm that puts PLANAR ROMAN DOMINATION into $\mathcal{FPT}$. From the standpoint of parameterized algorithmics, this is an interesting algorithm, since it "recycles" most of the rules and terminology that was earlier developed for PLANAR DOMINATING SET in [1], [12].

There, we introduced the notion of a *black and white graph*. The vertex set V of G is partitioned into two disjoint sets B and W of *black* and *white* vertices, respectively, i.e., $V = B \uplus W$. Black vertices are those vertices which still need to be dominated, while white vertices are already dominated, but it is still possible to place two armies on such a vertex in order to protect the neighboring vertices. In each step of the search tree, we would like to branch according to a low degree black vertex.

Formally, this means that we solve an annotated version of ROMAN DOMINATION, namely on black and white graphs. We propose to use the following reduction rules:

(R1) Delete an edge between white vertices.

(R2) Delete a pendant white vertex, i.e., a vertex of degree one.

(R4) If there is a white vertex u of degree 2, with two black neighbors u_1 and u_2 connected by an edge $\{u_1, u_2\}$, then delete u.

(R5) If there is a white vertex u of degree 2, with black neighbors u_1, u_3, and there is a black vertex u_2 and edges $\{u_1, u_2\}$ and $\{u_2, u_3\}$ in G, then delete u.

(R6) If there is a white vertex u of degree 2, with black neighbors u_1, u_3, and there is a white vertex u_2 and edges $\{u_1, u_2\}$ and $\{u_2, u_3\}$ in G, then delete u.

(R7) If there is a white vertex u of degree 3, with black neighbors u_1, u_2, u_3 for which the edges $\{u_1, u_2\}$ and $\{u_2, u_3\}$ are present in G (and possibly also $\{u_1, u_3\}$), then delete u.

The peculiar numbering is in accordance with our rule numbering scheme for PLANAR DOMINATING SET in [12] and should make clear that we actually must only replace one of the rules with some additional branching in our algorithm, in order to get rid of pendant black vertices.

Lemma 4. *The reduction rules are sound.*

Proof. (R1), (R2) are immediate.

(R4): Let $G = (V, E)$ be a black and white graph and $G' = (V', E')$ be obtained from G by applying (R4) once. Hence, there are vertices u, u_1, u_2 in V as described in (R4). If R' is a valid Roman domination function of G', then R' can be extended to a valid Roman domination function R' on V by setting $R'(u) = 0$. Obviously, $R'(V') = R'(V)$. If R is a valid Roman domination function of G, then R restricted to V' will be valid if $R(u) = 0$. Then, $R(V') = R(V)$. The case $R(u) = 1$ need not be considered, since u is white. If $R(u) = 2$, then $R(u_1) + R(u_2) \leq 1$, since otherwise by redefining $R(u) := 0$ a smaller valid Roman domination function can be obtained. However, if $R(u) \leq 1$, then $R(u_1) = 0$ or $R(u_2)$. Assuming $R(u_1) = 0$, we can obtain a valid Roman domination function by setting $R(u) := 0$ and $R(u_1) := 2$ without changing the overall value. Hence, after the indicated modifications, R restricted to V' will be valid, and $R(V') = R(V)$.

(R5), (R6), (R7) can be argued in a similar fashion.   ∎

A careful check of the reduction rules as developed for PLANAR DOMINATING SET show that all are valid but one, namely rule (R3) in [12], which is dealing with a black vertex x of degree one (it is not clear if one army should be put on x or two armies on the neighbor of x). That particular rule is not used in the (non-trivial) proof of the following theorem from [1], [12], where "reduced" refers to all reduction rules from [12] but (R3).

Theorem 3. *If $G = (B \uplus W, E)$ is a planar black and white graph that is reduced, then there exists a black vertex $u \in B$ with $\deg_G(u) \leq 7$.*

A simple search tree algorithm would now pick a black vertex v of smallest degree and branch according to if $R(v) = 1$ or if $R(u) = 2$ for some $u \in N[v]$; this branching reduces the parameter by two for each u; according to Thm. 3, $N[v]$ contains at most eight vertices. Solving the corresponding recurrence $T(k) \leq T(k-1) + 8T(k-2)$ for the size of the search tree shows the following assertion:

Theorem 4. PLANAR ROMAN DOMINATION *can be solved in $\mathcal{O}^*(3.3723^k)$ time.*
                                                                                    ∎

The $\mathcal{O}^*(\cdot)$ notation has by now become standard in exact algorithms. It is meant to not only suppress constants (as the more familiar $\mathcal{O}(\cdot)$-notation does) but also polynomial parts of the functions.

5   ROMAN DOMINATION on Graphs of Bounded Treewidth

In this section, we reconsider the problem of determining the minimum Roman domination set on graphs of bounded treewidth. This problem has been previously attacked in [20], but their algorithm is not quite correct, as we will explain. Then, we apply this treewidth-based algorithm to obtain $\mathcal{O}(c^{\sqrt{k}})$ algorithms for PLANAR ROMAN DOMINATION. Details on on tree decompositions can be found in [18] and are provided in an appendix.

On graphs of bounded treewidth, many otherwise combinatorially hard problems can be efficiently solved by dynamic programming. Given a so-called *nice tree decomposition* of a graph, we have to specify the operations in four different types of nodes, see [3], [18], [22]. Generally speaking, these operations are rather straightforward for all types of nodes but the join nodes. Therefore, we focus on that node type. Recall that a join node has two children nodes, and all three corresponding bags contain the same vertices. In the dynamic programming, to each node a table is associated that stores all possible combinations of "vertex states" together with their optimal value. With ROMAN DOMINATION, we need to store <u>four</u> states per vertex (only three are used in [20]):

- 0,1,2 are the values that the Roman domination function is assumed to assign to a particular vertex.
- $\hat{0}$ also tells us that the Roman domination function assigns 0 to that vertex.

The difference in the semantics of 0, $\hat{0}$ is the following: the assignment of 0 means that the vertex is already dominated at the current stage of the algorithm, and $\hat{0}$ means that, at the current stage of the algorithm, we still ask for a domination of this vertex. Let us only point to the following additional complication when dealing with join nodes: if we update an assignment that maps vertex x onto 0, it is not necessary that both children assign 0 to x; it is sufficient that one of the two branches does, while the other assigns $\hat{0}$. A naive implementation of what we said in the previous sentence would amount in spending $\mathcal{O}(16^{\text{tw}(G)})$ time for the join node processing. However, the "monotonicity trick" observed in [1] also works for this problem. Namely, for every vertex x in the parent bag, we consider the following cases:

- either 2, 1 or 0 is assigned to x; then, the same assignment must have been made in the two children;
- or $\hat{0}$ is assigned to x; then, we have two possible assignments in the child nodes: 0 to x in the left child and $\hat{0}$ to x in the right child or vice versa.

Theorem 5. MINIMUM ROMAN DOMINATION, *parameterized by the treewidth* $\text{tw}(G)$ *of the input graph* G, *can be solved in time* $\mathcal{O}(5^{\text{tw}(G)}|V(G)|)$.

This also generalizes Dreyer's result on trees [11–Sec. 2.9]. Besides having a corrected version of the $\mathcal{PTAS}$ for MINIMUM ROMAN DOMINATION explained in [20], we can also state an $\mathcal{O}^*(c^{\sqrt{k}})$ algorithm for PLANAR ROMAN DOMINATION. To get such an algorithm, we link ROMAN DOMINATION with DOMINATING SET:

Lemma 5. *If* $D \subseteq V$ *is a Roman domination set for* $G = (V, E)$ *(with respect to a Roman domination function* R, *i.e.,* $D = D_R$*), then* D *is also a dominating set. Moreover, if* $\sum_{x \in D_R} R(x) \leq k$, *then* $|D| \leq k$.

Theorem 6. *[Fomin and Thilikos [13]] If* G *is a planar graph which has a dominating set of size* k, *then* G *has treewidth of at most* $4.5^{1.5}\sqrt{k} \leq 9.55\sqrt{k}$.

Corollary 1. PLANAR ROMAN DOMINATION *can be solved in time*

$$\mathcal{O}^*\left(5^{4.5^{1.5}\sqrt{k}}\right) = \mathcal{O}^*\left(2^{22.165\sqrt{k}}\right).$$

6   A Dual Version of ROMAN DOMINATION

We finally mention that the following version of a parametric dual of ROMAN is in $\mathcal{FPT}$ by the method of kernelization, relying on [7–Proposition 4(e)]: given a graph G and a parameter k_d, is there a Roman domination function R such that $|R^{-1}(1)| + 2|R^{-1}(0)| \geq k_d$?

The definition of a dual of ROMAN DOMINATION might look a bit funny at first glance: But since ROMAN DOMINATION is a sort of weighted version of DOMINATING SET, it is not quite clear what the notion of a parametric dual should be in this case. With our definition, we have the possibly desirable property that (G, k_d) is a YES-instance of this variant of a dual of ROMAN DOMINATION iff $(G, 2|V(G)| - k_d)$ is a YES-instance of ROMAN. In other words, R is maximum for this dual version of ROMAN iff R is minimum for ROMAN.

Theorem 7. *Our version of parametric dual of* ROMAN DOMINATION *allows for a problem kernel of size* $(7/6)k_d$, *measured in terms of vertices. Hence, this problem is in* $\mathcal{FPT}$.

Proof. Note that we can easily get rid of all isolates with a first reduction rule: If x is an isolate, assign zero to x and decrease the parameter k_d by two.

As a second reduction rule, we claim that if $k_d < (6/7)|V(G)|$, then we can answer YES. Of course, this gives the claimed problem kernel.

Assume to the contrary that (G, k_d) is a NO-instance and that $k_d < (6/7)$ $|V(G)|$. Hence, for any optimum Roman domination function R for G,

$$|R^{-1}(1)| + 2|R^{-1}(0)| < k_d < (6/7)|V(G)|.$$

Hence, $|R^{-1}(0)| < (3/7)|V(G)|$. This is also true for any optimum Roman domination function R that also minimizes $|R^{-1}(1)|$ (as a second priority). This contradicts [7–Proposition 4(e)].

This shows that also this dual version of ROMAN DOMINATION is in $\mathcal{FPT}$. ∎

Notice that this results parallels the situation found with DOMINATING SET [9].

7   Conclusion

This paper contains a number of technical results concerning a parameterized view on ROMAN DOMINATION. Besides these technical results, we like to communicate the following messages:

- As can be seen from the W[2] completeness section, the "Turing way" to parameterized complexity is often quite amenable and may offer advantages over the standard approach as exhibited in [10].
- Strive to obtain structural results when developing algorithms: this turned out to be very beneficial for PLANAR ROMAN DOMINATION, since the results obtained for PLANAR DOMINATING SET could be "recycled."

References

1. Alber, J., Fan, H., Fellows, M.R., Fernau, H., Niedermeier, R., Rosamond, F., and Stege, U.: Refined Search Tree Techniques for the PLANAR DOMINATING SET Problem. In Proc. 26th MFCS, LNCS, Springer **2136** (2001) 111–122 Long version to appear in Journal of Computer and System Sciences
2. Benecke, S.: Higher Order Domination of Graphs. Master's Thesis, Department of Applied Mathematics of the University of Stellebosch, South Africa, (2004)

3. Bodlaender, H.L.: Dynamic Programming on Graphs with Bounded Treewidth. In Proc. 15th ICALP, LNCS **317** (1988) 105–119
4. Cesati, M.: The Turing Way to Parameterized Complexity. Journal of Computer and System Sciences **67** (2003) 654–685
5. Cesati, M., and Di Ianni, M.: Computation Models for Parameterized Complexity. Mathematical Logic Quarterly **43** (1997) 179–202
6. Chen, Y., and Flum, J.: Machine Characterization of the Classes of the W-Hierarchy. In Proc. 17th CSL, LNCS, Springer **2803** (2003) 114–127
7. Cockayne, E.J., Dreyer Jr., P.A., Hedetniemi, S.M., and Hedetniemi, S.T.: Roman Domination in Graphs. Discrete Mathematics **278** (2004) 11–22
8. Cockayne, E.J., Grobler, P.J.P., Gründlingh, W.R., Munganga, J., and van Vuuren, J.H.: Protection of a Graph. Utilitas Mathematica **67** (2005) 19–32
9. Dehne, F., Fellows, M., Fernau, H., Prieto, E., and Rosamond, F.: NONBLOCKER SET: Parameterized Algorithmics for MINIMUM DOMINATING SET. This volume.
10. Downey, R.G., and Fellows, M.R.: Parameterized Complexity. Springer (1999)
11. Dreyer Jr., P.A.: Applications and Variations of Domination in Graphs. PhD thesis, Rutgers University, New Jersey, USA, PhD Thesis (2000)
12. Fernau, H.: Parameterized Algorithmics: A Graph-Theoretic Approach. Habilitationsschrift, Universität Tübingen, Germany (2005) Submitted
13. Fomin, F.V., and Thilikos, D.M.: Dominating Sets in Planar Graphs: Branch-Width and Exponential Speed-up. In Proc. 14th SODA (2003) 168–177
14. Goddard, W.D., Hedetniemi, S.M., and Hedetniemi, S.T.: Eternal Security in Graphs. J. Combin. Math. Combin. Comput., to appear.
15. Haynes, T.W., Hedetniemi, S.T., and Slater, P.J.: Fundamentals of Domination in Graphs. Marcel Dekker (1998)
16. Henning, M.A.: Defending the Roman Empire from Multiple Attacks. Discrete Mathematics **271** (2003) 101–115
17. Henning, M.A., and Hedetniemi, S.T.: Defending the Roman Empire: a New Strategy. Discrete Mathematics **266** (2003) 239–251
18. Kloks, T.: Treewidth. Computations and Approximations, LNCS, Springer **842** (1994)
19. Liedloff, M., Kloks, T., Liu, J., and Peng, S.-L.: Roman Domination over Some Graphs Classes. To appear in the Proc. WG, Springer (2005)
20. Pagourtzis, A., Penna, P., Schlude, K., Steinhöfel, K., Taylor, D.S., and Widmayer, P.: Server Placements, Roman Domination and Other Dominating Set Variants. In 2nd IFIP International Conference on Theoretical Computer Science IFIP TCS, Kluwer (2002) 280–291
21. Stewart, I.: Defend the Roman Empire! Scientific American, Dec. (1999) 136–139
22. Telle, J.A., and Proskurowski, A.: Practical Algorithms on Partial *k*-Trees with an Application to Domination-Like Problems. In F. Dehne et al. (eds), Algorithms and Data Structures, Proc. 3rd WADS'93, LNCS **709** (1993) 610–621

Sedna: A Native XML DBMS

Andrey Fomichev, Maxim Grinev, and Sergey Kuznetsov

Institute for System Programming of Russia Academy of Sciences,
B. Kommunisticheskaya, 25, Moscow 109004, Russia
{fomichev, grinev, kuzloc}@ispras.ru
http://modis.ispras.ru

Abstract. Sedna is an XML database system being developed by the MODIS team at the Institute for System Programming of the Russian Academy of Sciences. Sedna implements XQuery and its data model exploiting techniques developed specially for this language. This paper describes the main choices made in the design of Sedna, sketches its most advanced techniques, and presents its overall architecture. In this paper we primarily focus on physical aspects of the Sedna implementation.

1 Introduction

Although XQuery is already a powerful and mature language for XML data querying and transformation, it is still a growing language. The authors of XQuery point out two principal directions of the XQuery evolution [4]: (1) extending it with data update facilities, and (2) growing it to a programming language. Thus, future XQuery is going to be a language for querying, updating and general-purpose programming. Implementing XQuery, researchers have been often focused on some of these aspects from the logical viewpoint[1] while an advanced industrial-strength implementation requires considering all three aspects as a single whole providing a physical layer that efficiently supports all these aspects. The layer is primarily based on data organization and memory management techniques. Query processing requires support for vast amounts of data that can exceed main memory and thus requires processing in secondary storage (i.e. on disk). Update processing requires a compromise between data organizations optimized for querying and updating. Using XQuery as a programming language requires fast processing in main memory without essential overheads resulting from support for external memory. In this paper we give an overview of our native XML DBMS implementation named Sedna focusing on its physical layer that provides efficient support for all the three aspects mentioned above.

The paper is organized as follows. Section 2 presents an overview of the system including its architecture, query optimization and concurrency control techniques. Section 3 describes principal mechanisms underlying the Sedna storage system,

---

[1] We have also contributed to this work by developing a set of logical optimization techniques for XQuery [5], [6], [7].

J. Wiedermann et al. (Eds.): SOFSEM 2006, LNCS 3831, pp. 272–281, 2006.

namely data organization and memory management. In Section 4, we discuss execution of XQuery queries over the Sedna storage system. We conclude in Section 5.

2 Sedna

2.1 Overview

Sedna is designed with having two main goals in mind. First, it should be the full-featured database system. That requires support for all traditional database services such as external memory management, query and update facilities, concurrency control, query optimization, etc. Second, it should provide a run-time environment for XML-data intensive applications. That involves tight integration of database management functionality and that of a programming language.

Developing Sedna, we decided not to adopt any existing database system. Instead of building a superstructure upon an existing database system, we have developed a native system from scratch. It took more time and effort but gave us more freedom in making design decisions and allowed avoiding undesirable run-time overheads resulting from interfacing with the data model of the underlying database system.

We take the XQuery 1.0 language [1] and its data model [2] as a basis for our implementation. In order to support updates we extend XQuery with an update language named XUpdate. Our update language is very close to [13].

Sedna is written in Scheme and C++. Static query analysis and optimization is written in Scheme. Parser, executor, memory and transaction management are written in C++. Supported platforms are Windows and Linux.

2.2 Architecture

Architecture of the Sedna DBMS is rather traditional (Fig.1) and consists of the following components. The *governor* serves as the "control center" of the system. It knows which databases and transactions are running and controls them. The *listener* component listens for clients and creates an instance of the *transaction* component for each client and sets up the direct connection between the client and the transaction component. From this point client's session is supported by the transaction component that encapsulates the following query execution components: parser, optimizer, and executor. The *parser* translates the query into its *logical representation*, which is a tree of operations close to the XQuery core. The *optimizer* takes the query logical representation and produces the optimized *query execution plan* which is a tree of low-level operations over physical data structures. The execution plan is interpreted by the *executor*. Each instance of the *database manager* encapsulates a single database and consists of database management services such as the *index manager* that keeps track of indices built on the database, the *buffer manager* that is responsible for the interaction between disk and main memory, and the *transaction manager* that provides concurrency control facilities.

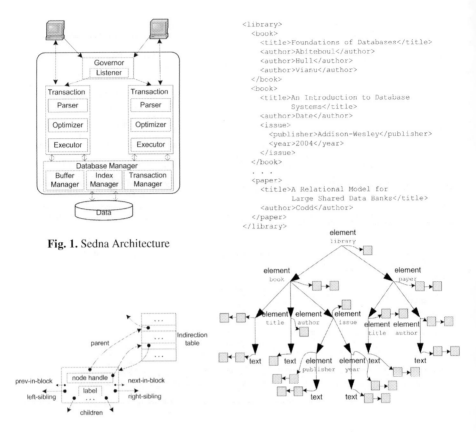

Fig. 1. Sedna Architecture

Fig. 3. Common Structure of Node Descriptor

Fig. 2. Data Organization

2.3 Optimization

In Sedna, we have implemented a wide set of rule-based query optimization techniques for XQuery. The cost-based optimization is the subject of future work.

Function inlining technique [8] allows replacing calls to user-defined functions with their bodies. Function inlining eliminates function call overhead and allows us to optimize in static the inlined function body together with the rest of the query. This essentially facilitates the application of the other optimization techniques. We have implemented an inlining algorithm that can properly handle non-recursive functions and structurally recursive functions. The algorithm reasonably terminates infinite inlining for recursive functions of any kind that makes the algorithm applicable to any XQuery query.

Predicate push down XML element constructors [6] changes the order of operations to apply predicates before XML element constructors. It allows reducing the size of intermediate computation results to which XML element constructors are applied. This kind of transformation is of great importance because XML element constructor is an expensive operation, the evaluation of which requires deep copy of the element content. *Projection of transformation* [6] statically applies XPath expressions to element constructors. It allows avoiding redundant computation of costly XML element constructors.

Query simplification using schema is useful when a query is written by the user that has vague notion about XML document schema. Making query formulation more accurate allows avoiding redundant data scanning that is peculiar to such queries. This optimization technique is based on the XQuery static type inference.

Making query formulation as declarative as possible allows the optimizer to widen search space with optimal execution plans. The technique is the adaptation of analogous SQL-oriented technique [9] that is aimed at unnesting subexpressions into joins.

Join predicates normalization consists in rewriting joins predicates into conjunctive normal form to take the advantage of using different join algorithms, but not only nested loop join. To achieve this goal we extract subexpressions like XPath statements from join predicates and place them outside join operations, where they are evaluated only once.

Identifying iterator-free subexpressions in the body of iterator-operations reduces the computation complexity of the query by putting subexpressions which do not contain free occurrences of iterator outside the body of the iterator-operation.

2.4 Concurrency Control

Sedna supports multiple users concurrently accessing data. To ensure serializability of transactions we use a well-known strict two phase locking protocol. For now, the locking granule is the whole XML document. In many cases locking of the whole XML document is not needed and this leads to the decreasing of concurrency. This is the reason why we are going towards a new fine-granularity locking method. The main idea behind our method is to use descriptive schema of the XML document for locking subtrees of the XML document according to the path query issued by the user [17], [18]. The notion of descriptive schema (that is a basis of our storage system) is introduced in the next section.

3 Storage System

3.1 Data Organization

Designing data organization, we would like it to be efficient for both queries and updates.

Designing data organization in Sedna we have made the following main decisions to speed up query processing. First, *direct* pointers are used to represent relationships between nodes of an XML document such as parent, child, and sibling relationships. An overview of pointers and their structures is given in Section 3.2. Second, we have developed a *descriptive schema driven storage strategy* which consists in clustering nodes of an XML document according to their positions in the descriptive schema of the document. In contrast to prescriptive schema that is known in advance and is usually specified in DTD and XML Schema, descriptive schema is dynamically generated (and increasingly maintained) from the data and presents a concise and accurate structure summary of these data. Formally speaking, every path of the document has exactly one path in the descriptive schema, and every path of the descriptive schema is a path of the document. As it follows from the definition, descriptive schema for XML is always a tree. Using descriptive schema instead of prescriptive one gives the following advantages: (1) descriptive schema is more accurate then prescriptive one; (2) it allows us to apply this storage strategy for XML documents which come with no prescriptive schema.

The overall principles of the data organization are illustrated in Fig. 2. The central component is the descriptive schema that is presented as a tree of schema nodes. Each schema node is labeled with an XML node kind name (e.g. element, attribute, text, etc.) and has a pointer to data blocks where nodes corresponding to the schema node are stored. Some schema nodes depending on their node kinds are also labeled with names. Data blocks belonging to one schema node are linked via pointers into a bidirectional list. Node descriptors in a list of blocks are partly ordered according to document order. It means that every node descriptor in the block **i** precedes every node descriptor in the block **j** in document order, if and only if **i** < **j** (i.e. the block **i** precedes the block **j** in the list).

Nodes are ordered between blocks in the same list in document order. Within a block nodes are unordered[2] that reduces overheads on maintaining document order in case of updates.

In our storage we separate node's structural part and text value. The text value is the content of a text node or the value of an attribute node, etc. The essence of text value is that it is of variable length. Text values are stored in blocks according to the well-known slotted-page structure method [10] developed specifically for data of variable length. The structural part of a node reflects its relationship to other nodes (i.e. parent, children, sibling nodes) and is presented in the form of *node descriptor*.

The common structure of node descriptors for all node kinds is shown in Fig. 3. The **label** field contains a label of *numbering scheme*. The main purpose of a numbering scheme is to provide mechanisms to quickly determine the structural relationship between a pair of nodes. Numbering scheme in Sedna is close to the one described in [11] and supports dynamic updates when order is a concern.

The **node handle** is discussed in Section 3.1.1. The meaning of the **left-sibling** and **right-sibling** pointers is straightforward. The **next-in-block** and **prev-in-block** pointers are used to link nodes within the block to allow reconstructing document order as was mentioned above. The **next-in-block** and **prev-in-block** pointers allow reconstructing document order among nodes corresponding to the same schema node, whereas the **left-sibling** and **right-sibling** pointers are used to support document order between sibling nodes.

Storing pointers to all children in the node descriptor may result in the node descriptor the size of which exceeds the size of block. To avoid this, we store only

---

[2] The order within a block can be reconstructed using pointers as described below.

pointers to the first children by the descriptive schema. Let us illustrate this by the example of the **library** element in Fig. 2. It has two books and one paper as child elements. In the descriptive scheme the **element library** schema node has only two children. In spite of the actual number of books and papers, the node descriptor for the library element has exactly two children pointers. These are pointers to the first **book** element and the first **paper** element. To traverse all the child **book** elements of the **library** element, we use the pointer to the first **book** element and then follow the **next-in-block** pointers (if all the children do not fit one block, we go to the next block via the interblock pointer). Having only pointers to the first children by schema allows us to save up storage space and, that is more important, to make node descriptors a fixed size. The latter is of crucial importance for efficient execution of updates because it simplifies managing free space in blocks. However, this approach leads to the following problem. If a node is inserted into the document for which there is no corresponding schema node, we have to rebuild all node descriptors in blocks belonging to the parent schema node of the inserted node. To solve this problem we maintain node descriptors to be of a fixed size only within one block by storing the number of children pointers in the header of all blocks. The number informs us that all node descriptors stored in the block have exactly this number of children pointers.

Using direct pointers is the main source of problems for efficient update execution. To make the data organization good for updates, we should minimize the number of modifications caused by the execution of an update operation. Let us consider an update operation that moves a node. This operation is invoked by the procedure of block's splitting as a result of inserting a node into the overfilled block. If the node to be moved has children, they all must be modified to change their **parent** pointers to the node. The solution is to use indirect pointers, that is implemented via *indirection table*, to refer to the parent.

In conclusion of this section we would like to sum up the features of our data organization that are designed to improve update operations:

- Node descriptors have a fixed size within a block;
- Node descriptors are partly ordered;
- The parent pointer of node descriptor is indirect.

Node Handle. Implementation of some operations and database mechanisms requires support for *node handle* that is immutable during the whole life-time of the object and can be used to access the node efficiently. For instance, node handle can be used to refer to the node from the index structures. As discussed in Section 4, node handle is also necessary for the proper implementation of update operations. As mentioned above, execution of some update operations (e.g. insert node) might lead to block splitting that in turn results in moving nodes. Therefore, pointers to nodes do not possess the property of immutability. Although the label of numbering scheme is immutable and allows uniquely identifying the node, it requires document tree traverse to get the node by the label. Our implementation of node handle is shown in Fig. 3. We exploit the indirection table that is also used to implement indirect pointers to parent. Node handle is the pointer to the record in the indirection table which contains the pointer to the node.

3.2 Memory Management

As discussed in Section 3.1, one of the key design choices concerning the data organization in Sedna is to use direct pointers to present relationships between nodes. Therefore, traversing the nodes during query execution results in intensive pointer dereferencing. Making dereferencing as fast as possible is of crucial importance to achieve high performance. Although using ordinary pointers of programming languages powered by the OS virtual memory management mechanism is perfect for performance and programming effort required, this solution is inadequate for the following two reasons. First, it imposes restrictions on the address space size caused by the standard 32-bit architecture that still prevails nowadays. Second, we cannot rely on the virtual memory mechanism provided by OS in case of processing queries over large amounts of data because we need to control the page replacement (swapping) procedure to force pages to disk according to the query execution logic [14].

To solve these problems we have implemented our own memory management mechanism that supports 64-bit address space (we refer to it as Sedna Address Space - SAS for short) and manages page replacement. It is supported by mapping it onto the process virtual address space (PVAS for short) in order to use ordinary pointers for the mapped part. The mapping is carried out as follows. SAS is divided into layers of the equal size. The size of layer has been chosen so that the layer fits PVAS. The layer consists of pages (that are those in which XML data are stored as described in Section 3.1). All pages are of the equal size so that they can be efficiently handled by the buffer manager. In the header of each page there is the number of the layer the page belongs to. The address of an object in SAS (that is 64-bit long) consists of the layer number (the first 32 bits) and the address within the layer (the second 32 bits). The address within the layer is mapped to the address in PVAS on an equality basis. So we do not use any additional structures to provide the mapping. The address range of PVAS (to which the layers of SAS are mapped) is in turn mapped onto main memory by the Sedna buffer manager using memory management facilities provided by OS.

Dereferencing a pointer to an object in SAS **(layer_num, addr)** is performed as follows. **addr** is dereferenced as an ordinary pointer to an object in PVAS. This may result in a memory fault that means there is no page in main memory by this address of PVAS. In this case buffer manager reads the required page from disk. Otherwise the system checks whether the page that is currently in main memory belongs to the **layer_num** layer. If it is not so, the buffer manager replaces the page with the required one. It is worth mentioning that the unit of interaction with disk is not a layer but a page so that main memory may contain pages from different layers at the same time.

The main advantages of the memory management mechanism used in Sedna are as follows:

- Emulating 64-bit virtual address space on the standard 32-bit architecture allows removing restrictions on the size of database;
- Overheads for dereferencing are not much more than for dereferencing ordinary pointers because we map the layer to PVAS addresses on an equality basis;

– The same pointer representation in main and secondary memory is used that allows avoiding costly pointer swizzling (i.e. the process of transformation of a pointer in secondary memory to the pointer that can be used directly in main memory is called).

4 Query Execution

In this section we discuss XQuery query execution over the storage system described in the previous section.

The set of physical operations also provides support for updates. The statement of XUpdate is represented as an execution plan which consists of two parts. The first part selects nodes that are target for the update, and the second part perform the update of the selected nodes. The selected nodes as well as intermediate result of any query expression are represented by direct pointers. The update switches to indirect pointers presented as node handles. It is necessary because the sequential updating of the selected nodes might invalidate pointers to them by performing a number of move operations. Switching to node handles fully avoids this problem.

4.1 Query Execution Aspects

In this section we would like to emphasize the query processing aspects that are specific to our executor.

Element Constructors. Besides the well-known heavy operations like joins, sorting and grouping, XQuery has a specific resource consuming operation - XML element constructor. The construction of an XML element requires deep copy of its content that leads to essential overheads. The overheads grow significantly when a query consists of a number of nested element constructors. Understanding the importance of the problem, we propose *suspended element constructor*. The suspended element constructor does not perform deep copy of the content of the constructed element but rather stores a pointer to it. The copy is performed on demand when some operation gets into the content of the constructed element. Using suspended element constructor is effective when the result of the constructor is handled by operations that do not analyze the content of elements. Our previous research [6] allows us to claim that for a wide class of XQuery queries there will be no deep copies at all. Most XQuery queries can be rewritten in such a way that above the element constructors in the execution plan there will be no operations that analyze the content of elements.

Different Strategies for XPath Queries Evaluation. Using descriptive schema as an index structure allows us to avoid tree traverse and speed up query execution. Let us consider the following XPath query: title. We call it *structural path query*, because it exploits only information about structure in such a way that we do not need to make any tests depending on data to evaluate this query. Structural path queries are ideal to be evaluated using descriptive schema. We start evaluation of the query with traversing the descriptive schema for the context document (See Fig. 2). The result of traverse is two schema nodes that contain pointers to the lists of blocks with the data we are looking for. Simply passing through the first list of blocks and then through the second one we may break document order, so before outputting the result the *merge operation* is performed. The merge operation receives several lists of blocks as an input and produces the sequence of node descriptors, which are ordered with respect to document order. The merge operation uses labels of the numbering scheme to reconstruct document order. The computation complexity of this operation is $O(\sum n_i)$ comparisons of labels, where n_i is the number of node descriptors in the i-th list of blocks.

The second query */library/book[issue/year=2004]/title* requires more effort to be evaluated. As for the previous queries we can select */library/book* elements using the descriptive schema, then apply the predicate and the rest of the query using pointers in data. But it seems to us the following algorithm could be more attractive. Firstly, we evaluate the structural path query */library/book/issue/year/text()*. Secondly, we apply the predicate (we select only those nodes, for which the text is equal to 2004). And at last, we apply *../../../title* to the result of the previous step. The idea is that we select blocks to which the predicate applies on the first step omitting blocks with book elements. Then we apply the predicate which potentially cuts off lots of data and then go up the XML hierarchy to obtain the final result.

4.2 Combining Lazy and Strict Semantics

All queries formulated to databases have one thing in common - they usually operate with great amounts of data even if results are small. So query processors have to (should) deal with intermediate huge data sets efficiently. To accommodate these needs the iterative query execution model, which avoids unnecessary data materialization, has been proposed. Being developed for relational DBMSs it is general enough to be adapted for other data models. We did this for XQuery in [12]. Keeping in mind that XQuery is a functional language, iterative model can be regarded as an implementation of lazy semantics. On the other hand, it is generally accepted [15] that computation efficiency of implementation of strict semantics for a programming language is higher comparing with implementation of lazy semantics for this language. As far as we consider XQuery as a general-purpose programming language that can be used for expressing application logic, implementing lazy semantics only has bad impact on overall executor performance. To let the XQuery implementation be efficient for both query and application logic processing we combine these two evaluation models. We have developed the XQuery executor, which keeps track of amounts of data being processed and automatically switches from the lazy to strict modes and vice versa at run-time.

The query evaluation starts in the lazy mode having the execution plan constructed. The overheads of the lazy model strongly correlates with a number of function calls made during the evaluation process. The more function calls are made, the more copies of function bodies are performed. The goal is to find the tradeoff between the copying of function body and the materializing of intermediate results of function's operations. The mechanism is as follows. Every function call is a reason to switch to strict mode if the sizes of arguments are relatively small. Vice versa, the large input sequence for any physical operation in the strict mode is a subject to switch this operation to the lazy mode.

5 Conclusion

In this paper we have presented an overview of the Sedna XML DBMS focusing on its physical layer. Sedna is freely available at our web site [16] and readers are encouraged to download it and have a look at it themselves.

References

1. XQuery 1.0: An XML Query Language, W3C Working Draft, 04 April 2005, http://www.w3.org/TR/2005/WD-xquery-20050404/
2. XQuery 1.0 and XPath 2.0 Data Model, W3C Working Draft, 04 April 2005, http://www.w3.org/TR/2005/WD-xpath-datamodel-20050404/
3. XQuery 1.0 and XPath 2.0 Functions and Operators, W3C Working Draft, 04 April 2005, http://www.w3.org/TR/2005/WD-xpath-functions-20050404/
4. Fernandez, M.F., Simeon, J.: Growing XQuery. ECOOP 2003: 405-430
5. Grinev, M.: XQuery Optimization Based on Rewriting (2003) Available at www.ispras.ru/~grinev
6. Grinev, M., Pleshachkov, P.: Rewriting-Based Optimization for XQuery Transformational Queries. Available at www.ispras.ru/~grinev
7. Grinev, M., Kuznetsov, S.: Towards an Exhaustive Set of Rewriting Rules for XQuery Optimization: BizQuery Experience. In Proc. ADBIS Conference, 2002
8. Grinev, M., Lizorkin, D.: XQuery Function Inlining for Optimizing XQuery Queries. In Proc. ADBIS Conference (2004)
9. Dayal, U.: Of Nests and Trees: A Unified Approach to Processing Queries that Contain Nested Subqueries, Aggregates, and Quantifiers. In Proc. VLDB Conference (1987)
10. Silberschatz, A., Korth, H., Sudarshan, S.: Database System Concepts. Third Edition, McGraw-Hill (1997)
11. Wu, X., Lee, M.L., Hsu, W.: A Prime Number Labeling Scheme for Dynamic Ordered XML Trees. Proceedings of ICDE'04
12. Antipin, K., Fomichev, A., Grinev, M., Kuznetsov, S., Novak, L., Pleshachkov, P., Rekouts, M., Shiryaev, D.: Efficient Virtual Data Integration Based on XML. In Proc. ADBIS Conference (2003)
13. Lehti, P.: Design and Implementation of a Data Manipulation Processor for an XML Query Language. Technische Universitt Darmstadt Technical Report No. KOM-D-149, http://www.ipsi.fhg.de/~lehti/diplomarbeit.pdf, (August 2001)
14. Chou, H.-T., DeWitt, D. J.: An Evaluation of Buffer Management Strategies for Relational Database Systems, Proceedings of VLDB (1985)
15. Ennals, R., Jones, S.P.: Optimistic Evaluation: an Adaptive Evaluation Strategy for Non-Strict Programs. Proceedings of the ICFP'03, August 25-29, 2003, Uppsala, Sweden
16. Sedna XML DBMS - http://modis.ispras.ru/Development/sedna.htm
17. Pleshachkov, P., Chardin, P., Kuznetsov, S.: XDGL: XPath-Based Concurrency Control Protocol for XML Data. BNCOD 2005: 145-154
18. Pleshachkov, P., Chardin, P., Kuznetsov, S.: A Locking Based Scheduler for XML Databases. SEBD 2005: 356-367

Optimal Memory Rendezvous of Anonymous Mobile Agents in a Unidirectional Ring

L. Gąsieniec[1], E. Kranakis[2], D. Krizanc[3], and X. Zhang[1]

[1] Department of Computer Science,
University of Liverpool, Liverpool L69 7ZF, UK
[2] Carleton University School of Computer Science,
1125 Colonel By Drive Ottawa, Ontario K1S 5B6, Canada
[3] Computer Science Group, Mathematics Department,
Wesleyan University, Middletown, CT 06459, USA

Abstract. We study the rendezvous problem with $k \geq 2$ mobile agents in a n-node ring. We present a new algorithm which solves the rendezvous problem for any non-periodic distribution of agents on the ring. The mobile agents require the use of $O(\log k)$−bit-wise size of internal memory and one indistinguishable token each. In the periodic (but not symmetric) case our new procedure allows the agents to conclude that rendezvous is not feasible. It is known that in the symmetric case the agents cannot decide the feasibility of rendezvous if their internal memory is limited to $\omega(\log \log n)$ bits, see [15]. In this context we show new space optimal deterministic algorithm allowing effective recognition of the symmetric case. The algorithm is based on $O(\log k + \log \log n)$-bit internal memory and a single token provided to each mobile agent. Finally, it is known that both in the periodic as well as in the symmetric cases the rendezvous cannot be accomplished by any deterministic procedure due to problems with breaking symmetry.

1 Introduction

The mobile agent *rendezvous* problem is a search optimization problem, whereby a number of autonomous deterministic agents starting from two (or more) given nodes of a network are required to rendezvous at some node eventually, so as to optimize either the number of steps or the memory used by the robots or a tradeoff of both. The mobile agents are autonomous entities that move along nodes of the network acting on the basis of collected information and the rules provided by a given protocol.

There are instances where the rendezvous problem is easy, e.g., if the nodes of the network have distinct identities, in which case the mobile agents can move to a node with a specific pre-assigned identity. However, even in this case the problem becomes more difficult to solve if the agents do not have enough memory to "remember" and distinguish identities. In general, solutions of the rendezvous problem are challenging under conditions that delimit what the mobile agents can do and/or know about the status of the overall system. We are interested

J. Wiedermann et al. (Eds.): SOFSEM 2006, LNCS 3831, pp. 282–292, 2006.
© Springer-Verlag Berlin Heidelberg 2006

in studying trade-offs between the use of memory and time required by mobile agents to rendezvous in a ring.

There is a variety of interesting scenarios under consideration that may involve 1) (minimum) number of tokens used by the mobile agents, 2) knowledge of the status of the network and presence of other mobile agents in the system (e.g., number of mobile agents participating in the rendezvous problem, feasibility of rendezvous for a given starting configuration), 3) knowledge of inter-agent distances at the start, etc. For example, under some conditions the rendezvous task is impossible to accomplish. The mobile agents will either execute the code of their rendezvous algorithm indefinitely (less favourable solution) or they will stop eventually claiming that the rendezvous is not feasible. Thus it is crucial to be able to determine conditions under which the rendezvous can be accomplished or at least the agents can conclude that the rendezvous is not possible.

Communication model. A number of mobile agents are situated at the nodes of a unidirectional synchronous ring. Each mobile agent marks its original position (node) by an indistinguishable token just after initiation of the rendezvous process. An original distribution (marked by the tokens) of agents on the ring can be either: *symmetric*, when the distances between the agents are uniform; *periodic*, when the distances between the consecutive agents form a periodic (cyclic) pattern; or *non-periodic* otherwise. During the execution of the algorithm, at the beginning of any time unit a mobile agent occupies some node of the ring. And during this time unit it may decide to: 1) stay at its current position, 2) move to the next position, 3) detect the presence of one or more agents at the node it is currently occupying, and 4) detect the presence of one or more tokens at the node it is currently occupying. We say that one or more mobile agents rendezvous when they meet at the same node. Mobile agents may communicate and exchange information with each other only when they rendezvous.

In this paper we study the rendezvous problem with $k \geq 2$ mobile agents in a n-node ring. We use the following model of communication. The ring and the agents are anonymous. The links in the ring are unidirectional and there is a sense of direction [13]. The ring consists of n nodes but this size is neither known to the nodes of the ring nor to the agents. The nodes of the ring are identical, i.e., they do not have distinct identities. The k participating agents use indistinguishable tokens only once to mark their original positions in the ring. The agents move along the ring in synchronous steps. We assume that all agents start to traverse the ring at the same time and they execute the same deterministic algorithm. The agents may communicate and exchange information with one another only when they meet each other at some node. Moreover, when an agent finds a token that has been released at a node in the ring it can not distinguish it from its own token(s) or from the token(s) of the other mobile agents (this is equivalent to identifying tokens with *erasable marks*).

Related work. There has been considerable literature on the rendezvous problem. The problem initiated with the work of Alpern (see the survey [2]). Research conducted over the years by Alpern and various collaborators [1], [3],

[4], [5], [17] concentrated on the optimization problem for probabilistic search in operations research. Additional research with emphasis on either optimization on rendezvous as a competitive game was also conducted by Pikounis and Thomas [18], Anderson and Essegaier [6], Anderson and Fekete [7], Anderson and Weber [8], Baston and Gal [10], [11], Chester and Tutuncu [12].

Here we are interested in time-memory trade-offs for achieving rendezvous as well as for detecting the feasibility of rendezvous. The main concern in all rendezvous algorithms is how to "break symmetry". In previous works mentioned above, symmetry in the rendezvous problem is typically broken either by using randomized algorithms or by mobile agents running different deterministic algorithms [3], e.g., based upon distinct identities. Baston and Gal [10] consider the case where agents may mark their starting points but they still rely on randomization or different deterministic algorithms to achieve rendezvous. The current token model used to break symmetries was initiated by Sawchuk [19].

Several possibility and impossibility results on the rendezvous problem for two mobile agents were considered in Kranakis et al. [14], whereby two mobile agents on an n node ring can use identical tokens to break the symmetry. In Flocchini et al. [15] it is proved that the agent rendezvous problem has no solution when both values of k and n are unknown. Since we assume that $k \leq n$ this implies that agents require at least $\log k$ bits to store the value k. Flocchini et al. also show that rendezvous is feasible iff the original distribution of the distances between agents on the ring is non-periodic. Further, they show that any deterministic algorithm for an n-node unidirectional ring using a single token to mark the starting positions of the agents requires $\Omega(\log \log n)$ memory to recognize if rendezvous is feasible. They present several unconditional and conditional solutions to the agents rendezvous problem with different memory and time requirements. In particular, they provide an algorithm that performs rendezvous when it is possible or recognises that rendezvous is not possible. This requires $O(k \log \log n)$ bits of memory per agent. This result is not optimal for non-constant k.

Results and organization of the paper. In this paper we show a new deterministic rendezvous algorithm based on the use of optimal $O(\log k + \log \log n)$-bit memory. The paper is organised as follows. In Section 2 we present a new rendezvous algorithm which performs rendezvous when it is possible or recognises the periodic (non-symmetric) input case. This algorithm requires $O(\log k)$ bits of memory per agent. Note that in the symmetric case this algorithm will not halt. In Section 3 an algorithm for identifying symmetric distributions of mobile agents is given. This algorithm requires $O(\log k + \log \log n)$ bits of memory per agent. In both cases we provide analysis and proof of correctness. Together, the algorithms provide an optimal memory solution to the rendezvous problem on the ring.

2   Efficient Rendezvous of Agents

In this section we give a detailed description of the communication model, the task to be performed as well as our new algorithm. The k anonymous agents

$A_1, A_2, \ldots, A_k$ are placed on an anonymous directed $n-$node ring R, where, the distance between agents A_i and A_{i+1} is denoted by S_i, for all $i = 1, \ldots, k$. Equivalently (depending on the context) we will also refer to distances $S_1, \ldots, S_k$ as segments, see Figure 1. Note that reference to agent A_j is always understood as $A_{(j-1 \bmod k)+1}$. All agents are anonymous (indistinguishable) and each of them possesses local memory limited to $\log k$ bits. Moreover, each agent A_i is allowed to leave a mark T_i (indistinguishable token) at its original position on the ring. We assume here that the actions of all agents are totally synchronised. I.e., the agents wake up at the same time and later proceed in perfectly synchronised time units, called also *time steps*. During each step an agent decides whether to move to the next node (in clockwise direction) or to remain stationary according to the algorithm and the content of its $O(\log k)-$size memory. Later we show that each agent uses exactly $2\log k + 2$ bits of its internal memory. At the conclusion of each time step the content of the local memory is updated. We also assume that the agents detect one another only when they meet at some node of the ring. When an agent moves back to its starting point, we say that the it has accomplished a full turn or a traversal of the ring.

The main task considered here is *to rendezvous* all participating agents (if possible) at one of the nodes of the ring R at some specific moment in time. *The outcome* of the rendezvous process depends on the size of the local memory of each agent. When the memory is limited to $O(\log k)$ bits then if the the distribution of the agents on the ring is: 1) *symmetric* - the agents run forever; 2) *periodic* (but not symmetric) - the agents do not rendezvous, though they eventually learn that the initial distribution is periodic and they stop; 3) otherwise, the rendezvous is always accomplished. In case when internal memory of each participating agent is limited to $O(\log k + \log\log n)$ bits agents are able to learn that the initial distribution is symmetric, and they stop having this knowledge.

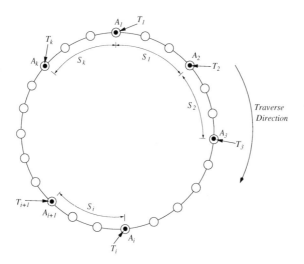

Fig. 1. Basic facts about the model

Further details. In this paper, we introduce a new rendezvous mechanism which is based on *variable speed* of agents. The use of different speeds by agents performing similar tasks, such as *leader election*, can be found in [16]. In our mechanism, a current speed of an agent A_i depends on the relative index of segment S_j, see Figure 1, as follows. We say that agent A_i traverses with speed $V_i(j)$ if it uses segment S_{i+j} to calculate its speed. And when this happens, A_i always moves to the next node during each time step while being in S_{i+j} (we say that the agent goes with the *full speed* 1 in S_{i+j}); and it alternates moves with stationary steps (the agent goes with the speed $1/2$) in all other segments.

There are three possible states in which the agents find themselves while moving: a *runner state*, a *marker state* and a *loser state*. An agent is called a *runner*, a *marker* and a *loser* in these states respectively. All agents start to traverse the ring while being in the *runner state* or in other words being *runners*. While being a *runner* agent A_i traverses the ring using Algorithm Rendezvous. Agent A_i becomes a *marker* when it is caught by A_{i-1}. When this happens, A_i loses its self-control and becomes the slave of agent A_{i-1}. From now on, A_i follows instructions only from its master A_{i-1}. When agent A_i is caught by A_j, for $j \neq i - 1$, agent A_i becomes a *loser*. In other words, agent A_i is switched off until a winning agent picks it up at the final stage of the rendezvous process.

The utilisation of the internal memory limited to $2 \log k + 2$ bits per each agent is done as follows: **State:** 2 bits of memory are used to store an agent's state. I.e., 0∗ means the agent is a *runner*, 10 means it is a *marker*, and 11 means it is a *loser*. **Position bits:** the first chunk of $\log k$ bits is used to count the number (modulo k) of tokens an agent passed from its original position. This value is always between 0 and $k-1$. As soon as this value turns to 0, the agent knows that it is back in its starting position, i.e., a full turn has been accomplished. **Speed indicator:** the second chunk of $\log k$ bits informs an agent in which segment the full speed should be used. This value is also within range $0, \ldots, k-1$. In particular, in round i this value is i and the agent uses full speed on the $(i+1)$th segment counting from its starting position. When this value turns back to 0, the agent is aware of the fact that it already tried all available speeds. And when this happens, it goes to stage (2) where this part of the internal memory is used to count the number of agents for which the rendezvous has been accomplished.

The algorithm. In this section we present our new rendezvous algorithm. Each of the participating agents executes the following code splitting the rendezvous procedure into three consecutive stages. During Stage (0) every running agent is expected either to catch its direct predecessor or to be caught by one of its successors. We show later that if the initial distribution is not symmetric every agent accomplishes Stage (0) eventually. Otherwise all agents remain in Stage (0) for ever. In the next section we also show how to recognise this situation with the use of $O(\log \log n)$ bits of extra memory. Stage (1) is used to eliminate (switch off) all agents apart from one who eventually gathers all (switched off) agents in its original position. We prove that this rendezvous process is entirely successful if the initial distribution is not periodic. In the periodic case there is more than one winner. The final stage is used to collect all losers (including their markers) by the winner. If the winning agent manages to collect all $(k-1)$ other agents it knows (and this knowledge is passed on collected agents too) that the rendezvous process was accomplished successfully. Otherwise the agents know that the case is periodic. Finally note that since we deal with anonymous agents the indices of agents, segments, and tokens are relative. The code of the algorithm follows.

Algorithm Rendezvous (A_i)

STAGE (0)
    Run with the speed $V_i(0)$ until:
    (*state bits* of A_i are set to 00, *position bits* start to count tokens.)
    (1) if A_i catches A_{i+1}
        (1.a) A_i overpowers A_{i+1} to create its *marker* M_i;
        (Change A_{i+1}'s *state* from 00 to 10.)
        (1.b) A_i moves with M_i to T_i, and leaves M_i there;
        (When *position bits* turn back to 0, A_i knows that it is back at T_i.
        Also, *position bits* of the *marker* are set to 0.)
        (1.c) go to Stage(0.5);
    (2) if A_i is caught or meets a marker of another agent A_i gets switched off.
    (In the symmetric case, all the agents remain in Stage (0) for ever.)

If the sequence of segments S_i is not uniform there are at least two neighboring agents, A_i and A_{i+1}, that will traverse the ring using two different speeds $V_i(0) > V_{i+1}(0)$. In this case, after every full turn, agent A_i gets closer to agent A_{i+1} by at least one position on the ring. Since the original distance between respective tokens T_i and T_{i+1} is less than n we know that agent A_i will catch A_{i+1} (if A_i is not caught earlier by its predecessor) within the first n full turns, which correspond to $O(n^2)$ units of time.

STAGE (0.5)
    Leave the marker M_i at the position containing T_i, and
    run with the full speed for one full turn.
    (1) When A_i catches another agent, switches it off;
    (2) Go to Stage (1).

After agent A_i moves to Stage (0.5), it leaves its marker M_i at the node containing token T_i and immediately it makes one full turn with full speed (one node per time unit). Note that during n time units (full turn), all other agents who are still in Stage (0) will be switched off (if they do not manage to find their own marker on time) either by being caught or by encountering the marker of another agent already being in Stage (0.5). The main purpose of Stage (0.5) is to ensure that on its completion by any agent (including the most advanced one) all other agents are either switched off or they are at least in Stage (0.5). This allows to assume that the largest time difference between the events in which two agents enter Stage (1) is never larger than n, see Figure 3.

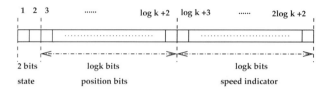

Fig. 2. Utilisation of the memory

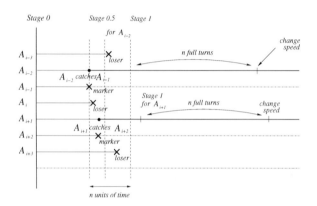

Fig. 3. Progress through Stage (0.5)

STAGE (1)

For the round $j = 0, 1, \dots (k-1)$ run with speed $V_i(j)$.
(The *speed indicator* counts from 0 to $k-1$ informing
agent A_i when it should use full speed to traverse.)
    (1) When A_i meets again its *marker* M_i, it moves M_i one position
ahead;
    (Agent A_i identifies its *marker* by comparing their position bits.)
    (2) When A_i catches another agent, A_i switches it off;
    (Change the *state* of the caught agent to 11.)
    (3) Until M_i is back to T_i, then $j = j + 1$;
    (*) If A_i is caught by another agent, then it gets switched off.

After entering Stage (1), agent A_i traverses the ring using k variable speeds
$V_i(j)$, for $j = 0, \dots, k-1$, based on sizes of consecutive segments following
token T_i (i.e., the original location of A_i). More precisely, the ring traversal in
Stage (1) is split into k consecutive rounds (see main loop for), s.t., during the
l^{th} round the speed $V_i(l)$ is used for exactly n full turns. Note that full turns
are counted with the help of *position bits* (1st chunk of $\log k$ bits in the internal
memory) of marker M_i, see Step (1) in the body of the main loop and Figure 2).
Similarly, a current (relative to the original) segment location of agent A_i is
also identified by properly updated position bits in its memory. A switch from
one speed to another is recorded via addition of 1 modulo k to the number
represented by the last $\log k$ bits in the internal memory. We say that agent A_i

accomplishes Stage (1) successfully if it runs all rounds of this stage without being caught by another agent. This process requires $O(kn^2)$ units of time. The following lemma holds.

Lemma 1. *On the successful completion of Stage (1) an agent A_i becomes either a unique winner (non-periodic case) or one of multiple winners (periodic case).*

Proof: Consider the non-periodic case and behaviour of two arbitrary agents A_i and A_j who managed to progress to Stage (1). Note that patterns of segments following initial positions of the agents must be different; otherwise we would have the periodic case. Thus there will be a round (with n full turns) in which the agents will use different speeds. And during this round one of the agents will have to catch the other if not caught by someone else in the meantime. In other words any agent entering Stage (1) will have a chance to challenge any other agent in one of the k rounds. And since during each challenge one of the competing agents gets switched off, after k rounds only one survivor is left alive on the ring. This is the winner who will accomplish the rendezvous process in Stage (2). Note that this dueling process is feasible because the maximum time difference between the entry of two agents to the Stage (1) is limited to at most n units of time. And since each rounds is based on n full turns there will be enough time to challenge any two agents.

We know that in the periodic case the rendezvous of agents governed by any deterministic procedure is not feasible. In this case the agents entering Stage (1) are partitioned into several classes of abstraction. The nodes in one class are represented by the same pattern of segments. Note that these agents will never compete (challenge each other) during the k consecutive rounds. However they will (potentially) challenge agents belonging to different classes. As a consequence of this at the end of Stage (1) there will be survivors in at most one class of abstraction. The survivors will enter Stage (2) when they will learn that the rendezvous is not feasible. This process takes n units of time.

STAGE(2) CLEANING-UP STAGE

The survivor A_i makes yet another full turn and collects all switched off agents left on the ring.
If the number of collected agents is $(k-1)$, agents know that rendezvous is successful.
Otherwise, agents recognise the periodic case.
(In this stage, agents do not need to calculate their speed anymore, so they use their *speed indicators* to count collected agents.)

Theorem 1. *The use of $O(\log k)$ bits of memory per each participating agent enables rendezvous of k agents in the non-periodic case. Moreover, in the periodic (but non-symmetric) case agents learn that the rendezvous is not feasible.*

The time complexity of the rendezvous process is dominated by Stage (1) and it is bounded by $O(kn^2)$.

3   How to Identify the Symmetric Distribution

If the distribution of k agents on the ring is entirely symmetric, then there is no deterministic algorithm that can complete the rendezvous task. So, it is important to be able to test the initial distribution of the agents for symmetry.

Handling the symmetric case. In this section we show how to recognise the symmetric case with a help of extra $O(\log \log n)$ memory bits. It has been proved in [15] that this is the minimal memory required to recognise the symmetric case. So our algorithm uses asymptotically optimal size of internal memory also in the symmetric case.

The algorithm is based on the use of a sequence of prime numbers and a simplified version of the Chinese Remainder Theorem (see Apostol [9]). The main line of our reasoning is that for any two numbers $0 < n_1 < n_2 < n$ the sequence of remainders (of integer division by consecutive prime numbers) of length $C \cdot \frac{\log n}{\log \log n}$, for small constant C must differ eventually. Otherwise the number $0 < n_2 - n_1 < n$ would have more than $C \cdot \frac{\log n}{\log \log n}$ distinct prime divisors which is not possible for C large enough.

Note that a value of the largest prime in the sequence is linear in $\log n$. In fact we can either consider remainders based on prime numbers, or alternatively we can use a testing procedure based on a sequence of initial integers $1, \ldots, O(\log n)$, which includes all primes required by the symmetry testing procedure.

The algorithm is split into consecutive rounds. During the ith round based on the ith prime (integer) every agent performs a full turn and calculates the remainder of division of each $|S_i|$ by the prime (integer). If the remainder is the same within each segment, the next prime is taken and the test is performed within each segment with the new prime, etc. If the remainders are uniform across all primes the agents know that the case is symmetric. If at any time of this process different remainders (based on the same prime) are discovered (i.e., the case is not symmetric), the testing process is halted (at the end of the round) and all agents proceed (at the very same moment) to Stage (0).

The pseudo-code of the symmetry test algorithm follows.

(0) Place token T_i at the starting position and set the flag to *symmetric-case*. (Then start traversing the ring with the full speed in rounds based on consecutive prime numbers.)

(1) Loop for $prime = 2, 3, 5, \ldots, p_{O(\frac{\log n}{\log \log n})}$ and flag = *symmetric-case*.

    (1.1) Visit consecutive segments $S_i, S_{i+1}, \ldots, S_{i-1}$ and

        (1.1.1) Set the counter of steps to 0;

        (1.1.2) Traverse each segment adding after each move one modulo *prime* to the counter of steps;

        (1.1.3) At the end of each segment test whether current content of the counter (representing the value of the remainder) is consistent with its content at all previous segments; (to implement this test we need one extra counter based on

$O(\log \log n)$ bits to remember a uniform value of reminders computed in previous segments)

(1.1.4) If the answer is negative, set the flag to *non-symmetric-case*.

Finally note that to implement this process each agent needs at most $O(\log k + \log \log n)$ bits of memory, since all values computed during the symmetry test procedure do not exceed neither k nor $\log n$. The time complexity of this test in $O(n \frac{\log n}{\log \log n})$.

Theorem 2. *The use of $O(\log k + \log \log n)$ bits of memory per each participating agent enables rendezvous of k agents in the non-periodic case. Moreover, in both periodic and symmetric cases agents learn that the rendezvous is not feasible.*

References

1. Alpern, S.: Asymmetric Rendezvous on the Circle. Dynamics and Control **10** (2000) 33–45
2. Alpern, S.: Rendezvous Search: A Personal Perspective. LSE Research Report, CDAM-2000-05, London School of Economics (2000)
3. Alpern, S., and Gal, S.: The Theory of Search Games and Rendezvous. Kluwer Academic Publishers (2003)
4. Alpern, S., and Howard, J.V.: Alternating Search at Two Locations. LSE OR Working Paper, 99.30 (1999)
5. Alpern, S., and Reyniers , D.: The Rendezvous and Coordinated Search Problems. Proceedings of the 33rd Conference on Decision and Control, Lake Buena Vista, FL (December 1994)
6. Anderson, E.J., and Essegaier, S.: Rendezvous Search on the Line with Indistinguishable Players. SIAM J. of Control and Opt. **33** (1995) 1637–1642
7. Anderson, E.J., and Fekete, S.: Two-Dimensional Rendezvous Search. Operations Research **49** (2001) 107–188
8. Anderson, E.J., and Weber, R.R.: The Rendezvous Problem on Discrete Locations. Journal of Applied Probability **28** (1990) 839–851
9. Apostol, T.M.: Introduction to Analytical Number Theory. Springer Verlag (1997)
10. Baston, V., and Gal, S.: Rendezvous on the Line When the Players' Initial Distance is Given by an Unknown Probability Distribution. SIAM Journal of Control and Optimization **36** 6 (1998) 1880–1889
11. Baston, V., and Gal, S.: Rendezvous Search When Marks are Left at the Starting Points. Naval Research Logistics **47** 6 (2001) 722–731
12. Chester, E., and Tutuncu, R.: Rendezvous Search on the Labeled Line, Old title: Rendezvous Search on Finite Domains, Preprint, Department of Mathematical Sciences, Carnegie Mellon University (2001)
13. Flocchini, P., Mans, B., and Santoro, N.: Sense of Direction in Distributed Computing. Theoretical Computer Science **291** 1 (2003) 29–53
14. Flocchini, P., Kranakis, E., Krizanc, D., Santoro, N., and Sawchuk, C.: The Rendezvous Search Problem with More Than Two Mobile Agents. Preprint (2002)
15. Flocchini, P., Kranakis, E., Krizanc, D., Santoro, N., and Sawchuk, C.: Multiple Mobile Agent Rendezvous in a Ring. LATIN'2004 599–608

16. Frederickson, G.N., and Lynch, N.A.: Electing a Leader in a Synchronous Ring. Journal of the ACM **1** 34 (1987) 98–115
17. Lim, W.S., and Beck A., and Alpern, S.: Rendezvous Search on the Line with More Than Two Players. Operations Research **45** (1997) 357–364
18. Pikounis, M., and Thomas, L.C.: Many Player Rendezvous Search: Stick Together or Split and Meet?, Working Paper 98/7, University of Edinburgh, Management School (1998)
19. Sawchuk, C.: Mobile Agent Rendezvous in the Ring. PhD Thesis, Carleton University (2004)

The Knowledge Cartography – A New Approach to Reasoning over Description Logics Ontologies

Krzysztof Goczyła, Teresa Grabowska,
Wojciech Waloszek, and Michał Zawadzki

Gdańsk University of Technology, Department of Software Engineering,
ul. Gabriela Narutowicza 11/12, 80-952 Gdansk, Poland
{kris, tegra, wowal, michawa}@eti.pg.gda.pl

Abstract. The paper presents a new method for representation and processing ontological knowledge - Knowledge Cartography. This method allows for inferring implicit knowledge from both: terminological part (TBox) and assertional part (ABox) of a Description Logic ontology. The paper describes basics of the method and gives some theoretical background of the method. Knowledge Cartography stores and processes ontologies in terms of binary signatures, which gives efficient way of querying ontologies containing numerous individuals. Knowledge Cartography has been applied in KASEA - a knowledge management system that is being developed in course of a European integrated research project called PIPS. Results of efficiency experiments and ideas of further development of the system are presented and discussed.

1 Introduction

Rapid development of Internet reveals new needs for exploring and processing data that are stored in resources of the global Web. There is a steady interest among researches (particularly - knowledge engineers) in providing theoretical backgrounds and building practically applicable prototypes of systems that would be able to efficiently integrate, use and exploit Web resources. These systems should be able to assimilate the newly acquired data with the data that already have been acquired and stored in data and knowledge bases. It is clear that data coming from different sources cover only partially a given area of interest, so it is of utmost importance that a powerful data acquisition system should be equipped with a reasoning engine that could infer new facts, not explicitly stated in the data.

To this aim, a knowledge representation method is necessary. In this paper, we present a novel method of knowledge representation called Knowledge Cartography. This method is based on Description Logic (DL) [1] - a decidable part of first-order logic that is aimed at describing terminology systems. Description Logic (actually, one of DL dialects, because DL is in fact a family of formalisms of different levels of expressiveness) became a basis of OWL (*Web Ontology Language*, [2]) that is a standard recommended by W3C Consortium for development of Web ontologies. In this context, the work presented in this paper, contributes

J. Wiedermann et al. (Eds.): SOFSEM 2006, LNCS 3831, pp. 293–302, 2006.

to the *Semantic Web* initiative [3] that strives for development of standard technologies for knowledge management over the Web, particularly for making Web sources semantics machine-readable.

The Knowledge Cartography, primarily proposed by one of the authors of this paper, W. Waloszek, has been applied in a prototype knowledge management system called KASEA (*Knowledge Signatures Analyzer*). KASEA is a part of a system PIPS (*Personal Information Platform for Life and Health Services*) [4] that is being developed within a 6th European Union Framework Programme integrated project (priority "e-Health") involving 17 partners from 12 countries, mainly from EU. PIPS's main goal is to create a Web infrastructure to support health and promote healthy life style among European communities. PIPS concentrates on providing health-related assistance to its users: citizens, patients and healthcare professionals. PIPS serves citizens and patients by helping them in making decisions concerning their everyday practices and deciding whether they should consult their doctors. PIPS can also be used by healthcare professionals and can provide them with health-related knowledge and advise about course of therapies.

PIPS system must efficiently process large (particularly – in terms of number of individuals) ontologies. The KASEA system allows both for inferring and for storing the inferred results (in this way it somehow resembles the InstanceStore system [5] that also stores results of its inferences but in quite different way). The price we pay for this is a slight reduction of expressiveness of queries that can be submitted to the system and longer time of ontology loading. These limitations, however, turned out not to be critical for the system clients.

The rest of the paper is organized as follows. Section 2 describes the basics of Knowledge Cartography. Section 3 illustrates implementation issues of KASEA. Section 4 presents results of performance analysis and tests in comparison with other DL reasoners. Section 5 summarizes the paper by discussing limitations of the presented approach and proposing the ways of its further development.

2   The Knowledge Cartography

Motivation behind the Knowledge Cartography is based on the three assumptions:

1. Terminological part of the knowledge base (TBox) is updated so rarely that it might be considered constant in time.
2. A knowledge base is queried much more often than updated (by updating we understand addition of new ABox assertions). Therefore performance of information retrieval is crucial, while performance of updating is less critical.
3. A knowledge base should be able to hold and efficiently process information about large numbers of individuals.

On the basis of these assumptions a cartographic approach has been developed. It aims at storing in the knowledge base as many conclusions about concepts and individuals as possible. The conclusions can be quickly retrieved in the process of query answering and remain valid due to the fact that terminology cannot be updated. By proper organisation of the knowledge base (see Sec. 3.1) the same conclusions can be applied to any number of individuals, facilitating information retrieval and reducing size of the base.

2.1 A General Idea

The Knowledge Cartography takes its name after a map of concepts. A map of concepts is basically a description of interrelationships between concepts in a terminology. The map is created in the course of knowledge base creation. A map of concepts can be graphically represented in a form similar to a Venn diagram (Fig. 1). Each atomic region (i.e. a region that does not contain any other region) represents a unique valid intersection of base concepts. By valid we mean an intersection that is satisfiable with respect to a given terminology. Intersections of concepts that are not allowed by terminological axioms are excluded from the map (as in Fig. 1b, where two additional axioms eliminated four regions from the map). Cartographer calculates a number of valid atomic regions n and assigns each atomic region a subsequent integer number from the range $[1, n]$. Because any region in the map consists of some number of atomic regions it can be represented by an array of binary digits of length n with "1"s in positions mapped to contained atomic regions and "0"s elsewhere.

Using this technique we can assign any concept in the terminology a *signature* – an array of binary digits representing a region covered by the concept in the map. In this way we can describe any combination of complement, union and intersection of described concepts by simply mapping these operations to Boolean negation, disjunction and conjunction.

Formally, we define a function s from concepts to elements of a Boolean algebra $\mathbb{B}^n = \{0,1\}^n$. The only condition that should be met by the function s to have all desired characteristics is:

$$s(C) \leq s(D) \Leftrightarrow C \sqsubseteq D \tag{1}$$

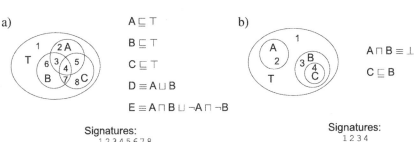

Fig. 1. A map of concepts (a) with two terminological axioms added (b)

In any such function atomic regions are mapped to atoms of the algebra, i.e. arrays of "0"s with a sole "1". Moreover, for any concepts C and D the following equalities hold:

$$s(\neg C) = \neg s(C),\ s(C \sqcap D) = s(C) \wedge s(D),\ s(C \sqcup D) = s(C) \vee s(D) \quad (2)$$

After determination of s function one can solve any TBox reasoning problem (after reducing it to subsumption [1] on the basis of (1)) by signature calculations. Namely:

- query about equivalence of concepts C and D can be performed by checking whether $s(C) = s(D)$,
- query about subsumption of concepts C and D can be performed by checking whether $s(C) \leq s(D)$,
- query about disjointness of concepts C and D can be performed by checking whether $s(C) \wedge s(D) = \{0\}^n$.

It can be proven that for any $\mathcal{ALC}$ terminology $\mathcal{T}$ that does not contain $\exists R.C$ and $\forall R.C$ constructors we can create the function s for which (1) and (2) hold.

Following the (1) we can notice that the order of the range of s should be equal to the number of terminologically unequivalent concepts that can be expressed. With introduction of $\exists R.C$ and $\forall R.C$ constructors the latter number can easily reach infinity (namely $\aleph_0$) rendering direct use of signatures infeasible.

Because of this fact, we have made an important decision restricting the use of $\exists R.C$ and $\forall R.C$ constructors in queries. The only concepts of the form $\exists R.C$ and $\forall R.C$ that can be used in queries are those explicitly included in the ontology. In that way we restrict the number of expressible terminologically unequivalent concepts. This restriction limits capabilities of the system, but our experiences show that this limitation is not critical for knowledge base users.

The same techniques as for TBoxes can be applied to ABox reasoning. We can assign each individual a in ABox a signature of the most specific concept (we denote this concept C_a; this concept need not to be defined explicitly in the terminology).

After determination of signatures for individuals we can reduce ABox reasoning problems to TBox reasoning problems which in turn can be solved by signature calculations. For example, an instance checking problem (check if an individual a is a member of a concept C) can be reduced to a question whether the concept C_a is subsumed by the concept C.

2.2   The Map Creation Algorithm

The key algorithmic problem in Knowledge Cartography is determination of function s, i.e. map of concepts. We define this problem as follows: for input $\mathcal{ALC}$ terminology $\mathcal{T}$ for each atomic concept and each concept of the form $\exists R.C$ ($\forall R.C$ are converted to the equivalent form $\neg \exists R.\neg C$), called together *mapped concepts*, generate the sequence of bits describing its signature.

The problem itself cannot be polynomial, unless $P = NP$, because of its reducibility to CNF-satisfiability. However use of some optimization techniques can make this process efficient for real-life ontologies.

For creation of signatures we base on the fact that atomic regions are mapped to the atoms of Boolean algebra being a range of the function s. Atomic regions can be viewed simply as valid intersections of all mapped concepts or their complements in the terminology, i.e. all possible complex concepts of the form:

$$L_1 \sqcap L_2 \sqcap \cdots \sqcap L_n \tag{3}$$

where n is the number of the mapped concepts and L_i is a placeholder for i-th mapped concept or its complement.

Using this approach we may view a terminology as a set of first-order logic formulae, mapped concepts as variables, and reduce the problem to finding a truth table for the terminology. Each satisfiable combination of variable values may be treated as an atomic region.

From among many techniques available we decided to exploit Ordered Binary Decision Diagrams (henceforth OBDD) originally proposed by Bryant in [7]. In our approach we systematically build a tree of the whole terminology by combining it with logical "AND" operation with the tree generated for formulae corresponding to consequent axioms. Axioms are converted into first order logic formulae in accordance with [7] but the method is somehow simplified because of the fact that concepts of the form $\exists R.C$ and $\forall R.C$ are represented as a single variable. Each new mapped concept is given a new variable name.

For example, the axiom:

$$Momo \equiv Person \sqcap \forall hasChild.Man \sqcap \exists hasChild.Man$$

would be converted to the form:

$$Momo \equiv Person \sqcap \neg \exists hasChild.\neg Man \sqcap \exists hasChild.Man$$

and consequently to the formula:

$$c_1 \leftrightarrow (c_2 \wedge \neg e_1 \wedge e_2)$$

The outline of the main part algorithm is presented below:

Data: Terminology $\mathcal{T}$ in $\mathcal{ALC}$
Result: OBDD T for terminology $\mathcal{T}$
1 Initiate T to OBDD of any true formula;
2 **for** *each axiom A from $\mathcal{T}$* **do**
3   Convert A to the formula F in the way described above;
4   Generate the OBDD U for the formula F;
5     $T := T \wedge U$ (where $\wedge$ denotes conjunction of two OBDD trees [7]);
6 **end**

Direct application of the algorithm to specific terminologies may lead to generation of spurious atomic regions, as shown in Fig. 2a. According to the terminology an individual cannot belong to $\exists R.B$ not belonging to $\exists R.A$ (because each member of B is a member of A). In order to avoid this effect we perform postprocessing.

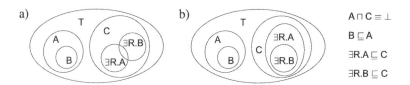

Fig. 2. Incorrect (a) and correct (b) assignment of roles to regions

The postprocessing produces a tree T' on the basis of T. The postprocessing may be basically brought down to checking whether for each combination of values of variables e_i concerning the role R and satisfiable in accordance with T it is possible to create a set of individuals that would satisfy the combination. In the example from Figure 2a the following family of atomic intersections is satisfiable in accordance to T:

$$\neg A \sqcap \neg B \sqcap C \neg \exists R.A \sqcap \exists R.B \ldots$$

But this region is excluded from T' during post-processing because the following family of concepts:

$$\neg A \sqcap B \sqcap \ldots$$

is not satisfiable in accordance with T (there cannot exist any individual that belongs to B and does not belong to A).

The outline of the post-processing algorithm is presented below:

Data: OBDD T produced in the course of processing
Result: OBDD T' with some regions excluded
1 Initiate T' to T.
2 **repeat**
3   **for** *each role R from T* **do**
4   **for** *each combination of values of e_i satisfiable in accordance with T'* **do**
5   Check whether it is possible to create a set of individuals that, being role R fillers of some individual a, would make a satisfy the intersection of $\exists R.C$ and $\neg \exists R.C$ implied by values of e_i.
6   **if** *there is no such set* **then**
7   Create the formula F making combination of values unsatisfiable.
8   Generate the OBDD U for the formula F.
9                 $T' := T' \wedge U$
10   **end**
11   **end**
12   **end**
13 **until** *no changes to T' have been made.*

It can be shown that the postprocessing is sound and complete, i.e. all intersections it excludes are invalid and there is no invalid intersection it does not exclude.

3   The KaSeA System

The Cartographic Approach has been successfully exploited in the PIPS system. The Knowledge Inference Engine (KIE), a vital component of the KaSeA system, exploits Knowledge Cartography to inferring and storing inferred information. KIE allows for processing a terminology (TBox) and assertions (ABox). Information is stored in a relational database (PostgreSQL 8.0 has been exploited in the most up-to-date version of KIE).

In the following we present scenarios that take place in situations of database update (*Tell*) and query (*Ask*) in the context of the previously described database schema. KIE is able to handle queries expressed in the DIGUT language [8], a special language for querying the KaSeA system, based on DIG/1.1 [9].

Tell queries that can be handled by the KaSeA system are concept assertion of the form $C(a)$ and role assertions of the form $R(a, b)$.

In processing of a concept assertion $C(a)$, C has to be an expression built of concepts used in the terminology. Constructors of the form $\exists R.C$ are allowed only if a signature for this constructor has been determined. The course of actions is as follows:

---

1 Calculate a signature $s(C)$;
2 If a is not in the database add it and assign it a signature $s(C)$. End the procedure.;
3 Otherwise combine the signature of C_a with $s(C)$ using logical AND operation;
4 If a signature of C_a has been changed update the neighbourhood of a (see below);

In processing of role assertions of the form $R(a, b)$ only neighbourhood update is performed.

Necessity of updating neighbourhood is a consequence of the fact that changing our knowledge about membership of the individual a may change our knowledge about the individuals related to a. In the current version of the KaSeA system a simple mechanism of *positive* and *negative role checking* has been applied. In *positive role checking* every pair (a, b) related with R is checked against all defined concepts of the form $\exists R.C$. If b is a member of the concept C the signature of C_a is combined with $s(\exists R.C)$ using logical AND operation. In *negative role checking* every pair (a, b) related with R is also checked against all defined concepts of the form $\exists R.C$. If a is a member of the concept $\exists R.C$ the signature of C_b is combined with $s(\neg C)$ using logical AND operation.

This process is recursively repeated if a signature of any individual has been changed. The process has to end in a finite number of steps because of the fact that the number of individuals is finite and each update may only decrease the number of "1"s in signatures of individuals being processed.

Almost all *Ask* operations can be brought down to subsumption checking. For example instance retrieval problem for the concept C can be viewed as finding all individuals a such that C_a is subsumed by C. In the course of subsumption checking section counters are exploited to do the preliminary selection of "candidate" signatures. Then bitwise Boolean operations are performed in order to check whether two signatures are in $\leq$ relation.

4   Performance Results

The space and time complexity of processing a terminology by Cartographer is in the worst case exponential. Indeed, the maximum number of regions that the space can be divided into by k concepts is 2^k, which results in signatures of such a length. The corresponding terminology would consist of k concepts that are not related to each other at all. However, such a case is very rare in practical terminologies (if found at all). Specifically, this would mean that any subset of concepts may have common instances, because no pair of concepts is declared disjoint. For instance, consider the terminology $\mathcal{T}$ containing one root concept and three direct subconcepts (axioms 1, 2, and 3 below):

1. $Bird \sqsubseteq Animal$ 4. $Bird \sqcap Fish \equiv \bot$
2. $Fish \sqsubseteq Animal$ 5. $Bird \sqcap Mammal \equiv \bot$
3. $Mammal \sqsubseteq Animal$ 6. $Fish \sqcap Mammal \equiv \bot$

In this terminology, $Bird$, $Fish$ and $Mammal$ are unrelated, which means that we could declare one individual to be simultaneously a bird and a fish. Such a terminology would create a domain space with 9 regions (Fig. 3a). Let us add three disjoints to $\mathcal{T}$ (axioms 4, 5, and 6 above). The number of regions in the domain space decreased to 5 (Fig. 3b). Actually, $\mathcal{T}$ is now a pure tree taxonomy, which reflects reality among animals.

For taxonomies the signature size grows linearly with k. The theoretical processing time is proportional to $k \log k$ for taxonomies except of inherently quadratic ($O(k^2)$) signature generation phase (the algorithm has to generate k signatures of length proportional to k). The results of our experiments showing the observed time complexity of map generation algorithm are presented in Table 1 (all tests were performed on a PC with Pentium IV 2GHz and 2GB RAM). The time was independent on the order of axioms in terminologies, as special heuristics has been used to estimate the best possible ordering.

The ABox queries processing performance of our Knowledge Inference Engine has been tested and compared with several freely available tools: Jena 2 [3] [10], FaCT [12], Racer [13]. The results of the tests are presented in Table 2 (FaCT is not included in the table because of its lack of support for ABoxes).

The main difference between analysed reasoning algorithms is related to time of loading an ontology (ABox tell queries). The time of loading ontology is longer

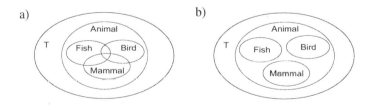

Fig. 3. The division of a domain space for the exemplary ontology: a) without disjoints, and b) with disjoints

Table 1. Results of efficiency experiments concerning signature generation for pure tree taxonomies

Number of concepts in taxonomy	Processing and postprocessing time [s]	Signature generation time [s]
3357	72	<1
82706	380	12
184086	857	115
545450	1386	2253

Table 2. Results of efficiency experiments. Hyphens denote that the activity could not be completed within 2 hours.

	Loading time [s]			Query-processing time [s]		
Size of ABox	400	1000	3800	400	1000	3800
Jena	1	22	-	6	250	-
RACER	3	4	5	58	-	-
Cartographer	43	122	465	<1	<1	1

for KIE. In return we obtain a very short time of response. While RACER was unable to answer an instance retrieval query when 1000 individuals have been loaded, KIE could process the same query for 11000 individuals in 1.4 seconds.

5 Further Development

Our present work concentrates on overcoming limitations of the KASEA system. The most notable ones are: restriction on use of $\exists R.C$ concepts in queries and the shortcomings of neighbourhood update mechanism.

Although the former limitation may seem inherent to Cartographic representation we work on overcoming it by using signatures with variable length. The range of the function s becomes in this way infinite, but longer signatures are assigned to complex concepts that are unlikely to appear in client queries.

The latter limitation comes out from the fact that neighbourhood update mechanism is not fully OWA (Open World Assumption) compliant. Consider the ontology in Figure 4. It can be easily noticed that there are only two possible cases of membership of a and b individuals: a can be a *Man* and b a *Woman* or alternatively a can be a *Woman* and b a *Man*. In both the cases c is a member of *Bisexual*. That fact will not be inferred by the KASEA system because in the processing of *Tell* queries only signatures of direct neighbours are taken into consideration.

Man $\equiv \neg$*Woman*	*loves*(*a*, *b*)
$\exists$*loves.Man* $\sqsubseteq$ *Woman*	*desires*(*c*, *a*)
$\exists$*loves.Woman* $\sqsubseteq$ *Man*	*desires*(*c*, *b*)
Bisexual $\equiv \exists$*desires.Woman* $\sqcap$ $\exists$*desires.Woman*	

Fig. 4. An exemplary ontology showing limitations in OWA support of the KASEA system

Our present work concentrates on overcoming the above limitations. Moreover we are gradually extending expressiveness of the KASEA system constructs in order to support such constructs as cardinality constraints, symmetric, transitive and functional roles so that KIE could be able to reason at least over the whole $\mathcal{SHIQ}$ (a DL dialect that OWL is based on). We are also working on extending signature analysis on roles. Another research focuses on knowledge distribution and embedding trust issues into the knowledge base.

References

1. Baader, F.A., McGuness, D.L., Nardi D., Patel-Schneider P.F.: The Description Logic Handbook: Theory, Implementation, and Applications, Cambridge University Press (2003)
2. OWL - Web Ontology Language Guide. W3C, 2004, available at the address http://www.w3.org/TR/2004/REC-owl-guide-20040210/
3. A Semantic Web Framework for Java, http://jena.sourceforge.net/
4. Goczyła, K., Grabowska, T., Waloszek, W., Zawadzki, M.: Issues Related to Knowledge Management in e-health System, (in Polish). In: Software Engineering - New Challenges, J. Grski, A. Wardziski (eds), WNT 2004, Chap. XXVI 358–371
5. Bechhofer, S., Horrocks, I., Turi, D.: Implementing the Instance Store, available at CEUR http://sunsite.informatik.rwth-aachen.de/Publications/CEUR-WS/Vol-115/
6. Goczyła, K., Grabowska, T., Waloszek, W., Zawadzki, M.: The Cartographer Algorithm for Processing and Querying Description Logics Ontologies. Lecture Notes in Artificial Intelligence, Advances in Web Intelligence, (June 2005) 163–169
7. Bryant, R.E.: Graph-Based Algorithms for Boolean Function Manipulation, IEEE Transaction on Computers (1986)
8. DIGUT Interface Version 1.3. KMG@GUT Technical Report, 2005, available at http://km.pg.gda.pl/km/digut/1.3/DIGUT_Interface_1.3.pdf
9. Bechhofer, S.: The DIG Description Logic Interface: DIG/1.1, University of Manchester, February 7, 2003
10. Reynolds, D.: Jena 2 Inference Support, 2004, also available at WWW site http://jena.sourceforge.net/inference/index.html
11. Horrocks, I., Patel-Schneider, P.F.: Optimising Propositional Modal Satisfiability for Description Logic Subsumption, (1998), file available at the following Internet site: http://www.cs.man.ac.uk/ horrocks/ Publications/download/1998/aisc98.ps.gz.
12. Horrocks, I.: FaCT Reference Manual v1.6, August 1998, Included in FaCT archive from http://www.cs.man.ac.uk/horrocks/FaCT/
13. Haarslev, V., Mller, R.: RACER User's Guide and Reference Manual, September 17, 2003 http://www.cs.concordia.ca/ haarslev/racer/racer-manual-1-7-7.pdf

Complexity and Exact Algorithms for Multicut*

Jiong Guo[1], Falk Hüffner[1], Erhan Kenar[2],
Rolf Niedermeier[1], and Johannes Uhlmann[2]

[1] Institut für Informatik, Friedrich-Schiller-Universität Jena,
Ernst-Abbe-Platz 2, D-07743 Jena, Germany
{guo, hueffner, niedermr}@minet.uni-jena.de
[2] Wilhelm-Schickard-Institut für Informatik, Universität Tübingen,
Sand 13, D-72076 Tübingen, Germany
{kenar, johannes}@informatik.uni-tuebingen.de

Abstract. The MULTICUT problem is defined as: given an undirected graph and a collection of pairs of terminal vertices, find a minimum set of edges or vertices whose removal disconnects each pair. We mainly focus on the case of removing vertices, where we distinguish between allowing or disallowing the removal of terminal vertices. Complementing and refining previous results from the literature, we provide several NP-completeness and (fixed-parameter) tractability results for restricted classes of graphs such as trees, interval graphs, and graphs of bounded treewidth.

1 Introduction

Motivation and previous results. MULTICUT in graphs is a fundamental network design problem. It models questions concerning the reliability and robustness of computer and communication networks. Informally speaking, the problem is, given a graph, to determine a minimum size set of either edges or vertices such that the deletion of this set disconnects a prespecified set of *pairs of terminal vertices* in the graph. In most cases, the problem is NP-complete. There are many results and variants for MULTICUT and we refer to Costa, Létocart, and Roupin [2] for a recent survey.

The major part of the literature deals with the "edge deletion variant" of MULTICUT (EDGE MULTICUT) [2, 6, 7, 8] whereas our main focus here lies on the "vertex deletion variant" (VERTEX MULTICUT). Relatively little seems to be known for VERTEX MULTICUT problems; we are only aware of two recent investigations [3, 9]. Călinescu, Fernandes, and Reed [3] introduced two variants of VERTEX MULTICUT:

UNRESTRICTED VERTEX MULTICUT (UVMC)
Input: An undirected graph $G = (V, E)$, a collection H of pairs of vertices $H \subseteq V \times V$, and an integer $k \geq 0$.

---

* Research supported by the Deutsche Forschungsgemeinschaft (DFG), Emmy Noether research group PIAF (fixed-parameter algorithms), NI 369/4.

J. Wiedermann et al. (Eds.): SOFSEM 2006, LNCS 3831, pp. 303–312, 2006.

Task: Find a subset V' of V with $|V'| \leq k$ whose removal separates each pair of vertices in H.

The vertices appearing in the vertex pairs in H are called *terminals* and, throughout this paper, we use S to denote the set of terminals, i.e., $S := \bigcup_{(u,v) \in H} \{u, v\}$. By way of contrast, in the case of RESTRICTED VERTEX MULTICUT the removal of terminal vertices is not allowed.

RESTRICTED VERTEX MULTICUT (RVMC)
Input: An undirected graph $G = (V, E)$, a collection H of pairs of vertices $H \subseteq V \times V$, and an integer $k \geq 0$.
Task: Find a subset V' of V with $|V'| \leq k$ that contains no terminal and whose removal separates each pair of vertices in H.

Călinescu et al. show that RVMC is NP-complete in bounded-degree trees and the "easier" UVMC is polynomially solvable in trees but becomes NP-complete in bounded-degree graphs of treewidth two. Moreover, they give a polynomial-time approximation scheme (PTAS) for UVMC in bounded treewidth graphs. Marx [9] extends the results for UVMC (which he calls MINIMUM TERMINAL PAIR SEPARATION) by providing an $O(2^{k\ell} \cdot k^k \cdot 4^{k^3} \cdot |G|^{O(1)})$ time algorithm for UVMC in general graphs, where k is an upper bound on the vertices to be removed and ℓ is the number of terminal pairs. In other words, UVMC is fixed-parameter tractable (FPT) with respect to the combined parameter (k, ℓ).

Our results. We continue and complement the work of Călinescu et al. [3] and Marx [9] as follows: We show that the NP-complete RVMC in trees is fixed-parameter tractable with respect to the parameter k (number of vertex deletions) with the modest running time $O(2^k \cdot |G| \cdot \ell)$ (again, ℓ is the number of terminal pairs). Whereas in trees UVMC is polynomial-time solvable but RVMC is NP-complete [3], we have the surprising result that UVMC is NP-complete in interval graphs but RVMC is polynomial-time solvable here.[1] We also strengthen the NP-completeness result for RVMC in trees of Călinescu et al. by showing that NP-completeness already holds for maximum-vertex-degree-three trees whereas their result only holds for maximum vertex degree four. Note that RVMC is clearly polynomial-time solvable in paths, that is, trees with maximum vertex degree two. Moreover, we show that RVMC in general graphs is NP-complete even in case of only three terminal pairs, hence excluding fixed-parameter tractability with respect to the parameter "number of terminal pairs". By way of contrast, we show that RVMC can be solved in $O(|S|^{|S|+\omega+1} \cdot |G|)$ time on graphs of treewidth ω, where S denotes the set of terminal vertices; thus, RVMC is fixed-parameter tractable with respect to the combined parameter "treewidth" and "terminal set size". Observe that there is no hope for fixed-parameter tractability exclusively with respect to the parameter $|S|$ or ω. This fixed-parameter tractability result directly transfers to UVMC as well; indeed, it also works for

---

[1] More specifically, the NP-completeness result for UVMC even holds in interval graphs of pathwidth four.

Table 1. Complexity of MULTICUT problems for several graph classes. For the parameters, $|S|$ is the number of terminals, k is the number of deletions, and ω is the treewidth of the input graph. In a row with a parameter, "NP-c" implies hardness even for some constant parameter value.

Graph class	Parameter	EMC	UVMC	RVMC
Interval graphs		NP-c [6]	NP-c (Thm. 4)	P (Thm. 5)
Trees		NP-c [6]	P (Sect. 2)	NP-c [3]
	k	FPT [8]	—	FPT (Thm. 2)
General graphs		NP-c [4]	NP-c [3]	NP-c [3]
	k	open	open	open
	$|S|$	NP-c [4]	FPT [9]	NP-c (Thm. 6)
	ω	NP-c [6]	NP-c [3]	NP-c [3]
	ω & $|S|$	FPT (Thm. 9)	FPT (Cor. 1)	FPT (Thm. 8)

the EDGE MULTICUT (EMC) variant. Finally, for EDGE MULTICUT we also prove NP-completeness in caterpillar graphs with maximum vertex degree five.

Table 1 summarizes most of the presented results.

Preliminaries. We introduce some additional terminology. By default, we consider only undirected graphs $G = (V, E)$ without self-loops. A graph is an *interval graph* if we can label its vertices by intervals of the real line such that there is an edge between two vertices iff their intervals intersect. A tree is called *caterpillar* if all vertices with degree at least three have at most two neighbors of degree two or greater. For any graph $G = (V, E)$, we can construct its *line graph* as $(E, \{\{e_1, e_2\} \in E \mid e_1 \cap e_2 \neq \emptyset\})$. We use $G[V']$ to denote the subgraph of G induced by the vertices $V' \subseteq V$. A set of vertices $V' \subseteq V$ is called *vertex separator* if $G[V \setminus V']$ has more connected components than G.

A *tree decomposition* of G is a pair $\langle \{X_i \mid i \in I\}, T \rangle$, where each X_i is a subset of V, called *bag*, and $T = (I, F)$ is a tree with node set I and edge set F. The following must hold: $\bigcup_{i \in I} X_i = V$; for every edge $\{u, v\} \in E$, there is an $i \in I$ such that $\{u, v\} \subseteq X_i$; and for all $i, j, l \in I$, if j lies on the path between i and l in T, then $X_i \cap X_l \subseteq X_j$. The *width* of $\langle \{X_i \mid i \in I\}, T \rangle$ is $\max\{|X_i| \mid i \in I\} - 1$. The *treewidth* of G is the minimum width over all tree decompositions of G. A *path decomposition* is a tree decomposition where T is a path.

A problem of size n is called *fixed-parameter tractable* (FPT) with respect to a parameter k if it can be solved in $f(k) \cdot n^{O(1)}$ time, where f is a function solely depending on the parameter k.

Due to the lack of space, some proofs had to be omitted.

2   Trees

UNRESTRICTED VERTEX MULTICUT in trees is trivially solvable in $O(|V| \cdot |H|)$ time: Root the tree at an arbitrary vertex. Then, compute the least common ancestors for all terminal pairs in H and sort these ancestors in a list L according to the decreasing order of their depth in the rooted tree. Finally, while $L \neq \emptyset$, remove the first element of L and its corresponding vertex from T and delete all separated terminal pairs from H and their least common ancestors from L. The solution is then the removed vertices. We omit further details.

Călinescu et al. [3] show that RVMC is NP-complete in trees with maximum vertex degree four by giving a reduction from EMC in binary trees. It is easy to observe that RVMC on trees with maximum vertex degree two, i.e., paths, can be solved in polynomial time. The complexity of RVMC in trees with maximum vertex degree three remained open. Here we close this gap.

Theorem 1. RESTRICTED VERTEX MULTICUT *in trees with maximum vertex degree three and pathwidth two is NP-complete.*

Proof. The reduction is from the NP-complete VERTEX COVER problem, which for a graph $G = (V = \{v_1, v_2, \ldots, v_n\}, E)$ and $k \geq 0$ asks whether there is a set of vertices $V' \subseteq V$ with $|V'| \leq k$ such that for every edge $\{v, w\} \in E$ at least one of v and w is in V'. Construct the tree $T = (W, F)$ with

$$W := \{l_i, a_i, r_i \mid 1 \leq i \leq n\} \cup \{p, q\}$$

and

$$F := \{\{l_i, a_i\}, \{a_i, r_i\} \mid 1 \leq i \leq n\} \cup \{\{r_i, r_{i+1}\} \mid 1 \leq i < n\} \cup \{\{r_n, p\}, \{p, q\}\}.$$

As the set of terminal pairs H we take for each vertex $v_i \in V$ the pair (r_i, q) and, moreover, for each edge $\{v_i, v_j\} \in E$, we add (l_i, l_j). See Fig. 1 for an example of the construction.

It is easy to show that the VERTEX COVER instance has a solution with no more than k vertices iff the constructed RVMC instance can be solved by removing at most $k + 1$ vertices. The constructed tree clearly has maximum vertex degree three and a path decomposition with pathwidth equal to two. $\square$

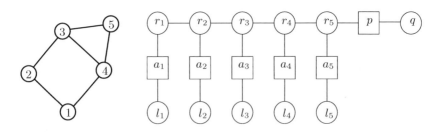

Fig. 1. An example for the reduction from VERTEX COVER to RVMC. The left figure is a VERTEX COVER instance and the right is the corresponding RVMC instance with $H = \{(l_1, l_2), (l_2, l_3), (l_3, l_4), (l_4, l_1), (l_3, l_5), (l_4, l_5)\} \cup \{(r_i, q) \mid 1 \leq i \leq 5\}$. Only the rectangular vertices can be deleted (all others are terminals).

In the following, we show that RVMC in trees can be solved in $O(2^k \cdot |V| \cdot |H|)$ time, where k denotes the allowed number of vertex removals. The basic idea is to modify the above polynomial-time algorithm for UVMC in trees into a depth-bounded search tree algorithm.

Let $T = (V, E)$ be the input instance and $S := \bigcup_{(u,v) \in H} \{u, v\}$ the set of terminals. The first step is to "contract" edges with both endpoints being terminals: For an edge $\{u, v\}$ with $u, v \in S$, we have $(u, v) \notin H$, since otherwise the instance is not solvable. Delete both u and v and the edge between them from T; insert a new vertex w into T and set $N(w) := N(u) \cup N(v) \setminus \{u, v\}$. Furthermore, replace each u and v in H by w. It is easy to see that this step does not change the solution.

Then, the search tree algorithm proceeds as the polynomial-time algorithm for UVMC in trees: root T in an arbitrary vertex, compute the least common ancestors of all terminal pairs and sort them by decreasing depth in a list L. While $L \neq \emptyset$, consider the first element u of L, which is the least common ancestor of a terminal pair (v, w). If u is a nonterminal, then remove it and update L and T; otherwise, there are two cases: If $u = v$ or $u = w$, then we delete the neighbor of u that lies on the path from u to w or v. This neighbor has to be a nonterminal due to the first step. Otherwise, we have $u \neq v$ and $u \neq w$. Then u has two nonterminals as neighbors lying on the path between v and w and we branch into two cases, in each case removing one of the two neighbors.

Finally, if there is a node in the search tree where $L = \emptyset$ and at most k vertices have been removed, then we have a solution. It is easy to observe that the depth of the search tree is bounded by k and its size is $O(2^k)$.

Theorem 2. RESTRICTED VERTEX MULTICUT *in trees can be solved in* $O(2^k \cdot |V| \cdot |H|)$ *time, where k is the number of allowed vertex removals.*

3 Interval Graphs

As mentioned in the introduction, RVMC is at least as hard as UVMC in general graphs and many special graph classes: From an instance of UVMC we can obtain an RVMC instance by adding for each terminal s a new degree-1 vertex s' adjacent only to s. Each terminal pair (s, t) is substituted by (s', t'). Then, solving RVMC in this new instance is equivalent to solving UVMC in the original instance. However, the class of interval graphs is an exception, that is, UVMC is NP-complete in interval graphs while RVMC is solvable in polynomial time:

Unrestricted Vertex Multicut in Interval Graphs. To show the NP-completeness of UVMC in interval graphs, we first show that EDGE MULTICUT is NP-complete in caterpillars and then reduce EMC in caterpillars to UVMC in interval graphs. We use a reduction from 3-SAT, which is similar to the reduction used to show the NP-completeness of EMC in binary trees [3–Theorem 6.1].

Theorem 3. EDGE MULTICUT *in caterpillars with maximum vertex degree five is NP-complete.*

The second reduction from EMC in caterpillars with maximum vertex degree five to UVMC in interval graphs with pathwidth four is—analogous to [3]— executed by constructing the line graph of the caterpillar:

Theorem 4. UNRESTRICTED VERTEX MULTICUT *in interval graphs with pathwidth at least four is NP-complete.*

Restricted Vertex Multicut in Interval Graphs. In contrast to EMC[2] and UVMC, which are NP-complete for interval graphs even with bounded pathwidth, we now give a dynamic programming algorithm solving RVMC in interval graphs in polynomial time.

For an interval graph $G = (V, E)$, we can construct a path decomposition in $O(|V| + |E|)$ time such that each bag one-to-one corresponds to a maximal clique of G (see Booth and Lueker [1]). The minimal vertex separators of G are the intersections of two neighboring bags in the path decomposition and are also cliques. The following lemma shows that the minimal vertex separators are crucial for solving RVMC in interval graphs.

Lemma 1. *Any optimal solution of RVMC in interval graphs consists of a selection of the minimal vertex separators, that is, for each vertex v in an optimal solution C for RVMC in an interval graph G, there is a minimal vertex separator Y of G such that $v \in Y$ and $Y \subseteq C$.*

Based on Lemma 1, we only consider the minimal vertex separators of G. Note that we exclude the vertex separators containing terminals since such vertex separators cannot be contained in an optimal solution for RVMC. Let $Y_1, Y_2, \ldots, Y_r$ with $r \leq |V|$ be the minimal vertex separators obtained by the path decomposition of G. For each $1 \leq i \leq r$ we define $P_i \subseteq H$ as the set containing the terminal pairs that are disconnected in $G[V \setminus Y_i]$. Let $H_i := \bigcup_{1 \leq j \leq i} P_j$. Note that $H_r = H$; otherwise, the given instance has no solution. Due to the third property of the path decomposition (see Sect. 1), the minimal separators can be linearly ordered such that they fulfill the following *"consistency condition"*: $Y_i \cap Y_l \subseteq Y_j$ for all Y_i, Y_j, Y_l with $i \leq j \leq l$. In addition, the sets P_i associated with Y_i, $1 \leq i \leq r$, fulfill also this consistency condition.

Now, we can formulate RVMC as a covering problem: Solving RVMC in interval graphs is equivalent to finding a subset Z of $\{1, 2, \ldots, r\}$ with $\bigcup_{i \in Z} P_i = H$ and $|\bigcup_{i \in Z} Y_i| \leq k$. Observe that, although at first sight they are very similar, there is a decisive difference to the classical SET COVER problem.[3] In our case, we have two subset systems, one is the set H and its subsets $P_1, P_2, \ldots, P_r$ and the other is V and its subsets $Y_1, Y_2, \ldots, Y_r$. Each P_i is associated with the subset of V with the same index, i.e., Y_i. The task is to select some sets

---

[2] EMC is NP-complete even in stars [6], which are interval graphs with pathwidth one.

[3] The in general NP-complete SET COVER problem can be solved in polynomial time on instances where the subsets in the subset collection can be linearly ordered such that they fulfill the consistency condition described above [10].

from $\mathcal{P} := \{P_1, P_2, \ldots, P_r\}$ to cover H. However, instead of minimizing the number of selected subsets from $\mathcal{P}$ as in SET COVER, we minimize $|\bigcup_{P_i \in \mathcal{P}'} Y_i|$ where $\mathcal{P}'$ denotes the set of the selected subsets from $\mathcal{P}$.

Observe that the minimal separators are not pairwise disjoint, i.e., there may be two Y_i and Y_j with $i \neq j$ and $Y_i \cap Y_j \neq \emptyset$. On the one hand, this forbids assigning to each P_i a weight equal to $|Y_i|$ and solving a "weighted" version of SET COVER, since $|\bigcup_{P_i \in \mathcal{P}'} Y_i|$ is not always equal to $\sum_{P_i \in \mathcal{P}'} |Y_i|$. On the other hand, for two separators Y_i and Y_j with $i \neq j$ and $Y_i \cap Y_j \neq \emptyset$, the selection of Y_j may affect the decision concerning the selection of Y_i and vice versa.

The key idea of the algorithm for this special covering problem is to exploit the consistency property of the minimal separators Y_i and their associated sets P_i: Order the minimal vertex separators Y_i and the associated sets P_i linearly such that they fulfill the consistency property. Then, the algorithm processes this linear ordering from $i = 1$ to $i = r$. At each i, it computes the best "local solution" to cover H_i by using only $P_1, \ldots, P_i$. As mentioned above, the selection of Y_j with $j > i$ may affect the decision concerning the selection of Y_i. To cope with this, the algorithm computes not only one local solution but $r - i + 1$ values for each i. The first value B_i represents the best local solution under the assumption that no j with $i < j \leq r$ and $Y_j \cap Y_i \neq \emptyset$ will be added into the global solution. Each of the other $r - i$ values $F_{i,j}$ represents, for each $i < j \leq r$, the best local solution under the assumption that j but no l with $i < l < j$ and $Y_l \cap Y_i \neq \emptyset$ will be added to the global solution. Note that due to the consistency condition, $F_{i,j}$ is equal to the best local solution under the assumption that j and l will be added to the global solution for any $l > j$.

When reaching r, there are at most two cases to consider: r is in the global solution or it is not. If it is not, then the local solution B_{r-1} turns out to be the global solution; otherwise, $|Y_r| + \min_{1 \leq i < r} \{ F_{i,r} \mid (H \setminus P_r) \subseteq H_i \}$ is the global solution.

In the following, we give the formal description of the algorithm.

For each i, $1 \leq i \leq r$, we will compute B_i and $F_{i,j}$, $i < j \leq r$, such that the following invariants hold:

$$B_i = \min\{ |\bigcup_{l \in Z} Y_l| \mid Z \subseteq \{1, \ldots, i\} \text{ and } H_i = \bigcup_{l \in Z} P_l \},$$

$$F_{i,j} = \min\{ |\bigcup_{l \in Z} (Y_l \setminus Y_j)| \mid Z \subseteq \{1, \ldots, i\} \text{ and } H_i = \bigcup_{l \in Z} P_l \}.$$

In order to simplify the presentation, we introduce $Y_0 := \emptyset$, $P_0 := \emptyset$, $H_0 := \emptyset$, $B_0 := 0$, and $F_{0,j} := 0$ for all $1 \leq j \leq r$. We start with the initialization $B_1 := |Y_1|$ and for all $1 < j \leq r$ let $F_{1,j} := |Y_1 \setminus Y_j|$.

When reaching i with $1 < i < r$, we consider two cases.

Case 1. $P_i \nsubseteq P_{i-1}$.
We set

$$B_i := |Y_i| + \min_{0 \leq l < i} \{ F_{l,i} \mid (H_i \setminus P_i) \subseteq H_l \};$$

$$F_{i,j} := |Y_i \setminus Y_j| + \min_{0 \leq l < i} \{ F_{l,i} \mid (H_i \setminus P_i) \subseteq H_l \}, \text{ for each } i < j \leq r.$$

This computation is correct since we have to take i to have a local solution. Then, B_i is set equal to the sum of $|Y_i|$ and the minimum of the local solutions to cover $H_i \setminus P_i$ under the assumption that i is already a part of the solution. The value of $F_{i,j}$ is set analogously.

Case 2. $P_i \subseteq P_{i-1}$.
We set

$$B_i := \min\{\, B_{i-1}, |Y_i| + \min_{0 \leq l < i}\{\, F_{l,i} \mid (H_i \setminus P_i) \subseteq H_l \,\}\};$$

$$F_{i,j} := \min\{\, F_{i-1,j}, |Y_i \setminus Y_j| + \min_{0 \leq l < i}\{\, F_{l,i} \mid (H_i \setminus P_i) \subseteq H_l \,\}\}, \text{ for each } i < j \leq r.$$

In this case, we choose the minimum of the two alternatives of adding i to the solution or not. Therefore, the correctness follows from the correctness of Case 1.

Theorem 5. RESTRICTED VERTEX MULTICUT *in interval graphs can be solved in* $O(|V|^2 \cdot |H|^2)$ *time.*

4   General Graphs and Bounded Treewidth

In this section, we present a fixed-parameter algorithm for RVMC in general graphs with treewidth and the number of terminals as parameters. Marx [9] shows that UVMC is fixed-parameter tractable with respect to the number of vertex removals and the number of terminal pairs.

As shown in Theorem 1, RVMC is NP-complete for tree networks with bounded vertex degree and bounded pathwidth. Therefore, we cannot hope for a fixed-parameter algorithm with only treewidth or pathwidth as parameter. Moreover, in the following theorem we show that RVMC is not fixed-parameter tractable with respect to the number of terminals. For the proof, we give a reduction from EMC to RVMC that preserves the number of terminals and the number of terminal pairs. The theorem follows then from the fact that EMC is NP-complete for more than two input terminal pairs [4].

Theorem 6. RESTRICTED VERTEX MULTICUT *is NP-complete if there are at least six terminals.*

Now we know that there is no hope for a fixed-parameter algorithm for RVMC with respect to the single parameter treewidth or number of terminals. In the following, we present the fixed-parameter algorithm for RVMC with treewidth *and* the number of the terminals as parameters. The basic idea of this algorithm comes from the observation that any solution of RVMC divides the input graph into at least two connected components such that any two terminals of an input terminal pair are not in the same connected component. Based on this observation, the algorithm consists of two phases. The first phase enumerates all possible partitions of the terminal set that separate all input terminal pairs. It is easy to observe that there are at most $O(|S|^{|S|})$ many partitions of the terminal set S. To check whether a partition separates the given terminal pairs in H can be done in $O(|H|)$ time. Then, the run time of the first phase is $O(|S|^{|S|} \cdot |H|)$. The second phase of the algorithm, for each partition, uses dynamic programming on the tree decomposition to compute the minimum number of vertex removals dividing the input graph into connected components such that each set in this partition is contained in a connected component and no two sets are contained in the same connected component. To simplify the presentation, we give an equivalent formulation of the task of the second phase:[4]

COLORING EXTENSION

Input: An undirected graph $G = (V, E)$, a set of terminals $S \subseteq V$, and a pre-coloring $L_S : S \to C$ with the colors from a set C where $|C| \leq |S|$.
Task: Find an extension $L_{G,S}$ of L_S with the colors from $C \cup \{r\}$ where $r \notin C$ such that
1. for every $s \in S$, $L_{G,S}(s) = L_S(s)$,
2. for every edge $\{u, v\} \in E$, either $L_{G,S}(u) = L_{G,S}(v)$ or $L_{G,S}(u) = r$ or $L_{G,S}(v) = r$, and
3. the cost $|\{v \in V \mid L_{G,S}(v) = r\}|$ is minimized.

Assume we have a fixed partition of the terminal set. If we assign to every terminal in a set of this partition a color from C, then a solution of the coloring problem ensures that every path between two terminals with different initial colors has to pass through at least one vertex v with $L_{G,S}(v) = r$. This implies that the removal of the vertices with color r separates the sets, which is a solution for the RVMC problem.

Theorem 7. *Given an undirected graph $G = (V, E)$ with a tree decomposition of width ω, COLORING EXTENSION with the terminal set $S \subseteq V$ pre-colored by the color set C can be solved in $O((|C| + 1)^{\omega+1} \cdot (|V| + |E|))$ time.*

In summary, the first phase of the algorithm for RVMC enumerates all possible partitions of the terminal set S that separate all input terminal pairs. In the second phase, for each partition, the algorithm colors the terminal set according the partition by using at most $|S|$ colors and, then, calls the dynamic programming algorithm for the COLORING EXTENSION problem. The minimum of the outputs of the dynamic programming algorithm for all partitions is then the optimal solution for RVMC. By a simple traceback phase, one can easily construct the set of the vertices to be removed. The main theorem then follows directly from the correctness and run times of the two phases.

Theorem 8. *Given an undirected graph $G = (V, E)$ with a tree decomposition of width ω, RESTRICTED VERTEX MULTICUT can be solved in $O(|S|^{|S|+\omega+1} \cdot (|V| + |E|))$ time, where S is the terminal set.*

UVMC can be reduced to RVMC with the same number of terminals and the same treewidth (Sect. 3). Therefore, the above algorithm also works for UVMC.

---

[4] A similar coloring problem is defined by Erdős and Székely [5]. Note that here we have a different cost function.

Corollary 1. *Given an undirected graph $G = (V, E)$ with a tree decomposition of width ω,* UNRESTRICTED VERTEX MULTICUT *can be solved in $O(|S|^{|S|+\omega+1} \cdot (|V| + |E|))$ time, where S is the terminal set.*

Actually, the same approach can also be applied to EMC. Here, the goal is to minimize the number of the "color-changing" edges, whose endpoints have different colors, while extending a coloring of the terminal set. The dynamic programming on the tree decomposition is almost the same. We omit the details.

Theorem 9. *Given an undirected graph $G = (V, E)$ with a tree decomposition of width ω,* EDGE MULTICUT *can be solved in $O(|S|^{|S|+\omega+1} \cdot (|V| + |E|))$ time, where S is the terminal set.*

References

1. Booth, K.S., and Lueker, G.S: Testing for the Consecutive Ones Property, Interval Graphs, and Graph Planarity Using PQ-Tree Algorithms. Journal of Computer and System Sciences **13** (1976) 335–379
2. Costa, M., Létocart, L., and Roupin, F.: Minimal Multicut and Maximal Integer Multiflow: a Survey. European Journal of Operational Research **162** 1 (2005) 55–69
3. Călinescu, G., Fernandes, C.G., and Reed, B.: Multicuts in Unweighted Graphs and Digraphs with Bounded Degree and Bounded Tree-Width. Journal of Algorithms **48** (2003) 333–359
4. Dahlhaus, E., Johnson, D.S., Papadimitriou, C.H., Seymour, P.D., and Yannakakis, M.: The Complexity of Multiterminal Cuts. SIAM Journal on Computing **23** 4 (1994) 864–894
5. Erdős, P.L., and Székely, L.A: Evolutionary Trees: an Integer Multicommodity Max-Flow-Min-Cut Theorem. Advances in Applied Mathematics **13** (1992) 375–389
6. Garg, N., Vazirani, V., and Yannakakis, M.: Primal-Dual Approximation Algorithms for Integral Flow and Multicut in Trees. Algorithmica **18** 1 (1997) 3–20
7. Guo, J., and Niedermeier, R.: Exact Algorithms and Applications for Tree-Like Weighted Set Cover. To appear in Journal of Discrete Algorithms (2005)
8. Guo, J., and Niedermeier, R.: Fixed-Parameter Tractability and Data Reduction for Multicut in Trees. Networks **46** 3 (2005) 124–135
9. Marx, D.:. Parameterized Graph Separation Problems. In Proc. 1st IWPEC, LNCS, Springer **3162** (2004) pages 71–82 Long version to appear in Theoretical Computer Science.
10. Veinott, A.F., and Wagner, H.M.: Optimal Capacity Scheduling. Operations Research **10** (1962) 518–532

Using Extensible Heterogeneous Database Transformers

Furman Haddix and Kalyan Pydipati

Department of Computer Science, Texas State University-San Marcos
fh10@txstate.edu, kalyan_pydipati@yahoo.com

Abstract. Transforming a heterogeneous data model to another heterogeneous data model involves mapping of structural information and data layout. For performing the transformation processes this paper presents a flexible and extensible approach for heterogeneous database transformation using XML. Basics steps involved are forward transformation and reverse transformation. Between these two steps lie two XML documents; one representing the database structure; the other representing the database data. The XML documents define tags for representing an arbitrary database thus making the representation independent of the source and target database management systems. The advantage of having standard XML representations for the database model is that it can be easily extended to support new database models with a maximum of two transformers per database management system.

1 Introduction

We present a flexible and extensible approach to transforming databases in one management system paradigm to databases in another management system paradigm; for example, the source database might be relational, while the target database is object-oriented. The transformation is divided into a forward transformation and a reverse transformation. The principal interface between the forward and reverse transformations is two Data Type Documents (DTDs): The structure DTD and the data DTD. The structure DTD defines a set of XML tags for embedding the structural information of a database independent of its management system format. The data DTD defines a set of XML tags for embedding data of a database independent of its data representation format. A data-type mapping DTD defines tags for embedding data-type mapping information between heterogeneous database models, for example, XML and relational. A forward transformation transforms the database structure and data of the source heterogeneous database to the hierarchical structure of XML documents specified by the structure DTD and the data DTD. A reverse transformation transforms the database structure and data represented by the XML documents to the destination heterogeneous database structure and data.

There have been numerous prior research efforts in mapping between different data models. Lee *et al.* [8] specify two algorithms, NET and COT to translate relational schemas to XML schemas using various semantic constraints. They used XSchema (XML representation), a language independent formalism. Fong *et al.* [4] provide a methodology of translating the conceptual schema of a relational database into an

J. Wiedermann et al. (Eds.): SOFSEM 2006, LNCS 3831, pp. 313–322, 2006.

XML schema through an EER (extended entity relationship) model. Baru [1] proposes an X-Database system to support import and export of XML documents from relational repositories. The base of this system is an XML-Schema file that describes the logical model of interchanged information. Hohenstein [5] proposes data migration between relational and object-oriented database systems using the Federation Approach. Given any relational database, a migration program filing an object-oriented database is generated. The other direction is automated the same way. Jahnke *et al.* [6] describe an integrated design environment that supports the migration process and overcomes major drawbacks of comparable approaches. They employed structure-oriented editors for the representation and manipulation of the SQL and the ODMG schema. These structure-oriented editors internally store an abstract syntax tree representation of the edited schemas. Mani and Lee [9] studied various steps for translating XML to relational models while maintaining semantic constraints. Their work is based on the theory of regular tree grammars, which proves a useful formal framework for understanding various aspects of XML schema languages. Bohannon *et al.* [3] propose LegoDB, a cost-based XML-to relational mapping engine that addresses the problem of storing XML documents in relational databases. LegoDB explores a space of possible mappings and selects the best mapping for a given application (defined by an XML Schema, XML data statistics, and an XML query workload). Bierman [2] proposes OIFML, a XML based language defined to dump and load the current state of ODMG-complaint databases. In this paper, he defined a new XML document type, OIFML, and showed how it can be used to specify ODMG-objects.

2 Methodology

In order to transform an arbitrary source database structure and data to an arbitrary destination database model, we interpret the database structural information and the format of data stored in the source database. We capture the database structural and data format information in XML documents that are processed according to the database structure and data format of the destination database. The tag definitions of these XML documents are independent of the source database. Conceptually, the database structure consists of a principal entity representing some particular aspect of the real world. In relational databases, a table represents the real world entity; in object-oriented databases a class; and in native XML, a database element represents the real world entity. This principal entity exhibits properties, attributes and keys.

The database data is organized according to the format specified by the database structure. For a relational database, database data is stored in tables of rows of columns. For an object-oriented database, data is stored in attributes of objects. For a native XML database, data is stored in attributes of elements. A structure DTD defines a set of tags to constrain the database structural information in a hierarchical order of an XML document which is independent of the database paradigm. The structure DTD can be extended to support new database formats by adding new tag definitions according to the new database theoretical base, thus enabling less overload for transforming the database between the existing database formats and the new database format. The tag definitions of the structure DTD are capable of representing relational, object-oriented and native XML database paradigms. The data DTD defines a set of tags to hold the database data in the hierarchical order of a XML document independent of the source database paradigm.

The transformation process consists of two stages: Forward transformation and reverse transformation. The forward transformation translates the source database structure and data into XML documents. The reverse transformation is translates the XML structure and data documents into the formats of the destination database management system. Fig. 1 shows the transformation process. An extended description of this process may be found at [10]. A less detailed explanation forms the balance of this chapter.

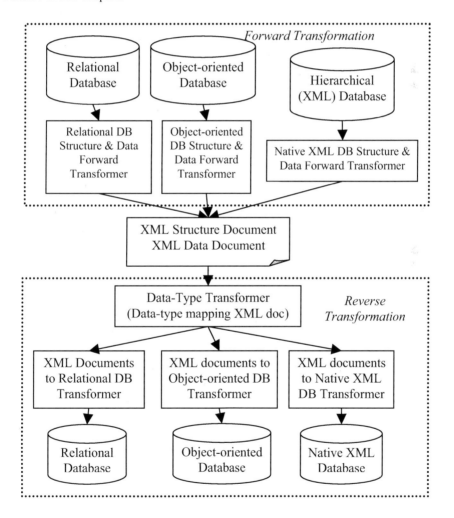

Fig. 1. Overview of database transformation process

2.1 Forward Transformation

In a forward transformation, heterogeneous data structure and data are mapped to the hierarchical structure of XML documents specified by the structure DTD and the data DTD. The hierarchical structure for storing the database structure information is generated according to the tag constraints specified in the structure DTD. The hierarchical structure for storing database data is generated according to the tag constraints specified in the data DTD. Fig. 2 illustrates the forward transformation process. The following paragraphs describe the principal components of this process:

Front End GUI: The Front End GUI consists of a series of java swing windows; each window providing a set of options. The user specifies the direction of transformation, the DBMS type, and related essential information.
Structure Extractor: The Structure Extractor retrieves structural information from the source database.

If the source database is a relational database, the Structure Extractor retrieves information table and column information, such as the names of columns, size of columns, data type of columns, if columns are NULL, if columns have values generated automatically and the key information. Extracted information is stored in a Hash table so that the Structure Transformer, GUI Builder, and Data Extractor can use the information later in the process.

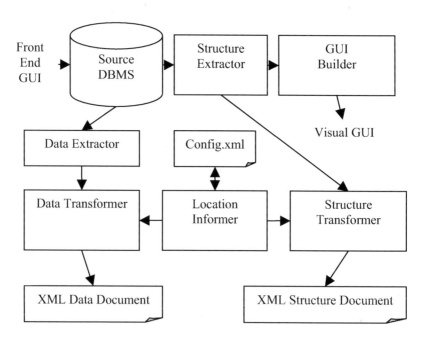

Fig. 2. Architecture of Forward Transformation

If the source database is an object-oriented database, the structure extractor parses java class files, and extracts class names, names of variables, data type of variables, object references, and method definitions. Extracted information is stored in a Hash table so that the Structure Transformer and GUI Builder can use it in later parts of the transformation.

If the source database is a hierarchical database, structure extractor extracts required XML schemas from the hierarchical database. It parses the XML schema and extracts XML schema ELEMENTS, attributes of the ELEMENTS, child elements of the ELEMENTS, data types of the attributes, data types of the child elements, and keys defined on the ELEMENTS. Extracted information is stored in a Hash table so that the Structure Transformer, GUI Builder, and Data Extractor can use the data in later parts of the transformation.

GUI Builder: The GUI Builder generates logical diagrams to represent the structure of the source database. For a relational database, it generates an ER diagram to represent table structures and their relationships. For an object-oriented database, it generates UML class diagrams to represent the class structure and relationships. For a hierarchical database it generates UML class diagrams to represent different elements of the schema and their relationships.

Data Extractor: The Data Extractor extracts the data associated with each component of the database such as tables, objects, and XML documents, and stores it in a hash table. For a relational database, it extracts all rows related to the tables. For an object-oriented database, it retrieves all required objects and their data. For hierarchical database, it retrieves and parses the XML document.

Visual GUI: The Visual GUI displays the logical diagrams built by GUI Builder. Visual GUI is built on top of JGraphpad [7].

Location Informer: The function of the Location Informer is to provide information about the location of XML structure and data documents and data type-mapping XML documents.

Database Structure Transformer: The Database Structure Transformer generates the XML structure document from the information stored in the hash table. The document is stored at the location given by the Location Informer.

Database Data Transformer: The Database Data Transformer uses the information stored in the Hash table for generating the XML data document and stores the generated file at the location provided by Location Informer.

Source DBMS and Target DBMS: The transformation tool supports the following DBMS.
- Relational databases: SQL Server, Oracle, and My SQL
- Object-oriented database: Ozone
- Native XML database: IPEDO

Relational Database to XML Documents Mapping. The mapping of relational database structure and data to XML documents consists of structural mapping and data mapping.

Structural mapping maps table structure information. This includes table descriptions, relationship between tables, and keys defined on tables. Table descriptions consist of table names and column descriptions. Column description consists of data types, size, and other properties, including allowing NULL values, default values, and auto increment.

In data mapping, data contained within rows and columns of a relational table are mapped to the hierarchical structure of an XML document specified by a data DTD. This row column information is stored in tags specified by a data DTD.

Object-Oriented Database to XML Documents Mappings. Object-oriented database structure and data must be mapped to the hierarchical structure of XML documents specified by the structure DTD and data DTD.

A class is the main component of an object-oriented database structure. Structural mapping, maps the class structure to the hierarchical structure of an XML document specified by a structure DTD. Class structure consists of class name, variable names, and data types and default values for variables, and inheritance and associations between classes.

Native XML Database to XML Documents Mapping. A hierarchical database (Native XML database) consists of XML documents as the storage unit. Data is embedded within tags of an XML document and the tag hierarchy defined in the XML schema.

2.2 Reverse Transformation

In the reverse transformation process, database structure and data represented by XML documents are mapped to the database structure and data according to the destination database. The first step is to generate the database structure which includes data type mapping of source database data type naming conventions to destination database data type naming conventions; the second step is to generate the database data. Fig. 3 illustrates the reverse transformation process. The principal components of this process are described in the following paragraphs.

Datatype Transformer: The Datatype Transformer maps data types between heterogeneous databases using data type mapping XML document.

Reverse Structure Transformer: The Reverse Structure Transformer derives the structure of the target DBMS from the structure DTD. For a relational database, it generates XML files containing SQL CREATE statements embedded within XML tags. For an object-oriented database, it generates XML files containing class declarations, variables, and methods embedded within XML tags. For a hierarchical database, it generates the XML Schema document.

Structure Inserter: The Structure Inserter generates the database structure in the target DBMS from the XML files created by the Reverse Structure Transformer. For a relational database it executes the SQL CREATE statements embedded within the tags of the XML document to create table structures in relational database. For an object-oriented database it executes the driver program, which inserts the class structures into the Ozone database. For a hierarchical database, it inserts the XML Schema into the IPEDO database.

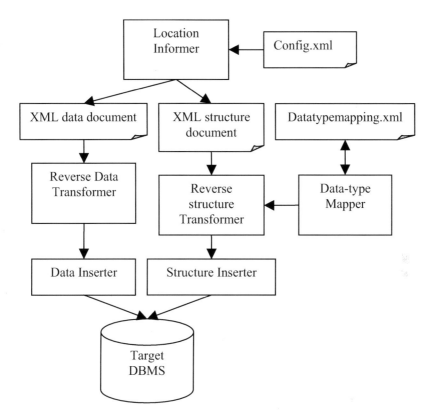

Fig. 3. Reverse transformation consists of two stages: structure mapping and data mapping

Reverse Data Transformer: The Reverse Data Transformer populates the structure of the DBMS from the data DTD. For a relational database, it generates Insert statements embedded within XML tags. For an object-oriented database, it generates object creation statements embedded within XML tags. For a hierarchical database, it generates the XML data document.

Data Inserter: The purpose of the data inserter is to insert the data into the database structure generated in the target DBMS.

Reverse structure mapping. In reverse structure mapping, the database structure information represented by the XML structure document is interpreted and processed to generate the destination database structure.

Component Description tag attributes mapping: With the *Component* tag *name* attribute mapping for relational databases, table names take the value of the *name* attribute of the *Component* tag; for object-oriented databases, class name represents the value of the *name* attribute of the *Component* tag; for hierarchical databases, XML schema element *name* attribute represents the value of the *name* attribute of the *Component* tag.

Attribute tag mappings: For relational databases, table columns are created for each *Attribute* tag of the *AttributeList* tag. Mapping of the *Attribute* tag attributes is as follows: the name of the column represents the value of the *name* attribute of the *Attribute* tag; the data type of the column takes the value of the *datatype* attribute of the *Attribute* tag, the size of the column is determined based on the datatype and the other properties are set according to appropriate attribute values.

For object-oriented databases, for each class, variables are declared for each *Attribute* tag of the *AttributeList* tag. Mapping of the *Attribute* tag attributes is as follows: name of the variable is the value of *name* attribute of the *Attribute* tag, data type of the variable is the value of *datatype* attribute of *Attribute* tag, and get and set methods are defined for each variable.

For hierarchical databases, each top-level element corresponds to the *ComponentDescription* tag, child elements are created for each *Attribute* tag of the *AttributeList* tag. Mapping of the *Attribute* tag attributes is as follows: the name of the child element is the value of *name* attribute of *Attribute* tag and the type of the child element is the value of the *datatype* attribute of the *Attribute* tag.

Key mappings: The XML structure document provides three tags for representing keys. These tags are *PrimaryKey* for primary keys, *ForeignKey* for representing foreign keys, and *UniqueKey* for unique keys.

For relational databases, we define primary keys, foreign keys and unique keys on the columns of relational tables according to each tag description. In primary key tag mapping, column definitions of tables are updated to primary keys using the value of the *name* attribute of the *PK* tags. In foreign key tag mapping, column definitions of tables are updated to foreign keys using the value of *name, referComponent* and *referField* attributes of the *FK* tag. In unique key tag mapping, column definitions of tables are updated to unique keys using the value of the *name* attribute of the *UK* tag.

For object-oriented databases, programming languages do not have appropriate constructs for defining keys, unless provided by the DBMS vendor.

For hierarchical databases, we transform the key definitions to appropriate tags of XML schema. In primary key tag mapping, for each PK tag, a *key* tag is defined in *topelement* declaration of the XML schema, the *name* attribute of *key* tag is set by appending "PK" to the value of the *name* attribute of PK tag, the *field* attribute of *xpath* tag within the *key* tag is set to the value of the *name* attribute of the PK tag. In foreign key tag mapping, for each FK tag, the corresponding *keyref* tag is defined in the *topelement* declaration of the XML schema. The *name* attribute of the *key* tag is set by appending "FK" to the value of the *name* attribute of the FK tag. The *refer* attribute of *keyref* tag is set to the value of the primary key defined for the element represented by the value of *referComponent*, the *field* attribute of the *xpath* tag within the *keyref* tag is set to the value of the *name* attribute of the FK tag. In unique key tag mapping, for each UK tag, a *unique* tag is defined in the topelement declaration of the XML schema; the *name* attribute of the *unique* tag is set by appending "UK" to the value of the *name* attribute of the UK tag, and the *field* attribute of the *xpath* tag within the *unique* tag is set to the value of the *name* attribute of the UK tag.

Inheritance tag mapping: Relational databases do not provide support for inheritance. Therefore we resolve the inheritance structure defined in the XML structure document as follows: for each child table we will add column definitions of its parent table.

Object-oriented databases provide inheritance through the use of keywords. Depending on programming language used, parent classes are inherited using language-specific keywords. XML schema provides inheritance support through the use of keywords like *extension* and *restriction*. All child tags use these keywords to inherit their parents.

Relationship tag mapping: The *Relationship* tag holds information about how each component is related to the other components. For relational databases, relationships are automatically created when we update the column definitions using the key definitions provided by XML structure document. For object-oriented databases, class references are created for each class existing in the relationship tag. For a hierarchical database, corresponding *key* and *keyref* tags are created.

Reverse Data Mapping. In the case of a relational database, each *ComponentData* tag maps to the relational table, and the name of the relational table is the value of the *name* attribute of the *ComponentData* tag. Each *ObjectData* tag forms the rows of the relational table, and each *Contains* tag attribute values are mapped to corresponding row-column position.

For an object-oriented database, each *ComponentData* tag maps to class definition, the name of the class is the value of the *name* attribute of the *ComponentData* tag. For each *ObjectData* tag, an object for the class is instantiated whose variable values are set according to the attribute of the *Contains* tag.

For a hierarchical database, XML elements are generated for each *ObjectData* tag with data embedded in the child tags.

3   Conclusion

In this research we proposed a generic framework for automated database transformation between heterogeneous databases using XML as intermediate format. We learned that each data model has its own theoretical base for representing components, attributes of components, data type conventions, size of attributes, relationships between components.

Based on these criteria for data models, we were able to successfully evolve the structure DTD and data DTD. Structure DTD and data DTD define generic tags for representing heterogeneous database structure and data independent of its underlying paradigm. Along with these DTDs we defined several mapping techniques from heterogeneous databases to the hierarchical structure of XML documents specified by the structure DTD and the data DTD and vice versa.

References

1. Baru, C.: XViews: XML Views of Relational Schemas. Technical Report, San Diego Supercomputer Center, University of California San Diego, October 7, 1999
2. Bierman, G.M.: Using XML as an Object Interchange Format. Technical Report, Department of Computer Science, University of Warwick, May 17, 2000
3. Bohannon, P., Freire, J., Roy, P., and Simeon, J.: From XML Schema to Relations: A Cost-Based Approach to XML Storage, Technical Report, Bell Laboratories, 2001

4. Fong, J., Pang, F., Bloor, C.: Converting Relational Database into XML Document. The 12th International Workshop on Database and Expert Systems Applications, Munich Germany, September 03 - 07, 2001.
5. Hohenstein, U.: Supporting Data Migration between Relational and Object-Oriented Databases Using a Federation Approach. 2000 International Database Engineering and Applications Symposium (IDEAS'00), Yokohama, Japan, September 18 - 20, 2000
6. Jahnke, J., Schäfer, W., and Zündorf, A.: A Design Environment for Migrating Relational to Object Oriented Database Systems. 1996 International Conference on Software Maintenance (ICSM '96), Monterey, CA, November 04 - 08, 1996
7. JGraph open source project: JGraphpad, 2001, http://jgraph.sourceforge.net/index.html
8. Lee, D., Mani, M., Chiu, F., and Chu, W.W.: NeT & CoT: Translating Relational Schemas to XML Schemas using Semantic Constraints. In 11th ACM Int'l Conf. on Information and Knowledge Management (CIKM), McLean, VA, USA, November 2002
9. Mani, M., Lee, D.: XML to Relational Conversion Using Theory of Regular Tree Grammars, VLDB Conference, 28th Proceedings, 2002
10. Pydipati, K.: Heterogeneous Database Transformation using XML, Thesis for the Degree Master of Computer Science, Texas State University, August 2003

P-Selectivity, Immunity, and the Power of One Bit

Lane A. Hemaspaandra[1,*] and Leen Torenvliet[2]

[1] Department of Computer Science,
University of Rochester, Rochester, NY 14627, USA
http://www.cs.rochester.edu/u/lane
[2] ILLC, University of Amsterdam,
1018 TV 24 Amsterdam, The Netherlands
http://staff.science.uva.nl/~leen/index.php

Abstract. We prove that P-sel, the class of all P-selective sets, is EXP-immune, but is not EXP/1-immune. That is, we prove that some infinite P-selective set has no infinite EXP-time subset, but we also prove that every infinite P-selective set has some infinite subset in EXP/1. Informally put, the immunity of P-sel is so fragile that it is pierced by a single bit of information.

The above claims follow from broader results that we obtain about the immunity of the P-selective sets. In particular, we prove that for every recursive function f, P-sel is DTIME(f)-immune. Yet we also prove that P-sel is not $\Pi_2^p/1$-immune.

1 Introduction

This paper studies whether the class of P-selective sets is so complex as to be immune to various uniform and nonuniform classes. A set B is *P-selective* ([18]; among the other early key papers that started the study of P-selectivity are [19], [20], [21], [12]) exactly if there is some polynomial-time computable function h such that, for each x and y, it holds that

1. $h(x,y) \in \{x, y\}$, and
2. if either x or y belongs to B then $h(x,y) \in B$.

There are many reasons for studying the P-selective sets. Among those reasons are that the P-selective sets can give insight into the relative power of polynomial-time reductions, the P-selective sets are related to heuristic search in which at each stage one merely wants to know "between these two alternatives, which is more likely to succeed," the study of selectivity can provide insights into seemingly unrelated areas (the nondeterministic analog of P-selectivity was used to show that if NP has unique solutions then the polynomial hierarchy collapses [6]), the P-selective sets are the most intensely studied of a broad range of classes

---

* Supported in part by grant NSF-CCF-0426761. Work done in part while visiting the University of Amsterdam.

J. Wiedermann et al. (Eds.): SOFSEM 2006, LNCS 3831, pp. 323–331, 2006.

of "partial information" classes [15], and the P-selective sets are particularly interesting in that they seem to have conflicting results on their complexity – in some ways they are complex and in some ways they are easy. For a far more detailed presentation of the motivations for studying the P-selective sets, see [10, Preface].

Let us turn to the last-mentioned theme. Are the P-selective sets complex or are they easy? In some senses they are known to be simple, e.g., if SAT is P-selective then P = NP, the P-selective sets are in the extended low hierarchy, and the P-selective sets all have small circuits (belong to P/poly). In some senses, they are known to be hard, e.g., every tally set (no matter how difficult) polynomial-time Turing reduces to some P-selective set.

The focus of the present paper is on whether the P-selective sets are so hard as to be immune to standard uniform and nonuniform complexity classes. A class $\mathcal{C}$ is said to be *immune* to a class $\mathcal{D}$ exactly if there is some infinite set in $\mathcal{C}$ that has no infinite subset that belongs to $\mathcal{D}$. Informally put, no $\mathcal{D}$ set can recognize an infinite number of the elements of $\mathcal{C}$'s "difficult" set without incorrectly claiming that nonelements of that set belong to that set – in some sense, $\mathcal{D}$ cannot "approximate well from the inside" the hard set. Immunity is a so-called "strong separation," and clearly $\mathcal{C}$ being $\mathcal{D}$-immune always implies that $\mathcal{C} - \mathcal{D} \neq \emptyset$ (see Figure 1a). (This paper provides an example for which the converse fails. Though such failure is not common, at least one example is widely known: Not all r.e. sets are recursive, but each infinite r.e. set has an infinite recursive subset. Another – admittedly relativized – example is that with probability one relative to a random oracle the high levels of the boolean hierarchy separate from the boolean hierarchy's second level [2], yet regardless of the oracle, each infinite set in the boolean hierarchy contains an infinite subset from the second level of the boolean hierarchy [3].)

It is very often the case in complexity theory that when two classes can be (absolutely or with some oracle) separated, then they can be (absolutely or with some other oracle) separated with immunity. Nonetheless, we will show that such an extension is impossible in some cases regarding the P-selective sets. In particular, it is known that P-sel $\not\subseteq$ EXP/n (although it also is known that P-sel $\subseteq$ NP/$n + 1$) [9]. Nonetheless, this result cannot possibly be extended to immunity, as we note that every infinite P-selective set has an infinite $\Pi_2^p/1$ (and thus certainly EXP/1) subset.

So, as mentioned above, P-sel is not immune to sufficiently powerful nonuniform classes. Nonetheless, we show that P-sel *is* immune to any nice time-bounded class. In particular, we show that for any recursive function f, P-sel is DTIME(f)-immune.

In fact, we will show a bit more. Building on the result of [9] that for any recursive function f, P-sel is not contained in DTIME(f)/n (a result that this paper shows cannot possibly be extended to immunity), Hemaspaandra, Hempel, and Nickelsen [4] showed that for any recursive function f, A-P-sel is not contained in DTIME(f)/n (also a result that this paper shows cannot possibly be extended to immunity), where A-P-sel is the class of all sets that are P-selective

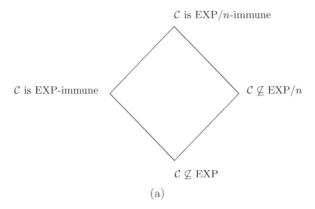

$\mathcal{C}$ is EXP/n-immune

$\mathcal{C}$ is EXP-immune $\mathcal{C} \nsubseteq$ EXP/n

$\mathcal{C} \nsubseteq$ EXP

(a)

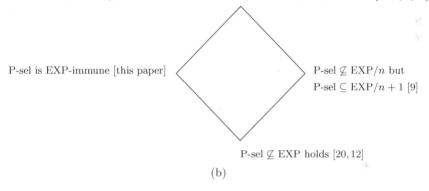

P-sel is EXP/n-immune and P-sel is EXP/n + 1-immune both FAIL [this paper]

P-sel is EXP-immune [this paper]   P-sel $\nsubseteq$ EXP/n but
                                          P-sel $\subseteq$ EXP/n + 1 [9]

P-sel $\nsubseteq$ EXP holds [20, 12]

(b)

Fig. 1. (a) Lattice of separation strengths comparing a class $\mathcal{C}$ with EXP and EXP/n. (b) P-sel versus EXP, in the context of separation-vs-immunity and n or $n + 1$ advice bits.

via some selector function that itself is associative (it is known that all such sets are contained in P/n + 1 [4]). We will show that for any recursive function f, P/$1 \cap$ A-P-sel is DTIME(f)-immune.

Thus, from our results it follows that in many cases the immunity of the P-selective set hinges on a single bit (per length). For example, P-sel is EXP-immune but P-sel is not EXP/1-immune. We know of no other natural examples of standard classes whose immunity relative to a class is pierced by the very first extra bit of information.

2   Definitions

Recall that a set B is *P-selective* exactly if there is some polynomial-time computable function h such that, for each x and y, it holds that (a) $h(x, y) \in \{x, y\}$ and (b) if either x or y belongs to B then $h(x, y) \in B$ [18]. We say that such a function h is a P-selector function for B. P-sel is defined as $\{A \mid A$ is

P-selective}. If B is P-selective via some P-selector function that is associative, we way that B is *associatively P-selective* (equivalently, $B \in$ A-P-sel) [4].

As mentioned in the introduction, a class $\mathcal{C}$ is said to be *immune* to a class $\mathcal{D}$ exactly if there is some infinite set in $\mathcal{C}$ that has no infinite subset that belongs to $\mathcal{D}$ (see [16], and introduced into complexity theory at least as early as [1], see also [17]).

As is standard, Π_2^p denotes coNP^{NP} and EXP denotes $\bigcup_{k>0} \text{DTIME}(\mathcal{O}(2^{n^k}))$.

Karp–Lipton advice classes – which capture the power of a given complexity class when augmented by a certain number of bits of free, nonuniform "advice" at each length – are defined in the standard way ([11]; for uniformity, we take the wording of the following definition directly from [7]). In particular, phrased very informally, a class A/g captures the power of the class A when it is helped, on each input string x, by being given a $g(|x|)$-bit "advice" string whose value depends only on $|x|$.

Definition 1.

1. *For any set A and any function g, A/g denotes the class of all sets L such that for some function r satisfying $(\forall n)\,[|r(n)| = g(n)]$ it holds that*

$$L = \{x \mid \langle x, r(|x|) \rangle \in A\}.$$

2. *For any class $\mathcal{C}$ and any function g, $\mathcal{C}/g$ denotes*

$$\{L \mid (\exists C \in \mathcal{C})\,[L \in C/g]\}.$$

3   Results

As mentioned in the introduction, it is known that for any recursive function f, P-sel (and even A-P-sel) is not contained in DTIME$(f)/n$ [9], [4]. The following two results show that this nonuniform result cannot possibly be extended to immunity, but that its uniform analog does extend to the case of immunity.

Theorem 1. *For each recursive function f, P-sel (and indeed even P/$1 \cap$ A-P-sel) is DTIME(f)-immune.*

Theorem 2. P-sel *is not $\Pi_2^p/1$-immune.*

Corollary 1. *If* P $=$ NP, *then* P-sel *is not* P/1-*immune.*

Corollary 2. P-sel *is not* EXP/1-*immune.*

We will prove Theorem 2 first, as it is the easier to prove.

Proof of Theorem 2.   Consider an arbitrary infinite P-selective set B. Let h be a P-selector function for B. Without loss of generality, we may assume that h is commutative – otherwise replace it with $h(\min(x,y), \max(x,y))$, which remains a P-selector for B and is clearly commutative. At each length n, consider the tournament induced by this selector function on the strings in Σ^n. By the induced tournament, we mean the graph on the strings in Σ^n such that between each pair of distinct strings x and y there is an edge in exactly one direction, namely, if $f(x, y) = x$ then the edge points from x to y. We say a node w of a tournament is a *king* if each node in the tournament can be reached from w via paths of length at most two. By an old result of Landau, each nonempty tournament has a king [13]. Hemaspaandra, Ogihara, Zaki, and Zimand [8] proved that testing whether a given string is a king of a tournament can be done in Π_2^p.[1] Note that if any string at length n belongs to B, then certainly each king of length n belongs to B. Thus, infinite set B has an infinite $\Pi_2^p/1$ subset. In particular, our $\Pi_2^p/1$ set works as follows: The one bit regarding length n says whether $B \cap \Sigma^n \neq 0$, and our Π_2^p set, on input $\langle z, b \rangle$, $z \in \Sigma^*$, $b \in \{0, 1\}$, accepts exactly if advice bit b is one and the string z is a king in the tournament induced by f on the strings in $\Sigma^{|z|}$. $\square$

We now turn to our main result, namely, Theorem 1: For each recursive function f, P-sel (and indeed even A-P-sel) is DTIME(f)-immune.

As mentioned earlier, for each recursive function f, P-sel (and even A-P-sel) has been separated previously, though not with immunity, from DTIME(f) [9],[4]. Each of those proofs works by direct diagonalization. Unfortunately, due to the fact that machines can "play possum" (can for long periods of time accept no strings), direct diagonalization does not seem to work for the more demanding case of separation with immunity. To handle this, we differ from those previous papers, and create immunity, by employing an injury-free "waiting"/priority-type construction. Our construction is a rather unusual one in that, though some requirements may remain active and unsatisfied forever, we ensure that at each stage we simultaneously satisfy all active requirements that can be satisfied via acting just at the current, relevant length. In short, we given a "waiting"/priority-type argument that is so egalitarian as to not need explicit priorities. While doing so, we integrate the strengths of each of the earlier proofs mentioned above, namely, we retain the gap-like approach of [9] and part of the scheme of [4] for assuring associativity, and for purposes of clarity, comparison, and connection, where possible we retain as far as we can their notations and arguments. However, note that our proof creates a simpler framing structure: By putting all strings at a length in or out as a block, we avoid not just explicit priorities, but also we avoid the issues of "left cut"ing (or in [4], "right cut"ing) that are central to the earlier work, since (unlike those earlier proofs that truly needed them) here they would just be needlessly entangling the proof and argument.

---

[1] Indeed, though we do not need these facts here, king-testing in tournaments in fact is Π_2^p-*complete* [5], and kings have also played a key role in proving the first-order definability of – and thus upper-bounding the complexity of – the reachability problem for certain nonsuccinctly specified restricted graph types [14]. Also, we mention that [8] itself proves some immunity claims, most particularly that P-sel is not bi-immune to the class of weakly-P-rankable sets, and that P-sel is not immune to the class of weakly-$FP^{\Sigma_2^p}$-rankable sets. However, due to the nature of the notion of weak-rankability (which we do not define here), those nonimmunity results seem to be of no help regarding obtaining the current result.

Proof of Theorem 1.   Let f be a recursive function. Then there will always exist a strictly increasing recursive function f' such that: (a) for each n, $f'(n) > \max(f(n), 2)$, and (b) for some Turing machine M that computes f' it holds that for each n the machine computes $f'(n)$ using at most $f'(n)^{\mathcal{O}(1)}$ steps. Fix such a function f'.

Let $\ell_1 = 2$. For each $i \geq 1$, let $\ell_{i+1} = 2^{2^{2^{2^{2^{f'(\ell_i)}}}}}$. Let $\mathcal{L} = \{\ell_1, \ell_2, \ldots\}$. Our set B will have the following properties: (a) $B \in \mathrm{DTIME}(2^{2^{f'(n)}})$, (b) $x \in B \implies |x| \in \mathcal{L}$, and (c) $(|x| = |y| \wedge x \in B) \implies y \in B$.

We must and will also ensure that B is an infinite set.

Note that any set satisfying (c) is in P/1, since at each length it will contain either all strings or no strings, and so one bit of advice easily suffices to accept the set. So, in our particular case, $B \in \mathrm{P}/1$. (In fact, even the P interpreter is overkill. The complexity is even lower, at least if one's pairing function from the definition of advice classes is such that it doesn't really require the full power of P to decode its subparts.)

Any set B satisfying (a), (b), and (c) is associatively P-selective. This follows by an argument given (though not in the explicit context of the f'-based gaps we use above) in [4], and for completeness, we argue that B is in A-P-sel. Let $\widehat{\mathcal{L}}$ denote $\{x \mid |x| \in \mathcal{L}\}$. Our selector function for B will be

$$h(x, y) = \begin{cases} \max(x, y) & \text{if } ||\{x, y\} \cap \widehat{\mathcal{L}}|| = 0 \\ \{x, y\} \cap \widehat{\mathcal{L}} & \text{if } ||\{x, y\} \cap \widehat{\mathcal{L}}|| = 1 \\ \min(x, y) & \text{if } ||\{x, y\} \cap \widehat{\mathcal{L}}|| = 2 \wedge |x| = |y| \\ \min(x, y) & \text{if } ||\{x, y\} \cap \widehat{\mathcal{L}}|| = 2 \wedge |x| \neq |y| \wedge \min(x, y) \in B \\ \max(x, y) & \text{if } ||\{x, y\} \cap \widehat{\mathcal{L}}|| = 2 \wedge |x| \neq |y| \wedge \min(x, y) \notin B. \end{cases}$$

In the second line here, by $\{x, y\} \cap \widehat{\mathcal{L}}$ we, in a slight abuse of type rules, mean the unique element in the named 1-element set, rather than the set itself. It is clear that h is in P since, if $||\{x, y\} \cap \widehat{\mathcal{L}}|| = 2 \wedge |x| \neq |y|$, then – since $B \in \mathrm{DTIME}(2^{2^{f'(n)}})$ and the lengths in $\widehat{\mathcal{L}}$ are quadruple-exponentially spaced – we given x and y can brute-force test "$\min(x, y) \in B$?" in time polynomial in $|\max(x, y)|$. It is also clear that h is a P-selector function for B. To see that h is associative, first notice that h, which is clearly commutative, has the following properties. When both of h's inputs belong to B, h outputs the (lexicographically) smaller input. When exactly one input belongs to B, h outputs that one. And when neither input belongs to B, h outputs the lexicographically smallest input whose length equals the largest value in $\mathcal{L}$ that is the length of one of the inputs if any input belongs to $\widehat{\mathcal{L}}$, and otherwise h outputs the larger input. In light of these observations, it is clear that when for any a, b, and c the function h is applied twice in any of the 12 possible ways (six possible orderings of $a/b/c$ and two possible groupings for each, though due to commutativity some are instantly seen as the same), the result is the same, namely, if at least one of $a/b/c$ belongs to B then the result is the lexicographically smallest string in $\{a, b, c\} \cap B$. If none of $a/b/c$ belong to B, then the result is the lexicographically smallest string of length $\max(\{|a|, |b|, |c|\} \cap \mathcal{L})$ if $\{|a|, |b|, |c|\} \cap \mathcal{L} \neq \emptyset$, and otherwise is $\max(a, b, c)$. So h is associative.

Let M_1, M_2, M_3, ... be a simple enumeration of Turing machines such that this enumeration has the properties that (a) $\bigcup_k L(M_k) \supseteq \text{DTIME}(f')$, and (b) for each k and each y, the running time of machine M_k on input y is at most $2^{kf'(|y|)}$ steps. And let our enumeration be such that each language in $\text{DTIME}(f')$ is accepted by infinitely many machines from this enumeration (this keeps us from having to worry about problems if a few small values of k might seem to cause tension with respect to our $B \in \text{DTIME}(2^{2^{f'(n)}})$ constraint).

We now turn to the stage construction that will define B. Our construction proceeds in stages. Let requirement R_i be defined as "$L(M_i) \not\subseteq B$." Once we start trying to satisfy a requirement, it will be said to be active (until we mark it, if ever, as satisfied).

At stage k, we will define which strings of length ℓ_k are in B. At stage k, we will have as active all requirements $R_1, \ldots, R_{k/2}$, other than those that we have marked as being satisfied.

At the start of stage k, we will rebuild the history of this construction, and in doing so, will determine which strings are in B at each interesting (i.e., member of $\widehat{\mathcal{L}}$) length of B that is strictly less than ℓ_k, and – rather crucially – will also determine which requirements were, during that part of the construction, marked as being satisfied. (Since this involves objects that are at most quadruple-exponentially smaller than our input, it his not hard to see that this will not interfere with the goal of ensuring that $B \in \text{DTIME}(2^{2^{f'(n)}})$.) After doing so, we seek to extend B at the current length, ℓ_k, in such a way as to satisfy at least one active requirement. So, for each M_i corresponding to an active requirement, see if there is any string of the current length that the machine accepts. Let I denote the set of all M_i's corresponding to active requirements for which there is such a string. If $I \neq \emptyset$, we will leave B at the current length completely empty, and for each $i \in I$ we will mark R_i as satisfied (M_i accepts a string that is not in B, so M_i certainly does not accept a subset of B).

On the other hand, if $I = \emptyset$ then we will put into B all strings of of length ℓ_k. Note that since, through stage k, we have activated no more than $k/2$ requirements, this case ($I = \emptyset$) happens at least half the stages, and so our set B will indeed be an infinite set.

Note that each requirement eventually becomes active. There are two cases. If in some stage after the point where it becomes active the requirement is one of those that can be satisfied, then it be marked as satisfied then. Otherwise, it (say, R_i) indeed will never be marked as satisfied, but that means – since there were only finitely many stages that occurred before the point where R_i became active – that $L(M_i)$ contains only a finite number of strings at lengths in the set $\mathcal{L}$, and so certainly is not an *infinite* subset of B. Thus, for each i, we know that it will be the case that $L(M_i)$ cannot be an infinite subset of B.   □

We start to wind up by giving an example of how these theorems can be applied to a concrete class. Theorem 1 on its surface applies to a class defined by a single time-function, f. Note that for natural time classes, the class is defined by an infinite collection of functions that in general have no single function that majorizes them (since each may have bigger and bigger constants). Nonetheless, to inherit our result it suffices to majorize each almost everywhere, and so our result is inherited by all standard time-bounded and space-bounded classes. For example, consider EXP. From the fact that P-sel is immune to DTIME(2^{2^n}) it is easy to see that P-sel is immune to EXP. This holds because if a set B has an infinite subset in EXP, it clearly (regardless of what huge constants may apply to the EXP algorithm) has an infinite subset in DTIME(2^{2^n}), e.g., by having the time 2^{2^n} machine accept no strings at all except when n has become so large that 2^{2^n} is so much bigger than the exponential bound of the EXP machine that our machine can easily simulate the EXP machine. So, we have that P-sel is clearly EXP-immune (and, for that matter, EEEEEXP/immune too). Combining this observation with the known result that P-sel is contained in EXP/$n + 1$ (even NP/$n + 1$) but is not contained in EXP/n [9], Figure 1b now as an example presents (in light of Corollary 2) what regular and strong separations hold for EXP with respect to n and $n + 1$ bits of advice.

On the other hand, we leave as an open issue whether Theorem 1 can be extended to show that P-sel is RECURSIVE-immune. Note that our result shows something weaker, namely, that for each recursive function f, P-sel is immune to DTIME(f); though trivially

$$\text{RECURSIVE} = \bigcup_{\{f \,|\, f \text{ is a recursive function}\}} \text{DTIME}(f),$$

our result nonetheless does not imply that P-sel is RECURSIVE-immune, and the proof technique does not seem to generalize to yield that.

Finally, we mention that our result is not really specific to P-selectivity, but that the natural analogs exist for other selectivity types (based on the corresponding complexity for generating and evaluating king-ness in their induced tournaments), e.g., EXP-sel is immune to DTIME(f) for each recursive function f, and yet EXP-sel is not EXP/1-immune (as one can, still within EXP-time, brute-force king-finding in tournaments based even on EXP-selectors).

References

1. Berman, L.: On the Structure of Complete Sets. In Proceedings of the 17th IEEE Symposium on Foundations of Computer Science, IEEE Computer Society (October 1976) 76–80
2. Cai, J.: Probability one Separation of the Boolean Hierarchy. In Proceedings of the 4th Annual Symposium on Theoretical Aspects of Computer Science, Springer-Verlag, Lecture Notes in Computer Science **247** (1987) 148–158
3. Cai, J., Gundermann, T., Hartmanis, J., Hemachandra, L., Sewelson, V., Wagner, K., and Wechsung, G.: The Boolean Hierarchy I: Structural Properties. SIAM Journal on Computing **17** 6 (1988) 1232–1252
4. Hemaspaandra, L., Hempel, H., and Nickelsen, A.: Algebraic Properties for Selector Functions. SIAM Journal on Computing **33** 6 (2004) 1309–1337

5. Hemaspaandra, E., Hemaspaandra, L., and Watanabe, O.: The Complexity of Kings. Technical Report TR-870, Department of Computer Science, University of Rochester, Rochester, NY, June 2005

6. Hemaspaandra, L., Naik, A., Ogihara, M., and Selman, A.: Computing Solutions Uniquely Collapses the Polynomial Hierarchy. SIAM Journal on Computing 25 4 (1996) 697–708

7. Hemaspaandra, L., and Ogihara, M.: The Complexity Theory Companion. Springer-Verlag (2002)

8. Hemaspaandra, L., Ogihara, M., Zaki, M., and Zimand, M.: The Complexity of Finding Top-Toda-Equivalence-Class Members. Theory of Computing Systems. To appear. Preliminary version available in Proceedings of 6th Latin American Symposium on Theoretical Informatics (Springer-Verlag, 2004)

9. Hemaspaandra L., and Torenvliet, L.: Optimal Advice. Theoretical Computer Science 154 2 (1996) 367–377

10. Hemaspaandra, L. and Torenvliet, L.: Theory of Semi-Feasible Algorithms. Springer-Verlag (2003)

11. Karp, R., and Lipton, R.: Some Connections between Nonuniform and Uniform Complexity Classes. In Proceedings of the 12th ACM Symposium on Theory of Computing, ACM Press, April 1980, 302–309. An extended version has also appeared as: Turing Machines that Take Advice, L'Enseignement Mathématique, 2nd series 28 (1982) 191–209

12. Ko, K.: On Self-Reducibility and Weak P-Selectivity. Journal of Computer and System Sciences 26 2 (1983) 209–221

13. Landau, H.: On Dominance Relations and the Structure of Animal Societies, III: The Condition for Score Structure. Bulletin of Mathematical Biophysics 15 2 (1953) 143–148

14. Nickelsen, A., and Tantau, T.: On Reachability in Graphs with Bounded Independence Number. In Proceedings of the 8th Annual International Computing and Combinatorics Conference, Springer-Verlag, Lecture Notes in Computer Science 2387 (August 2002) 554–563

15. Nickelsen, A. and Tantau, T.:. Partial information classes. SIGACT News, 34(1):32–46, 2003.

16. Rogers, H., Jr.: The Theory of Recursive Functions and Effective Computability. McGraw-Hill (1967)

17. Schöning, U. and Book, R.: Immunity, Relativization, and Nondeterminism. SIAM Journal on Computing 13 (1984) 329–337

18. Selman, A.: P-Selective Sets, Tally Languages, and the Behavior of Polynomial Time Reducibilities on NP. Mathematical Systems Theory 13 1 (1979) 55–65

19. Selman, A.: Some Observations on NP Real Numbers and P-Selective Sets. Journal of Computer and System Sciences 23 3 (1981) 326–332

20. Selman, A.: Analogues of Semirecursive Sets and Effective Reducibilities to the Study of NP Complexity. Information and Control 52 1 (1982) 36–51

21. Selman, A.: Reductions on NP and P-Selective Sets. Theoretical Computer Science 19 3 (1982) 287–304

Transparent Migration of Database Services

Krzysztof Kaczmarski

Warsaw University of Technology
k.kaczmarski@mini.pw.edu.pl

Abstract. Database services are tightly connected to network nodes, in present distributed query processing. We believe that dynamic changes of data and services environment are unpreventable. Currently, moving services to other locations, while continuing operations' execution without notifying their clients (service migration), is not supported. We analyze requirements for transparent migration of database services, in this paper. We also sketch a solution based on so called migration agents and middle layer for abstract network communication. We emphasize the importance of the research in the wide area heterogeneous networks, Grid databases and mobile solutions, in the conclusion.

1 Introduction

A database service in OGSA [17] may be of the two general kinds: *data access component* and *data integration component*. Tasks of a component of the latter kind consist in integration and transformation of data according to certain requests. Such a service may not be assigned to any particular network node or data repository, but may be automatically moved by a Distributed Query Processing Service [16] around the network to find optimal working conditions (the fastest node in reasonable distance between data source and a user). Therefore, service creation is often dynamic in nature, according to the client's requests.

The traditional roles of permanently working server and querying client are evolving. In dynamic agent-based networks this change goes even further: agent systems offer new ability to build autonomously communicating software moving around computer networks. Combination of agent systems and dynamic services, creates new quality in database services, which are serving their clients as before in traditional architectures, but are no longer limited by any particular network node.

This ability is crucial for dynamically changing networks, where nodes' availability may change unexpectedly. For example, some machines are going down every day in wide area networks like PlanetLab consisting of more than 580 machines all over the world.

Similarly, Grid databases deal with an important assumption on high independence of participating nodes. It is then possible that an administrator of a node forces a service migration due to machine's servicing procedure. In such situations, service clients have to react properly – messages in network protocol cannot be lost or broken. This feature is currently not supported by standard services' interfaces over TCP/IP protocol.

J. Wiedermann et al. (Eds.): SOFSEM 2006, LNCS 3831, pp. 332–340, 2006.
© Springer-Verlag Berlin Heidelberg 2006

Such dynamically changing environments were rarely concerned to be a background for distributed database system. However, modern agent systems, Grid databases, distributed query processing and emerging OGSA-DAI standard, which defines dynamic creation of database services [16], force us to reconsider those assumptions.

A new solution of database services usage, in unpredictably changing networks, is presented in this paper. In such an environment, stability of a service requires ability to move it. However, database services often based on views of different kinds may have state unlike normal Web Services, which are stateless. Additionally, if they perform long lasting computation in case of aggregating queries or joins in large distributed databases, they cannot be moved anytime. Our transparent service migration also overcomes this problem. As a result we get possibility to use a service and do not focus on a place where it operates or will operate in the future. Service location is orthogonal to basic clients' interests.

It means that new highly reliable grid database services should operate in an abstract layer, which hides all unimportant networking aspects and thus creates a new quality in client application development. Similar revolution on the level of data objects is used in CORBA. Apart from other limitations, it hides data location and thus enables higher data processing sophistication. It is widely accepted that we need the same approach in Web services, particularly in database services.

Summarizing, the advantages of using our migrating services would be: advanced network architecture transparency, higher level of network programming and database processing, better reliability, availability, continuity and quality of services, plus accommodation of dynamically changing environments.

The paper proposes a feasible solution to the sketched problem and is organized as follows. The next section discusses related research and summarizes motivation of this work. Section 3 describes our approach, while section 4 concludes.

2   Related Research and Motivation

There are many systems that create abstract layers on existing networks. One of the most spectacular is Ocean Store [15] – a persistent distributed data repository accessible from everywhere. Users simply put their data inside the store and the system is responsible for finding space for it, making replicas, managing it and migrating in case of network problems. It hides all implementation, network architecture and data storage details that are not important for users. It is based on another important project: PlanetLab [18], which creates a uniform access method to distributed machines and hides administration and authorization details (adding new user action is automated).

In Globus Toolkit project [8], a distributed computation and data storage system, certain tools are responsible for automatic execution of a job in the best possible place. Users just have to describe it in a dedicated language [5], supply binaries, point to required data and the system does the rest. All jobs are queued [4] and invoked again in case of failures, which are invisible for users. Globus is a good abstraction layer designed to run jobs in Grid systems but not supporting service continuity in case of migration and rather for computing applications not long working services.

These three projects and OGSA-DAI data virtualization [16] as well as many other initiatives, prove that creation of high-level access methods and virtual abstractions is still an important topic in which much has to be done. Also service mobility and availability in case of mobile devices, which may switch between heterogeneous networks like GSM, WLAN or BlueTooth is in the center of our interest. Services should be available at any time and any place [11].

Processes migration itself is a broad area with many tools and theories. There are two major groups of solutions. Solutions within the first one, based on process checkpoints, propose dedicated programming languages, interfaces or libraries to support threads' migration [2]. For example, Sumatra [1], a widely known solution dedicated for Java programs, puts certain checkpoints inside an application, stores them together with current state and execution counter, and then uses them to restore the thread in case of a system failure. Systems of this kind are focused on process recovery, which means persistent threads, not on process migration, which requires also persistent network connections. After the migration, an application must somehow reestablish network transmission – migration is not transparent. We claim that is one of the major problems of processes migration. Fortunately it is not completely abandoned. JADE [9] system offers a common and standardized [7] platform for migration and intercommunication of agents. Usually, they are small applications that behave in a special way and are enabled for transparent mobility. From our point of view their most important feature is that they may communicate regardless to their locations. We use it to organize migration of our database services.

Within the second group of solutions, process migration tools like Mosix [14] based on Linux and similar, extended operating systems are used offering more advanced possibilities. They modify system's kernel or virtual machine and are able to perform transparent migration of a lightweight running process to another machine within a cluster and thus distribute computations. All network connections are controlled by the system in a centralized manner that may be a source of potential communication overhead.

Finally, LAMS is a system designed to perform a transparent Web Services migration [13]. It supports automatic transfer of all service's files but it assumes that the service is stateless. The big advantage of LAMS is that it also changes DNS entries for the service, thus if a client uses a domain name server lookup, the service will be found in the new location automatically.

After noticing problems of transparent migration of database services and finding existing solutions and standards inadequate we show our proposal in this field. The motivation of this paper is thus to create a framework for transparent migration of database services. To achieve this goal, we try to put together several of the described related technologies avoiding their drawbacks. The result is a significantly new quality in distributed databases integration.

3   Transparent Service Migration Layer

We say, that a service migration layer has desired level of transparency if:

1. services are unaware of its existence, concrete network locations, etc.,
2. services may be moved to another location anytime in a transparent manner while their availability and continuity is maintained,

3. connected to services users are unaware of network nodes nor of any concrete service location,
4. users do not notice migration and do not have to modify his/her behavior if a service is moved,
5. migration layer is orthogonal to other features of system functionality which is not limited neither on service's nor on client's side,

The abstract layer creates kind of a cloud in which network architecture details disappear. Only the service itself stays in the center of user's interest (Fig. 1). There should be no limitation in combining several migration layers allowing clients to migrate.

On the other hand, transparency of layer architecture should also assure independence of applications and the migration layer, which may change as network infrastructure or protocols change. All networking aspects that are not important for a user are hidden between mobility agents and client façade library.

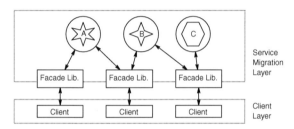

Fig. 1. A transparent service migration system – general architecture. Client applications are hidden behind façade libraries. Mobility agents (circles) wrap services 'A', 'B', 'C'.

3.1 Service Migration Problems

In this paper, we address seamless service mobility [11], rather than user or terminal mobility. In case of our database services, the service migration mechanism has to assure that:

1. service's state will be maintained and unchanged,
2. service's data (files, registers, logs, etc.) will be moved or at least remain accessible,
3. service's network connections will be sustained and all sent data will not be lost.

This goal is not easy to achieve taking into account that nowadays we face different communication domains, heterogeneous networks, different platforms, different access and connection methods, authorization, message filtering and firewalls. Also the destination for the migration cannot be random but has to fulfill certain service's requirements. Fig. 2 presents relationships between agent, node, service and metadata constraining them. A candidate node has to fulfill capabilities required by a service. Node's metadata description must allow an agent to choose, accept or reject it according to at least the following parameters: virtual machine type and version; available network transport; local storage support; computational power; system resources; available privileges.

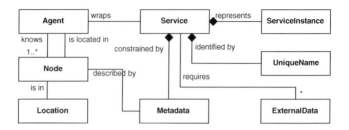

Fig. 2. The data required by mobility agent. Metadata contain description of both service working constraints and node capabilities. If they fit, the service may be located at the particular node.

Only complete consistency between node's capabilities and service's requirements assure correct migration to that node. Neither JDL job description [5] used in Globus Toolkit project, nor JADE mobility ontology [10] is not enough for these purposes – a more powerful metadata standard must be developed.

3.2 Architecture

Two notions define the network layer within which our services may migrate. The first one is the user-side *façade library*. Its task is to make service migration fully transparent for the service users. As it was explained earlier, one should not focus on network as it is only a means to communicate, but rather concentrate on available services. Broken network connections, changed service's locations and other network related topics should be taken away from application's developer. For example, a service must not be searched using a concrete IP address but rather using its location independent unique name or its semantic description.

The second dimension of transparent services migration is the service wrapper, which we call a *mobility agent*. These perform two general tasks: assure transparent service migration and wrap services' network connections. An agent working on JADE [9] platform is a kind of vehicle that moves around the network with a service inside. It performs all necessary actions to find a new place, prepare migration, perform migration, restore service's state in the new place and reopen network connections. After that, a service is ready to continue operations without any obstacles. Each client has exactly one façade but may connect to arbitrarily many services. Separation of JADE mobile agent and the service is necessary as it was explained earlier.

3.3 Mobility Agent

The agent is autonomous from a service it wraps and is able to undertake independent decisions. Migration to another server may be triggered by several events:

- system signal informing on machine malfunction or halting procedure,
- system signal requesting freeing more system resources,
- detecting not enough system resources,
- user's request to move to another location due to other reasons.

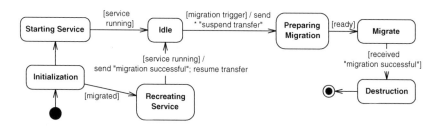

Fig. 3. Mobility agent - states. After the migration is complete, a new agent is created at initialization state.

If one of the migration causing events occurs, the agent transits to *preparing migration* state and migration procedure begins (Fig. 3):

1. Find new server, establish a connection and authorize (supported by multi-agent environment);
2. Contact all clients façades, halt transmissions, stop the service and serialize its state;
3. Inform all connected client façade libraries about migration destination;
4. Transfer all necessary files, logs, checkpoint data and agent binaries;
5. Initialize agent in a new destination (supported by multi-agent environment);
6. Recreate the service state and all network connections in a new destination;
7. Inform client façade libraries about the successful migration;
8. Let the service continue its operations;
9. Delete all old local data and destroy service process;
10. Remove the agent from the old location (supported by multi-agent environment).

A service is not working between steps (2) and (8). The length of this time period may vary depending on the size of necessary data transfer or connection problems. The client application cannot recognize the reason of temporal service inactivity, since it is hidden behind façade library. It may be interpreted as network delays or periodical communication problems. However, this time should be as short as possible due to database locks and transaction management. Distributed system is highly dependent on these mechanisms and prolonging this unavailability state, especially in case of system-critical services, could halt whole database for unacceptable long time.

Serialization of service's state and its recreation (steps 2 and 6) is done by dedicated tools. Agent implementation may choose here between many known software tools with different capabilities. The state should be recreated without any changes and special behavior of the service application.

Service migration requires also transferring all of its local files (4). Service must list all its necessary files in dedicated agent's register before it starts operations (Fig. 2). This may be done by the service itself or by its administrator through service meta-description. The bigger files are the longer transition procedure lasts. A big improvement may be achieved by storing all data in a distributed storage like Ocean Store [15]. In such a case, the service do not create or use any local files but forwards all requests to the store, which handles them automatically. The storage is accessed in the same way from all places, so after migration data access remains the same. The distributed storage mechanism may decide to move data closer to the new destination, if it finds it reasonable.

Old service destruction must be done after the successful migration, that is, after the system is sure that the service is running properly in the new destination. These two tasks may be easily handled by JADE platform *beforeMove* and *afterMove* methods. The first one is invoked in the old location, and the second one in the new location just after the agent is successfully moved. The old instance of the agent and the new one have to agree, that the service is safely running and all the network connections are recreated. This agreement may be done by JADE inter-agent messages. After it is done step 9 and 10 are performed.

3.4   Client Façade Library

Client façade library is necessary in order to achieve full transparency of service location and hide network details. Its goals are following:

1. Find the service in the network upon its name or other description;
2. Wrap network transfer and hide service migration;
3. Perform necessary authorizations and assure secure connection to an agent.

In order to open a connection to a service, client supplies service's name, thus unique naming is an important topic, which has to be resolved by a consortium agreement [6] or other standardization initiatives. Service's name must be different than a name of an agent within the migration layer. An agents' name is used only for communication inside the layer between façade and the agent and between agents, while service's name is used for accessing it by clients.

Wrapping the network transfer and hiding network details by our façade is similar to Client Stub in SUMA meta-system [3]. The library takes control over all network operations and creates a more abstract network access. Client applications are no longer limited by direct IP addresses or hosts' names. They only know what is to be done and how to name it. The rest of the communication is done by the façade. If a service is about to migrate the library suspends transmission and after a migration reestablishes connection and continues data transfer (Fig. 4). The façade may buffer

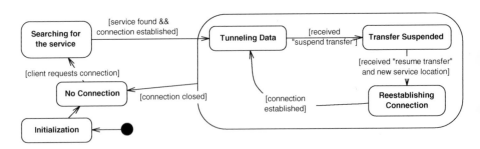

Fig. 4. States of the façade library for each service's connection

data transfer until the service is ready to receive it, so client application does not recognize any changes. The library knows the new service location from the mobility agent and thus must be connected to the migration layer.

4 Conclusions and Future Work

At present, database services are tightly connected to certain network nodes, which is unfortunate in case of dynamic changes of the network environment. Besides, there is generally no way of abstracting from service's location and there is also no tool allowing clients to move a service to another (safe) location and continue performing operations without client notification. As a consequence, service migration (and location) is not supported.

We propose to solve the problem using a new network communication layer that hides all network details and create a new paradigm of communication between clients and services. To this goal, we propose to use multi-agent systems like JADE which enable us to discover new places and, what is the most important, supplies us with universal communication mechanism between agents working on servers.

We have presented a way of transparent migration of database services between servers - in the Internet and other networks. The ability to move services without notification of their users is important for achieving high level of abstraction and transparency. Database services nature makes this task more complex due to their required high reliability, their state, and critical network connectivity. A database service is wrapped by an agent and a client is hidden behind a facade; agent's tasks are to find a new service location and perform safe migration. Our approach opens a new area in this field and creates a new data processing paradigm decreasing the required effort to produce both reliable database services and client applications.

Some of the concrete advantages of transparent database services migration are:

1. Improved reliability and availability - services may move to another machine in case of server malfunctioning in a transparent manner;
2. Dynamic job distribution in cases when more computation power is needed; a client may ask an agent not only to migrate but also to clone and thus distribute query processing - the same may be requested by a DQP service;
3. Transparent optimization of job's scenario - selected mobile services working on the same task like in case of distributed query processing, may migrate transparently to be closer to data while other ones are not aware of such movement;
4. Higher culture of data processing - abstract communication layer between clients and services increases quality and improves their design and implementation.

Our prototype grid object database system is already working. It supports data transformation services based on updatable object views [12]. The system is unique due to its transparent data integration and transformation and, what is the most important, supports data updates which is unusual among other database views mechanisms. We are now working on a stable extension allowing transparent migration of these services over the nodes within PlanetLab slices using JADE multi-agent platform as described in the paper.

Current server and service description languages are not fully adequate to present useful and convenient solutions we are looking for – we plan to continue the work. Our future work will also focus on analysis of the working system behavior in different network settings and under different load and environmental conditions. Also, new metadata for network servers and services, allowing agents to find a new proper place for a service, is under development.

References

1. Acharya, A., Ranganathan, M., and Saltz J.: Sumatra: A Language for Resource-Aware Mobile Programs. Mobile Object Systems: Towards the Programmable Internet **1222**, (1997), 111-130
2. Bouchenak, S., Hagimont, D., and De Palma, N.: Efficient Java Thread Serialization. Proceedings of the 2nd International Conference on Principles and Practice of Programming in Java, ACM ICPS **42** (2003) 35-39
3. Cardinale, Y., and Hernández, E.: Checkpointing Facility on a Metasystem, LNCS **2150**, (2001) 75-79
4. Condor,G: A Computation Management Agent for Multi-Institutional Grids. J. Frey, T. Tannenbaum, I. Foster, M. Livny, S. Tuecke. Cluster Computing, **5** 3 (2002) 237-246
5. Data Grid. Job Description Language. Workload Management Work Package. Technical Specification, 2003. http://server11.infn.it/workload-grid/
6. Foster, I., and Kesselman, C.: The Grid: Blueprint for a New Computing Infrastructure. Morgan Kaufmann Publishers (2004)
7. FIPA – Foundation for Intelligent Physical Agents. http://www.fipa.org/
8. The Globus Toolkit. The Globus Alliance. http://www.globus.org/
9. JADE – Java Agent Development Framework. TILAB, 2005. http://jade.tilab.com.
10. JADE Programmers Guide. TILAB, 2005. http://jade.tilab.com/doc/index.html
11. Jørstad, I., Van Thanh, D., and Dustdar, S.: An Analysis of Service Continuity in Mobile Services. Proceedings of the Thirteenth IEEE International Workshops on Enabling Technologies: Infrastructure for Collaborative Enterprises. Italy, Modena (2004)
12. Kozankiewicz, H.: Updatable Object Views. Ph.D. Thesis. The Institute of Computer Science, The Polish Academy of Science, Warsaw (2004). zamiast tego dałbym pracę konferencyjną
13. Mifsud, T., and Stanski, P.: Peer-2-Peer Nomadic Web Services Migration Framework. 2nd Asian International Mobile Computing Conference, Langkawi Island, Malaysia 2002
14. Mosix. Cluster and Grid Management. http://www.mosix.org/
15. The OceanStore Project. Providing Global-Scale Persistent Data. UC Berkeley Computer Science Division. http://oceanstore.cs.berkeley.edu
16. Open Grid Services Architecture Data Access and Integration Documentation. Service Based Distributed Query Processor. www.ogsadai.org.uk, www.ogsadai.org.uk/dqp
17. Open Grid Services Architecture. The project's website. http://www.globus.org/ogsa/
18. PlanetLab. An open platform for developing, deploying, and accessing planetary-scale services. PlanetLab Consortium. http://www.planet-lab.org

Merging and Merge-Sort
in a Single Hop Radio Network⋆

Marcin Kik

Institute of Mathematics and Computer Science,
Wrocław University of Technology,
ul. Wybrzeże Wyspiańskiego 27, 50-370 Wrocław, Poland
kik@im.pwr.wroc.pl

Abstract. We present two merging algorithms on a single-channel single-hop radio network without collision detection. The simpler of these algorithms merges two sorted sequences of length n in time $4n$ with energetic cost for each station $\approx \lg n$. The energetic cost of broadcasting is constant. This yields the merge-sort for n elements in time $2n \lg n$, where the energetic cost for each station is $\frac{1}{2} \lg^2 n + \frac{7}{2} \lg n$ (the energetic cost of broadcasting is only $2 \lg n$), which seems to be suitable for practical applications due to its simplicity and low constants. We also present algorithm for merging in time $O(n \lg^* n)$ with energetic cost $O(\lg^* n)$.

1 Introduction

A *radio network* consists of processing units (called *stations*) which communicate with each other by broadcasting radio messages. There are two important complexity measures of the radio network algorithms: *time* and *energy consumption*. Most of energy is consumed by broadcasting and listening to messages. The stations are often powered by batteries. If a single station fails due to battery exhaustion, then the whole task performed by the network may also fail. Therefore we want to implement algorithms in such a way that the maximal energy used by a single station is minimized. There are many problems concerning self-organization of the network (such as leader election and initialization [8], [5], [6]) that are nontrivial even in the single-hop networks. We may also need to process or organize data distributed among the stations (for example some measurements made by the stations). Some of the typical examples of such problems are finding minimum, maximum, median [10], average value [7], or sorting [11].

We consider a network of n numbered stations $s_1, \ldots, s_n$ communicating through a single radio channel. Each station s_i knows the value n, its own number i and stores a single key in its variable $key[s_i]$. We want to sort the keys within the network. (The keys are *sorted* if, for each pair of stations, the station with

---

⋆ Partially supported by KBN, grant number 3T11C 011 26 in year 2004 and by the European Union within the 6th Framework Programme under contract 001907 (DELIS).

J. Wiedermann et al. (Eds.): SOFSEM 2006, LNCS 3831, pp. 341–349, 2006.

a lower number holds the lower key.) All stations are synchronized. Time is divided into *slots*. Within a single time slot a single message can be broadcast. We consider *single-hop* network: Message broadcast by any station can be received by any other station. A single message contains $O(\max\{B, \lg n\})$ bits, where B is the number of bits of a single key. (Typically $B = \Theta(\lg n)$.) Broadcasting and listening in a single time slot requires a unit of *energetic cost*. Each station has limited memory. It can contain a constant number of words of $O(\max\{B, \lg n\})$ bits each. By *energetic cost of the algorithm* we mean the maximal energy dissipated by a single station. We do not assume the existence of the "wake up mechanism" with a low power paging channel, as described in [10], [11]. Each station predicts its next time slot for listening or broadcasting using only its internal clock and state.

There exists an algorithm [9] that sorts n elements in time $O(n)$ with energetic cost of broadcasting $O(1)$. However the energetic cost of listening in this algorithm is $\Theta(n)$. A comparator network can also be transformed into algorithm for single-hop networks: each comparator is simulated in two consecutive time slots, when two endpoints of the comparator exchange their values. The time of such algorithm (in single channel) is two times the number of comparators, and the energetic cost is not greater than two times the depth of the network. Thus the AKS sorting network [1] can be transformed into (impractical) sorting algorithm with time $O(n \lg n)$ and energetic cost $O(\lg n)$ and the Batcher networks [2] can be transformed into sorting algorithms with time $O(n \lg^2 n)$ and energetic cost $O(\lg^2 n)$. However, in radio network, a single message can be listened by many stations and the messages may contain other information besides the keys. Singh and Prasanna [10], [11] proposed algorithm sorting in time $O(n \lg n)$ with energetic cost $O(\lg n)$ by implementing quick-sort and selecting the median as the partitioning element in each recursive call with energetically balanced implementation of asymptotically optimal selection algorithm [3]. It is sophisticated and the constants involved are large (although not as large as in the AKS network) (see simulation results in [11]).

1.1   Result

We present two merging procedures. The first one merges two sequences of length n in time $O(n)$ with energetic cost of listening $O(\lg n)$ and of broadcasting $O(1)$. It can be used for implementation of sorting in time $O(n \lg n)$ and energetic cost of listening $O(\lg^2 n)$ and of broadcasting $O(\lg n)$ based on the classical merge-sort algorithm (see [4]). Although the asymptotic energetic cost of listening for sorting is worse than that obtained by Singh and Prasanna, it seems to be more suitable for practical implementations due to the low constants and simplicity. The energetic cost of broadcasting in merging is only $O(1)$ and in merge-sort is $O(\lg n)$. This is important since in practice broadcasting requires more energy than listening. The second presented merging algorithm works in time $O(n \lg^* n)$ with energetic cost of listening and broadcasting $O(\lg^* n)$. To the knowledge of the author it is not known whether there exists merging algorithm with asymptotically lower energetic cost or whether there is any non-constant lower bound for energetic cost of merging. This algorithm can also be used for merge-sorting in time in time $O(n \lg n \lg^* n)$ with energetic cost $O(\lg n \lg^* n)$. Implementations of the simulations of these algorithms can be found at [12].

Theorem 1. *There exist algorithms that merge two sorted sequences of length m on a single hop radio network without collision detection:*

- *in time $4m$ with energetic cost of listening $\lceil \lg(m+1) \rceil + 1$ and of broadcasting 2.*
- *in time $O(m \lg^* m)$ with energetic cost of listening and broadcasting $O(\lg^* m)$*

2   Merging

For simplicity of description we assume that all the keys are pairwise distinct. Let T_m denote a balanced binary tree consisting of the nodes $1, \ldots, m$: If $m = 2^k - 1$, for some integer $k > 0$, then T_m is a complete binary tree. If $m = 2^k - 1 - l$, for some positive integer $l < 2^{k-1}$, then the l rightmost leaves are missing. The nodes are placed in T_m in the *inorder* order (i.e. for each node x the nodes in its left subtree are less than x and the nodes in its right subtree are greater than x). By $l(m, x)$ (respectively $r(m, x)$), for $1 \leq x \leq m$, we denote the left (respectively right) child of node x in T_m. (A non-existing child is represented by NIL.) By $p(m, x)$ we denote the index of node x in T_m in *preorder* ordering. (I.e. the *preorder* index of the root is 1, then the nodes on the second level are indexed from left to right, then on the third level, and so on.) We also assume that $p(m, NIL) = NIL$. An example of T_m for $m = 6$ is given in Figure 1. Note that the height (number of levels) of T_m is $\min\{k : 2^k - 1 \geq m\} = \lceil \lg(m+1) \rceil$ (where "lg" denotes "$\log_2$"). For $m \geq 1$, we define a sequence $h(m, 0), h(m, 1), \ldots$ as follows:

$$h(m, i) = \begin{cases} m & \text{if } i = 0 \\ \lceil \lg(h(m, i-1) + 1) \rceil & \text{if } i \geq 1 \end{cases} \tag{1}$$

Let $l^*(m) = \min\{i : h(m, i) \leq 2\}$. Note that $l^*(m) = O(\lg^* m)$. (Note also, that $l^*(m) \leq 4$, for $m \leq 2^{127} - 1$.) The functions $l(m, x)$, $r(m, x)$, $p(m, x)$, $h(m, i)$ and $l^*(m)$ can be computed internally by each station.

We want to merge two sorted sequences of keys stored in stations $\langle a_1, \ldots, a_m \rangle$ and $\langle b_1, \ldots, b_m \rangle$ into a single sorted sequence of length $2m$ stored in $\langle a_1, \ldots, a_m,$

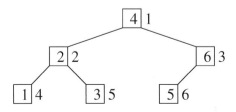

Fig. 1. Tree T_6. Right to the nodes are their *preorder* indexes

procedure Rank($\langle a_1, \ldots, a_m \rangle$, $\langle b_1, \ldots, b_m \rangle$)
Each station a_i does: $timer[a_i] \leftarrow 1$; $rank[a_i] \leftarrow 0$;
for *time slot* $d \leftarrow 1$ *to* m **do**
| let x be such that $p(m, x) = d$; (* d is preorder index of x *)
| station b_x broadcasts $\langle k \rangle$, where $k = key[b_x]$;
| each station a_j with $timer[a_j] = d$ listens and does:
| **if** $key[a_j] < k$ **then**
| | $timer[a_j] \leftarrow p(m, l(m, x))$; (* preorder index of left child of x *)
| **else**
| | $timer[a_j] \leftarrow p(m, r(m, x))$; (* preorder index of right child of x *)
| | $rank[a_j] \leftarrow x$;

Algorithm 1. Procedure Rank

procedure Merge($\langle a_1, \ldots, a_m \rangle$, $\langle b_1, \ldots, b_m \rangle$)
Rank($\langle a_1, \ldots, a_m \rangle$, $\langle b_1, \ldots, b_m \rangle$);
Rank($\langle b_1, \ldots, b_m \rangle$, $\langle a_1, \ldots, a_m \rangle$);
All stations a_i and b_i do: $idx[a_i] \leftarrow i + rank[a_i]$; $idx[b_i] \leftarrow i + rank[b_i]$;
(* for $1 \leq i \leq m$ let $c_i = a_i$ and $c_{m+i} = b_i$ *)
for *time slot* $t \leftarrow 1$ *to* $2m$ **do**
| station c_i with $idx[c_i] = t$ broadcasts $\langle k \rangle$, where $k = key[c_i]$;
| station c_t listens and does: $new[c_t] \leftarrow k$;
Each station c_i does: $key[c_i] \leftarrow new[c_i]$;

Algorithm 2. Procedure Merge

$b_1, \ldots b_m \rangle$. Procedure Rank (see Algorithm 1) computes the rank of each element of the first sequence in the second sequence. (By the *rank* of a_i in $\langle b_1, \ldots, b_m \rangle$ we mean the number of elements b_j with $key[b_j] < key[a_i]$.) The result of Rank for each a_i is in $rank[a_i]$. Note that it is a parallel implementation of the classical bisection algorithm, where each station a_i predicts when its next bisecting key will be broadcast by some b_j. The bisecting keys are broadcast in appropriate order, since in *preorder* each key is preceded by all the keys from the higher levels of T_m. The time of Rank is m slots. The energetic cost of broadcasting is 1. (Each b_i broadcasts once.) The energetic cost of listening is $\lceil \lg(m + 1) \rceil$, since each a_i listens at most once at each level of T_m. Rank can be used for merging two sorted sequences as in the procedure Merge (Algorithm 2). The time of Merge($\langle a_1, \ldots, a_m \rangle$, $\langle b_1, \ldots, b_m \rangle$) is $4m$. The energetic cost of listening is $\lceil \lg(m + 1) \rceil + 1$. (Each station listens at most $\lceil \lg(m + 1) \rceil$ times in one of the Rank procedures and once in the "for" loop.) The energetic cost of broadcasting is 2: Each station broadcasts at most twice (in one of the Rank procedures and in the "for" loop). Thus the total energetic cost is $\lceil \lg(m + 1) \rceil + 3$. (This could be compared to the time $\approx 2 \cdot m \lg m$ and energetic cost $\approx 2 \lg m$ of merging procedures obtained by the transformation of Batcher merging comparator networks [2].) Note that the algorithm is correct: The key $key[a_i]$ is preceded by $idx[a_i] - 1 = i - 1 + rank[a_i]$ keys in the sorted sequence of keys from both sequences. (The same holds for each $key[b_i]$.) Since the keys are pairwise distinct, no two elements c_i have the same $idx[c_i]$ and there are no transmission collisions in the "for" loop.

2.1 Reducing the Asymptotic Energetic Cost of Merging to $O(\lg^* m)$

We reduce the asymptotic energetic cost of listening. Instead of computing the ranks of each a_i in $\langle b_1, \ldots, b_m \rangle$, we first compute the ranks of some stations b_j (*b-splitters*) in $\langle a_1, \ldots, a_m \rangle$. The b-splitters split the sequence $\langle b_1, \ldots, b_m \rangle$ into blocks (*b-blocks*) of size $h(m, 1)$. The energetic cost of computing the rank of each b-splitter is balanced among all stations in its b-block. Then the stations $a_1, \ldots, a_m$ are grouped so that the stations of each group are ranked in separate b-block. Then we split $\langle a_1, \ldots, a_m \rangle$ into a-blocks of size $h(m, 2)$ which compute the rank of their a-splitters (it is enough, to find the rank of a-splitter in its corresponding b-block) and regroup the stations $b_1, \ldots, b_m$ into separate a-blocks. We iterate this procedure while the sizes of the blocks decrease rapidly. We define an auxiliary procedure Regroup (see Algorithm 3)Let $g(m, i) = \lceil \frac{m}{h(m,i)} \rceil$ and $\alpha(m, i, j, k) = (j - 1) \cdot h(m, i) + k$. By $c_{i,j,k}$ and $d_{i-1,j,k}$ we denote the stations from $\{a_1, \ldots, a_m\}$ and $\{b_1, \ldots, b_m\}$ as follows. For $1 \le k \le h(m, i)$:

$$c_{i,j,k} = \begin{cases} a_{\alpha(m,i,j,k)} & \text{if } \alpha(m, i, j, k) \le m, \\ b_{\alpha(m,i,j,k)-m} & \text{if } \alpha(m, i, j, k) > m. \end{cases}$$

For $1 \le k \le h(m, i-1)$: for $\alpha(m, i-1, j, k) \le m$, let $d_{i-1,j,k} = b_{\alpha(m,i-1,j,k)}$ and, for $\alpha(m, i-1, j, k) > m$, $d_{i,j,k}$ does not exist (it is treated as if $key[d_{i,j,k}] = +\infty$).

For $1 \le j \le g(m, i)$, $c_{i,j,1}$ is jth *a-splitter* and, for $k > 1$, $c_{i,j,k}$ is a *slave* of $c_{i,j,1}$. For parameter $i > 1$, we assume that the stations $a_1, \ldots a_m$ are grouped between the b-splitters $d_{i-1,1,1}, \ldots, d_{i-1,g(m,i-1),1}$ as follows. For any a_l and $j = group[a_l]$:

- If $1 \le j \le g(m, i - 1) - 1$ then $key[d_{i-1,j,1}] < key[a_l] < key[d_{i-1,j+1,1}]$.
- If $j = 0$ then $key[a_l] < key[b_1]$. (Note that $b_1 = d_{i-1,1,1}$)
- If $j = g(m, i - 1)$, then $key[a_l] > key[d_{i-1,g(m,i-1),1}]$.

Note that, for parameter $i = 1$, we do not have any assumptions. In this case $g(m, i - 1) = 1$ and each a_l has $group[a_l] = 1$. The task of Regroup is grouping of the stations $b_1, \ldots, b_m$ between the splitters $c_{i,1,1}, \ldots, c_{i,g(m,i),1}$.

We divide the code into fragments (*phases*) and analyze each phase separately. Each station has a *clock* variable t, that is increased after each time slot. In Phase 1 the rank of each splitter $c_{i,j,1}$ in $\langle b_1, \ldots, b_m \rangle$ is computed. Each splitter $d_{i-1,j',1}$ together with its slaves forms a binary tree $T_{h(m,i-1)}$. These trees are scanned level by level: first all the nodes of all the trees at level 1 (i.e. roots), then all the nodes of all the trees at level 2, and so on. The number of levels (the height of $T_{h(m,i-1)}$) is $h(m, i)$. To compute the rank of $c_{i,j,1}$ we have to consider only the tree corresponding to $group[c_{i,j,1}]$. At level l each station listens at most once and corrects its $rank'$ and $timer$. (The new value of $timer$ is either NIL or *preorder* index of some $b_{i'}$ on the next level.) Between the levels l and $l + 1$, after all stations $b_{i'}$ on level l in all

procedure Regroup(i, $\langle a_1, \ldots, a_m \rangle$, $\langle b_1, \ldots, b_m \rangle$)
(* Phase 1 *)
Each station $c_{i,j,1}$ does: **begin**
   | $group'[c_{i,j,1}] \leftarrow group[c_{i,j,1}]$; $key'[c_{i,j,1}] \leftarrow key[c_{i,j,1}]$; $timer[c_{i,j,1}] \leftarrow 1$;
   | $rank'[c_{i,j,1}] \leftarrow 0$;
end
for $l \leftarrow 1$ **to** $h(m, i)$ **do**
   | (* l denotes level in $T_{h(m,i-1)}$ *)
   | **for** $v \leftarrow 2^{l-1}$ **to** $\min\{2^l - 1, h(m, i-1)\}$ **do**
   | | (* v – preorder index on level l *)
   | | let x be such that $p(h(m, i-1), x) = v$;
   | | **for** $g \leftarrow 1$ **to** $g(m, i-1)$ **do**
   | | | $d_{i-1,g,x}$ (if exists) broadcasts $\langle k' \rangle$, where $k' = key[d_{i-1,g,x}]$;
   | | | Each $c_{i,j,l}$ with $group'[c_{i,j,l}] = g$ and $timer[c_{i,j,l}] = v$ listens and
   | | | does:
   | | | **if** *there was no message or* $key'[c_{i,j,l}] < k'$ **then**
   | | | |_ $timer[c_{i,j,l}] \leftarrow p(h(m, i-1), l(h(m, i-1), x))$;
   | | | **else**
   | | | | $timer[c_{i,j,l}] \leftarrow p(h(m, i-1), r(h(m, i-1), x))$;
   | | | |_ $rank'[c_{i,j,l}] \leftarrow \alpha(m, i-1, g, x)$; (* index of $d_{i-1,g,x}$ *)
   | | |_ all stations increase clock t;
   | | **if** $l < h(m, i)$ **then**
   | | | (* not last level – TRANSFER TO THE NEXT SLAVES *)
   | | | **for** $j \leftarrow 1$ *to* $g(m, i)$ **do**
   | | | | $c_{i,j,l}$ broadcasts $\langle t', r', g, k' \rangle$ where $t' = timer[c_{i,j,l}]$, $r' = rank'[c_{i,j,l}]$,
   | | | | $g = group'[c_{i,j,l}]$, and $k' = key'[c_{i,j,l}]$;
   | | | | $c_{i,j,l+1}$ listens and does: **begin**
   | | | | | $timer[c_{i,j,l+1}] \leftarrow t'$; $rank'[c_{i,j,l+1}] \leftarrow r'$; $group'[c_{i,j,l+1}] \leftarrow g$;
   | | | | | $key'[c_{i,j,l+1}] \leftarrow k'$;
   | | | | **end**
   | | |_ |_ all stations increase clock t;
(* Phase 2 *)
Each station $c_{i,j,1}$ does: $winner[c_{i,j,1}] \leftarrow TRUE$;
for $j \leftarrow 1$ *to* $g(m, i)$ **do**
   | $c_{i,j,h(m,i)}$ broadcasts $\langle r' \rangle$ where $r' = rank'[c_{i,j,h(m,i)}]$;
   | $c_{i,j,1}$ and (if $j > 1$) $c_{i,j-1,1}$ listen;
   | $c_{i,j,1}$ does $rank[c_{i,j,1}] \leftarrow r'$;
   | $c_{i,j-1,1}$ (if exists) does: if $rank[c_{i,j-1,1}] = r'$ **then**
   | $winner[c_{i,j-1,1}] \leftarrow FALSE$;
   |_ all stations increase clock t;
(* Phase 3 *)
Each station b_l does: if $l = 1$ **then** $group[b_l] \leftarrow 0$ **else** $group[b_l] \leftarrow NIL$;
for $l \leftarrow 1$ **to** m **do**
   | **if** *exists* $c_{i,j,1}$ *with* $winner[c_{i,j,1}] = TRUE$ *and* $rank[c_{i,j,1}] = l - 1$ **then**
   | |_ $c_{i,j,1}$ broadcasts $\langle j \rangle$;
   | b_l listens and does: **if** *there was a message* **then** b_l does $group[b_l] \leftarrow j$;
   |_ all stations increase clock t;
(* Phase 4 *)
for $l \leftarrow 1$ **to** $m - 1$ **do**
   | b_l broadcasts $\langle g \rangle$ where $g = group[b_l]$;
   | **if** $group[b_{l+1}] = NIL$ **then** b_{l+1} listens and does: $group[b_{l+1}] \leftarrow g$;
   |_ all stations increase clock t;

Algorithm 3. Procedure Regroup

the trees have broadcast their messages, the collected information and the task of further computation is transferred from each $c_{i,j,l}$ to the next slave $c_{i,j,l+1}$. The time slot of this transfer is known in advance, since the size of each level is known. The time of Phase 1 is $O(m)$ since the number of all stations $c_{i,j,k}$ and $d_{i-1,j',k'}$ is $O(m)$ and in each time slot a different one of them broadcasts. The energetic cost is $O(1)$, since each $c_{i,j,k}$ listens once and broadcasts once and each $d_{i-1,j',k'}$ broadcasts once. After Phase 1 each $c_{i,j,h(m,i)}$ stores in $rank'[c_{i,j,h(m,i)}]$ the rank of $c_{i,j,1}$ in $\langle b_1, \ldots, b_m \rangle$. (The value $rank'[c_{i,j,1}]$ is deliberately initiated to 0 at the beginning of Phase 1: If $i > 1$ and $group[c_{i,j,1}] \geq 1$ then $key[c_{i,j,1}]$ is compared to at least one lesser key, since $key[d_{i-1,group[c_{i,j,1}],1}] < key[c_{i,j,1}]$. If $i = 1$ or $group[c_{i,j,1}] = 0$, this ensures that we do not start with too large $rank'[c_{i,j,1}]$.) In Phase 2 each splitter $c_{i,j,1}$ learns its rank and computes Boolean value $winner[c_{i,j,1}]$. A splitter $c_{i,j,1}$ is a $winner$ if it is the last splitter with given $rank$. Time of Phase 2 is $g(m,i)$ and energetic cost is $O(1)$. In Phase 3 each winner $c_{i,j,1}$ informs its successor b' in $\langle b_1, \ldots b_m \rangle$ about its block number j (i.e. new group number for b'). The uninformed stations b_l with $l > 1$ end up with $group[b_l] = NIL$. (b_1 ends up with $group[b_1] = 0$ or higher.) The time of Phase 3 is m and energetic cost is $O(1)$. In Phase 4 each b_l with $group[b_l] = NIL$ learns its proper group number from its predecessor. After Phase 4 each station b_l with $group[b_l] = j$, knows that it is ranked somewhere between $c_{i,j,1}$ and $c_{i,j+1,1}$. The time of Phase 4 is $m - 1$ and energetic cost is $O(1)$. The time of Regroup is $O(m)$ and the energetic cost is $O(1)$, since the time of each phase is $O(m)$ and energetic cost of each phase is $O(1)$.

---

procedure Rank'($\langle a_1, \ldots, a_m \rangle$, $\langle b_1, \ldots, b_m \rangle$)
if $m \geq 2$ **then**
 Each a_i does: $group[a_i] \leftarrow 1$;
 for $i \leftarrow 1$ **to** $\lceil l^*(m)/2 \rceil + 1$ **do**
  Regroup($2i - 1$, $\langle a_1, \ldots, a_m \rangle$, $\langle b_1, \ldots, b_m \rangle$);
  Regroup($2i$, $\langle b_1, \ldots, b_m \rangle$, $\langle a_1, \ldots, a_m \rangle$);
 (* RANK EACH b_j IN $\langle a_1, \ldots, a_m \rangle$ *)
 Each station b_j does: $rank[b_j] \leftarrow 0$;
 for $i \leftarrow 1$ **to** m **do**
  a_i broadcasts $\langle k \rangle$, where $k = key[a_i]$;
  each b_j with $group[b_j] = \lceil i/2 \rceil$ listens and does:
  if $k' < key[b_j]$ **then** $rank[b_j] \leftarrow i$;
  all stations increase clock t;
 DO SYMMETRICAL RANKING OF EACH a_j IN $\langle b_1, \ldots, b_m \rangle$
else a_1 and b_1 simply compare-exchange their keys

Algorithm 4. Procedure Rank'

We apply Regroup in the procedure Rank' (Algorithm 4) that ranks two sorted sequences of length m in each other in time $O(m \lg^* m)$ with energetic cost $O(\lg^* m)$. Note that in the last iteration of the first "for" loop we have $h(m, 2i - 1) =$

$h(m, 2i) = 2$. Thus we only need to rank each element in a block of size 2 of the other sequence. The number of iterations of the first "for" loop is $O(\lg^* m)$, and hence the time of it is $O(m \lg^* m)$ and the energetic cost is $O(\lg^* m)$. The time of the remaining part is $O(m)$ and energetic cost is $O(1)$. By replacing both invocations of Rank in Merge by a single Rank'($\langle a_1, \ldots, a_m \rangle$, $\langle b_1, \ldots, b_m \rangle$), we obtain an algorithm merging in time $O(m \lg^* m)$ with energetic cost (of both listening and broadcasting) $O(\lg^* m)$.

3   Merge-Sort

For simplicity, we assume that $n = 2^k$ for some positive integer k. The stations $c_1, \ldots, c_n$ contain initially unsorted sequence of keys $\langle key[c_1], \ldots, key[c_n] \rangle$. Merge-Sort (Algorithm 5) sorts the sequence stored in the network. Assume that we apply the first of the described merging algorithms. The time for merging two sequences of length $n/2$ is $4n/2 = 2n$. On the next level of recursion we have to merge two pairs of sequences of length $n/4$ in time $2 \cdot 4n/4 = 2n$. And so on. The number of levels is $\lg n$, thus the total sorting time is $2n \lg n$. The energetic cost is $\sum_{l=0}^{k-1}(\lceil \lg(2^l + 1) \rceil + 3) = \frac{1}{2} \lg^2 n + \frac{7}{2} \lg n$. For example, for $n = 2^{13} = 8192$, the bounds on time and energetic cost are 212992 and 130, respectively. If we apply the second merging algorithm, then the time of Merge-sort is $O(n \lg n \lg^* n)$ and the energetic cost of listening and broadcasting is $O(\lg n \lg^* n)$.

> **procedure** Merge-Sort($\langle c_1, \ldots, c_n \rangle$)
> **if** $m > 1$ **then**
> > Merge-Sort($\langle c_1, \ldots, c_{n/2} \rangle$)
> > Merge-Sort($\langle c_{n/2+1}, \ldots, c_n \rangle$)
> > Merge($\langle c_1, \ldots, c_{n/2} \rangle, \langle c_{n/2+1}, \ldots, c_n \rangle$)

Algorithm 5. Procedure Merge-Sort

Remark: The presented algorithms can be parallelized and accelerated $\Omega(k)$ times if we use k channels instead of one, where k is $O(\sqrt{n})$.

Acknowledgment. I would like to thank Mirosław Kutyłowski for helpful comments.

References

1. Ajtai, M., Komlós, J., and Szemerédi, E.: Sorting in $c \log n$ Parallel Steps. Combinatorica **3** (1983) 1–19
2. Batcher, K.E.: Sorting Networks and Their Applications. Proceedings of 32nd AFIPS (1968) 307–314
3. Blum., M., Floyd, R.W., Pratt, V., Rivest, R.L., and Tarjan, R.E.: Time Bounds for Selection. Journal of Computer System Sciences **7** 4 (1973) 448–461

4. Cormen, Th.H., Leiserson, Ch.E., and Rivest,R,L,: Introduction to Algorithms (1994)

5. Jurdziński, T., Kutyłowski, M., and Zatopiański, J.: Efficient Algorithms for Leader Election in Radio Networks. ACM PODC'2002, ACM Press, 51–57

6. Jurdziński, T., and Kutyłowski, M., and Zatopiański, J.: Energy-Efficient Size Approximation for Radio Networks with No Collision Detection. COCOON'2002, LNCS **2387**, Springer Verlag, Berlin (2002) 279–289

7. Kutyłowski, M., and Letkiewicz, D.: Computing Average Value in Ad Hoc Networks. MFCS'2003, LNCS **2747**, Springer Verlag, Berlin (2003) 511-520

8. Nakano, K., and Olariu, S.: Efficient Initialization Protocols for Radio Networks with No Collision Detection. ICPP 2000, IEEE Computer Society Press: New York (2000) 263–270

9. Nakano, K., Olariu, S.: Broadcast-Efficient Protocols for Mobile Radio Networks with Few Channels. IEEE Transactions on Parallel and Distributed Systems **10** (1999) 1276–1289

10. Singh, M., and Prasanna, V.K.: Optimal Energy Balanced Algorithm for Selection in Single Hop Sensor Network. SNPA ICC, May 2003

11. Singh, M., and Prasanna, V.K.: Energy-Optimal and Energy-Balanced Sorting in a Single-Hop Sensor Network. PERCOM, March 2003

12. Compendium of Large-Scale Optimization Problems. (DELIS, Subproject 3). http://ru1.cti.gr/delis-sp3/

On Optimal and Efficient in Place Merging

Pok-Son Kim[1,*] and Arne Kutzner[2]

[1] Kookmin University, Department of Mathematics, Seoul 136-702, Rep. of Korea
pskim@kookmin.ac.kr
[2] Seokyeong University, Department of E-Business, Seoul 136-704, Rep. of Korea
kutzner@skuniv.ac.kr

Abstract. We introduce a new stable in place merging algorithm that needs $O(m \log(\frac{n}{m}+1))$ comparisons and $O(m+n)$ assignments. According to the lower bounds for merging our algorithm is asymptotically optimal regarding the number of comparisons as well as assignments. The stable algorithm is developed in a modular style out of an unstable kernel for which we give a definition in pseudocode.

The literature so far describes several similar algorithms but merely as sophisticated theoretical models without any reasoning about their practical value. We report specific benchmarks and show that our algorithm is for almost all input sequences faster than the efficient minimum storage algorithm by Dudzinski and Dydek. The proposed algorithm can be effectively used in practice.

1 Introduction

Merging denotes the operation of rearranging the elements of two adjacent sorted sequences of size m and n, so that the result forms one sorted sequence of $m + n$ elements. An algorithm merges two sequences *in place* when it needs $O(1)$ bits additional space. It is regarded as *stable*, if it preserves the initial ordering of elements with equal value.

There are two significant lower bounds for merging. The lower bound for the number of assignments is $m + n$ because every element of the input sequences can change its position in the sorted output. As shown by Knuth in [1] the lower bound for the number of comparisons is $\Omega(m \log(\frac{n}{m} + 1))$, where $m \leq n$.

So far there are three publications about optimal stable in place merging. The work of Symvonis [2] shows how to get an optimal algorithm by combining several given concepts but contains no information about the involved asymptotic constants or implementation aspects. Geffert et. all present in [3] a rather complex algorithm together with its asymptotic constants, but there are no notes regarding any successful implementation or benchmarking. Chen [4] simplified Geffert's algorithm for the price of slightly worse asymptotic constants but also without any remarks about a concrete implementation. All three publications have some resemblance. They take the algorithm from Mannila and

* This work was supported by the Kookmin University research grant in 2005.

Ukkonen [5] as starting point, rely on the concept of an internal buffer introduced by Kronrod in [6] and develop a stable algorithm out of an unstable one. We will follow this path but with the focus on an improved stable algorithm as well as concrete benchmarking. The proposed stable algorithm can be effectively used in practice as shown by the fact that it can compete with the algorithm of Dudzinski and Dydek [7] that is used as foundation of the `merge_without_buffer` function contained in the C++ Standard Template Libraries (STL) [8].

Significant older works in the area of in place merging are the publications of Pardo [9], Salowe and Steiger [10] and Huang and Langston [11]. All algorithms introduced there are asymptotically optimal regarding the number of assignments, but lack in meeting the lower bound for comparisons. Another class of merging algorithms are the *minimum storage* algorithms presented in [7] and [12] which both rely on $O(\log^2(m+n))$ bits of extra storage. The latter two algorithms are effective in practice and simply structured, but they are not asymptotically optimal regarding the number of assignments.

We will begin with the introduction of our notation and some toolbox algorithms, followed by the presentation of an unstable core algorithm. Afterwards the unstable core algorithm is extended to an unstable in place algorithm which in turn is extended to a stable in place algorithm. We will report some benchmarks and finish with a short conclusion.

2   Notation/Algorithm Toolbox

We now introduce some notations that we will use throughout the paper. Let u and v two ascending sorted sequences. We define $u \leq v$ ($u < v$) iff. $x \leq y$ ($x < y$) for all elements $x \in u$ and for all elements $y \in v$. $|u|$ denotes the size of the sequence u. Unless stated otherwise, m and n ($m \leq n$) are the sizes of two input sequences u and v respectively.

Table 1. Complexity of the Toolbox-Algorithms

Algorithm	Arguments	Comparisons	Assignments
Hwang and Lin	u, v with $|u| \leq |v|$ let $m = |u|, n = |v|$	$m(t+1) + n/2^t$ where $t = \lfloor \log(n/m) \rfloor$	
(1) - ext. buffer (2) - m rotat.			$2m + n$ $n + m^2 + m$
Block Swapping	u, v with $|u| = |v|$	-	$3|u|$
Floating Hole	u, v with $|u| = |v|$ (element x is in front of u)	-	$2(|u| + 1)$
Block Rotation	u, v	-	$|u| + |v| + \gcd(|u|, |v|)$ $\leq 2(|u| + |v|)$
Binary Search	u, x (searched element)	$\lfloor \log |u| \rfloor + 1$	-
Insertion Sort	u, let $m = |u|$	$\frac{m(m-1)}{2} + (m-1)$	$\frac{m(m+1)}{2} - 1$

We will use six other algorithms as subcomponents. We now briefly introduce these algorithms and their complexity (A summary is given in Tab. 1):

(1) *Hwang and Lin* [13] introduced a merging-algorithm that is optimal regarding the number of comparisons as well as assignments. Unfortunately their algorithm is not in-place, it relies on an external buffer of size m when the merging shall be achieved by applying a linear number of assignments only. The algorithm granulates the longer input sequence into segments of size $2^{\lfloor \log(n/m) \rfloor}$ and uses a smart combination of a sequential search together with several binary searches for staying asymptotically optimal regarding the number of comparisons. Hwang and Lin's algorithm can be modified so that it works in place, but for the price of m^2 assignments. The modified form avoids the usage of an external buffer by using repeated rotations instead. Geffert et al. give a detailed description of that variant in [3].

(2) *Block Swapping* denotes the operation of exchanging the contents of two (not necessarily adjacent) blocks u and v with $|u| = |v|$. *Floating Hole* denotes a technique that can sometimes be applied in order to reduce the number of assignments necessary for achieving a block rearrangement. In our algorithms we will have to accomplish a rearrangement from $\ldots x u \, p \, v \ldots$ to $\ldots v x \, p \, u \ldots$, where x is a single element, u and v are blocks of equal size and p is some arbitrary subsequence. [3] gives a detailed description for both operations and their complexity.

(3) Let u and v be two adjacent blocks of not necessarily equal size. The circular rearrangement from $\ldots u v \ldots$ to $\ldots v u \ldots$, is called a *Block Rotation*. If we have an intermediate storage of one element only we need at least $|u| + |v| + \gcd(|u|, |v|)$ assignments for accomplishing a block rotation. Here $\gcd(a, b)$ denotes the greatest common divisor of two positive integers. An algorithm that meets this lower bound is presented in [7].

(4) *Binary Search* and *Insertion-Sort* are two standard algorithms described in almost all introducing literature about algorithms (e.g. [14]).

3 The Core Algorithm

We now give the definition of our unstable core algorithm that relies on extra storage of size $\lfloor \sqrt{m} \rfloor$ for local merges.

Algorithm 1: UNSTABLE-CORE-MERGE

Let $k = \lfloor \sqrt{m} \rfloor$ and $l = \lfloor m/k \rfloor$. We granulate the sequence u into blocks $u_0 u_1 \ldots u_l$, so that all blocks u_i with $0 < i \leq l$ have size k. The first block u_0 gets the size $m - l * k$. (u_0 is empty in the case $l * k = m$). Let $u_i = b_i x_i$ for all i ($0 \leq i \leq l$), where x_i corresponds to the last element of u_i. If u_0 is empty, then b_0 and x_0 are empty as well. We separate the sequence v into $l + 2$ sections $v = v_0 v_1 \ldots v_l v_{l+1}$ using the x_i ($0 \leq i \leq l$), so that we get for all i: $v_i < x_i \leq v_{i+1}$. Using these granulations of v and u we rearrange our input sequences to $b_0 v_0 x_0 b_1 v_1 x_1 \ldots b_l v_l x_l v_{l+1}$. Eventually we get the desired sorted result by local merging of all pairs $b_i v_i$ ($0 \leq i \leq l$). Please note that all x_i are at their final position after the rearrangement-step and do not need to be part of the local merges.

Algorithm 1. Unstable Core Algorithm

UNSTABLE-CORE-MERGE($A, first1, first2, last$)

```
 1   ▷ u is in A[first1 : first2 − 1], v is in A[first2 : last − 1]
 2   m ← first2 − first1; k ← ⌊sqrt(m)⌋; delta ← 0;
 3   if m mod k = 0
 4      then blockEnd ← first1 + k
 5      else blockEnd ← first1 + (m mod k)
 6
 7   while true
 8      do ▷ Processing of the current minimal block
 9         b ← BINARY-SEARCH(A, first2, last, A[blockEnd − 1])
10         to ← b − (first2 − blockEnd)
11         if to > first2
12            then BLOCK-ROTATION(A, blockEnd − 1, first2, b)
13            else FLOATING-HOLE(A, blockEnd, first2, b − first2)
14               delta ← (b − first2 + delta) mod k
15         HWANG-AND-LIN(A, first1, blockEnd − 1, to − 1)
16         first2 ← b; first1 ← to
17         if first1 ≥ first2
18            then break ▷ No more blocks to be placed - leave the while-loop
19
20         ▷ Search the next minimal block
21         t ← first1 + k − delta; e ← first2 − delta
22         if delta > 0
23            then startMin ← SEARCH-MINIMAL-BLOCK(A, k, t, e, e)
24            else startMin ← SEARCH-MINIMAL-BLOCK(A, k, t, e, first1)
25               t ← first1
26
27         ▷ Move the minimal block to the front of sequence q
28         if startMin = e
29            then BLOCK-SWAP(A, t, e, delta)
30               BLOCK-ROTATION(A, first1, t, first1 + k)
31            else BLOCK-SWAP(A, t, startMin, k)
32               BLOCK-ROTATION(A, first1, t, t + k)
33         blockEnd ← first1 + k
```

In order to keep the optimality the rearrangement must be achieved by applying a linear number of assignments only. The following technique can be used to do so. It is similar to the following method described by Mannila and Ukkonen in [5]:

The rearrangement happens in a sequential style, it starts with block u_0 (u_1 if u_0 is empty) and continues by placing the blocks in increasing order one by one. During the rearrangement all unprocessed blocks, this means blocks that are not moved to their final position, stay together as a group, but we allow that these blocks become interleaved and rotated as a complete segment.

Let us now assume that we have already successfully processed all blocks $u_0 \ldots u_j$ with $(0 \leq j < l)$. Then we have some sequence $p \; q \; v_{j+1} \ldots v_{l+1}$, where $p = b_0 v_0 x_0 b_1 v_1 x_1 \ldots b_j v_j x_j$ contains all blocks already processed and $q = c'' u_1' \ldots u_{l-j-1}' c'$ comprises the unprocessed blocks $u_{j+1} \ldots u_l$ in some interleaved form. Additionally, due to the rotation, one unprocessed block can be split into two parts, this is $c'c''$. To place the next block u_{j+1}, we have first to find the position of that block in q. Due to the increasing order of the elements in u, we have to find the block with the smallest elements in order to find b_{j+1}. We can do so by looking for the block with the smallest first and last element. Depending on the result of this search, we have to distinguish two different cases:

(*Case 1.*) The minimal block is $c'c''$: We split u_1' into $d'd''$, so that $|d'| = |c'|$ and $|d''| = |c''|$. Then we exchange c' and d' in order to get $q = c'' c' d'' u_2' \ldots u_{l-j-1}' d'$. Afterwards we rotate $c'' c'$ to $c' c''$ and get $q = u_{j+1} d'' u_2' \ldots u_{l-j-1}' d'$.

(*Case 2.*) The minimal block is in $u_1' \ldots u_{l-j-1}'$, let u_i' $(1 \leq i < l - j)$ be the minimal block. Then we exchange u_1' and u_i' in order to get $q = c'' u_i' u_2' \ldots u_1' \ldots u_{l-j-1}' c'$. Afterwards we rotate $c'' u_i'$ to $u_i' c''$ and get $q = u_{j+1} c'' u_2' \ldots u_1' \ldots u_{l-j-1}' c'$.

Hence, after moving u_{j+1} to the front position we have some sequence $p \; b_{j+1} x_{j+1} q' v_{j+1} \ldots v_{l+1}$ $(q = b_{j+1} x_{j+1} q')$. Now we will move v_{j+1} to its final position just in front of x_{j+1}. Once more we have to distinguish two cases:

(*Case 1.*) $|v_{j+1}| \geq |q'|$: We use a rotation in order to get $v_{j+1} x_{j+1} q'$ out of $x_{j+1} q' v_{j+1}$.

(*Case 2.*) $|v_{j+1}| < |q'|$: We split q' into $q_1' q_2'$ so that $|q_1'| = |v_{j+1}|$ and use a floating-hole operation to get $v_{j+1} x_{j+1} q_2' q_1'$ out of $x_{j+1} q_1' q_2' v_{j+1}$. Please note that $q_1' q_2'$ is a rotated form of q' merely.

Table 2. Pseudocode Definitions of the Toolbox Algorithms

Pseudocode Definition	Description of the Arguments
Hwang-And-Lin$(A, first1, first2, last)$	u is in $A[first1 : first2 - 1]$, v is in $A[first2 : last - 1]$
BSearch$(A, first, last, x)$	delivers the position of the **first** occurrence of x in $A[first : last-1]$
Block-Swap$(A, pos1, pos2, len)$	u is in $A[pos1 : pos1 + len]$, v is in $A[pos2 : pos2 + len]$
Floating-Hole$(A, pos1, pos2, len)$	u, v as in Block-Swap, element x in $A[pos - 1]$
Block-Rotate$(A, first1, first2, last)$	u, v as in Hwang-And-Lin

Alg. 1 gives an implementation for the Unstable-Core-Merge algorithm in pseudocode. Table 2 comprises the pseudocode definitions for all toolbox algorithms. The pseudocode conventions are taken from [14].

Theorem 1. *The* UNSTABLE-CORE-MERGE *algorithm needs* $O(m \log(\frac{n}{m} + 1))$ *comparisons and* $O(m + n)$ *assignments.*

Proof. The $l + 1$ calls of Hwang and Lin's algorithm need less than $\Sigma_{i=0}^{l}(q_i \log(\frac{p_i}{q_i} + 1)) + q_i = O(m \log(\frac{n}{m} + 1))$ comparisons and $\Sigma_{i=0}^{l}(2q_i + p_i) \leq 2m + n$ assignments, where $p_i = \max\{|u_i|, |v_i|\}$ and $q_i = \min\{|u_i|, |v_i|\}$. Further, since $\lfloor \sqrt{m} \rfloor (\lfloor \log n \rfloor + 1) \leq \sqrt{m}(\log n + 1) = m \cdot \frac{\log n}{\sqrt{m}} + \sqrt{m} \leq m \cdot (\log n - \log m) + \sqrt{m} = O(m \log \frac{n}{m})$, the $l+1$ calls of the binary search need $O(m \log(\frac{n}{m} + 1))$ comparisons. The l searches of the minimal block consume $\Sigma_{i=1}^{l} 2i \leq m + \sqrt{m} \leq 2m$ comparisons. The l extractions of the minimal block need $l(7k) \leq 7m$ assignments. The $l + 1$ movements of the minimal block need less than $\Sigma_{i=0}^{l} 4|v_i| \leq 4n$ assignments. So, altogether we have $O(m \log(\frac{n}{m} + 1))$ comparisons and $O(m + n)$ assignments. $\qquad\square$

3.1 Extending the Core Algorithm to an Unstable in Place Algorithm

The UNSTABLE-CORE-MERGE algorithm is asymptotically optimal, but it demands an extra storage of size $O(\lfloor \sqrt{m} \rfloor)$. We will now apply a technique called *internal buffer* for reducing the necessary extra storage to $O(1)$. The notion internal buffer is due to Kronrod and was first proposed in [6]. The basic idea is to use some particular area of the input sequences repeatedly as buffer and to accept that the area elements are disordered by this usage. At the end the internal buffer is sorted by applying some sorting algorithm and afterwards the buffer elements are merged by some way. Using this approach we now derive an unstable in-place algorithm from our core algorithm:

Algorithm 2: UNSTABLE-IN-PLACE-MERGE (u, v)
We split the input sequence u into $u_1 u_2$ so that $|u_1| = \lfloor \sqrt{m} \rfloor$. Let x be the last element of u_1. By applying a binary search we separate v into $v_1 v_2$, so that $v_1 < x \leq v_2$. We rearrange $u_1 u_2 v_1 v_2$ to $u_1 v_1 u_2 v_2$ using a block rotation. Then we merge u_2 and v_2 using the UNSTABLE-CORE-MERGE algorithm (Alg. 1), where the embedded calls of Hwang and Lin's algorithm use the segment u_1 as buffer area. Because the elements of u_1 can be disordered during the last step, we afterwards sort them using Insertion-Sort. Finally we use the rotation based variant of Hwang and Lin's algorithm for merging the two segments u_1 and v_1.

Theorem 2. *The* UNSTABLE-IN-PLACE-MERGE *algorithm needs* $O(m \log(\frac{n}{m} + 1))$ *comparisons and* $O(m + n)$ *assignments.*

Proof. We have simply to count the additional operations. The unique additional binary search and call of Hwang and Lin's algorithm trivially doesn't change the asymptotic number of comparisons. Hwang and Lin's call poses $|v_1| + |u_1|^2 + |u_1| = O(m + n)$ additional assignments. The final insertion sort needs $O(m)$ comparisons as well as assignments (see Table 1). So altogether the algorithm performs $O(m \log(\frac{n}{m} + 1))$ comparisons and $O(m + n)$ assignments. $\qquad\square$

A merging algorithm is called *semi-stable* when it preserves the initial ordering of equal elements of at least one of either input-sequences. It is easy to check that none of the applications of toolbox algorithms in UNSTABLE-IN-PLACE-MERGE changes the initial ordering of equal elements in v.

Corollary 1. UNSTABLE-IN-PLACE-MERGE *is semi-stable.*

4 Deriving a Stable in Place Algorithm

The lack of stability in UNSTABLE-IN-PLACE-MERGE is caused (1) by the block extraction in the lines 27-32 of Alg. 1 and (2) the usage of the first elements $\lfloor \sqrt{m} \rfloor$ of u as internal buffer. The block extraction raises stability-problems because there might be two blocks containing equal elements. Such two blocks can't be distinguished during the search of the minimal block and so we can't reconstruct their initial order. We will fix these problems as follows:

We extract $2 \lfloor \sqrt{m} \rfloor$ *distinct* elements out of u and create 2 buffers of size $\lfloor \sqrt{m} \rfloor$ by moving these elements to the front of u. Please note that we can disorder and afterwards sort these buffers without losing stability. The first buffer will be used by the embedded calls of Hwang and Lin's algorithm, the second buffer will be used to keep track of the order of unprocessed blocks in u. To keep track we will apply a technique called *movement imitation* that is described by Symvonis in [2]. Movement imitation means that we establish a 1-to-1 correspondence between elements of the movement imitation buffer (mi-buffer) and u-blocks as shown in Fig. 1. Each time when we change the order of the u-blocks during the processing or extraction of a minimal block, we imitate this reordering in the mi-buffer. Hence, we can find the minimal block by searching for the minimal element in the mi-buffer.

Algorithm 3: STABLE-IN-PLACE-MERGE (u, v)
We take the UNSTABLE-IN-PLACE-MERGE algorithm as basis and apply the following modifications:

(1) We start by extracting two buffers of size $\lfloor \sqrt{m} \rfloor$ (mi-buffer and buffer for local merges) at the beginning of u, where all buffer-elements are distinct. Such buffer extraction can happen by performing $O(m)$ comparisons and $O(m)$ assignments as described by Pardo in [9]. (2) We replace the search for the minimal block

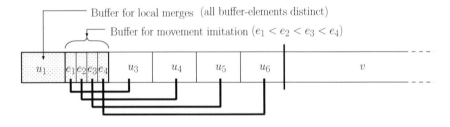

Fig. 1. Partitioning scheme (here for $|u| = 24$)

(lines 23-24 in Alg. 1) by a procedure using the mi-buffer. (3) Any u-block reordering must be imitated in the mi-Buffer. (4) We need a counter variable that counts the number of unprocessed blocks for maintaining the size of the mi-Buffer. (5) At the end we must sort and merge the two buffers extracted in the beginning, this replaces 2 corresponding tasks in the unstable algorithm.

Theorem 3. *The* STABLE-IN-PLACE-MERGE *algorithm needs* $O(m \log(\frac{n}{m} + 1))$ *comparisons and* $O(m + n)$ *assignments.*

Proof. We have to check the effect of all modifications applied to the unstable in place algorithm. The extraction of a buffer of size $2 \lfloor \sqrt{m} \rfloor$ in u needs $O(m)$ additional comparisons and $O(m)$ additional movements. The repeated search of the minimal block needs $\Sigma_{i=1}^{l} i \leq m$ comparisons. The management of the mi-buffer causes less than $l \cdot 2 \lfloor \sqrt{m} \rfloor \leq 2m$ assignments. For the final sorting and merging the same argumentation can be applied as in Theorem 2.   □

There might be the case that there are less than $2 \lfloor \sqrt{m} \rfloor$ distinct elements in u and so, due to the lack of a buffer of appropriate size, the above algorithm fails. In order to give a solution for this case we first slightly extend the rotation-based variant of Hwang and Lin's algorithm as follows:

Instead of directly inserting an element x as in the original algorithm, we first extract a maximal segment of elements equal to x by a simple linear search. Afterwards we treat this segment as one element. This extension causes m additional comparisons at most but allows us to express the number of necessary assignments depending on the number of different elements in u.

Lemma 1. *Let p and q two ascending sorted sequences with $p \leq q$. The rotation-based variant of Hwang-and-Lin's algorithm extended by the extraction of maximal segments of equal elements needs $2(\lambda|p| + |q|)$ many assignments at most, where λ is the number of distinct elements in p.*

Based on the above extension we handle the case of too few distinct elements as follows:

Let us assume that we could extract a buffer of λ distinct elements, where $\lambda < 2 \lfloor \sqrt{m} \rfloor$ and that this buffer extraction divides u into $u_1 u_2$ where u_1 contains the λ buffer elements. We granulate u_2 into λ blocks of size $k = \lfloor \frac{m-\lambda}{\lambda} \rfloor$ and one segment containing λ elements at most. We apply the stable merging algorithm using this modified block size and for the local merges we use the variant of Hwang and Lin's algorithm introduced above that doesn't rely on any internal buffer.

Theorem 4. *In the case of λ distinct elements in u, where $\lambda < 2 \lfloor \sqrt{m} \rfloor$, two adjacent sorted sequences can be merged stable, in place and asymptotically optimal.*

Proof. The only significant modification compared to the STABLE-IN-PLACE-MERGE algorithm concerns the size of the u-blocks and the number of different elements in all u-blocks. It is easy to verify that this keeps the algorithm asymptotically optimal.   □

5   Experimental Results

We did some benchmarking with the algorithms developed here, in order to get an impression of their practical value. We compared the stable and unstable variant with the RECMERGE algorithm proposed by Dudzinsky and Dydek in [7] as well as the well known standard algorithm that needs linear extra storage. Table 3 contains a summary of our results. Each entry shows a mean value of 30 runs with different data. We took a state of the art hardware platform with 2.4 Ghz processor speed and 512MB main memory, all coding was done in the C programming language.

Table 3. Practical comparison of various merge algorithms

n	m	Unstab.-In-Pl.-Merge		Stab.-In-Pl.-Merge		Recmerge		Standard alg.	
		#comp	t_e	#comp	t_e	#comp	t_e	#comp	t_e
2^{21}	2^{21}	7373277	721	6359488	891	4631976	1172	4194166	180
2^{21}	2^{18}	1572372	185	1448275	210	1268154	550	2359280	95
2^{21}	2^{15}	290180	70	277387	90	255641	240	2129916	80
2^{21}	2^{12}	48638	60	47501	80	44238	200	2100313	80
2^{23}	2^{9}	8588	260	8538	330	8064	721	8383203	340
2^{23}	2^{6}	1257	301	1271	320	1195	611	8287178	330
2^{23}	2^{3}	176	411	180	250	172	421	7381470	330
2^{23}	2^{0}	24	70	24	110	23	101	6537757	327

t_e : Execution time in ms, #comp : Number of comp., m, n : Lengths of inp. seq.

Despite their rather complex inner structure, the algorithms proposed here are surprisingly fast. The stable variant is almost always a bit slower than the unstable one, so stability seems to have a price. Additionally we observed that our algorithm is almost always a bit faster than RECMERGE. The latter algorithm is not optimal regarding the number of assignments. Hence, our algorithm would be the best selection in practice, particularly if you have to cope with input sequences of big size.

6   Conclusion

We could show that optimal stable in place merging is not merely a theoretical model but effectively usable in practice. Although our stable algorithm is fairly complex, it is fast, for almost all inputs even faster than the algorithm of Dudzinski and Dydek that is used as foundation of the `merge_without_buffer` function contained in the C++ Standard Template Libraries. The reason for this performance can be seen in the algorithm's structure. The kernel provides only a mechanism for $\sqrt{m}$ calls of Hwang-and-Lin's algorithm. So most of the work is done by Hwang-and-Lin's algorithm that is well known for its efficiency.

A serious question that still remains is the role of the subalgorithms as driving factor of the overall running time. E.g. there are several rotation algorithms and

Bentley shows in [15] that the best one from the theoretical point of view is not always the best one in practice. Another question is whether there exists a structurally more homogeneous and less complex algorithm with the same characteristics regarding optimality. Even an easy structured minimum storage algorithm that is optimal regarding both aspects (comparisons and assignments) would be interesting, but is not known so far. We lead these questions to further research in this area.

References

1. Knuth, D.E.: The Art of Computer Programming. Sorting and Searching Addison-Wesley **3** (1973)
2. Symvonis, A.: Optimal Stable Merging. Computer Journal **38** (1995) 681–690
3. Geffert, V., Katajainen, J., and Pasanen, T.: Asymptotically Efficient in-Place Merging. Theoretical Computer Science **237** (2000) 159–181
4. Chen, J.: Optimizing Stable in-Place Merging. Theoretical Computer Science **302** (2003) 191–210
5. Mannila, H., and Ukkonen, E.: A Simple Linear-Time Algorithm for in Situ Merging. Information Processing Letters **18** (1984) 203–208
6. Kronrod, M.A.: An Optimal Ordering Algorithm without a Field Operation. Dokladi Akad. Nauk SSSR **186** (1969) 1256–1258
7. Dudzinski, K., and Dydek, A.: On a Stable Storage Merging Algorithm. Information Processing Letters **12** (1981) 5–8
8. C++ Standard Template Library: (http://www.sgi.com/tech/stl)
9. Pardo, L.T.: Stable Sorting and Merging with Optimal Space and Time Bounds. SIAM Journal on Computing **6** (1977) 351–372
10. Salowe, J., and Steiger, W.: Simplified Stable Merging Tasks. Journal of Algorithms **8** (1987) 557–571
11. Huang, B.C., and Langston, M.: Practical in-Place Merging. Communications of the ACM **31** (1988) 348–352
12. Kim, P.S., and Kutzner, A.: Stable Minimum Storage Merging by Symmetric Comparisons. In Albers, S., Radzik, T., (eds), Algorithms – ESA 2004. Lecture Notes in Computer Science, Springer **3221** (2004) 714–723
13. Hwang, F., and Lin, S.: A Simple Algorithm for Merging Two Disjoint Linearly Ordered Sets. SIAM J. Comput. **1** (1972) 31–39
14. Cormen, T., Leiserson, C., Rivest, R., and Stein, C.: Introduction to Algorithms. 2nd edn. MIT Press (2001)
15. Bentley, J.: Programming Pearls. 2nd edn. Addison-Wesley, Inc (2000)

A Personalized Recommendation System Based on PRML for E-Commerce

Young Ji Kim[1], Hyeon Jeong Mun[2], Jae Young Lee[3], and Yong Tae Woo[2]

[1] Dept. of Computer Science, Kosin University, Pusan, Korea
yjkim@hibrain.net
[2] Dept. of Computer Engineering, Changwon National University, Changwon, Korea
{mun, ytwoo}@changwon.ac.kr
[3] Dept. of Mathematical and Computer Sciences,
Colorado School of Mines, Colorado, U.S.A
jaelee@mines.edu

Abstract. We propose a new personalized recommendation technique, which dynamically recommends products based on user behavior patterns for E-commerce. It collects and analyzes user behavior patterns from XML-based E-commerce sites using the PRML (Personalized Recommendation Markup Language) approach. The collected information is saved as PRML instances and an individual user profile is built from the PRML instances of the user using a CBR (Case-Based Reasoning) learning technique. When a new product is introduced, the system compares, for a user, the preference information saved in the user profile and the information about the new product and produces a recommendation that best fits the user preference.

1 Introduction

Web personalization can be defined as the process of customizing the contents and structure of a Web site to the specific and individual needs of each user taking advantage of the user's navigational behavior [1]. A personalized recommendation system, which is widely used in E-commerce, analyzes user's behavioral patterns and recommends new products that best match the individual user's preference [2]. There are various approaches to develop recommendation systems such as rule-based filtering techniques that use demographic information [3], collaborative filtering techniques that use other user's rating value with similar preference [4], content-based filtering techniques that compare a user profile and product description [5], and item-based filtering methods that analyze association among products [6]. However, existing methods have following drawbacks. First, some users are concerned about privacy issues and, thus, do not enter personal information or enter incorrect information [5]. Second, it is not easy to dynamically incorporate time-varying aspects of user preference in the recommendation algorithms [5], [7], [8]. Third, existing log files, such as CLF, do not contain enough personal information to be utilized by personalized recommendation systems [9]-[11]. Fourth, existing methods

J. Wiedermann et al. (Eds.): SOFSEM 2006, LNCS 3831, pp. 360–369, 2006.
© Springer-Verlag Berlin Heidelberg 2006

are tailored to particular applications and are not appropriate for web-based recommendation systems that have to manage various types of web contents. Finally, they lack ability to analyze user behavior patterns from XML contents and to dynamically generate and recommend web contents.

In this paper, we propose a new personalized recommendation technique that is based on PRML. User's behavioral patterns are collected from XML-based E-commerce sites and user profiles are built from them. Then, personalized recommendations are created by comparing the similarity between the information about new products and personal preference in the user profile. The personal preferences in the user profile are continuously updated using a CBR-based learning technique to reflect the changes of user's preference and recommendations can be made dynamically over time. Fig. 1 shows the configuration of the proposed system.

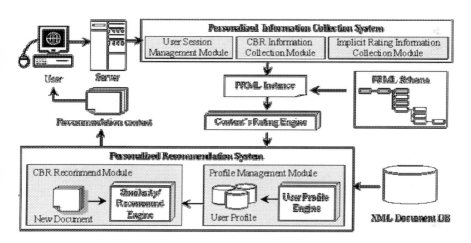

Fig. 1. Configuration of personalized recommendation system

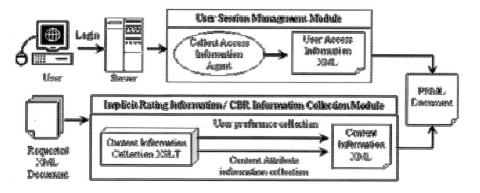

Fig. 2. Configuration of personal information collection system

2 Personal Information Collection System

The PICS (Personal Information Collection System) first collects user's behavioral patterns while a user is connected to a XML-based web site and, then, it implicitly extracts user's preference on the contents of the web site. There are three major modules in the PICS. Fig. 2 shows the configuration of the PICS.

The user session management module manages user sessions, where a session is defined as the duration between a user login and the logout. The implicit rating information module implicitly collects user's preference on the XML contents the user accessed. The CBR information collection module collects attribute information of the web contents.

2.1 User Session Management Module

The purpose of the user session management module is to effectively identify and manage user information. User information is collected for each user session, from a login to the logout. First, an agent is created at the server side that collects user access information. The collected information includes the user ID, session ID, and the connection IP address. Also it includes the URL of the web site the user accessed, the size of the requested document, and the server status. So, the module collects all the information that is typically collected in traditional log information in CLF. The module removes all unnecessary image data and Javascript pages to reduce the log information size. Then, the collected information is converted to PRML instances using the PRML Schema. The PRML instances are summarized into user identification information and log information and stored in a XML database. Fig. 3 shows the schema diagram of user identification information.

Fig. 3. Schema structure of individual user identification section

2.2 Implicit Rating Information Module

This module implicitly collects rating information from XML-based web sites utilizing hierarchical characteristics of XML documents[12]. First, elements in the XML documents are assigned different weights based on their importance in the documents and these weights are stored in the element weight databases. Whenever a user visits a web site, the module collects the XML elements in the XML contents which the user accessed and stores them as PRML instances. This information, combined with the user information, is used to create personalized rating information. This approach is more effective in collecting user's preference than existing methods that use the duration of time the user is connected or user behavioral pattern from a web log. Fig. 4 shows the diagram that depicts how implicit rating information is collected.

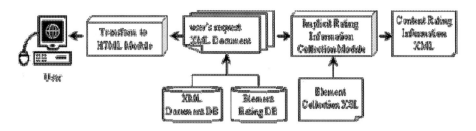

Fig. 4. Configuration of implicit rating collection technique

2.3   CBR Information Collection Module

This module collects CBR attribute information to extract user's preference on web site contents. To effectively reflect the characteristics of XML documents, we define intra-attribute weights and inter-attribute weights [13]. Intra-attribute weights represents weights among different attribute values of the same attribute, and inter-attribute weights represents the weights among different attributes. The collection of attributes and attribute values that are accessed by a user represents the user's preference on the contents of a XML-based web site. This information is stored as PRML instances along with the user's implicit rating information. Fig. 5 shows the configuration of the CBR information collection technique. Fig. 6 shows the schema diagram of the implicit rating Information module and the schema structure of the CBR information collection module.

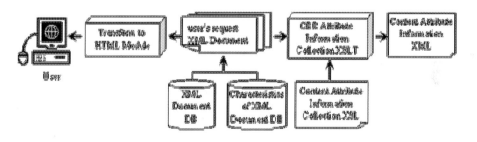

Fig. 5. Configuration of CBR attribute collection technique

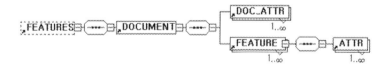

Fig. 6. Schema structure for implicit rating and CBR attribute information collection section

3   Personalized Recommendation System

The Personalized Recommendation System uses a CBR-based learning technique. It creates user profiles based on the web contents the users accessed and the profiles are saved in the user profile database. When new products are introduced, it computes the similarity between a user's preference in the user profile and each new product. It, then, recommends to the user the new products with top *n* similarities. The proposed CBR-based recommendation system is illustrated in Fig. 7 As shown in the figure, it consists of three major components – personalized rating information calculation module, user profile creation module, and contents recommendation module.

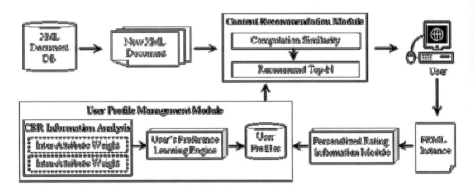

Fig. 7. Configuration of recommender system using CBR technique

3.1   Personalized Rating Information Calculation Module

This module computes the rating information of the contents a user accessed using the information recorded in the PRML instances of implicit rating information. The resulting value of this computation represents the user preference on the XML contents the user visited.

The rating information of a web content a user accessed is computed using the element weights that are stored in the element weight database and the collection of elements in the content. In the element weight database, each element is given a level weight in addition to an element weight. The level weight of an element is determined by its position in the hierarchy of the XML documents, and is adopted to reflect the hierarchical characteristics of XML-based web contents[12]. The collection of elements in a web content is obtained from PRML instances that were collected by the implicit rating information module of the PCIS. First, all the elements collected by the implicit rating information module are divided into groups based on their contents. Next, for each content, element weights and level weights of the elements in the content are retrieved from the element weight database. Then, rating information of the content is computed as

$$R_c = \sum_{e \in V} l_e \cdot k_e \tag{1}$$

Here, V is the set of elements in the XML content the user accessed, l_e is the level weight of the element e, and k_e is the element weight of e. The implicit rating information, R_c, represents the user's preference on that particular content.

3.2   User Profile Management Module

A user profile is represented as a tuple $P = (u, A, R, D)$, where u is a user ID, A is the set of attributes in the web contents, R is a set of intra-attribute weights, and D is a set of inter-attribute weights[13]. Let A be $\{A_1, A_2, \cdots, A_n\}$, and let each attribute A_i have m attribute values $\{a_{i1}, a_{i2}, \cdots, a_{im}\}$. The intra-attribute weights R of A_i is $\{r_{i1}, r_{i2}, \cdots, r_{im}\}$. r_{ij} represents how much a user prefers the attribute value a_{ij} to other attribute values, and is defined as:

$$r_{ij} = \frac{k_{ij}}{\sum_{p=1}^{m} k_{ip}}, \quad i = 1, 2, \cdots, n, \text{ and } j = 1, 2, \cdots, m. \tag{2}$$

Here, k_{ij} is the number of times a_{ij} is accessed. The inter-attribute weights D of A is $\{d_1, d_2, \cdots, d_n\}$. Here, again, each d_i represents how much A_i is preferred by the user, and is defined as:

$$d_i = \max_{1 \le j \le m}(r_{ij}) - \frac{1}{m}\sum_{j=1}^{m} r_{ij}, \quad i = 1, 2, \cdots, n. \tag{3}$$

If d_i is large, that implies the attribute A_i is more important to the user than other attributes. Note that both r_{ij} and d_i are determined from the user profile.

3.3   Contents Recommendation Module

Unlike the collaborative filtering technique that uses other users' rating information, the proposed recommendation technique analyzes individual user's behavioral pattern to generate recommendation for the user. This approach is based on Case-Based reasoning technique. We utilize nearest-neighbor approach to compute the similarities between the user profile and the attributes of new products. When computing the similarities, we use intra-attribute weights and inter-attribute weights. When new products are introduced, the similarity between a new product and the profile of a user is computed in the following way. Let P be the user profile and I be a new product with the same set of attributes $A = \{A_1, A_2, \cdots, A_n\}$ and the same attribute domains. Then, the similarity between P and I can be computed as:

$$Similarity(P, I) = \sum_{i=1}^{n}(d_i \cdot \sum_{j=1}^{m} f(a_{ij}, a'_{ij}) \cdot r_{ij}) \tag{4}$$

Here, a_{ij} is the attribute value of A_i in P, a'_{ij} is that of I, and $f(a_{ij}, a'_{ij})$ returns 1 if $a_{ij} = a'_{ij}$ and 0 otherwise. Note that for an attribute A_i only one a_{ij} matches a'_{ij} and $\sum_{j=1}^{m} f(a_{ij}, a'_{ij}) \cdot r_{ij}$ returns the r_{ij} of the $a_{ij} (= a'_{ij})$ that appears in I. The contents recommendation module, then, recommends the products (or contents) to a user based on the similarities between the products and the user's profile, e.g., products with top n similarities [13].

While collaborative filtering methods, which are considered more effective than other existing methods, use the profiles of other users in creating recommendations for a user, the proposed method uses the profile of the user himself/herself. So, the recommendation created by the proposed method reflects the user's preference more accurately. Furthermore, the profile of a user is continuously learned to reflect the change of user's preference on products in the E-commerce site.

4 Experimental Results

To verify the effectiveness of the proposed method, we conducted experiments with data collected from a recruitment web site for the duration of one week. This web site is accessed by about 70,000 users and the size of web log file collected each day is approximately 250MB. In our experiments, during the one week, total 824 users accessed 1,144 XML contents on the web site and each user accessed on average 10 XML contents. We analyzed the web log and created a user profile database. Then, we generated recommendations for 1,484 new contents.

4.1 XML Schema Diagram

Fig. 8 shows the schema diagram of the XML contents of the recruitment site, which were accessed by the users.

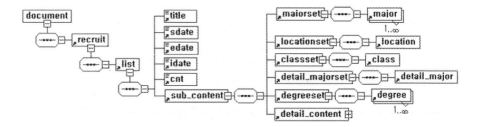

Fig. 8. A schema structure of experimental XML content

4.2 Personal Information Collection Experiment

From the XML web contents which a user visited, we collected implicit rating information and CBR attribute information. Then, we stored the information as PRML instances. Fig. 9 shows an example a personalized PRML instance that was created by our experiment. As shown in the Fig. 9, we do not lose any important information in the PRML compared with the CLF. Furthermore, we can observe that user identification information, which is not easily collected by CLF, is more effectively captured in the PRML instances. Note that the PRML instances facilitate real-time collection of log information.

We also assigned a level weight and an element weight to each element and stored them in the element database. A level weight is determined by the depth of the element in the XML document hierarchy and an element weight reflects the importance of the element. Table 1 shows an example of level weights and element weights stored in the database.

```
<?xml version="1.0" encoding="UTF-8"?>
<PRML xmlns:xsi="http://www.w3.org/2001/XMLSchema-instance"
        xsi:noNamespaceSchemaLocation="http://www.hibrain.net/prml/PRML.xsd">
  <USER ID="gdhong">
    <SESSIONID ID="JHPWDWORDS"/>
    <IPADDR IP="203.246.6.121"/>
    <AGENT TYPE="Mozilla/4.0"/>
    <REQUEST_SET>
      <REQUEST>
        <REQUEST_URL URL="RECRUIT_VIEW"/>
        <TIME DATE="2005/06/26 10:23:22"/>
        <BYTES SIZE="1024"/>
        <HTTPCODE METHOD = "GET" NAME="HTTP/1.0" STATUS_CODE="200"/>
        <FEATURES>
          <DOCUMENT CLASS="1" VALUE="recruit" DOC_ID="1234">
            <DOC_ATTR ELEM="list"/>
            <DOC_ATTR ELEM="sub_content"/>
            <DOC_ATTR ELEM="detail_content"/>
            <FEATURE VALUE="major"><ATTR VALUE="database"/><FEATURE>
            <FEATURE VALUE="recruit type"><ATTR VALUE="faculty"/></FEATURE>
            <FEATURE VALUE="place"><ATTR VALUE="LA/><FEATURE>
          </DOCUMENT>
        </FEATURES>
      </REQUEST>
    </REQUEST_SEt>
  </USER>
</PRML>
```

Fig. 9. An example of personalized PRML instance

Table 1. An example of element weight database

Element	list	sub_content	detail_content	resume	company	reference	act
Level	1	2	3	4	5	5	5
Weight	1	3	5	5	5	5	5

4.3 Personalized Recommendation System Experiment

Personalized Rating Information Calculation. For each XML contents a user visited, we computed rating information of the contents using the implicit rating information stored in the PRML instances. Here, as discussed in Section 3.1, we use level weight and element weight of each element in the contents, which are stored in the element weight database.

User profile creation. Among the web contents whose CBR attribute information is stored as PRML instances, we selected those whose rating information is high and used them to create user profiles. A user profile consists of user ID, all attributes and their values in the contents, intra-attribute weights, and inter-attribute weights. We also included in the profile total number of web contents accessed and how many times an attribute value is accessed. The intra-attribute weights and inter-attribute weights were computed using the Equations (2) and (3).

Personalized recommendation. Then, we generated personalized recommendations by comparing the user profiles and XML contents of new products using the similarity measure defined in Equation (4) and selecting top *n* products in terms of their similarity measures.

4.4 Experiment for Effectiveness of Recommendation System

We compared the proposed method with a collaborative filtering technique and a rule-based demographic technique using MAE (Mean Absolute Error) and ROC (Receiver Operating Characteristic) measures. The   result is shown in Fig. 10. We can see that the proposed method outperforms the other methods for all measures.

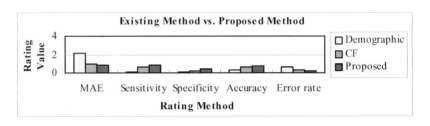

Fig. 10. Experimental Results

5 Conclusion

We proposed a new personalized recommendation system that utilizes the PRML approach. A user profile is built based on the behavioral patterns of a user. In building a user profile, we defined the inter-attribute weights and intra-attribute weights, which effectively represent the preference of the user on attributes of web contents. This profile is saved in the user profile database and is continuously learned to reflect the change of user's preferences in the E-commerce site. When new products are introduced, we compute the similarity between each new product and the profile of a user and recommend the products with top n similarities. Our experiment showed that the proposed method is more effective than existing methods.

Acknowledgements. This work was supported by the Korea Research Foundation Grant funded by Korean Government (D00039). We thank the anonymous reviewers for their valuable comments.

References

1. Eirinaki, M., Vazirgiannis M.: Web Mining for Web Personalization. ACM Transaction on Internet Technology **3** 1 (2003) 1-27
2. Sarwar, B., Karypis, G., Konstan, J., Riedl, J.: Analysis of Recommender Algorithms for E-Commerce. Proceedings of ACM Conference on E-Commerce (2000) 158-167
3. Pazzani, M.: A Framework for Collaborative, Content-Based and Demographic Filtering. Artificial Intelligent Review (1999) 394-408
4. Renick, P., Iacovou, N., Suchak, M., Bergstrom, P., Riedl, J.: GroupLens: An Open Architecture for Collaborative Filtering of Netnews. Proceedings of ACM Conference on Electronic Commerce (1994) 175-186

5. Claypool, M., Gokhale, A., Miranda, T., Murnikov, P., Netes, D., Sati, M.: Combining Content-Based and Collaborative Filters in an Online Newspaper. Proceedings of ACM SIGIR Workshop on Recommender Systems (1999)
6. Sarwar, B., Karypis, G., Konstan, J., Riedl, J.: Item-Based Collaborative Filtering Recommendation Algorithms. Proceedings of WWW Conference (2001) 285-2957
7. Schafer, J.B., Konstan, J., Riedl, J.: Recommender Systems in E-Commerce. Proceedings of ACM Conference on Electronic Commerce (1999) 158-166
8. Claypool, M., Brown, D., Le P., Waseda, M.: Inferring User Interest. Technical Report WPI-CS-TR-01-97 (2001)
9. Spiliopoulou, M., Pohle, C., Faulstich, L. C.: Improving the Effectiveness of a Web Site with Web Usage Mining. Proceedings of WEBKDD (1999) 142-162
10. Mobasher, B., Dai, H., Luo, T., Nakagawa, M., Sun, Y., Wilshire, J.: Discovery of Aggregate Usage Profiles for Web Personalization. Proceedings of WEBKDD (2000)
11. Mobasher, B., Cooley, R., Srivastava, J.: Automatic Personalization based on Web Usage Mining. Communications of ACM (2000) 142-151
12. Mun, H.J., Ok, S.H., Woo, Y.T.: An Automatic Rating Technique Based on XML Document. In Paul, D. B., Peter, B., & Ricardo. C. (Eds.), Adaptive Hypermedia and Adaptive Web-Based Systems. Lecture Notes in Computer Science, Springer-Verlag, Malaga, Spain **2347** (2002) 424-427
13. Kim, Y. J., Ok, S. H., Woo, Y. T.: A Case-Based Recommender System using Implicit Rating Techniques. In Paul, D. B., Peter, B., & Ricardo. C. (Eds.), Adaptive Hypermedia and Adaptive Web-Based Systems. Lecture Notes in Computer Science, Springer-Verlag, Malaga, Spain **2347**. (2002) 522-526

An Efficient Index Scheme for XML Databases

Young Kim, Sang-Ho Park, Tae-Soon Kim, Ju-Hong Lee, and Tae-Su Park

School of Computer Science and Information Engineering,
Inha University, Incheon, Korea
{youngjin, parksangho, kts429, taesu}@datamining.inha.ac.kr,
juhong@inha.ac.kr

Abstract. Finding efficient and useful ways to search and index XML documents is a popular research topic in the field of computer and information science today. The path-based indexing method shows disadvantages of performance degradation when performing join operations of ancestor-descendent relationships and searching for middle and lower level nodes. To alleviate these disadvantages, a numbering scheme based indexing technique was proposed. This technique shows better performance in a variety of queries. However, a numbering scheme based indexing method is necessary to assign numbers to all nodes of all XML documents. It occurs the problem of both search overhead and disk space usage for indexes. In this paper, we propose a novel method that can efficiently construct and manage common paths of all XML documents. The proposed method stores similar structured XML documents more efficiently. In addition, it supports both insertion and deletion of XML documents more flexible.

1 Introduction

The problem of managing and querying XML documents poses interesting challenges to database researchers. XML is composed of what has been termed semi-structured data containing a large variety of different structures of varying data types; in fact, XML documents can be viewed as an ordered tree and have a rather complex internal structure. Therefore, for XML query processing of ordered tree, an efficient index scheme is required. The major challenges of the most indexing scheme [2], [7], [9], [16] were concentrated on storing large volume of XML documents and processing complex queries efficiently. This representation are based upon path [1], [8], [11], [15] or numbering schemes [4], [5], [12], [14]. Path based indexing schemes encode all possible paths from root node to leaf node into one simple path [1], [8], [11], [15], while a numbering scheme based indexing method encodes every XML nodes into a pair *<preorder, postorder>* [4], [5], [12], [14]. The path based indexing scheme is an efficient approach when processing a simple path queries, but inefficient when processing a join operation of an ancestor-descendant relationship. The numbering based indexing scheme guarantees average performance in all various cases including above two cases, because it requires the only comparison operations among pairs, such as *<preorder, postorder>* or *<order, size>* assigned to each node.

J. Wiedermann et al. (Eds.): SOFSEM 2006, LNCS 3831, pp. 370–378, 2006.

Nevertheless, it is not efficient only when processing queries for a large number of nodes, because many self-join operations are required.

To resolve this problem, we suggest efficient indexing scheme using both Node-Range and Pre-Order List indexes which based on a numbering scheme. The main contributions of this paper are summarized as following: First of all, XPath is analyzed rapidly. Second, the storage for indexes is managed effectively. Third, the retrieval range using Pre-Order List is reduced. Fourth, insertion and deletion are performed efficiently.

The rest of the paper is organized as follows. Section 2 reviews related work. Section 3 proposes a new indexing scheme and explains the query processing through use of an example. Section 4 presents performance results. Section 5 concludes the paper.

2   Related Work

XML documents are represented as a tree, in which every node can also be a duplicate path. All paths should be traversed to retrieve specific XML data or a full XML document. To resolve this problem, Goldman [11] suggested the DataGuide indexing method that summarizes all paths in the database including XML documents, starting from root, as simple paths, and then using the integration path for duplicate paths. This method reduces the portion of the database required to be scanned for path queries, useful for navigating the semi-structured graph from the root.1-index/2-index/T-index methods [15] derived from the DataGuide indexing method. Index Fabric [8] adopted Patricia Trie [13] to reduce the cost of path operation. Patricia Trie is encoded through eliminating duplicated characters and storing distinct characters tagged with position information. Index Fabric concentrated on reducing the range influenced by the path operation through encoding of all paths that started from the root node, adding data in each path to form a Patricia Trie. As a result, in querying a simple path, the retrieval performance is enhanced, since XML documents are retrieved through encoded paths, from root to leaf. This method is not efficient when retrieving the intermediate and leaf nodes as well as performing the join operation of ancestor-descendant relationships ('//'). Here, the double slash '//' represents the ancestor-descendant relationship. A single slash '/' represents a parent-child relationship. To enhance the efficiency of the join operation, the refined path includes frequently used paths in index storage. This also is not suitable for processing various types of queries. The problem is such that the DBA should specify all possible types of queries. Xpath performs the join operation of ancestor-descendant relationships frequently. Indexing methods based on the numbering scheme were developed to process various queries efficiently, [4], [5], [12], [14]. In a numbering scheme, all nodes are numbered in form $<d_1,d_2,d_3>$, where d_1 is preorder, d_2 is postorder, and d_3 is the level. The indexing method based on numbering schemes performs query processing by only comparing the numbers assigned to each XML document. This is achieved by following the following conditions:

For any two distinct node m and n,

- m is a descendant of n iff $n.d_1 < m.d_1$ and $n.d_2 > m.d_2$
- m is an ancestor of n iff $n.d_1 > m.d_1$ and $n.d_2 < m.d_2$.
- m is a child of n iff $n.d_3+1 = m.d_3$

However, in performing insert operations of intermediate or leaf nodes, all nodes assigned with a pair of numbers needs to be reassigned. This problem needs to be resolved. XISS[12,14] replaced a pair *<preorder, postorder>* assigned to all nodes by a pair *<order, size>*, where *size* is the information about the number of containable data and extensible ranges satisfying the condition that n is a descendant of m if $order(m) < order(n)$ and $order(n)+size(n) <= order(m) + size(m)$. This method can index a document easily, even when inserting various structural XML documents. Maintaining a pair *<order, size>* for each node of the XML document causes the inefficiency of index space. A high retrieval overhead is also caused from various self-join operations. Each of XML documents is indexed according to the number of nodes included in XPath queries. So, many join operations and comparison operations equal the number of XML documents required. As the size of data increases and the number of nodes in query increases, the retrieval performance decreases. This apparently occurs when many data comparison operations are required.

3   Indexing Method Using Node-Range of Integration Path

To manage XML documents efficiently, we proposed a novel indexing method using node-range integration paths. The contribution can be summarized as follows: First, the index size is small. Second, the overhead is low. Third, comparing the number of XML documents is not required.

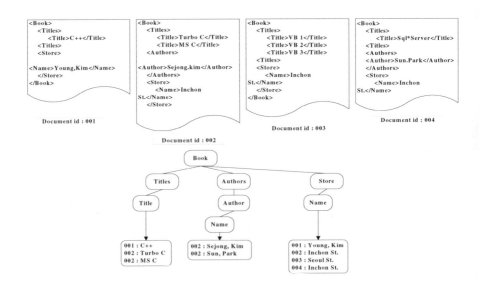

Fig. 1. Construction of Integration paths

As shown in Figure 1, common nodes of all XML paths are integrated with a path and additional indexes. Pairs of *<ID, data>* are managed on each leaf node, where *ID* is the identification number of XML documents and data is XML data. The result traversed only through integration paths numbered, provides the result table range information.

Inserting XML documents provide three attributes, *<preorder, postorder, node-range>* to each node of integration path, using Numbering scheme technique, as shown in Figure 2. Nodes of integration paths are lined up in the order of the Pre-Order List. Each list maintains the name of data table containing the leaf node data. Given XPath, we restrict the retrieval range of data and retrieve only data tables.

As shown in Figure 3 the suggested system is constructed with four principle components, the Name Index, Pre-Order List, Doc_id_TB, and Data Table. Name Index(A) is used to analyze the XPath query using integration paths. Pre-Order List(B) builds all integration path information in the order of preorder and stores this data in the table names. Doc_id_TB(C) stores the ID of XML documents contained in the data table. Data Table(D) store real XML documents. When XML documents are

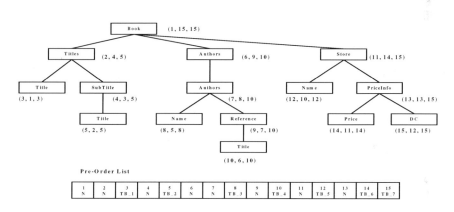

Fig. 2. Index system using Integration Path

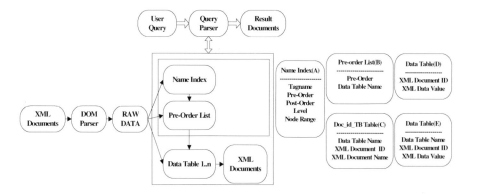

Fig. 3. Architecture of Index System

```
Node : n, Range of Pre-Order List : x
[ Calculate Node Range ]
if n.pos = ROOT then
    n.noderange = n.postorder
else
    if n.rightsibling is true then
        n.noderange = rightsibling.preorder - 1
    else
        n.noderange = n.parent.noderange
    end if
[ Range calculation of Pre-Order List data table using Node
Range ]
n.preorder <= x and x <= n.noderange and x.data_flg = 'Y'
```

Fig. 4. Node-Range calculation algorithm

```
XPath Query : /Book//Titles[.= 'Visual C++']
(Comparison of the Ancestor-descendant relationship and the
data value)
(XISS)
SELECT i1.doc_id, i1.value
FROM Element_ix e1, Element_ix e2, Value_ix i1
WHERE e1.doc_id = e2.doc_id
  AND    e2.doc_id = i1.doc_id
  AND    e1.tagname = 'Book'
  AND    e2.tagname = 'Titles'
  AND e1.order < e2.order AND (e1.order + e1.size) >= e2.order
  AND e2.order < e3.order AND (e2.order + e2.size) >= i1.order
  AND e1.level < e2.level
  AND i1.value = 'Visual C++'
(Pre-Order List)
(1)SELECT    e2.preorder, e2.noderange
 FROM    NameIndex e1, NameIndex e2
 WHERE e1.tagname = 'Book' AND e2.tagname = 'Titles'
  AND e1.preorder<e2.preorder AND e1.postorder>e1.postorder)
  AND e1.level < e2.level
(2) Result of Pre-Order List :
<3,3>, <5,5>, <10,10> => "TB_1", "TB_2", "TB_4"
(3)SELECT * FROM TB_1 WHERE Values = 'Visual C++'UNION
SELECT * FROM TB_2 WHERE Values = 'Visual C++' UNION
SELECT * FROM TB_4 WHERE Values = 'Visual C++'
```

Fig. 5. Comparison of XISS and Pre-Order List

inserted, we store the simple path and data of the XML document in temporary raw data format, using a DOM parser, the information *<preorder, postorder, node-range>* is obtained by comparing with the existing information in Name Index, and using the

Node-range resulting from the analysis of XPath in order to access Pre-Order List rapidly. Figure 4 shows how to calculate the Node-range.

Pre-Order List(B) in Figure 3 is a dynamic array stored in the order of preorder of Name Index(A). As storage in minimal, each item in the array only has the preorder of Name Index and the name of the data table. When processing a query for XPath, our suggested method obtains the lowest preorder and node range using the Name Index, accessing Pre-Order List(B) directly for the table name, and operating an XML document using the name of the data table. Figure 5 shows an example of a query like "Book//Title[.='Visual C++']".

As shown in Figure 5, given an XPath query in the form of "Book//Title[.='Visual C++']", the method using Pre-Order List is processed in three steps. First, three data range <3,3>, <5,5>, <10,10> of a given query are obtained. Second, three data ranges are obtained at the second step to get the name of data table accessed. Finally, the join operations are performed using the tables name.

4 Experimental Evaluation

In this section, we evaluate the efficiency of our proposed indexing method. The Pass-Based indexing methods were not very efficient when join operations among intermediate nodes or the operation for ancestor-descendant relationships is performed. We implemented the Pre-Order List in a disk-based dynamic array, comparing and evaluating the results of our method compared to the representative XISS method of numbered scheme indexing. The experimental results indicated that our proposed indexing method was more efficient than the XISS indexing methods.

All of the experiments were run under a Window2000 Server on a 2.0GHz Pentium 4 CPU with main memory of 512MB and a hard disk size of 60GB. We used MS-SQL Server 2000 as the relational databases, Visual Basic 6.0 and T-SQL as development languages, and MSXML(DOM) as a parser for extracting both internal data and the data structure of the XML documents.

We used three types of experimental structural property datasets for our experiments. The first dataset(A) consisted of statutory XML documents for business ends. It had two properties, the number of nodes included in the XML documents was small, but the number of documents was large. The second dataset(B) consisted of XML documents obtained from a Shakespeare play. This dataset was distinct in that the number of nodes was high and the data was very large. The third dataset(C) consisted of synthetic data. It had three kinds distinct properties, it had many duplicate nodes, the data size was large and it had considerable depth. Table1 shows the details.

We used three types of retrieval queries for the ancestor-descendant relationship, simple pass query, join operation queries and conditional operation queries. The experimental results showed that our proposed method was much more efficient when compared to XISS, especially in performing join operation of ancestor-descendant relationship and conditional queries. And it managed the index space efficiently, because our proposed method didn't require numbering of each of data table or amalgamated passes.

Table 1. Characteristics of the XML documents

	Experiment Dataset(A)	Experiment Dataset(B)	Experiment Dataset(C)
Numer of documents	9,495	38	200
Numer of nodes of total documents	725,538	150,059	2,741,100
Size of Documents	287MB	13 MB	251 MB
Numer of average elements per a document	24	90	58
Numer of average data per a document	52	3,967	13,647
maximum depth of documents	5	6	20

Experimental Query Type_1
Q1:/laws/contents /information management/title (**Simple Path**)
Q2: / laws /announcement revision/relevant ordinance (**Without Simple Path**)
Q3:/laws/announcement revision/ordinance/revision data 0 (**Simple Path**)
Q4:/ laws /common ordinance (**ancestor-descendant relationship**)
Q5: /laws/title (**ancestor-descendant relationship +duplicate nodes**)
Q6: / laws //text//title (**multiple ancestor-descendant relationship**)
Q7:/ laws //relevant ordinance /title (**ancestor-descendant relationship + Simple Path**)
Q8:/ laws /contents/information management /title [.='Local Taxes regulations'] (**ancestor-descendant relationship +condition**)
Q9: / laws //common ordinance[.='ministry of agriculture & forestry '] (**ancestor-descendant relationship +condition**)
Q10:/ laws //relevant ordinance/title [.='Clear Air ACT'] (**ancestor-descendant relationship +condition**)
Q11: / laws /announcement revision/relevant ordinance [.='trade transaction regulations] (**ancestor-descendant relationship +condition**)
Q12:/ laws //text//title [.'正富支侵'] (**ancestor-descendant relationship +condition**)

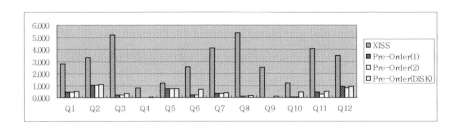

Experimental Query Type_2
Q1: /PLAY/INDUCT/TITLE (Without Simple Path)
Q2: /PLAY/PROLOGUE (Without Simple Path)
Q3: /PLAY//ACT/SCENE (Without Simple Path)
Q4: /PLAY//SPEECH (ancestor-descendant relationship)
Q5: /PLAY//INDUCT/SPEECH (ancestor-descendant relationship)
Q6: /PLAY//SCENE/SPEECH (Simple Path +ancestor-descendant relationship)
Q7: /PLAY//SPEECH/TITLE (multiple ancestor-descendant relationship)
Q8: /PLAY//shashi[.='ACT'] (ancestor-descendant relationship +condition)
Q9:/PLAY//SCENE/TITLE[.='SCENE'] (ancestor-descendant relationship +condition)

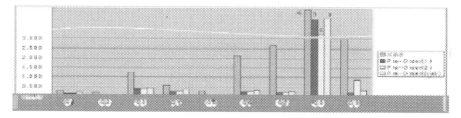

Experimental Query Type_3
Q1: /A/D/E/C/B/E/E/E/F/E (Without Simple Path)
Q2: /A/B/B/C/B (Without Simple Path)
Q3: /A//B//C (ancestor-descendant relationship)
Q4: /A//D//C//B//E (ancestor-descendant relationship + Simple Path)
Q5: /A//D//C//B//E//F (ancestor-descendant relationship + Simple Path)
Q6: /A/D/E//B//E//F/F (Simple Path + ancestor-descendant relationship)
Q7: /A/D/E//B/E/E//F/F (multiple ancestor-descendant relationship)
Q8:/A//F//E[.='addchannel'] (ancestor-descendant relationship +condition)
Q9:/A/D/E//B/E/F[.='kbEnglish'] (ancestor-descendant relationship +condition)

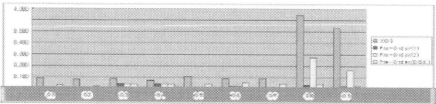

Fig. 6. Performance Evaluation

5 Conclusion

The path-based indexing methods have been an unqualified success when performing the retrieval of intermediate and leaf nodes, and the join operation of ancestor-descendant relationships. The numbering scheme based indexing method guaranteed average performance for all operations. However, under this scheme, all nodes of the XML document, data, and attribute should be numbered. This incurred a high retrieval overhead and wasted storage space.

In this paper, we suggest a novel indexing method to resolve this problem. We used integration paths to reduce the storage space for indexes, three attributes *<preorder, postorder, node-range>* and an additional Pre-Order List to enhance the efficiency of retrieval. The suggested methods were efficient even when inserting new XML documents. Finally, through experimental results with XISS, it has been shown that our method is more efficient than others.

Acknowledgments. This work was supported by INHA University Research Grant.

References

1. Abiteboul, S., Quass, D., McHugh, J., Widom, J., and Wiener, J.: The Lorel Query Language for Semistructured Data. Int, J. on Digital Libraries 1 1 (1997) 68-88
2. Boag, S. Chamberlin, D., Fernandez, M., Florescu, D., Robie, J., and Simeon, J.: An XML Query Language(XQuery). http://www.w3.org/TR/xquery/ (2004)
3. Bruno, N., Koudas, N., and Srivastava, D.: Holistic Twig Joins: Optimal XML Pattern Matching. In Proc. of the ACM SIGMOD (2002) 310-321
4. Chen, Y., Davidson, S., and Zheng, Y.: BLAS: An Efficient XPath Processing System. In Proc. of the ACM SIGMOD (2004) 47-58
5. Chien, S., Vagena, Z., Zhang, D., Tsotras, V., and Zaniolo, C.: Efficient Structural Joins on Indexed XML Documents. In Proc. of the VLDB (2002) 263-274
6. Chung, C., Min, J., and Shim, K.: APEX: An Adaptive Path Index for XML Data. In Proc. of the ACM SIGMOD (2002) 121-132
7. Clark, J., and DeRose, S.: XML Path Language(XPath). Version 1.0 w3c recommendation. Technical Report REC-xpath-1999 1116, World Wide Web Consortium (1999)
8. Cooper, B., Sample, N., Franklin, M., Hjaltason, G., and Shadmon, M.: A Fast Index for Semistructured Data. In Proc. of the VLDB (2001) 341-350
9. Deutsch, A., Fernandez, M., Florescu, D., Levy, A., and Suciu, D.: XML-QL: A Query Language for XML. http://www.w3.org/TR- /1998/Note-XML-QL-19980819/ (1998)
10. Dietz, P.: Maintaining Order in a Linked List. In Proc. of the Fourteenth Annual ACM Symposium on Theory of Computing (1982) 122-127
11. Goldman, R., and Widom, J.: DataGuides: Enabling Query Formulation and Optimization in Semistructured Databases. In Proc. of the VLDB (1997) 436-445
12. Harding, P., Li, Q., and Moon, B.: XISS/R: XML Indexing and Storage System Using RDBMS. In Proc. of the VLDB (2003) 1073-1076
13. Knuth, D.: The Art of Computer Programming, Vol.III, Sorting and Searching. Third Edition. Addison Wesley, Reading, MA (1998)
14. Li, Q., Moon, B.: Indexing and Querying XML Data for Regular Path Expression. In Proc. of VLDB (2001) 361-370
15. Milo, T., Suciu, D.: Index Structures for Path Expressions. In Proc. of the ICDT (1997) 277-295
16. Robie, J., Lapp, J., and Schach, D.: XML Query Language (XQL). http://www.w3.org- / TrandS/QL/QL98/pp/xql.htm (1998)

On Separating Constant from Polynomial Ambiguity of Finite Automata⋆
(Extended Abstract)

Joachim Kupke

ETH Zurich, Zurich, Switzerland
joachim.kupke@inf.ethz.ch

Abstract. The degree of nondeterminism of a finite automaton can be measured by means of its ambiguity function. In many instances, whenever automata are allowed to be (substantially) less ambiguous, it is known that the number of states needed to recognize at least some languages increases exponentially. However, when comparing constantly ambiguous automata with polynomially ambiguous ones, the question whether there are languages such that the inferior class of automata requires exponentially many states more than the superior class to recognize them is still an open problem. The purpose of this paper is to suggest a family of languages that seems apt for a proof of this (conjectured) gap. As a byproduct, we derive a new variant of the proof of the existence of a superpolynomial gap between polynomial and fixed-constant ambiguity. Although our candidate languages are defined over a huge alphabet, we show how to overcome this drawback.

1 Introduction

Nondeterminism is a concept which – in spite of its pivotal importance regarding our conception of complexity and computation at large – computer science has failed to understand satisfactorily. The most widely known impact is our inability to answer the longstanding $P \neq NP$ question, and the most plausible reason is a considerable lack of tools we could employ in order to establish lower bounds on the running time of deterministic Turing machines.

But not only in the context of Turing machines, where the term "efficiency" usually relates to running time, which is hard to lower-bound, does nondeterminism confront us with enormous trouble. Even with regular languages there are lots of open questions when it comes to examining sets of nondeterministic finite automata. One of these questions is how hard it is to compute the minimal number of states a nondeterministic automaton must use in order to recognize a given language. We know that while for deterministic automata, we can answer the question within polynomial time, for nondeterministic automata, it gives rise to a PSPACE-complete problem [1]. This is caused by the fact that nondeterministic automata have plenty of possibilities to save states while the

---

⋆ This work was supported by SNF grant 200021-107327/1.

J. Wiedermann et al. (Eds.): SOFSEM 2006, LNCS 3831, pp. 379–388, 2006.

states in deterministic automata always form a refinement of the appropriate Nerode right-congruence relation. Hence, even where "efficiency" pertains to the number of states of finite automata (their so-called *succinctness*), we have failed to explain what the exact conjunctures are for improving efficiency by the introduction of nondeterminism. Note that if it comes to estimating the minimal number of states (or transitions, for that matter) in a nondeterministic automaton, a negative answer has been given recently [6] to the question of approximating this number efficiently.

A sensible approach is to limit the "amount" of nondeterminism in an automaton. The idea is that "more nondeterminism" is more likely to save states than "less nondeterminism." We will quantify nondeterminism by using an automaton's so-called ambiguity function which measures the number of accepting paths for input words of a certain length. Intuitively, this function grows faster for more nondeterministic automata. If it is bounded by a constant (however huge it may be), do automata require (substantially many) more states to recognize the same language than if it is not?

The answer given in [7] is yes, and, moreover, the languages presented there even require *exponential* ambiguity to be recognized by succinct automata. This gives rise to the question whether there are languages such that polynomial ambiguity is enough to yield succinct automata, but on the other hand, it should be hard (i.e., require many more states) to recognize these languages at an ambiguity that is bounded by a constant. The purpose of this paper is to give insights which will shed more light on this intriguing problem.

Note that considerable efforts have been made in order to use *communication complexity* as a means to describe ambiguity [3]. However, communication complexity, where one usually analyzes the behavior of two communicating computers on an arbitrarily-sized input (for a complete survey, see [2]), does not appear to be the method of choice when it comes to distinguishing unbounded from bounded ambiguity. This is explained in more detail in [4].

This paper is organized as follows: In Section 2, we will fix our notation and introduce basic notions. Section 3 will introduce a family of candidate languages, and we will prove that these cannot be recognized by succinct unambiguous automata. In Section 4, we will explore possibilities to decrease the size of the alphabet we use (which is unusually big), and in Section 5, miscellaneous properties our languages enjoy will be discussed.

2   Preliminaries

We begin with the most basic of our definitions. First of all, we introduce the notion of a finite automaton. Our definition may differ from those more commonly used in two aspects: On the one hand, we allow for multiple initial states, and on the other hand, we use binary vectors and matrices in order to represent sets of states and transitions between them. This will prove more convenient later.

Definition 1. In this work, a (nondeterministic) *finite automaton* is a quintuple $\mathcal{A} = (Q, \Sigma, I, \Delta, F)$ where

Q is a finite non-empty set of states,

Σ is a finite non-empty set of input symbols,

$I \in \{0, 1\}^Q$ is the initial state vector,

$F \in \{0, 1\}^Q$ is the final state vector, and

$\Delta \colon \Sigma \to \{0, 1\}^{Q \times Q}$ maps every input symbol to its transition matrix.

Let nfa be the set of all (nondeterministic) finite automata. For an automaton $\mathcal{A} \in$ nfa and a word $w \in \Sigma^*$, let $\mathrm{amb}_{\mathcal{A}}(w)$ denote the number of paths that $\mathcal{A}$ can follow from an initial to a final state while reading w. In particular, $L(\mathcal{A}) = \{w \in \Sigma^* \mid \mathrm{amb}_{\mathcal{A}}(w) > 0\}$. More formal definitions can be found in [5].

This slightly technical definition will alleviate the complexity of Definition 4.

Definition 2. Let $(\mathcal{A}_k)_{k=0}^\infty \in$ nfa$^{\mathbb{N}}$ be any sequence of automata where Q_k is the set of states of $\mathcal{A}_k$. Now, let $\#_{\mathcal{A}} \colon \mathbb{N} \to \mathbb{N}$ be defined by $\#_{\mathcal{A}}(k) := |Q_k|$.

When comparing classes of automata, we only consider those classes that are not artifically deprived of their power to recognize regular languages.

Definition 3. A class of finite automata $\mathcal{F} \subseteq$ nfa is said to be *full* iff for every regular language L there is an automaton $\mathcal{A} \in \mathcal{F}$ such that $L(\mathcal{A}) = L$.

Definition 4. Let $f \colon \mathbb{N} \to \mathbb{N}$ be some function. Two full classes of finite automata $\mathcal{F}_1$ and $\mathcal{F}_2$ are said to be *f-separable* iff there exists a sequence of languages $(L_k)_{k=0}^\infty \in (\Sigma^*)^{\mathbb{N}}$ and there exists a sequence of automata $(\mathcal{B}_k)_{k=0}^\infty \in \mathcal{F}_2^{\mathbb{N}}$ such that for all $k \in \mathbb{N}$, we have $L(\mathcal{B}_k) = L_k$, $\#_{\mathcal{B}} \in \mathcal{O}(k)$, and for every sequence of automata $(\mathcal{A}_k)_{k=0}^\infty \in \mathcal{F}_1^{\mathbb{N}}$ satisfying $L(\mathcal{A}_k) = L_k$ for all $k \in \mathbb{N} \setminus \{0\}$, we have $\#_{\mathcal{A}} \in \Omega(f)$. In this case, we write $\mathcal{F}_1 \prec_f \mathcal{F}_2$.

It is well-known [8][1] that dfa $\prec_{2^n}$ nfa where dfa is the class of *deterministic* finite automata. In other words, nondeterminism allows finite automata to be exponentially more succinct than their deterministic counterparts to recognize the same language. The same holds for interesting intermediate classes, where in some sense, the amount of nondeterminism is bounded.

Definition 5. Let $\mathcal{A} \in$ nfa. Its *ambiguity function* (or simply *ambiguity*) is $\mathrm{amb}_{\mathcal{A}} \colon \mathbb{N} \to \mathbb{N}$; $\mathrm{amb}_{\mathcal{A}}(n) := \max\{\mathrm{amb}_{\mathcal{A}}(w) \mid w \in \Sigma^*, |w| \le n\}$.

Intuitively, the ambiguity of an automaton is the number of accepting computations on input words of a given maximum length. A multitude of functions can

---

[1] Please note that it is not the author's intention to wrongly credit [8] with the original *discovery* of this theorem, which has become folklore some time in prehistoric computer science (i.e., around 1960).

be realized as ambiguity functions, but we are only interested in their asymptotic behavior. The overall idea is that ambiguity functions of faster growth signify more nondeterministic automata, while those of slower growth signify less nondeterministic automata. This constitutes a gradual measurement from nondeterminism to determinism rather than a classification. However, only classes of automata can be separated (using Definition 4). In this paper, we will be concerned with the following classes of automata.

Definition 6. We define *un*ambiguous *f*inite *a*utomata, *c*onstantly *a*mbiguous *f*inite *a*utomata, and *p*olynomially *a*mbiguous *f*inite *a*utomata.[9]

$$\mathsf{unfa} := \{\mathcal{A} \in \mathsf{nfa} \mid \forall n \in \mathbb{N} : \mathrm{amb}_{\mathcal{A}}(n) \le 1\}$$
$$\mathsf{cafa} := \{\mathcal{A} \in \mathsf{nfa} \mid \mathrm{amb}_{\mathcal{A}} \in \mathcal{O}(1)\}$$
$$\mathsf{pafa} := \{\mathcal{A} \in \mathsf{nfa} \mid \mathrm{amb}_{\mathcal{A}} \notin \bigcup_{b>1} \Omega(b^n)\}$$

The last definition is sound because it is known [3] that the ambiguity function of an automaton is either a polynomial or an exponential function.

Fact 7 ([7]). $\mathsf{dfa} \prec_{2^n} \mathsf{unfa} \prec_{2^n} \mathsf{cafa}$ $\mathsf{pafa} \prec_{2^n} \mathsf{nfa}$

It is a longstanding question whether also $\mathsf{cafa} \prec_{2^n} \mathsf{pafa}$ holds. It is tempting to assume that language sequences like $(BRIDGE_k)_{k=1}^{\infty}$ where

$$BRIDGE_k := \{w = w_1 \ldots w_n \in \{a, b\}^* \mid \exists j \in \{1, \ldots, n-k\} \colon w_j \ne w_{j+k}\}$$

were natural candidates to show $\mathsf{cafa} \prec_{2^n} \mathsf{pafa}$. In fact, $\{a, b\}^* \setminus BRIDGE_k$ is the set of all finite prefixes of $\{w^\omega \mid w \in \{a, b\}^k\}$, and intuitively, the index j can be found in unboundedly many places, given a sufficiently long input word. A natural automaton $\mathcal{B}_k \in \mathsf{pafa}$ with $L(\mathcal{B}_k) = BRIDGE_k$ can be depicted as:

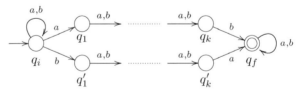

However, there are also succinct automata $\mathcal{A}_k \in \mathsf{cafa}$ with $L(\mathcal{A}_k) = BRIDGE_k$. The automaton $\mathcal{A}_k$ can be represented as follows:

Note that its ambiguity is in fact bounded by k. Even for long words, there are no more than k ways of accepting them: For every word, $\mathcal{A}_k$ guesses a residuum

$1 \le r \le k$ (by guessing an appropriate final state), and then, among the symbols with index $\in \{r, r+k, r+2k, \ldots\}$, it unambiguously guesses the last symbol that is not equal to its k-th successor.

Using communication complexity [3], it is however easy to show that unambiguous automata which recognize $BRIDGE_k$ have an exponential number of states (in k). Therefore, $(BRIDGE_k)_{k=1}^\infty$ can be used to show unfa $\prec_{2^n}$ cafa.

We shall suggest a sequence of languages that seems apt to take the place of $(L_k)_{k=1}^\infty$ in Definition 4 to establish cafa $\prec_{2^n}$ pafa.

3   The Candidate Languages

One of the things noteworthy about languages like $BRIDGE_k$ is that if information is to be carried over a bounded-length infix, small constantly ambiguous automata can usually be found to do this job. Inspired by [10], we will therefore define languages whose complexity is not derived from such a property.

Definition 8. Let $k \in \mathbb{N} \setminus \{0\}$, and let $\Sigma_k := \{M \in \{0,1\}^{k \times k} \mid M_{ij} = 0$ for all $1 \le j < i \le k\}$, the set of upper triangular Boolean matrices of dimension $k \times k$. Let $\iota\colon \Sigma_k^* \to \mathbb{N}^{k \times k}$ be defined such that $\iota(w)$ is the product of the matrices which the symbols of w represent. Let $CONN_k := \{w \in \Sigma_k^* \mid (\iota(w))_{1k} > 0\}$.

There is a very intuitive way of thinking about $CONN_k$: Regard every symbol as adjacency matrix of a bipartite graph with node set $\{\overline{1}, \ldots, \overline{k}\} \cup \{\underline{1}, \ldots, \underline{k}\}$. In fact, this is the alphabet used in [10]. But since our matrices are triangular, these bipartite graphs have edges $(\overline{i_1}, \underline{i_2})$ only for $i_1 \le i_2$, i.e., all edges are either horizontal or downward askew (assuming left-to-right reading direction). This modification is crucial since it guarantees that there are canonical automata of sub-exponential (i.e., polynomial) ambiguity (see Remark 9).

For the sake of intuition, imagine that nodes $\overline{1}, \ldots, \overline{k}$ are aligned vertically in a left column and that nodes $\underline{1}, \ldots, \underline{k}$ are aligned vertically in a right column. When collating n symbols, we identify neighboring nodes. As a consequence, we regard a word $w \in \Sigma_k^n$ as an $(n+1)$-partite graph with node set $\{(i,j) \mid 1 \le i \le k$ and $0 \le j \le n\}$. There is an edge between $(i_1, j-1)$ and (i_2, j) iff the j-th symbol in w has a one in the (i_1, i_2)-entry.

Now, words belong to $CONN_k$ iff their corresponding $(|w|+1)$-partite graph connects nodes $(1,0)$ and $(k, |w|)$ (see Figure 1).

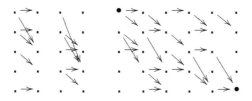

Fig. 1. Two symbols and a word in $CONN_k$

Remark 9. Clearly, there is a finite automaton $\mathcal{A}_k$ for $CONN_k$ with states $\{1, \ldots, k\}$, where there are transitions from state i_1 to state i_2 exactly for all symbols that contain the $(\overline{i_1}, i_2)$ edge in their representation as bipartite graphs. Indeed, $\mathcal{A}_k \in$ pafa for all $k \in \mathbb{N}$ because Σ_k contains triangular matrices only.

Using the following slightly technical definition, it is relatively easy to prove that in order to recognize $CONN_k$, either a huge number of states or at least *some* ambiguity is necessary.

Definition 10. Let $\mathcal{L}$ be a family of languages over a fixed alphabet Σ. The XOR-closure of $\mathcal{L}$ is defined to be

$$\langle \mathcal{L} \rangle := \{\{w \in \Sigma^* \mid |\{L \in \mathcal{S} \mid w \in L\}| \text{ is an odd number}\} \mid \mathcal{S} \subseteq \mathcal{L}\},$$

i.e., the set of all possible symmetric differences (XOR combinations) of the languages in $\mathcal{L}$.

Remark 11. Clearly, $\langle\langle \mathcal{L} \rangle\rangle = \langle \mathcal{L} \rangle$ for all language families $\mathcal{L}$. Also note that $\langle \mathcal{L} \rangle$ is infinite iff $\mathcal{L}$ is. For finite $\mathcal{L}$, note that $|\langle \mathcal{L} \rangle|$ is a power of two. More specifically,

$$|\langle \mathcal{L} \rangle| \leq 2^{|\mathcal{L}|}.$$

Lemma 12. Let $\mathcal{A} = (Q, \Sigma_k, I, \Delta, F) \in$ unfa with $L(\mathcal{A}) = CONN_k$. Then, $|Q| \geq 2^k - 1$.

Proof. Let $\mathcal{M} := \{\sigma \in \Sigma_k \mid \sigma_{ij} = 0 \text{ for all } 1 < i \leq k \text{ and all } 1 \leq j \leq k\}$ and
$\mathcal{N} := \{\tau \in \Sigma_k \mid \tau_{ij} = 0 \text{ for all } 1 \leq i \leq k \text{ and all } 1 \leq j < k\}$.

That is, matrices $\sigma \in \mathcal{M}$ are defined by their first row, and matrices $\tau \in \mathcal{N}$ are defined by their last column. Let us order the matrices in $\mathcal{M}$ [$\mathcal{N}$] lexicographically, such that $\sigma^{(i)}$ [$\tau^{(i)}$] denotes the matrix with the binary representation of i in the first row [last column] (see Figure 2 for an example).

It is enough to look at words $w \in \mathcal{MN} = \{\sigma\tau \in \Sigma_k^2 \mid \sigma \in \mathcal{M} \text{ and } \tau \in \mathcal{N}\}$ and at whether they are elements of $CONN_k$ in order to show that unambiguous automata for $CONN_k$ require at least $2^k - 1$ states.

To do so, for every state $q \in Q$ which is reachable via a σ-transition for some $\sigma \in \mathcal{M}$, consider the set $N_q := \{\tau \in \mathcal{N} \mid (\Delta(\tau) \cdot F)(q) = 1\}$, the set of symbols τ from $\mathcal{N}$ which yield a transition from q to a final state. For states $q \in Q$ which are not reachable via a σ-transition, set $N_q := \emptyset$.

Fig. 2. The graph representation of $\sigma^{(13)}, \tau^{(18)} \in \Sigma_5$; $\tau^{(18)} \notin N_{13}$ because the bit-wise AND of 13 and 18 equals 0

We further set $\qquad \mathfrak{N} := \langle \{N_q \mid q \in Q\} \rangle.$

By Remark 11, we have $\quad |\mathfrak{N}| = |\langle \{N_q \mid q \in Q\} \rangle| \leq 2^{|\{N_q \mid q \in Q\}|} \leq 2^{|Q|}.$

For technical reasons, set $\overline{\mathfrak{N}} := \langle \{\mathcal{N} \setminus N_q \mid q \in Q\} \cup \{\mathcal{N}\} \rangle,$

for which we have $\mathfrak{N} \subseteq \overline{\mathfrak{N}}$ because the languages $\mathcal{N} \setminus N_q$, which generate $\overline{\mathfrak{N}}$, can be written as the symmetric difference (or XOR combination) of $\mathcal{N}$ and N_q, and $\mathcal{N} \in \overline{\mathfrak{N}}$. Since we also have that $\overline{\mathfrak{N}} \subseteq \langle \mathfrak{N} \cup \{\mathcal{N}\} \rangle$, we may conclude $|\mathfrak{N}| \geq \frac{1}{2}|\overline{\mathfrak{N}}|$, and thus
$$2 \cdot 2^{|Q|} \geq |\overline{\mathfrak{N}}|. \qquad (\star)$$

Using just the combinatorial properties of the language $CONN_k$ (or $CONN_k \cap \mathcal{MN}$, to be precise), we can construct the family $\overline{\mathfrak{N}}$ independently from $\mathcal{A}$:

For every number ℓ with $0 \leq \ell < 2^k$, consider the set (recall Figure 2)

$$
\begin{aligned}
N_\ell &:= \{\tau \in \mathcal{N} \mid I \cdot \Delta(\sigma^{(\ell)}) \cdot \Delta(\tau) \cdot F > 0\} \\
&= \{\tau \in \mathcal{N} \mid I \cdot \Delta(\sigma^{(\ell)}) \cdot \Delta(\tau) \cdot F = 1\} \\
&= \{\tau \in \mathcal{N} \mid \sigma^{(\ell)}\tau \in CONN_k\},
\end{aligned}
$$

which we will use to construct a hierarchy of language families as follows:

$$
\begin{aligned}
\mathfrak{N}_{2^k} &:= \langle \emptyset \rangle = \{\emptyset\} \\
\mathfrak{N}_\ell &:= \langle \mathfrak{N}_{\ell+1} \cup \{\mathcal{N} \setminus N_\ell\} \rangle = \langle \{\mathcal{N} \setminus N_i \mid i \geq \ell\} \rangle \quad \text{for all } 0 \leq \ell < 2^k.
\end{aligned}
$$

It is obvious that we have $\qquad \mathfrak{N}_{2^k} \subseteq \mathfrak{N}_{2^k-1} \subseteq \cdots \subseteq \mathfrak{N}_1 \subseteq \mathfrak{N}_0, \qquad (\star\star)$

and, of course, $\mathfrak{N}_0$ is finite.

Noting that $N_{2^k-1} = \mathcal{N}$, it is evident that $\mathfrak{N}_0 = \overline{\mathfrak{N}}$. It only remains to be shown that the hierarchy $(\star\star)$ is strict since according to Remark 11, the cardinalities of all $\mathfrak{N}_\ell$ must be powers of two, thus, $|\mathfrak{N}_0| = 2^{2^k}$, and $(\star)$ yields: $|Q| \geq 2^k - 1$.

In order to see the strictness of the hierarchy $(\star\star)$, we note that $\sigma^{(\ell)}\tau^{(2^k-1-\ell)} \notin CONN_k$ for all ℓ because the binary representations of ℓ and $2^k - 1 - \ell$ are complementary. For the same reason, $\sigma^{(i)}\tau^{(2^k-1-\ell)} \in CONN_k$ for all $i > \ell$. This yields $\tau^{(2^k-1-\ell)} \in \mathcal{N} \setminus N_\ell$. Now, $\mathcal{N} \setminus N_\ell \in \mathfrak{N}_\ell$, but $\mathcal{N} \setminus N_\ell \notin \mathfrak{N}_{\ell+1}$ because $\tau^{(2^k-1-\ell)} \notin L$ for all $L \in \mathfrak{N}_{\ell+1}$: Suppose that there existed $L \in \mathfrak{N}_{\ell+1}$ with $\tau^{(2^k-1-\ell)} \in L$. Hence, $\tau^{(2^k-1-\ell)}$ is an element of an odd number of languages $\mathcal{N} \setminus N_i$ with $i > \ell$, but $\tau^{(2^k-1-\ell)} \in N_i$ for all $i > \ell$, so it is an element of none of the complement languages. $\qquad \square$

Remark 13. Just as with $(BRIDGE_k)_{k=1}^\infty$, it is possible to use $(CONN_k)_{k=1}^\infty$ in order to show a gap between polynomial ambiguity and *fixed-constant* ambiguity [3]. Contrary to the class cafa where ambiguity is bounded only with respect to n (the length of the input word) and not to k (the index in the language family), a sequence of automata $(\mathcal{A}_k)_{k=1}^\infty$ is said to have fixed-constant ambiguity iff there is a constant c such that $\mathrm{amb}_{\mathcal{A}_k}(w) \leq c$ for all words w and all indices k. (Note that *"fixed-constant"* does *not* constitute a class akin to those of Definition 6.) This result can be generalized to the case where constants need not be fixed but must not grow too fast with respect to k [4]. Again, this generalization is also possible using $CONN_k$.

Fig. 3. Simulating arbitrary symbols with $K_k \cup Z_k$

4   Decreasing the Alphabet Size

It is striking that $CONN_k$ is defined over alphabets not only of a non-constant but even of a gigantic size: Since Σ_k contains all triangular Boolean matrices of size $k \times k$, we have $|\Sigma_k| = 2^{\binom{k+1}{2}}$. However, we can get rid of most of the symbols in Σ_k without any impact on whether the resulting subsets of $CONN_k$ can still be used to show cafa $\prec_{2^n}$ pafa.

Definition 14. Let Γ and Λ be sub-alphabets of Σ_k. Γ is said to be Λ-*full* iff for all $\sigma \in \Lambda$, there is a word $w \in \Gamma^*$ such that $\sigma = \iota(w)$, i.e., all matrices from Λ can be simulated by a product of matrices from Γ.

First, we will see that we can restrict ourselves to those symbols which differ from the unit matrix in exactly one entry. In their bipartite graph representation, these may either be symbols that connect all $\bar{i}$ with the corresponding $\underline{i}$ but one, which they "white out." Or, these may be symbols that, again contain all $(\bar{i}, \underline{i})$ edges, but also exactly one $(\overline{i_1}, \underline{i_2})$ edge (with $i_1 < i_2$).

Definition 15. Let $\kappa_\ell^{(k)}$ be the $k \times k$ unit matrix except in the ℓ-th diagonal entry (let it be zero there), and let $\chi_{i_1 i_2}^{(k)}$ be the $k \times k$ unit matrix except in the (i_1, i_2) entry (let it be one there).
Let $K_k := \{\kappa_\ell^{(k)} \mid 1 \le \ell \le k\}$ and $Z_k := \{\chi_{i_1 i_2}^{(k)} \mid 1 \le i_1 < i_2 \le k\}$.

Lemma 16. $K_k \cup Z_k$ is Σ_k-full. (For an idea for a proof, see Figure 3.)
This means we can restrict ourselves to the analysis of the effect of the symbols in K_k and Z_k. Note that $|K_k \cup Z_k| = k + \binom{k}{2} = \binom{k+1}{2}$, which already constitutes a tremendous decrease of the alphabet size. We can still do better, though [5].

5   Miscellaneous Aspects of Ambiguity in Automata

It is worth noting that there is a very simple syntactic criterion as to whether any given automaton has exponential (i.e., super-polynomial), polynomial (i.e., unbounded), or constant ambiguity. Since we are dealing with separating polynomial (unbounded) ambiguity from constant one, we recall a result from [11]:

Lemma 17. Let $\mathcal{A} = (Q, \Sigma, I, \Delta, F) \in$ pafa, and let $\mathcal{A}$ have no superfluous (non-reachable or non-productive) states. Then, $\mathcal{A} \not\in$ cafa iff there are two distinct states $q_1, q_2 \in Q$ and there exists a word $w \in \Sigma^*$ such that q_1 is reachable from q_1 via w, q_2 is reachable from q_1 via w, and q_2 is reachable from q_2 via w.

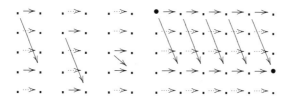

Fig. 4. Three Zs from Z_5 and the fifth power of the leftmost Z

In the automata $\mathcal{A}_k \in \mathsf{pafa}\backslash\mathsf{cafa}$ from Remark 9, all pairs of distinct states play the role of the preceding lemma. Most notably, consider the symbols from the set Z_k from Lemma 16. The reader may notice that the notation "Z_k" was chosen deliberately: Its symbols resemble the shape of a mirrored Z (see Figure 4).

Indeed, powers of these (mirrored) "Zs" are to blame for why automata need unbounded ambiguity in order to recognize $CONN_k$: Since the decision to shift from the corresponding upper row in the $(|w| + 1)$-partite graph (as defined in Remark 9) to the corresponding lower row can be deferred arbitrarily often, it seems mandatory that every automaton that recognizes $CONN_k$ have unbounded ambiguity unless it keeps track of sufficiently much information – as does the deterministic automaton for $CONN_k$: It simply keeps track of the exact subset of reachable nodes from $\{1, \ldots, k\}$.

Unfortunately, these intuitive attempts to (eventually) prove $\mathsf{cafa} \prec_{2^n} \mathsf{pafa}$ have failed so far. It seems misled to try and shrink the relevant alphabet as long as we are unable to say anything useful about the capabilities of constantly ambiguous automata with respect to $CONN_k$.

Definition 18. Let S be some set and let $M\colon S \times S \to \{0, 1\}$ be a binary matrix over $S \times S$. M is called *idempotent* iff M^2 and M have the same non-zero pattern, i.e., iff for all $s, t \in S$, we have

$$M(s, t) = 1 \iff \exists u \in S\colon M(s, u) = M(u, t) = 1.$$

Fact 19. All the symbols/matrices in $K_k \cup Z_k$ are idempotent.

The last observation means that in any automaton $\mathcal{A}$ with $L(\mathcal{A}) = CONN_k \cap (K_k \cup Z_k)^*$ where $\Delta(\sigma)$ is not idempotent for any $\sigma \in \Sigma_k$, we can make it idempotent. Simply compute all powers $(\Delta(\sigma))^i$ of $\Delta(\sigma)$ until the pattern of non-zeros becomes stable (which happens after finitely many steps, of course). Let $\Delta'(\sigma)$ be the Boolean matrix with zeros wherever all the matrices $(\Delta(\sigma))^i$ have zero entries (and ones in the other entries). We may replace Δ by Δ' because $\mathcal{A}$, by definition of $CONN_k$, must not notice the difference: Wherever a symbol σ from Z_k (or K_k) is replaced by a (non-empty) power of itself, this has no consequences as to the membership in $CONN_k$ of words which σ is a factor of.

Hence, without loss of generality, all matrices $\Delta(\sigma)$ should be idempotent. The layout of a proof to $\mathsf{cafa} \prec_{2^n} \mathsf{pafa}$ should look like this: Suppose, there is an automaton $\mathcal{A}$ with $o(2^k)$ states which recognizes $CONN_k$. Then, show that $\mathcal{A} \notin \mathsf{cafa}$, i.e., show that it fulfills the criteria of Lemma 17.

To have the transition matrices of $\mathcal{A}$ be idempotent is a strong constraint: For all (useful) transitions $(q_1, q_2) \in \Delta^{-1}(\sigma)$, we have either $(\Delta(\sigma))(q_1, q_1) = 1$ or $(\Delta(\sigma))(q_2, q_2) = 1$ (but not both, since then, $\mathcal{A} \notin$ cafa). If we think of the matrices $\Delta(\sigma)$ as adjacency matrices of bipartite graphs again, this means there are lots of horizontal edges and Zs that are deprived of one horizontal edge. Hence, the task is to emulate the behavior of Zs with these "half-Zs," which sounds as if it could be a provably hard task.

References

1. Hopcroft, J., Motwani, R., Ullman, J.: Introduction to Automata and Language Theory. Addison-Wesley, 2000
2. Hromkovič, J.: Communication Complexity and Parallel Computing. Springer '97
3. Hromkovič, J., Karhumäki, J., Klauck, H., Seibert, S., Schnitger, G.: Measures on Nondeterminism in Finite Automata. In: Proc. ICALP 2000, LNCS **1853**, Springer (2000) 199–210
4. Kupke, J.: Limiting the Ambiguity of Non-Deterministic Finite Automata. Diploma Thesis, RWTH Aachen (2002). Available online at:
   http://www-i1.informatik.rwth-aachen.de/~joachimk/ltaondfa.ps
5. Kupke, J.: On Separating Constant from Polynomial Ambiguity of Finite Automata. http://www.ite.ethz.ch/people/jkupke/publications/oscfpaofa.ps
6. Gramlich, G., and Schnitger, G.: Minimizing NFAs and Regular Expressions. In: Proc. STACS 2005, LNCS **3404**, Springer (2005) 399–411
7. Leung, H.: Separating Exponentially Ambiguous Finite Automata from Polynomially Ambiguous Finite Automata. SIAM J. Comp. **27** (1998) 1073–1082
8. Moore, F.: On the Bounds for State-Set Size in the Proofs of Equivalence between Deterministic, Nondeterministic, and Two-Way Finite Automata. IEEE Trans. Comput. **20** (1971) 1211–1214
9. Ravikumar, B., and Ibarra, O.: Relating the Type of Ambiguity of Finite Automata to the Succinctness of Their Representation. SIAM J. Comp. **18** (1989) 1263–1282
10. Sipser, M.: Lower Bounds on the Size of Sweeping Automata. J. Comp. and Sys. Sci. **21** 2 (1980) 195–202
11. Weber, A., Seidl, H.: On the Ambiguity of Finite Automata. MFCS 1986, LNCS **233** Springer (1986) 620–629

Reliable Broadcasting
Without Collision Detection[*]
Extended Abstract

Jarosław Kutyłowski[1] and Filip Zagórski[2]

[1] International Graduate School of Dynamic Intelligent Systems,
University of Paderborn
[2] Institute of Mathematics and Computer Science,
Wrocław University of Technology

Abstract. We propose a dynamic, ad-hoc communication network consisting of mobile units that can warn about traffic jams on motorways.

Our goal is to provide a practical, low cost solution. Therefore we consider very simple wireless communication hardware, without collision detection, with very small bandwidth and a probabilistic model of link failure.

We provide a complete system architecture. For this purpose we design and analyze solutions for size approximation, leader election and broadcasting. Our algorithms are fine-tuned for fast operation in a practical setting. We provide both a theoretical and experimental evaluation of our solutions.

Our contribution is much different from the previous work, where either pure theoretical models with a pure theoretical analysis are provided or algorithms working in practical models are evaluated only through simulations.

1 Introduction

Communication in ad-hoc networks has been a broadly studied topic recently. A wide range of algorithms for routing [6], broadcasting [8],[7], MAC protocols [2] and algorithms for leader election [5], [3] and size approximation [4] have been proposed. Usually, the authors consider networks, where the number of participating nodes is a parameter n that can take arbitrary values. So the focus is on solutions that achieve good performance in parameters that depend on n.

A typical approach in the literature is to use layered solutions, where routing and broadcasting algorithms are layered on top of MAC protocols, which themselves use leader election algorithms for proper operation. This ensures ease of design and maintenance as each layer is responsible for assuring only a few properties. However, it degrades performance to some extent. This is a minor issue

---

[*] Partially supported by the EU within the 6th Framework Programme under contract 001907 (DELIS).

J. Wiedermann et al. (Eds.): SOFSEM 2006, LNCS 3831, pp. 389–398, 2006.

for modern communication hardware (e.g. WLAN) operating with high bandwidths. However, this becomes a significant problem, if we work with extremely simple hardware and a low-bandwidth communication channel. Moreover, we have to design algorithms having good performance for small parameter values, asymptotical behavior is less important.

Problem Statement. Our goal is to design an ad-hoc communication system for cars traveling along a motorway so that they can be warned about conditions ahead (like jams, accidents, ...). Certainly, there are hundreds of ways, in which one can deploy such a warning system. However our goal is to find a low-cost solution with a minimal number of resources used, and working in an environment with many faults. (Of course, the system will be designed in a much more general setting, we start with a concrete scenario in order to justify some parameter choices.)

We assume that no infrastructure can be used for the system – it consists solely of mobile nodes installed on mobile cars. The proposed system relies on very limited communication hardware with the following properties:

- transmission range is r,
- only one frequency channel is available for transmission,
- the available bandwidth is practically in the order of a few Kbits per second,
- the transmitters are synchronized,
- a transmission can be properly received, if it has been sent by a node within distance r from the receiver and no other transmitters are active during this time within the interference range of $2r$, i.e. no collision has occurred.
- collision detection is limited: only a sender of a message can check whether his message has been sent successfully, other nodes cannot distinguish between a collision, random noise and lack of transmission,
- transmissions are unreliable – i.e. a collision free transmission is received by a node with a constant probability p_r (this models imperfections of the wireless channel).

We design a complete system fulfilling the above goals and provide both theoretical and experimental analysis. The core of the system are algorithms for size approximation, leader election and broadcasting. These algorithms cooperate tightly to ensure that messages propagate fast along the motorway. In detail, we present:

- the overall system architecture for the interaction of all necessary algorithms (Section 2),
- a size approximation algorithm which runs in linear time with respect to the maximum number of stations in a sector (Section 3),
- a leader election algorithm which elects a leader in logarithmic time in terms of the maximum number of stations in a sector (Section 4),
- a reliable broadcasting algorithm (Section 5).

Section 6 concludes the paper with the results of an experimental evaluation.

Due to space limitations a proofs of several lemmas have been omitted in this version of the paper and can be found in the full version.

2   System Architecture

The main functionality of the system is provided by a broadcasting algorithm (BA) which passes information from a traffic jam to other stations on the road. For the broadcasting algorithm, the road has been conceptually divided into geographical sectors of relatively small length, which is the half of the transmission range. This implies that cars must be able to determine the sector they are currently in (e.g. by utilizing GPS).

For the communication to work properly, we assume that all transmitters are synchronized. As there is only one frequency available for communication, a time-division protocol is used in order to split available transmission time.

It may not be allowed for all sectors to broadcast their message at the same time since the interferences would cause an excess of collisions. Thus each sector is allowed to transmit only in specific time slots. These time slots are allocated in such a way, that only sectors in a sufficient distance transmit in parallel. Thus each BCAST slot (as shown in Fig. 1) is divided into a constant number of sub-slots in which appropriate sectors can transmit. The same applies for size approximation and leader election.

Periodically, the number of nodes in each sector is estimated by the size approximation algorithm (SA). This estimation is used by the leader election algorithm (LEA). Before each time slot used for broadcasting there is a time slot devoted to leader election, so that during broadcasting there is a leader in each in each sector. Figure 1 illustrates this division.

Fig. 1. Static time division between algorithms

The only algorithm utilizing communication between sectors is the broadcast algorithm. Size approximation and leader election work locally within respective sectors. This implies that these algorithms work in a one-hop wireless network.

3   Size Approximation

In this section we present an algorithm estimating the number of stations in a single-hop radio network. We assume that an upper bound on number of stations in a sector is known to each station (the number of cars in a sector is limited – this follows from physical sizes!). We do not demand from the nodes to have unique IDs.

In contrast to many previous solutions we do not pay attention to energy cost of our algorithms (i.e. the number of time slots, when a station transmits or listens to the communication channel), since in our case we have a large amount of energy available from the car's electrical system. Our aim is to get algorithms which are fast and reliable. We are interested in achieving good results for a small number of stations, without considering asymptotic complexity.

Multi-Round Algorithm. We call a transmission proper (or successful), if it does not collide with any other transmission. We divide stations in two groups: active stations and inactive stations. Inactive stations are those which are allowed to listen only. Active stations listen, too, but they can also transmit messages. (Simultaneous transmitting and listening is feasible in our case, since transmitter and receiver can be installed on different parts of a car.)

In our algorithm, the goal is that every station has exactly one successful transmission during the algorithm. Then we take the number of successful transmissions as an estimated number of stations within the sector. We will show that with high probability the number of successful transmissions is equal to the number of stations in the sector, if parameters are suitably chosen. In the following paragraphs we assume that the maximum number of stations in a sector is equal to N_{max}, the actual number of stations is N and, as a result of the algorithm each station knows n, an approximation of N.

The algorithm runs for a duration of f rounds, each consisting of M_j single-bit transmission slots. At the beginning, all stations are active. All stations (both active and inactive) listen all the time.

Before a round j, each active station i chooses uniformly and independently at random a transmission slot $T_{i,j} \in 1, \ldots, M_j$. Then, within round j, every active station i sends a single bit message in transmission slot $T_{i,j}$. When there are no collisions with other transmissions, i.e. $T_{i,j} \neq T_{k,j}$ for every $i \neq k$, the message is received properly by every station.

Every station counts the number of proper transmissions in each round. A station which has succeeded (i.e. its transmission was successful) becomes inactive. Active stations, which did not manage to successfully transmit in round j, remain active.

After f rounds, every station computes an estimation of the number of stations as the number of successful transmissions from all rounds.

Analysis of One Round. Now we shall investigate the properties of one round of the Multi-Round Algorithm. Based on that knowledge, we can set an optimal number and length of rounds.

Expected Number of Successful Transmissions. Let S^j denote the number of successful transmissions in the jth round.

Lemma 1. *Let N_j denote the number of active stations in the jth round. Let M_j be the number of transmission slots of the jth round. Then the expected number of new inactive stations after the j-th round is $N_j(1 - 1/M_j)^{N_j-1}$.* □

Optimal Length of Rounds. Now we investigate an optimal trade-off between the number of transmission slots for a given round and the expected number of successful transmissions. For a fixed number of stations we want to maximize the expected number of successes per transmission slot for each round of the algorithm.

Consider the function $\mu(m,n) = n(1 - \frac{1}{m})^{n-1}$ equal to the expected number of successful transmissions in one round, assuming there are exactly n active stations in the given round and m time slots reserved for that round. Defining a price function $p(m,n) = \frac{\mu(m,n)}{m}$ describing the average number of successes per step and finding its minimum we obtain the result $m = n$. Thanks to this, we have an indication on how to set the number of transmission slots per round to achieve a good time efficiency.

To obtain a sequence of round lenghts we set $M_1 = N_{max}$, and for the next rounds, we set the number of time slots equal to the expected number of active stations $M_{i+1} = M_i - \mu(M_i, N_i) = M_i - \mu(M_i, M_i)$.

Deviation from Expectation. The previous analysis bases only on expectations and is thus insufficient. In Lemma 2 we limit the deviation of S^j from its expectation. Its proof can be found in the full version of the paper.

Lemma 2.

$$\Pr[E[S^j]^2 - S^j \geq \lambda] \leq \exp\left(-\frac{\lambda^2 N^2(2M-1)}{2(M-1)^2(N^2 - E[S^j]^2)}\right). \tag{1}$$

□

By Lemma 2 we estimate how many stations will become inactive after one round with high probability. We define $\lambda(m,n,\delta)$ to be a number λ such that Eq. 1 is satisfied for $M = m$, $N = n$ and probability not greater than δ. With this in mind, we can redefine the price function $p(m,n) = \frac{\mu(m,n)-\lambda(m,n,\delta)}{m}$. Choosing for each round such a length M_j that $p(M_{j-1}, N_{j-1})$ is maximized and setting $N_j = N_{j-1} - (\mu(M_j, N_{j-1}) - \lambda(M_j, N_{j-1}, \delta))$ we obtain a sequence of round lengths $\{M_1, \ldots, M_k\}$ which allow the algorithm to count the number of nodes precisely with probability greater than $1 - k\delta$. Unfortunately the bound on the deviation as presented in Lemma 2 is not applicable for $N \leq 10$ as it is not tight enough to produce reasonable results.

Link Unreliability. In the proofs we have omitted the problem of link unreliability to avoid complex analysis. Because every node hears proper transmission with probability p_r, the expected estimated value is $\geq p_r N$.

Evaluation. Here we give some calculated examples of the time efficiency of the proposed algorithms. We assume a maximum of 100 stations in one sector and try to minimize the time needed for the size approximation in such a setting. The analysis based on expectations gives us a sequence of round lengths $\{100, 63, 40, 25, 16, 10, 6, 4\}$ with a total length of 264 time slots. Obviously the analysis taking deviations into account suggests us to allocate more time slots, in detail this is $\{140, 106, 90, 75, 78, 55, 48\}$ with a total length of 592 slots.

We have performed 100000 independent experiments for the worst case of $n = 100$ and the second sequence of round's lengths. In all cases the precise number of nodes was computed by the algorithm. In the same setting, the first sequence achieves a probability of 0.45 to estimate the number of stations perfectly.

4   Leader Election

The algorithm consists of one-bit transmission slots, called steps. During one step each node transmits messages with probability $1/n$, where n denotes the node's estimation of the total number of nodes in the sector. The first node, which successfully transmits its message becomes the leader.

During the remaining steps every node that knows that a leader has been elected sends messages in each step in order to prevent the other stations from becoming a leader.

For the analysis of the leader election algorithm see the full version of this paper.

5   Broadcast

The broadcast algorithm works as follows. The key role of the stations in each sector is to forward messages to the next sector. The only active station in each sector in a given point of time is the leader of this sector. Thus it is his responsibility to resend a received message. Leaders should resend a message so that a sector as a whole resends the message a predefined constant number of times.

Each node remembers the messages it has seen coming from the previous sector (those which should be forwarded). It also remembers all messages it has heard from the leader of its section, which it has not heard from the previous sector. It remembers also for each message how many times it was heard from a leader of its sector. If a message is resent often enough (a constant number of times), the node marks it as processed. The message is also marked as processed when the station leaves the sector.

Analysis. Due to the properties of the communication model, the analysis of the broadcast algorithm is probabilistic. The reliability of the algorithm is measured in terms of the probability of successful transmission of a message between two distant sectors in a given time.

The key problem which underlies the broadcast reliability is the link unreliability. After a transmission from sector S only a fraction of all stations in sector $S + 1$ knows about the transmitted message and can transmit it to the next sector.

In order to simplify the analysis we make two assumptions. First, we disregard node mobility (in terms of nodes leaving and joining a sector). We will show that a message is with high probability transmitted to the next sector within two time slots. Even with low bandwidth for transmissions these two time slots correspond to a fraction of a second – only a small number of stations can change sectors in this time. The experimental evaluation presented in Section 6 takes node mobility fully into account. Second, we assume that only one message is traveling through the system.

We are going to analyze what happens when a message reaches some sector S, i.e. it is transmitted by sector $S - 1$. The number of stations which have heard this transmission is described by the binomial distribution with success probability p_r (recall that p_r denotes the probability of hearing a successful transmission) and n trials. Then the probability that exactly k of n stations received a message correctly is equal to $\binom{n}{k}p_r^k(1 - p_r)^{n-k}$. The probability that this message is retransmitted by sector S in the next broadcast slot is equal to $\frac{k}{n}$, as we assume that the leader election algorithm chooses uniformly at random one of the stations and k of n stations know about the message.

So the probability that a message is passed from the Sth sector to the $S + 1$st sector, after there has been a transmission from the sector $S - 1$, is equal to:

$$\sum_{k=0}^{n} \binom{n}{k} p_r^k (1 - p_r)^{n-k} \frac{k}{n} = \frac{1}{n}(1 - p_r)^n \sum_{k=0}^{n} \binom{n}{k} k \left(\frac{p_r}{1 - p_r}\right)^k = p_r \ .$$

Let us describe this value by $P_1^{p_r,n}$. With $P_k^{p_r,n}$ we describe the probability that a message is passed successfully from sector S to sector $S + 1$ for the first time in the kth broadcast slot ($k - 1$ previous steps were unsuccessful).

The problem with values $P_k^{p_r,n}$ is that they are hard to compute. Thus in Lemma 4 we develop an approximation for them, based on auxiliary Lemma 3.

Lemma 3. *For every i, n and every series k_i it holds*

$$\left(1 - \sum_{i=1}^{l} \frac{k_i}{n} \prod_{j=1}^{i-1}\left(1 - \frac{k_j}{n}\right)\right) = \prod_{j=1}^{l}\left(1 - \frac{k_j}{n}\right) \ . \qquad \square$$

Lemma 4. *For all l and n,*

$$\sum_{i=1}^{l} P_i^{p_r,n} \geq \sum_{k=0}^{n}\sum_{i=1}^{l} \binom{n}{k} p_r^k (1 - p_r)^{n-k} \frac{k}{n}\left(1 - \frac{k}{n}\right)^{i-1} \ . \qquad \square$$

Lemma 5. *For all $p_r \in (0,1)$ there exists a constant c such that for all $n \geq 1$ and $l \geq 1$ the following inequality holds:*

$$\sum_{k=0}^{n}\sum_{i=1}^{l} \binom{n}{k} p_r^k (1 - p_r)^{n-k} \frac{k}{n}\left(1 - \frac{k}{n}\right)^{i-1} \geq c \sum_{i=1}^{l} p_r(1 - p_r)^{i-1} \ .$$

Proof. The inequality has been numerically evaluated for all $l \geq 1$ and $n \geq 1$. c is an increasing function of n and l for all $n \geq 1$ and $l \geq 2$. For $l = 1$ the sums are equal. Thus c can be chosen as the value required for $l = 2$ for the smallest n used practically. $\square$

Now, we are ready to investigate the reliability of the algorithm. We will consider random variables $F(i,j)$, where $F(i,j)$ is the probability that a message travels from the sector S to sector $S + i$ in exactly j broadcast slots. It is easy to see that the following recursive equation holds

$$F(i,j) = \begin{cases} \sum_{k=i-1}^{j-1} F(i-1,k)P_{j-k}^{p_r,n} \, , & \text{if } i > 1 \\ P_j^{p_r,n} \, , & \text{if } i = 1 \, . \end{cases}$$

Of course, $F(i,j) = 0$ for $j < i$.

We are interested in finding the value of $\sum_{t=0}^{m} F(i, i+t)$, which defines the probability that a message travels the requested distance in $i + m$ or less transmission slots. Unfortunately, the values $F(i,j)$ are hard to compute (mainly because of $P_{j-k}^{p_r,n}$). Thus we will substitute $F(i,j)$ with $T(i,j)$. We define

$$T(i,j) = \begin{cases} \sum_{k=i-1}^{j-1} T(i-1,k)p_r(1-p_r)^{j-k-1} \, , & \text{if } i > 1 \\ (1-p_r)^{j-1}p_r & , & \text{if } i = 1 \, . \end{cases}$$

In Lemma 6, we show that the series $T(i,j)$ is a lower bound for $F(i,j)$.

Lemma 6. *For given p_r, and c from Lemma 5, for all i,m*

$$\sum_{j=1}^{m} F(i,j) \geq c^i \sum_{j=1}^{m} T(i,j) \, . \qquad \square$$

By Lemma 6 we can use $T(i,j)$ instead of $F(i,j)$.

It is easy to see that $T(i,j) = w(i,j)p_r^i(1-p_r)^{j-i}$ as there should be exactly i successful transmissions and exactly $j - i$ failures. One can derive values $T(i,j)$ from $T(i-1,k)$, for $i - 1 \leq k \leq j - 1$. The following equality holds for $i \geq 2$:

$$T(i,j) = \sum_{k=i-1}^{j-1} T(i-1,k)(1-p_r)^{j-k-1}p_r \, .$$

Thanks to that, one can find the coefficient $w(i,j)$:

$$T(i,j+1) = \sum_{k=i-1}^{j} T(i-1,k)(1-p_r)^{j-k}p_r$$

$$= (1-p_r) \sum_{k=i-1}^{j-1} T(i-1,k)(1-p_r)^{j-k}p_r + p_rT(i-1,j)$$

$$= (1-p_r)T(i,j) + p_rT(i-1,j).$$

Now, while comparing coefficients w, we get $w(i, j+1) = w(i, j) + w(i-1, j)$, hence $w(i, j) = \binom{j-1}{i-1}$. Finally, we get

$$T(i, j) = \binom{j-1}{i-1} p_r^i (1 - p_r)^{j-i} .$$

Thus we can lower bound the value of

$$\sum_{t=0}^{x} P(i, i+t) \geq c^i \sum_{t=0}^{x} T(i, i+t) = c^i \sum_{t=0}^{x} \binom{i+t-1}{i-1} p_r^i (1 - p_r)^t .$$

Evaluation. With the assumption of $p_r = 0.9$ the value of c from Lemma 5 has to be set to 0.9818. This gives a probability of traveling a distance of 10 sectors within 20 slots of time equal to approximately 0.83. For practical parameters (sector length 250 meters and 10 broadcast time slots per second) this distance and time correspond to 2.5 kilometers and 2 seconds. If we additionally assume that there are at least 10 cars in each sector (for crowded traffic very common) then $c = 0.9909$ and thus the probability of traveling 10 sectors in 20 time slots increases to 0.91.

6   Experimental Evaluation

The system has been evaluated experimentally within an environment based on a cellular automaton of the Helbing type (see [1]), which simulates the behavior of cars on a road.

The cellular automaton has been extended by allowing each car to run its own simulated wireless transceiver. Additionally each car is able to run the size approximation, leader election and broadcasting algorithms.

The goal of the simulator was to measure message travel time, leader election success rate and size approximation accuracy. The test environment consists of

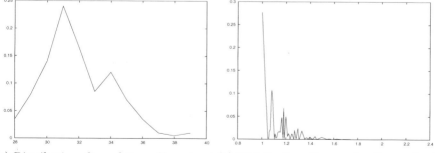

(a) Distribution of travel time of broadcast messages

(b) Distribution of approximation ratio of size approximation

Fig. 2. Reliability of algorithms in simulation

a road of 6.75 km length, thus being divided into 27 sectors. Every 3 seconds a broadcast is issued by the last sector and is forwarded by the broadcasting algorithm to the first sector. Figure 2(b) shows the distribution of the travel time of messages from the last sector to the first one. As there are 10 broadcast time slots in each second, the most common travel time of 31 time slots corresponds to 3.1 seconds. The p_r parameter has been set to 0.9.

The cars on the road travel with a maximum speed of 135 km/h, with a density of 0.3 and all other cellular automaton parameters as suggested in [1].

The leader election success rate is equal to 0.99959 and the size approximation accuracy is shown in Fig. 2(a). For every invocation the leader election algorithm was allowed to run for 20 rounds and the size approximation algorithm was allowed to run for 264 rounds, divided into 8 rounds as suggested in Section 3.

References

1. Helbing, D., and Schreckenberg, M.: Cellular Automata Simulating Experimental Properties of Traffic Flow. Physical Review E **59** 3 (March 1999)
2. Jurdak, R., Videira Lopes, C., and Baldi, P.: A Survey, Classification and Comparative Analysis of Medium Access Control Protocols for Ad Hoc Networks. IEEE Communications Surveys and Tutorials **6** 1 (First Quarter 2004) 2–16
3. Jurdziński, T., Kutyłowski, M., and Zatopiański, J.: Efficient Algorithms for Leader Election in Radio Networks. In PODC '02: Proceedings of the Twenty-First Annual Symposium on Principles of Distributed Computing, New York, NY, USA, ACM Press (2002) 51–57
4. Jurdziński, T., Kutyłowski, M., and Zatopiański, J.: Energy-Efficient Size Approximation of Radio Networks with no Collision Detection. In COCOON '02: Proceedings of the 8th Annual International Conference on Computing and Combinatorics, London, UK, Springer-Verlag (2002) 279–289
5. Malpani, N., Welch, J.L., and Vaidya, N.: Leader Election Algorithms for Mobile Ad Hoc Networks. In DIALM '00: Proceedings of the 4th International Workshop on Discrete Algorithms and Methods for Mobile Computing and Communications, New York, NY, USA, ACM Press (2000) 96–103
6. Ramanathan, S., and Steenstrup, M.: A Survey of Routing Techniques for Mobile Communications Networks. Mob. Netw. Appl. **1** 2 (1996) 89–104
7. Vollset, E., and Ezhilchelvan, P.: A Survey of Reliable Broadcast Protocols for Mobile Ad-Hoc Networks. Technical Report CS-TR-792, University of Newcastle upon Tyne (2003)
8. Williams, B., and Camp, T.: Comparison of Broadcasting Techniques for Mobile Ad Hoc Networks. In Proceedings of the ACM International Symposium on Mobile Ad Hoc Networking and Computing (MOBIHOC) (2002) 194–205

Semi-strong Static Type Checking of Object-Oriented Query Languages*

Michał Lentner[1], Krzysztof Stencel[2], and Kazimierz Subieta[3,1]

[1] Polish-Japanese Institute of Information Technology, Warsaw, Poland
[2] Institute of Informatics, Warsaw University, Warsaw, Poland
[3] Institute of Computer Science PAS, Warsaw, Poland

Abstract. We propose a new semi-strong approach to types and static type checking in object-oriented database query and programming languages. Many features of current object-oriented query/programming languages, such as naming, ellipses, automatic coercions and irregularities in data structures, cause that current formal strong type systems are irrelevant to practical situations. There is a need for semi-strong, but still efficient type checking. We treat types as syntactic qualifiers (signatures) attached to objects, procedures, modules and other data/program entities. In our approach a type inference system is based on decision tables involving signatures and producing type checking decisions. A type checker is based on data structures which statically model run-time structures and processes: a metabase, a static environment stack, a static result stack and a type inference decision tables. To discover several type errors in one run we use the mechanism for restoring the state of the type checker after a type error.

1 Introduction

Apparently, strong type checking of object-oriented or XML-oriented query languages integrated with programming languages is exhausted by the current state-of-the-art. There are thousands of papers on types. Many of them deal with bulk types typical for databases and database programming languages, including query languages. There are also many practical proposals of type systems implemented in object-oriented programming languages (e.g. C++ or Java) as well as in research prototypes, e.g. PS-Algol, DBPL, Galileo, Napier-89, Fibonacci, etc. (see overviews [2], [3]). A strong typing system (however, criticized [1]) has also been proposed within the ODMG standard [7] for object databases. Although typing was not the main concern of the SQL-99 standard, it contains many pages devoted to types. Recently the XQuery standard proposal is also claimed to be strongly typed and corresponding typecheckers have been developed (see e.g. [8]).

However, there are features of query/programming languages and environments that make implementation of types difficult. Taking into account such issues as

---

* This paper presents a part of the research preceding the 6th Framework European Project eGov Bus, IST-026727-STP.

J. Wiedermann et al. (Eds.): SOFSEM 2006, LNCS 3831, pp. 399–408, 2006.

400 M. Lentner, K. Stencel, and K. Subieta

mutability, collection cardinality constraints, collection kinds, type equivalence based on type names, inheritance and multiple inheritance, dynamic object roles and dynamic inheritance, modules, export and import lists, etc. causes that the type notion is tangled with so many details and peculiarities that typical type systems known e.g. from functional languages become idealistic and impractical. Moreover, irregularities in data structures (null values, repeating data, variants/unions, unconstrained data names), ellipses and automatic coercions occurring in queries cause that strong typing should be relaxed to be efficient for the programmers.

Indeed, strong type checking professionals are trying to convince the community that all what should be done is already done. On the other hand, the typing solutions of the ODMG standard and challenging implementation of types in XQuery cause another impression. Developers of many web and database programming tools ignore types totally because the theories are obscure and implementation is too difficult. If it is so good in theory, why it is so bad in practice? We have checked this fundamental question by implementation of a strong type checker within our recent project ODRA, an object-oriented database server devoted to Web and grid applications. ODRA is based on the query/language SBQL, incomparably more powerful than ODMG OQL (because of its algorithmic power) and Xquery (because of updating facilities and views). SBQL is not only a very powerful object-oriented query language, it is also extended by imperative constructs of programming languages (a la Oracle PL/SQL or SQL-99), programming abstractions such as procedures, functions and methods, and database abstractions such as stored procedures and updateable views.

The report [6] and this paper present the first inferences concerning this experience. First, we have concluded that many theories are good guidelines, but eventually must be corrected by practical considerations. Second, strong typing systems presented by the theories are too strong and must be relaxed to meet reality. Therefore we propose a new semi-strong approach to the problem. Third, the major issues in the typing systems are not theoretical, but practical development of solutions that meet the typical programmer's psychology. Psychology is hardly formalized, thus a lot of solutions in our typing system is dependent on (sometimes random) decisions which anticipate further behaviour of the programmers.

To make our contribution more clear, we present the following example from the ODMG standard. The problem concerns auxiliary names or "synonyms" or "iteration variables" in languages such as SQL and OQL. Consider the following OQL query, p. 104 [7]:

select * **from** *Students* **as** *x*, *x.takes* **as** *y*, *y.taught_by* **as** *z*
where *z.rank* = "full professor"

The query defines three names *x, y, z*, considered "iteration variables". According to the scope rules (p. 112), their scope is limited to this query (they have no meaning outside it). But it appears (p. 105) that the type returned by this query is:

bag<struct (*x:Students*, *y:Section*, *z:Professor*)>

The semantic qualification of these names is changed: instead of being "iteration variables" they become structure field labels. Because the output of the query can be used in another (outer) query, these names can be used outside the query where they have been defined (which is inconsistent with the assumed scope rules).

This example shows very basic questions:

(1) Which formal model makes it possible to change iteration variables into structure field labels?
(2) What is the real scope for x, y, z?
(3) How the semantics can be correctly formalized?
(4) How this situation can be correctly statically typed?
(5) Which of the currently known typing systems can handle such situations?

In our formalization of SBQL [11] we have shown that intuitions of the ODMG are correct. We have precisely defined the semantics of the **as** operator, but this semantics has no precedents in programming languages. The resulting type is as shown above, however, the scope of variables x, y, z is restricted in a way that is different from any kind of textual query/program parentheses (a query, a program block, a procedure, a module, etc.). Obviously, the type inference engine should approximate run-time calculations during parse/compilation time. However, because such a semantic situation is unknown in programming languages, the answer for (5) is negative: no currently known typing systems is proper. The answer for (4) is (in particular) the subject of our research: we show how this case can be correctly typed.

This is one of many examples showing that current trends in object-oriented and XML-oriented databases and query languages go far beyond the proposals of strong polymorphic typing systems that are known from previous years. Even apparently innocent concept of *collection* (bulk type) causes difficulties. In particular, it is normal e.g. in SQL that a collection with one value v is considered equivalent to the value v (see nested *select* clauses in SQL). This kind of coercion requires shifting some type checks to run time. Careful analysis has shown that collections (especially heterogeneous ones) are in contradictions with the fundamental for object-orientedness substitutability and open-close principles. In XML technologies (DTD and XML Schema) the collection concept is replaced by the cardinality constraint concept, which makes quite a big difference for static typing systems (bulk types are type constructors, while cardinalities are attributes of internal type signatures). Again, we didn't find any static typing system dealing with cardinalities rather than collections. Such cases have convinced us that static strong typing requires nowadays a quite new approach. We call it *semi-strong typechecking* (after semi-structured data concept). A thorough description of the approach and implementation can be found in [6].

Data schemata partly release programming languages from keeping type information. Run-time libraries or programs read this information from schemata stored by databases. In this way types become neutral to programming languages. This assumption is the basis of the type systems of CORBA [10] and ODMG [7]. Some hybrid solutions are proposed which consists in textual mapping of types (defined e.g. in CORBA IDL) to types specific to a programming language. In our approach we assume that the semi-strong type checking mechanism is directly based on the database schema. We do not consider how our type system can be mapped to a typical object-oriented programming language such as C++ or Java. Because our typing system is much more sophisticated, this probably would not be an easy task.

Our idea follows the Stack-Based Approach [12], [11], which explains the mechanism of query evaluation for object-oriented databases through concepts well-known in programming languages. It involves three basic architectural elements: an object store, an environment stack and a result stack. The idea of a static type checker consists in simulating actions of the above three run-time structures during the compile time. This concept (executing programs on abstract data to obtain information about them) is the underlying intention of abstract interpretation, which was first proposed in [4] and some other work has been done later [9].

A static type checker consists of the following architectural elements: a metabase (a counterpart of an object store), a static environment stack, a static result stack and type inference decision tables for all operators introduced in a given query/programming language.

A particular row of a decision table contains signatures of the given operator arguments and the decision, which is one of the three items: (1) it determines the resulting signature for the given operator and signatures of its arguments; (2) it qualifies situation as a type error; (3) it qualifies the situation as impossible to check statically and adds run-time coercions and/or pushes the type check to run-time.

Type inference decision tables make type soundness a straightforward issue, provided that the description of query operators indeed matches their run-time behavior. Our approach facilitates accommodating non-standard ad-hoc features of practical languages better than conventional type systems, since the operational semantics can be modeled more directly. Such ad-hoc features are very useful in semi-structured processing.

Our semi-strong approach to typing is very different from everything what till now has happened in the domain. The approach is supported by experimental implementation in the ODRA system, where we have shown that the idea is implementable, efficient and has many advantages over current proposals for database typing systems. The comparison with similar existing proposals is difficult due to incompleteness and inconsistency (hence, non-implementability) of some proposals, much higher functionality and power of SBQL in comparison to e.g. ODMG OQL and XQuery, totally different formal background, unknown implementation features of majority of other proposals, etc. The black-box comparison convinced us that our approach offers for the designers of database languages much more flexible typing mechanisms that cover object-oriented, semi-structured and Web-oriented technologies.

The rest of the paper is organized as follows. In section 2 we present database schemata and metabases compiled from the schemata. Section 3 introduces the idea of type inference decision tables. Section 4 describes the type checking procedure. Section 5 concludes.

2   Database Schema and Metabase

A type system for a database is necessary to express the information on the conceptual and logical structure of the data store. The information is commonly referred to as the *database schema*. Fig.1 presents an example schema in an UML-like notation that can be easily transformed into e.g. ODMG ODL-like specification. Although basically the query engine is independent of the database schema, we need it to reason statically about type correctness of queries and programs. We also need it for other reasons, in particular, to enforce type constraints inside the object store, to resolve some binding ambiguities, to reason about ellipses, dereferences and coercions occurring in queries, and to optimize queries.

A schema has two forms: *external* (as presented for programmers, e.g. Fig.1) and *internal* (as used by the type inference engine). There is a lot of syntactic freedom concerning the external schema form and this issue we consider important but secondary. In this paper we are interested in an internal schema, which will be called *metabase*. A metabase represents schema information in a form of well-structured data (a graph), allowing for querying and for modification. A metabase statically models and reflects the data store and itself it looks like a data store. This idea is similar to DataGuides of Lore [5]. Fig.2 presents a metabase compiled from the schema depicted in Fig.1.

A node of a metabase graph represents some data entity (entities) of the object store: object(s), attribute(s), link(s), procedure, class, method, view, and perhaps others. Each node itself is a complex object having its non-printable identifier (we call it *static identifier*) which uniquely identifies the node. In this paper we assume a meta-language convention that the node describing entities named n has the identifier denoted i_n. The convention has no meaning for semantics and implementation of the static typing mechanism.

For simplification in this paper we "stick" representation of a complex object with representantation of its direct class. This does not lead to ambiguity, because on the run-time environment stack the section with binders to a complex object has always a twin, neighbouring section with binders to properties of its direct class. Such sticking of metabase nodes implies similar sticking of these two sections on the static environment stack, thus simplifies the metabase and implementation.

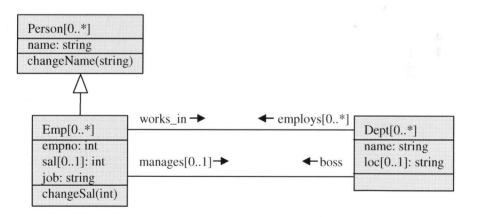

Fig. 1. An example database schema

As a complex object, a node of a metabase contains several attributes. In this paper we distinguish the following ones: **name**, **kind** (atomic, complex, link, procedure, method, class, etc.), **type** (an atomic type of objects described by the node; this attribute is not present in nodes describing complex and link objects, because their types are composed from types of other entities), **card** (cardinality). Cardinalities will be written as *i..j*, where *i* is the minimal number of described objects and *j* is the maximal number of them. If the number of described objects is unlimited, *j* has the value *. Cardinalities 0..0 and 1..1 will be written 0 and 1, and 0..* will be written as *.

There could be other attributes of the node, in particular, mutability (perhaps, subdivided into update-ability, insert-ability, delete-ability), a collection kind (bag, sequence, array, etc.), type name (if one would like to assume type equivalence based on type names, as e.g. in Pascal), and perhaps others. For simplicity of presentation in this paper we omit them, but they can be easily involved into type inference decision tables and then introduced in implementation.

Edges in the metabase are of three kinds: (1) an ownership which connects subobjects with their owner, (2) the range of a link object and (3) the inheritance.

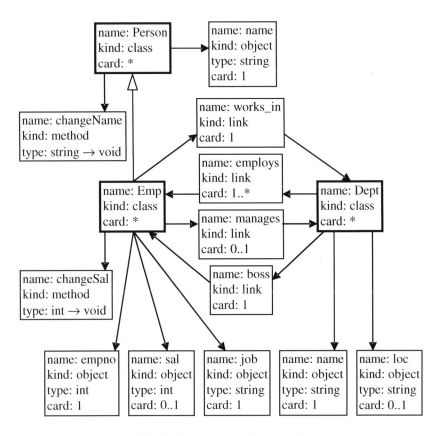

Fig. 2. An example metabase graph

In Fig.2 we distinguish (1) and (2) edge kinds by the attribute **kind**. Note that assuming some predefined (the same) name for all nodes, the metabase can be easily represented as an object store built according to the store model. In this way the metabase can be queried through SBQL.

3 Type Inference Decision Tables

The query engine processes *values* which can also be object references. The purpose of introducing static stacks is precise simulation of the actual computation. The static stacks contain *signatures* which are descriptions of values used during the actual computation. The set of signatures S is recursively defined together with the set of signature components SC. These two sets are the smallest sets which satisfy the following conditions:

1. Names of atomic types (e.g. int, float, string, date, etc.) belong to SC.
2. All static identifiers of the metabase graph nodes (e.g. i_{Emp} and i_{Dept}) belong to SC. Identifiers of graph nodes represent types defined in the database schema. Static identifiers are signatures of references to store objects.
3. If x belongs to S and n is an external name, then the pair $n(x)$ belongs to SC. Such a pair will be called *static binder*.
4. If $n \geq 1$, x_1, $x_2, ..., x_n$ belong to SC, c is a cardinality, and o is an ordering tag, then $(x_1, x_2, ..., x_n)[c]o$ belong to S.

The last point defines collections of structures, but it also encompasses individual items which are just singleton structures. Although the set of cardinalities may be arbitrary, in our research we have limited it to {0..0, 0..1, 1..1, 0..*, 1..*}. Its elements have an obvious meaning. Therefore, collections are treated the same way as individual and optional items. It is just the matter of cardinality. The ordering tag is one of {**o**, **u**} which stand for ordered and unordered respectively.

All signatures are thus uniform. Each of them determines a content, a cardinality and an ordering. As it can be seen all three aspects are orthogonal. Such signatures can be further orthogonally augmented with mutability tags, store locations (in distributed environments), etc.

During the static type check we use rules to infer the type of complex expressions from types of their subexpressions. These rules have the form of type inference decision tables. Such a table is established for each operator of the query/programming language. The decision tables for all the non-algebraic operators are generalized, i.e. each row of the table represents some collection (usually infinite) of real cases. Such generalized decision tables will be called *meta-rules*.

For example, let us consider the navigation (the dot operator) and query $q_L.q_R$. The type of this query depends on the types of the queries q_L and q_R.

The type of q_L	The type of q_R	The type of $q_L.q_R$
$(x_1, x_2, ..., x_n)[c]o$	$(y_1, y_2, ..., y_m)[d]p$	$(y_1, y_2, ..., y_m)[c \otimes d](o \wedge p)$

In this table $c \otimes d$ is the product of c and d, which is obtained by the multiplication of lower and upper bounds of the cardinalities c and d: $[e..f] \otimes [g..h] = [e*g..f*h]$. The meaning of the conjunction of o and p is obvious. The resulting collection (even empty or singleton) is ordered if and only if both argument collections are ordered.

In general, development of type inference decision tables presents a kind of art with no tips from theories. The art is based on precise understanding of the language semantics and the sense of programmers' psychology. The devil is within a lot of detailed decisions concerning particular rows of the tables.

4 Static Type Checking

The general architecture of the type checker is presented in Fig.3. Shaded shapes are program modules, while dashed lines surround data structures which are used and created by the modules. The *query parser* takes a *query* as a text supplied by a *client* and compiles it to produce an *abstract syntax tree* of the query. This syntax tree is analysed, decorated and sometimes modified by the *type checker*. If the type checking is successful (the query is correct), the query is executed by the *query engine*. The query engine operates on two stacks and on the data store.

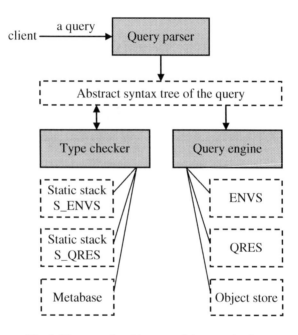

Fig. 3. The general architecture of the type checker

Analogously, the type checker which is to simulate the execution of the query operates on corresponding static structures (the static environment stack S_ENVS, the static result stack S_QRES and the metabase). The type checker uses the information known during the parsing and does not retrieve any information from the data store. The static stacks contain, in particular, signatures of objects from the data store. The type checker processes the signatures exactly in the same way as the query engine could later process the concrete object from the data store, if they were not optimized.

The procedure *static_type_check* is the heart of the type checker and operates on the syntactic tree of a query, both static stacks and the metabase. This procedure is an abstract implementation of our type checker. It performs the computation on signatures just as if they were actual data. During the signature computation, the procedure accomplishes the following actions:

- Checks the type correctness of the syntactic tree of a query by simulating the execution of this query on the static stacks S_ENVS and S_QRES.
- Generates messages on type errors.
- Augments the syntactic tree in order to resolve ellipses.
- Augments the syntactic tree with automatic dereferences and coercions.
- Augments the syntactic tree with dynamic type checks, if the type correctness cannot by asserted statically. Such augmenting means that type checks are postponed until run-time.
- Possibly modifies the static stacks in order to restore the process after a type error has been encountered. These modifications are driven by rules which define most probable result types in certain cases. They allow detecting more than one error during one type check pass.

Before the function *static_type_check* is run, the stack S_ENVS must contain the static base section which consists of the static binders to all static root identifiers (i.e. static identifiers of objects which are starting points for querying). For each static root identifier i_n defined in the schema, the base section of S_ENVS will contain the signature $(n(i_n))[0..*]\mathbf{u}$. For the schema presented on Fig. 1 the base section of S_ENVS will consists of $(Person(i_{Person}))[0..*]\mathbf{u}$, $(Emp(i_{Emp}))[0..*]\mathbf{u}$ and $(Dept(i_{Dept}))[0..*]\mathbf{u}$.

The structure of the procedure *static_type_check* is driven by the abstract syntax of queries. For each kind of a query (literal, name, unary operator, algebraic operator, non-algebraic operator) it contains a section which describes how to check the type of a query built from this kind of operator.

5 Conclusions

We have proposed a new semi-strong approach to static type checking assuming the practitioners' viewpoint. Many interrelated aspect of a strong type checking mechanism, irregular, arbitrary choices that must be taken during the development, dependencies on programmers' psychology, and other factors have caused our loss of believe that any academic type theory could bring an essential support in the development of strong static type systems for object-oriented database query/programming languages.

Our type system consists of a metabase, a static environment stack, a static result stack and type inference rules. The rules are represented as decision tables and are defined for all the operators occurring in the language. We have described an appropriate static type checking procedure and explained how this procedure can be used to correct certain type errors in queries and to recover a type checking process from wrong state that may occur after a type error. Such restorations allow detecting more than one error during one type check pass. The procedure makes it also possible to resolve some ellipses, to accomplish some type coercions and to insert dynamic type checking actions into a run-time query/program code.

We have validated our semi-strong approach to typing on our experimental object-oriented database system ODRA devoted to Web and grid applications, where we have shown that the approach is implementable and efficient.

References

1. Alagic, S.: The ODMG Object Model: Does it Make Sense? Proc. OOPSLA Conf. (1997) 253-270
2. Atkinson, M., and Buneman, P.: Types and Persistence in Database Programming Languages. ACM Computing Surveys **19** 2 (1987) 105-190
3. Atkinson, M., Morrison, R.: Orthogonally Persistent Object Systems. The VLDB Journal **4** 3 (1995) 319-401
4. Cousot, P., and Cousot, R.: Abstract Interpretation: A Unified Lattice Model for Static Analysis of Programs by Construction or Approximation of Fixpoints. POPL (1977) 238-252
5. Goldman, R., and Widom, J.: DataGuides: Enabling Query Formulation and Optimization Semistructured Databases. 23th International Conference on Very Large Data Bases (1997) 436-445
6. Hryniów, R., Lentner, M., Stencel, K., and Subieta, K.: Types and Type Checking in Stack-Based Query Languages. Institute of Computer Science PAS Report 984, Warszawa, March 2005, ISSN 0138-0648 (60 pages), http://www.si.pjwstk.edu.pl/-publications/en/publications-2005.html
7. Cattell, R.G.G., Barry, D.K., Berler, M., Eastman, J., Jordan, D., Russell, C., Schadow, O., Stanienda, T., and Velez, F.: The Object Data Standard: ODMG 3.0, Morgan Kaufman (2000)
8. Fankhauser, P., and Lehti, P.: XQuery by the Book - an Implementation Based on Rigid Formal Semantics. http://www.idealliance.org/papers/xml02/dx_ xml02 /papers/05-01-04/05-01-04.html
9. Kahrs, S.: Polymorphic Type Checking by Interpretation of Code, LFCS report ECS-LFCS-92-238, University of Edinburgh, Laboratory for Foundations of Computer Science (1992)
10. Object Management Group: OMG CORBA/IIOP™ Specifications. http://www.omg.org/-technology/documents/corba_spec_catalog.htm (2002)
11. Subieta, K.: Theory and Construction of Object Query Languages, Publishers of the Polish-Japanese Institute of Information Technology (2004) (in Polish. 522 pages)
12. Subieta, K., Kambayashi, Y., and Leszczyłowsk, J.: Procedures in Object-Oriented Query Languages, Proc. of VLDB (1995) 182-193

Building a Fuzzy Transformation System[*]

Ginés Moreno

Department of Computer Science,
University of Castilla-La Mancha 02071 Albacete, Spain
Gines.Moreno@uclm.es

Abstract. Multi-adjoint logic programming represents a very recent, extremely flexible attempt for introducing fuzzy logic into logic programming. Inspired by previous approaches largely used in other (*crisp*) declarative paradigms, in this paper we propose the development of a fold/unfold based transformation system for optimizing such kind of fuzzy logic programs. We prove that our set of transformation rules composed by definition introduction, folding, unfolding and facting, enjoys strong correctness properties (i.e. the semantics of computed substitutions and truth degrees is preserved) and it is able to significantly improve the execution of goals against transformed programs. To the best of our knowledge, this is the first approach to the construction of a complete transformation system in a fuzzy logic setting.

1 Introduction

Program transformation is an optimization technique for computer programs that, starting with an initial program $\mathcal{P}_0$, derives a sequence $\mathcal{P}_1, \ldots, \mathcal{P}_n$ of transformed programs by applying *elementary transformation rules* such as folding and unfolding (i.e., contraction and expansion of sub-expressions of a program using the definitions of this program or of a preceding one) thus generating more efficient code. The basic idea is to divide the program development activity, starting with a (possibly naive) problem specification written in a programming language, into a sequence of small transformation steps. The development of useful fold/unfold based transformation systems was first introduced in [4] to optimize functional programs and then used for logic programs [16].

More recently, in [2], [13] we have described a complete set of fold/unfold transformation rules (based on *needed narrowing*) for lazy functional–logic programs, which combine the best properties of both declarative paradigms. Sophisticated strategies for guiding the optimal application of such rules in order to produce significant benefits on transformed programs (for instance, by avoiding the construction of intermediate data structures, redundant computations, and so on) can be found too in [1], [12]. Having into account all these hopeful and suggestive precedents, the main goal of the present work consists in the adaptation of such transformation methodology to a fuzzy logic setting.

---

[*] This work has been partially supported by the EU, under FEDER, and the Spanish Science and Education Ministry (MEC) under grant TIN 2004-07943-C04-03.

J. Wiedermann et al. (Eds.): SOFSEM 2006, LNCS 3831, pp. 409–418, 2006.

Multi-adjoint logic programming [9]-[11] is an extremely flexible framework combining fuzzy logic and logic programming. Informally speaking, a multi–adjoint logic program can be seen as a set of rules each one annotated by a truth degree and a goal is a query to the system plus a substitution (initially the identity substitution, denoted by *id*). In the multi–adjoint logic programming framework, goals are evaluated, in a given program, in two separate computational phases. During the *operational* one, *admissible steps* (a generalization of the classical *modus ponens* inference rule) are systematically applied by a backward reasoning procedure in a similar way to classical resolution steps in pure logic programming, thus returning a computed substitution together with an expression where all atoms have been exploited. This last expression is then interpreted under a given lattice during what we call the *interpretive* phase, hence returning a pair ⟨*truth degree*; *substitution*⟩ which is the fuzzy counterpart of the classical notion of computed answer traditionally used in pure logic programming.

Let us now formally introduce a short summary of the main features of this language (we send the interested reader to [9, 10, 11] for a complete formulation). We work with a first order language, $\mathcal{L}$, containing variables, function symbols, predicate symbols, constants, quantifiers, $\forall$ and $\exists$, and several (arbitrary) connectives to increase language expressiveness:

$\&_1, \&_2, \ldots, \&_k$	(conjunctions)	$\vee_1, \vee_2, \ldots, \vee_l$	(disjunctions)
$\leftarrow_1, \leftarrow_2, \ldots, \leftarrow_m$	(implications)	$@_1, @_2, \ldots, @_n$	(aggregations)

Although the connectives $\&_i$, $\vee_i$ and $@_i$ are binary operators, we usually generalize them as functions with an arbitrary number of arguments. In the following, we often write $@_i(x_1, \ldots, x_n)$ instead of $@_i(x_1, @_i(x_2, \ldots, @_i(x_{n-1}, x_n) \ldots))$. Moreover, the truth function for any conjunction operator verifies $[\![\&_i]\!](1, v) = [\![\&]\!](v, 1) = v$, for all $v \in L$ and $i = 1, \ldots, n$; whereas any n-ary aggregation operator $[\![@]\!] : [0, 1]^n \to [0, 1]$ is required to be monotonous and fulfills $[\![@]\!](1, \ldots, 1) = 1$ and $[\![@]\!](0, \ldots, 0) = 0$.

Additionally, our language $\mathcal{L}$ contains the values of a multi–adjoint lattice, $\langle L, \preceq, \leftarrow_1, \&_1, \ldots, \leftarrow_n, \&_n \rangle$, equipped with a collection of adjoint pairs $\langle \leftarrow_i, \&_i \rangle$, where each $\&_i$ is a conjunctor[1] intended to the evaluation of *modus ponens*. In general, the set of truth values L may be the carrier of any complete bounded lattice but, for readability reasons, in the examples we shall select L as the set of real numbers in the interval $[0, 1]$.

A *rule* is a formula $A \leftarrow_i \mathcal{B}$, where A is an atomic formula (usually called the *head*) and $\mathcal{B}$ (which is called the *body*) is a formula built from atomic formulas $B_1, \ldots, B_n$ — $n \geq 0$ —, truth values of L and conjunctions, disjunctions and aggregations. Rules with an empty body are called *facts*. A *goal* is a body submitted as a query to the system. Variables in a rule are assumed governed by universal quantifiers.

Roughly speaking, a multi–adjoint logic program is a set of pairs $\langle \mathcal{R}; \alpha \rangle$, where $\mathcal{R}$ is a rule and α is a *truth degree* (a value of L) expressing the confidence which

---

[1] It is noteworthy that a symbol $\&_j$ of $\mathcal{L}$ does not always need to be part of an adjoint pair.

the user of the system has in the truth of the rule $\mathcal{R}$. Often, we will write "$\mathcal{R}$ with α" instead of $\langle \mathcal{R}; \alpha \rangle$. Observe that, truth degrees are axiomatically assigned (for instance) by an expert.

The structure of the paper is as follows. In Section 2, we summarize the main operational features of the programming language we use in this work, by defining its procedural semantics and establishing a clean separation between the operational and the interpretive phase of a computation. In Section 3 we not only define, relate and illustrate our set of fuzzy transformation rules, but we also formally prove the strong correctness properties of the complete transformation system. Finally, in Section 4 we give our conclusions and propose future work.

2   Procedural Semantics

The procedural semantics of the multi–adjoint logic language $\mathcal{L}$ can be thought as an operational phase followed by an interpretive one. Similarly to [7], in this section we establish a clear separation between both phases.

The operational mechanism uses a generalization of *modus ponens* that, given a goal A and a program rule $\langle A' \leftarrow_i B, v \rangle$, if there is a substitution $\theta = mgu(\{A = A'\})^2$, we substitute the atom A by the expression $(v \&_i B)\theta$. In the following, we write $\mathcal{C}[A]$ to denote a formula where A is a sub-expression (usually an atom) which arbitrarily occur in the —possibly empty— context $\mathcal{C}[]$. Moreover, expression $\mathcal{C}[A/A']$ means the replacement of A by A' in context $\mathcal{C}[]$. Also we use $Var(s)$ for referring to the set of distinct variables occurring in the syntactic object s, whereas $\theta[Var(s)]$ denotes the substitution obtained from θ by restricting its domain, $Dom(\theta)$, to $Var(s)$.

Definition 1 (Admissible Steps). *Let $\mathcal{Q}$ be a goal and let σ be a substitution. The pair $\langle \mathcal{Q}; \sigma \rangle$ is an* state *and we denote by $\mathcal{E}$ the set of states. Given a program $\mathcal{P}$, an* admissible computation *is formalized as a state transition system, whose transition relation $\rightarrow_{AS} \subseteq (\mathcal{E} \times \mathcal{E})$ is the smallest relation satisfying the following* admissible rules *(where we always consider that A is the selected atom in $\mathcal{Q}$):*

1) $\langle \mathcal{Q}[A]; \sigma \rangle \rightarrow_{AS} \langle (\mathcal{Q}[A/v \&_i B])\theta; \sigma\theta \rangle$ *if $\theta = mgu(\{A' = A\})$, $\langle A' \leftarrow_i B; v \rangle$ in $\mathcal{P}$ and B is not empty.*

2) $\langle \mathcal{Q}[A]; \sigma \rangle \rightarrow_{AS} \langle (\mathcal{Q}[A/v])\theta; \sigma\theta \rangle$ *if $\theta = mgu(\{A' = A\})$, and $\langle A' \leftarrow_i; v \rangle$ in $\mathcal{P}$.*

3) $\langle \mathcal{Q}[A]; \sigma \rangle \rightarrow_{AS} \langle (\mathcal{Q}[A/\bot]); \sigma \rangle$ *if there is no rule in $\mathcal{P}$ whose head unifies to A.*

Formulas involved in admissible computation steps are renamed before being used. Note also that rule 3 is introduced to cope with (possible) unsuccessful

---

^{2} Let $mgu(E)$ denote the *most general unifier* of an equation set E (see [8] for a formal definition of this concept).

admissible derivations. When needed, we shall use the symbols $\to_{AS1}$, $\to_{AS2}$ and $\to_{AS3}$ to distinguish between computation steps performed by applying one of the specific admissible rules. Also, when required, the exact program rule used in the corresponding step will be annotated as a super–index of the $\to_{AS}$ symbol.

Definition 2. *Let $\mathcal{P}$ be a program and let $\mathcal{Q}$ be a goal. An* admissible derivation *is a sequence $\langle \mathcal{Q}; id \rangle \to_{AS}^{*} \langle \mathcal{Q}'; \theta \rangle$. When $\mathcal{Q}'$ is a formula not containing atoms, the pair $\langle \mathcal{Q}'; \sigma \rangle$, where $\sigma = \theta[\mathcal{V}ar(\mathcal{Q})]$, is called an* admissible computed answer *(a.c.a.) for that derivation.*

We illustrate these concepts by means of the following example.

Example 1. Let $\mathcal{P}$ be the following program and let $([0, 1], \leq)$ be the lattice where $\leq$ is the usual order on real numbers.

$$\begin{aligned}
&\mathcal{R}_1 : p(X) &&\leftarrow_{\text{prod}} q(X, Y) \&_{\text{G}}\, r(Y) &&\text{with} &&\alpha = 0.8 \\
&\mathcal{R}_2 : q(a, Y) &&\leftarrow_{\text{prod}} s(Y) &&\text{with} &&\alpha = 0.7 \\
&\mathcal{R}_3 : q(Y, a) &&\leftarrow_{\text{luka}} r(Y) &&\text{with} &&\alpha = 0.8 \\
&\mathcal{R}_4 : r(Y) &&\leftarrow_{\text{luka}} &&\text{with} &&\alpha = 0.6 \\
&\mathcal{R}_5 : s(b) &&\leftarrow_{\text{luka}} &&\text{with} &&\alpha = 0.9
\end{aligned}$$

The labels prod, G and luka mean for *product logic*, *Gödel intuitionistic logic* and *Lukasiewicz logic*, respectively. That is, $[\![\&_{\text{prod}}]\!](x, y) = x \cdot y$, $[\![\&_{\text{G}}]\!](x, y) = min(x, y)$, and $[\![\&_{\text{luka}}]\!](x, y) = max(0, x + y - 1)$.

In the following admissible derivation for the program $\mathcal{P}$ and the goal $\leftarrow p(X) \&_{\text{G}} r(a)$, we underline the selected expression in each admissible step:

$$\begin{aligned}
\langle \underline{p(X)} \&_{\text{G}} r(a); id \rangle \;\; &\to_{AS1}{}^{\mathcal{R}_1} \langle (0.8 \&_{\text{prod}} (\underline{q(X_1, Y_1)} \&_{\text{G}} r(Y_1))) \&_{\text{G}} r(a); \sigma_1 \rangle \\
&\to_{AS1}{}^{\mathcal{R}_2} \langle (0.8 \&_{\text{prod}} ((0.7 \&_{\text{prod}} \underline{s(Y_2)}) \&_{\text{G}} r(Y_2))) \&_{\text{G}} r(a); \sigma_2 \rangle \\
&\to_{AS2}{}^{\mathcal{R}_5} \langle (0.8 \&_{\text{prod}} ((0.7 \&_{\text{prod}} 0.9) \&_{\text{G}} \underline{r(b)})) \&_{\text{G}} r(a); \sigma_3 \rangle \\
&\to_{AS2}{}^{\mathcal{R}_4} \langle (0.8 \&_{\text{prod}} ((0.7 \&_{\text{prod}} 0.9) \&_{\text{G}} 0.6)) \&_{\text{G}} \underline{r(a)}; \sigma_4 \rangle \\
&\to_{AS2}{}^{\mathcal{R}_4} \langle (0.8 \&_{\text{prod}} ((0.7 \&_{\text{prod}} 0.9) \&_{\text{G}} 0.6)) \&_{\text{G}} \underline{0.6}; \sigma_5 \rangle,
\end{aligned}$$

where:

$$\begin{aligned}
\sigma_1 &= \{X/X_1\}, \\
\sigma_2 &= \{X/a, X_1/a, Y_1/Y_2\}, \\
\sigma_3 &= \{X/a, X_1/a, Y_1/b, Y_2/b\}, \\
\sigma_4 &= \{X/a, X_1/a, Y_1/b, Y_2/b, Y_3/b\}, \text{ and} \\
\sigma_5 &= \{X/a, X_1/a, Y_1/b, Y_2/b, Y_3/b, Y_4/a\}.
\end{aligned}$$

So, since $\sigma_5[\mathcal{V}ar(\mathcal{Q})] = \{X/a\}$, the a.c.a. associated to this admissible derivation is: $\langle (0.8 \&_{\text{prod}} ((0.7 \&_{\text{prod}} 0.9) \&_{\text{G}} 0.6)) \&_{\text{G}} 0.6; \{X/a\} \rangle$.

Let us now explain the interpretive phase. If we exploit all atoms of a goal, by applying admissible steps as much as needed during the operational phase, then it becomes a formula with no atoms which can be then directly interpreted in the multi–adjoint lattice L.

Definition 3 (Interpretive Step). *Let $\mathcal{P}$ be a program, $\mathcal{Q}$ a goal and σ a substitution. We formalize the notion of interpretive computation as a state transition system, whose transition relation $\rightarrow_{IS} \subseteq (\mathcal{E} \times \mathcal{E})$ is defined as the least one satisfaying: $\langle Q[@(r_1, r_2)]; \sigma \rangle \rightarrow_{IS} \langle Q[@(r_1, r_2)/[\![@]\!](r_1, r_2)]; \sigma \rangle$, where $[\![@]\!]$ is the truth function of connective @ in the lattice $\langle L, \preceq \rangle$ associated to $\mathcal{P}$.*

Definition 4. *Let $\mathcal{P}$ be a program and $\langle Q; \sigma \rangle$ an a.c.a., that is, Q is a goal not containing atoms. An interpretive derivation is a sequence $\langle Q; \sigma \rangle \rightarrow_{IS}^* \langle Q'; \sigma \rangle$. When $Q' = r \in L$, being $\langle L, \preceq \rangle$ the lattice associated to $\mathcal{P}$, the state $\langle r; \sigma \rangle$ is called a fuzzy computed answer (f.c.a.) for that derivation.*

Usually, we refer to a *complete derivation* as the sequence of admissible/interpretive steps of the form $\langle Q; id \rangle \rightarrow_{AS}^* \langle Q'; \sigma \rangle \rightarrow_{IS}^* \langle r; \sigma \rangle$ (sometimes we denote it by $\langle Q; id \rangle \rightarrow_{AS/IS}^* \langle r; \sigma \rangle$) where $\langle Q'; \sigma[Var(\mathcal{Q})] \rangle$ and $\langle r; \sigma[Var(\mathcal{Q})] \rangle$ are, respectively, the a.c.a. and the f.c.a. for the derivation.

Example 2. We complete the previous derivation of Example 1 by executing the necessary interpretive steps in order to obtain the fuzzy computed answer (f.c.a.) with respect to lattice $([0, 1], \leq)$:

$$\langle (0.8 \&_{\mathtt{prod}}((0.7 \&_{\mathtt{prod}} 0.9) \&_{\mathtt{G}} 0.6)) \&_{\mathtt{G}} 0.6; \{X/a\} \rangle \quad \rightarrow_{IS}$$
$$\langle (0.8 \&_{\mathtt{prod}}(\overline{0.63 \&_{\mathtt{G}} 0.6})) \&_{\mathtt{G}} 0.6; \{X/a\} \rangle \quad \rightarrow_{IS}$$
$$\langle (0.8 \&_{\mathtt{prod}} 0.6) \&_{\mathtt{G}} 0.6; \{X/a\} \rangle \quad \rightarrow_{IS}$$
$$\langle 0.48 \&_{\mathtt{G}} 0.6; \{X/a\} \rangle \quad \rightarrow_{IS}$$
$$\langle 0.48; \{X/a\} \rangle$$

Then the f.c.a for this complete derivation is the pair $\langle 0.48; \{X/a\} \rangle$.

3 Fuzzy Transformation Rules

In this section, our aim is to define a set of program transformations rules which is strongly correct, i.e., sound and complete w.r.t. the semantics of fuzzy computed answers (that is, truth degrees and substitutions).

Let us first give the rule for the introduction of new predicate definitions in a similar style to [16], in which the set of definitions is partitioned into "old" and "new" predicates. In the following, we consider a fixed transformation sequence $(\mathcal{P}_0, \ldots, \mathcal{P}_k)$, $k \geq 0$.

Definition 5 (Definition introduction). *We may get program $\mathcal{P}_{k+1}$ by adding to $\mathcal{P}_k$ a new rule called "definition rule" (or "eureka") of the form[3]: $p(\overline{x_n}) \leftarrow \mathcal{B}$ with $\alpha = 1$, such that:*

1. *p is new, i.e., it does not occur in the sequence $\mathcal{P}_0, \ldots, \mathcal{P}_k$,*
2. *$\overline{x_n}$ is the set of variables appearing in $\mathcal{B}$, and*
3. *every non-variable symbol occurring in $\mathcal{B}$ belongs to $\mathcal{P}_0$.*

---

[3] Observe that the $\leftarrow$ symbols does not need to be labeled with any sub-index due to the fact that the truth degree associated to eurekas are always the maximum one 1.

We say that p is a new *predicate symbol, and every predicate symbol belonging to $\mathcal{P}_0$ is called an* old *predicate symbol.*

The introduction of a new eureka definition is virtually always the first step of a transformation sequence. Determining which definitions should be introduced is a clever task (which justifies the name "eureka" for the new rules) which falls into the realm of *strategies* (see [15] for a survey). In general, the main idea consists in producing a new rule whose body contains a subset of predicates appearing in the body of a program rule whose definition is intended to be improved by subsequent transformation steps.

Example 3. Consider now the program $\mathcal{P}$ of Example 1 as the initial one $\mathcal{P}_0$ of a transformation sequence. Inspired by its first rule whose (whole) definition we want to enhance, we can build the eureka rule $\mathcal{R}_6 : new(X, Y) \leftarrow q(X, Y) \&_G r(Y)$ with $\alpha = 1$, and then, the next program in the sequence is $\mathcal{P}_1 = \mathcal{P}_0 \cup \{\mathcal{R}_6\}$.

Let us now introduce the folding rule, which roughly speaking consists in the compression of a piece of code into an equivalent call. Our definition is closely related to the *reversible folding* rule defined for pure logic programs in [5].

Definition 6 (Folding). *Let $\mathcal{R} : (A \leftarrow_i B \text{ with } \alpha = v) \in \mathcal{P}_k$ be a non-eureka rule (the "folded rule") and let $\mathcal{R}' : (A' \leftarrow B' \text{ with } \alpha = 1) \in \mathcal{P}_k$ be an eureka rule (the "folding rule") such that, there exist a substitution σ verifying that $B'\sigma$ is contained in B. We may get program $\mathcal{P}_{k+1}$ by folding rule $\mathcal{R}$ w.r.t. eureka $\mathcal{R}'$ as follows: $\mathcal{P}_{k+1} = (\mathcal{P}_k - \{\mathcal{R}\}) \cup \{A \leftarrow_i B[B'\sigma/A'\sigma] \text{ with } \alpha = v\}$.*

There are two points regarding our last definition which are worth noticing:

- The condition which says that the folded rule $\mathcal{R}$ is a non-eureka rule whereas $\mathcal{R}'$ is an eureka rule is useful to avoid the risk of *self-folding*, that is, the possibility of folding a rule w.r.t. itself, hence producing a wrong rule with the same head and body which may introduce infinite loops on derivations and destroy the correctness properties of the transformation system.
- The substitution σ of Definition 6 is not a unifier but just a matcher, similarly to many other folding rules for logic programs, which have been defined in a similar "functional style" (see, e.g., [3, 5, 15, 16]). Moreover, it has the advantage that it is easier to check and can still produce effective optimizations at a lower cost.

Example 4. Continuing with Example 3, the goal now is to link the eureka definition (which will be afterwards improved by means of unfolding steps) to the original program. This is done by simply folding $\mathcal{R}_1$ w.r.t. eureka $\mathcal{R}_6$, thus obtaining $\mathcal{P}_2 = (\mathcal{P}_1 - \{\mathcal{R}_1\}) \cup \{ \mathcal{R}_7 : p(X) \leftarrow_{\text{prod}} new(X, Y) \text{ with } \alpha = 0.8 \}$.

On the other hand, the unfolding transformation can be seen as the inverse of the previous folding rule, and it has been traditionally considered in pure logic programming as the replacement of a program clause C by the set of clauses obtained after applying a (SLD-resolution) symbolic computation step in all its possible forms on the body of C [15]. As detailed in [6], we have adapted this transformation to deal with multi–adjoint logic programs by defining it in terms of admissible steps. However, in the following definition we increase the power of the transformation by also allowing interpretive steps in its formulation[4].

Definition 7 (Unfolding). *We may get program* $\mathcal{P}_{k+1}$ *by unfolding (the non-unit) rule* $\mathcal{R} : (A \leftarrow_i B \text{ with } \alpha = v) \in \mathcal{P}_k$ *as follows:* $\mathcal{P}_{k+1} = (\mathcal{P}_k - \{\mathcal{R}\}) \cup \{A\sigma \leftarrow_i \mathcal{B}' \text{ with } \alpha = v \mid \langle \mathcal{B}; id \rangle \rightarrow_{AS/IS} \langle \mathcal{B}'; \sigma \rangle\}$.

There are some remarks to do regarding our definition:

- Similarly to the classical SLD–resolution based unfolding rule presented in [16], the substitutions computed by admissible steps during the unfolding process, are incorporated to the transformed rules in a natural way, i.e., by applying them to the head of the rule.
- On the other hand, regarding the propagation of truth degrees, we solve this problem in a very easy way: the unfolded rule directly inherits the truth degree α of the original rule.

We illustrate the use of unfolding by means of the following example.

Example 5. The next phase in our transformation sequence is devoted to improve the eureka definition by means of unfolding steps. If we want to unfold now rule $\mathcal{R}_6$, we must firstly build the following one–step admissible derivations:

$$\langle \underline{q(X,Y)}\&_G r(Y); id \rangle \quad \rightarrow_{AS1}{}^{\mathcal{R}_2} \quad \langle (0.7\&_{prod}s(Y_0))\&_G r(Y_0); \{X/a, Y/Y_0\} \rangle, \text{ and}$$
$$\langle \underline{q(X,Y)}\&_G r(Y); id \rangle \quad \rightarrow_{AS1}{}^{\mathcal{R}_3} \quad \langle (0.8\&_{luka}r(Y_1))\&_G r(a); \{X/Y_1, Y/a\} \rangle.$$

So, the resulting rules are:

$$\mathcal{R}_8 : new(a, Y_0) \leftarrow ((0.7\&_{prod}s(Y_0))\&_G r(Y_0)) \text{ with } \alpha = 1, \text{ and}$$
$$\mathcal{R}_9 : new(Y_1, a) \leftarrow ((0.8 \&_{luka} r(Y_1)) \&_G r(a)) \text{ with } \alpha = 1.$$

Moreover, by performing now a $\rightarrow_{AS2}$ admissible step on the body of rule $\mathcal{R}_8$, we obtain the new rule $\mathcal{R}_{10} : new(a, b) \leftarrow ((0.7\&_{prod}0.9)\&_G r(Y_0))$ with $\alpha = 1$. Finally, a new unfolding step (based again in the second type of admissible step) on rule $\mathcal{R}_{10}$ generates the rule $\mathcal{R}_{11} : new(a, b) \leftarrow ((0.7\&_{prod}0.9)\&_G 0.6)$ with $\alpha = 1$.

On the other hand, we can now apply an interpretive step to unfold rule $\mathcal{R}_{11}$, obtaining $\mathcal{R}_{12} : new(a, b) \leftarrow (0.63\&_G 0.6)$ with $\alpha = 1$, which, after the last (interpretive) unfolding step finally becomes $\mathcal{R}_{13} : new(a, b) \leftarrow 0.6$ with $\alpha = 1$.

So, after these five unfolding steps, the resulting program is the set of rules $\mathcal{P}_7 = \{\mathcal{R}_2, \mathcal{R}_3, \mathcal{R}_4, \mathcal{R}_5, \mathcal{R}_7, \mathcal{R}_9, \mathcal{R}_{13}\}$.

---

[4] This last case case remembers the so-called *interpretive unfolding* formalized in [7].

Our last transformation rule is not previously known in the literature on program transformation and declarative programming, with the unique exception of [7], where we have proposed an equivalent characterization called IU2 (that is, the second variant of interpretive unfolding) in a fuzzy setting. The idea now is similar to apply an interpretive step to the body of program rules, but, in contrast with unfolding, not only the truth degrees of the transformed rules differs from the original ones, but also, and what is better, the transformation is able to simplify program rules by directly eliminating its bodies, and hence, producing facts.

Definition 8 (Facting). *We may get program $\mathcal{P}_{k+1}$ by facting rule $\mathcal{R} : (A \leftarrow_i r \text{ with } \alpha = v) \in \mathcal{P}_k$, where $r \in L$, as follows: $\mathcal{P}_{k+1} = (\mathcal{P}_k - \{\mathcal{R}\}) \cup \{A \leftarrow \text{ with } \alpha = [\![\&_i]\!](v, r)\}$.*

Example 6. Let's perform now a facting step on rule $\mathcal{R}_{13}$. Since, as said before, the truth function for any conjunction operator verifies $[\![\&]\!](1, v) = [\![\&]\!](v, 1) = v$, then $[\![\&]\!](1, 0.6) = 0.6$, which implies that $\mathcal{R}_{14} : new(a, b) \leftarrow$ with $\alpha = 0.6$.

So, the final program $\mathcal{P}_8$ of our transformation sequence contains the original rules $\mathcal{R}_2, \mathcal{R}_3, \mathcal{R}_4$ and $\mathcal{R}_5$ together with:

$$\begin{array}{llll}
\mathcal{R}_7 : & p(X) & \leftarrow_{\text{prod}} new(X, Y) & \text{with} \quad \alpha = 0.8 \\
\mathcal{R}_9 : & new(Y_1, a) \leftarrow & (0.8 \,\&_{\text{luka}}\, r(Y_1)) \,\&_{\text{G}}\, r(a) & \text{with} \quad \alpha = 1 \\
\mathcal{R}_{14} : & new(a, b) & \leftarrow & \text{with} \quad \alpha = 0.6
\end{array}$$

and now, the derivation showed in Example 1 and continued in Example 2 can be simulated in $\mathcal{P}_8$ in a shorter way (mainly due to the use of rule $\mathcal{R}_{14}$), with only three admissible steps (instead of five) and two interpretive steps (instead of four), that is, almost the half of its length, which illustrates the benefits obtained by fold/unfold on the transformed program:

$$\begin{array}{ll}
\langle \underline{p(X)}\&_{\text{G}}r(a); id\rangle & \rightarrow_{AS1}{}^{\mathcal{R}_7} \; \langle(0.8\&_{\text{prod}}\underline{new(X_1, Y_1)})\&_{\text{G}}r(a); \{X/X_1\}\rangle \\
& \rightarrow_{AS2}{}^{\mathcal{R}_{14}} \; \langle(0.8\&_{\text{prod}}0.6)\&_{\text{G}}\underline{r(a)}; \{X/a, X_1/a, Y_1/b\}\rangle \\
& \rightarrow_{AS2}{}^{\mathcal{R}_4} \; \langle(0.8\&_{\text{prod}}0.6)\&_{\text{G}}0.6; \{X/a, X_1/a, Y_1/b, Y_2/a\}\rangle \\
& \rightarrow_{IS} \; \langle \underline{0.48\&_{\text{G}}0.6}; \{X/a, X_1/a, Y_1/b, Y_2/a\}\rangle \\
& \rightarrow_{IS} \; \langle 0.48; \{\underline{X/a}, X_1/a, Y_1/b, Y_2/a\}\rangle.
\end{array}$$

As expected, by simply taking into account the bindings associated to the variables of the original goal, we have obtained the same f.c.a $\langle 0.48; \{X/a\}\rangle$ of Example 2.

To finish this section, we present the main property of our transformation system.

Theorem 1. *(Strong Correctness of the Transformation System)*
Let $(\mathcal{P}_0, \ldots, \mathcal{P}_k)$ be a transformation sequence where each program in the sequence, except the initial one $\mathcal{P}_0$, is obtained from the immediately preceding one by applying definition introduction, folding, unfolding or facting, and let Q be a goal with no new predicate symbols. Then, $\langle Q; id\rangle \rightarrow^*_{AS/IS} \langle r; \theta\rangle$ in $\mathcal{P}_0$ iff $\langle Q; id\rangle \rightarrow^*_{AS/IS} \langle r; \theta'\rangle$ in $\mathcal{P}_k$, where $\theta' = \theta[Var(Q)]$.

Proof. [Sketch]
We treat separately the strong correctness of each fuzzy transformation rule:

- Since we only consider goals without new predicate symbols, the definition introduction rule does not affect our claim (remember that it only generates rules defining new predicate symbols).
- Moreover, the strong correctness of our present unfolding/facting rules follows from their equivalences with the operational/interpretive unfolding rules described in [6], [7].
- Finally, due to the reversibility of our folding rule, (that is, if a program rule $\mathcal{R}'$ is obtained by folding a rule $\mathcal{R}$, then $\mathcal{R}$ can be generated again by simply unfolding $\mathcal{R}'$) then, its strong correctness directly follows from the strong correctness of unfolding.

4   Conclusions and Future Work

This paper must be thought as a first step in the development of a transformation system for fuzzy logic programs, by considering one of the most recent and flexible languages in the field which is based in the multi-adjoint logic approach presented in [11]. Helped by our previous experiences in the study of fuzzy variants of unfolding rules (see [6], [7]), which have inspired the present unfolding and facting operations, we have also designed a definition introduction and a folding rule to obtain a strongly sound and complete transformation system.

We have used a very simple, but effective strategy to guide the generation of transformation sequences in order to produce more efficient residual programs. Basically, the proposed heuristic proceeds in three stages as follows:

1. We first generate an eureka based on the body of a program rule $\mathcal{R}$ whose definition is intended to be improved.
2. Then, by means of a folding step, we link the new predicate to $\mathcal{R}$.
3. Finally, the eureka definition is improved as much as wanted by means of unfolding and facting steps.

As we have previously done in other declarative settings [1], [2], [12], [13], but focusing now in the fuzzy field, for the future we are interested in defining more sophisticated variants of folding rules (for instance, those non-reversible ones with the capability of generating recursive eureka definitions by folding rules belonging to different programs in a transformation sequence) and more powerful transformation strategies, such as composition, tupling, and so on [15], [16].

In the limit, we also think that all these proposals admit a future adaptation to the fully integrated field of *functional–fuzzy–logic* programming, by considering languages as the one we are nowadays designing in [14].

References

1. Alpuente, M., Falaschi, M., Moreno, G., and Vidal, G.: An Automatic Composition Algorithm for Functional Logic Programs. In V. Hlaváč, K.G. Jeffery, and J. Wiedermann (eds): Proc. of the 27th Annual Conference on Current Trends in Theory and Practice of Informatics, SOFSEM'2000, Springer LNCS **1963** (2000) 289–297
2. Alpuente, M., Falaschi, M., Moreno, G., and Vidal, G.: Rules + Strategies for Transforming Lazy Functional Logic Programs. Theoretical Computer Science **311** (2004) 479–525
3. Bossi, A., and Cocco, N.: Basic Transformation Operations which Preserve Computed Answer Substitutions of Logic Programs. Journal of Logic Programming **16** (1993) 47–87
4. Burstall, R.M., and Darlington, J.: A Transformation System for Developing Recursive Programs. Journal of the ACM **24** 1 (1977) 44–67
5. Gardner, P.A., and Shepherdson, J.C: Unfold/Fold Transformation of Logic Programs. In J.L. Lassez and G. Plotkin (eds), Computational Logic, Essays in Honor of Alan Robinson, the MIT Press, Cambridge, MA (1991) 565–583
6. Julián, P., Moreno, G., and Penabad, J.: On Fuzzy Unfolding. A Multi-Adjoint Approach. Fuzzy Sets and Systems, Elsevier **154** (2005) 16–33
7. Julián, P., Moreno, G., and Penabad, J.: Operational/Interpretive Unfolding of Multi-adjoint Logic Programs. In F. López-Fraguas (ed), Proc. of V Jornadas sobre Programación y Lenguajes, PROLE'2005, Granada, Spain, September 14-16, University of Granada (2005) 239–248
8. Lassez, J.-L., Maher, M.J., and Marriott, K.: Unification Revisited. In J. Minker (ed.), Foundations of Deductive Databases and Logic Programming, Morgan Kaufmann, Los Altos, Ca. (1988) 587–625
9. Medina, J., Ojeda-Aciego, M., and Vojtáš, P.: Multi-Adjoint Logic Programming with Continuous Semantics. In Proc. of Logic Programming and Non-Monotonic Reasoning, LPNMR'01, Springer LNAI **2173** (2001) 351–364
10. Medina, J., Ojeda-Aciego, M., and Vojtáš, P.: A Procedural Semantics for Multi-adjoint Logic Programing. In Proc. of Progress in Artificial Intelligence, EPIA'01, Springer LNAI **2258** (2001) 290–297
11. Medina, J., Ojeda-Aciego, M., and Vojtáš, P.: Similarity-Based Unification: a Multi-Adjoint Approach. Fuzzy Sets and Systems, Elsevier **146** (2004) 43–62
12. Moreno, G.: Automatic Optimization of Multi-Paradigm Declarative Programs. In F.J. Garijo, J.C. Riquelme, and M. Toro (eds), Proc. of the 8th Ibero–American Conference on Artificial Intelligence, IBERAMIA'02, Springer LNAI **2527** (2002) 131–140
13. Moreno, G.: Transformation Rules and Strategies for Functional-Logic Programs. AI Communications, IO Press (Amsterdam) **15** 2,3 (2002) 163–165
14. Moreno, G., and Pascual, V.: Programming with Fuzzy–logic and Mathematical Functions. In I. Bloch, A. Petrosino, and A. Tettamanzi (eds), Proc. of the 6th International Whorshop on Fuzzy Logic and Applications, WILF'05, University of Milan, Crema (Italy), 10 pages. Springer LNCS (to appear) (2005)
15. Pettorossi, A., and Proietti, M.: Rules and Strategies for Transforming Functional and Logic Programs. ACM Computing Surveys **28** 2 (1996) 360–414
16. Tamaki, H., and Sato, T.: Unfold/Fold Transformations of Logic Programs. In S. Tärnlund (ed.), Proc. of Second Int'l Conf. on Logic Programming (1984) 127–139

News Generating
Via Fuzzy Summarization of Databases

Adam Niewiadomski

Institute of Computer Science, Technical University of Lodz,
ul. Wólczańska 215, 93-005, Łódź, Poland
aniewiadomski@ics.p.lodz.pl

Abstract. The paper focuses on a practical use of knowledge extraction mechanisms in mining databases. The fuzzy-based methods that enable the linguistic interpretation of large sets of numerical data, are presented. In particular, generating the so-called *linguistic summaries of databases*, exemplified by *About half of records have very high values of attribute A*, in sense of Yager [1] with further improvements [2], [3] is described.

The original contribution by the author is the class of algorithms, based on linguistic summaries, which enable automated generating of brief textual news or comments to be published in press and/or WWW. The obtained messages describe quantitative dependencies among chosen values or attributes. Moreover, the produced results are expressed in semi-natural language which makes them readable for an average user. Finally, a prototype implementation on sample data is described.

1 Motivation and Problem Study

Human skills of grasping large numbers of data are naturally limited. On the other hand, the amount of information stored and processed electronically has been growing exponentially in recent years. Collecting and managing data in many areas, like financial or military politics, mass-media, security and rescue systems, etc., definitely must be supported by information technologies, due the amount of data which is impossible to be grasped manually by a human in a reasonable time.

Therefore, needed data must be not only found and retrieved but also finally reproduced in easy-to-use, compact, and human-consistent forms, e.g. statistical characteristics or natural language (NL). However, statistical methods, although precise, may seem to be too terse to describe data communicatively. Moreover, the results obtained this way are understandable and practicable for rather small groups of specialized people, like analysts, managers, etc. [1].

Thus, in this approach, we propose to apply the so-called *linguistic summaries of databases* which are based on soft-computing methods, in particular, on fuzzy logic. A sample linguistic summary of a database (in sense of Yager) is of the form *Few cars are cheap and very fast*, where the linguistic terms *few*, *cheap*, and *very fast* are handled by fuzzy sets and by operations on them [4], [5], [6].

J. Wiedermann et al. (Eds.): SOFSEM 2006, LNCS 3831, pp. 419–429, 2006.

Some very interesting approaches of reporting large datasets via ordinary-fuzzy-sets-based tools are given by Kacprzyk and Zadrożny [7] and by Kacprzyk and Strykowski [8].

In this paper, the idea of linguistic summarization of databases is originally adapted to generate NL messages which are used as press comments, memos, news, etc. The foundations of fuzzy sets and of linguistic summarization are recalled in sections 2 and 3, respectively. Then, in Section 4, the original authors contribution – the algorithms which generate news – are introduced. Finally, an application on sample data is presented in Section 5.

2   Fuzzy-Based Linguistic Interpretation of Data

2.1   Fuzzy Sets

In the classic set theory, a set A in a universe $\mathcal{X}$ can be represented by its characteristic function $\chi_A \colon \mathcal{X} \to \{0, 1\}$. Such a construction suggests that an element belongs to the set or does not, and *tertium non datur*. Nevertheless, it frequently happens in modelling elements of NL that the so-called *partial belongingness* of an element to a set must be considered. The concept of a *fuzzy set* represented by its *membership function* (MF) was introduced by Zadeh in 1965; it extends the set of values of a characteristic function to the $[0, 1]$ interval [4]. The generalization enables modelling of linguistic statements like *old man, very fast car*, which are inherently imprecise, but understandable in NL. Formally, a fuzzy set A in a universe of discourse $\mathcal{X}$ is defined as:

$$A = \{< x, \mu_A(x) > \colon x \in \mathcal{X}, \mu_A \colon \mathcal{X} \to [0, 1]\} \tag{1}$$

where μ_A is *the membership function of A*; its value for $x \in \mathcal{X}$ is interpreted as *the membership level* (or *degree*) of x to A.

2.2   Linguistic Variables

Linguistic variable (LV) is an ordered quintuple $< L, V(L), \mathcal{X}, G, M >$, where: L is the name of the variable; $V(L)$ is the set of its linguistic values; $\mathcal{X}$ is the universe of discourse in which the fuzzy sets modelling the values of L are determined; G is a grammatical/syntactical rule which enables generating names of values (labels) of L; M is a semantic rule which associates the meaning of a value of L with a fuzzy set in $\mathcal{X}$. A sample linguistic variable is $L = age\_of\_worker$, and $V(L) = \{$novice, young, middle-aged, experienced, old$\}$, where the given labels are associated with fuzzy sets in $\mathcal{X} = [15, 80]$ — the set of numbers expressing employees' age in years.

Many operations on LVs, especially composing their values with AND, OR, and other connectives, are defined on the base of functions called *the triangular norms* [9], [10]. Popular *t*-norms are minimum, or the algebraic product; they are used as models for the AND connective in linguistic summaries, e.g. *Few cars are fast* AND *cheap*.

2.3   Linguistic Quantifiers

Natural human tendencies to use imprecise quantities instead of crisp figures may be particularly observed in expressing cardinalities of sets and amounts of objects. The corresponding NL statements are called *linguistic quantifiers*, e.g. MOST, VERY FEW, BETWEEN 1 AND 3, etc.

The most known method of modelling of linguistic quantifiers is Zadeh's *fuzzy quantification* [6], and we follow this approach in summarizing databases. Numerous models of linguistic quantifiers are described in [11], [12] and in [13]. The most recent works on linguistic quantification are presented by Glöckner and Knoll [14].

Two kinds of the Zadeh fuzzy quantifiers can be distinguished: **absolute** which are fuzzy sets in a positive universe of discourse, e.g. OVER 190, ABOUT 1000, LESS THAN 10, and **relative** which are fuzzy sets in $[0,1]$ and express amounts as ratios to the cardinality of the whole universe; e.g. ABOUT $1/4$, ALMOST ALL, FEW. Both kinds are usually represented as *possibility distributions* on $\mathcal{R}^+ \cup \{0\}$ and on $[0,1]$, respectively [15].

In general, fuzzy quantifying in Zadeh's approach is linked to a special case of LV. When a LV L is to express imprecise quantities of objects and its $\mathcal{X}$ is included in $\mathcal{R}^+ \cup \{0\}$ then $V(L)$ consists of *fuzzy linguistic quantifiers* Q_i, $i = 1, \ldots, k$. $Q_1, \ldots, Q_k$ are modelled by fuzzy sets in $\mathcal{X}$, if absolute, or in $[0,1]$, if relative. In addition, fuzzy sets which are the models for linguistic fuzzy quantifiers must be normal and convex; cf. [10].

3   Linguistic Summaries of Databases

3.1   Preliminaries

In order to obtain compact and communicative (though not strictly precise) information about the content of a given database, natural language sentences which describe amounts of elements manifesting properties of interest, can be generated. Such sentences are called *linguistic summaries of databases*. The basic Yager approach to linguistic summaries [1], [16], and its further extensions [2], [3] are presented in this section.

Yager's Summaries (Y). Let us define the set of objects $\mathcal{Y} = \{y_1, \ldots, y_m\}$, the set of attributes $V = \{V_1, \ldots, V_n\}$. Let $\mathcal{X}_1, \ldots, \mathcal{X}_n$ be the domains of $V_1, \ldots, V_n$, respectively. Attributes from V describe objects from $\mathcal{Y}$; it is denoted as $V_j(y_i)$ – a value of attribute V_j for object y_i. Hence, a database $\mathcal{D}$ which collects information about $\mathcal{Y}$, is in the form of

$$\mathcal{D} = \{< V_1(y_1), \ldots, V_n(y_1) >, \cdots, < V_1(y_m), \ldots, V_n(y_m) >\} = \{d_1, \ldots, d_m\} \quad (2)$$

where $d_1, \ldots, d_m$ are the records which describe objects $y_1, \ldots, y_m$, respectively, such that $d_i \in \mathcal{X}_1 \times \ldots \times \mathcal{X}_n$. $S_1, \ldots, S_n$ are fuzzy sets in $\mathcal{X}_1, \ldots, \mathcal{X}_n$, respectively.

$S_1, \ldots, S_n$ are the labels for linguistic values of $V_1, \ldots, V_n$, respectively. Let Q be a fuzzy quantifier. A linguistic summary of $\mathcal{D}$ is in the form of

$$Q \ P \ \text{are/have} \ S_j \ [T] \tag{3}$$

where

$$T = \mu_Q \left(\frac{\sum_{i=1}^m \mu_{S_j}\left(V_j(y_i)\right)}{m} \right) \tag{4}$$

if Q is relative (for an absolute Q the denominator equals 1 instead of m). P is the subject of summary, and S_j is the summarizer, $j = 1, \ldots, m$. $T \in [0,1]$ is called *degree of truth* or *truth of the summary* and is interpreted as a quality measure of a summary: the closer to 1 it is, the more reliable the summary is.

George and Srikanth's Summaries (G). George and Srikanth [2] proposed building summarizers of a few fuzzy sets using a t-norm (originally, the minimum), in contrary to the Yager approach in which summarizers are built of single fuzzy sets. Thus the MF of the so-called *composite summarizer* $S = S_1$ AND $\ldots$ AND S_n is of the form

$$\mu_S(d_i) = \min_{j=1,2,\ldots,n} \left\{ \mu_{S_j}\left(V_j(y_i)\right) \right\}, \ i = 1, 2, \ldots, m \tag{5}$$

and the formula for T is still (4) in which S_j is replaced with S. A sample (G) summary is: *Almost none of my friends is young* AND *reach*.

Kacprzyk and Zadrożny's Summaries (K). Kacprzyk and Yager [3] proposed generating summaries in which one of summarizers is chosen as the so-called *query* (denoted as w_g):

$$Q \ \text{objects from} \ \mathcal{Y} \ \text{being/having} \ w_g \ \text{are/have} \ S \ [T] \tag{6}$$

The form of μ_S is:

$$\mu_S(d_i) = \min_{j=1,2,\ldots,n} \left\{ \mu_{S_j}\left(V_j(y_i)\right) \ t \ \mu_{w_g}\left(V_g(y_i)\right) \right\}, i = 1, \ldots, m \tag{7}$$

where the cofactor $\mu_{w_g}\left(V_g(y_i)\right)$ means that only the tuples with non-zero memberships to w_g — $\mu_{w_g}\left(V_g(y_i)\right) > 0$ — are considered in the final result; other records are not considered. The T index is:

$$T = \mu_Q \left(\frac{\sum_{i=1}^m \mu_S(d_i)}{\sum_{i=1}^m \mu_{w_g}\left(V_g(y_i)\right)} \right) \tag{8}$$

(for relative quantifiers only). The mechanism, apart from the meaningful cost reduction, provides also more specific and informative summaries.

3.2   Quality Measures for Linguistic Summaries

The indices presented in this section were first defined by Traczyk [17] to determine the quality of knowledge mined from textual datasets due to lengths of sentences expressing facts, or due to shapes of fuzzy sets modelling properties. These indices are originally reformulated by Kacprzyk, Yager, and Zadrożny [18] and applied in linguistic summaries by Kacprzyk and Strykowski [8]. Therefore, *imprecision* (denoted as T_2), *covering* (T_2), *appropriateness* (T_4), and *length* (T_5) of a linguistic summary are determined. The indices are expressed with real numbers from $[0, 1]$, and it strictly corresponds to the set of truth values in fuzzy logic. Thus, it is crucial to determine exactly their semantic interpretation.

Degree of Truth. The degree of truth is the very first measure of quality of a summary. It was introduced by Yager [1]. In its basic form, T_1 has been the only index allowing to determine how precise a summary is; see (4).

Degree of Imprecision. The degree of imprecision, T_2, is a very intuitive criterion which describes how imprecise the summarizer used in a summary is. It is, at first, required to define the degree of fuzziness for a fuzzy set S_j in $\mathcal{X}_j$:

$$in(S_j) = \frac{|\{x \in \mathcal{X}_j : \mu_{S_j}(x) > 0\}|}{|\mathcal{X}_j|} \qquad (9)$$

The degree of imprecision is given as

$$T_2 = 1 - \left(\prod_{j=1}^{n} in(S_j)\right)^{1/n} \qquad (10)$$

The semantics of this index shows that the flatter μ_{S_j} is, the closer to unity $in(S_j)$ is, hence, the less precise the feature S_j. If the degrees of fuzziness for $S_1, \ldots, S_n$ grow, and, in consequence, the geometric average in (10) increases, then the precision of the summary decreases.

Degree of Covering. The degree of covering is based on the t_i function:

$$t_i = \begin{cases} 1, & \text{if } \mu_S(d_i) > 0 \text{ and } \mu_{w_g}\left(V_g(y_i)\right) > 0 \\ 0, & \text{otherwise} \end{cases} \qquad (11)$$

and on the h_i function

$$h_i = \begin{cases} 1, & \text{if } \mu_{w_g}\left(V_g(y_i)\right) > 0 \\ 0, & \text{otherwise} \end{cases} \qquad (12)$$

Thus, T_3 is in the form of

$$T_3 = \frac{\sum_{i=1}^{m} t_i}{\sum_{i=1}^{m} h_i} \qquad (13)$$

The degree of covering determines how many objects in the database corresponding to the query w_g are covered by the summary.

Degree of Appropriateness. If a summarizer S is represented by the family of fuzzy sets $\{S_1, \ldots, S_n\}$, the summary may be divided into n partial summaries based on attributes $S_1, \ldots, S_n$, respectively. The degree of appropriateness is based on the r index computed for S_j as

$$r_j = \frac{\sum_{i=1}^m g_i}{m} \tag{14}$$

where

$$g_i = \begin{cases} 1, \text{ if } \mu_{S_j}\left(V_j(y_i)\right) > 0 \\ 0, \text{ otherwise} \end{cases} \tag{15}$$

The degree of appropriateness is in the form of

$$T_4 = \left| \prod_{j=1}^n r_j - T_3 \right| \tag{16}$$

and it is said to be the most relevant degree of validity of summaries.

Length of Summary. The index of quality called *a length of a summary*, denoted as T_5, is defined as

$$T_5 = 2 \cdot \left(\frac{1}{2} \right)^{card(S)} \tag{17}$$

where $card(S)$ is the number of features. Thus, T_5 indicates that the longer the summary is, the smaller its correctness. All the presented indices can be used to determine a reliable quality measure for the summary:

$$T = T(T_1, T_2, T_3, T_4, T_5; w_1, w_2, w_3, w_4, w_5) = \sum_{i=1}^5 w_i \cdot T_i \tag{18}$$

where: $w_1 + w_2 + w_3 + w_4 + w_5 = 1$.

4 Automated Generating of News

The general schema of the system which generates textual messages on a given database, is depicted in Fig. 1. As it is seen, the process is not performed automatically at all; similarly to systems that support medical diagnosis, each artificially made decision must be corrected/verified/rejected by a human expert. Input data from a database, from user's and expert's entries, are processed by the summaries generator block via the algorithms described in this section.

We assume that the database is constructed according to the most popular model, i.e. relational. The symbolical form of the database is given by (2). Let a set of k linguistic quantifiers $\{Q_1, \ldots, Q_k\}$ (e.g. MANY, FEW, ABOUT HALF), and a set of l linguistic variables $\{L_1, \ldots, L_l\}$ (e.g. L_1=''age of worker'', L_2=''salary'') be given. Each linguistic variable (LV) is represented by the set of its values:

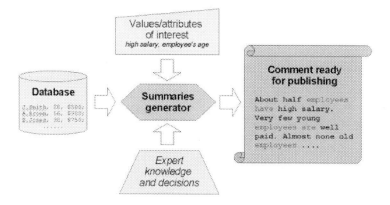

Fig. 1. The process of generating press comments

$V(L_p) = \{S_{p,1}, \ldots, S_{p,n_p}\}$, $p = 1, \ldots, l$ (e.g. $V(L_2)$={LOW, MEDIUM, HIGH}, thus $n_2 = 3$). Let us denote $n = n_1 + \ldots + n_l$ as the number of all single summarizers possible to be used by the generator.

Three algorithms which build comments: 1) on z summarizers, $z = 1, \ldots, n$, 2) on two attributes represented by linguistic variables: $L_p, L_q, p \neq q$, $p, q = 1, \ldots, l$, and 3) on b, $b = 1, \ldots, l$ are described in the three following subsections, respectively.

4.1 Commenting on z Summarizers

Let us assume that a brief textual message about dependencies among $z \in \mathbb{N}$ features is to be generated. These z features are values of the LVs $L_1, \ldots, L_l$, thus $z = 1, \ldots, n$. For instance, we choose HIGH from "salary" and YOUNG from "age of worker" (so z would equal 2). In general, the number of possible summaries generated from z summarizers is:

$$k\binom{z}{0}\left[\binom{z}{1} + \cdots + \binom{z}{z}\right] + k\binom{z}{1}\left[\binom{z-1}{1} + \cdots + \binom{z-1}{z-1}\right] + \cdots + k\binom{z}{z-1}\left[\binom{1}{1}\right] =$$
$$= k\binom{z}{0}\left(2^z - 1\right) + \ldots + k\binom{z}{z-1}\left(2^1 - 1\right) = k\sum_{i=0}^{z-1}\binom{z}{i}\left(2^{z-i} - 1\right) \tag{19}$$

The comment to this formula must be given under the assumption that we treat Yager's form (Y) of a summary as a special case of George and Srikanth's form (G). In consequence, Kacprzyk and Zadrożny's (K) form of a summary (with a w_g query) is a further generalization of (G), or, in other words, (G) is a special case of (K) in which $w_g = \emptyset$. Hence, the form of the first element, $\binom{z}{0}[\binom{z}{1} + \cdots + \binom{z}{z}] = \binom{z}{0}(2^z - 1)$, comes from the fact that we choose 0 of z summarizers to build w_g and $i = 1, \ldots, z$ summarizers to build S. The next one, $\binom{z}{1}(2^{z-1} - 1)$ is related to the choice of exactly one summarizer for w_g and $i = 1, \ldots, z - 1$ summarizers for S, etc.

Formula (19) is valid under the assumption that only the AND connective is used to build composite summarizers or queries, e.g. "high salary AND young"; see (5). Nevertheless, it is worth mentioning that summarizers can be also joined with other connectives, like OR, etc.

```
// generating (Y) summaries
1. for each single summarizer S ∈ {S₁,...,Sᵤ}
      1.1. for each quantifier Qₕ, h = 1,...,k
           if (Qₕ is absolute)
```
$$\text{compute } T_h = \mu_{Q_h}\left(\sum_{j=1}^{m} \mu_S(d_j)\right)$$
```
           else       // i.e. if Qₕ is relative
```
$$\text{compute } T_h = \mu_{Q_h}\left(\frac{\sum_{j=1}^{m} \mu_S(d_j)}{m}\right)$$
```
      1.2. compute T_{h_max} = max_{h=1,...,k} Tₕ, remember h_max
      1.3. generate summary in the form of
```
$$Q_{h_{max}} \ P \text{ is/have } S \ [T_{h_{max}}]$$

```
// generating (G) summaries
2. for each non-singleton and non-empty Ŝ ⊆ {S₁,...,Sᵤ}
      2.1. determine μ_S(d_j) = min_{S_i ∈ Ŝ} μ_{S_i}(d_j)
      2.2. for each quantifier Qₕ, h = 1,...,k
           compute T_{1,h} analogously to step 1.1.
      2.3. compute T_{1,h_max} = max_{h=1,...,k} T_{1,h}, remember h_max
```
$$2.4. \text{ compute } T_2 = 1 - \left(\prod_{S_i \in \hat{S}} \frac{card(\{x \in \mathcal{X}_i : \mu_{S_i}(x) > 0\})}{card(\mathcal{X}_i)}\right)^{1/card(\hat{S})}$$
$$2.5. \text{ compute } T_4 = \left|\prod_{S_i \in \hat{S}} \frac{\sum_{d \in D} g(d)}{m}\right|,$$
```
           where g is given by (15)
```
$$2.6. \text{ compute } T_5 = 2 \cdot \left(\tfrac{1}{2}\right)^{card(\hat{S})}$$
$$2.7. \text{ compute } T = w_1 \cdot T_{1,h_{max}} + w_2 \cdot T_2 + w_4 \cdot T_4 + w_5 \cdot T_5$$
```
      2.8. generate summary in the form of
```
$$Q_{h_{max}} \ P \text{ are/have } \hat{S} \ [T]$$

```
// generating (K) summaries
3. for each non-empty query S_w ⊊ {S₁,...,Sᵤ}
   and for each non-empty summarizer Ŝ ⊆ {S₁,...,Sᵤ} \ S_w
      3.1. determine μ_{S_w}(d_j) = min_{S_g ∈ S_w} μ_{S_g}(d_j)
      3.2. determine D ⊇ D_w = {d ∈ D : μ_{S_w}(d) > 0}
      3.3. for each d ∈ D_w determine μ_{Ŝ}(d) = min_{S_i ∈ Ŝ} μ_{S_i}(d)
```
$$3.4. \text{ for each } h = 1,...,k \text{ compute } T_{1,h} = \mu_{Q_h}\left(\frac{\sum_{d \in D_w} \mu_{\hat{S}}(d)}{\sum_{d \in D_w} \mu_{S_w}(d)}\right)$$
```
      3.5. choose T_{1,h_max} analogously to step 1.2.
      3.6. compute T₂ analogously to 2.4.
```
$$3.7. \text{ compute } T_3 = \frac{\sum_{d \in D_w} t(d)}{\sum_{d \in D_w} h(d)} \text{ where } t \text{ and } h$$
```
           are given by (11) and (12), resp.
```
$$3.8. \text{ compute } T_4 = \left|\prod_{S_i \in \hat{S}} \frac{\sum_{d \in D_w} g(d)}{m} - T_3\right|,$$

```
    where function g is given by (15)
3.9. compute T_5 analogously to 2.6.
3.10. compute T = T_{1,h_max} + Σ_{i=2}^5 w_i T_i
3.11. generate summary in the form of
    Q_{h_max}  P being/having S_w are/have Ŝ [T]
```

Ad. 2. In generating (G) summaries which are based on at most z summarizers, the algorithm determining all the non-singleton and non-empty subsets of $\{S_1, \ldots, S_z\}$ is required; the number of such subsets is exactly $2^z - 1 - z$. In the implementation, the problem is resolved via generating binary forms of all natural numbers between 0 and $2^z - 1$; the forms are taken as characteristic vectors of the sought subsets.

Ad. 2.1. When generating (G) summaries, the minimum operation can be replaced, in general, by a t-norm; see Section 2.2.

Ad. 2.4. The $\mathcal{X}_i$ set is the domain of the S_i fuzzy set.

Ad. 2.6. $w_1 + w_2 + w_4 + w_5$ must equal 1.

Ad. 3.10. $w_1 + w_2 + w_3 + w_4 + w_5$ must equal 1.

4.2   Commenting on Two Attributes

This variant of generating messages may be applied when dependencies between two attributes with respect to all their values are to be referred. We model these attributes with the LVs L_p and L_q, $p \neq q$, $p, q = 1, 2, \ldots, l$, therefore, the summaries which use all the sets $S_{p,1}, \ldots, S_{p,n_p}$ and $S_{q,1}, \ldots, S_{q,n_q}$ are to be generated. In this case, the general number of possible summaries is:

$$\underbrace{k(n_p + n_q)}_{(Y)} + \underbrace{k n_p n_q}_{(G)} + \underbrace{2k n_p n_q}_{(K)} \tag{20}$$

The first element describes the number of possible Yager summaries; it refers to the number of values of L_p and to a single summarizer which is a value of L_q. The second element is also related to the number of values of L_p and L_q, because (G) summaries are generated for composite summarizers in the form of $S_{p,i}$ AND $S_{q,j}$, where $i = 1, \ldots, n_p$, and $j = 1, \ldots, n_q$. The third element, (K), describes the number of summaries which use two features, $S_{p,i}$ and $S_{q,j}$, as a query and a summarizer, respectively or *vice versa* — that is why it is multiplied by 2. The technical details of the algorithm are omitted, but its general idea is analogous to the one presented in Section 4.1.

4.3   Commenting on b Attributes

The algorithm given in Section 4.2 can be generalized to obtain comments on dependencies and trends among $b = 1, \ldots, l$ attributes (the case for $b = 2$ is described above). It would require to perform the two following modifications in the algorithm given in Section 4.1: 1) The substitution: $z := \binom{n_1}{1} \cdots \binom{n_b}{1}$ (where $n_1, \ldots, n_b$ are the numbers of values in linguistic variables describing the chosen attributes), and 2) the condition that each of z summarizers is a value of separated linguistic variable.

5 Implementation

The prototype news generator is implemented on .NET platform in the C#
language. A sample database consists of 5000 records in the form of <ID,
seniority, profit, salary> and is implemented with MS Access. Three linguistic variables are applied to interpret numerical values of the fields of records
(except of ID): L_1 = "seniority", $V(L_1)$={ *beginner, intermediate, experienced* },
L_2 = "profit", $V(L_2)$={ *low, medium, high* }, L_3 = "salary", $V(L_3)$={ *low, medium,
high* } with trapezoidal membership functions in the domains $[0, 40]$ for L_1,
$[1000, 7000]$ for L_2, and $[2000, 14000]$ for L_3. Three fuzzy relative quantifiers
are determined in the $[0, 1]$ domain: Q_1 = "few", $\mu_{Q_1}(x) = x$, Q_2 = "about half",
$\mu_{Q_2}(x) = -|2x - 1| + 1$, Q_3 = "many", $\mu_{Q_3}(x) = -x + 1$. The weights for
the quality measures are $w_1 = w_2 = w_4 = w_5 = \frac{1}{4}$ for (G) summaries and
$w_1 = w_2 = w_3 = w_4 = w_5 = \frac{1}{5}$ for (K) summaries. The sample news generated
via the algorithm described in Section 4.1 is presented below:

> (Y) About half of employees are intermediates [0.98].
> Many employees have medium salary [0.71]. (G) About half
> of employees are intermediates and have medium salary
> [0.53]. (K) Many intermediate employees have medium salary
> [0.61]. About half of employees which have medium salary
> are intermediates [0.59].

6 Conclusions and Further Work Directions

The presented paper is focused on fuzzy-based methods applied to linguistic
interpretation of large datasets. The linguistic summaries of databases in the
sense of Yager with their later improvements, are presented. The methods are
the foundations necessary to construct the system which generates short textual and natural language reports on databases. The original algorithms, which
mechanise the reporting of large datasets, provide linguistically formulated and
user-friendly results, are introduced. An effective application which automatically generates news or messages to be published as press or WWW comments,
is presented.

The extension of the Yager approach, based on Interval-Valued Fuzzy Sets, is
successfully presented by Niewiadomski in [19] and [20]. The analysis of further
generalizations which may employ the so-called Type-2 Fuzzy Sets are made
in [21] and are currently being developed.

References

1. Yager, R.: A New Approach to the Summarization of Data. Information Sciences
   (1982) 69–86
2. George, R., Srikanth, R.: Data Summarization Using Genetic Algorithms and Fuzzy
   Logic. In Herrera, F., Verdegay, J., eds.: Genetic Algorithms and Soft Computing.
   Physica–Verlag, Heidelberg (1996) 599–611

3. Kacprzyk, J., Yager, R.R.: Linguistic Summaries of Data Using Fuzzy Logic. Int. J. of General Systems (2001) 133–154
4. Zadeh, L.A.: Fuzzy Sets. Information and Control (1965) 338–353
5. Zadeh, L.A.: The Concept of Linguistic Variable and Its Application for Approximate Reasoning (i). Information Sciences (1975) 199–249
6. Zadeh, L.A.: A Computational Approach to Fuzzy Quantifiers in Natural Languages. Computers and Maths with Applications (1983) 149–184
7. Kacprzyk, J., Yager, R.R., Zadrożny, S.: Fuzzy Linguistic Summaries of Databases for an Efficient Business Data Analysis and Decision Support. In Abramowicz, W., Żurada, J., eds.: Knowledge Discovery for Business Information Systems. Kluwer Academic Publisher B. V., Boston (2001) 129–152
8. Kacprzyk, J., Strykowski, P.: Linguistic Data Summaries for Intelligent Decision Support. In: Proceedings of EFDAN'99. (4-th European Workshop...). (1999) 3–12
9. Dubois, D., Prade, H.: Fuzzy Sets and Systems. Theory and Applications. Academic Press, Inc., NY (1980)
10. Kacprzyk, J.: Fuzzy Sets in System Analysis. PWN, Warsaw (1986) (in Polish).
11. Thiele, H.: On t-Quantifiers and s-Quantifiers. In: Proceedings of the Twenty-Fourth International Symposium on Multiple-Valued Logic. (1994) 264–269
12. Thiele, H.: On Fuzzy Quantifiers. In: Fuzzy Logic and its Applications to Engineering, Information Science and Intelligent Systems. Kluwer Academic Publishers (1995)
13. Novak, V.: Fuzzy Sets and Their Applications. Adam Hilger (1989)
14. Glöckner, I., Knoll, A.: A Formal Theory of Fuzzy Natural Language Quantification and Its Role in Granular Computing. In Pedrycz, W., ed.: Granular Computing: An Emerging Paradigm. Physica-Verlag (2001) 215–256
15. Liu, Y., Kerre, E.E.: An Overview of Fuzzy Quantifiers, Part i: Interpretations. Fuzzy Sets and Systems (1998) 1–21
16. Yager, R.R., Ford, M., Canas, A.J.: An Approach to the Linguistic Summarization of Data. In: Proceedings of 3rd International Conference IPMU, Paris, France. (1990) 456–468
17. Traczyk, W.: Evaluation of Knowledge Quality. System Science (1997)
18. Kacprzyk, J., Yager, R.R., Zadrożny, S.: A Fuzzy Logic Based Approach to Linguistic Summaries of Databases. Int. J. of Appl. Math. and Comp. Sci. (2000) 813–834
19. Niewiadomski, A.: Interval-Valued Linguistic Variables. An Application to Linguistic Summaries. In Hryniewicz, O., Kacprzyk, J., Koronacki, J., Wierzchoń, S.T., eds.: Issues in Intelligent Systems. Paradigms. EXIT Academic Press, Warsaw (2005) 167–184
20. Niewiadomski, A.: Interval-Valued Quality Measures for Linguistic Summaries. EXIT Academic Press, Warsaw (2005) (in print).
21. Niewiadomski, A.: On Two Possible Roles of Type-2 Fuzzy Sets in Linguistic Summaries. Lecture Notes on Artificial Intelligence **3528** (2005) 341–347

Improving Web Sites with Web Usage Mining, Web Content Mining, and Semantic Analysis

Jean-Pierre Norguet[1], Esteban Zimányi[1], and Ralf Steinberger[2]

[1] Department of Computer & Network Engineering,
CP 165/15, Université Libre de Bruxelles,
50 av. F.D. Roosevelt, 1050 Brussels, Belgium
{jnorguet, ezimanyi}@ulb.ac.be
[2] European Commission – Joint Research Centre,
Via E. Fermi 1, T.P. 267, 21020 Ispra (VA), Italy
Ralf.Steinberger@jrc.it

Abstract. With the emergence of the World Wide Web, Web sites have
become a key communication channel for organizations. In this context,
analyzing and improving Web communication is essential to better satisfy
the objectives of the target audience. Web communication analysis is
traditionnally performed by Web analytics software, which produce long
lists of audience metrics. These metrics contain little semantics and are
too detailed to be exploited by organization managers and chief editors,
who need summarized and conceptual information to take decisions. Our
solution to obtain such conceptual metrics is to analyze the content of the
Web pages output by the Web server. In this paper, we first present a list
of methods that we conceived to mine the output Web pages. Then, we
explain how term weights in these pages can be used as audience metrics,
and how they can be aggregated using OLAP tools to obtain concept-
based metrics. Finally, we present the concept-based metrics that we
obtained with our prototype WASA and SQL Server OLAP tools.

1 Introduction

The ease and speed with which information exchange and business transactions
can be carried out over the Web has been a key driving force in the rapid
growth of the Web and electronic commerce. In this context, improving Web
communication is essential to better satisfy the objectives of both the Web site
and its target audience, and Web usage mining [17], a relatively new research
area, has gained more attention. The strategic goals of Web usage mining are
prediction of the user's behaviour within the site, comparison between expected
and actual Web site usage, and adjustment of the Web site with respect to
the interests of its users. Web analytics [19] is the part of Web usage mining
that has the most emerged in the corporate world. Web analytics focuses on
improving Web communication by mining and analyzing Web usage data to
discover interesting metrics and usage patterns.

From the huge amount of usage data collected by Web servers, Web analytics software produce many detailed reports. The usefulness of these reports

J. Wiedermann et al. (Eds.): SOFSEM 2006, LNCS 3831, pp. 430–439, 2006.

depends on the report viewers in the organization. While Web designers are interested in detailed reports, organization managers are only interested in summary dashboards that show the number of visitors and a list of the most viewed pages, and the Web site chief editor needs concept-based results to redefine the publishing rules. In addition, the temporal evolution of the Web site content and the volatility of the scripted pages are not considered by Web analytics software.

To solve these issues, our approach aims at analyzing the content of the Web pages output by the Web server in order to obtain concept-based metrics. In Section 2, we present a list of methods that we conceived to mine the output pages, whatever the Web site technologies. In Section 3, we describe the content processing that we apply to the pages. From the term occurrences in the pages, we define the term-based consultation and we discuss some results obtained with our prototype WASA. Then, we group the terms into meaningful concepts using the concept hierarchies of ontologies. By the means of hierarchical aggregation, we define a set of concept-based metrics and we compute them with OLAP tools. In Section 4, we present and discuss the results obtained with our prototype WASA and SQL Server OLAP. In Section 5, we describe the results exploitation process. In Section 6, we expose the limitations of the metrics and our future work. Finally, in Section 7 we discuss how our approach compares with related work and we conclude in Section 8.

2   Output Page Mining

The first step in our approach is to mine the Web pages that are output by the Web server. We have conceived a number of methods, each of them being located at some point in the Web environment.

- In the Web server, log files can be coupled to a content journal that stores the evolution of the Web site content.
- In the Web server, a plugin can store the pages after they have been sent to the browser.
- On an Ethernet wire, a network monitor can capture the TCP/IP packets and reassemble the Web pages.
- On the client machine, an embedded program can run inside the page and send the content to a mining server.

This makes a number of mining methods that can be used alone or in combination. Each method has its advantages. Log file parsing combined with content journaling is easy to setup, runs in batch, and offers good performance. Dynamic Web sites require the use of a Web server plugin, a network monitor, or a client-side miner. Web server plugins are usually installed in secure Web sites, and network monitors elsewhere because of the lower risk. For the pages composed on the client-side, like XML/XSL pages, a client-side miner is required. As far as we can see, this set of methods can mine the pages output from any Web site.

3   Concept-Based Audience Metrics

Once the output pages have been mined, they can be processed in order to extract meaningful content. This processing is well-known in information retrieval [2]. Content processing includes unformatting, tokenization, stopword removal, stemming, and term selection. From P_d the set of Web pages mined during day d, content processing ultimately produces a list of stemmed terms s_i that appear with a frequency which we call $Consultation(s_i, d)$. The consultation represents the number of times the term s_i has been displayed on visitors' screens during day d. To neutralize the fluctuation of the metrics along time, the consultation can be divided by the total number of pages views. In this sense, term-based consultation is similar to the term frequency in the vector model [16].

To experiment this notion of consultation, we developed a prototype called WASA[1]. We ran WASA for the academic year 2003-2004 on our department's Web site cs.ulb.ac.be, which contains about 2,000 Web pages and receives an average of 100 page requests a day. The result is a list of 30,000 terms and their daily consultation. Term-based consultation is very promising but the list of terms is too long and suffers from polysemy and synonymy. These observations call for the grouping of terms into meaningful concepts.

The main difficulty in grouping the terms is to define groups that match semantic fields for the human mind. Such groups can be found in *ontologies* [7]. If we define an ontology $\Omega := (S, r_0, R, \sigma)$ where S is a set of terms, r_0 is a partial order relation on S, R is a set of relation names, and $\sigma \to \mathcal{P}(S \times S)$ is a function, then meaningful term groups can be found in the hierarchy obtained by restricting the ontology (S, r_0, R, σ) to (S, r_0) [20]. For each term s_i in S, we define the associated concept C_i as the aggregation of the term s_i and its subterms s'_j in the hierarchy: $C_i := \{s_i\} \cup \{\ldots, s'_j, \ldots\}$. The consultation of a concept is the sum of the consultation of the term and of the consultation of the subterms:

$$Consultation(C_i, d) := Consultation(s_i, d) + \sum_{s'_j} Consultation(s'_j, d) \quad (1)$$

If a term is a leaf in the hierarchy, it has no subterms and therefore $C_i = \{s_i\}$. In this case, $Consultation(C_i, d) = Consultation(s_i, d)$. As the term consultation is known, the consultation of the concepts can be recursively aggregated from the leaf terms up to the root. Similarly, we define the presence of a concept by adding the frequency of the terms and of the subterms in the online Web pages during day d:

$$Presence(C_i, d) := Presence(s_i, d) + \sum_{s'_j} Presence(s'_j, d), \quad (2)$$

with $Presence(s_i, d) = \int_d Presence(s_i, t)\, dt$. The interest into a concept is defined as the division of the two:

$$Interest(C_i, d) := \frac{Consultation(C_i, d)}{Presence(C_i, d)} \quad (3)$$

---

[1] WASA stands for Web Audience Semantic Analysis.

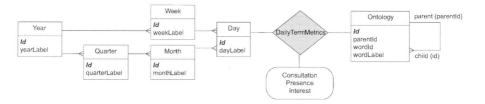

Fig. 1. OLAP cube with two dimensions: Time and Ontology

Recursive aggregation of the term-based metrics into concept-based metrics can be computed by OLAP tools. Our multidimensional model (OLAP cube) is represented in Figure 1. The notation used in the figure was introduced in [9]. In our cube, we define two dimensions: Time and Ontology. The time dimension has two important levels: Week and Day. Metrics by week neutralize the weekly patterns, which contain unsignificant information. More levels can be added depending on the needs (year, months, quarters, . . .). The ontology dimension is modeled as a *parent-child dimension* to support ontologies with any number of levels. Other dimensions could be added like physical geography, site geography, Web geography, pages, users, internal referrers, external referrers, or other variations of the time dimension. The cube fact table contains daily term consultation and presence, which are provided by our prototype WASA. The cube measures are consultation, presence, and interest, where the interest measure is a calculated member defined as the division of the first two measures.

4   Experimentation

To test our approach, we introduced our cube into SQL Server, along with the audience data computed by our prototype WASA for our department's Web site and the ACM classification. After cube processing, queries can be formulated on any combination of dimensions and measures. For example, if we display the ontology dimension vertically and the metrics horizontally, we can expand the concepts to see detailed results of the subconcepts (Figure 2). The cube can be queried and browsed with the SQL Server built-in module, from a Microsoft Excel PivotTable, or from any OLAP client like Mondrian/JPivot. With Microsoft Excel, we can produce a variety of charts to visualize cube-queried results. For example, we produced a multi-line chart where each curve represents the visitors' consultation of the top ACM concepts (Figure 3). This chart is easy to relate to the problem domain. For example, Computing Methodologies, Software, and Information Systems rank in the top, as many students follow these courses. Also, a peak of interest in Theory of Computation can be observed at the beginning of the academic year, when the 1st-year students starts following the corresponding course in the computers room. Finally, the average consultation falls down during the various periods of examination: August-September, January-February, and May-June. We can also produce a bar chart representing

		Data ▾		
Level 02	▾ Level 03	Consultation	Presence	Interest
Computer Applications		2708.459184	583792.6282	46.39419981
Computer Systems Organization		12817.90958	2931785.46	43.72048964
Computing Methodologies		22518.35586	10057223.39	22.39023136
Computing Milieux		11996.16535	3672462.928	32.66517751
Data		6579.186259	1133266.697	58.05505689
General Literature		336.0899529	70145.62587	47.91317331
Hardware		5241.491734	1446659.252	36.23169539
Information Systems	Database Management	22756.03891	5449485.45	41.75814235
	Information Interfaces and Presentation	5800.806073	950737.2194	61.01376863
	Information Storage and Retrieval	5743.399621	2150755.4	26.70410416
	Information Systems Applications	2400.736092	1287511.649	18.64632521
	Models and Principles	1700.907825	350728.1293	48.49647584
Information Systems Total *		38401.88853	10189217.85	37.68875011
Mathematics of Computing		7684.084663	1502851.178	51.13004385
Software		18059.03443	3566113.109	50.64066641
Theory of Computation		10783.28339	1674443.972	64.39918904
Grand Total *		137125.9489	36827962.09	37.23419412

Fig. 2. Browsing the ACM classification and associated metrics in SQL Server

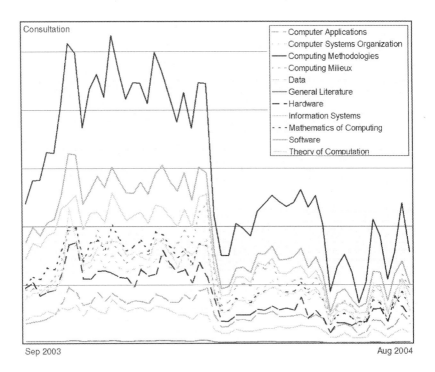

Fig. 3. Consultation of the ACM classification top concepts on the cs.ulb.ac.be Web site during the 2003-2004 academic year

the various metrics for each of the top concepts. This kind of chart allows to compare the metrics of the various concepts, as well as the different metrics together. For example, we produced a chart for our department's Web site and the ACM classification (Figure 4). The top 3 consulted concepts are: (1) Information Systems, (2) Computing Methodologies, and (3) Software. However, these concepts are major topics in the Web site, which is confirmed by high presence

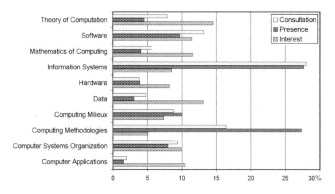

Fig. 4. Consultation, presence and interest metrics for the top concepts in the ACM classification

values. Therefore, high consultation values are not representative of the visitors' interest, what is indicated by low interest values. The top 3 concepts of interest are: (1) Theory of Computation, (2) Data, and (3) Mathematics of Computing. We can see that the ranking of the concepts can dramatically change according to the considered metrics, and that these should be interpreted carefully.

To test the influence of the ontology on concept-based metrics, we ran WASA on our (computer science) department's Web site with two ontologies: Eurovoc, the European Commission's thesaurus, and the ACM classification. Eurovoc knowledge domain is extremely generic, from sociology to science, while the ACM classification knowledge domain is focused on computer science. With more than 5 times less terms than Eurovoc, the ACM classification covers much better the Web site knowledge domain. This coverage can be quantified by the percentage r_Ω of the ontology terms that appear in the output pages:

$$r_\Omega := \frac{\text{card}\,(S \cap P_{\max})}{\text{card}\,(S)} \tag{4}$$

where $P_{\max}$ is the set of distinct terms in the output pages mined during the maximal period of time. For our department's Web site, the ACM classification coverage is 16% while the Eurovoc coverage is only 0.75%. This indicates how the meaning of the results improves with the ontology coverage of the Web site knowledge domain. A similar problem with Eurovoc has been observed in [18].

5   Exploitation

As concept-based metrics are extremely intuitive, they can be exploited at the highest levels of the organization, in order to take more effective decisions [10]. As concept-based metrics target different roles than classical Web analytics software, the exploitation process must be re-organized. With concept-based metrics,

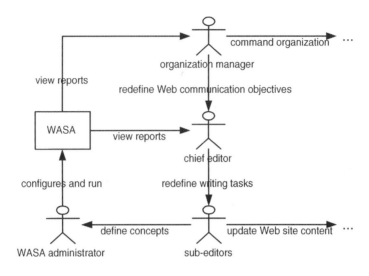

Fig. 5. Concept-based metrics exploitation life cycle

the chief editor and the sub-editors define the concepts relevant to the Web site knowledge domain. The tool administrator encodes these concepts into WASA, which generates the concept-based metrics reports. These reports are distributed to the organization manager and to the chief editor. With concept-based metrics, the organization manager is provided with an intuitive view of what messages are delivered through the Web site. He can then redefine the organization strategy according to the visitors' interests, adapt the other communication channels, and eventually request the chief editor to better adapt the Web site communication to the organization objectives. The chief editor on his part can redefine the publishing orders, dispatch the reports to the sub-editors, and redefine the writing tasks (Figure 5).

6   Future Work

Our future work will aim to study the benefits of improving ontology coverage. First, we will evaluate a manual approach. The researchers in our department will enrich the ACM classification with terms of the department's Web site. Each researcher will browse the Web pages under his/her responsability and select the most relevant terms of his domain knowledge. At the end, the chief editor will validate the enrichments. This method will ensure an optimal improvement of the ontology coverage, the effect of which will be evaluated by running WASA on the enriched ontology. Furthermore, this manual enrichment will be compared against automatic and semi-automatic techniques.

The results obtained by our approach will be validated against WebTrends in a particular case of Web site where the results obtained by WebTrends should be comparable to those obtained by WASA. Indeed, if the Web site directories match the ontology concepts, the hits by directories obtained by WebTrends should be comparable to the interest by concept obtained by WASA.

Although the complexity of our algorithms are linear, we will test the scalability of our prototype WASA on our university's Web site[2], which contains a very high number of pages (about 50,000) and receives a very high number of page requests (about 200,000 a day).

Finally, variations of the metrics inspired from the vector model [16], as well as evaluators for ontology coverage of Web site knowledge domain [8], should be experimented.

7 Related Work

In the recent years, Web analytics software have shown little evolution. The most interesting feature introduced is page grouping with respect to a concept. For example, in the most popular Web analytics tool WebTrends, the pages can be grouped into *content groups*, which can be defined either by enumeration or regular expressions over the URI [21]. In the subsequent content-groups report, WebTrends shows the score of each content group, computed by aggregating the hits of the composing pages. The report is more intuitive than the page-views report, but the quality of the results depends on the page-grouping operation, which is not assisted by the software. Also, the temporal evolution of the pages remains ignored. Finally, content groups are groups of entire pages, with no finer-grained data units. Another attempt in the corporate world to consider more semantics has been to map back-end product data to an id parameter in URLs, like in IBM Tivoli Web Site Analyzer [12]. However this solution is limited to e-commerce Web sites and remains site specific.

In the research world, the closest approach to ours is reverse clustering analysis [15], an algorithm based on self-organizing feature maps. This algorithm integrates Web Usage Mining and Web Content Mining by integrating Web logs and Web site text. The result of this integration is a list of pages representing the most popular Web pages in the site. The pages are prioritized with regard to a score called "square vicinity". Although the results help to improve the content of a Web site, the approach suffers from a list of drawbacks. First, the text content which is part of the analysis process does not appear in the results, which are consequently prived from the corresponding intuitivity. Second, although the page list is limited to a fraction of the Web site, it remains proportional to the site size and can therefore lack summarization. Third, the technique handles static Web sites only, which excludes the many dynamic Web sites from being analyzed. Finally, the experimental performances and the algorithm complexity do not guarantee the scalability of the approach.

The Information Scent model aims to infer an intuitive representation of the user need from the user actions [5]. In particular, the IUNIS algorithm inputs a sequence of visited pages and outputs a weighted vector of terms describing

---

[2] http://www.ulb.ac.be/

the visitor's interest. These vectors are quite intuitive, but can be very vague without context. In addition, the analysis is more user-centric than site-centric. Finally, the scalability of the algorithm is not proven; the cited paper presents results for single visits over a few pages, and does not discuss performance, which makes it unclear how the algorithm can handle 50,000 visits over 50,000 pages.

Most of the other Web usage mining research efforts have focused on other research paths, like usage pattern analysis [4], personalization [11], system improvement [1], site structure modification [13], marketing business intelligence [3], and usage characterization [14]. In these research paths, Web analytics concerns have been mostly left aside.

Finally, many other research projects are somehow related to Web usage mining, as unveiled in a recent survey [6]. To the best of our knowledge, our approach is the first to analyze the content of output Web pages to provide site-wide concept-based metrics in order to represent the user needs of any Web site, whatever the Web server technologies.

8   Conclusion

In this paper we have presented our solution to answer the need for summarized and conceptual audience metrics in Web analytics. We first described the various techniques that we conceived to mine the Web pages output by a Web server, showing a set of combinable options that should be applicable for any Web server. Then, we defined three term-based metrics: consultation, presence, and interest. We have seen that these metrics are much more interesting if the terms are grouped into meaningful concepts. Our first experiments on automated term-grouping algorithms showing disappointing results, we reuse the term groups that are naturally present in the concept hierarchies of ontologies. OLAP tools can be used to aggregate the term-based metrics into concept-based metrics. The OLAP cube can be queried from any OLAP-enabled visualization interface. According to our first experiments with the WASA prototype and SQL Server, concept-based metrics prove intuitive enough to support the decision-making process of Web site editors and organization managers. The condition to the wide adoption of concept-based metrics in Web analytics software is the generalization of custom ontologies for Web sites. The availability of large generic ontologies and the development of ontology enrichment techniques and tools, as well as the growing interest into the Semantic Web, should fill the gap with the continuous and growing development of suitable ontologies.

References

1. Aggarwal, C.C., and Yu, P.S.: On Disk Caching of Web Objects in Proxy Servers. In Proc. of the 6th Int. Conf. on Information and Knowledge Management, CIKM'97 (1997) 238–245
2. Baeza-Yates, R., and Ribeiro-Neto, B.: Modern Information Retrieval. Addison-Wesley (1999)

3. Büchner, A.G., and Mulvenna, M.D.: Discovering Internet Marketing Intelligence through Online Analytical Web Usage Mining. SIGMOD Record **27** 4 (1998) 54–61

4. Chen, M.-S., Han, J., and Yu, P.S.: Data Mining: An Overview from a Database Perspective. IEEE Trans. Knowl. Data Eng. **8** 6 (1996) 866–883

5. Chi, E.H., Pirolli, P., Chen, K., and Pitkow, J.E.: Using Information Scent to Model User Information Needs and Actions and the Web. In Proc. of the SIGCHI on Human Factors in Computing Systems (2001) 490–497

6. Facca, F.M., and Lanzi, P.L.: Mining Interesting Knowledge from Weblogs: a Survey. Data Knowl. Eng. **53** 3 (2005) 225–241

7. Fensel, D.: Ontologies: A Silver Bullet for Knowledge Management and Electronic Commerce. Springer-Verlag (2000)

8. Lozano-Tello, A., and Gómez-Pérez, A.: Ontometric: A Method to Choose the Appropriate Ontology. J. Database Manag. **15** 2 (2004) 1–18

9. Malinowski, E., and Zimányi, E.: OLAP Hierarchies: A Conceptual Perspective. In Proc. of the 16th Int. Conf. on Advanced Information Systems Engineering, CAiSE'04, LNCS **3084** Springer-Verlag, (2004) 477–491

10. March, J.G., Simon, H.A., and Guetzkow, H.S.: Organizations. Cambridge Mass. Blackwell, second edition (1983)

11. Mobasher, B., Cooley, R., and Srivastava, J.: Automatic Personalization Based on Web Usage Mining. Communications of the ACM **43** 8 (2000) 142–151

12. Moeller, M., Cicaterri, C., Presser, A., and Wang, M.: Measuring e-Business Web Usage, Performance, and Availability. IBM Press (2003)

13. Perkowitz, M., and Etzioni, O.: Towards Adaptive Web Sites: Conceptual Framework and Case Study. Artif. Intell. **118** 1-2 (2000) 245–275

14. Pirolli, P., and Pitkow, J.E.: Distributions of Surfers' Paths through the World Wide Web: Empirical Characterizations. World Wide Web **2** 1-2 (1999) 29–45

15. Ríos, S.A., Velásquez, J.D., Vera, E.S., Yasuda, H., and Aoki, T.: Using SOFM to Improve Web Site Text Content. In Proc. of First Int. Conf. on Advances in Natural Computation, ICNC 2005, Part II (2005) 622–626

16. Salton, G., and McGill, M.J.: Introduction to Modern Information Retrieval. McGraw-Hill (1983)

17. Srivastava, J., Cooley, R., Deshpande, M., and Pang-Ning, T.: Web Usage Mining: Discovery and Applications of Usage Patterns from Web Data. SIGKDD **1** 2 (2000)

18. Steinberger, R., Pouliquen, B., and Ignat, C.: Exploiting Multilingual Nomenclatures and Language-Independent Text Features as an Interlingua for Cross-Lingual Text Analysis Applications. In Proc. of the 4th Slovenian Language Technology Conf., Information Society 2004 (2004)

19. Sterne, J.: Web Metrics: Proven Methods for Measuring Web Site Success. John Wiley & Sons (2002)

20. Stumme, G., and Maedche, A.: Fca-Merge: Bottom-up Merging of Ontologies. In Proc. of the 17th Int. Joint Conf. on Artificial Intelligence, IJCAI 2001 (2001) 225–234

21. Wahli, U., Norguet, J.P., Andersen, J., Hargrove, N., and Meser, M.: Websphere Version 5 Application Development Handbook. IBM Press (2003)

Automatic Distribution of Sequential Code Using JavaSymphony Middleware

Saeed Parsa and Vahid Khalilpoor

Faculty of Computer Engineering,
Iran University of Science and Technology
Parsa@iust.ac.ir

Abstract. In this paper the design and implementation of a framework, called jDistributor, for automatic conversion of sequential code into distributed program code is described. Optimal distribution of the program code is attained by applying a specific hierarchical clustering algorithm to partition the code into components with almost the same amount of speed up. To speed up the execution of the components, inter-component method calls are converted into non-blocking remote calls, when appropriate. All the inter-component remote calls are carried out through a component, called Proxy. The Proxy uses an Object Manager component to construct remote objects. A component called Synchronizer receives the values of reference parameters and the return value from remote methods. All the inter-component communications are handled by a connector component, which is based on a javaSymphony infrastructure.

1 Introduction

Recent advents in networking and PCs technologies have commoditized power and stability to such an extent as to make them, collectively, suitable alternatives to supercomputers for running computationally intensive applications in a reasonable amount of time. Solutions for computationally intensive classes of problems, previously the domain of expensive supercomputers, may now be easily implemented through heterogeneous networked computers. On the other hand, high-performance distributed applications are difficult to create in large part because the programmer must manually partition and distribute the application to maximize locality and minimize communication. There are many software tools such as ProActive [1], cJVM [2], JavaParty [3], Jada [4] and JavaSymphony [5] that try to overcome developmental complexities of distributed and parallel programs. However, in most of these software tools, you need to deal with a programmer to build an efficient and true distributed system. It is argued that system software, not the programmer, should partition and distribute applications [6]. Application partitioning in an object oriented environment is the task of breaking up the functionality of an application into distinct set of objects that can operate concurrently. If an application can not be partitioned in the way, the distribution is not beneficial.

In this paper we introduce a framework called jDistributor. This framework harnesses the processing power of idle computers or computing systems in networks by automatically distributing the user application across available resources. This

J. Wiedermann et al. (Eds.): SOFSEM 2006, LNCS 3831, pp. 440–450, 2006.

system accepts a sequential Java source code, extracts an apposite class dependency graph by using CHA, RTA and FRTA [8]. If the classes of the Java code are separated amongst different stations, then the amount of processing time may be reduced in comparison to when the code is processed on one single station. Afterwards, the amount of time saved by separating any two classes is written over the edge which connects the two classes in the program class dependency graph. We shall call this amount of time saved "Distribution Gain."

Our proposed approach to compute the Distribution Gain is described in section 2.1. The resulting class dependency graph is then clustered using our new hierarchical clustering algorithm, described in Section 2.2. Since each cluster is expected to be assigned to a separate station, the objective of the clustering algorithm is to balance the Distribution Gain amongst the clusters and minimize inter-cluster interactions.

To facilitate inter-cluster communications over the network a new architecture including, five code blocks described in Section 3 are augmented to each cluster. Finally, JavaSymphony library is used to automatically convert the original program into a distributed program. The architecture of the distributed code is described in Section 3. A case study is presented in Section 4.

2 Suitable Partitioning

In order to distribute a given program over the network, the program code should be partitioned. Each partition is then assigned to a separate station. Here, the suitable number of stations is computed using a new hierarchical clustering algorithm. To achieve this, we have developed an interactive clustering environment which allows the user to run the clustering method step by step, view the clustering results and move the graph nodes to different clusters.

2.1 Clustering Criteria

A hierarchical clustering algorithm within the jDistributor is applied to the class dependency graph which is extracted from the serial code, to be distributed over the network. Here, the major issue is to define the clustering criteria such that the distributed code runs faster than its corresponding sequential code, meanwhile minimizing intra-cluster communication and synchronization overheads over the network. To accomplish this, a new relation to compute Distribution Gain is suggested in this Section. For each remote invocation, the Distribution Gain, *alpha*, is calculated as shown below in Figure 1.

T_C = Remote invocation elapsed time
Td = Called method execution time
T_S = Elapsed time between the call statement
      And the first use of the call results
Alpha = $(T_S > (2*T_C + T_d))$? T_d :

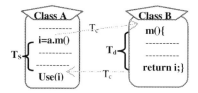

Fig. 1. Estimation of Distribution Gain

In Figure 1, a parameter called *alpha* is calculated for each method call from class A to class B. The parameter *alpha* indicates the Distribution Gain for remote method calls where the caller and the callee classes belong to different clusters. It means that by distributing A and B in different clusters, we expect to execute the caller, *alpha* unit of time, faster.

Since class, A, can make several calls to methods of class B, we have to add the calculated *alpha* values for each call to obtain a total *alpha* value for pair A and B. The *alpha* value eventually is assigned to the edge between A and B in the class dependency graph. In Figure 1, *Ts* indicates the time elapsed to reach the first position where the results of the remote call to method m() in class B is required, *Td* is the execution time of the remote method, m() and *Tc* indicates the network delay. Obviously the higher the number of method calls between the two classes, the higher the network delay will be. Considering the definition of these three parameters, the Distribution Gain achieved by assigning A and B to two different stations over the network may be estimated as follows:

$$alpha_{A,B} = \sum_{i=1}^{n} alpha_i - (n * \beta + T_c) \text{, for all method calls, i = 1 to n, from A to B} \tag{1}$$

In the above relation, n is the number of method calls from class A to class B and *Tc* indicates the network delay. Apparently, if the method calls reside within loops with symbolic bounds, the value of n can not be determined statically. This is a known problem in symbolic analysis of programs [9]. Using a dynamic approach such as profiling it is possible to have a rough estimation of the loop bounds [10]. The amount of *Tc* is increased by a coefficient, β, as the number of method calls is increased. If the value of *alpha* is greater than zero, the distribution is beneficial; otherwise the distribution is not useful. The maximum speed up is achieved when T_s equals $(T_d + 2T_c)$. The value of Td and Ts can be estimated using any algorithm for estimating execution time for a sequence of statements.

2.2   Interactive Clustering Environment

After labeling the edges of the class dependency graph with the Distribution Gains, described in the previous section, the resulting labeled graph is clustered. The idea has been to assign each cluster to a distinct station across the network. To achieve load balancing amongst the clusters, we have developed an agglomerative hierarchical clustering algorithm. Unlike the existing agglomerative approaches [11], which use a greedy approach to select combining clusters, we combine the pair of clusters for which the overall Distribution Gain is maximum. The sum of the Distribution gains written over the edges connecting the clusters together is the overall Distribution Gain of the clusters. Our specific hierarchical clustering algorithm is shown in Figure 2.

Before combining clusters, the distribution gain for the combined cluster should be recalculated in order to find out whether the combination is beneficial. For instance, if the two classes p and q are to be assigned to a same cluster. Then in the best case the distribution gain achieved between the cluster containing p and q and the cluster containing a class i is:

$$S_{p+q,\ i} = S_{p,i} + S_{q,i}$$

where Sp,i is the amount of distribution gain achieved by assigning the two classes p and i to two different stations each containing a cluster. In the worst case the amount of distribution gain is:

$$S_{p+q, i} = \min(S_{p,i}, S_{q,i}) - T_c$$

where Tc is the communication cost. In general the distribution gain, $S_{p+q,i}$, can be estimated as the average of distribution gains for the best and worst cases. Hence, the similarity between any two merged clusters, p + q, and another cluster, i, can be computed as follows:

$$S_{p+q,i} = \frac{(S_{p,i} + S_{q,i}) + \min(S_{p,i}, S_{q,i}) - T_c}{2} \qquad (2)$$

Obviously, as the number of method calls between the clusters is increased the amount of network traffic delay, T_c, is increased. In relation (2) the number of method calls between the clusters p+q and cluster i affects the amount of network traffic delay, T_c, by a factor β. Hence, as the number of remote method calls between the clusters is increased, the Distribution Gain, or in other words the amount of time saved by distributing the clusters is reduced.

```
NumClusters = Number of classes
Assign each class in the class dependency graph to a distinct clsuter
While NumClusters >1 do Begin MaxGain = 0;
    For ClusterI=1 to NumClusters do For ClusterJ=1 to NumClusters do
      Begin OverallGain= the overal gain achieved if clusteri is combined with cluster j
      If  maxGain < OverallGain  then
        Begin maxGain=OverallGain; Prevclusteri = clusteri;  prevclusterj=clusterj; end;
        else If  maxGain=OverallGain  and   NumberOfMethodcallsBetwwen(ClusterI , ClusterJ)<
            NumberOfMethodcallsBetwwen (Cluster c1 , Cluster c2)   then
        Begin maxGain=OverallGain; Prevclusteri = clusteri; prevclusterj=clusterj; end;  end;
      closestClusters = [Cluster c1,Cluster c2];   CalculateNewDistance(closestClusters);
      Replace(closestClusters ,  Cluster c1, Cluster c2); End
```

Fig. 2. Hierarchical clustering algorithm

2.3 Data Dependency Analysis

Accurate and efficient data dependency analysis is an important cornerstone of any parallelizing compiler. Data dependency analysis is performed on sequential code to identify the inherent parallelism within the code [12]. Here, the analysis is only applied to determine asynchronous intra-module method invocations. Using a data analysis approach, a def-use chain [12] can be constructed to find the first locations within a program code where the values affected by a remote method call are required. Restricting dependency analysis to remote method calls within each cluster, obviously, reduces the analysis time.

2.4 Distributed Program Architecture

The idea has been to automatically translate serial source code into distributed code. The overall layered architecture of the distributed code is shown in Figure 3. As shown in Figure 3, in order to distribute a serial code, each component or cluster of the code is augmented with a number of code blocks described bellow:

- Proxy: This code block acts as an interface for each cluster. Remote invocations are performed through the Proxy component. The Proxy component is further described in Section 3.1.
- Synchronizer: Asynchronous remote calls are controlled via a Synchronizer code block. The Synchronizer is fully described in Section 3.2.
- Object Manager: This component manages creation of objects. Object Manager creates an object and assigns it a GUID (global unique identifier) whenever an object creation request arrives from a remote cluster. The object manager is described in Section 3.3.
- Connector: The Connector object is responsible for sending and receiving events between clusters. Several implementations may exist for this component depending on the middleware used to deliver remote method calls.

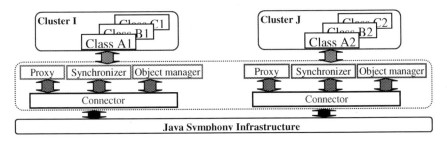

Fig. 3. The main components of the proposed environment of classes

2.5 Proxy

A *Proxy* component is created for each cluster to communicate with the other clusters. The *Proxy* component performs outgoing inter-cluster invocations. Bellow in Figure 4 is the class definition of the *Proxy*.

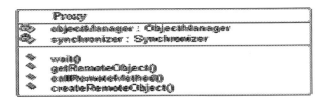

Fig. 4. Proxy class definition

To achieve this, a method of the *Proxy* code block called callRemoteMethod, described below, is invoked, is used to carry out remote method calls:

```
Public void callRemoteMethod(String ClassName, String objectName, String  methodName,
                  ,String returnName,Object[] params,String []signature)
{Jsobject remoteObject; ResultHandle result; remoteObject=objectManager.getObjectHandeler(
       String            ClassName,            String            objectName);
    result=remoteObject.ainvoke(methodName,params);
        synchronizer.addMethodCall(  esult,objectname,methodName,returnName,params,
    ignature);}
```

Fig. 5. A method to support remote calls

As it can be seen in the above method definition, the name of the remote object, objectName, the name of the class to which the object belongs, ClassName and the name of the variable in which the results of the remote call is to be stored, are all passed to the callRemoteMethod method. The list of the actual parameters to be passed to the method, methodName, is kept in an array of objects called Params.

The callRemoteMethod accesses the remote object through its handle. To access the handle, the getObjectHandler method of the Object manager component is invoked. The handle addresses a Java Symphony method, aInvoke, which is then used by the callRemoteMethod to invoke the remote method, methodName. After, the remote method is invoked, aInvoke creates a handler, ResultHandlert, to check the status of the remote method execution. The ResultHandler is then used by the Synchronizer component, described in Section 3.3, to access the return value and the parameter objects affected by the remote method.

The Wait method of the proxy component checks the status of a remote method via its handler object in a loop. This is achieved by calling the getResult method of the JavaSymphony object library.

```
public Object wait(String ClassName,String ObjectName,String MethodTime, String []signature)
    {ResultHandle result   = sychronizer.getResultHandeler(ClassName,objectname,
                methodName,signature);  return(result.getResult()); }
```

To receive the value returned by a remote method the wait method is used as follows:

```
ReturnValue =( Return Type) Proxy.wait(ClassName,ObjectName,MethodName,signature);
```

In order to wait for the value of a variable, par, which is already passed as a reference parameter to a remote method, MethodName, another method which is also called wait is invoked. The method is declared as follows:

```
public Object Wait(String ClassName, String ObjectName, String MethodName, String []signature,
            String par) { resultHandle resHandle= synchronizer.getResultHanlde(ClassName,
    ObjectName,MethodName,signature); int aramIndex=synchronizer.getParamIndex(ClassName,
    ObjectName,MethodName,signature,var);  return(resHandle.getParam(paramIndex)); }
```

The wait method invokes the gertParam method to receive the value of the reference parameter, par. To receive the value of a variable, V, from a remote method call the wait method is used as follows:

```
V =( param Type) Proxy.wait(ClassName,ObjectName,MethodName,signature, param 'V');
```

2.6 Object Manager

Object manager is a class, providing three methods to create, remove and access remote objects. Below is the interface definition of the object manager class.

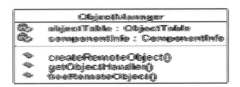

Fig. 6. Object manager class definition

In the above class definition, the method createRemoteObject constructs a new remote object and returns a handle including a unique identifier to access the object and its methods. Object handles are also associated with the information about the location of the object and the location where the object originates. Below is a JAVA code implementation of the method:

```
public void createRemoteObject(String className,String objectName,Object[] params)
    { int componentIndex=componentInfo.getComponent(className);
      if(componentIndex>0)
        {JSObject obj = new JSObject(className,params,v1.getVA(componentIndex);
        objectTable.addObject(obj,className,objectName);   } }
```

Fig. 7. Remote objects constructor

In the above code, to create a remote object, a JavaSymplony method called JSObject is invoked. This method calls GetRemotClassLocation method of the JavaSymphony class ComponentsInfo to find the location of the class of the object and constructs the remote object in that location and then returns a handle to access the remote object. The handle, the name and the class name of the remote object are all kept in a table which is an instance of the class objectTable.

2.7 Synchronizer

The addMethodCall() method of the Synchronizer component retains the signature, the name of the variable which receives the return value and the names of all of the reference parameters of an asynchronous remote method call in a table called CallMethodsTable. The getResultHandle() method of the component calls a method called gerParam to receive the return values and the value of the reference parameters of a remote method call.

Fig. 8. Synchronizer class definition

2.8 Connector

The Connector code block uses JavaSymphony middleware to transfer data and commands between clusters. To create a remote object a JavaSymphony class called jsobject is used as follows:

JSObject remoteObject=new JSObject("ClassName", ConstructorParameters, VA)

Remote method calls can be carried out through the ainvoke method of the JSObject class as follows:

resultHandle result=remoteObject.ainvoke(methodName,params);

The getParam and getResult methods of the resultHandle class can be used to receive the results of asynchronous remote calls.

2.9 Translation of Serial into Distributed Code

The application of the code blocks, described above, to convert an ordinary serial remote call to an asynchronous remote call is shown in the following example.

```
1.  public class A{ private  static Keyboard keyboard=new Keyboard();
3.     // The following line is inserted into the serial code to define a proxy object
4.     private static Proxy proxy=new Proxy();
5.     public static void main(String [] args)throws Exception{
6.     int i=0,j=1,k=0;  String s1,s3;  char[] s2=new char[10];
7.     // Below the CreateRemoteObject is called to create an object called "b" of class "B"
8.     proxy.createRemoteObject("B","b",null);
9.     while(i!=j) {i=keyboard.readInt(); j=keyboard.readInt(); s1=keyboard.readString();
10.    System.out.println("\n\n"+s1);
11.    // The following asynchronous method call susbtitutes:  k=b.set(s1,i,j,s2);
12.    proxy.callRemoteMethod("B","b","set",new Object[]{s1,new Integer(i),new integer(i),s2}
13.       ,new String[]{"s1",null,null,"s2"},new String[]{"String","Integer","Integer","char[]"});
14.    System.out.println("Start index "+i);  System.out.println("End index "+j);
15.    // The following code is inserted into the original code to wait for the results of a remote call
16.    k=((Integer)proxy.Wait("B","b","set",new String[]
17.                    {"String","Integer","Integer","char[]"})).intValue();
18.    System.out.println("char num "+ k);
19.    //The following line of code is inserted in the original code to wait for the results of a remote call
20.    if(k%2==0)    {s2=(char[])proxy.Wait("B","b","set",newString[]
21.                    {"String","Integer","Integer","char[]"}, s2");
22.    //The following asynchronous method call substitutes: s3=b.reverse(s2,k);
23.       proxy.callRemoteMethod("B","b","reverse",new Object[]{s2,new Integer(k)},new String[]
24.       {"s2",null},new String[]{"String","Integer"});
25.    //The following two lines are inserted in the original code to wait for the results of a remote call
26.    s3=(String)proxy.Wait("B","b","reverse",new String[]{"String","Integer"});
27.    s2=(char[])proxy.Wait("B","b","reverse",new String[]{"String","Integer"},"s2");
28.    } else { // The following line of code is inserted in the original code to wait for the results
29.       s2=(char[])proxy.Wait("B","b","set",new String[]
30.       {"String","Integer","Integer","char[]"},"s2"); s3=String.valueOf(s2);  }
31.    System.out.println(s3);
32.    s1=(String)proxy.Wait("B","b","set",new String[]{"String","Integer","Integer",
33.       "char[]"},"s1");  }  }
```

Fig. 9. An example of a distributed code

3   A Case Study: TSP

In order to evaluate the applicapability of the jDistributor environment the java code for the traveling salesman problem was automatically converted into a corresponding distributed code and executed over a network of 3 personal computers. Below in Figure 10 the execution time of the serial and the distributed code for the TSP are compared. The execution time is shown in minutes: seconds: milliseconds.

The TSP program includes three major classes called TSPShortPath, TSPMinimal and GraphMaker to find the shortest path, build a minimal spanning tree and handle graphs, respectively. The TSPminimalTree class includes three classes kruskal, prim and TreeMaker to build a minimal spanning tree for the input graph.

Graph No.		Execution Time	
Nodes	Edges	Serial	Distributed
20	40	0:0:573	0:7:357
40	81	0:1:383	0:7:810
60	122	0:3:246	0:8:163
80	163	0:11:214	0:11:109
100	204	0:19:773	0:14:741
120	245	0:43:517	0:30:722
140	286	0:25:362	1:0:871
160	327	2:25:721	1:45:227
180	368	3:54:871	2:48:280
200	409	6:0:143	4:21:412
220	450	9:36:655	7:20:343
240	491	16:37:653	12:54:142

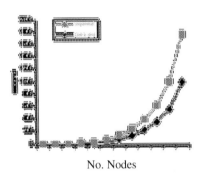

No. Nodes

Fig. 10. A comparison of the execution time of the TSP serial and distributed code

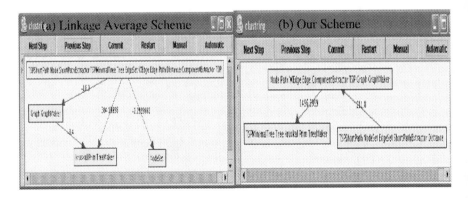

Fig. 11. Clustering of the TSP weighted class dependency graph

The results of applying both our scheduling scheme and the linkage average scheme [11] to cluster the class dependency graph of the TSP distributed code are shown in Figures 11.a and 11.b, respectively. Each cluster, in Figure 11, is shown with a rectangle which contains the names of all the classes residing in that cluster. All the edges connecting the clusters are labelled with Distribution Gains. The overall Distribution Gain using our approach is 1708 which is much more than the Distribution Gain for the linkage approach which is 355.

As shown in Figure 11, within the jDistributor environment our hierarchical clustering algorithm can be executed step by step, by pressing the two buttons 'Next Step' and 'Previous Step'. To move a node from one partition to another partition the 'Manual' button should be pressed.

4 Conclusions

Optimal distribution of a program code over network can be achieved by clustering its class dependency graph and assigning each cluster to a distinct station over the network. The clustering objective can be to balance the amount of time saved, by concurrent execution of the caller and callee in inter-cluster method invocations across the clusters. The type and number of instructions between two positions of the program code can be used as a measure to estimate the execution time. To locate the very first positions within the caller, where the results of a method call are required, dependency analysis techniques may be employed.

Within the proposed architecture, remote calls are carried out through a code block called Proxy. In order to reduce the network communication overhead, objects can be created remotely. Remote objects are created using the object manager component. To synchronize the concurrent execution of the caller and callee a component called synchronizer is presented in this paper. The experimental results show that jDistributor is a reliable environment to transform a serial Java code into an efficient distributed code.

References

1. Baude, F.C., Caromel, D., and Morel, M.: From Distributed Objects to Hierarchical Grid Components. International Symposium on Distributed Objects and Applications (DOA), Catania, Sicily, Italy, 3-7 November 2003 (ProActive)
2. Aridor, Y., and Teperman, M.F.A.: cJVM: a Cluster Aware JVM. Proceedings of the First Annual Workshop on Java for High-Performance Computing in Conjunction with the 1999 ACM International Conference on Supercomputing (ICS), Rhodes, Greece June 20, 1999
3. Haumacher, B., Moschny, T., Reuter, J., and Tichy, W.F.:Transparent Distributed Threads for Java. IPDPS 2003, Nice, France, April 22-26, 2003, IEEE Computer Society (2003)
4. http://www.cs.unibo.it/~rossi/jada/
5. Jugravu, A., and Fahringer, T.: JavaSymphony: A New Programming Paradigm to Control and to Synchronize Locality, Parallelism and Load Balancing for Parallel and Distributed Computing. Concurrency and Computation: Practice and Experience: Concurrency Commutate: Pract.Exper. (2000)
6. Fahringer, T.: JavaSymphony: A System for Development of Locality-Oriented Distributed and Parallel Java Applications. IEEE Intl. Conf. on Cluster Computing, CLUSTER 2000, Chemnitz, Germany,Dec. 2000
7. Hunt, G.C., and Scott, M.L.: The Coign Automatic Distributed Partitioning System. 3th Symposium on Operating Systems Design and Implementation (1999)

8. Parsa, S., and Bousherian, O.: The Design and Implementation of a Framework for Automatic Modularization of Software Systems. Journal of Supercomputing **32** 1 (January 2005)
9. Efficient Symbolic Analysis for Parallelizing Compilers and Performance Estimation. The Journal of Supercomputing **12** 3 (May 1998) 227-252
10. Suresh, D.C., and Najar, W.A.: Profiling Tools for Hardware/Software Partitioning of Embeded Applications. Proc. ACM Symp. On LCTES, June 2003
11. Arnold, G.M.: Cluster Analysis. 4th edn B. S. Everitt, S. Landau and M. Leese, 2001 London, Arnold viii + 238 pp., £40.00 ISBN 0-340-76119-9
12. Zima, H.: Supercompilers for Parallel and Vector Computers, ACM Press (1990)

Unifying Framework for Message Passing*

Tomas Plachetka

Comenius University, Bratislava, Slovakia

Abstract. Theoretical models are difficult to apply for the analysis of practical message passing systems used today. We propose a model which can be used for such an analysis. Our framework for message passing is in many ways similar to the framework for transactional database systems. The abstract message passing system is defined in our framework independently of hardware, operating system and means of communication. The interface between the application and the message passing system consists of four basic abstract message passing operations. The application can be written in any programming language, provided that the application's communication primitives can be translated into semantically equivalent sequences of the basic message passing operations. We prove that a restricted version of our model is as powerful as the unbounded asynchronous channel model. We also prove that MPI, the Message Passing Interface, is in some sense weaker than our restricted model and therefore also than the unbounded asynchronous channel model.

1 Introduction

The reason for the introduction of a unifying framework is that we know of no theoretical message passing model which can be directly mapped onto contemporary practical systems. For instance, the abstract channel model [1], [7] has been used in computer languages and software libraries which support parallel computation, e.g. [9], [4], [7]. Nevertheless, the mapping of the abstract channel model onto a computer network is not apparent for the following reason. A *channel* is an unbounded first-in-first-out data structure which stores messages sent to the channel by a sender process; a receiver process removes the messages from the channel, or blocks if the channel is empty. The wires in computer networks have no capacity—either the receiver or the sender processes can store messages, but not the wire between them. Therefore channels cannot be directly mapped onto wires and vice versa. We propose a model which uses neither channels nor wires. It uses an abstraction of communication which can be efficiently mapped onto different communication mechanisms provided by contemporary networking and shared-memory systems. Mutual simulations of various abstract models are summarised in the *invariance thesis: "'Reasonable' machines can simulate each other with a polynomially bounded overhead in time and a constant overhead in space."* [12]. We will show that our model is 'reasonable' in this sense.

---

* This work was partially supported by the grant APVT-20-018902.

J. Wiedermann et al. (Eds.): SOFSEM 2006, LNCS 3831, pp. 451–460, 2006.

Our framework fits into the framework for transactional database systems which is well-accepted among academic researchers and implementors of the systems [3], [2], [5]. The latter defines a clean interface between a database transaction and a database system. This interface consists of only four basic operations which operate on database records: READ, WRITE, INSERT and DELETE (the last two operations are often omitted in database textbooks which silently assume that the database is non-empty and its cardinality does not change). The semantics of these basic operations is defined independently of the actual database programming language (e.g. SQL). It is only required that the application's language primitives can be automatically translated into equivalent sequences of the basic operations. This allows for the programming of database transactions without any knowledge as to how the four basic operations are implemented, independently of whether the database system is centralised or distributed and independently of the hardware or the operating system used to run the database system. This also gives rise to the development of important abstract theories such as serialisability and recovery which help the implementors of database systems to optimise their systems by reordering the basic operations in the system, while adhering to the semantics of the basic operations. Altogether, the framework for transactional database systems is a standard with a solid scientific background which helps to make complex database systems robust and reliable. In our opinion, this all holds for our message passing framework— only the set of the basic operations is different. The basic database operations work with database records, whereas the basic message passing operations work with messages.

This paper is organised as follows. Section 2 describes the components of our framework and formally defines its main component, the message passing system. This definition induces the semantics of basic message passing operations. We prove in Section 3 that a restricted version of our model can simulate the unbounded asynchronous channel model and vice versa within the bounds of the invariance thesis. This means that our restricted model is as powerful as other abstract models. We then prove that MPI, the Message Passing Interface [11], [10] cannot simulate our restricted model within the bounds of the invariance thesis and is therefore weaker than the asynchronous channel model. The same holds for other practical systems—we chose MPI as it is becoming a de facto industrial standard for programming parallel applications. Section 4 concludes the paper.

2   Components of the Message Passing Framework

This section describes the roles of the components used in our framework. Fig. 1 depicts the relationships between the components. *Process* communicates with other processes only by submitting basic message passing operations to the message passing system. (We will assume throughout this paper that the set of processes does not change with time; we only make this restriction for the sake of simplicity.) A process can be a process in the POSIX sense but our framework does not require

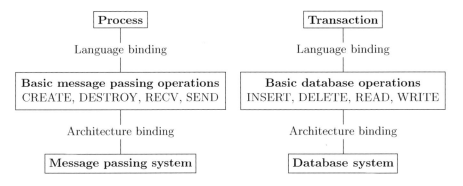

Fig. 1. Left: Components of the message passing framework; Right: Components of the database framework

that. The system regards a process as a single entity with a unique identifier from which it reads a stream of basic message passing operations. A process corresponds to a transaction in the database framework. *Language binding* translates communication primitives used in processes (e.g. a broadcasting primitive, a barrier primitive etc.) into semantically equivalent sequences of basic message passing operations. The use of synchronous and asynchronous communication primitives in processes does not influence the semantics of basic message passing operations. The interface between the processes and the message passing system consists of four types of *basic message passing operations* which work with messages: CREATE, DESTROY, RECV, SEND. The semantics of the basic message passing operations is induced by the definition of the message passing system. The representation and contents of messages is arbitrary and does not influence the semantics of the basic operations. *Architecture binding* maps the semantics of the basic message passing operations onto a specific architecture of the message passing system. This mapping may for example include routing algorithms for distributed architectures with different network topologies, algorithms which guarantee faults tolerance; etc. Architecture binding hides similar mechanisms from processes and guarantees that the semantics of the basic operations does not depend on the actual implementation of the system. *Message passing system* is an abstract component which reads basic message passing operations and executes them as it is defined in the rest of this section.

Definition 1 (Submission of a basic message passing operation). *Submission of a basic operation denotes the act of passing the operation from a process (or the language binding layer) to the message passing system.*

Definition 2 (Representation of basic message passing operations). *All basic message passing operations are tuples $[op, x, Y, m, f, s, t]$, where $op \in$ {CREATE, DESTROY, SEND, RECV}; x is the identifier of the process which submits the operation; Y is a set of process identifiers; m is a message; f is a boolean function defined on messages (a filter); s is either a reference to* *a semaphore object which can be accessed by the message passing system, or* NULL; *t is the time stamp of the submission of the operation (i.e. the time when the operation has been read by the message passing system).*

Definition 3 (Scope of a process). *The* scope *of a process is a memory space where messages relating to the process are stored. A message can only be accessed (i.e. read from, written into, shrunk or expanded) by the process in the scope of which the message is stored. A process can create and destroy messages only by submitting* CREATE *and* DESTROY *operations. The system creates, destroys and accesses messages in scopes of processes only as it is defined in this section. In addition, the system stores operations which it has read in the scope of the process which submitted the operation.* $SC(x)$ *will denote the scope of the process* x *and* $SC(*)$ *will denote the union of the scopes of all the processes.*

To keep things simple, we will deliberately mix messages with pointers to messages in the field m. It is obvious where in the text m denotes a message and where it denotes a reference to a message.

Definition 4 (Processing of submitted operations). *The system may at any one time either read one operation or execute one operation. The system only reads those operations which have been submitted. Every submitted operation is only read once by the system. When the system reads an operation, then it updates the operation's time stamp and stores the operation in the scope of the process which submitted the operation. At any time* t, *the system can only execute an operation which is stored in* $SC(*)$ *at the time* t. *The system may postpone the execution of a submitted operation (i.e. operations are not necessarily executed by the system in the order in which they are submitted).*

Definition 5 (Matching operations). *We will say that two basic message passing operations*
$BO_1 = [op_1, x_1, Y_1, m_1, f_1, s_1, t_1]$, $BO_2 = [op_2, x_2, Y_2, m_2, f_2, s_2, t_2]$, *(or* $BO_2 = [op_1, x_1, Y_1, m_1, f_1, s_1, t_1]$, $BO_1 = [op_2, x_2, Y_2, m_2, f_2, s_2, t_2]$, *respectively) are a matching pair (we will also say that* BO_1 *is an operation matching the operation* BO_2 *and vice versa) iff*

$$(op_1 = \text{SEND} \wedge op_2 = \text{RECV} \wedge x_1 \in Y_2 \wedge x_2 \in Y_1 \wedge f_2(m_1) \wedge$$

$$(\forall BO_1' = [op_1', x_1', Y_1', m_1', f_1', s_1', t_1'] \in SC(*) : (BO_1' \equiv BO_1 \vee$$

$$op_1' \neq \text{SEND} \vee x_1' \notin Y_2 \vee x_2 \notin Y_1' \vee \neg f_2(m_1') \vee t_1' \geq t_1)) \wedge$$

$$(\forall BO_2' = [op_2', x_2', Y_2', m_2', f_2', s_2', t_2'] \in SC(*) : (BO_2' \equiv BO_2 \vee$$

$$op_2' \neq \text{RECV} \vee x_1 \notin Y_2' \vee x_2' \notin Y_1 \vee \neg f_2'(m_1) \vee t_2' \geq t_2)))$$

Informally, a send operation $BO_1 = [SEND, x_1, Y_1, m_1, f_1, s_1, t_1]$ matches a receive operation $BO_2 = [RECV, x_2, Y_2, m_2, f_2, s_2, t_2]$ iff the set of recipients Y_1 contains x_2, the set of senders Y_2 contains x_1, the filtering function f_2 accepts the message m_1 and neither BO_1 nor BO_2 can be replaced with an older operation so that all the previous properties hold.

The definition of matching operations can be weakened if we do not require the messages sent from a process to another process to be received in the same order by the latter process. In such a case, the time-stamps are ignored and the predicate in the definition 5 becomes

$$(op_1 = \text{SEND} \land op_2 = \text{RECV} \land x_1 \in Y_2 \land x_2 \in Y_1 \land f_2(m_1))$$

We will use the definition with message ordering (i.e. Definition 5) in the sequel.

Definition 6 (Execution of CREATE operations). *The execution of an operation* $[\text{CREATE}, x, Y, m, f, s, t]$ *consists of the following actions performed in an atomic step:*

1. *The system creates a new message* m *in* $SC(x)$.
2. *If* $s \neq \text{NULL}$ *then the system performs* semaphore_signal(s).
3. *The system removes this operation from* $SC(x)$.

Definition 7 (Execution of DESTROY operations). *The execution of an operation* $[\text{DESTROY}, x, Y, m, f, s, t]$. *consists of the following actions performed in an atomic step:*

1. *The system removes* m *from* $SC(x)$.
2. *If* $s \neq \text{NULL}$ *then the system performs* semaphore_signal(s).
3. *The system removes this operation from* $SC(x)$.

Definition 8 (Execution of RECV and SEND operations). *The system may execute an operation* $BR = [\text{RECV}, x, Y, m, f, s, t]$ *at time* t *only if a matching operation* $BS = [\text{SEND}, x', Y', m', f', s', t']$ *exists in* $SC(*)$ *at the time* t. *If the system decides to execute* BR *then it must also execute the matching* BS *in the same atomic step which consists of the following actions:*

1. *The system creates a new message* m *in* $SC(x)$.
2. *The system copies the contents of the message* m' *into the contents of the message* m.
3. *The system removes the message* m' *from* $SC(x')$.
4. *If* $s \neq \text{NULL}$ *then the system performs* semaphore_signal(s).
5. *If* $s' \neq \text{NULL}$ *then the system performs* semaphore_signal(s').
6. *The system removes* BS *from* $SC(x')$.
7. *The system removes* BR *from* $SC(x)$.

Definition 9 (Progress of processing). *The system will eventually read every submitted operation and it will eventually execute all* CREATE *and* DESTROY *operations which have been read. Moreover, if a matching operation pair exists in* $SC(*)$ *at any time* t *then the system will eventually execute at least one of the operations of that matching pair.*

The last part of Definition 9 is expressed cautiously in order to support alternative definitions of matching operations. For example, replace Definition 5 with the definition which uses no time-stamps and consider the following scenario. A pair of matching operations BS and BR exists in $SC(*)$ at time t. Before either of these operations is executed, another send operation BS' which also matches BR, is stored into $SC(*)$. Then the "at least one" part of Definition 9 allows the system to execute either the pair BR, BS or the pair BR, BS'.

3 Computational Power of Models

We will say that a program which uses primitive statements of a model A is *correct* iff all possible executions of the program with the same input yield the same output. We will say that a *model B can simulate a model A* iff an arbitrary correct program which uses primitive statements of the model A can be written as a functionally equivalent program which uses primitive statements of the model B. The functional equivalence means that for any input, B computes the same output as A; and B terminates iff A terminates (a program terminates iff all its processes terminate). We will only consider imperative programs with a single thread of control in every process and we will use the C-like notation to write the programs. We will say that two models are *of the same computational power* iff they can simulate each other within the bounds of the invariance thesis from Section 1. If a model B can simulate a model A within these bounds but not the other way around then we will say that B is *computationally stronger* than A (or that A is *computationally weaker* than B).

3.1 Asynchronous Unbounded Channel Model

We will shortly describe the asynchronous unbounded channel model (a more formal definition can be found e.g. in [7]). A channel is an unbounded FIFO queue which stores messages. An application program consists of a constant number of parallel processes which communicate exclusively via channels. The number of channels can be arbitrary but the set of channels does not change in run-time. The processes use only two communication primitives with the usual semantics: PUT(ch, m) inserts the message m into the channel ch. GET(CH, m) (where CH denotes a set of channels) atomically reads a message from a channel $ch \in CH$, stores the message into the variable m and then it removes the message from the channel ch. Each channel can be accessed by any number of processes but only one process can access a channel at any time. PUT never blocks; GET blocks until it has not read a message. It is guaranteed that if a channel ch is non-empty at some time and some GET(CH, m) with $ch \in CH$ is blocked at that time then some (not necessarily the same) blocked GET(CH', m') with $ch \in CH'$ will eventually read a message and unblock.

3.2 Our Restricted Model

We will make the following restrictions in our model from Section 2. All the messages will be tuples $[c, m]$, where c (context) belongs to some finite set C and m is of an arbitrary data type. If $M \equiv [c, m]$ then $M[1]$ will denote c and $M[2]$ will denote m. The only filtering functions in basic message passing operations will be $f_{CH}(M) = $ TRUE iff $M[1] \in CH$, $CH \subset C$ (i.e. only testing a context prefix of messages for a membership in CH, $CH \subset C$, will be allowed). All processes will submit CREATE operations only in the following context (i.e. only a blocking CREATE will be allowed): {new(s); semaphore_init(s, 0); [CREATE, x, NULL, M, NULL, s, t]; semaphore_wait(s); delete(s);}. All the processes will submit RECV operations only in the following context (i.e. only a blocking RECV will be allowed): {new(s); semaphore_init(s, 0); [$RECV, x, Y$, M, f, s, t]; semaphore_wait(s); delete(s);}. All irrelevant fields in the 7-tuples representing basic message passing operations will be NULL.

3.3   The MPI Model

The MPI model [11] uses many primitives, but we will only describe those which are relevant for the comparison with the two previous models. MPI does not use the channel abstraction. It uses point-to-point message addressing which is similar to the one of our restricted model. MPI has a primitive MPI_Recv which blocks until it receives a message and it has a nonblocking send primitive, MPI_Isend. Unlike our model, MPI requires the process to free the memory occupied by the message sent used in MPI_Isend. However, the process must not free this memory before the recipient has received the message—in MPI's terminology, before the MPI_Isend completes. In order to detect this completion, each MPI_Isend must be paired either with MPI_Wait which blocks until the MPI_Isend completes, or with nonblocking MPI_Test which returns a value indicating whether the MPI_Isend has completed. As we will show, this pairing requirement makes the MPI model weaker than the previous two models. Note that our model allows for this kind of synchronisation (deferred synchronisation), as a process may include a semaphore s in a send operation and perform semaphore_wait(s) later. Nevertheless, our model does not require the process to do this.

3.4   Mutual Simulations of Models

Theorem 1. *Our restricted model can simulate the channel model and vice versa with a constant overhead factor in both time and space.*

Proof. We will show that our restricted model can simulate the channel model, with a constant overhead factor in both time and space. Consider a program $PROG_1$ which uses the PUT and GET communication primitives of the channel model. We will construct a program $PROG_2$ which is functionally equivalent with $PROG_1$ but only uses the basic message passing operations of our restricted model. Messages in $PROG_2$ will be tuples [ch, m], where ch is a channel identifier in $PROG_1$ and m is a message in $PROG_1$. The program $PROG_2$ will consist of the same processes as $PROG_1$. Let P_* denote the union of all the processes. Replace in each process x in $PROG_2$ each occurrence of PUT(ch, m); with {new(s); semaphore_init(s, 0); [CREATE, x, NULL, m', NULL, s, t]; semaphore_wait(s); delete(s); $m' = [ch, m]$; [SEND, x, P_*, m', NULL, NULL, t];}. Replace in each process x in $PROG_2$ each occurrence of GET(CH, m); with {new(s); semaphore_init(s, 0); [RECV, x, P_*, m', f_{CH}, s, t]; semaphore_wait(s); delete(s); $m = m'[2]$; [DESTROY, x, NULL, m', NULL, NULL, t];}. It follows directly from the definitions of the models that the programs $PROG_1$ and $PROG_2$ are functionally equivalent and that the replacements only incur a constant overhead in both time and space.

We will now prove that the channel model can simulate our restricted model within the bound. Consider a program $PROG_1$ which uses the basic message passing operations of our restricted model. We will construct a program $PROG_2$ which only uses the channel communication primitives PUT and GET. The program $PROG_2$ will consist of the same processes as $PROG_1$. The channel identifiers in $PROG_2$ will be tuples $[c, Y]$ where $c \in C$ and Y is a set of processes (this tuple can be encoded as an integer if the channel model requires it). Replace in each process x in $PROG_2$ each occurrence of the sequence {new(s); semaphore_init(s, 0); [CREATE, x, NULL, m, NULL, s, t]; semaphore_wait(s); delete(s);} with new(m);. Replace in each process x in $PROG_2$ each occurrence of [DESTROY, x, Y, m, NULL, NULL, t]; with delete(m);. Replace in each process x in $PROG_2$ each occurrence of [SEND, x, Y, m, NULL, NULL, t]; with {PUT($[m[1], Y]$, m); delete(m);}. Replace in each process x in $PROG_2$ each occurrence of the sequence {new(s); semaphore_init(s, 0); [RECV, x, Y, m, f, s, t]; semaphore_wait(s); delete(s);} with GET(CH, m);, where CH is the set of all the channels $ch = [c, m]$ for which $f(ch) = $ TRUE. Note that the set CH can be computed in constant time as the set of first message components c is known and finite and $f([c, m])$ only depends on c. It follows directly from the definitions of the models that the programs $PROG_1$ and $PROG_2$ are functionally equivalent and that the replacements only incur a constant overhead in time and space.   □

Theorem 2. *The MPI model cannot simulate our restricted model within the bounds of the invariance thesis.*

Proof. Consider the following program in our model which consists of processes $p0$ and $p1$ ($P0$ will denote the set containing $p0$, $P1$ will denote the set containing $p1$ and f_{TRUE} will denote a function which always returns TRUE).

```
p0(FILE *inp0)
{
  while (! feof(inp0))
  {
    new(s);
    semaphore_init(s, 0);
    [CREATE, p0, NULL, m, NULL, s, t];
    semaphore_wait(s);
    delete(s);
    m=fgetc(inp0);
    [SEND, p0, P1, m, NULL, NULL, t];
    printf("sent");
  }
}
```

```
p1(FILE *inp1)
{
  while (! feof(inp1))
  {
    new(s);
    semaphore_init(s, 0);
    [RECV, p1, P0, m, fTRUE, s, t];
    semaphore_wait(s);
    delete(s);
    printf("received %c", m);
    [DESTROY, p1, NULL, m, NULL,
    NULL, t];
    fgetc(inp1);
  }
}
```

It is easy to verify that this program is correct. We will now prove that it cannot be simulated by a program which uses MPI primitives MPI_Recv, MPI_Isend, MPI_Wait and MPI_Test without breaching the bounds of the invariance thesis. (The rest of MPI's primitives apparently does not help in the simulation of the program above.) The process $p1$ receives $n1$ messages from the process $p0$, where $n1$ is the number of characters in the input stream $inp1$ (this number is unknown until the entire stream $inp1$ has been read). This can only be accomplished by calling MPI_Recv $n1$ times in the $p1$. In the process $p0$, MPI_Isend must obviously be called $n0$ times, where $n0$ is the number of characters in the input stream $inp0$. These $n0$ calls must be paired with $n0$ either MPI_Wait or MPI_Test calls in $p0$, otherwise the memory overhead of the MPI program for $n0 = n1$ would depend on $n1$ and would therefore exceed a constant factor. (We recall that even if $p0$ submits SEND operations faster than $p1$ or vice versa, the system is allowed to postpone the reading of these operations until the previous operations of that process have been executed—therefore the program above can be executed in constant memory for $n0 = n1$. Generally, the space complexity of the program above is $c + |n0 - n1|$, where the constant c depends on neither $n0$ nor $n1$.) MPI_Wait cannot be used in any of the $n1$ pairings because the MPI program would not terminate for $n0 > 0$ and $n1 = 0$, whereas the program above would. This implies that MPI_Test must be used in all the $n1$ pairings. In each of these pairings, the nonblocking MPI_Test must be repeatedly called until the corresponding MPI_Isend completes, otherwise the memory overhead would exceed a constant factor. However, in this case the MPI program would not terminate for $n0 > 0$ and $n1 = 0$, whereas the program above would.   □

4   Conclusions

We presented a framework for message passing which defines an interface between message passing applications and message passing systems. We proved that its restricted version is as powerful as the unbounded asynchronous channel model (our unrestricted model is apparently at least as powerful). We also proved that the MPI model is less powerful than these models. The substantial difference between the models is that the MPI standard only supports so-called deferred synchronous communication [8]. Statements such as "MPI has full asynchronous communication" [6] are false. This deviation of the MPI standard from theoretical models has negative consequences for efficiency and portability of parallel applications which build on the MPI standard.

Our framework can serve as a well-founded specification of message passing systems. We stress that this specification only defines the semantics of the basic message passing operations (which should be provided by any message passing system), not the means of their implementation. For instance, the implementation of the operations for distributed architectures does not require a global clock despite of the time-stamps in Definition 5. We implemented the framework as a message passing library for several operating systems and network types. Our implementation is thread-safe and polling-free (it uses no busy waiting).

References

1. Andrews, G.A.: Concurrent Programming, Principles and Practice. Benjamin/ Cummings Publishing Company (1991)
2. Bacon, J.: Concurrent Systems (Operating Systems, Database and Distributed Systems: An Integrated Approach). Addison-Wesley-Longman (1998)
3. Bernstein, A.J., and Lewis, P.M.: Concurrency in Programming and Database Systems. Jones and Bartlett Publishers (1993)

4. Galletly, J.: Occam 2. Pitman Publishing (1990)
5. Gray, J., and Reuter, A.: Transaction Processing: Concepts and Techniques. Morgan Kaufmann (1993)
6. L.P. Hewlett-Packard Development Company: HP MPI User's Guide, eight edition (2003)
7. Peyton Jones, S.L., Gordon, A., and Finne, S.: Concurrent Haskell. In 23rd ACM Symposium on Principles of Programming Languages (1996) 295–308
8. Liebig, C., and Tai, S.:   Middleware-Mediated Transactions.   In G. Blair, D. Schmidt, and Z. Tari (eds), Proc. of the 5th International Symposium on Distributed Objects and Applications (DOA'01), IEEE Computer Society (2001) 340–350
9. Mitchell, D.A.P., Thompson, J.A., Manson, G.A., and Brookes, G.R.: Inside The Transputer. Blackwell Scientific Publications (1990)
10. MPI Forum. MPI-2: Extensions to the Message Passing Interface (1997)
11. MPI Forum. MPI: Message Passing Interface, Version 1.1 (1998)
12. van Emde Boas, P.: Machine Models and Simulation. In Handbook of Theoretical Computer Science, Volume A: Algorithms and Complexity (A), Elsevier and MIT Press (1990) 1–66

Appendix

Semantics of Semaphores

Throughout the paper, we assume the standard semaphore semantics as it is defined in [ISO/IEC 9945-1: 1990 Information Technology. Portable Operating System Interface (POSIX), Part 1: System Application Program Interface, C language]. Although we are convinced that most readers are familiar with the notion of semaphores, we provide this appendix in order to avoid misunderstandings concerning the notation.

A semaphore object is an abstract synchronisation object which keeps an internal variable $count$. (The formal definition of semaphores allows for an arbitrary representation of $count$, provided that the semantics of the semaphore's operations remains unchanged.) The call new(s) creates a semaphore object referred to as s and semaphore_init(s, c) sets the variable $count$ belonging to s to c. The call delete(s) destroys the semaphore s.

The call semaphore_wait(s) acquires the semaphore. Its semantics corresponds to the semantics of Dijkstra's operation $P(s)$: if the variable $count$ of s is 0 then the calling process blocks in the call, otherwise the variable $count$ of s is decreased by 1 and the calling process continues. The testing and decreasing of the variable $count$ is an atomic operation.

The call semaphore_signal(s) signals the semaphore and its semantics corresponds to the semantics of Dijkstra's operation $V(s)$: the $count$ of s is increased by 1. Moreover, if there is at least one process which is blocked on the semaphore s then one of these blocked processes unblocks and attempts to acquire the semaphore as if it has called that semaphore_wait(s) once again.

Heuristics on the Definition of UML Refinement Patterns

Claudia Pons

LIFIA – Computer Science Faculty – University of La Plata and CONICET,
La Plata, Buenos Aires, Argentina
cpons@info.unlp.edu.ar

Abstract. In this article we present a strategy to formalize frequently occurring forms of refinement that take place in UML model construction. Such strategy consists in recognizing a set of well founded refinement structures in a formal language which are then immersed into a UML-based development, giving origin to a set of UML refinement patterns. Apart from providing semi-formal evidence on the presence of refinement structures in object-oriented designs, this strategy made it possible to reveal hidden refinements and to discover weaknesses of the UML language that hinder the specification of refinement. An automatic tool is provided to support model refinement activities.

1 Introduction

Model Driven Development (MDD) [8][16], which prescribes the use of UML [14] as the standard modeling language, aims at introducing techniques for raising the level of abstraction to describe both the problem and its solution, and by clearly establishing methodologies to define the problem and how to move to its solution. The idea promoted by MDD is to use models at different levels of abstraction. A series of transformations are performed starting from a platform independent model with the aim of making the system more platform-specific at each refinement step. However, model transformations are frequently only viewed as a technique for generating models; little is said about guaranteeing the correctness of the generated models. In fact, model transformations should do more than just generate models; in addition, they should generate evidence that the generated models are actually correct. In particular, some of these transformations can be cataloged as refinements in the sense of formal languages [6], thus being amenable to formal verification.

Formal verification of model refinement can be fully exploited only if the language used to create the models is equipped with formal refinement machinery, making it possible to prove that a given model is a refinement of another one, or even to calculate possible refinements from a given model. This refinement machinery is present in most formal specification languages such as Object-Z [6], [21], B [10], and the refinement calculus [2]. Besides, some restricted forms of programming languages can also be formally refined [4]. But, in the standard specification language UML [14], the refinement machinery has not reach a mature state yet. Being UML a language widely used in software development, any effort made towards increasing the robustness of the UML refinement machinery becomes a valuable task which will also contribute to the improvement of MDD. To reach this goal, most researchers

J. Wiedermann et al. (Eds.): SOFSEM 2006, LNCS 3831, pp. 461–470, 2006.
© Springer-Verlag Berlin Heidelberg 2006

have used an "informal-to-formal" approach consisting in translating the graphical notation into a formal language equipped with refinement machinery. For example, the works of Davies and Crichton [5] Engels et al.[7] Astesiano and Reggio [1], Lano and Biccaregui [11], Ledang and Souquieres [12] among others. In this way, UML refinements become formally defined in terms of refinements in the target language. This approach is valuable, and in most cases it allows us to verify and calculate refinements of UML models. However, this approach is insufficient because it does not address the following problems: - *lack of notation to specify refinements (*although the UML Abstraction artifact allows for the explicit documentation of the refinement relationship in UML models, the available features of the Abstraction artifact are frequently insufficient to formally define the relationship); - *presence of hidden refinements:* an important amount of variations of abstraction/refinement remains unspecified, usually hidden under other notations. Those hidden refinements should be discovered and accurately documented [17], [18]; - *missing refinement methodology:* the formalization of the language itself is only the starting point; we also need a stepwise refinement methodology, based on a formal theory, consisting of refinement patterns, rules and guidelines.

We explored an alternative approach (i.e., a "formal-to-informal" approach) as a complement to the former. According to this approach a formally defined refinement methodology is immersed into a UML-based development. Concretely, well founded refinement structures in the Object-Z formal language provide inspiration to define refinement structures in the UML, which are (intuitively) equivalent to their respective inspiration sources.

The structure of this document is as follows: first, in sections 2 and 3 we describe the results of applying a "formal-to-informal" approach towards the improvement of the UML refinement machinery; we present an extract of a catalog of well-founded Object-Z refinement patterns, each of them giving origin to a list of several UML refinement patterns (each single Object-Z refinement pattern can be analyzed from a number of perspectives, which give rise to a number of UML refinement structures, one for each perspective). Finally, sections 4 discusses related work and conclusions.

2   Object Decomposition Pattern

Description: Composition is a form of abstraction: things are composed of smaller things, and this recursively; the composite represents its components in sufficient detail in all contexts in which the fact of being composed is not relevant and conversely decomposition is a form of refinement: an abstract element is described in more detail by revealing its interacting internal components.

Example: in a flight booking system (figure 1), each flight is abstractly described by its overall capacity and the quantity of reserved seats in its cabin (i.e., class FlightC), then a refinement is produced (i.e.,class FlightD) by specifying in more detail the fact that a flight contains a collection of seats in its interior. In this case seats are described as individual entities whit their own attributes and behavior (a seat has an identification number and a Boolean attribute indicating whether it is reserved or not). In both specifications a Boolean attribute is used to represent the state of the

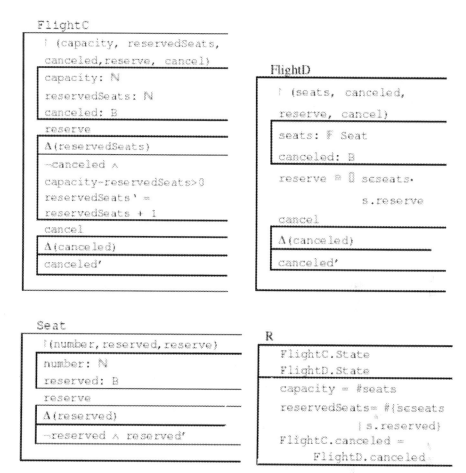

Fig. 1. Refinement induced by Decomposition in Object-Z Classes

flight (open or canceled). The available operations are `reserve` to make a reservation of one seat and `cancel` to cancel the entire flight. The retrieve relation R establishes the connection between both specifications. The refined version of the operation `reserve` selects a seat, ready to be reserved, in a non-deterministic way.

UML Realizations of the Pattern: In this section we describe one UML instantiations of the Object Decomposition Pattern: Object Decomposition in Class Diagrams; other instantiations of the pattern are observed for example in Collaboration and Interaction Diagrams. The OCL language [15], [20] has been used to specify the operation's pre and post conditions. The mapping attached to the abstraction relationship is expressed in an OCL-like language (a discussion on the mapping's language issue is included bellow). Figure 2 shows a refinement of the class FlightC, which was obtained by specifying in detail the fact that a flight contains a collection of seats. The refinement mapping (expressed in pseudo-OCL) states the connection between abstract and refined attributes.

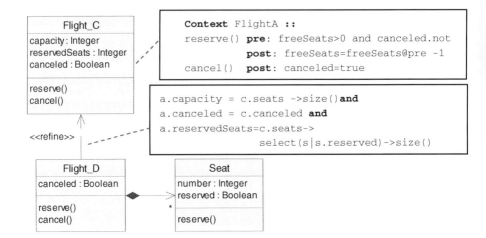

Fig. 2. Refinement induced by Decomposition in UML Class Diagram

Formalization: By applying the definition of downward simulation in Object-Z [6], it is possible to verify the refinement, in the following way:

Initialization:
∀FlightD.State · FlightD.init ⇒(∃ FlightC.State · FlightC.init ∧ R)

Applicability:
∀FlightC.State;FlightD.State · R ⇒ (pre reserveC ⇒ pre reserveD)
∀FlightC.State;FlightD.State · R ⇒ (pre cancelC ⇒ pre cancelD)

Correctness
∀FlightC.State;FlightD.State;FlightD.State'·
           R ∧ pre reserveC ∧ reserveD ⇒ ∃.FlightC.State'· R' ∧ reserveC
∀FlightC.State;FlightD.State;FlightD.State'·
           R ∧ pre cancelC ∧ cancelD ⇒ ∃.FlightC.State'· R'∧ cancelC

Discussion:
Issues on hidden refinement: In UML, decomposition is not considered as a form of model refinement. This pattern reveals a particular case of hidden refinement: UML models with composite association implicitly specify refinement relationship. See [18] for a detailed discussion on this issue.

Issues on the specification of delegation: The behavior of the class FlightC was specified in figure 2 as follows:

```
Context FlightC :: reserve()
pre: capacity-reservedSeats>0 and not canceled
post: reservedSeats=reservedSeats@pre + 1
```

In general, the structural decomposition of an object is accompanied by a behavioral decomposition realized through delegations. In the abstract specification it seems that the object carries out its tasks by itself, but in the refined version we can observe that the object delegates sub-tasks to its constituent objects. Let us present the OCL specification of the constituent class Seat:

```
Context Seat :: reserve()
pre:  not reserved
post: reserved
```

To specify the behavior of the refined class FlightD we need to write an OCL expression that is (intuitively) equivalent to the simple following Z expression, which makes a non-deterministic choice of a seat to be reserved:

reserve ≙ ⫿ s ∈ seats • s.reserve

The most approximated OCL expression we obtain is:

```
Context FlightD :: reserve()
pre:  seats -> select (s| not s.reserved) -> notEmpty()
post: let s=seats->any(s| not s.reserved) in s^reserve()
```

In this pattern we face the OCL restriction that non query operations, such as the reserve() operation, are not allowed to be referred to within OCL expressions. Without this facility the specification of delegation in OCL is only possible through the use of OCL Message expressions, allowing us to express messages sent between objects through the hasSent operator ^ [17, pg.29-31]. These expressions are little appropriate for building specifications because they talk about explicit communication between objects instead of describing the effects of the communication in a declarative form. The expression s^reserve() in the specification of operation FlightD::reserve() evaluates true if a reserve() message was sent to s during the execution of the operation. Moreover, the fact that a method has been called during the execution of an operation, does not assure that its effects were accomplished. The only thing we can assure is that sometime during the execution of FlightD::reserve(), the operation reserve() has been called over the Seat instance s. Furthermore, to specify that the operation has already returned we should use the OCL operation hasReturned(), however this introduces annoying complication on the specification.

Issues on the syntax to specify the retrieve relation: Graphically, the abstraction mapping describing the relation between the attributes in the abstract element and the attributes in the concrete element is attached to the refinement relationship; however, OCL expressions can only be written in the context of a Classifier, but not of a Relationship. Then, if we want to use the OCL to express the abstraction mapping we need to determine which the context of the expression is. On the Z side, the context of the abstraction mapping is the combination of the abstract and the concrete states; however, a combination of Classifiers is not an OCL legal context; consequently we might write the mapping in the context of the abstract (or the concrete) classifier only, in the following way:

```
Context a:FlightC
def: mapping(c : FlightD) : Boolean =
  a.capacity = c.seats ->size() and a.canceled = c.canceled
  and a.reservedSeats=c.seats ->select(s|s.reserved)->size()
```

The transformation from the pseudo-OCL expressions in figures 2 to their corresponding legal OCL expressions above can be generically defined in the following way: let d be a refine relationship with meta-attributes d.supplier (the abstract classifier), d.client (the concrete classifier) and d.mapping.body (the pseudo OCL expression specifying the mapping). We derive a Boolean operation definition in the context of the abstract classifier:

```
Context a: anAbstractElement
def:mapping(c:aConcreteElement):Boolean=aBoolOclExpression
```

Where anAbstractElement, aConcreteElement and aBoolOclExpression are replaced by d.supplier.name, d.client.name and d.mapping.body respectively.

Issues on the verification process: Verification heuristics can be defined for this refinement pattern. On the one hand, to verify the refinement conditions we can translate the UML diagram back to Object-Z using already developed strategies such as the one proposed by Kim and Carrington in [9]. Then, verification is carried out on the formal specification. Alternatively, we might remain on the UML+OCL side by defining refinement conditions in OCL in a similar style to the Object-Z refinement conditions [6].

3 Non-atomic Operation Refinement Pattern

Description: In the refinements we have analyzed so far the abstract and concrete classes have been conformal, i.e., here has been a 1-1 correspondence between the abstract and concrete operations. Conformity can be relaxed allowing the abstract and concrete specifications to have different sets of observable operations. This case takes place when the abstract operation is refined not by one, but by a combination of concrete operations, thus allowing a change of granularity in the specification.

Example: the flight booking system specified in the schema BookingSystemD in figure 3 records a sequence of flights which can be reserved through the system; then the schema BookingSystemE defines a refinement of operation reservation into *checkPassenger ⅋checkFlight recordReservation.*

UML Realizations of the Pattern: This section contains the description of one of the instantiation of the Non-Atomic operation Refinement Pattern - non-atomic operation refinement in class diagrams. This pattern can also be instantiated in Use Case, Interaction and Activity diagrams, among others. Figure 4 contains an example of non-atomic operation refinement in a class diagram; the refinement relationship specifies that the abstract class BookingSystemD has been refined by the more concrete class BookingSystemE; in particular, the abstraction mapping states that operation reservation() has been refined by the combination of three concrete operations.

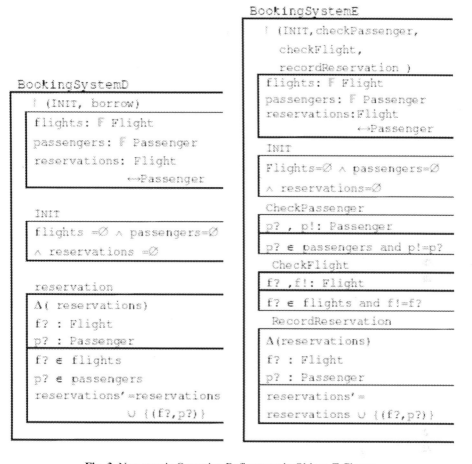

Fig. 3. Non-atomic Operation Refinement in Object_Z Classes

Discussion:

Issues on the syntax to specify the retrieve relation: It was already discussed in the definition of previous patterns, that although in the diagram the mapping specifying the relation between the abstract operation `reservation ()` and its refinement is attached to the refinement relationship, the mapping should be actually defined in the context of some of the involved classes, as follows:

```
Context a: BookingSystemD
def: mapping(c : BookingSystemE) : Boolean =
     c^checkPassenger()and c^checkFlight()and
     c^recordReservation() implies a^reservation()
```

Issues on the syntax to specify composition of behaviors: It is possible to express that reservation() is realized as the combination of the three operations, however message expressions do not provide the way to specify execution order. The fact that the reservation should be checked before being recorded cannot be expressed.

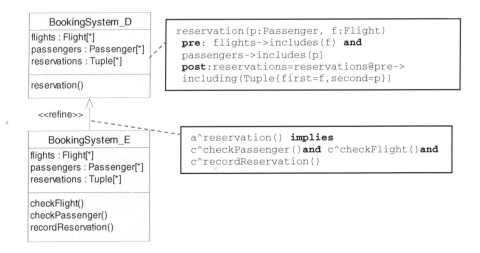

Fig. 4. Non-atomic Operation Refinement in UML Class Diagrams

Although we agree that other UML artifacts (such as Interactions) can be used to specify this concern, we believe that OCL suffers from the lack of an operation calculus (like the one of Z) allowing us to specify sequential and parallel composition of operations. Besides, the operational semantics of the OCL hasSent operation (^) given in [15] does not fit the intended semantics of a refinement mapping which declares the equivalence of both behaviors without talking about the actual execution of them.

4   Conclusion

The aim of this work is not to formalize UML refinements in Object-Z, but to substantiate a number of intuitions about the nature of possible refinement relations in UML, and even to discover particular refinement structures that designers do not perceive as refinements in UML. Focusing on the refinement structures of Object-Z we obtained a compact catalog of refinement patterns that can be applied during the UML modeling process; each graphical refinement pattern being based on a formal refinement pattern.

Similar proposal were presented in [3], where Boiten and Bujorianu explore refinement indirectly through unification; the formalization is used to discover and describe intuitive properties on the UML refinements. On the other hand, Liu, Jifeng, Li and Chen in [13] use a formal specification language to formalize and combine UML models. Then, they define a set of refinement laws of UML models to capture the essential nature, principles and patterns of object-oriented design, which are consistent with the refinement definition.

The strategy we propose in this article apart from providing formal evidence on the presence of refinement structures in object-oriented designs made it possible to reveal hidden refinements and to discover weaknesses of the UML language that prevent designers from specifying frequently occurring forms of refinement. Besides, the understanding of refinement patterns is more precise, since each pattern is described from both an intuitive and a mathematical point of view. Finally, the overall contribution of this research is to clarify the abstraction/refinement relationship in UML models, providing basis for tools supporting the refinement driven modeling process. In this direction we are building ePLATERO [19] that is a plug-in to the Eclipse development environment, based on the heuristics that have been proposed in this article. ePlatero will assist a variety of activities related to refinement, such as explicit documentation, semi-automatic discovering of hidden refinements, refinement-step checking, constraint refinement and refinement patterns application.

References

1. Astesiano, E., and, Reggio, G.: An Algebraic Proposal for Handling UML Consistency. Workshop on Consistency Problems in UML-based Software Development,. Blekinge Institute of Technology Research Report (2003)
2. Back, R. and, von Wright, J.: Refinement Calculus: a Systematic Introduction, Graduate Texts in Computer Science, Springer Verlag. (1998)
3. Boiten, E.A., and Bujorianu, M.C.: Exploring UML Refinement through Unification. Proceedings of the UML'03 Workshop on Critical Systems Development with UML, J. Jurjens, B. Rumpe, et al., (eds) -TUM-I0323, Technische Universitat Munchen, September 2003
4. Cavalcanti, A., and Naumann, D.: Simulation and Class Refinement for Java. In Proceedings of ECOOP 2000 Workshop on Formal Techniques for Java Programs (2000)
5. Davies, J., and Crichton, C.: Concurrency and Refinement in the Unified Modeling Language. Electronic Notes in Theoretical Computer Science, Elsevier **70** 3 (2002)
6. Derrick, J., and Boiten, E.: Refinement in Z and Object-Z. Foundation and Advanced Applications. FACIT, Springer (2001)
7. Engels, G., Küster, J., Heckel, R., and Groenewegen L.: A Methodology for Specifying and Analyzing Consistency of Object Oriented Behavioral Models. Procs. of the IEEE International Conference on Foundation of Software Engineering. Vienna (2001)
8. Kent, S.: Model Driven Engineering. Integrated Formal Methods: Third International Conference, Turku, Finland, May 15-17, 2002. LNCS **2335**, Springer-Verlag (2003)
9. Kim, S., and Carrington, D.: Formalizing the UML Class Diagrams using Object-Z, Proceedings UML´99 Conference, Lecture Notes in Computer Sciencie **1723** (1999)
10. Lano, K.: The B Language and Method. FACIT. Springer (1996)
11. Lano, K., Biccaregui, J.: Formalizing the UML in Structured Temporal Theories, 2nd. ECOOP Wrk. on Precise Behavioral Semantics, TUM-I9813, Technische U. Munchen (1998)
12. Ledang, H., and Souquieres, J.: Integration of UML and B Specification Techniques: Systematic Transformation from OCL Expressions into B. Proceedings of Asia-Pacific SE Conference 2002. IEEE Computer Society. Australia. December 4-6, 2002
13. Liu, Z., Jifeng H., Li, X. Chen Y.: Consistency and Refinement of UML Models. Third International Workshop, Consistency Problems in UML-based Software Development III. Satellite event of <<UML>> 2004. Lisbon, Portugal, October 11, 2004
14. UML 2.0. The Unified Modeling Language Superstructure version 2.0 – OMG Final Adopted Specification. August 2003. http://www.omg.org.

15. OCL 2.0. OMG Final Adopted Specification. October 2003
16. Object Management Group, *MDA Guide*, v1.0.1, omg/03-06-01, June 2003
17. Pons, C., Pérez, G., Giandini, R., Kutsche, and Ralf-D.: Understanding Refinement and Specialization in the UML. 2nd International Workshop on MAnaging SPEcialization/Generalization Hierarchies (MASPEGHI). In IEEE ASE 2003, Canada (2003)
18. Pons, C. and Kutsche, R-D.: Traceability Across Refinement Steps in UML Modeling. Workshop in Software Model Engineering, 7th International Conference on the UML, Lisbon, Portugal. October 11, 2004.
19. Pons C., Giandini R., Pérez G., Pesce P., Becker V., Longinotti J., and Cengia J.: Precise Assistant for the Modeling Process in an Environment with Refinement Orientation. In UML Modeling Languages and Applications: UML 2004 Satellite Activities, Revised Selected Papers. Lecture Notes in Computer Science **3297**, Springer, Oct., 2004. The tool can be downloaded from http://sol.info.unlp.edu.ar/eclipse
20. Richters, M., and Gogolla M.: OCL-Syntax, Semantics and Tools. in Advances in Object Modelling with the OCL. Lecture Notes in Computer Science **2263**, Springer (2001)
21. Smith, G.: The Object-Z Specification Language. Advances in Formal Methods. Kluwer Academic Publishers. ISBN 0-7923-8684-1. (2000)

The Complexity of Problems on Implicitly Represented Inputs*

Daniel Sawitzki**

University of Dortmund, Computer Science 2,
D-44221 Dortmund, Germany
daniel.sawitzki@cs.uni-dortmund.de

Abstract. Highly regular data can be represented succinctly by various kinds of implicit data structures. Many problems in P are known to be hard if their input is given as circuit or Ordered Binary Decision Diagram (OBDD). Nevertheless, in practical areas like CAD and Model Checking, symbolic algorithms using functional operations on OBDD-represented data are well-established. Their theoretical analysis has mostly been restricted to the number of functional operations yet. We show that P-complete problems have no symbolic algorithms using a polylogarithmic number of functional operations, unless P=NC. Moreover, we complement PSPACE-hardness results for problems on OBDD-represented inputs by fixed-parameter intractability results, where the OBDD width serves as the fixed parameter.

1 Introduction

Algorithms on (weighted) graphs G with node set V and edge set $E \subseteq V^2$ typically work on adjacency lists of size $\Theta(|V| + |E|)$ or on adjacency matrices of size $\Theta(|V|^2)$. But in many of today's application areas, graphs occur which cannot be represented explicitly on current computers, or on which even efficient algorithms are not applicable. *Ordered Binary Decision Diagrams (OBDDs)* [2], [20] are a data structure for Boolean functions which is proven as succinct representation for structured and regular data.

Having an OBDD representation of a graph, we are interested in solving problems on it without extracting too much explicit information from it. Algorithms whose access to the input graph is mainly restricted to functional operations are called *implicit* or *symbolic* algorithms. In this way, OBDD-based methods are well-established heuristics for special problems in CAD and Model Checking (see, e.g., [10], [20]). These algorithms are observed to be very efficient in practical applications handling large inputs. However, their theoretical analysis has mostly been restricted to the *number* of functional operations up to the present.

Recent research tries to develop theoretical foundations on OBDD-based algorithms. On the one hand, this includes the development of symbolic methods

---

* Extended version available at http://ls2-www.cs.uni-dortmund.de/~sawitzki/.
** Supported by DFG grant We 1066/10-2.

J. Wiedermann et al. (Eds.): SOFSEM 2006, LNCS 3831, pp. 471–482, 2006.

for fundamental graph problems like topological sorting [21] and the computation of connected components [7], [8], maximum flows [11], [16], and shortest paths [15], [18]. On the other hand, we need more sophisticated analysis techniques to explain the practical success of symbolic algorithms.

In order to represent a directed graph $G = (V, E)$ by an OBDD, we consider its *characteristic Boolean function* χ_G, which maps binary encodings of node pairs to 1 if and only if they correctly reflect G. This representation is known to be not larger than classical ones. Nevertheless, we hope that advantageous properties of G lead to small, that is sublinear OBDD size. Nunkesser and Woelfel [13] show that OBDD representations of various kinds of P_4-sparse and interval graphs can be essentially smaller than explicit representations.

Problems typically get harder when their input is represented implicitly. For circuit representations, this is shown in [1], [6], [14]. Because OBDDs may be exponentially larger than circuits, these results do not directly carry over to problems on OBDD-represented inputs. Feigenbaum et al. [5] prove that the *Graph Accessibility Problem* is PSPACE-complete on OBDD-represented graphs. First efficient upper bounds on time and space of symbolic graph algorithms on special inputs have been presented by Sawitzki [16], [18] and Woelfel [21]. These results rely on restrictions on the complete-OBDD width of occurring OBDDs. The representational power of complete OBDDs with bounded width is discussed in [17].

The design of symbolic graph algorithms often pursues the aim of obtaining polylogarithmic runtime w. r. t. $|V|$ on special input instances. This requires two conditions: A small number of executed OBDD operations *and* small size of *all* occurring OBDDs. We contribute hardness results related to both conditions.

The paper is organized as follows: Section 2 formalizes symbolic algorithms working on the characteristic Boolean function of an input string. This framework enables us to describe a simulation of symbolic algorithms by parallel algorithms in Section 3, which implies that P-complete problems have no symbolic algorithms using a polylogarithmic number of functional operations, unless P=NC. For none of the existing OBDD-based symbolic algorithm analyses so far, a restriction on the input OBDD width suffices to prove efficiency. This would correspond to a fixed-parameter tractable algorithm with the input's OBDD width as parameter. For various fundamental graph problems, such algorithms do not exist unless P=PSPACE, which is shown in the second part of the paper. After foundations on OBDDs in Section 4, we discuss the fixed-parameter tractability of critical operations on OBDDs in Section 5. So we are able to prove implicit versions of several graph problems to be fixed-parameter intractable in Section 6. Finally, Section 7 gives conclusions on the work.

2   A Framework for Symbolic Algorithms

In order to formalize what typically makes a symbolic algorithm, we introduce *Symbolic Random Access Machines*. A classical Random Access Machine (RAM) gets its input as a binary string $I \in \{0,1\}^*$ on a read-only input tape and presents its output O on a write-only output tape.

For $\mathbb{B} := \{0,1\}$, let us denote the ith character of a binary string $x \in \mathbb{B}^n$ by x_i and let $|x| := \sum_{i=0}^{n-1} x_i 2^i$ identify its value. The class of Boolean functions $f \colon \{0,1\}^n \to \{0,1\}$ will be denoted by B_n. We define the *characteristic Boolean function* $\chi_I \in B_n$ of some $I \in \mathbb{B}^N$ by $\chi_I(x) := I_{|x|}$ for $n := \lceil \log_2 N \rceil$, $x \in \mathbb{B}^n$, and $I_N, \ldots, I_{2^n-1} := 0$.

Definition 1. *A Symbolic Random Access Machine (SRAM) $\mathcal{M}$ corresponds to a classical RAM without input and output tapes. In addition to its working registers $R = R_0, R_1, \ldots$ (containing integers), it has symbolic registers $S = S_0, S_1, \ldots$ which contain Boolean functions initialized to the zero function. The input I is presented to $\mathcal{M}$ as characteristic Boolean function χ_I in S_0. Finally, $\mathcal{M}$ presents its output O as χ_O in S_0.*

Besides the usual RAM instructions, an SRAM $\mathcal{M}$ offers the following operations on registers (resp. functions) S_i and S_j:

- *Request the number n of Boolean variables all functions S_i are defined on (initially $\lceil \log_2 N \rceil$).*
- *Increase the variable count n by some amount $\Delta n \in \mathbb{N}$.*
- *Set $S_i := S_j$.*
- *Evaluate S_i due to some variable assignment $a \in \mathbb{B}^n$.*
- *Compute the negation $\overline{S_i}$.*
- *Compute $S_i \otimes S_j$ for some binary infix operator $\otimes \in B_2$.*
- *Replace a variable x_k for S_i by a constant $c \in \mathbb{B}$.*
- *Swap two variables x_k, x_ℓ for S_i, i.e., $S'(x_0, \ldots, x_k, \ldots, x_\ell, \ldots, x_n) := S_i(x_0, \ldots, x_{k-1}, x_\ell, x_{k+1}, \ldots, x_{\ell-1}, x_k, x_{\ell+1}, \ldots, x_{n-1})$.*
- *Decide whether $S_i = S_j$.*
- *Compute the number $|S_i^{-1}(1)|$ of satisfying variable assignments.*
- *Write all satisfying variable assignments $S_i^{-1}(1)$ into R.*
- *Compute the subset of $\{x_0, \ldots, x_{n-1}\}$ on which S_i essentially depends on.*
- *Set S_0 to some function $f \in B_n$ represented in R due to some standard encoding (e.g., as polynomial, circuit, or OBDD). The encoding must enable to be evaluated in linear sequential time w.r.t. its length.*

Each operation costs one unit of time.

(The last operation enables to create fundamental building block functions having some short description. Quantifications and variable replacements by functions can be implemented by a constant number of negations and binary operators.)

This model is independent of a concrete data structure for Boolean functions; it is chosen with the aim of showing *lower bounds* on the number of functional operations. It covers what is considered as a symbolic resp. implicit algorithm in most of the literature. Depending on the type of input data (e.g., graphs) the definition of χ_I may vary; due to its interchangeability in this context, this does not affect our results.

3   Parallel Simulation of Symbolic Algorithms

It is known from P-completeness theory that P-complete, FP-complete, resp. quasi-P-complete problems cannot be solved by PRAMS in parallel time $\mathcal{O}(\log^k N)$ using $\mathcal{O}(N^k)$ processors for problem size N and some constant k, unless P=NC (see, e.g., [9]). Sieling and Wegener [19] present NC-algorithms for all important OBDD operations. We use a simpler approach which suits better for our purpose to prove the first main result of this paper.

Theorem 1. *An SRAM $\mathcal{M}$ using time $t_{\mathcal{M}}(N)$ and at most $k \log N$ Boolean variables on implicitly represented inputs $I \in \mathbb{B}^N$ can be simulated by a CREW-PRAM $\mathcal{M}'$ in parallel time $\mathcal{O}((t_{\mathcal{M}}(N))^2 \cdot \log^2 N)$ using $\mathcal{O}(N^k)$ processors working on the explicit representation of I.*

Proof. Each assignment $a \in \mathbb{B}^n$ of the $n \leq k \log N$ Boolean variables the functions of $\mathcal{M}$ can be defined on at any point in time is handled by its own processor P_a which locally saves the value $S_i(a)$ for all symbolic registers S_i used so far. Hence, $2^n = \mathcal{O}(N^k)$ processors are used. At the beginning, P_a reads cell $|a|$ on the input tape and sets $S_0(a)$ accordingly. Common RAM instructions are executed only on P_0. Symbolic operations are simulated in parallel time $\mathcal{O}(t_{\mathcal{M}}(N) \cdot \log^2 N)$ each (proved in the paper's extended version). Finally, S_0 contains χ_O and each processor P_a writes $S_0(a)$ into position $|a|$ on the output tape.   □

Corollary 1. *Unless P=NC, (strongly) P-complete, FP-complete, and quasi-P-complete problems cannot be solved by SRAMs in (pseudo-)polylogarithmic time $\mathcal{O}(\log^k(N))$ ($\mathcal{O}(\log^k(N) \cdot \log^k(M))$) using at most $k \log N$ Boolean variables, where N is the input size, M is the maximum magnitude of all numbers in the input, and k is constant.*

We briefly add an inapproximability result. Let $\mathcal{A}$ be a strongly quasi-P-complete integer-valued combinatorial maximization problem whose optimal solution value is polynomially bounded both in the input size N and the input's largest number M. Analog to Theorem 10.3.4 in [9] it follows:

Proposition 1. *If $\mathcal{A}$ has a fully polynomial symbolic approximation scheme, it can be solved by an SRAM in pseudopolylogarithmic time $\mathcal{O}(\log^k(N) \cdot \log^k(M))$ using $\mathcal{O}(\log N)$ Boolean variables, k constant.*

Corollary 2. *$\mathcal{A}$ has no fully polynomial symbolic approximation scheme using $\mathcal{O}(\log N)$ Boolean variables, unless P=NC.*

We have proved that none of the many P-complete problems can be solved by symbolic algorithms using a polylogarithmic number of functional operations and $\mathcal{O}(\log N)$ variables, unless P=NC. All existing symbolic methods known to the author use less than $10 \log_2 N$ variables, which is a usual restriction to keep concrete data structures small. In particular, there is neither an NC algorithm nor a P-completeness proof for the unit capacity maximum flow problem yet [9], which gives a hint why not even the best known symbolic methods [16] for this problem can guarantee polylogarithmic behavior on all the instances.

In the remainder of the paper, we will consider the complexity of problems on OBDD-represented inputs, which makes it necessary to give some foundations on this well-established data structure. Hence, the terms "implicit", "symbolic", and "OBDD-based" will be used interchangeable.

4   Ordered Binary Decision Diagrams

A Boolean function $f \in B_n$ defined on variables $x_0, \ldots, x_{n-1}$ can be represented by an *Ordered Binary Decision Diagram (OBDD)* [2]. An OBDD $\mathcal{G}$ is a directed acyclic graph consisting of *internal nodes* and *sink nodes*. Each internal node is labeled with a Boolean variable x_i, while each sink node is labeled with a Boolean constant. Each internal node is left by two edges one labeled 0 and the other 1. A *function pointer* p marks a special node that represents f. Moreover, a permutation $\pi \in \Sigma_n$ called *variable order* must be respected by the internal nodes' labels on every path from p to a sink. For a given variable assignment $a \in \mathbb{B}^n$, we compute the function value $f(a)$ by traversing $\mathcal{G}$ from p to a sink labeled with $f(a)$ while leaving each node labeled with x_i via its a_i-edge.

An OBDD with variable order π is called π-OBDD. The minimal-size π-OBDD for a function $f \in B_n$ is known to be canonical and will be denoted by π-OBDD$[f]$. Its size $\text{size}(\pi\text{-OBDD}[f])$ is measured by the number of its nodes. We adopt the usual assumption that all OBDDs occurring in symbolic algorithms have minimal size, since all essential OBDD operations produce minimized diagrams. On the other hand, finding an optimal variable order leading to the minimum size OBDD for a given function is known to be NP-hard. Independent of π it is $\text{size}(\pi\text{-OBDD}[f]) \leq (2 + o(1))2^n/n$ for any $f \in B_n$.

Efficient Algorithms on OBDDs.   OBDDs offer algorithms (called *OBDD operations* in the following) for nearly all the symbolic operations of Definition 1, which are efficient w.r.t. the size of involved OBDDs. The satisfiability of f can be decided in time $\mathcal{O}(1)$. The negation $\overline{f}$, the replacement of a variable x_i by some constant c (i.e., $f_{|x_i=c}$), and computing $|f^{-1}(1)|$ are possible in time $\mathcal{O}(\text{size}(\pi\text{-OBDD}[f]))$. The set $f^{-1}(1)$ of f's minterms can be obtained in time $\mathcal{O}(n \cdot |f^{-1}(1)|)$. Whether two functions f and g are equivalent (i.e., $f = g$) can be decided in time $\mathcal{O}(\text{size}(\pi\text{-OBDD}[f]) + \text{size}(\pi\text{-OBDD}[g]))$. The most important OBDD operation is the *binary synthesis* $f \otimes g$ for $f, g \in B_n$, $\otimes \in B_2$ (e.g., $\wedge$, $\vee$), which corresponds to the binary operator of SRAMs; in general, it produces the result π-OBDD$[f \otimes g]$ in time and space $\mathcal{O}(\text{size}(\pi\text{-OBDD}[f]) \cdot \text{size}(\pi\text{-OBDD}[g]))$. The synthesis is also used to implement *quantifications* $(\mathcal{Q}x_i)f$ for $\mathcal{Q} \in \{\exists, \forall\}$. Hence, computing π-OBDD$\big[(\mathcal{Q}x_i)f\big]$ takes time $\mathcal{O}(\text{size}^2(\pi\text{-OBDD}[f]))$ in general.

Nevertheless, a sequence of only n synthesis operations may cause an exponential blow-up on OBDD sizes, in general. The book of Wegener [20] gives a comprehensive survey on different types of Binary Decision Diagrams.

Representing Graphs by OBDDs.   In Section 2, we defined characteristic functions χ_I for inputs I of general problems. The next sections' results will mostly be connected to decision problems on graphs $G = (V, E)$ with N nodes $v_0, \ldots, v_{N-1}$. Hence, we adapt the definition of χ_I to $\chi_G(x, y) = 1 :\Leftrightarrow (|x|, |y| < N) \wedge (v_{|x|}, v_{|y|}) \in E$, where $x, y \in \mathbb{B}^n$ and $n := \lceil \log_2 N \rceil$, which is common in the literature. Undirected edges are represented by symmetric directed ones. It can be easily seen that this is equivalent to the definition of χ_I in Section 2 if I is the row-wise adjacency matrix.

Symbolic graph algorithms typically use intermediate functions defined on a constant number $k > 2$ of variable vectors $x^{(1)}, \ldots, x^{(k)} \in \mathbb{B}^n$ mostly interpreted as node numbers or components of them. Therefore, reordering a function's arguments becomes an important operation:

Definition 2. *Let* $\rho \in \Sigma_k$ *and* $f \in B_{kn}$ *be defined on variable vectors* $x^{(1)}, \ldots, x^{(k)} \in \mathbb{B}^n$. *The argument reordering* $\mathcal{R}_\rho(f) \in B_{kn}$ *w. r. t.* ρ *is defined by* $\mathcal{R}_\rho(f)\big(x^{(1)}, \ldots, x^{(k)}\big) = f\big(x^{(\rho(1))}, \ldots, x^{(\rho(k))}\big)$.

In order to enable efficient argument reorderings (see Lemma 3), it is common to use k-*interleaved* variable orders, denoted by $\pi_{k,n}^\tau$, which read bits of same significance en bloc:

$$\pi_{k,n}^\tau := \left(x_{\tau(0)}^{(1)}, \ldots, x_{\tau(0)}^{(k)}, x_{\tau(1)}^{(1)}, \ldots, x_{\tau(1)}^{(k)}, \ldots \ldots, x_{\tau(n-1)}^{(k)} \right) ,$$

where τ is the local order of every $x^{(1)}, \ldots, x^{(k)}$. The order $\pi_{k,n}^{\mathrm{id}}$ is called *natural* in the following.

5   Fixed-Parameter Tractable OBDD Operations

Feigenbaum et al. have proved some fundamental graph problems to be hard if the input is represented as OBDD. That is, there is no hope of beating classical algorithms on explicit inputs in general. However, symbolic methods for maximum flows [16], shortest paths [18], and topological sortings [21] could be proved to have polylogarithmic runtime when the input graphs are of special structure. The analysis technique relies on the *complete-OBDD width* of Boolean functions:

Definition 3. *An OBDD for* $f \in B_n$ *is called* complete *if every path from its function pointer to a sink has length* n.

That is, complete OBDDs are not allowed to skip variable tests. The minimal-size complete π-OBDD for $f \in B_n$ is also known to be canonical [20] and will be denoted by π-OBDD$_c[f]$ in the following.

Definition 4. *The* complete-OBDD width *of a function* $f \in B_n$ *w. r. t. a variable order* $\pi \in \Sigma_n$ *is the maximum number of OBDD nodes labeled with the same variable in* π-OBDD$_c[f]$.

Clearly, it is $\mathrm{size}(\pi\text{-OBDD}[f]) \leq \mathrm{size}(\pi\text{-OBDD}_c[f]) = \mathcal{O}(nw)$ for any $f \in B_n$ with complete-OBDD width w and variable order π. On the other hand, it is $\mathrm{size}(\pi\text{-OBDD}_c[f]) \leq n \cdot \mathrm{size}(\pi\text{-OBDD}[f])$ (see, e. g., [20]).

We now briefly introduce the concept of fixed-parameter tractability. For a comprehensive introduction, the reader is referred to the book of Downey and Fellows [4].

Definition 5.

(1) Let Γ be a finite alphabet. A parameterized problem *Π is a map $\Pi\colon \Gamma^*\times\mathbb{N} \to \Gamma^*$. The second component k of a problem instance $(I,k) \in \Gamma^* \times \mathbb{N}$ is called the* problem parameter.

(2) An algorithm for a parameterized problem Π is called fixed-parameter tractable *(FPT), if it solves Π in time $\mathcal{O}(N^\alpha \cdot \beta(k))$ on any instance $(I,k) \in \Gamma^N \times \mathbb{N}$ for a constant α and an arbitrary function $\beta\colon \mathbb{N} \to \mathbb{N}$.*

That is, Π can be solved in polynomial time for fixed k. Recent symbolic algorithm analyses [16], [18], [21] use that critical OBDD operations which may cause OBDDs to grow are fixed-parameter tractable, where the complete-OBDD width serves as the fixed parameter.

Let $f^{(1)}, f^{(2)} \in B_n$ be defined on variables $x_0, \ldots, x_{n-1}$; assume $f^{(1)}$ resp. $f^{(2)}$ has complete-OBDD width w_1 resp. w_2 w.r.t. some variable order $\pi \in \Sigma_n$.

Lemma 1 (Binary synthesis). *The binary synthesis result π-OBDD$[f^{(1)} \otimes f^{(2)}]$, $\otimes \in B_2$, is computed in time $\mathcal{O}\big(nw_1w_2 \log(nw_1w_2)\big)$ and space $\mathcal{O}\big(nw_1w_2\big)$ and has a complete-OBDD width of at most w_1w_2.*

Often, symbolic algorithms contain quantification sequences over $\Omega(n)$ variables of some variable vector (e.g., a graph node encoding). While each single one is efficient, a sequence of length $\Omega(n)$ may cause an exponential blow-up in general. Hence, we consider the properties of quantifications over a subset of variables.

Lemma 2 (Quantification). *Let $X \subseteq \{x_0, \ldots, x_{n-1}\}$. The quantification result π-OBDD$\big[(QX)f^{(1)}\big]$, $Q \in \{\exists, \forall\}$, is computed in time $\mathcal{O}\big(|X|n2^{2w_1} \log(n2^{2w_1})\big)$ and space $\mathcal{O}\big(|X|n2^{2w_1}\big)$ and has a complete-OBDD width of at most 2^{w_1}.*

Let $f^{(3)} \in B_{kn}$ be defined on variable vectors $x^{(1)}, \ldots, x^{(k)} \in \mathbb{B}^n$; assume $f^{(3)}$ has complete-OBDD width w_3 w.r.t. a variable order $\pi_{k,n}^\tau$, $\tau \in \Sigma_n$. Let $\rho \in \Sigma_k$.

Lemma 3 (Argument reordering). *The argument reordering result $\mathcal{R}_\rho(f^{(3)})$ of $f^{(3)}$ w.r.t. ρ is computed in time $\mathcal{O}\big(nw_3k3^k\big)$ and space $\mathcal{O}\big(nw_33^k\big)$ and has a complete-OBDD width of at most w_33^k.*

(Proofs of Lemmas 1–3 can be found in the paper's extended version.)

As a final building block we introduce *multivariate threshold functions*, which are used to implement weighted comparisons.

Definition 6 ([21]). *Let $f \in B_{kn}$ be defined on variable vectors $x^{(1)}, \ldots, x^{(k)} \in \mathbb{B}^n$. Function f is called k-variate threshold function iff there are $W \in \mathbb{N}$, $T \in \mathbb{Z}$, and $\alpha_1, \ldots, \alpha_k \in \{-W, \ldots, W\}$ such that*

$$f\left(x^{(1)}, \ldots, x^{(k)}\right) = \left(\sum_{i=1}^{k} \alpha_i \cdot \left|x^{(i)}\right| \geq T\right) \ .$$

The corresponding class of functions is denoted by $\mathbb{T}_{k,n}^{W}$.

Clearly, each of the relations $>$, $\leq$, $<$, and $=$ can be composed of $\mathcal{O}(1)$ multivariate threshold functions.

Lemma 4 ([21]). *Functions* $f \in \mathbb{T}_{k,n}^{W}$ *have complete OBDDs of width* $\mathcal{O}(k^2 W)$ *using the natural variable order* $\pi_{k,n}^{\mathrm{id}}$.

Having considered all critical OBDD operations which may enlarge their operands, Lemmas 1–4 imply a general result on the fixed-parameter tractability of bounded sequences of operations.

Theorem 2. *Let* $f \in B_{kn}$ *be defined on variable vectors* $x^{(1)}, \ldots, x^{(k)} \in \mathbb{B}^n$ *for a constant* k. *Assume* f *has complete-OBDD width* w *w. r. t. the variable order* $\pi_{k,n}^{\mathrm{id}}$. *Let* $\mathcal{S}$ *be a sequence of* $\mathcal{O}(1)$

- *operations as introduced in Section 4 and*
- *quantifications over variable subsets* $X \in \mathbb{B}^n$

applied on f, *functions from* $\mathbb{T}_{k,n}^{\mathcal{O}(1)}$, *and intermediate results generated by the current prefix of* $\mathcal{S}$.

Each function generated by $\mathcal{S}$ *has a complete-OBDD width of at most* $\beta(w)$ *w. r. t.* $\pi_{k,n}^{\mathrm{id}}$ *for some appropriate function* $\beta \colon \mathbb{N} \to \mathbb{N}$. *So* $\mathcal{S}$ *can be implemented as an FPT algorithm on* $\pi_{k,n}^{\mathrm{id}}$*-OBDD[f] with parameter* w, *runtime* $\mathcal{O}(n\gamma(w) \log(n))$, *and space* $\mathcal{O}(n\gamma(w))$ *for some appropriate function* $\gamma \colon \mathbb{N} \to \mathbb{N}$.

Using this result it is possible to prove that some OBDD-based graph algorithms have polylogarithmic runtime w. r. t. N on special instances [16], [18], [21]. Nevertheless, for none of these analyses it is sufficient to restrict only the input's complete-OBDD width; for example, the symbolic shortest paths algorithm in [18] requires also the output to have constant complete-OBDD width. This motivates the question if there are any FPT algorithms for fundamental graph problems whose parameter is associated solely to the input OBDD.

Starting from a PSPACE-hardness result in [5–Theorem 16], we show in the next section that such algorithms do not exist for some basic graph problems, unless P=PSPACE. This will incorporate FPT reductions build upon Theorem 2 which assure that the fixed parameter grows independently of N.

6   Fixed-Parameter Intractability Results

The *Graph Accessibility Problem (GAP)* is defined as follows: Given a directed graph $G = (V, E)$, decide whether there is a directed path from some source $s \in V$ to some terminal $t \in V$. Due to Theorem 16 in [5], the GAP is PSPACE-complete if G is represented by an OBDD for χ_G.

The reduction generates an OBDD representing the configuration graph $G_\mathcal{M}$ of a polynomially space bounded Turing machine $\mathcal{M}$ with some input $I \in \mathbb{B}^*$. The OBDD for $\chi_{G_\mathcal{M}}$ checks for each local pair $(X, Y, Z), (X', Y', Z')$ of three consecutive tape positions of the configuration encodings if they are consistent with a computation step. From the construction in [5] it directly follows that the complete-OBDD width of $\chi_{G_\mathcal{M}}$ w.r.t. the natural 2-interleaved variable order $\pi^{\text{id}}_{2,p(|I|)}$ is constant (i.e., independent of $|I|$), where $p(|I|)$ is a polynomial number of Boolean variables used to encode one configuration. Hence, an FPT algorithm for GAP on OBDDs would be able to decide in polynomial time w.r.t. $|I|$ if there is a path between the start and accepting configuration – we have our first fixed-parameter intractability result:

Corollary 3 (from Theorem 16 in [5]). *The GAP on OBDD-represented graphs has no FPT algorithm with the fixed parameter being the input's complete-OBDD width, unless P=PSPACE.*

(In the following, we always assume that the fixed-parameter is the input's complete-OBDD width.)

In [18], the *All-Pairs Shortest-Paths Problem (APSPP)* on OBDD-represented graphs is investigated assuming a canonical generalization to graphs with edge weights $c \colon E \to \mathbb{N}$ by $\chi_G(x, y, a) = 1 :\Leftrightarrow c(v_{|x|}, v_{|y|}) = |a|$. An FPT algorithm is presented whose fixed parameter depends also on the output's complete-OBDD width. This additional condition is necessary (unless P=PSPACE) because the GAP can be trivially reduced to a shortest path problem. Similarly easy, the GAP can be reduced to the *Maximum Flow Problem*.

Proposition 2. *Neither the APSPP nor the Maximum Flow Problem on OBDD-represented graphs has an FPT algorithm, unless P=PSPACE.*

Analog to Theorem 3.2(1) in [3], the result $G_\mathcal{M}$ generated in the PSPACE-hardness proof for GAP can be modified to three fundamental problems on undirected graphs: *Acyclicity*, *Connectivity*, and the GAP in undirected planar graphs, *UPGAP*. In doing so, the OBDD width is not essentially enlarged (proved in the paper's extended version).

Theorem 3. *Acyclicity, Connectivity, and the UPGAP have no FPT algorithms on OBDD-represented graphs with 2-interleaved natural variable order, unless P=PSPACE.*

Last but not least, we transfer a selection of reductions from [1], [3], [12] to symbolic OBDD-based reductions which satisfy the preconditions of Theorem 2 and, hence, are transitive FPT reductions (see, e.g., [4–Definition 9.3]). We write $\mathcal{A} \leq_{\text{S-FPT}} \mathcal{B}$ if such a reduction exists for decision problems $\mathcal{A}$ and $\mathcal{B}$.

Theorem 4.

(1) Connectivity $\leq_{\text{S-FPT}}$ Eulerian-Cycle,
(2) UPGAP $\leq_{\text{S-FPT}}$ Bipartiteness,
(3) UPGAP $\leq_{\text{S-FPT}}$ Planarity.

Proof. We describe reductions from $\chi_G \in B_{2n}$ to $\chi_{G'}$ for $G = (V, E)$, $V = \{v_0, \ldots, v_{N-1}\}$, $N = 2^n$, and $G' = (V', E')$.

Part (1): We set $V' := V \cup \{u_{ij} \mid 0 \le i < j < N\} \cup \{a_i, b_i \mid 0 \le i < N\}$. E' contains E, $\{v_i, a_i\}$, $\{a_i, b_i\}$, and $\{b_i, v_i\}$ for all i, and $\{v_i, u_{ij}\}$, $\{u_{ij}, v_j\}$ iff $\{v_i, v_j\} \in E$. Note that all nodes in V' have even degree and G' is connected iff G is connected. Hence, G' has an Eulerian cycle iff G is connected.

We define $\chi_{G'}$ on $4(n+1)$ variables with order $\pi^{\mathrm{id}}_{4,n+1}$. A node number $x \in \mathbb{B}^{2(n+1)}$ consists of two concatenated variable vectors of length $n+1$ each. Bits $x_{n-1} \ldots x_0$ encode the index i, bits $x_{2n} \ldots x_{n+1}$ encode the index j for nodes $u_{i,j}$, and the remaining bits x_n and x_{2n+1} encode the node type (i.e., v, u, a, or b). We denote these three components of a node number x by $i(x)$, $j(x)$, resp. $T(x)$ and define

$$
\begin{aligned}
\chi_{G'}(x, y) := & \big[(T(x) = T(y) = v) \wedge \chi_G(i(x), i(y))\big] \\
& \vee \big[(T(x) = v) \wedge (T(y) = a) \wedge (i(x) = i(y))\big] \\
& \vee \big[(T(x) = a) \wedge (T(y) = b) \wedge (i(x) = i(y))\big] \\
& \vee \big[(T(x) = b) \wedge (T(y) = v) \wedge (i(x) = i(y))\big] \\
& \vee \big[(T(x) = v) \wedge (T(y) = u) \wedge (i(x) = i(y)) \wedge \chi_G(i(y), j(y))\big] \\
& \vee \big[(T(x) = u) \wedge (T(y) = v) \wedge (j(x) = j(y)) \wedge \chi_G(i(x), j(x))\big] \;,
\end{aligned}
$$

where tests $T(x) = v, u, a, b$ check x_n and x_{2n+1} and ensure $|j(x)| = 0$ for $T(x) \ne u$.

Part (2): We set $V' := (V \cup E) \times \{1, 2\} \cup \{w\}$. E' contains edges $\{(v, r), (e, \ell)\}$ for $e \in E$, $v \in V \cap e$, and $r = \ell$. Moreover, E' contains $\{(s, 1), (s, 2)\}$, $\{(t, 1), w\}$, and $\{(t, 2), w\}$ for source and terminal $s, t \in V$. G' contains an odd cycle (i.e., is not bipartite) iff G contains a path between s and t.

We define $\chi_{G'}$ on $4(n+2)$ variables with order $\pi^{\mathrm{id}}_{4,n+2}$. A node number $x \in \mathbb{B}^{2(n+2)}$ consists of two concatenated variable vectors of length $n+2$ each. The additional bits x_n, x_{n+1}, x_{2n+2}, and x_{2n+3} are used to encode the node type (i.e., v, e, or w) and the copy index (i.e., 1 or 2). We denote $x_{n-1} \ldots x_0$ by $i(x)$, $x_{2n+1} \ldots x_{n+2}$ by $j(x)$, the type by $T(x) \in \{v, e, w\}$, and the copy index by $c(x) \in \{1, 2\}$.

$$
\begin{aligned}
\chi_{G'}(x, y) := & \\
& \big[(T(x) = v) \wedge (T(y) = e) \wedge (i(x) = i(y)) \wedge (c(x) = c(y)) \wedge \chi_G(i(y), j(y))\big] \\
& \vee \big[(T(x) = e) \wedge (T(y) = v) \wedge (j(x) = j(y)) \wedge (c(x) = c(y)) \wedge \chi_G(i(x), j(x))\big] \\
& \vee \big[(T(x) = T(y) = v) \wedge (v_{|i(x)|} = v_{|i(y)|} = s) \wedge (c(x) \ne c(y))\big] \\
& \vee \big[(T(x) = v) \wedge (T(y) = w) \wedge (v_{|i(x)|} = t)\big] \;,
\end{aligned}
$$

where tests against $T(x)$ and $c(x)$ check the additional bits x_n, x_{n+1}, x_{2n+2}, and x_{2n+3} and ensure $|j(x)| = 0$ for $T(x) = v$ as well as $|i(x)|, |j(x)| = 0$ for $T(x) = w$.

Part (3): We set $V' := V \cup \{w_1, w_2, w_3\}$ and define $w_4 := s$ and $w_5 := t$. E' is obtained by adding the edges of the complete graph on $w_1, \ldots, w_5$ to E except of the edge $\{w_4, w_5\}$. Because G is planar, G' is planar iff there is no path between $s = w_4$ and $t = w_5$. Now the definition of $\chi_{G'}$ in terms of binary operators and comparisons is straightforward and left to the reader.

Final thoughts: In order to obtain an undirected graph G', we set $\chi_{G'}(x, y) := \chi_{G'}(x, y) \vee \chi_{G'}(y, x)$. Additional singletons appearing due to the node encoding do not affect any of the three considered graph properties. We have seen that $\chi_{G'}$ can be expressed in terms of a constant number of disjunctions, conjunctions, negations, and argument reorderings applied to the original χ_G, multivariate threshold functions from $\mathbb{T}_{\mathcal{O}(1),\mathcal{O}(n)}^{\mathcal{O}(1)}$, and intermediate results. Due to Theorem 2, all three reductions can be implemented as an OBDD-based FPT algorithm on the $\pi_{2,n}^{\mathrm{id}}$-OBDD for χ_G. □

Because Theorem 3 satisfies the preconditions on the variable order of Theorem 2, we conclude:

Corollary 4. *None of the problems Bipartiteness, Eulerian-Cycle, and Planarity on OBDD-represented graphs has an FPT algorithm, unless P=PSPACE.*

In contrast to this paper's exemplary applications of the symbolic FTP reduction technique, more sophisticated reductions (e. g., to the *Bipartite Perfect Matching Problem* [3]) require quantifications and more complex multivariate threshold functions.

7 Conclusions

The complexity of problems on implicitly represented inputs has been considered from two different points of view: First, the number of Boolean operations as a lower bound on the over-all runtime of typical symbolic algorithms. Unless P=NC, no P-complete problem can be solved by $\mathcal{O}(\log^k N)$ operations on functions defined on $\mathcal{O}(\log N)$ variables.

Then, we turned to lower bounds on the concrete over-all runtime of OBDD-based graph algorithms. While the hardness of some basic problems in this scenario was already known, we showed that even the restriction to inputs with constant complete-OBDD width does not yield polylogarithmic algorithms w. r. t. $|V|$, unless P=PSPACE. While applied to a selection of fundamental problems yet, the technique of symbolic FPT reductions can be used for various further problems on OBDD-represented inputs by substituting existing constant depth reductions and projections used for circuit representations (which are more powerful in general, see [20–Section 4.12]).

We conclude that symbolic resp. OBDD-based algorithms, though very successful in practical applications, have quite limited capabilities on many polynomially solvable problems, even for strongly restricted instances.

Acknowledgments. Thanks to Detlef Sieling and Ingo Wegener for proofreading and discussions.

References

1. Balcázar, J.L., and Lozano, A.: The Complexity of Graph Problems for Succinctly Represented Graphs. In WG 1989, LNCS **411**, Springer, (1989) 277–285
2. Bryant, R.E.: Graph-Based Algorithms for Boolean Function Manipulation. IEEE Transactions on Computers **35** (1986) 677–691
3. Chandra, A.K., Stockmeyer, L., and Vishkin, U.: Constant Depth Reducibility. SIAM Journal on Computing **13** 2 (1984) 423–439
4. Downey, R.G., and Fellows, M.R.: Parameterized Complexity. Springer, Berlin Heidelberg New-York (1999)
5. Feigenbaum, J., Kannan, S., Vardi, M.Y., and Viswanathan, M.: Complexity of Problems on Graphs Represented as OBDDs. In STACS 1998, LNCS **1373**, Springer (1998) 216–226
6. Galperin, H., and Wigderson, A.: Succinct Representations of Graphs. Information and Control **56** (1983) 183–198
7. Gentilini, R., Piazza, C., and Policriti, A.: Computing Strongly Connected Components in a Linear Number of Symbolic Steps. In SODA 2003, ACM Press (2003) 573–582
8. Gentilini, R., and Policriti, A.: Biconnectivity on Symbolically Represented Graphs: A Linear Solution. In ISAAC 2003, LNCS **2906**, Springer (2003) 554–564
9. Greenlaw, R., Hoover, H.J., and Ruzzo, W.L.: Limits to Parallel Computation. Oxford University Press, New York (1995)
10. Hachtel, G.D., and Somenzi, F.: Logic Synthesis and Verification Algorithms. Kluwer Academic Publishers, Boston (1996)
11. Hachtel, G.D., and Somenzi, F.: A Symbolic Algorithm for Maximum Flow in 0–1 Networks. Formal Methods in System Design **10** (1997) 207–219
12. Jones, N.D., Lien, Y.E., and Laaser, W.T.: New Problems Complete for Nondeterministic Log Space. Mathematical Systems Theory **10** (1976) 1–17
13. Nunkesser, R., and Woelfel, P.: Representation of Graphs by OBDDs. To appear in ISAAC 2005
14. Papadimitriou, C.H., and Yannakakis, M.: A Note on Succinct Representations of Graphs. Information and Control **71** (1986) 181–185
15. Sawitzki, D.: Experimental Studies of Symbolic Shortest-Path Algorithms. In WEA 2004, LNCS **3059**, Springer (2004) 482–497
16. Sawitzki, D.: Implicit Flow Maximization by Iterative Squaring. In SOFSEM 2004, LNCS **2932**, Springer (2004) 301–313
17. Sawitzki, D.: On Graphs with Characteristic Bounded-Width Functions. Technical Report, University of Dortmund (2004)
18. Sawitzki, D.: A Symbolic Approach to the All-Pairs Shortest-Paths Problem. In WG 2004, LNCS **3353**, Springer (2004) 154–167
19. Sieling, D., and Wegener, I.: NC-Algorithms for Operations on Binary Decision Diagrams. Parallel Processing Letters **3** (1993) 3–12
20. Wegener, I.: Branching Programs and Binary Decision Diagrams. SIAM, Philadelphia (2000)
21. Woelfel, P.: Symbolic Topological Sorting with OBDDs. In MFCS 2003, LNCS **2747**, Springer (2003) 671–680

How Many Dots Are Really Needed for Head-Driven Chart Parsing?[*]

Pavel Smrž[1] and Vladimír Kadlec[2]

[1] Faculty of Information Technology, Brno University of Technology,
Božetěchova 2, 612 66 Brno, Czech Republic
smrz@fit.vutbr.cz
[2] Faculty of Informatics, Masaryk University,
Botanická 68a, 602 00 Brno, Czech Republic
xkadlec@fi.muni.cz

Abstract. This paper presents an improved form of head-driven chart parser that is appropriate for large context-free grammars. The basic method – HDddm (Head-Driven dependent dot move) – is introduced first. Both variants that improve the basic approach are based on the same idea – to reduce the number of chart edges by modifying the form of items (dotted rules). The first one "unifies" the items that share the analyzed part of the relevant rule (thus, only one dot is needed to mark the position before and after the covered part). The second method applies the inverse strategy, it "eliminates" the parts that have not been covered yet (no dot needed). All the discussed alternatives are described in the form of parsing schemata. We also shortly mention a tricky technique (employing a special trie-like data structure developed originally for Scrabble) that enables minimizing the extra information needed in the algorithms. We demonstrate the advantages of the described methods by the significant decrease in the number of edges for charts. The results are given for the standard set of testing grammars (and respective inputs) as well as for a large and highly ambiguous Czech grammar.

1 Introduction

Parsing algorithms for context-free (CF) grammars play a crucial role in the field of general parsing. Either their basic form is directly employed (usually for parsing a context-free backbone for the grammars based on one of the modern formalisms), or an extension of a standard parsing algorithm is proposed that can deal with more complex features of the particular grammar form. Moreover, the leading position of CF parsing is further strengthened by the interest it got from (speech-recognition) language modeling community in last years [1].

Various methods have been designed for CF parsing and new variants and enhancements emerge every year. To enable the efficient processing, modern

[*] This work was partially supported by the Grant Agency of the Czech Republic under the project 201/05/2781 and by the Ministry of Education of the Czech Republic, Research Plan MSM 6383917201.

J. Wiedermann et al. (Eds.): SOFSEM 2006, LNCS 3831, pp. 483–492, 2006.

parsing algorithms employ sophisticated structures to store intermediate parsing results. The most popular data structure for this purpose is chart.

Chart is a table of all viable strings. The dotted rules (items) are used to represent the state of the analysis. Dots stay on boundary between the analyzed and non-analyzed parts of items. If the parsing procedure is unidirectional only, (left to right or vice versa), only one dot is needed.

There are many advanced techniques aiming at refinement of basic chart parsing algorithms. This paper deals with one of the head-driven approaches that showed to be beneficial for parsing Czech as a free word order language [2].

In the experiments that are behind the effort discussed in this paper, a special attention is paid to parser robustness. If no complete parse is found for an input (e.g. from a speech recognizer in a dialogue system) a special technique is employed to efficiently retrieve a set of the most probable maximal subtrees (chunks) to provide a partial analysis of the input. Therefore, we are not able to apply the most popular (and, in general case, efficient) approach to head-driven parsing – head-corner chart parser [3], [4] that would prune chart edges that could be needed in our later processing of incomplete parse. Moreover, the head-driven bottom-up algorithm discussed in the paper is also more suitable for our research on incremental parsing. Nevertheless, the refinements depicted in the text are directly applicable to the head-corner case.

As the paper is rather technical (we take advantage of parsing schemata [5] – an algebraic method appropriate for description of key ideas in parsing algorithms) we will give a short overview of the content here.

The following section brings a basic version of the algorithm that presents a slight improvement over a known chart parsing technique. Next sections discuss two modifications of the basic method aiming at reduction of edges in the resulting chart. The first method eliminates those parts of the dotted rules that were already analyzed, the second, in reverse, keeps only the analyzed part of items. Though the approaches work in reverse, both mean a significant decrease of the number of edges. The optimization technique has been previously used for other variants of chart parsing, its application for head-driven approaches is original.

A smaller number of chart edges does not need to entail a more efficient parsing. We briefly mention a technique optimizing the search in grammar rules (their right-hand sides) that exploits sophisticated data structures. A standard trie structure is sufficient for the first refinement. The second case requires an efficient procedure enabling bidirectional search for paths starting from any symbol on the right-hand side of grammar rules. Such a procedure (designed originally for generating possible moves in Scrabble) has been employed in the second case.

Optimization of parsing need not to have a dramatic effect on an overall performance if one needs to parse grammars with a relatively small number of rules only. However, we aim at applications where very large (and highly ambiguous) grammars are a rule. The Czech grammar used in the described experiment contains approximately 10,000 rules and, if only the feature agreement in noun groups is expanded to the CF backbone [6], we work with more than 30,000 CF grammar rules. The enormous number of rules is also typical for the "treebank grammars" automatically extracted from syntactically annotated corpora and used for training stochastic parsers.

The results of the refinements discussed in the paper are demonstrated on both, the mentioned Czech grammar as well as the PT grammar generated from the Penn Treebank. The latter is a part of a standard set of testing grammars that are available together with the respective inputs on the Internet. Thus, we were able to test the designed methods on all the grammars from the standard set.

The last section summarizes the size of the resulting chart (in terms of the number of edges) for parsing on the test set. The effect of both optimizations can be significant in some cases (less than 50 % edges in the chart). The paper concludes with future directions of our research.

1.1 Terminology and Notation

The input grammar will be designated by $G = \langle N, \Sigma, P, S \rangle$, where N is a finite set of nonterminals, Σ a finite set of terminals, P a set of rules and S the starting symbol of the grammar.

The i-th word of the input sequence, designed by w_i, represents one terminal in the grammar G, $w_i \in \Sigma$. (Note that $w_i \in \Sigma$ applies only for known words. There is usually a special mechanism to handle "out of vocabulary words".) The number of input words is n.

Upper-case letters (A, B, etc.) will designate nonterminals, lower case letters (i, j, k) will be used for natural numbers, Greek letters ($\alpha, \beta, \ldots$) for (possibly empty) strings of symbols. The empty string is denoted by ϵ.

We will underline the head symbol of each grammar rule, e. g. X is the head in the rule $A \rightarrow B\underline{X}C$. It can be defined formally as a function assigning a natural number (the position of the head on the right-hand side) to each grammar rule. The head of ϵ-rules is defined as ϵ.

2 HDddm Parsing

This section describes the base version of the head-driven algorithm (HD). As in other "head-oriented" approaches in parsing, the direction of the parsing process is not unidirectional (e. g., from left to right). It starts at the head of the given grammar rule and processes it bidirectionally to the first and to the last rule symbols.

The HDddm parsing technique was described in [7]. Similarly to [4] and [8], it improves the process of viable hypotheses confirmation. HDddm (head-driven with dependent dot move) refers to the fact that the move of one "dot" in the head-driven parsing step is dependent on the opposite move of the other one.

The algorithm can be described as parsing system [5]. A parsing system $\mathbb{P}$ is a triple $\mathbb{P} = \langle \mathcal{I}, H, D \rangle$, in which:

- $\mathcal{I}$ is a set of items called *domain* or *item set* of $\mathbb{P}$;
- H is a finite set of items (not necessarily a subset of $\mathcal{I}$), the *hypotheses* of $\mathbb{P}$;

– D is a set of *deduction steps* of the form

$\eta_1, ..., \eta_k \vdash \xi$,

with $\eta_i \in \mathcal{I} \cup H$ for $0 \le i \le k$ and $\xi \in \mathcal{I}$. The items $\eta_1, ..., \eta_k$ are called the *antecedents*, ξ the *consequent* of the deduction step.

The parsing schemata for the HDddm parsing technique, $\mathbb{P}_{HD} = \langle \mathcal{I}_{HD}, H, D_{HD} \rangle$ is defined as follows. The domain $\mathcal{I}_{HD}$ is given as:

$$\mathcal{I}^{HD(i)} = \{[A \to \alpha_\bullet \beta X \gamma_\bullet \delta, i, j] \mid$$
$$A \to \alpha \beta \underline{X} \gamma \delta \in P, 0 \le i \le j \le n\},$$

$$\mathcal{I}^{HD(ii)} = \{[A \to {}_\bullet{}_\bullet, i, i] \mid$$
$$A \to \epsilon \in P, 0 \le i \le n\},$$

$$\mathcal{I}_{HD} = \mathcal{I}^{HD(i)} \cup \mathcal{I}^{HD(ii)}.$$

The hypotheses set H encodes the input sequence. For input $w_1 \ldots w_n$ we take:

$$H = \{[w, i-1, i] \mid w \equiv w_i, 0 \le i \le n\}.$$

The set of deduction steps D_{HD} is defined as follows:

$$D^{Init} = \{[w, i-1, i] \vdash [A \to \alpha_\bullet w_\bullet \beta, i-1, i]\} \cup$$
$$\{\vdash [A \to {}_\bullet{}_\bullet, i, i]\},$$

$$D^{Pred} = \{[A \to {}_\bullet \alpha_\bullet, i, j] \vdash$$
$$[B \to \beta_\bullet A_\bullet \gamma, i, j]\},$$

$$D^{Scan(i)} = \{[A \to \alpha_\bullet \beta_\bullet w \delta, i, j], [w, j, j+1] \vdash$$
$$[A \to \alpha_\bullet \beta w_\bullet \delta, i, j+1]\},$$

$$D^{Scan(ii)} = \{[w, i-1, i], [A \to \alpha w_\bullet \beta_\bullet, i, j] \vdash$$
$$[A \to \alpha_\bullet w \beta_\bullet, i-1, j]\},$$

$$D^{Complete(i)} = \{[A \to \alpha_\bullet \beta_\bullet B \delta, i, j], [B \to {}_\bullet \gamma_\bullet, j, k] \vdash$$
$$[A \to \alpha_\bullet \beta B_\bullet \delta, i, k]\},$$

$$D^{Complete(ii)} = \{[B \to {}_\bullet \gamma_\bullet, i, j], [A \to \alpha B_\bullet \beta_\bullet, j, k] \vdash$$
$$[A \to \alpha_\bullet B \beta_\bullet, i, k]\},$$

$$D_{HD} = D^{Init} \cup D^{Pred} \cup D^{Scan(i)} \cup D^{Scan(ii)} \cup$$
$$D^{Complete(i)} \cup D^{Complete(ii)}.$$

String γ in *Complete* steps can be empty (ϵ).

Note that the left dot in the edge cannot move leftwards until the right dot moves to the right. This is precisely the difference between HDddm and the technique described in [4]. The parser never creates edges like $[A \rightarrow \alpha_\bullet \beta \underline{X} \gamma_\bullet \delta, i, j]$ for non empty β. This approach avoids a redundant work during the analysis.

For the sake of brevity, a simplified form of the algorithm is given here. Various optimizations are possible. For example, the real implementation of the algorithm benefits from an approach that would call for CKY items $([A, i, j])$ in the above definitions (see [8] for details).

3 Head-Driven Algorithm with One Dot in Items

The idea comes from [9] (for Earley's algorithm), it has been applied to the left-corner algorithm in [10]. In these cases, the optimization is based on the observation that the nonterminals that are on the left of the dot in an Earley "one dot" item play no role in the parsing algorithm. The approach can be adapted for the HD algorithm so that nonterminals *between* the dots in a HD item can be "forgotten".

The algorithm with one dot in items (iHD) can be described as parsing system $\mathbb{P}_{iHD} = \langle \mathcal{I}_{iHD}, H, D_{iHD} \rangle$. The domain $\mathcal{I}_{iHD}$ is given as:

$$\mathcal{I}^{iHD(i)} = \{[A \rightarrow \alpha_\bullet \delta, i, j] \mid$$
$$A \rightarrow \alpha \beta \underline{X} \gamma \delta \in P, 0 \leq i \leq j \leq n\},$$

$$\mathcal{I}^{iHD(ii)} = \{[A \rightarrow _\bullet, i, j] \mid A \rightarrow \alpha \in P,$$
$$\text{possibly } \alpha \equiv \epsilon, 0 \leq i \leq j \leq n\},$$

$$\mathcal{I}_{iHD} = \mathcal{I}^{iHD(i)} \cup \mathcal{I}^{iHD(ii)}.$$

We replace the HD item of the form $[A \rightarrow \alpha_\bullet \beta_\bullet \delta, i, j]$ with an iHD item $[A \rightarrow \alpha_\bullet \delta, i, j]$. This approach leads to a lower number of items in the resulting chart. The hypotheses set H is the same as for $\mathbb{P}_{HD}$. The set of deduction steps D_{iHD} is given as:

$$D^{Init(i)} = \{[w, i - 1, i] \vdash [A \rightarrow \alpha_\bullet \beta, i - 1, i] \mid$$
$$A \rightarrow \alpha \underline{w} \beta \in P\},$$

$$D^{Init(ii)} = \{\vdash [A \rightarrow _\bullet, i, i] \mid A \rightarrow \epsilon \in P\},$$

$$D^{Pred} = \{[A \rightarrow _\bullet, i, j] \vdash [B \rightarrow \alpha_\bullet \beta, i, j] \mid$$
$$B \rightarrow \alpha \underline{A} \beta \in P\},$$

$$D^{Scan(i)} = \{[A \rightarrow \alpha_\bullet w \delta, i, j], [w, j, j + 1] \vdash$$
$$[A \rightarrow \alpha_\bullet \delta, i, j + 1]\},$$

$$D^{Scan(ii)} = \{[w, i, i + 1], [A \rightarrow \alpha w_\bullet, i + 1, j] \vdash$$
$$[A \rightarrow \alpha_\bullet, i, j]\},$$

$$D^{Complete(i)} = \{[A \to \alpha_\bullet B\delta, i, j], [B \to \bullet, j, k] \vdash$$
$$[A \to \alpha_\bullet \delta, i, k]\},$$

$$D^{Complete(ii)} = \{[B \to \bullet, i, j], [A \to \alpha B_\bullet, j, k] \vdash$$
$$[A \to \alpha_\bullet, i, k]\},$$

$$D_{iHD} = D^{Init(i)} \cup D^{Init(ii)} \cup D^{Pred} \cup D^{Scan(i)} \cup$$
$$D^{Scan(ii)} \cup D^{Complete(i)} \cup D^{Complete(ii)}.$$

The deduction steps are similar to the HD steps. Note that an item $[A \to \bullet, i, j]$ represents now the situation that an arbitrary rule with left-hand side A has been recognized between positions i and j.

As in the previous case, we employ the refined version where the left dot moves left only if the right one is already after the rightmost symbol. The same is true for the replacement of $[A \to \bullet, i, j]$ items by CKY item $[A, i, j]$. The above definition would be more complex. We use the CKY items in the following algorithm.

4   Simplified Items, No Dots Needed

The algorithm described in the previous section cuts out the already analyzed part represented by β in HD items $[A \to \alpha_\bullet \beta_\bullet \delta, i, j]$.

However, the opposite approach is possible as well. One can realize that the remaining parts of the rule (left nonterminal A and the parts α and δ) are given by the grammar. Thus, only the analyzed parts are stored in the chart. We apply this general idea from [11] for the HDddm parsing.

Note that the dots in items occurring in the following definitions play no role in the algorithm. We keep them for better readability only and for a comparison with previous algorithms.

The head-driven algorithm with simplified items (sHD) can be described as parsing system $\mathbb{P}_{sHD} = \langle \mathcal{I}_{sHD}, H, D_{sHD} \rangle$. The domain $\mathcal{I}_{sHD}$ is defined as:

$$\mathcal{I}^{sHD(i)} = \{[_\bullet \beta X \gamma_\bullet, i, j] \mid$$
$$A \to \alpha \beta \underline{X} \gamma \delta \in P, 0 \le i \le j \le n\},$$

$$\mathcal{I}^{CKY} = \{[A, i, j] \mid A \to \alpha \in P,$$
$$\text{possibly } \alpha \equiv \epsilon, 0 \le i \le j \le n\},$$

$$\mathcal{I}_{sHD} = \mathcal{I}^{sHD(i)} \cup \mathcal{I}^{CKY}.$$

Item $[_\bullet \beta_\bullet, i, j]$ denotes that:

- β covers the input sequence between i and j;
- there exists grammar rule $A \to \alpha \beta \gamma \in P$ with the head in β.

CKY item $[A, i, j]$ represents complete (inactive) item as discussed in the previous section. Notice the difference between $[A, i, j]$ and $[\bullet A \bullet, i, j]$.

Table 1. A comparison of the three discussed variants of the HD algorithm on the number of edges of the resulting chart

Grammar	HD	iHD	% of HD	sHD	% of HD
ATIS	882,673	793,370	89.8%	390,860	44.2%
ATIS (H)	401,782	362,568	90.2%	139,935	34.8%
PT	1,227,500	510,175	41.5%	456,736	37.2%
CT	638,276	606,591	95.0%	381,115	59.7%
Czech	994,402	915,004	92.0%	496,129	49.8%

Deduction steps D_{sHD} are given as:

$$D^{Init(i)} = \{[w, i-1, i] \vdash [_\bullet w_\bullet, i-1, i] \mid A \to \alpha \underline{w} \beta \in P\},$$

$$D^{Init(ii)} = \{\vdash [A, i, i] \mid A \to \epsilon \in P\},$$

$$D^{Pred} = \{[A, i, j] \vdash [_\bullet A_\bullet, i, j] \mid B \to \alpha \underline{A} \beta \in P\},$$

$$D^{Scan(i)} = \{[_\bullet \beta_\bullet, i, j], [w, j, j+1] \vdash [_\bullet \beta w_\bullet, i, j+1] \mid A \to \alpha \beta w \gamma \in P\},$$

$$D^{Scan(ii)} = \{[w, i, i+1], [_\bullet \beta_\bullet, i+1, j] \vdash [_\bullet w \beta_\bullet, i, j] \mid A \to \alpha w \beta \in P\},$$

$$D^{Complete(i)} = \{[_\bullet \beta_\bullet, i, j], [B, j, k] \vdash [_\bullet \beta B_\bullet, i, k] \mid A \to \alpha \beta B \delta \in P\},$$

$$D^{Complete(ii)} = \{[B, i, j], [_\bullet \beta_\bullet, j, k] \vdash [_\bullet B \beta_\bullet, i, k] \mid A \to \alpha B \beta \in P\},$$

$$D^{Complete(iii)} = \{[_\bullet \alpha_\bullet, i, j] \vdash [A, i, j] \mid A \to \alpha \in P\},$$

$$D_{sHD} = D^{Init(i)} \cup D^{Init(ii)} \cup D^{Pred} \cup D^{Scan(i)} \cup D^{Scan(ii)} \cup D^{Complete(i)} \cup D^{Complete(ii)} \cup D^{Complete(iii)}.$$

5 Data Structures Employed in the Implementation

To implement an efficient parsing algorithm, we need appropriate data structures to store the needed information. Especially the *Complete* steps in the discussed algorithms ask for a special handling. The appropriate data structure has to efficiently represent (parts of) the right-hand sides of grammar rules. For example, the sHD algorithm needs to identify fully analyzed rules in step $D^{Complete(iii)}$ above.

The trie [12] structure showed to be the most suitable candidate for storing the right-hand side of grammar rules. It is true especially for parsing with our grammar of Czech where the average number of right-hand side symbols in the rules is rather high.

Chappelier and Rajman [13] apply trie to store Earley-like simplified items. The same approach works for the basic variant of our algorithm as well as for iHD. We could take advantage of the free implementation of finite-state automaton and the routines for their searching described in [14].

It is much more difficult to come up with an appropriate data structure to efficiently search rules in the case of the last parsing method (sHD). The removal of the non-analyzed parts from the sHD items requires a bidirectional search from the inside of the right-hand side. A sophisticated data structure for this purpose has been found in GADDAG [15]. Originally, it was designed for generating possible moves in an implementation of the game Scrabble. It allows bidirectional path starting from each letter (a symbol on the right-hand side in our case) of each word (a grammar rule) in the lexicon (a grammar).

6   Grammars Used in Tests and Results of Experiments

The performed tests that are described in this section are based on the data (testing grammars and respective inputs) provided at `http://www.cogs.susx.ac.uk/lab/nlp/carroll/cfg-resources/` (The web pages resulted from discussions at the Efficiency in Large Scale Parsing Systems Workshop at COLING 2000, where one of the main conclusions was the need for a bank of data for standardization of parser benchmarking.)

ATIS, PT and CT in the following results refer to the standard grammars from the benchmarking site. As the original data do not provide information about heads of the rules, a simple heuristics has been employed for setting the heads in these cases. If a rule contains terminals, the left-most one is chosen as the head. Otherwise, a distance measure from terminals is computed for all the right-hand side nonterminals (how many derivations are needed to get a rule with a terminal) and the left-most one with the smallest "terminal distance" is taken as the head. Note, that the heuristics does not work too well for ATIS as the grammar contains many rules with the same nonterminal on the left-hand side and the right-hand side starting with the same terminal.

ATIS (H) is a variant of the ATIS grammar where the position of the heads has been set to the best position according to the chart size (for the HDddm algorithm). The optimization of the head positions has been described in [16].

The other grammar referred in the results is the Czech grammar that serves as a base for our robust parser. It is the second form of the grammar generated directly from the metagrammar form [17]. It contains 10,000 rules and is highly ambiguous.

The PACE (PArser Comparison and Evaluation) testing environment [18] has been used to compute the reported result. It enables to evaluate just the contribution of the changed parts of the parsing method and to "freeze" all the rest.

The benefits of the discussed HD refinements are demonstrated by the reduction of edges in the resulting charts. Table 1 summarizes the results. It is obvious that the improved HD parsing methods significantly reduces the size of the resulting chart. The average decrease of the number of chart edges is about 50 %.

A special attention should be also paid to the two variants of the ATIS grammar. The optimal positions of heads bring a slight downgrade for the iHD algorithm but a considerable improvement for sHD. Also note that the PT grammar is the only one in our experiments where the iHD improvement proved a substantial effect.

7   Conclusions and Future Directions

The iHD and sHD algorithms process and store exactly inverse information, but both approaches are functional. The degree of their help depends on the grammar, positions of heads and the input. The sHD method made about 50 % reduction of the number of edges without any change in the algorithm. Just the items took a different form.

A reduction of the chart size does not necessarily imply a more efficient parser. As the complete incorporation of the discussed refinements into our system is not finished yet we do not present a comparison of running times for the discussed methods. However, the preliminary results that we are able to obtain clearly demonstrate that the data structures discussed above really allow to work with the more complex items efficiently enough to overcome the basic method with the standard items.

The described improvements of the HD algorithm do not prevent all other refinements designed for the original form of items (see, e. g., [5] and [8]). Moreover, the modified items can be directly taken for the head-corner algorithm. Such combinations are the topic for our future research.

References

1. Chelba, C., Jelinek, F.: Exploiting Syntactic Structure for Language Modeling. In Boitet, C., Whitelock, P. (eds), Proceedings of the Thirty-Sixth Annual Meeting of the Association for Computational Linguistics and Seventeenth International Conference on Computational Linguistics, San Francisco, California, Morgan Kaufmann Publishers (1998) 225–231
2. Smrž, P., Horák, A.: Probabilistic Head-Driven Chart Parsing of Czech Sentences. In: Proceedings of the Third International Workshop on Text, Speech and Dialogue-TSD 2000, Brno (Czech Republic) (2000) 81–86
3. Kay, M.: Head Driven Parsing. In: Proceedings of International Workshop on Parsing Technologies, Pittsburg (1989)
4. Satta, G., Stock, O.: Head-Driven Bidirectional Parsing: A Tabular Method. In: Proceedings of IWPT'1989, Pitsburg (1989) 43–51
5. Sikkel, K.: Parsing Schemata: A Framework for Specification and Analysis of Parsing Algorithm. Springer, Berlin (1996)

6. Smrž, P., Horák, A.: Large Scale Parsing of Czech. In: Proceedings of Efficiency in Large-Scale Parsing Systems Workshop, COLING'2000, Saarbrucken: Universitaet des Saarlandes (2000) 43–50

7. Horák, A., Kadlec, V., Smrž, P.: Enhancing Best Analysis Selection and Parser Comparison. In: Text, Speech and Dialogue: Proceedings of the 5th International Workshop TSD 2002, Brno, Czech Republic, Springer Verlag, Lecture Notes in Artificial Intelligence, **2448** (2002)

8. Sikkel, K., op den Akker, R.: Predictive Head-Corner Parsing. In: Proceedings of IWPT'1993, Tilburg/Durbuy (1993) 267–276

9. Leermakers, R.: A Recursive Ascent Earley Parser. Information Processing Letters **41** 2 (1992) 87–91

10. Moore, R.C.: Improved Left-Corner Chart Parsing for Large Context-Free Grammars. In: Proceedings of the 6th IWPT, Trento, Italy (2000) 171–182

11. Nederhof, M.J., Satta, G.: An Extended Theory of Head-Driven Parsing. In: Meeting of the Association for Computational Linguistics (1994) 210–217

12. Fredkin, E.: Trie Memory. CACM **3** 9 (1960) 490–499

13. Chappelier, J.C., Rajman, M.: A Practical Bottom-up Algorithm for On-line Parsing with Stochastic Context-Free Grammars. In: Technical Report No 98/284, Département Informatique, EPFL, Lausanne, Switzerland (1998)

14. Daciuk, J., Watson, R.E., Watson, B.W.: Incremental Construction of Acyclic Finite-State Automata and Transducers. In: Finite State Methods in Natural Language Processing, Bilkent University, Ankara, Turkey (1998)

15. Gordon, S.A.: A Faster Scrabble Move Generation Algorithm. Software – Practice and Experience **24** 2 (1994) 219–232

16. Kadlec, V.: Optimizing Head Positions for Head-Driven Chart Parsing. In: The Seventh International Conference on Text, Speech and Dialogue – TSD 2004, Brno, Czech Republic (2004) (submitted for review).

17. Smrž, P., Horák, A.: Implementation of Efficient and Portable Parser for Czech. In: Text, Speech and Dialogue: Proceedings of the Second International Workshop TSD 1999, Berlin, Springer-Verlag Lecture Notes in Artificial Intelligence **1692** (1999) 105–108

18. Kadlec, V., Smrž, P.: PACE - Parser Comparison and Evaluation. In: Proceedings of the 8th International Workshop on Parsing Technologies, IWPT 2003, Le Chesnay Cedex, France, INRIA, Domaine de Voluceau, Rocquencourt (2003) 211–212

Ontology Acquisition for Automatic Building of Scientific Portals*

Pavel Smrž[1] and Vít Nováček[2]

[1] Faculty of Information Technology, Brno University of Technology,
Božetěchova 2, 612 66 Brno, Czech Republic
smrz@fit.vutbr.cz
[2] Faculty of Informatics, Masaryk University,
Botanická 68a, 602 00 Brno, Czech Republic
xnovacek@fi.muni.cz

Abstract. Ontologies are commonly considered as one of the essential parts of the Semantic Web vision, providing a theoretical basis and implementation framework for conceptual integration and information sharing among various domains. In this paper, we present the main principles of a new ontology acquisition framework applied for semi-automatic generation of scientific portals. Extracted ontological relations play a crucial role in the structuring of the information at the portal pages, automatic classification of the presented documents as well as for personalisation at the presentation level.

1 Introduction

Ontology acquisition framework described in this paper is a part of PortaGe – an ongoing project aiming at semi-automatic generation of scientific web portals. We would like to briefly introduce basic characteristics of the project that influenced our decisions in the area of ontology learning.

The generator of scientific web portals is meant as an extension of the existing tools such as Google Scholar (http://scholar.google.com) or CiteSeer (http://citeseer.ist.psu.edu/). A typical user is a young researcher or a PhD student that looks for relevant information (knowledge) in a subfield (s)he needs to fathom. The interest in the subject is supposed to be long-term, so the user would be notified about new publications, projects, events, calls, etc. in the field.

The current search engines employ user-specified keywords and phrases as the major means of their input. Digital libraries, such as ACM DL (http://portal.acm.org/dl.cfm) or Springer DL (http://arxiv.org/), add a detailed metainformation level and are able to find publications of a given author, from a given journal, conference proceedings etc. However, these services are not able

* This work was partially supported by the Ministry of Education of the Czech Republic, Research Plan MSM 6383917201, and by the Grant Agency of the Czech Academy of Sciences, Project 1ET100300419.

J. Wiedermann et al. (Eds.): SOFSEM 2006, LNCS 3831, pp. 493–500, 2006.
© Springer-Verlag Berlin Heidelberg 2006

to relate the information to the context of the search. They cannot evaluate what "relevant" means in a particular case.

PortaGe builds a web portal for a domain given by initial data. In addition to the standard keywords, known authors, journals, conferences or projects characterizing the subject field, the user can provide seed documents and conference/project web pages relevant for the current search and select apt nodes in the current ontology (automatically extracted from the given and retrieved documents). The tool combines responses from several information sources:

- search results from Google Scholar;
- articles and papers found in digital libraries (currently available ACM DL and Springer Link);
- information from freely accessible web services (arxiv.gov and ResearchIndex);
- metainformation about hard-copies (books, journals, proceedings) in the faculty library and other traditional repositories.

Besides the ontology acquisition by means of text mining which is tackled in the next sections, the essential components of PortaGe include: efficient local document classification and indexing, extraction of metainformation from the documents, citation analysis (from ResearchIndex), metasearch in digital libraries, analysis of "Publications" web pages, meta-data annotation of web resources, merging of information, continuous search and source-change analysis. The personalization of the portal driven by ontologies is discussed in the next section.

The rest of the paper is organized as follows: The role ontologies play in PortaGe and the consequences in the form of requirement specification for the automatic acquisition system are presented in the next section. Section 3 describes fundamentals of OLE – a new ontology acquisition framework and OLITE – its essential part designed primarily for the extraction of detailed semantic relations from unstructured plain-text data. A brief comparative overview of other relevant approaches and related works is given in Section 4. We conclude the paper by proposing future directions for our research.

2   Ontologies in the Scope of PortaGe

Several components of PortaGe take advantage of domain-specific as well as general ontologies. This impacts the way the automatic ontology acquisition has been implemented. The particular needs have determined the methods and techniques that could be applied for the extraction of semantic relations. The following paragraphs briefly introduce the role of ontologies in PortaGe and summarize the defined requirements.

Ontologies found their place in a couple of areas within PortaGe:

1. The basic role consists in the definition of portal structures. The core ontology contains concepts of publishers, books and book series, journals and

their special issues, conferences, conference tracks workshops, projects, research teams, authors, papers, web pages, etc. PortaGe supposes that the most of this can be shared among various scientific fields (different disciplines slightly yet differ in the conceptualisation of their research areas). For a particular domain, it needs to be extended by individual instances of journals, conferences, etc. It is one of the tasks of an ontology extraction engine.

2. Ontologies also help to classify the content of documents in PortaGe. This is important especially for very narrow subfields with a limited number of documents that can be applied for training of the standard classifiers. The automatic classification process can base its decision on the knowledge extracted from other documents in a previous run, such as the fact that a particular method is used for machine learning in other fields.

3. As stated above, it is difficult to define a context of the search when using the standard search engines. Ontologies provide mechanisms for a comprehensive context specification. In PortaGe, the user can restrict the search for documents reflecting certain semantic relations based on the ontology, e.g. limit the output to the documents discussing "context-free grammars" as a "tool-for" "analysis of protein sequences". The OLE framework interlinks individual pieces of such knowledge with lexico-syntactic patterns able to identify the relations in the retrieved documents.

4. The discussion of the PortaGe system has assumed a single individual user of the generated portals so far. However, the multi-user environment is much more realistic in many circumstances. For example, imagine a typical scenario of a team leader that supervises several PhD students. He creates a general web portal that covers various subfields of the area in focus. Individual students work on their particular topics, interact with the system and extend its coverage in the given subfield. The last role of the ontologies in PortaGe that will be mentioned here deals with the personalisation of general portals. The system uses ontologies to evaluate what "relevant" information means for a particular user. Based on user profiles PortaGe defines rules to identify "the best" information for an individual user. A novice (in the given research domain) can ask for introductory documents, others prefer new information (the documents that appeared/were found in the last month), need a general summary of used methods (usually the most referenced documents), or focus on the relevance only. The user profiles and the ontologies also cover the availability of the resources for a particular user (e. g. a preference for a general introductory book from the local library available for loan this weekend), user-specified amount of documents that should be presented (e. g. two new documents every Friday) and processing time requirements (the detailed analysis of a new bunch of documents will not be available until tomorrow morning).

Taking into account the given functions of ontologies in PortaGe, the following basic requirements on the ontology acquisition must be considered:

– Ideally, the process of ontology acquisition should run without any need of human assistance. On the other hand, the user must be able to influence the learning, refine the extracted, select relevant information and modify the stored data manually.

- In general, the amount of the processed resources can be very high (thousands of documents). The implementation of the ontology learning must be computationally efficient and robust.
- The produced ontologies must reflect the stepwise development of the Porta-Ge system. If there is no current need for a particular kind of knowledge, the extraction (which often needs detailed analysis and is therefore resource demanding) should be postponed to later phases.

3   Architecture of the Ontology Extraction Framework

OLE – the ontology acquisition framework described in this section has been developed in order to support the PortaGe project with instant ontological background. PortaGe ontologies are supposed to grow continuously when processing new resources provided by external tools.

Table 1. A fragment of a miniontology extracted from bioinformatics texts

type of the relation	subject	object	relevance
used_for	SCFG	RNA secondary structure prediction	0.66
described_in	CKY algorithm	Cocke-Kasami-Younger	0.81
is_a	ribosomal frameshifting	RNA function	0.73
abbr_means	HMM	Hidden Markov Models	0.69
abbr_means	SCFG	Stochastic Context-Free Grammars	0.62
is_a	RNA	molecule	0.45
is_a	protein	molecule	0.45

The framework comprises several modules and related system components:

- OLITE module is responsible for processing the plain text resources (e. g. articles and conference papers from a given domain) and creating very simple ontologies from the extracted information. Presently, the relations are extracted according to specific patterns. However, any other method of information extraction can be easily incorporated as an independent plug-in.
- PALEA is the module responsible for learning of new semantic relations' patterns; the patterns are induced from the same resources as those used by OLITE. This component employs the methods described in [10] and [18] for learning new patterns.
- OLEMAN is intended to merge the outputs of the OLITE module – miniontologies – and update the PortaGe domain ontology with the resulting one. The uncertain information representation techniques [23] are used in this phase. Crisp ontology merging and alignment is based on the algorithms described in [4], [8], [9], [11] or [22]. Moreover, fuzzy ontology representation and alignment framework is currently one of the main subjects of our intensive research.

The OLE parts are implemented as stand-alone modules. However, a server version is supposed to be developed for the final integration within the PortaGe project.

The OLITE module forms a crucial part of the entire system. The following paragraphs characterize the main processing steps performed by this component. The resources are first preprocessed by the subsystem. The main reasons for this are:

- the amount of input data must be reduced to its relevant subset only in order to increase the computational efficiency;
- at least some shallow syntactic structure must be imposed upon the reduced data before trying to extract the semantic relations.

The preprocessing must be as fast as possible, so no sophisticated (and time consuming) linguistic techniques, such as deep syntactic analysis, cannot be used. The input data are preprocessed in the following steps: sentence splitting, reduction to the relevant sentences only, sentence tokenization, POS tagging and lemmatization of the tokenized sentence, and chunking of the tagged sentences. We use our own custom preprocessing tools developed with support of NLTK toolkit (see [1]) instead of ready-made platforms (such as GATE, see [7]). This approach allows us to port the system easily for different languages, not only English. After the successful preprocessing, the extraction patterns are applied.

The OLITE module structure is devised so that it is able to adopt any extraction algorithm independently in the form of a specific plug-in. Such a plug-in is responsible for the concept extraction then, precise (or fuzzy) annotation by some class or property and passing of gained information further to the other parts of the module in order to build an output miniontology.

A fragment of the miniontology resulting from a test run of the extraction module is presented in Table 1. The semantic relations have been learned from a testing set of documents from the bioinformatics field. The relevance measure is computed by an algorithm inspired by C-value/NC-value method described in [12].

The extracted information is stored in a universal internal format that can be passed to the alignment module in order to be merged with the current ontology (also loaded in this format). The format is extensively expressive and universal with respect to efficient encoding of various relations and uncertainty representation[1]. The updated ontology (or even the output miniontology) file can be directly produced by applying translation rules. These rules are implemented as an independent plug-in (likewise the extraction algorithm itself) responsible for producing the output file in a desired format. Currently, the OWL DL format is supported, but OLITE is able to produce any other format this way (such as BayesOWL, see [23]).

---

[1] The research behind proposal and implementation of this format will be presented in another paper.

4   Related Work

The OLE project dissociates from the frameworks concentrated on facilitation of the manual (or expert-guided) ontology engineering activities, such as Protégé [15], WebODE [2] or OntoEdit [19]. The main reason is the infeasibility of the development and management of many different domain-specific ontologies needed for the full function of PortaGe.

Several automatic ontology acquisition systems have been developed in the last decade. One of them is OntoLT [5] implemented as a plug-in for the Protégé ontology editor. Its focus on the linguistic analysis for knowledge extraction is shared by our tool. However, our approach is able to extract deep semantic relations that seem to be out of scope of OntoLT. In this respect, PortaGe also differs from another ontology learning system – the Mo'K Workbench [3] based on clustering techniques for concept taxonomy building.

The OntoLearn [13, 21] and KnowItAll [10] systems incorporate the extraction of semantic relations, as well as we do. In KnowItAll, there is a notion of uncertainty introduced in the form of so called web-scale probability assessment to the extractions made, although it is not included in the ontology structure itself. On the contrary, the system proposed by T. T. Quan et al. in [20] deals with uncertain information implicitly and on the well defined fuzzy-logic basis. Their system is oriented to meta-information representation, which is supposed to be helpful when building scholarly semantic web. Our system attempts to represent the whole conceptual structure of a domain in an uncertain ontology. Such an ontology can be used for improvement of full-text search in the PortaGe portal documents, relevance measuring, resource categorization and even for domain meta-information representation.

A different perspective of the uncertain information is present in Text2Onto [6] – a successor of the former TextToOnto [17], [16] system. The learned knowledge is represented at a meta-level within Probabilistic Ontology Model (POM). The independence brought by the use of POM is not necessary in our case as the output to other knowledge representation formalisms can be easily added in the form of plug-ins.

The OLE tools are designed as an open platform, which is easy to be amended by different extraction techniques or output modes of creation of ontologies. The pattern-based extraction of semantic relations is described in [14], [10], or [18]. The concept clustering techniques are introduced in the terascale knowledge acquisition efforts ([18]) and in [20] (fuzzy concept clustering). All these techniques can be easily adopted by the OLITE module to supplement the dynamic pattern learning and application (being under research within the PALEA module).

5   Conclusions and Future Directions

The ontology acquisition framework is presented in the context of automatic creation of web portals by means of the PortaGe system. The paper discussed the importance of ontologies for scientific portals. The preliminary results indicate that the ontologies automatically extracted by the OLE system provide valuable resource of semantic data that are necessary for the function of PortaGe.

A lot of work still needs to be done on both the tools, the PortaGe system and the OLE tool. Our future research will focus on the design and implementation of advanced mechanism covering uncertainty in the acquired ontologies. We will also work on a qualitative evaluation of the scientific portals generated by PortaGe. They would be employed for example for e-learning of PhD students at our universities.

References

1. NLTK: Natural Language Toolkit – Technical Reports (2005)   Available at: http://nltk.sourceforge.net/tech/index.html
2. Arpirez, J.C., Corcho, O., Fernandez-Lopez, M., and Gomez-Perez, A.: Webode in a Nutshell. AI Magazine **24** 3 (2003) 37–47
3. Bisson, G., Nedellec, C., and Canamero, L.: Designing Clustering Methods for Ontology Building - The Mo'K Workbench. In Proceedings of the ECAI Ontology Learning Workshop (2000) 13–19
4. Bouquet, P., Serafini, L., and Zanobini, S.: Semantic Coordination: a New Approach and an Application. In ISWC 2003: Second International Semantic Web Conference. Proceedings, Springer-Verlag Berlin Heidelberg (2003) 130–145
5. Buitelaar, P., Olejnik, D., and Sintek, M.: OntoLT: A Protégé Plug-in for Ontology Extraction from Text. In Proceedings of the International Semantic Web Conference (ISWC) (2003)
6. Cimiano, P., and Voelker, J.: Text2Onto – a Framework for Ontology Learning and Data-Driven Change Discovery. In Proceedings of the 10th International Conference on Applications of Natural Language to Information Systems (NLDB'05) (2005)
7. Cunningham, H., Maynard, D., Bontcheva, K., and Tablan, V.: GATE: A Framework and Graphical Development Environment for Robust NLP Tools and Applications. In Proceedings of the 40th Anniversary Meeting of the Association for Computational Linguistics (2002)
8. Doan, A., Madhavan, J., Dhamankar, R., Domingos, P., and Halevy, A.: Learning to Match Ontologies on the Semantic Web. The VLDB Journal **12** 4 (2003) 303–319
9. Ehrig, M., and Staab, S.: Qom - Quick Ontology Mapping. In ISWC 2004: Third International Semantic Web Conference. Proceedings (2004) 683–697
10. Etzioni, O., Cafarella, M., Downey, D., Kok, S., Popescu, A.-M., Shaked, T., Soderland, S., Weld, D.S., and Yates, A.: Web-Scale Information Extraction in Knowitall: (Preliminary Results). In WWW '04: Proceedings of the 13th International Conference on World Wide Web, New York, NY, USA, ACM Press (2004) 100–110
11. Euzenat, J.: An api for Ontology Alignment. In ISWC 2004: Third International Semantic Web Conference. Proceedings (2004) 698–712
12. Frantzi, K.T., Ananiadou, S., and Tsujii, J.: The c-Value/nc-Value Method of Automatic Recognition for Multi-Word Terms. In Proceedings of Second European Conference ECDL '98, Springer-Verlag Berlin Heidelberg (1998) 585–604
13. Gangemi, A., Navigli, R., and Velardi, P.: Corpus Driven Ontology Learning: a Method and Its Application to Automated Terminology Translation. IEEE Intelligent Systems (2003) 22–31

14. Hearst, M.A.: Automatic Acquisition of Hyponyms from Large Text Corpora. In Proceedings of the 14th Conference on Computational Linguistics, Morristown, NJ, USA, Association for Computational Linguistics (1992) 539–545
15. Knublauch, H.: Ontology Driven Software Development in the Context of the Semantic Web: An Example, Scenario with Protégé/owl. In Proceedings of 1st International Workshop on the Model-Driven Semantic Web (MDSW2004) (2004)
16. Maedche, A., and Staab, S.: Ontology Learning. In S. Staab and R. Studer (eds), Handbook on Ontologies, Springer (2004) 173–189
17. Maedche, A., and Staab, S.: Ontology Learning for the Semantic Web. IEEE Intelligent Systems **16** 2 (2001) 72–79
18. Hovy, E., Pantel, P., Ravichandran, D.: Towards Terascale Knowledge Acquisition. In Proceedings of Conference on Computational Linguistics (COLING-04) (2004) 771–777
19. Sure, Y., Erdmann, M., Angele, J., Staab, S., Studer, R., and Wenke, D.: Ontoedit: Collaborative Ontology Development for the Semantic Web. In ISWC 2002: First International Semantic Web Conference. Proceedings, Springer-Verlag Berlin Heidelberg (2002) 221–235
20. Cao, T.H., Quan, T.T., and Hui, S.C.: Automatic Generation of Ontology for Scholarly Semantic Web. In ISWC 2004: Third International Semantic Web Conference. Proceedings, Springer-Verlag Berlin Heidelberg (2004) 726–740
21. Velardi, P., Navigli, R., Cuchiarelli, A., and Neri, F.: Evaluation of OntoLearn, a Methodology for Automatic Population of Domain Ontologies. In P. Buitelaar, P. Cimiano, and B. Magnini (eds), Ontology Learning from Text: Methods, Applications and Evaluation. IOS Press (2005)
22. Widhalm, R., and Mueck, T.A.: Merging Topics in Well-Formed xml Topic Maps. In ISWC 2003: Second International Semantic Web Conference. Proceedings, Springer-Verlag Berlin Heidelberg (2003) 64–79
23. Pan, R., Peng, Y., Ding, Z.: Bayesowl: A Probabilistic Framework for Uncertainty in Semantic Web. In Proceedings of Nineteenth International Joint Conference on Artificial Intelligence (IJCAI05) (2005)

Improved ROCK for Text Clustering Using Asymmetric Proximity

Shaoxu Song and Chunping Li

School of Software, Tsinghua University, 100084 Beijing, China
song-sx03@mails.tsinghua.edu.cn, cli@tsinghua.edu.cn

Abstract. The ROCK algorithm can be applied to text clustering in large databases. The effectiveness of ROCK, however, is limited, because of the high dimensionality of textual data and traditional proximity measure of documents. In this paper, we propose an improved approach to strengthen the discriminative feature of text documents, which uses asymmetric proximity. Instead of the links count in ROCK, we propose a novel concept of link weight overlaps to measure the proximity between two clusters. The IROCK (Improved ROCK) algorithm performs clustering analysis based on the overlap information of asymmetric proximities between text objects. We carry on the clustering process in an agglomerative hierarchical way. To demonstrate the effectiveness of IROCK, we perform an experimental evaluation on real textual data. A comparison with ROCK and classical algorithms indicates the superiority of our approach.

Keywords: Data Mining, Text Clustering.

1 Introduction

Clustering is a process of grouping a set of physical or abstract objects into classes with high inner proximity. For text clustering, data objects are always semi-structured or unstructured, like text and hypertext documents. Due to the high dimensionality and polysemy of words, the nearest distance neighbors of a document belong to different classes in some cases [9]. Methods, such as TFx-IDF [8], ROCK (RObust Clustering using linKs) [2] and CHAMELEON [4], try to strengthen the discriminative features of objects to improve the effectiveness of clustering. Instead of traditional proximity measures like distance, ROCK presents a concept of clustering that is based on links between data points. The notion of links between text documents helps us overcome the problem that some nearest neighbors belong to different classes.

However, ROCK ignores the information about the closeness of two clusters while emphasizing their inter-connectivity [3]. Furthermore, traditional proximity measures are relied on when finding initial neighbors and links. In the specific case of textual data, we should consider the discriminative feature of document objects in clustering. Current existing approaches (including ROCK) can hardly deal with the special textual correlation. For example, some specialized articles

J. Wiedermann et al. (Eds.): SOFSEM 2006, LNCS 3831, pp. 501–510, 2006.

may be dedicated to one topic (i.e. *basketball*) in a single document, while some summarized articles may include several topics (i.e. *sports* like *basketball* and *football*) in one document. Traditional symmetry measures cannot tell the difference between summarized articles and specialized ones. On the other hand, *NIKE*, known as a famous sports sponsor, is always mentioned together with *football* and *basketball*. Although *NIKE* may not appear in a *sports* topic based article, *NIKE* and *sports* are correlated. Also it is hard to find this correlation with existing methods.

In this paper, we define the proximity of documents in a more natural way. The discriminative features of text documents are described with an asymmetric approach. For example, *sports* has a high similarity to *basketball*, because all about *basketball* are also about *sports*. In contrast, *basketball* has a low similarity to *sports*, because *sports* may include other subjects like *football*. We discuss this example more specifically in Section 3. Based on this discriminative rule, we obtain a natural asymmetric description of correlation between documents. In order to use asymmetric proximity for text clustering, we propose an improved version of ROCK, named IROCK. Instead of links count, IROCK considers the weight of directed links. We define the proximity between a pair of text objects(clusters) to be the overlaps of common link weights.

The basic outline of this paper is as follows. Section 2 briefly introduces the general idea of the ROCK algorithm. In Section 3 we propose our definition of asymmetric proximity and link weight overlap for IROCK. Section 4 gives a description of the IROCK algorithm process for text clustering. Section 5 reports an experimental evaluation on real textual data and shows the quality of IROCK. Finally, Section 6 is a summary of our study.

2   ROCK Approach

The clustering model of ROCK is based on the notion of neighbors and links. To use ROCK for text clustering, we need to find initial neighbors and links of documents. Simply speaking, a document's neighbors are those documents that are considerably similar to it. *Euclidean Distance* and *Cosine Measure* are commonly used as proximity measures between documents.

In this paper, documents are represented by *vector-space model*. Each text document d is represented by a vector of weights of p terms:

$$d_i = (w_{i1}, \ldots, w_{ip}) \tag{1}$$

where d_i is the vector of document i, w_{ik} is the weight of term k in document i. Then, the similarity between documents can be quantified by the correlation, ϕ_{ij}, which is so-called the *Cosine Measure*:

$$\phi_{ij} = \frac{\sum_{k=1}^{p} w_{ik} w_{jk}}{\sqrt{\sum_{k=1}^{p} w_{ik}^2 \sum_{k=1}^{p} w_{jk}^2}} \tag{2}$$

where ϕ_{ij} is the cosine similarity value between documents i and j. Clearly, a measure based on cosine similarity can be used when all terms are measured on the same scale. For a critical review, see [1].

Clustering documents only based on the similarity between them is not strong enough to distinguish two "not so well-separated" clusters because it is possible for documents in different clusters to be neighbors. But it is very unlikely that pairs of documents that have many common neighbors belong to different clusters. ROCK defines $link(d_i, d_j)$ to be the number of common neighbors between d_i and d_j. The link-based ROCK can correctly identify overlapping clusters.

ROCK is an hierarchical clustering algorithm and uses a goodness function to determine the best pair of clusters to merge at each step. The *goodness measure* $g(C_i, C_j)$ for merging clusters C_i, C_j is defined as

$$g(C_i, C_j) = \frac{link(C_i, C_j)}{(n_i + n_j)^{f(\theta)} - n_i^{f(\theta)} - n_j^{f(\theta)}} \tag{3}$$

where n_i, n_j are the sizes of clusters C_i and C_j, $f(\theta) = 1 + 2\frac{1-\theta}{1+\theta}$, θ is an input parameter, $link(C_i, C_j)$ stores the number of cross links between clusters C_i and C_j, which is $\sum_{d_q \in C_i, d_r \in C_j} link(d_q, d_r)$. The pair of clusters for which the above goodness measure is maximal is the best pair of clusters to be merged at any given step.

For text clustering, ROCK is adept at dealing with text clusters that are not so well-separated by using cross links. However, ROCK ignores the information about the proximity of two clusters while emphasizing their inter-connectivity. Our work is dedicated to propose a novel measure of similarity and links between text objects. We introduce our improved approach named IROCK in the following sections.

3   IROCK Clustering Strategy

In IROCK, we use asymmetric proximity to strengthen the discriminative features of text documents and we use link weight overlaps instead of links to measure correlation of text objects.

3.1   Neighbors

Considering the case illustrated in the example in Section 1, IROCK uses an asymmetric proximity measure to find neighbors. Assume that the common terms of two documents d_i and d_j are s. If the weight of s in d_j is large, then the asymmetric similarity from d_i to d_j is high; and if the weight of s in d_i is small, then the asymmetric similarity from d_j to d_i is low. More precisely,

$$\overrightarrow{\phi}(d_i, d_j) = \frac{\sum_{k=1}^{p} |w_{ik} - |w_{ik} - w_{jk}||}{\sum_{k=1}^{p} w_{jk}} \tag{4}$$

where $\overrightarrow{\phi}(d_i, d_j)$ is the direct similarity value from document d_i to d_j, w_{ik} is the weight value of term k in document d_i. Clearly, the similarity between documents is asymmetric, i.e., $\overrightarrow{\phi}(d_i, d_j) \neq \overrightarrow{\phi}(d_j, d_i)$.

Now we can define the neighbors in IROCK clustering. Given a threshold η, the neighbors of document d_i are those documents d_j for which the following formula holds:

$$\overrightarrow{\phi}(d_i, d_j) \geq \eta \tag{5}$$

All links from d_i to the others are considered in IROCK, if the weights of these links are larger than the minimum proximity threshold η.

3.2   Overlaps

Instead of the common links count in ROCK, we consider the weights of these links. IROCK defines ϕ_{ik} to be the link weight from d_i to d_k, i.e., $\overrightarrow{\phi}(d_i, d_k)$. A directed graph with link weights is constructed to describe the correlation of text objects. We define $\varphi(d_i, d_j)$ to be the overlap of common link weights

$$\varphi(d_i, d_j) = \sum_{k=1}^{p} \left| \phi_{ik} - |\phi_{ik} - \phi_{jk}| \right| \tag{6}$$

where ϕ_{ik} denotes a weighted link from d_i to d_k that satisfies the minimum weight threshold η, p is the total number of objects. If the $\varphi(d_i, d_j)$ is large, both d_i and d_j are similar to the same objects. It is more probable that d_i and d_j belong to the same cluster. From the definition of link weight overlaps, we can overcome the shortcoming of ROCK, which ignores the proximity information.

3.3   Textual Correlation

Let us look at the example in Section 1 again. Fig. 1 shows an asymmetric proximity description of the example case. Gray points denote articles, and directed links are the asymmetric proximity between them. The words append the gray points mean the topic of the text objects. The real numbers append to the directed links are the weigh of them, which denote the asymmetric similarity value between two text objects.

As mentioned in Section 1, the correlation between *NIKE* and *sports* is hard to find. ROCK tries to solve this problem by counting the common neighbors, for instance, *football* and *basketball* are the common neighbors of *NIKE* and *sports*. Consequently, the value of $link(d_{NIKE}, d_{sports})$ is 2, whereas it ignores the link weights to their neighbors. Our approach considers the overlaps of these link weights as the correlation between text objects. The value of ϕ_{ik} is the link weight from d_i to d_k, i.e., $\overrightarrow{\phi}(d_{NIKE}, d_{football}) = 0.7$ as shown in the figure. Then the overlap of common link weights can be computed by formula (6), i.e. $\varphi(d_{NIKE}, d_{sports}) = 1.4$.

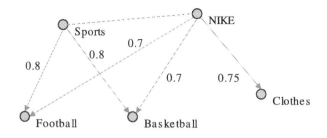

Fig. 1. Example of asymmetric proximity

4   Algorithm Description

In the preprocessing work, stop words are removed and documents are represented by a *vector-space model* using TFxIDF. After modeling the data, a sparse matrix about document asymmetric proximity is constructed. We need to mention that the matrix is not a triangular matrix, because of the asymmetry of document proximity. All link weight overlaps can be computed from this matrix.

4.1   Goodness Measure

IROCK, as ROCK, belongs to the class of agglomerative hierarchical clustering algorithms. It starts by placing each object in its own cluster and then merges these atomic clusters into larger and larger clusters until a certain termination condition is satisfied. Their merge strategy is to choose the pair of objects with highest goodness values. IROCK defines the goodness measure $g(C_i, C_j)$ for merging clusters C_i, C_j as follows.

$$g(C_i, C_j) = \frac{\sum_{d_q \in C_i, d_r \in C_j} \varphi(d_q, d_r)}{(n_i + n_j)^{f(\theta)} - n_i^{f(\theta)} - n_j^{f(\theta)}} \tag{7}$$

where n_i, n_j are the sizes of clusters C_i and C_j, $f(\theta) = 1 + 2\frac{1-\theta}{1+\theta}$, θ is an input parameter. In contrast to ROCK, we use the link weight overlap instead of cross link count to measure goodness. $\sum_{d_q \in C_i, d_r \in C_j} \varphi(d_q, d_r)$ is the link weight overlap between clusters C_i and C_j. According to the principle of clustering with high inner correlation and low exterior correlation, it seems intuitive that clusters with high link weight overlaps are good candidates for merging.

4.2   Clustering Algorithm

The IROCK algorithm performs clustering based on the overlap information of asymmetric proximities between text objects. The most significant work is to find clusters with high overlap of common nearest neighbors. Due to the asymmetry of text proximity, the "nearest" links of neighbors are directed.

IROCK Algorithm

```
Input:
    number of clusters k;
    p document vectors.
Output:
    k clusters.
Method:
    begin
        C := initial clusters;
        M := proximity matrix of p docs;
        O := all link weight overlaps;
        G := all goodness values;
        repeat
            [u, v] := max(G);
            w := merge(u, v);
            C := update(C, w, u, v);
            O := update(O, w, u, v);
            G := update(G, w, u, v);
        until size(C) <= k
    end.
```

Fig. 2. Clustering algorithm

The IROCK algorithm is presented in Fig. 2. As an initialization, each document is assigned to its own cluster in C. For the construction of the asymmetric proximity matrix M of p documents, formula (4) is used. Those proximity values that don't satisfy the minimum threshold η are removed. Based on the sparse proximity matrix, all link weight overlaps are computed in O by formula (6). Then formula (7) computes all goodness values G between objects. In each iteration, the core step is finding a pair of clusters with maximum goodness to merge. Clusters u and v, the best pair to merge, are removed from C, O and G. The new cluster w, consisting of u and v, is inserted into C, O and G by the update operation. The program stops when the number of clusters satisfies the given size value k.

5   Experiments

In this section we report an experimental evaluation of IROCK on real textual data. The experiments were performed on a Xeon server. The programs are implemented in java 1.5.

5.1   Data Sets

Pre-classified documents are needed to test and compare clustering algorithms. We used two different data sets: *RCV1* and *20Newsgroups*, which are widely used in text categorization.

RCV1. We work with the new version of Reuters corpus: *Reuters Corpus Volume I (RCV1)*. It is an archive of over 800,000 manually categorized newswire stories recently made available by Reuters Ltd. for research purposes. Topic codes are assigned to capture the major subjects of a story. They are organized in four hierarchical groups: CCAT(Corporate/Industrial), ECAT(Economics), GCAT(Government/Social), and MCAT(Markets). Sizes of the four categories are different (for further details see [7]).

20Newsgroups. The 20 Newsgroups[1] (20Ng) data set, collected by Lang [6], contains about 20,000 articles. Each newsgroup represents one class in the classification task. Each article is designated to one or more semantic categories and the total number of categories is 20, all of them are about the same size. Most of the articles have only one semantic tag, however, about 7% of them have two or more. We chose 4 topic categories in our experiments.

5.2   Evaluation Criteria

We evaluate our approach by classification accuracy, which has also been used in the works of [5] and [10]. Kohonen et al. define the classification error as "all documents that represented a minority newsgroup at any grid point were counted as classification errors." Our classification accuracy is very similar to Kohonen's, but we count the correct documents instead of errors. The article is correct, if one of the original labels assigned by data set matches the cluster label. The accuracy is the proportion of the number of correct articles to the number of all input news articles.

5.3   Evaluation

Comparison on Different Number of Clusters. Our first experiment was focused on evaluating the quality of the clustering solutions produced by ROCK and classical algorithms. IROCK as an improvement of ROCK was tested in this experiment. For classical algorithms, we chose K-Means. Initial centroids are selected by randomly choosing K documents, so we ran the program 10 times and chose the best results. These algorithms were compared on both *RCV1* and *20Newsgroups*.

For the experiments on the Reuters data set, we used 2000 documents which consist of 49% CCAT, 20% MCAT, 18% GCAT and 12% ECAT. The results of IROCK with $\theta = 0.045$, $\eta = 0.05$ and ROCK with $\theta = 0.02$, $\eta = 0.02$ are presented in Table 1. From the table we can learn that IROCK has a good ability to deal with data sets with differently sized clusters such as RCV1, and K-Means works poorer than ROCK on RCV1.

In 20 Newsgroups as a comparison, we used 2000 documents in 4 classes with the same size, i.e. "comp.os.ms-windows.misc", "comp.sys.mac.hardware",

---

[1] The 20 newsgroups data collection can be obtained from:
   http://kdd.ics.uci.edu/.

Table 1. Accuracy on RCV1 data

Number of Clusters	IROCK	ROCK	K-Means
8	0.777	0.628	0.605
16	0.779	0.686	0.669
50	0.836	0.848	0.749
100	0.860	0.859	0.798

Table 2. Accuracy on 20 Newsgroups data

Number of Clusters	IROCK	ROCK	K-Means
8	0.829	0.799	0.778
16	0.845	0.821	0.826
50	0.871	0.926	0.857
100	0.890	0.928	0.888

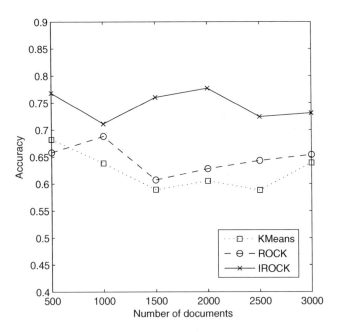

Fig. 3. Accuracy comparison in different data scales

"sci.crypt" and "sci.electronics". The results of IROCK with $\theta = 0.03$, $\eta = 0.03$ and ROCK with $\theta = 0.03$, $\eta = 0.04$ are given in Table 2. In the clustering, 7 single documents as outliers are generated by both ROCK and IROCK. For the experiment with same cluster sizes on *20 Newsgroups*, the performance of ROCK and K-Means are quite similar, whereas IROCK performs better than the other two approaches in the final results (i.e., 8 clusters), as on RCV1.

Comparison on Different Data Scale. This experiment compared the scalability of IROCK, ROCK and K-Means. All algorithms were performed on the same data set *RCV1* with different number of documents. The final number of clusters is set to 8.

Fig. 3 shows the results with parameter settings: $\theta = 0.045$, $\eta = 0.05$ in IROCK and $\theta = 0.02$, $\eta = 0.02$ in ROCK. In Fig. 3, we can see that ROCK has quite similar final results with K-Means, whereas IROCK achieves better than both ROCK and K-Means for different data sizes.

From the experiments above, we can see that IROCK has a notable effect in text clustering. Our improved approach performs better than both ROCK and classical K-Means, especially on data with different sizes of clusters like RCV1. The superiority of ROCK is not so remarkable when compared with K-Means.

6   Conclusions

In this paper, we have presented two new concepts: asymmetric proximity and link weight overlap to measure the correlation of text objects. Asymmetric proximity improves text clustering by strengthening discriminative features, which are difficult to describe in traditional proximity measures. Link weight overlap overcomes the shortcoming of ROCK in which the information about the closeness of two clusters is ignored while emphasizing on their inter-connectivity. Both of these techniques are adopted in the improved algorithm IROCK. The clustering process is based on the overlap information of asymmetric proximities between text objects.

Our experimental evaluation on real textual data sets demonstrates that the IROCK approach yields a better clustering quality than the original ROCK does. Furthermore, links based ROCK has a higher accuracy than classical K-Means in our experiments for text clustering. However, some inherent defects of agglomerative approaches still exist in IROCK, for instance, slow runtime performance. We hope to improve them in the future by using more sophisticated approaches.

Acknowledgement. This work was supported by Chinese 973 Research Project under grant No. 2004CB719401.

References

1. Cliff, A., Haggett, P., Smallman-Raynor, M., Stroup, D., and Williamson, G.: The Application of Multidimensional Scaling Methods to Epidemiologial Data. Statistical Methods in Medical Research **4** (1995) 345–366
2. Guha, S., Rastogi, R., and Shim, K.: ROCK: A Robust Clustering Algorithm for Categorical Attributes. Information Systems **25** 5 (2000) 345–366
3. Han, J., and Kamber, M.: Data Mining: Concept and Techniques. Morgan Kaufmann Publishers (2001)

4. Karypis, G., Han, E.H., and Kumar, V.: Chameleon: Hierarchical Clustering Using Dynamic Modeling. IEEE Computer **32** 8 (1999) 68–75

5. Kohonen, T., Kaski, S., Lagus, K., Salojärvi, J., Honkela, J., Paatero, V., and Saarela, S.: Self Organization of a Massive Document Collection. In IEEE Transactions on Neural Networks **11** 3 (2000) 574–585

6. Lang, K.: Newsweeder: Learning to Filter Netnews. In Proceedings of the 12th International Conference on Machine Learning, ICML95 (1995) 331–339

7. Lewis, D., Yang, Y., Rose, T., and Li, F.: Rcv1: A New Benchmark Collection for Text Categorization Research. Journal of Machine Learning Research **5** (2004) 361–397

8. Salton, G.: Automatic Text Processing–The Transformation, Analysis, and Retrieval of Information by Computer. Addison–Wesley (1989)

9. Steinbach, M., Karypis, G., and Kumar, V.: A Comparison of Document Clustering Techniques. In KDD Workshop on Text Mining (2000)

10. Wermter, S., and Hung, C.: Selforganising Classification on the Reuters News Corpus. In The 19th International Conference on Computational Linguistics (COLING 2002) (2002) 1086–1092

Compact Encodings for All Local Path Information in Web Taxonomies with Application to WordNet

Svetlana Strunjaš-Yoshikawa, Fred S. Annexstein, and Kenneth A. Berman

Department of ECE and Computer Science, University of Cincinnati,
Cincinnati OH 45220-0030, USA
strunjs@ececs.uc.edu, annexste@ececs.uc.edu,
berman@ececs.uc.edu

Abstract. We consider the problem of finding a compact labelling for large, rooted web taxonomies that can be used to encode all local path information for each taxonomy element. This research is motivated by the problem of developing standards for taxonomic data, and addresses the data intensive problem of evaluating semantic similarities between taxonomic elements. Evaluating such similarities often requires the processing of large common ancestor sets between elements. We propose a new class of compact labelling schemes, designed for directed acyclic graphs, and tailored for applications to large web taxonomies. Our labelling schemes significantly reduce the complexity of evaluating similarities among taxonomy elements by enabling the gleaning of inferences from the labels alone, without searching the data structure. We provide an analysis of the label lengths for the proposed schemes based on structural properties of the taxonomy. Finally, we provide supporting empirical evidence for the quality of these schemes by evaluating the performance on the WordNet taxonomy.

1 Introduction

New distributed-information applications are being built on datasets associated with large-scale, web-accessible taxonomies. These applications motivate the study of compact representations of portions of this data that will enable better communication, and more efficient inferencing and information sharing. In this paper we propose a new class of compact representations which are applied to the problem of encoding all local path information in a large-scale, hierarchical taxonomy. The information concerning all paths in a local region of a taxonomy is important for many applications, including effectively deriving inferences within the data, and for effectively computing various semantic similarity measures between elements in the taxonomy. For example, the semantic similarity measures studied in the literature [3] and [12] are based on identifying common ancestor sets within a hierarchy, and identifying nearest common ancestors, in particular. Computing such similarity measures is complicated due to the data intensive nature and complexity of deriving all local paths. The methods

J. Wiedemann et al. (Eds.): SOFSEM 2006, LNCS 3831, pp. 511–520, 2006.

and models that we present in this paper significantly reduces the complexity of evaluating similarities, since we compactly encode all the relevant local path information in a single node label. Evaluating similarities can then be efficiently computed directly from a pair of node labels, with no other information required.

In this paper we model hierarchical taxonomies using a rooted (single source) directed acyclic graph (or dag), and we model all the localized paths by all the directed paths from the root to a particular node in the dag. We show that there are common structural properties of the dags underlying several well known web taxonomies, and that we can exploit these properties when constructing our encodings.

Formal Problem Statement: Given a rooted dag $D = (V, E)$, the problem of all local path encoding is defined as follows: 1) produce a labelling L of the nodes of V, where each node v in V is represented by $L(v)$, a unique identifier in binary. 2) for each node v in V, produce an encoded binary string $E(v)$ so that all paths from root to v can be reconstructed from $E(v)$ only, where reconstruction means that for each path $r = v_1, v_2, \ldots, v_k = v$ from root r to node v we can present the associated sequences of node labels $L(v_1), L(v_2), \ldots, L(v_k)$ for each node on that path.

Our Design Methodology for All Local Path Encoding: Our methodology is divided into three stages. In the first stage we choose a spanning tree of the dag and produce a binary labelling of the edges of the spanning tree in such a way that the out edges associated with a node v are unique, and in addition we use the fewest bits possible to do this. Next, for each node v we concatenate the labels of the edges on the unique path from root to node v in the tree; let $L'(v)$ denote this string. This labelling does not necessarily satisfy the uniqueness criteria needed for L, and thus can not be used as valid encoding. However, as we will show, this is a quite compact labelling, requiring for each node v only $\lfloor \log n \rfloor + \sigma_v$ bits, where n is the number of nodes in the dag and σ_v is the depth of v in the spanning tree (see Theorem 1). In the next stage, we produce a valid encoding of the nodes by solving the problem of delimiting each of the edges in $L'(v)$. There are several methods that can accomplish this, and we show that by considering the structure of the dag improved solutions are possible. The final stage of our methodology involves creating the final encoding $E(v)$ by creating a list of edges that do not lie on the spanning tree, yet are on some path from root r to v. Again various schemes are possible for encoding such an edge list, and we present and analyze several alternatives.

1.1   The Structure of Web Taxonomies

Through empirical evidence we have found four specific structural properties that are found in well known web taxonomies and have bearing on the problem of compact representations of the path information. These structural properties characterize a class of dags having the following four statistical properties: i) large out-degree (Δ) range and variance, ii) small in-degree (δ) range and variance, iii) small depth (σ) range and variance, and iv) small range and variance

Table 1. Statistics for the WordNet 2.1, ODP and Mathematics International Taxonomies

Taxonomy	Size	Property	Max	Min	Avg	Var
WordNet 2.1	81426	Indegree	6	0	1.027	0.029
		OutDegree	619	0	1.027	43.82
		Depth	17	0	7.193	4.825
		Paths	12	1	1.433	0.566
ODP [6]	253215	OutDegree	314	—	0.999	—
		Depth	14	0	8.83	—
Math.International [9]	211	OutDegree	43	—	1.6	—
		InDegree	9	—	1.6	—
		Depth	11	0	7.9	—

in the number of paths (ρ) from the root. See Table 1 for these statistical values for two large-scale taxonomies, Wordnet 2.1 and ODP taxonomy.

When considering encodings for the local path information in dags with such statistical properties, we have found two key issues must be addressed. First is the issue of very large variance in the out-degree, and the second is the delimitation of lists of edge identifiers for representing paths. To wit, consider a dag that has a maximum out-degree Δ^* that is much larger than the average out-degree. The naive representation for identifying each edge out of a node is to use a fixed length $\lceil \log \Delta^* \rceil$ bit string. However, the possibility exists that this fixed length representation is quite wasteful as compared to the potential of a variable length encoding. For example, from the Wordnet statistics (see Table 1), we have that $\Delta^* = 619$. Therefore, at least 10 bits (or possibly 2 bytes) would be required for each edge encoded. Whereas statistics, on the average out-degree of the (internal) nodes, show that on average we should require only 7 bits (or 1 byte) for each edge.

As an alternative we can consider variable length encodings for the edges. However, variable length representations require a delimitation scheme that must be carefully constructed if it is to outperform a fixed length representation. We present several methods for the effective delimitation of edges. These various methods offer alternatives for fine tuning an encoding of all-paths information based upon structural parameter values of directed acyclic graphs.

We show a variable length encoding scheme so that when it is applied to any n-node tree enables a representation of each root to node v path that uses at most $\sigma_v + \lfloor \log(n) \rfloor$ bits, where σ_v is the depth of node v in the tree. This result, however, is before delimitation which, in general, results in a constant factor overhead increase in the length result above. We present a variety of delimitation schemes that can be tailored to specific dags and thus can minimize the constant factors involved. We have applied our methods to the Wordnet 2.1 taxonomy for nouns, and we have shown that for certain delimitation schemes, the constant factors involved are less than $\frac{4}{3}$ (see lines 1 and 3 of Table 2).

Our encoding methods are applied in experiments with the Wordnet 2.1 noun taxonomy [10]. For our experiments we restrict this taxonomy to the

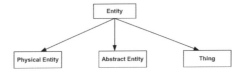

Fig. 1. The first two levels of the WordNet "is-a-hypernym-of" taxonomy

"is-a-hypernym-of" relation. A noun-concept a is said to be *a hypernym* of a noun-concept b, if b is a kind of a (e.g. 'animal' is a hypernym of 'dog'). This WordNet 2.1 taxonomy is a rooted taxonomy that has multiple inheritance in a limited extent, as seen from the indegree statistic in Table 1. The root of the taxonomy is the generic noun concept "entity", see Figure 1 for the top level of the hierarchy.

1.2 Related Work

Our focus in this paper is on encoding all local path information in rooted dags. Our methods build upon and extend previous approaches to the problem of tree labelling that support nearest common ancestor queries (NCA). An NCA u of nodes v and w in a dag D is an ancestor of both v and w, where u does not have descendants that are ancestors for both v and w. Labelling schemes for NCA queries have been shown to belong to a larger, more general family of graph labelling schemes that are called *informative labelling schemes* (see [11]). This family includes all label-based graph representations that will allow retrieving certain specific global properties using only local information. Properties that have been studied include, subsumption check, descendants, ancestors or NCAs, and graph distances [11].

In applications, labelling schemes for hierarchies such as Netscape Open Directory Portal have been considered in [6]. This approach is motivated by the problem of optimizing navigation through the Portal topic hierarchy. The labelling schemes are modelled to support subsumption, NCA, ancestor and descendant queries. Abiteboul et al. in [1] present two tree labelling schemes for answering ancestor queries in trees, with labels of size $\frac{5}{3}\log n + O(1)$ and $\frac{3}{2}\log n + O(\log\log n)$ bits respectively. These labelling schemes are applied to encoding XML trees, and they enable efficient execution of the ancestor queries in XML search engines.

Several papers have considered encoding of multiple inheritance with application to the design of compilers for handling subsumption (i.e., ancestor relations) in object-oriented languages, see e.g., [4], [5], [8]. These methods have been used to generate compact, fixed length codes by mapping types to subsets (of some base set) and thereby reduces the problem of testing type inclusion to testing subset inclusion. The effectiveness of these encoding methods for large, web-based hierarchies remains open.

Our results in this paper extend tree-based labellings, so that they are tailored to the case of the dag structure representing web taxonomies, such as WordNet.

We achieve logarithmic (or nearly logarithmic) label sizes, which are particularly effective for dags with limited depth and indegree. As we have noted above and in Table 1, many web taxonomies have small (logarithmic) depth and small (constant) indegree.

In Section 2, we describe the first phase of our encoding scheme which uses a prefix based approach to labelling trees: all nodes are labelled in such a way that for each node v there is a path to the root with each node on the path labeled with a prefix of vs label. We call this approach a 'greedy Dewey labelling' due to its natural relation to Dewey decimal classification commonly used for libraries. This first phase is called the "greedy Dewey labelling for trees (or, TGDL for short). In Section 3, we consider three potential delimiting schemes, applied to the first phase labelling. We analyze bounds on the label lengths required when applying each of these schemes. In section 4 we present the next phase of labelling which we call the extended greedy Dewey labelling for dags (or, EGDL for short). We show how the Dewey labelling and delimiting schemes can be used to extended to solve the problem of compact encoding of subgraphs of dags. Finally, in Section 5 we present empirical results of the application of our labelling schemes to the WordNet 2.1 taxonomy.

2   Greedy Labelling for Trees (TGDL)

Our labelling of rooted dags, underlying hierarchical taxonomies, includes two schemes: the first is called the Greedy Dewey Labelling for Trees (or TGDL) and the second is called the Extended Greedy Dewey Labelling for DAGs (or EGDL).

The TGDL labelling scheme is a prefix-based labelling scheme. The first phase of the TGDL labeling algorithm includes finding and extracting a Breadth-First (BF) tree T from a rooted dag D. After the BF tree is found, TGDL is performed as follows. The root r of the taxonomy (and the BF tree T) is labelled with the label TGDL$(r)=\epsilon$, where ϵ denotes an empty bit string. Each edge of the tree T is then assigned a GDL label which are obtained as follows. All children-edges $e_{c_1}, .., e_{c_j}$ of a parent node u are ordered in the non-decreasing order based on the size of the subtree rooted at the associated child. For each child-edge e_{c_i} of the node u, the GDL label is assigned uniquely, where the ith edge in the previously mentioned ordering is encoded with exactly $\lfloor \log_2(i+1) \rfloor$ bits.

Now using the GDL labellings of all the edges we recursively determine the TGDL labeling of all the nodes. For each non-root node v in the tree T, we set TGDL(v)=TGDL$(u)\cdot$ edel$(e_v)\cdot$GDL(e_v), where u is the parent of v in T, e_v is the edge from u to v, and edel(e_v) is some edge delimiting label (as yet unspecified). In the next section we consider delimiting schemes, which for now can be considered as encoding the length of the string GDL(e_v).

2.1   Analysis of the Length for the TGDL Labels

We perform an analysis of the TGDL labels length in two steps. In the first step, we assume that the edge delimiting labels are empty. This step is purely

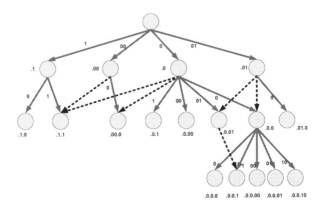

Fig. 2. TGDL labelling of nodes of tree given by solid edges. Non-tree edges are dashed, and dots in node labels denote edge delimiters.

theoretical and we use it primarily to estimate the lower bound of our labelling approach. In Section 3 we analyze the length of the TGDL labels given different schemes for creating the delimiting labels.

TGDL Labels Without Delimiters

Theorem 1. *Let T be a tree with n nodes. The TGDL algorithm labels each node v of T with at most $\sigma_v + \lfloor \log n \rfloor$ bits, where σ_v is the depth of v in T. Note this result ignores length of edge delimiters.*

Proof. Let n_u denote the size of the subtree of T rooted at node u. Consider any child-edge (u, v) in the tree T. The following expresses an upper bound number of bits used to GDL encode this edge: the expression:

$$\left\lfloor \log \frac{n_u}{n_v} + 1 \right\rfloor$$

This upper bound follows from the fact that the GDL labelling uses exactly $\lfloor \log(i+1) \rfloor$ bits to encode the edge incident to the ith largest subtree. For each i, the size of the ith largest subtree is less than the size of tree divided by i (i.e., $n_v < n_u/i$). Hence,

$$\lfloor \log(i+1) \rfloor \leq \left\lfloor \log \left(\frac{n_u}{n_v} + 1 \right) \right\rfloor \leq \left\lfloor \log \frac{n_u}{n_v} + 1 \right\rfloor.$$

Now consider any length-k tree path $v_0, v_1, \ldots, v_k$ from the root v_0 to the leaf node v_k. By definition, this path is of length σ_{v_k}. The total number of bits used to encode all edges on this path is bounded above by the sum:

$$\left\lfloor \log \frac{n_{v_0}}{n_{v_1}} \right\rfloor + 1 + \left\lfloor \log \frac{n_{v_1}}{n_{v_2}} \right\rfloor + 1 + \ldots + \left\lfloor \log \frac{n_{v_{k-1}}}{n_{v_k}} \right\rfloor + 1 \leq$$

$$\sigma_{v_k} + \left\lfloor \log \frac{n_{v_0}}{n_{v_1}} + \log \frac{n_{v_1}}{n_{v_2}} + \ldots + \log \frac{n_{v_{k-1}}}{n_{v_k}} \right\rfloor =$$

$$\sigma_{v_k} + \left\lfloor \log \frac{n_{v_0}}{n_{v_k}} \right\rfloor = \sigma_{v_k} + \lfloor \log n \rfloor$$

The proof of the theorem follows.

3   Delimiting Schemes

In this paper we analyze three different labelling schemes for edge delimiters, based on different methods for length encoding. The three delimiting schemes we investigated are called unary length encoding, fixed binary, and variable binary encoding.

3.1   Unary Length Encoding

In the unary length scheme, for a given edge e, the edge delimiting label for e is a bit string of length $|e| = |GDL(e)|$, $edel(e) = "(0)_{|e|-1}1"$, where $"(0)_{|e|-1}"$ denotes a $|e| - 1$ long zero bit string. The proof of the following corollary is immediate.

Corollary 1. *Let T be a tree with n nodes. If the unary length encoding scheme is used for encoding the edge delimiters, then the TGDL algorithm labels each node v of the tree with at most $2(\sigma_v + \lfloor \log(n) \rfloor)$ bits, where σ_v is the depth of v in T.*

3.2   Fixed Binary Length Encoding

In the fixed binary labelling scheme, an edge delimiter for some edge e is the binary representation of the length for GDL(e). All edge delimiters are encoded with the fixed number of bits chosen to be of sufficiently large length, and at most of length $\lceil \log \log(\Delta^* + 1) \rceil$, where Δ^* is the maximum node out-degree that is found in the given tree. We have the following corollary.

Corollary 2. *Let T be a tree with n nodes. If the fixed binary length encoding scheme is used for encoding the edge delimiters, then the TGDL algorithm labels each node v of the tree with at most $\sigma_v + \lfloor \log n \rfloor + \sigma_v \lceil \log \lfloor \log(\Delta^* + 1) \rfloor \rceil$ bits, where Δ^* is the maximum node out-degree in T, and σ_v is the depth of v in T.*

3.3   Variable Binary Length Encoding

In this labelling scheme, for a given node v_p and a given path $rv_1 \ldots v_p$ from the root to v_p in a tree T, each edge delimiter in this path is encoded with at most $\lceil \log \log(\Delta^*_{path_{v_p}} + 1) \rceil$ bits. $\Delta^*_{path_{v_p}}$ is the maximum node out-degree for the nodes on the given path. Additional bit string of length approximately of $\lceil \log \log \log(\Delta^* + 1) \rceil$ bits is preceding the edge encodings. This bit-string is used to determine the maximum length of the edge encoding in the given path. We have the following corollary.

Corollary 3. *Let T be a tree with n nodes. If the variable binary length encoding scheme is used for encoding the edge delimiters, then the TGDL algorithm labels each node v of the tree with at most $\sigma_v + \lfloor \log n \rfloor + \sigma_v \lceil \log \lfloor \log(\Delta^*_{pathv} + 1) \rfloor \rceil + \lceil \log \lceil \log \lfloor (\Delta^* + 1) \rfloor \rceil \rceil$ bits, where Δ^* is the maximum node out-degree in T, σ_v is the depth of v in T, and Δ^*_{pathv} is the maximum out-degree for nodes on the path from the root to v in T.*

4   Extended Greedy for DAGs(EGDL)

Our goal for extending the 'greedy Dewey' labelling from the last section in order to design a compact encoding for each node of a large taxonomy, represented with a dag. All relevant path information should be effectively computable using only the information in the encoding of the node. Since we are considering the path structure of a dag D, we are interested in encoding for each node v of D the path-induced subgraph of v in D, call this $PS(v)$. This subgraph is defined as the unique minimal subdigraph of D that contains all the paths in the dag from the root to node v. Since our TGDL labelling implicitly encodes nodes as breadth-first paths from the root, we see that to encode $PS(v)$ we require only information about the edges that do not appear in the breadth-first tree. Focusing our representation on the non-tree edges can have great advantage for web taxonomies, for as we have noted above it is apparent in a number of web taxonomies that the number of paths ρ_v, that are present from the root to a vertex v is typically bounded by a small number. It easily follows that the number of non-tree edges of any path-induced subgraph of D is smaller than the number of paths i.e., if m' is the number of non-tree edges in the subgraph $PS(v)$, then we have that $m' < \rho_v$. To generate the EGDL label for the node v, we simply concatenate together an edge list for all non-tree edges of the subgraph $PS(v)$.

Any edge of D can be represented by a pair of vertices. Therefore, in the EGDL labelling for D, each node v is represented as

$$EGDL(v) = ndel(v) \cdot TGDL(v) \cdot edge_{EGDL}(e_1) \cdot \ldots \cdot edge_{EGDL}(e_g),$$

where $edge_{EGDL}(e)$ is the EGDL encoding for the non-tree edges in $PS(v)$; and for each $e = (v_1, v_2)$.

$$edge_{EGDL}(e) = ndel(v_1) \cdot TGDL(v_1) \cdot ndel(v_2) \cdot TGDL(v_2),$$

The label $ndel(v)$ is a node delimiting label for v, and it can be implemented using the previously mentioned unary or fixed binary labelling schemes discussed in Section 3.

In the fixed binary labelling scheme, the node delimiter for v is encoded with at most $\lceil \log(\sigma^*) \rceil$ bits, where σ^* is the depth of the BF tree of D. The unary labelling scheme will label each node delimiter for v with at most $\sigma_v + 1$ bits, where σ_v is the depth of v in the BF tree. Note that node delimiters are non-empty for each node, including the root. Using the previously established values on the length labels, the following theorem is immediate.

Theorem 2. *Let m' be the number of non-tree edges in the subgraph $PS(v)$ of the dag D, and let σ^* be the depth of a BF tree of D. The Extended Greedy Dewey Labelling (EGDL) for a dag D labels each node with at most $O(m'(\sigma^* + \log(n)))$ bits.*

5 Experimental Results

In our experiments, we labelled the Wordnet 2.1 "hypernym of" taxonomy for nouns, using described TGDL and EGDL labelling algorithms. For encoding edge and node delimiters, we used two previously described delimiting schemes - the Unary Length Encoding and the Fixed Binary Length Encoding. Note that the TGDL labelling is applied to a breadth-first tree of the Wordnet taxonomy, whereas the EGDL scheme is applied to the full "hypernym-of" Dag.

We present statistics for the use of our encoding schemes applied to Word-Net 2.1 label lengths(see Table 2 and Figure 3). Note that the Unary Length

Table 2. Results of our encoding schemes applied to WordNet 2.1 taxonomy

Type of Encoding	Maximum Length	Avg. Length
Theorem 1 Bound	33	-
TGDL with Fixed Bin. Length Enc.	88	45.05
TGDL with Unary Length Enc.	40	24.24
EGDL with Fixed Bin. Length Enc.	611	64.90
EGDL with Unary Length Enc.	417	43.04

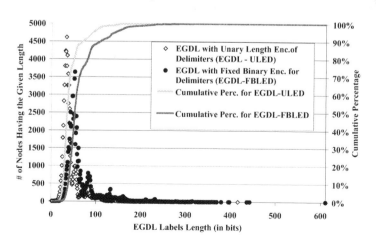

EGDL Length Distribution for WordNet

Fig. 3. Distribution of WordNet EGDL label length for fixed binary and unary encoding of delimiters

Encoding (for delimiters) almost matches the theoretical lower bound of our scheme (i.e., on the length of the TGDL without delimiters). The Fixed Binary Length Encoding for delimiters requires higher overheads. EGDL requires substantially more bits in the worst case, however, from Figure 3 we see that a very small number are near the maximum. The majority of nodes have the size of their EGDL labels significantly smaller, close to the average length (around length 50 bits).

References

1. Abiteboul, S., Kaplan, H., Milo, T.: Compact Labeling Schemes for Ancestor Queries. In Proceedings of 12th ACM-SIAM Symposium on Discrete Algorithms (2001) 547–556
2. Alstrup, S., Gavoille, C., Kaplan, H., Rauhe, T.: Nearest Common Ancestor: A Survey and a New Algorithm for a Distributed Environment. Theory of Computing Systems **37** (2004) 441–456
3. Budanitsky, A., Hirst, G.: Semantic Distance in WordNet: An Experimental, Application-Oriented Evaluation of Five Measures. Workshop on WordNet and Other Lexical Resources, Second Meeting of the North American Chapter of the Association for Computational Linguistics (2001)
4. Caseau, Y.: Efficient Handling of Multiple Inheritance Hierarchies. OOPSLA 93 (1993) 271–287
5. Caseau, Y. Habib, M., Nourine, L., Raynaud, O.: Encoding of Multiple Inheritance Hierarchies and Partial Orders. Computational Intelligence **15** (1999) 50–63
6. Christophides, V., Plexousakis, D., Scholl, M., and Tourtounis, S.: On Labeling Schemes for the Semantic Web. In Proceedings of the 13th World Wide Web Conference (2003) 544–555
7. Kaplan, H., Milo, T., Ronen, S.: A Comparison of Labeling Schemes for Ancestor Queries. In Proceedings of the 13th Annual ACM-SIAM Symposium on Discrete Algorithms (2000) 954–963
8. Krall, A., Vitek, J., Horspoool, R.N.: Near Optimal Hierarchical Encoding of Types. In Proceedings of Ecoop97, LNCS, SpringerVerlag **1241** (1997)
9. Maganaraki, A., Alexaki, S., Christophides, V., Plexousakis, D.: Benchmarking rdf Schemas for the Semantic Web. In Proc. of the First Inter. Semantic Web Conf. (ISWC'02) (2002) 132–147
10. Miller, G.: Wordnet: An On-Line Lexical Database. International Journal of Lexicography **3** 4 (1990)
11. Peleg, D.: Informative Labeling Schemes for Graphs. In 25th International Symposium on Mathematical Foundations of Computer Science (MFCS), In Lecture Notes in Comput. Sci., Springer, **1893** (2000) 579–588
12. Resnik, P. Semantic Similarity in a Taxonomy: An Information-Based Measure and its Application to Problems of Ambiguity in Natural Language, Journal of Artificial Intelligence Research **11** (1999) 95–130

Computational Complexity
of Relay Placement in Sensor Networks*

Jukka Suomela

Helsinki Institute for Information Technology HIIT,
Basic Research Unit, Department of Computer Science,
P.O. Box 68, FI-00014 University of Helsinki, Finland
jukka.suomela@cs.helsinki.fi

Abstract. We study the computational complexity of relay placement in energy-constrained wireless sensor networks. The goal is to optimise balanced data gathering, where the utility function is a weighted sum of the minimum and average amounts of data collected from each sensor node. We define a number of classes of simplified relay placement problems, including a planar problem with a simple cost model for radio communication. We prove that all of these problem classes are NP-hard, and that in some cases even finding approximate solutions is NP-hard.

1 Introduction

In this article, we study the problem of placing relay nodes in *wireless sensor networks*. Sensor networks [1]-[4] consist of a large number of sensor nodes which collect data. The collected data is routed via the network to a sink node. The nodes are battery powered, and when considering battery lifetime, radio communication is a key issue [5].

Falck *et al.* [6] formulate the problem of *balanced data gathering* in sensor networks. In this formulation, the utility function is a weighted sum of the minimum and average amounts of data gathered from the nodes before the batteries are drained. The goal is to collect a large total amount of data, but not at the cost of completely ignoring some parts of the monitored area. Falck *et al.* show that the problem of finding an optimal routing can be presented as a linear program.

If the optimum is not satisfactory, one solution could be to add a small number of new *relay nodes* to the network. The obvious question is how to determine the optimal locations of the relays. This is the *relay placement problem*. Falck *et al.* [6] consider this problem briefly in the context of balanced data gathering. However, the computational complexity of this problem has not yet been analysed.

We will formalise the relay placement problem in Section 2. We will define various special cases or simplified versions of the general relay placement problem.

---

* This work was supported in part by the Academy of Finland, Grant 202203, and by the IST Programme of the European Community, under the PASCAL Network of Excellence, IST-2002-506778. This publication only reflects the author's views.

J. Wiedermann et al. (Eds.): SOFSEM 2006, LNCS 3831, pp. 521–529, 2006.

We will then show in Section 3 that even these simplified versions are NP-hard, and we will show in Section 4 that in some cases even finding approximate solutions is NP-hard. Section 5 concludes this article.

2   Definitions of the Relay Placement Problems

An instance of the *balanced data gathering problem* [6], [7] is a tuple $B = (\lambda, S, R, \sigma, E, s, \tau, \rho)$. Here $\lambda \in [0, 1]$ is a balance parameter, S is a finite set of sensor nodes, R is a finite set of relay nodes, and σ is the sink node. The sets S, R and $\{\sigma\}$ are disjoint. Let $V = S \cup R \cup \{\sigma\}$. The function $E \colon V \to [0, \infty) \cup \{+\infty\}$ specifies the battery capacity of each node. The function $s \colon S \to [0, \infty) \cup \{+\infty\}$ specifies how much data is available at each sensor node. The parameter $\rho \in [0, \infty)$ is the cost of receiving one unit of data, and the function $\tau \colon V \times V \to [0, \infty) \cup \{+\infty\}$ maps a pair of nodes to the cost of sending one unit of data from the first node to the second one. The solution to the problem is a flow f, where $f_{\eta\kappa}$ is the amount of data transmitted from node $\eta \in V$ to node $\kappa \in V$. The value q_η denotes the amount of data gathered from a node $\eta \in S$. The utility of the flow is $\lambda \min_{\eta \in S} q_\eta + (1 - \lambda) \operatorname{avg}_{\eta \in S} q_\eta$.

An instance of the *relay placement problem* is a tuple $P = (\lambda, S, \mathcal{R}, \sigma, E, s, \tau, \rho)$; the set of all such tuples is $\mathcal{P}$. Here $\mathcal{R}$ is the set of *possible* relays, and the other parameters are as above. The sets S, $\mathcal{R}$, and $\{\sigma\}$ are disjoint. Let $\mathcal{V} = S \cup \mathcal{R} \cup \{\sigma\}$. The battery capacity function $E(\eta)$ must be defined for all possible nodes $\eta \in \mathcal{V}$, and the transmission cost function $\tau(\eta, \kappa)$ must be defined for all pairs of possible nodes $\eta, \kappa \in \mathcal{V}$. We will also assume that the location of the node, $l(\eta) \in \mathbb{R}^2$, is defined for all $\eta \in \mathcal{V}$. The solution is a finite subset R of possible relays $\mathcal{R}$. Given a relay placement instance P and its solution R, we can define the corresponding balanced data gathering instance $B = (\lambda, S, R, \sigma, E_{|V}, s, \tau_{|V \times V}, \rho)$, where $V = S \cup R \cup \{\sigma\}$. The utility of this solution, $U(P, R)$, is the maximum utility of B.

An instance of the *decision problem* is a tuple (P, N, u) where $P \in \mathcal{P}$, N is the number of relays, and u is the utility requirement. The answer to the decision problem is *yes* if and only if there is a solution R to the relay placement problem P such that $|R| = N$ and $U(P, R) \geq u$.

An instance of the *relay-constrained problem* is a pair (P, N) where $P \in \mathcal{P}$ and N is the number of relays. The solution is any $R \in \mathcal{R}$ with $|R| = N$. A solution R^* is optimal if it maximises $U(P, R^*)$. A solution $\tilde{R}$ is k-optimal if $U(P, \tilde{R}) \geq \frac{1}{k} U(P, R^*)$.

An instance of the *utility-constrained problem* is a pair (P, u) where $P \in \mathcal{P}$ and u is the utility requirement. The solution is any $R \in \mathcal{R}$ with $U(P, R) \geq u$. A solution R^* is optimal if it minimises $|R^*|$. A solution $\tilde{R}$ is k-optimal if $|\tilde{R}| \leq k|R^*|$.

A problem instance $P \in \mathcal{P}$ is *planar*, denoted by $P \in \mathcal{P}_P$, if the set of possible relays $\mathcal{R}$ is the plane $\mathbb{R}^2$, and $l(\eta) = \eta$ for all $\eta \in \mathcal{R}$. A problem instance $P \in \mathcal{P}$ has a *finite relay set*, denoted by $P \in \mathcal{P}_D$, if $\mathcal{R}$ is finite. A problem instance $P \in \mathcal{P}$ uses the *sensor upgrade model*, denoted by $P \in \mathcal{P}_U$, if $\mathcal{R} = l(S)$. Note that $\mathcal{P}_U \subseteq \mathcal{P}_D$.

A problem instance $P \in \mathcal{P}$ has *location-dependent* transmission costs, denoted by $P \in \mathcal{P}_L$, if $\tau(\eta, \kappa) = \tau'(l(\eta), l(\kappa))$ for some function τ'. A problem instance $P \in \mathcal{P}_L$ uses the *line-of-sight model*, denoted by $P \in \mathcal{P}_S$, if transmission costs can be defined by some parameters α, p, and O as follows: The finite set O consists of disjoint obstacles; each obstacle is a simple (i.e., not self-intersecting) polygon in the real plane. The transmission cost $\tau'(l_1, l_2)$ is infinite if the line segment $\overline{l_1 l_2}$ intersects some obstacle $o \in O$. Otherwise, $\tau'(l_1, l_2) = d_p(l_1, l_2)^\alpha$ where $d_p(\cdot, \cdot)$ denotes the distance measured using the p-norm[1]. A problem instance $P \in \mathcal{P}_S$ uses the *free space model*, denoted by $P \in \mathcal{P}_F$, if $O = \emptyset$.

A problem instance $P \in \mathcal{P}$ has *identical batteries*, denoted by $P \in \mathcal{P}_I$, if there is E such that $E(\eta) = E$ for all possible relays $\eta \in \mathcal{R}$.

We will denote $\mathcal{P}_x \cap \mathcal{P}_y$ by $\mathcal{P}_{xy}$, etc. One can construct a total of 32 relay placement problem classes: $\mathcal{P}, \mathcal{P}_P, \mathcal{P}_D, \ldots, \mathcal{P}_{UFI}$. We will denote the set of these classes by $\mathcal{P}^*$ and we will use $\mathcal{P}_x$ to refer an arbitrary member of $\mathcal{P}^*$.

3   All Problem Classes Are NP-Hard

PARTITION is a well-known NP-complete problem [13], [14]. An instance of the PARTITION problem consists of a list of positive integers, $(a_1, \ldots, a_n)$. A set $X \subseteq \{1, 2, \ldots, n\}$ is a feasible solution if $\sum_{i \in X} a_i = \sum_{i \notin X} a_i$. We will develop a polynomial reduction from PARTITION to $\mathcal{P}_{UFI}$ and $\mathcal{P}_{PFI}$.

Let a list of positive integers, $(a_1, \ldots, a_n)$, be given. We will assume that the sum of the integers is even; otherwise the answer to the problem would be trivially *no*. Construct a relay placement problem instance P as follows. First, define $a^* = \max a_i$, and $b = \frac{1}{2} \sum a_i$. Choose $\lambda = 0$, $p = 1$, $\alpha = 2$, and $\rho = 0$. Choose any values $z \geq (na^*)^{1/\alpha}$, $y \geq z + 1$, and $x \geq ny$.

Construct the problem geometry as shown in Fig. 1. Firstly, there are 2 sensors, η and η', with $E(\eta) = E(\eta') = bx^\alpha$, $s(\eta) = s(\eta') = b$, $l(\eta) = (z/2 + 1/2 + x/2, -z/2 - 1/2 - x/2)$, and $l(\eta') = -l(\eta)$. Then, there are n diagonal rows of nodes, each row corresponding to one integer in the PARTITION problem. The centre points of these rows are $l_i = ((2i - n - 1)y/2, (2i - n - 1)y/2)$. On each row, there are two sensors, κ_i and κ_i', with $E(\kappa_i) = E(\kappa_i') = a_i$, $s(\kappa_i) = s(\kappa_i') = 0$, $l(\kappa_i) = l_i + (z/2 + 1/2, -z/2 - 1/2)$, and $l(\kappa_i') = l_i - (z/2 + 1/2, -z/2 - 1/2)$. Furthermore, on each row there are two sensors, μ_i and μ_i', with $E(\mu_i) = E(\mu_i') = 0$, $s(\mu_i) = s(\mu_i') = 0$, $l(\mu_i) = l_i + (z/2, -z/2)$, and $l(\mu_i') = l_i - (z/2, -z/2)$. The only purpose of these nodes is to act as possible relay locations in the sensor upgrade model. Finally, on each row there is one sensor, ν_i, with $E(\nu_i) = z^\alpha$, $s(\nu_i) = 1$, and $l(\nu_i) = l_i$. The location of the sink is $l(\sigma) = (x/2 + y, x/2 + y)$ and the battery capacity of the sink is irrelevant as the reception cost is zero. For the battery capacity of the relays, choose any value $E \geq (a^* + 1)(2x + 2y)^\alpha$.

The total number of sensor nodes is $m = 5n + 2$, and the total amount of available data is $2b + n$ units. The utility of any solution is thus at most

---

[1] This simple power law has both theoretical [8] and practical [9]-[11] foundations, and non-Euclidean distance metrics may be a useful approximation in certain urban environments [12].

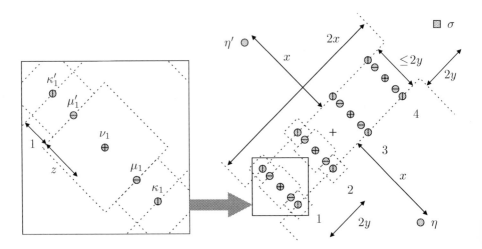

Fig. 1. Reduction from PARTITION to $\mathcal{P}_{UFI}$ and $\mathcal{P}_{PFI}$. In this example, the corresponding PARTITION problem instance consisted of four integers. The diagonal rows labelled with numbers 1–4 correspond to the four integers.

$U^* = (2b + n)/m$. We can now formulate the following decision problem instance: P is the relay placement problem instance constructed above, the number of relays N is n, and the utility requirement u equals U^*. We will show that this formulation is indeed a polynomial reduction from PARTITION to $\mathcal{P}_{UFI}$ and $\mathcal{P}_{PFI}$.

Lemma 1. *Constructing the problem instance is possible in polynomial time.*

Proof. We may choose $z = na^*$, $y = z + 1$, $x = ny$, and $E = (a^* + 1)(2x + 2y)^{\alpha}$. The total number of nodes in the constructed problem is $O(n)$. The parameters of each node can be calculated in polynomial time: keeping in mind that $\alpha = 2$, all expressions above only involve integer or rational numbers, and the size of each integer is polynomial in the size of the input.

Lemma 2. *If the answer to the PARTITION problem instance is yes, the answer to the relay placement problem instance constructed above is yes, both in the $\mathcal{P}_{UFI}$ and in the $\mathcal{P}_{PFI}$ formulation.*

Proof. Let X be a feasible solution to the PARTITION problem. Denote the set $\{1, \ldots, n\} \setminus X$ by X'. For each $i \in X$, place a relay on μ_i, transmit a_i units of data from η to κ_i, forward a_i units of data from κ_i to the relay at μ_i, transmit 1 unit of data from ν_i to the relay at μ_i, and forward $a_i + 1$ units of data from the relay at μ_i to the sink. For each $i \in X'$, place a relay on μ'_i, and construct flows as above for η' and κ'_i.

Lemma 3. *If the answer to the PARTITION problem instance is no, the answer to the relay placement problem instance constructed above is no, both in the $\mathcal{P}_{UFI}$ and in the $\mathcal{P}_{PFI}$ formulation.*

Proof. Let us assume that the answer to the relay placement problem instance is *yes*. This is possible only if all available data from all sensor nodes is forwarded to the sink node.

Let us first study the node ν_i for some i. Due to its limited battery capacity, the sensor has to send at least some of its data to a node whose distance is at most z units. No sink or sensor node with a positive battery capacity is available within the area of distance z from ν_i. Thus, at least one relay node has to be located in this area. As there are n such areas, all non-overlapping, there must be exactly one relay node in each area.

Let us denote by X the indexes of the areas where the relay is closer to η than to η'. Denote $\{1, \ldots, n\} \setminus X$ by X'. As the answer to the PARTITION problem was no, $\sum_{i \in X} a_i \neq \sum_{i \in X'} a_i$. Without loss of generality, we assume that $\sum_{i \in X} a_i < \sum_{i \in X'} a_i$. Clearly $\sum_{i \in X} a_i < b$. As b and a_i are integral, $\sum_{i \in X} a_i \leq b - 1$.

The sensor η has to send b units of data to other nodes. The node has enough energy resources for transmitting b units of data to the distance of exactly x units. If some part of the data was sent over a larger distance, another part would have to be sent to a node whose distance is less than x units; however, no sensor or sink node is available closer than this, and all relays are already tied to the proximity of nodes ν_i. Thus, the only possibility is to send all data to nodes κ_i, each exactly x units from the source node. Let the amount of data transmitted from η to κ_i be c_i. Clearly $\sum c_i = b$ and $c_i \geq 0$.

Now, $\sum_{i \in X} a_i \leq b - 1 = \sum (c_i - 1/n)$. At least one of the following holds: there is $i \in X$ such that $a_i \leq c_i - 1/n$, or there is $i \in X'$ such that $c_i \geq 1/n$. If neither holds, then $\sum_{i \in X} a_i > \sum_{i \in X} (c_i - 1/n) \geq \sum (c_i - 1/n)$, a contradiction.

Let us first assume that there is i such that $i \in X$ and $a_i \leq c_i - 1/n$. In this case the node κ_i would have to transmit at least $a_i + 1/n$ units of data to some other node. The distance to the closest node is at least 1 unit. Thus, the transmission cost is at least $a_i + 1/n$, exceeding the available battery capacity a_i, a contradiction.

On the other hand, if there is i such that $i \in X'$ and $c_i \geq 1/n$, the node κ_i would have to transmit at least $1/n$ units of data to some other node. As $i \in X'$, the distance to the closest relay node is at least $z + 1$ units. The only node less than $z + 1$ units from κ_i is ν_i, and it does not have any battery capacity for forwarding data. Thus, we need to transmit at least $1/n$ units of data to a distance of at least $z + 1$ units, requiring at least $(1/n)(z + 1)^\alpha$ units of energy. Here $(1/n)(z + 1)^\alpha \geq (1/n)((na^*)^{1/\alpha} + 1)^\alpha > (1/n)((na^*)^{1/\alpha})^\alpha = (1/n)(na^*) = a^* \geq a_i = E(\kappa_i)$. Again, a contradiction. Thus the assumption must be false.

Theorem 1. *The decision versions of all relay placement problem classes in $\mathcal{P}^*$ are NP-hard.*

Proof. From the list of problem definitions in Section 2 we see that for any relay problem class $\mathcal{P}_x$ in $\mathcal{P}^*$, either $\mathcal{P}_{UFI} \subseteq \mathcal{P}_x$ or $\mathcal{P}_{PFI} \subseteq \mathcal{P}_x$. The theorem follows from Lemmas 1, 2, and 3.

Theorem 2. *The decision version of the relay placement problem class $\mathcal{P}_D$ is NP-complete.*

Proof. Use (R, f) as a certificate for a *yes* instance of the decision problem.

4   For Some Problem Classes, Approximation Is NP-Hard

SET COVERING is another well-known NP-complete problem [13, 14]. An instance of the SET COVERING problem consists of a finite collection of finite sets, $\mathcal{A} = \{A_1, \ldots, A_n\}$, and a positive integer m. A subcollection $\mathcal{X} \subseteq \mathcal{A}$ is a feasible solution if $|\mathcal{X}| \leq m$ and $\bigcup \mathcal{X} = \bigcup \mathcal{A}$. We will now develop a polynomial reduction from SET COVERING to $\mathcal{P}_{DSI}$ and $\mathcal{P}_{PSI}$.

Let $\mathcal{A} = \{A_1, \ldots, A_n\}$ and m be given. Let $a = |\bigcup \mathcal{A}|$. Without loss of generality we will assume that $\bigcup \mathcal{A} = \{1, \ldots, a\}$. Construct a relay placement problem instance P as follows. Choose $\lambda = 1$, $p = 2$, $\alpha = 2$, and $\rho = 0$. Define $x = 4m$ and $y = 2x(a + n)$. Construct the problem geometry as shown in Fig. 2.

On the left-hand side of part (a), we have $a + 2n - 1$ triangular *nests*. The first $n - 1$ nests are empty. The next a nests, Λ_1 to Λ_a, correspond to integers $\{1, \ldots, a\}$, where the nest Λ_i contains the sensor node η_i, with $E(\eta_i) = 1$, $s(\eta_i) = 1$. The next nest, Λ_σ, contains the sink node σ. The last $n - 1$ nests are empty.

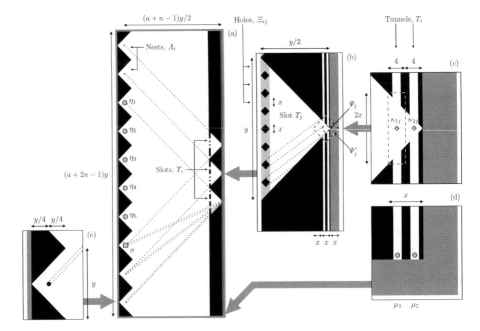

Fig. 2. Reduction from SET COVERING to $\mathcal{P}_{DSI}$ and $\mathcal{P}_{PSI}$. This figure illustrates the case of $m = 2$, $n = 3$, and $a = 5$. Some details are shown in a larger scale.

On the right-hand side, we have n triangular *slots*, Υ_1 to Υ_n. Each slot corresponds to one element of $\mathcal{A}$. Let us now have a closer look at one of these slots, let it be slot Υ_j. See Fig. 2 (b) for an illustration. On the leftmost side of the slot, we have $a + n - 1$ diamond-shaped obstacles. Between the diamond-shaped obstacles, we have $a + n$ holes. The first $n - j$ holes are unused. The next a holes, Ξ_{1j} to Ξ_{aj}, correspond to the sensors η_1 to η_a, and the next hole, $\Xi_{\sigma j}$ corresponds to the sink σ. Finally, there are $j - 1$ unused holes.

Let us now construct two diamond-shaped areas, Ψ_j and Ψ_j', as illustrated in Fig. 2 (b). All points $l \in \Psi_j$ satisfy the following conditions: for all i, there is a line of sight from l to η_i through Ξ_{ij}; and there is a line of sight from l to σ through $\Xi_{\sigma j}$. All points $l \in \Psi_j'$ satisfy the following conditions: for all i, if there is a line of sight from l to η_i, it necessarily passes through Ξ_{ij}; and if there is a line of sight from l to σ, it necessarily passes through $\Xi_{\sigma j}$.

Now, we will block the hole Ξ_{ij} if and only if $i \notin A_j$. Let us denote by X_l the set of indexes j such that η_j is still visible from the location l. We can make two observations: If $l \in \Psi_j$, then $X_l = A_j$. If $l \in \Psi_j'$, then $X_l \subseteq A_j$.

We will also need m narrow, vertical tunnels, T_1 to T_m, in the rightmost part of the construction; see parts (c) and (d) for an illustration. Each tunnel consists of a 1-unit-wide wall, a 2-unit-wide tunnel, and a 1-unit-wide wall, and we will refer to the *interior* of this 4-unit-wide area as T_i'. For each i, place a sensor node μ_i at the bottom of tunnel T_i, with $E(\mu_i) = 1$ and $s(\mu_i) = 1$. Note that all points in T_i are visible from μ_i, and no point outside T_i' is visible from μ_i.

At the intersection of the tunnel T_i and the slot Υ_j there is a possible relay location κ_{ij}. Note that this location is inside area Ψ_j. Finally, the construction is surrounded by four walls, shown in the figure in grey colour.

All relays have a battery capacity of 1 unit. We can now formulate the following relay-constrained optimisation problem instance: P is the relay placement problem instance constructed above, and the number of relays N is m.

Lemma 4. *Constructing this relay placement problem instance is possible in polynomial time.*

Proof. The construction involves generating a problem instance with $O(a + n)$ sensors, $O(nm)$ possible relays, and $O((a+n)n)$ quadrilateral or triangular obstacles. Calculating the parameters of each node and each obstacle can be performed in a polynomial time. The calculations only involve integers.

Lemma 5. *If the answer to the SET COVERING problem instance is yes, the optimal solution to the relay placement problem instance constructed above has a positive utility, both in the $\mathcal{P}_{DSI}$ and in the $\mathcal{P}_{PSI}$ formulation.*

Proof. Let $\mathcal{X}' = \{A_{c_1}, \ldots, A_{c_{m'}}\}$ be a solution to the SET COVERING problem, with $m' \leq m$. Choose, for example, $c_i = 1$ for all $i > m'$. Now $\mathcal{X} = \{A_{c_1}, \ldots, A_{c_m}\}$ is still a feasible solution. For each $i \in \{1, \ldots, m\}$, place a relay at κ_{ic_i}. This way all sensors can forward some data through relays.

Lemma 6. *If the answer to the SET COVERING problem instance is no, there is no solution with a positive utility, either in $\mathcal{P}_{DSI}$ or in $\mathcal{P}_{PSI}$.*

Proof. If the utility is positive, we have to gather some data from all sensors. For each i, there has to be at least one relay on T_i', let us call it ν_i. Thus, all m relays are bound to tunnels. Let $Y_i = X_{l(\nu_i)}$, and $\mathcal{Y} = \{Y_1, \ldots, Y_m\}$. To gather data from each η_j, we must have $\bigcup \mathcal{Y} = \bigcup \mathcal{A}$. If the relay ν_i is located in some Ψ_j', we choose $c_i = j$; otherwise the relay must be inside a tunnel, Y_i is $\emptyset$, and we can choose $c_i = 1$. For each i there is now a c_i such that $Y_i \subseteq A_{c_i}$. Define $\mathcal{Y}' = \{A_{c_1}, \ldots, A_{c_m}\}$. Now we have $\bigcup \mathcal{A} = \bigcup \mathcal{Y} \subseteq \bigcup \mathcal{Y}' \subseteq \bigcup \mathcal{A}$. Thus, $\mathcal{Y}'$ is a feasible solution to the SET COVERING problem instance.

Theorem 3. *Finding k-optimal solutions to the relay-constrained optimisation versions of problem classes $\mathcal{P}_x$ satisfying $\mathcal{P}_{DSI} \subseteq \mathcal{P}_x$ or $\mathcal{P}_{PSI} \subseteq \mathcal{P}_x$ is NP-hard.*

Proof. Let us assume that for some k, we have an oracle for solving the relay-constrained optimisation problems of class $\mathcal{P}_{DSI}$ or $\mathcal{P}_{PSI}$ k-optimally in constant time. We may then use the construction presented above to solve SET COVERING in polynomial time.

By Lemma 4, we may construct the relay placement problem instance in polynomial time. By Lemmas 5 and 6, the oracle will return a solution with a positive utility if and only if the answer to the SET COVERING problem is *yes*.

5 Conclusions

In this article, we have specified and studied a number of classes of relay placement problems. All classes have been proved NP-hard. For some important problem classes, approximation has been proved NP-hard as well. It is an open question whether it is possible to formulate a relay placement problem which is computationally tractable but still meaningful in practise. We may need to consider other utility functions in addition to the balanced data gathering formulation.

However, these results do not prevent us from optimising relay placement. One possibility is to use a heuristic approach [6], which is computationally effective. While it does not guarantee optimality, it may still be useful in practical problems. There are also algorithms for finding k-optimal solutions [15]. The time complexity of these algorithms may be high, but they have been successfully used for solving problem instances of moderate size.

Acknowledgements. Thanks to Patrik Floréen, Jyrki Kivinen, Tanja Säily, Jukka Kohonen, and Petteri Nurmi for discussions and comments.

References

1. Akyildiz, I.F., Su, W., Sankarasubramaniam, Y., and Cayirci, E.: Wireless Sensor Networks: a Survey. Computer Networks **38** (2002) 392–422
2. Al-Karaki, J.N., and Kamal, A.E.: Routing Techniques in Wireless Sensor Networks: a Survey. IEEE Wireless Communications **11** (2004) 6–28
3. Culler, D., Estrin, D., and Srivastava, M.: Guest Editors' Introduction: Overview of Sensor Networks. IEEE Computer **37** (2004) 41–49

4. Ephremides, A.: Energy Concerns in Wireless Networks. IEEE Wireless Communications **9** (2002) 48–59
5. Raghunathan, V., Schurgers, C., Park, S., and Srivastava, M.B.: Energy-Aware Wireless Microsensor Networks. IEEE Signal Processing Magazine **19** (2002) 40–50
6. Falck, E., Floréen, P., Kaski, P., Kohonen, J., and Orponen, P.: Balanced Data Gathering in Energy-Constrained Sensor Networks. In: Algorithmic Aspects of Wireless Sensor Networks: First International Workshop (ALGOSENSORS 2004, Turku, Finland, July 2004), Berlin Heidelberg, Springer-Verlag (2004) 59–70
7. Floréen, P., Kaski, P., Kohonen, J., and Orponen, P.: Exact and Approximate Balanced Data Gathering in Energy-Constrained Sensor Networks. Theoretical Computer Science (2005) To appear.
8. Rappaport, T.S.: Wireless Communications, Principles and Practice. Prentice Hall, Inc., Upper Saddle River (1999)
9. Andersen, J.B., Rappaport, T.S., and Yoshida, S.: Propagation Measurements and Models for Wireless Communications Channels. IEEE Communications Magazine **33** (1995) 42–49
10. Seidel, S.Y., and Rappaport, T.S.: 914 MHz Path Loss Prediction Models for Indoor Wireless Communications in Multifloored Buildings. IEEE Transactions on Antennas and Propagation **40** (1992) 207–217
11. Sohrabi, K., Manriquez, B., and Pottie, G.J.: Near Ground Wideband Channel Measurement in 800–1000 MHz. In: Proceedings of the 49th Vehicular Technology Conference (1999) 571–574
12. Goldsmith, A.J., and Greenstein, L.J.: A Measurement-Based Model for Predicting Coverage Areas of Urban Microcells. IEEE Journal on Selected Areas in Communications **11** (1993) 1013–1023
13. Karp, R.M.: Reducibility among Combinatorial Problems. In Miller, R.E., Thatcher, J.W., eds.: Complexity of Computer Computations, Plenum Press, New York (1972) 85–103
14. Garey, M.R., and Johnson, D.S.: Computers and Intractability: A Guide to the Theory of NP-Completeness. W. H. Freeman and Company, New York (2003)
15. Suomela, J.: Algorithms for k-Optimal Relay Placement in Sensor Networks (2005) Submitted for publication.

On the NP-Completeness of Some Graph Cluster Measures

Jiří Šíma[1,*] and Satu Elisa Schaeffer[2,**]

[1] Institute of Computer Science,
Academy of Sciences of the Czech Republic,
P. O. Box 5, 18207 Prague 8, Czech Republic
sima@cs.cas.cz

[2] Laboratory for Theoretical Computer Science,
Helsinki University of Technology,
P. O. Box 5400, FI-02015 TKK, Finland
elisa.schaeffer@tkk.fi

Abstract. Graph clustering is the problem of identifying sparsely connected dense subgraphs (clusters) in a given graph. Identifying clusters can be achieved by optimizing a fitness function that measures the quality of a cluster within the graph. Examples of such cluster measures include the conductance, the local and relative densities, and single cluster editing. We prove that the decision problems associated with the optimization tasks of finding clusters that are optimal with respect to these fitness measures are NP-complete.

1 Introduction

Clustering is an important issue in the analysis and exploration of data. There is a wide area of applications in data mining, VLSI design, parallel computing, web searching, relevance queries, software engineering, computer graphics, pattern recognition, gene analysis, etc. See also [13] for an overview. Intuitively clustering consists in discovering natural groups (clusters) of similar elements in a data set. The input data sets of current interesting application areas are very large, which motivates research on the complexity of finding and evaluating complete clusterings or single clusters, as such results will help to determine whether certain methods will be scalable for processing large data sets.

An important variant of data clustering is graph clustering where the similarity relation is expressed by a graph. The graph may either be a weighted graph with the similarity values captured by the edge weights, or an unweighted one, where the similarities have been thresholded or otherwise coded such that an edge is only placed between two vertices if the vertices are considered similar; the absence of an edge implies dissimilarity. In this paper, we restrict ourselves to unweighted, undirected graphs with no self-loops.

* Research partially supported by project 1M0545 of The Ministry of Education of the Czech Republic.
** Research supported by the Academy of Finland, grant 126235, and the Nokia Fndn.

J. Wiedermann et al. (Eds.): SOFSEM 2006, LNCS 3831, pp. 530–537, 2006.

We first recall some basic definitions from graph theory. Let $G = (V, E)$ be an *undirected* graph and denote by $E(S) = \{\{u, v\} \in E \mid u, v \in S\}$ the set of edges in a *subgraph* $G(S) = (S, E(S))$ *induced* by a subset of vertices $S \subseteq V$. We say that $S \subseteq V$ creates a *clique* of *size* $|S|$ if edges in $E(S) = \{\{u, v\} \mid u, v \in S, u \neq v\}$ join every pair of different vertices in S. Further denote by $d_G(v) = |\{u \in V \mid \{u, v\} \in E\}|$ the *degree* of vertex $v \in V$ in G. We say that graph G is a *cubic* graph if $d_G(v) = 3$ for every $v \in V$. Moreover, any subset of vertices $S \subseteq V$ creates a *cut* of G, that is a partition of V into disjoint sets S and $V \setminus S$. The *size* of cut S is defined as

$$c_G(S) = |\{\{u, v\} \in E \mid u \in S, v \in V \setminus S\}| \,, \tag{1}$$

and

$$d_G(S) = \sum_{v \in S} d_G(v) \tag{2}$$

denotes the sum of degrees in cut $S \subseteq V$.

A canonical definition of a graph cluster does not exist, but it is commonly agreed that a cluster should be a connected subgraph induced by a vertex set S with many internal edges $E(S)$ and few edges to outside vertices in $V \setminus S$ [5], [15]. In this paper we consider several locally computable fitness functions that are used for measuring the quality of a cluster within the graph. The prominent position among graph cluster measures is occupied by the *conductance* [4], [8], [9], [11], [15] which is defined for any cut $\emptyset \neq S \subset V$ in graph G as follows

$$\Phi_G(S) = \frac{c_G(S)}{\min(d_G(S), d_G(V \setminus S))}. \tag{3}$$

Furthermore, the *local density* $\delta_G(S)$ [23] (cf. the *average degree* [12]) of a subset $\emptyset \neq S \subseteq V$ in graph G is the ratio of the number of edges in subgraph $G(S)$ induced by S over the number of edges in a clique of size $|S|$ vertices, that is

$$\delta_G(S) = \frac{|E(S)|}{\binom{|S|}{2}} = \frac{2 \cdot |E(S)|}{|S| \cdot (|S| - 1)} \tag{4}$$

for S containing at least two vertices whereas we define $\delta_G(S) = 0$ for $|S| = 1$. Similarly, we define the *relative density* [19] of cut $\emptyset \neq S \subseteq V$ as follows

$$\varrho_G(S) = \frac{|E(S)|}{|E(S)| + c_G(S)}. \tag{5}$$

Yet another graph cluster measure which we call *single cluster editing* (cf. [21]) of a subset $S \subseteq V$ counts the number of edge operations (both additions and deletions) needed to transform S into an isolated clique:

$$\varepsilon_G(S) = \binom{|S|}{2} - |E(S)| + c_G(S). \tag{6}$$

Proposed clustering algorithms [4], [13], [19], [20] usually search for clusters that are optimal with respect to the above-mentioned fitness measures. Therefore the underlying optimization problems of finding the clusters that minimize the conductance or maximize the densities or that need a small single cluster editing are of special interest. In this paper we will formally prove that the associated decision problems for the conductance (Sect. 2), local and relative densities (Sect. 3), and single cluster editing (Sect. 4) are NP-complete. These complexity results appear to be well-known or at least intuitively credible, but not properly documented in the literature. However, such results are useful in choosing a fitness measure in the design or application of a clustering algorithm, and especially to justify the use of approximate methods as the amount of computation needed to identify the global optima cannot be expected to scale well for large problem instances.

2 Conductance

Finding a subset of vertices that has the minimum conductance in a given graph has been often stated to be an NP-complete problem in the literature [2], [4], [7], [9], [15], [17], [18]. However, we could not find an explicit proof anywhere. For example, the NP-completeness proof due to Papadimitrou [22] for the problem of finding the minimum *normalized cut* which is in fact the conductance of a weighted graph does not imply the hardness in the unweighted case. Thus we provide the proof in this section. The decision version for the conductance problem is formulated as follows:

Minimum Conductance (Conductance)
Instance: An undirected graph $G = (V, E)$ and a rational number $0 \leq \phi \leq 1$.
Question: Is there a cut $S \subset V$ such that $\Phi_G(S) \leq \phi$?

Theorem 1. Conductance *is NP-complete.*

Proof. Clearly, Conductance belongs to NP since a nondeterministic algorithm can guess a cut $S \subset V$ and verify $\Phi_G(S) \leq \phi$ in polynomial time. For the NP-hardness proof the following maximum cut problem on cubic graphs will be reduced to Conductance in polynomial time.

Maximum Cut for Cubic Graphs (Max Cut–3)
Instance: A cubic graph $G = (V, E)$ and a positive integer a.
Question: Is there a cut $A \subseteq V$ such that $c_G(A) \geq a$?

The Max Cut–3 problem was first stated to be NP-complete in [24] which became a widely used reference [10] although an explicit proof cannot be found there and we were unable to reconstruct the argument from the sketch. Nevertheless, the NP-completeness of Max Cut–3 follows from its APX-completeness presented in [1]. The following reduction to Conductance is adapted from that used for the minimum edge expansion problem [14].

Given a Max Cut–3 instance, i.e. a cubic graph $G = (V, E)$ with $n = |V|$ vertices, and a positive integer a, a corresponding undirected graph $G' = (V', E')$

for CONDUCTANCE is composed of two fully connected copies of the complement of G, that is $V' = V_1 \cup V_2$ where $V_i = \{v^i \mid v \in V\}$ for $i = 1, 2$, and $E' = E_1 \cup E_2 \cup E_3$ where $E_i = \{\{u^i, v^i\} \mid u, v \in V, u \neq v, \{u, v\} \notin E\}$ for $i = 1, 2$, and $E_3 = \{\{u^1, v^2\} \mid u, v \in V\}$. In addition, define the required conductance bound

$$\phi = \frac{1}{2n - 4}\left(n - \frac{2a}{n}\right). \tag{7}$$

The number of vertices in G' is $|V'| = 2n$ and the number of edges $|E'| = (2n - 4)n$ since

$$d_{G'}(v) = 2n - 4 \quad \text{for every } v \in V' \tag{8}$$

due to G being a cubic graph. It follows that G' can be constructed in polynomial time.

For a cut $\emptyset \neq S \subset V'$ in G' with $k = |S| < 2n$ vertices, denote by

$$S_i = \{v \in V \mid v^i \in S\} \quad \text{for } i = 1, 2 \tag{9}$$

the cuts in G that are projections of S to V_1 and V_2, respectively. Since $c_{G'}(S) = c_{G'}(V' \setminus S)$ it holds that $\Phi_{G'}(S) = \Phi_{G'}(V' \setminus S)$ according to definition (3). Hence, $k \leq n$ can be assumed without loss of generality when computing the conductance in G'. Thus,

$$\Phi_{G'}(S) = \frac{|S| \cdot |V' \setminus S| - c_G(S_1) - c_G(S_2)}{(2n - 4) \cdot |S|} \tag{10}$$

follows from condition (8) and the fact that G' is composed of two fully connected complements of G, which can be rewritten as

$$\Phi_{G'}(S) = \frac{1}{2n - 4}\left(2n - k - \frac{c_G(S_1) + c_G(S_2)}{k}\right). \tag{11}$$

Now we verify the correctness of the reduction by proving that the MAX CUT–3 instance has a solution if and only if the corresponding CONDUCTANCE instance is solvable. First assume that a cut $A \subseteq V$ exists in G whose size satisfies

$$c_G(A) \geq a. \tag{12}$$

Denote by

$$S^A = \{v^1 \in V_1 \mid v \in A\} \cup \{v^2 \in V_2 \mid v \in V \setminus A\} \subseteq V' \tag{13}$$

the cut in G' whose projections (9) to V_1 and V_2 are $S_1^A = A$ and $S_2^A = V \setminus A$, respectively. Since $|S^A| = n$ and $c_G(A) = c_G(V \setminus A)$ the conductance of S^A can be upper bounded as

$$\Phi_{G'}\left(S^A\right) = \frac{1}{2n - 4}\left(n - \frac{2c_G(A)}{n}\right) \leq \frac{1}{2n - 4}\left(n - \frac{2a}{n}\right) = \phi \tag{14}$$

according to equations (11), (12), and (7), which shows that S^A is a solution of the CONDUCTANCE instance.

For the converse, assume that the conductance of cut $\emptyset \neq S \subset V'$ in G' meets

$$\Phi_{G'}(S) \leq \phi. \tag{15}$$

Let $A \subseteq V$ be a maximum cut in G. For cut S^A defined according to (13) we prove that

$$\Phi_{G'}\left(S^A\right) \leq \Phi_{G'}(S) \tag{16}$$

which is rewritten to

$$\frac{1}{2n-4}\left(n - \frac{2c_G(A)}{n}\right) \leq \frac{1}{2n-4}\left(2n - k - \frac{c_G(S_1) + c_G(S_2)}{k}\right) \tag{17}$$

according to (14) and (11) where $k = |S| \leq n$ and S_1, S_2 are defined in (9). Since $2c_G(A) \geq c_G(S_1) + c_G(S_2)$ due to A being a maximum cut in G, it suffices to show

$$n - k + \left(\frac{1}{n} - \frac{1}{k}\right)(c_G(S_1) + c_G(S_2)) \geq 0 \tag{18}$$

which follows from $\frac{1}{n} - \frac{1}{k} \leq 0$ and $c_G(S_1) + c_G(S_2) \leq |S_1| \cdot n + |S_2| \cdot n = kn$. Thus,

$$\frac{1}{2n-4}\left(n - \frac{2c_G(A)}{n}\right) = \Phi_{G'}\left(S^A\right) \leq \Phi_{G'}(S) \leq \phi = \frac{1}{2n-4}\left(n - \frac{2a}{n}\right) \tag{19}$$

holds according to (14), (16), (15), and (7), which implies $c_G(A) \geq a$. Hence, A solves the MAX CUT–3 instance. □

3   Local and Relative Density

The decision version of the maximum density problem is formulated as follows:

Maximum Density (DENSITY)
Instance: An undirected graph $G = (V, E)$, a positive integer $k \leq |V|$, and a rational number $0 \leq r \leq 1$.
Question: Is there a subset $S \subseteq V$ such that $|S| = k$ and the density of S in G is at least r?

We distinguish between LOCAL DENSITY and RELATIVE DENSITY problems according to the particular density measure used which is the local density (4) and the relative density (5), respectively. Clearly, LOCAL DENSITY is NP-complete since this problem for $r = 1$ coincides with the NP-complete CLIQUE problem [16]. Also the NP-completeness of RELATIVE DENSITY can easily be achieved:

Theorem 2. RELATIVE DENSITY *is NP-complete.*

Proof. Obviously, RELATIVE DENSITY belongs to NP since a nondeterministic algorithm can guess a cut $S \subseteq V$ of cardinality $|S| = k$ and verify $\varrho_G(S) \geq r$ in polynomial time. For the NP-hardness proof the following minimum bisection problem on cubic graphs which is known to be NP-complete [6] will be reduced to RELATIVE DENSITY in polynomial time.

Minimum Bisection for Cubic Graphs (MIN BISECTION–3)
Instance: A cubic graph $G = (V, E)$ with $n = |V|$ vertices and a positive integer a.
Question: Is there a cut $S \subseteq V$ such that $|S| = \frac{n}{2}$ and $c_G(S) \leq a$?

Given a MIN BISECTION–3 instance, i.e. a cubic graph $G = (V, E)$ with $n = |V|$ vertices, and a positive integer a, a corresponding RELATIVE DENSITY instance consists of the same graph G, parameters $k = \frac{n}{2}$ and

$$r = \frac{3n - 2a}{3n + 2a}. \tag{20}$$

Now for any subset $S \subseteq V$ such that $|S| = k = \frac{n}{2}$ it holds that

$$|E(S)| = \frac{3|S| - c_G(S)}{2} = \frac{3n - 2c_G(S)}{4} \tag{21}$$

due to G being a cubic graph, which gives

$$\varrho_G(S) = \frac{3n - 2c_G(S)}{3n + 2c_G(S)} \tag{22}$$

according to (5). It follows from (20) and (22) that $\varrho_G(S) \geq r$ iff $c_G(S) \leq a$.   □

4   Single Cluster Editing

The problem of deciding whether a given graph can be transformed into a collection of cliques using at most m edge operations (both additions and deletions) which is called CLUSTER EDITING is known to be NP-complete [3], [21]. When the desired solution must contain exactly p cliques, the so called P–CLUSTER EDITING problem remains NP-complete for every $p \geq 2$. Here we study the issue of whether a given graph contains a subset S of exactly k vertices such that at most m edge additions and deletions suffice altogether to turn S into an isolated clique:

Minimum Single Cluster Editing (1–CLUSTER EDITING)
Instance: An undirected graph $G = (V, E)$, positive integers $k \leq |V|$ and m.
Question: Is there a subset $S \subseteq V$ such that $|S| = k$ and $\varepsilon_G(S) \leq m$?

Theorem 3. 1–CLUSTER EDITING *is NP-complete.*

Proof. Obviously, 1–CLUSTER EDITING belongs to NP since a nondeterministic algorithm can guess a subset $S \subseteq V$ of cardinality $|S| = k$ and verify $\varepsilon_G(S) \leq m$ in polynomial time. For the NP-hardness proof the MIN BISECTION–3 problem is used again (cf. the proof of Theorem 2) which will be reduced to 1–CLUSTER EDITING in polynomial time.

Given a MIN BISECTION–3 instance, i.e. a cubic graph $G = (V, E)$ with $n = |V|$ vertices, and a positive integer a, a corresponding 1–CLUSTER EDITING instance consists of the same graph G, parameters $k = \frac{n}{2}$ and

$$m = \frac{12a + n(n - 8)}{8}. \tag{23}$$

Now for any subset $S \subseteq V$ such that $|S| = k = \frac{n}{2}$ it holds that

$$\varepsilon_G(S) = \frac{|S| \cdot (|S| - 1)}{2} - \frac{3|S| - c_G(S)}{2} + c_G(S) = \frac{12c_G(S) + n(n - 8)}{8} \tag{24}$$

according to (6) and (21). It follows from (23) and (24) that $\varepsilon_G(S) \leq m$ iff $c_G(S) \leq a$.   □

5   Conclusion

In this paper we have presented the explicit NP-completeness proofs for the decision problems associated with the optimization of four possible graph cluster measures; namely the conductance, the local and relative densities, and single cluster editing. In addition, the results for relative density and single cluster editing are also valid for cubic graphs (by construction). In clustering algorithms, combinations of fitness measures are often preferred as only optimizing one may result in anomalies such as selecting small cliques or connected components as clusters. An open problem is the complexity of minimizing the *product* of the local and relative densities [20] (e.g. their sum is closely related to the edge operation count for the single cluster editing problem). Another important area for further research is the complexity of finding related approximation solutions [2].

References

1. Alimonti, P., Kann, V.: Some APX-Completeness Results for Cubic Graphs. Theoretical Computer Science **237** 1-2 (2000) 123–134
2. Arora, S., Rao, S., and Vazirani, U.: Expander Flows, Geometric Embeddings and Graph Partitioning. Proceedings of the STOC'04 Thirty-Sixth Annual ACM Symposium on Theory of Computing, New York: ACM Press (2004) 222–231
3. Bansal, N. Blum, A., and Chawla, S.: Correlation Clustering. Machine Learning **56** 1-3 (2004) 89–113
4. Brandes, U., Gaertler, M., and Wagner, D.: Experiments on Graph Clustering Algorithms. Proceedings of the ESA 2003 Eleventh European Symposium on Algorithms, LNCS, Berlin: Springer-Verlag **2832** (2003) 568–579
5. Broder, A., Kumar, S.R., Maghoul, F., Raghavan, P., Rajagopalan, S., Stata, R., Tomkins, A., and Wiener, J.: Graph Structure in the Web. Computer Networks **33** 1-6 (2000) 309–320
6. Bui, T.N., Chaudhuri, S., Leighton, F.T., and Sipser, M.: Graph Bisection Algorithms with Good Average Case Behavior. Combinatorica **7** 2 (1987) 171–191

7. Carrasco, J.J., Fain, D.C., Lang, K.J., and Zhukov, L.: Clustering of Bipartite Advertiser-Keyword Graph. The ICDM 2003 Third IEEE International Conference on Data Mining, Workshop on Clustering Large Data Sets, Melbourne, Florida (2003)
8. Cheng, D., Kannan, R., Vempala, S., and Wang, G.: A Divide-and-Merge Methodology for Clustering. Proceedings of the PODS 2005 Twenty-Fourth ACM Symposium on Principles of Database Systems, Baltimore, June 2005
9. Flake, G.W., Tsioutsiouliklis, K., and Tarjan, R.E.: Graph Clustering Techniques Based on Minimum-Cut Trees. Technical report 2002-06, NEC, Princeton, NJ (2002)
10. Garey, M.R., and Johnson, D.S.: Computers and Intractability: A Guide to the Theory of NP-completeness. San Francisco: W. H. Freeman & Co. (1979)
11. Gkantsidis, C., Mihail, M., and Saberi, A.: Conductance and Congestion in Power Law Graphs. Proceedings of the SIGMETRICS 2003 ACM International Conference on Measurement and Modeling of Computer Systems, New York: ACM Press (2003) 148–159
12. Holzapfel, K., Kosub, S., Maaß, M.G., and Täubig, H.: The Complexity of Detecting Fixed-Density Clusters. Proceedings of the CIAC 2003 Fifth Italian Conference on Algorithms and Complexity, LNCS **2653**, Berlin: Springer-Verlag (2003) 201–212
13. Jain, A.K., Murty, M.N., and Flynn, P.J.: Data Clustering: A Review. ACM Computing Surveys **31** 3 (1999) 264–323
14. Kaibel, V.: On the Expansion of Graphs of 0/1-Polytopes. Technical report arXiv:math.CO/0112146 (2001)
15. Kannan, R., Vempala, S., and Vetta, A.: On Clusterings: Good, Bad and Spectral. Proceedings of the FOCS'00 Forty-First Annual Symposium on the Foundation of Computer Science, New York: IEEE Computer Society Press (2000) 367–377
16. Karp, R.M.: Reducibility among Combinatorial Problems. In R.E. Miller and J.W. Thatcher (eds), Complexity of Computer Computations, New York: Plenum Press (1972) 85–103
17. Leighton, T., and Rao, S.: Multicommodity Max-Flow Min-Cut Theorems and Their Use in Designing Approximation Algorithms. Journal of the ACM **46** 6 (1999) 787–832
18. Lovász, L.: Random Walks on Graphs: A Survey. Bolyai Society Mathematical Studies, 2, Combinatorics, Paul Erdös is Eighty, Budapest: Bolyai Mathematical Society **2** (1996) 353–397
19. Mihail, M., Gkantsidis, C., Saberi, A., and Zegura, E.: On the Semantics of Internet Topologies. Technical Report GIT-CC-02-07, College of Computing, Georgia Institute of Technology, Atlanta, GA (2002)
20. Schaeffer, S.E.: Stochastic Local Clustering for Massive Graphs. Proceedings of the PAKDD 2005 Ninth Pacific-Asia Conference on Knowledge Discovery and Data Mining, LNCS **3518**, Berlin, Springer-Verlag (2005) 354–360
21. Shamir, R., Sharan, R., and Tsur, D.: Cluster Graph Modification Problems. Proceedings of the WG 2002 Twenty-eighth International Workshop on Graph-Theoretic Concepts in Computer Science, LNCS **2573**, Berlin: Springer-Verlag (2002) 379–390
22. Shi, J., and Malik, J.: Normalized Cuts and Image Segmentation. IEEE Transactions on Pattern Analysis and Machine Intelligence **22** 8 (2000) 888–905
23. Virtanen, S.E.: Properties of Nonuniform Random Graph Models. Technical Report HUT-TCS-A77, Laboratory for Theoretical Computer Science, Helsinki University of Technology, Espoo, Finland (2003)
24. Yannakakis, M.: Node- and Edge-Deletion NP-Complete Problems. Proceedings of the STOC'78 Tenth Annual ACM Symposium on Theory of Computing, New York: ACM Press (1978) 253–264

A Flexible Policy Architecture
for Mobile Agents

Suat Ugurlu and Nadia Erdogan

Istanbul Technical University, Computer Engineering Department,
Ayazaga, 34390 Istanbul, Turkey
suat@suatugurlu.com, erdogan@cs.itu.edu.tr

Abstract. Recent advances in distributed computing has lead software
agents to be mobile and/or composed of distributed resources. In order
to perform certain tasks, mobile agents may require access to resources
available on remote systems. Although appealing in terms of system design and extensibility, mobile agents are a security risk and require strong
access control. Further, the mobile code environment is fluid where resources located on a host may change rapidly, necessitating an extensible
security model. This makes difficult to dynamically change agent ability
and host security strategies in order to adapt to evolving conditions of
the execution environment. In this paper, we present the design and implementation of a policy-based secure mobile agent platform (SECMAP).
The platform makes use of agent and host policies for security and flexibility concerns. Its main strength is that it allows security policies to be
specified or modified dynamically at runtime, resulting in high adapt-
ability of agents and hosts to varying system state and requirements.

1 Introduction

Intelligent agents and multi-agent systems bring in a new approach to the design and implementation of complex distributed systems. Several multi-agent
systems have been implemented either as commercial products or in various
research projects, with varying success [1]-[7]. Reasons for the growing recognition of agent technology are the innovative solutions it provides to problems
of more traditionally designed distributed systems through mobility of code,
machine based intelligence, and improved network and data-management possibilities. Using mobile agent technologies provides potential benefits to applications, however, an agent's ability to move introduces significant security risks.
Both mobile agents during their life times and hosts executing mobile agents are
under security threats [8], [9].

Mobile code environments, however, have two important characteristics. They
are dynamic - mobile programs come and go rapidly, and the resources present
on a host may change. They are also unpredictable - administrators might not
know ahead of time the source, behavior, or requirements of the programs that
migrate to their host. There is no fixed set of resources that a host administers.
Further, because the different components of resources and mobile programs may

J. Wiedermann et al. (Eds.): SOFSEM 2006, LNCS 3831, pp. 538–547, 2006.

require different levels of protection, security models must support fine-grained access control. This paper describes a new mobile agent platform, Secure Mobile Agent Platform (SECMAP) and its policy architecture. Unlike other agent systems, SECMAP proposes a new agent model, the shielded agent model, for security purposes. A shielded agent is a highly encapsulated software component that ensures complete isolation against unauthorized access of any type. SECMAP presents a policy-driven framework to support adaptive and dynamic behavior of agents, providing a secure environment through host and agent policies. SECMAP allows dynamic manipulation of policy content, which results in an adaptive and flexible framework that eliminates the reprogramming of the agents on changing conditions.

2   SECMAP Architecture

A brief overview of SECMAP architecture[8] is necessary before the description of the policy architecture. We have used Java for the implementation of the execution environment because it offers several features that ease the development process. The main component of the architecture is a Secure Mobile Agent Server (SMAS) that is responsible of all agent related tasks such as creation, activation, communication, migration and execution of policies. The system comprises of several SMAS executing on each node which acts as a host for agents. A SMAS may operate in three modes according to the functionality it exhibits. It can be configured to execute in any of the three modes on a host through a user interface. A SMAS on a node can also operate in all three modes at the same time.

Standard Mode(S-SMAS): S-SMAS provides standard agent services such as agent creation, activation, inactivation, destruction, communication, and migration. It also includes a policy engine that checks agent activity and resource utilization according to the rules that are present in host and agent policy file. In addition, S-SMAS maintains a list of all active agents resident on the host and notifies the Master Browser SMAS anytime an agent changes state. Keeping logs of all agent activities is another important task S-SMAS carries out.

Master Browser Mode (MB-SMAS): When agents are mobile, location mappings change over time, therefore agent communication first requires a reference to the recipient agent to be obtained. In addition to supporting all functionalities of S-SMAS, MB-SMAS also maintains a name-location directory of all currently active agents in the system. This list consists of information that identifies the host where an agent runs and is kept up to date as information on the identities and status (active/inactive) of agents from other SMAS is received.

Security Manager Mode (SM-SMAS): In addition to supporting all functionalities of S-SMAS, SM-SMAS performs authentication of all SMAS engines and maintains security information such as DES keys and certificates. Any SMAS engine in the system has to be authenticated before it can start up as a trusted server. SM-SMAS holds an IP address and key pair for each of SMAS engine that wants to be authenticated. If the supplied key and the IP address of the requesting SMAS engine is correct then it is authenticated. The authenticated SMAS engine gets a ticket from the SM-SMAS and uses this ticket when communicating with other SMAS engines. A SMAS that receives a request from another SMAS refers to SM-SMAS to verify the validity of its ticket before proceeding with the necessary actions to fulfill the request.

SECMAP provides a secure communication framework for mobile agents [9]. Agent communication is secured by transferring encrypted message content by SSL protocol and is managed in a location transparent way. SECMAP also supports weak migration of agents between remote hosts.

2.1 SECMAP Agents

SECMAP requires agents to conform to a software architectural style, which is identified by a basic agent template given below. The agent programmer is provided a flexible development environment with an interface for writing mobile agent applications. He determines agent behavior according to the agent template given and is expected to write code that reflects the agent's behavior for each of the public methods. For example, code for the *OnCreate()* method should specify initial actions to be carried out while the agent is being created, or code for the *OnMessageArrive()* method should define agent reaction to message arrival.

```
public class Main extends Agent{
public void OnMessageArrive(){...}
public void OnCreate(){ ... }
public void OnActivate(){...}
public void OnInactivate(){... }
public void OnTransfer(){... }
public void OnEnd(){... }}
```

An instance of class *AgentIdentity* is defined for the agent on an initial creation. All agents in the system are referenced through their unique identities, which consist of three parts. The first part, a random string of 128 bytes length, is the unique identification number and, once assigned, never changes throughout the life time of the agent. The second part is the name which the agent has announced for itself and wishes to be recognized with. While the first two parts are static, the third part of the identity has a dynamic nature: it carries location information, that is, the address of the SMAS on which the agent is currently resident, and varies as the agent moves among different nodes. This dynamic approach to agent identity facilitates efficient message passing.

3 Security Policies

SECMAP provides a highly configurable security environment by supporting policy-driven integration of mobile agent activity with system level services and resources. Policies define how allocation of resources is to be carried out and how security should be ensured. A policy is represented by a number of rules, where each rule is triggered by an event and consists of an action if a condition is evaluated to true. Thus, a security policy specifies the conditions under which a request is to be granted. If a request does not violate a policy rule, it is allowed to proceed; if it does violate a policy rule, it is blocked. The system-wide security policies are defined by agent developers as well as by system administrators.

A mobile agent is expected to adapt itself to environmental changes immediately. Such dynamic behavior in mobile agent systems requires mechanism where agent reprogramming is not needed. Hosts also need to easily reconfigure their resources in order to provide more flexible environments for the mobile agents. SECMAP's approach to achieve such flexibility is by means of dynamic policies that allow the agent programmer to change his agent's abilities without reprogramming the agent and the system administrator to reconfigure the execution environment on changing conditions. Thus, SECMAP employs policies mainly for two reasons: security and dynamism. The platform supports the specification of two kinds of security policies.

Host Policy: Host policies are concerned with the security of the host and its execution environment. They ensure that the local resources of the host are protected from unauthorized actions by the agent, by either granting or denying agent requests according to local policies.

Agent Policy: Agent policies are specified by the creator of the agent and define the capabilities of the agent to carry out requests on remote hosts. Those access privileges may be dynamically updated on changes in policy content. Agent policies also serve to protect the agent against malicious hosts or other agents through restrictions on communication, migration, etc.

Java has a default *Security Manager* which is initially disabled for applications. The Security Manager is a single Java object that performs runtime checks on potentially unsafe method calls. Code in the Java library consults the Security Manager whenever an operation of this nature is attempted. Decisions made by the Security Manager take into account the origin of the requesting class. The Security Manager makes the final decision as to whether a particular operation is to be permitted or rejected. In case of a reject decision, the operation is prevented to proceed by generating a *Security Exception.*

SECMAP agent servers utilize a strong custom policy engine that is derived from Java's default security manager. It replaces Java's default policy manager with an infrastructure that presents a flexible configuration interface for policies to be defined and assigned to agents and hosts. Opposite to Java's static policy definitions, the infrastructure allows policy rules to be inspected and manually modified at runtime so that policies can be dynamically adjusted to new, changing requirements and circumstances.

A SECMAP agent can issue two kinds of calls; SMAS calls or JAVA API calls, as shown in Figure 1. Through SMAS calls, the agent announces its requests to migrate, to communicate (send or receive messages), or to publish itself through the agent interface. Both kinds of calls are intercepted by the *Policy Engine* to

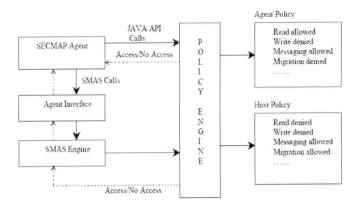

Fig. 1. The operation of the Policy Engine

check policy violations, and they are either allowed to proceed, or are blocked, according to agent and host policy definitions. Even though we are not able to catch every Java API call, we do intercept every call that Java's default security manager supports. These are;

- File system functions (read, write, delete)
- Networking functions (socket creation for listening and opening connection)
- Class loader functions
- Functions accessing system resources (print queues, clipboards, event queues, system properties, and windows)

The operation of the Policy Engine is as follows:

- An agent or the SECMAP platform itself makes a call to a potentially unsafe operation in the Java API, or an agent makes a communication or migration call.
- The call is intercepted by the Policy Engine to be checked for any policy violations.
- The Policy Engine determines the source of the call, if the call is issued by SECMAP, the operation is permitted to proceed, if the call is issued by an agent, the Policy Engine finds out its agent identity in order to refer to its specific policy definitions. In case the operation is permitted by the agent policy, the Policy Engine next refers to the host policy. If host policy permits the operation as well, then the Policy Engine allows the call to continue with a no-error return. On the other hand, if either agent policy or host policy, or both, do not permit the operation, Policy Engine returns a SecurityException, thus blocking the call.

3.1   Agent Policies

Each SECMAP agent is assigned an agent policy which includes "creator granted capabilities", when the agent is first deployed into the system by the agent programmer. The agent policy simply defines the types of actions that the agent can perform in its execution environment (Migration, messaging, writing to disk, reading from disk, etc.) Agent policies are maintained as encrypted XML files and carried with the agent itself as it moves between nodes. SECMAP keeps all of agent class files in a single zipped encrypted file and stores it together with the agent policy and data file in a secure place in the host disk. When an agent is to be activated, SMAS first loads the agent's classes and its final state information from its code and state files. Next, it creates an "Agent Policy" object for the agent. The *AgentShield* object that isolates the agent from its environment associates this policy object with the agent and updates the policy values from the agent's policy file before activating the agent. If agent policy is modified at runtime by the agent programmer, SMAS updates the agent policy file on host disk as well.

The platform presents a flexible graphical interface window for the agent owner to monitor his agents on the network and to manually change their policies if necessary to adapt to changing conditions at any time during execution. An agent policy can only be changed by the agent owner.

3.2   Host Policies

Host policies mainly serve security reasons by denying unauthorized agent access to host resources. Security and flexibility generally are not tolerant to each other; however, SECMAP policy architecture presents a flexible environment for mobile agents while it can still protect the host from intrusted agents that come from unknown sources. Host policy rules are defined considering two criteria: the agent owner and the agent source.

Agent Owner: Agent owner is the location where the agent is created and deployed into the system. It simply consists of the IP address of the host where the agent was created. The agent owner information is carried with the agent and does not change throughout its life time.

Agent Source: Agent source is the location from where the agent has migrated. It consists of the IP address of the host where the agent was running previously. This information is not carried with the agent since, on a migration request; the target agent server is provided with the information where agent is coming from and where it wants to move. The host administrator can define different host policy rules for different agent owners and agent sources.

As can be seen in the Figure 2, the administrator can assign different policies for different agent owners so that some agents whose owners are trusted will possess more rights than others whose owners are not trusted as much. It is possible to restrict all or particular actions of agents whose owners are not trusted. It is also possible to define rules that will enable the host to reject migration requests of agents from a specific agent owner or source. Sending to and receiving messages from intrusted agent sources can also be similarly restricted.

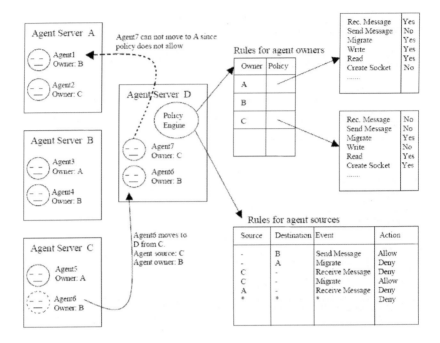

Fig. 2. A snap shot of agents and host policy rules at runtime

The platform provides the host administrator a flexible graphical window interface to specify host policies. Rules for both agent owners and for agent sources are checked for inconsistencies. For example if there is a rule stating that agents can not send messages to Agent Server B, then a new rule stating agents can send messages to Agent Server B will not be allowed to be defined.

Since there may be a large number of agent owners and agent sources in a network, it is not convenient for the administrator or agent programmer to define policy rules for each one of them separately. For example, the administrator may wish to grant certain rights to particular agent owners or sources while denying the rest, or he may wish to deny particular agent owners or sources while permitting the others. To ease rule specification in such conditions, there is a default policy rule at the end of the host policy that determines the course of action in case there is not a matching rule for a specific owner or source. This default rule is represented by the symbol "*" in Figure 2.

3.3 Performance Evaluation

While policies provide both security and execution time flexibility, one drawback may be a performance overhead being introduced. We have carried out tests in order to analyze the performance affect of policy usage in SECMAP. We've chosen "disk write" action of an agent as a sample operation. In terms of policy execution, the type of operation has no influence on the results obtained as the agent server's policy engine proceeds in exactly the same way for each type of operation. The tests are carried out on a PC with celeron 2.4 GHz CPU, 512 MB RAM.

We first carried out the test with all policy features disabled and computed the time required when access requests are not checked against policy rules. Next, we enabled the policy features and repeated the test with different numbers of policy rules, to see the influence of varying numbers of policy rules in the host policy on performance. Table 1 shows the result, the elapsed time measured for each test. The agent code executed for the tests is also given below.

```
1-   byte[] text = "Hello I am the helloworld agent".getBytes();
2-   FileOutputStream fo = null;
3-       for (int j = 1; j <= 10; j++) {
4-           long startTime = System.currentTimeMillis();
5-           for (int i = 1; i <= 50000; i++) {
6-               File a = new File("agentdata.txt");
7-               a.createNewFile(); //Policy engine interruption
8-               fo = new FileOutputStream(a);
9-               fo.write(text);
10-              fo.close(); }
11-          long endTime = System.currentTimeMillis();
12-          System.out.println("Elapsed Time = ");
13-          System.out.println(endTime - startTime);}
14-      }
```

When we analyze the results, we see that the use of policies brings a performance overhead of about %13 ((35823-31691)/31691) for operations which require a security check. This decrease in performance may be overlooked when the benefits of policy usage is considered. We also see that the number of rules in host policy has no effect on the performance attained. This is because policy rules are kept in a hash table in the memory and are searched for in a very time-effective manner.

Table 1. The elapsed time measured for each test

Test	Policy Disabled	Policy Enabled Number of Rules:1	Policy Enabled #Rules:10	Policy Enabled #Rules:30
1	31875ms	35562ms	35828ms	35032ms
2	30735ms	35735ms	33906ms	35500ms
3	29891ms	35781ms	36219ms	37171ms
4	34579ms	35469ms	37640ms	35110ms
5	29985ms	35813ms	34485ms	35937ms
6	28750ms	36531ms	36578ms	36500ms
7	36421ms	35281ms	35203ms	33625ms
8	32829ms	35250ms	37500ms	37906ms
9	31047ms	36672ms	35687ms	35016ms
10	30797ms	36140ms	35969ms	36781ms
Avg	31691ms	35823ms	35902ms	35858ms

4   Related Work

Several mobile agent systems have been proposed and developed up to now. They all have their software agent specific features. Although most of them have enough features for mobile agents to communicate with each other and migrate to remote hosts, a flexible policy-based management is not available in any. Because mobile agents require a dynamic environment where conditions and requirements may change rapidly, necessary changes should be done without reprogramming agents. SECMAP's policy architecture gives this opportunity to agent programmers and administrators. Gallery [10] introduces a framework to authorize mobile agents and determines whether or not a mobile agent should be executed on a particular platform. SECMAP includes both authentication and authorization mechanism while it is possible to give an agent detailed access rights. The work in[11] implements a policy-based solution to control only mobile agent mobility. In [12], the researchers have developed an authorization platform that supports definition and enforcement of history-based security policies, allowing hosts to decide on the authorization of an agent's action upon its past behaviour. As a whole, we see that work has focused on policy-based solutions for the problems in mobile environments with different approaches. A contribution of SECMAP is that, it not only supports mobile agent services in a secure way, but it also presents a policy-based management.

5   Conclusions and Future Work

This paper describes the policy architecure of a secure mobile agent platform. SECMAP provides an isolated, secure execution environment for mobile agents. It also presents a policy based management framework to protect system-level resources and agents against unauthorized access, as well. The policy architecture allows for dynamic manipulation of policy content, which results in an adaptive and flexible framework that eliminates the reprogramming of the agents on changing conditions.

Future work will concentrate on definition of policy rules that specify further details on rights granted, possibly narrowing the scope of rules. For example, it will be possible to restrict disk access rights to specific files. The only unsafe action for the host that an agent may perform and which we do not control with security policies is memory and CPU utilization functions. An agent may consume host memory and CPU time, running in an endless loop, and currently SECMAP doesn't have the capability to realize and stop this kind of action. We have already worked on some methods to measure the amount of memory that an agent is using and have obtained some good results. However, this kind of low level checks ended with different results in different JVM. After completing our work successfully, we plan to restrict the memory usage of agents using policies.

References

1. Voyager, http://www.recursionsw.com/products/voyager/voyager.asp
2. Aglets, http://www.trl.ibm.com/aglets/

3. http://www.genmagic.com/technology/odyssey.html
4. Stanford Univ., JATLite,
   http://www-cdr.stanford.edu /ProcessLink/ papers/ jat
5. http://www.cs.dartmouth.edu/ dfk/papers/gray:security-book.ps.gz
6. Bryce, C., and Vitek, J.: The JavaSeal Mobile Agent Kernel. Autonomous Agents and Multi-Agent Systems **4** (2001) 359–384
7. Concordia, http://www.merl.com/projects/concordia
8. Ugurlu, S., and Erdogan N.: An Overview of the SECMAP Secure Mobile Agent Platform. AAMAS05 – 2nd International Workshop on Safety and Security in Multiagent Systems (SASEMAS '05), Utrecht, The Netherlands (July 2005)
9. Ugurlu, S., and Erdogan, N.: A Secure Messaging Architecture for Mobile Agents. To appear in the LNCS proceedings of The 20th International Symposium on Computer and Information Sciences, Istanbul, Turkey (October 2005)
10. Gallery, E.: Towards a Policy Based Framework for Mobile Agent Authorisation in Mobile Systems. Mobile VCE Research Group, Royal Holloway, University of London (2003)
11. Montanari, R., Lupu, E., Stefanelli, C.: Policy-Based Dynamic Reconfiguration of Mobile-Code Applications. ISSN: 0018-9162, Computer **37** 7 (July 2004) 73
12. Dias, P., Riberio, C., Ferreira, P.: Enforcing History-Based Security Policies in Mobile Agent Systems. Fourth IEEE International Workshop on Policies for Distributed Systems and Networks (POLICY'03) (2003) 231

An Improved Digital Signature with Message Recovery Using Self-certified Public Keys Without Trustworthy System Authority

Eun-Jun Yoon and Kee-Young Yoo

Department of Computer Engineering, Kyungpook National University,
Daegu 702-701, South Korea
ejyoon@infosec.knu.ac.kr, yook@knu.ac.kr

Abstract. In 2005, Chang et al. proposed a digital signature scheme with message recovery using self-certified public keys without trustworthy system authority. The current paper demonstrates that Chang et al.'s authenticated encryption scheme (CCH-AEDSMR) is vulnerable to the known plaintext-ciphertext attack in that the attacker can easily recover all messages from the signature that sent between the signer and the specified receiver. We propose an improvement to the scheme in order to overcome this weakness.

Keywords: Cryptography, Self-certified public key, Message recovery, Digital signature, Known plaintext-ciphertext attack.

1 Introduction

A digital signature is very important in modern electronic data processing systems. A digital signature is analogous to an ordinary hand-written signature and it establishes both sender authenticity and data authenticity. The signer uses his private key to generate a signature for the given message, and the verifier uses the signer's public key to verify the signature. In order to provide integrity, authentication, and non-repudiation services, the digital signature schemes play an important role [1], [2], [3]. Confidentiality means that it is computationally infeasible for an adaptive adversary to obtain any secret information from a ciphertext. Authenticity (unforgeability) means that it is computationally infeasible for an adaptive adversary to masquerade as the sender in sending a message. Non-repudiation means that it is computationally feasible for a third party to settle a dispute between the sender and the receiver in the event the sender denies the fact that he is the originator of the message.

The digital signature schemes can be classified into two general classes: Digital signature schemes with an appendix; and digital signature schemes with message recovery [4]. In the signature schemes with message recovery, the message can be recovered from the signature but the message cannot be obtained from the signature in the signature schemes with an appendix. Due to message recovery properties, an authenticated encryption scheme is proposed by integrating

J. Wiedermann et al. (Eds.): SOFSEM 2006, LNCS 3831, pp. 548–555, 2006.

the public key cryptosystem and the digital signature scheme. With the exception of integrity, authentication, and non-repudiation services, the authenticated encryption scheme can provide confidentiality services for messages [5].

In 1991, Girault [6] introduced the notion of a self-certified public key. Recently, Tseng et al. [7] proposed a digital signature scheme with message recovery (TJC-DSMR) that is an extension of the self-certified public key system. Also, Tseng et al. presented two variations of the proposed digital signature scheme; one authenticated encryption scheme (TJC-AEDSMR) allows only the specified receiver to verify and recover messages while the other is an extension of the authenticated encryption scheme with message linkages (TJC-AEDSMRML). This is used to prevent message blocks from being reordered while larger messages are transmitted. Tseng et al. supposed that there exists a trusted system authority (SA).

In 2005, however, Chang et al. [8] pointed out that Tseng et al.'s schemes were vulnerable to SA's forgery attacks because the SA is not guaranteed to be honest in practice. Hence, Cange et al. proposed improved digital signature schemes (CCH-DSMR, CCH-AEDSMR, CCH-AEDSMRML) that provide the same properties as Tseng et al.'s method, without the assumption that the SA is trustworthy.

Nevertheless, the current paper demonstrates that Chang et al.'s authenticated encryption scheme (CCH-AEDSMR) is vulnerable to the known plaintext-ciphertext attack. That is, an attacker can easily recover all messages from the signature that are sent between the signer and the specified receiver. Furthermore, we propose improvements to the scheme in order to overcome this weakness.

The remainder of our paper is organized as follows: In Section 2, we review Chang et al.'s CCH-AEDSMR scheme. An outline of the known plaintext-ciphertext attack on Chang et al.'s CCH-AEDSMR scheme is proposed in Section 3. The improved scheme is presented in Section 4, while Section 5 discusses the security of the proposed scheme. Our conclusions are presented in Section 6.

2   Review of Chang et al.'s CCH-AEDSMR Scheme

In this section, we briefly review Chang et al.'s CCH-AEDSMR scheme [8], which allows only the specified receiver to verify and recover messages. Chang et al.'s CCH-AEDSMR scheme is divided into three phases: system initialization phase, signature generation phase, and message recovery phase.

2.1   System Initialization Phase

In the system initialization phase, the SA generates system parameters. First, the SA chooses two large primes p and q such that $p = 2p' + 1$ and $q = 2q' + 1$, where p' and q' are also primes. The SA computes $n = p \cdot q$ and selects a base element g of order $p' \cdot q'$. The SA makes p, q, p' and q' secret and publishes g, n, and a one-way hash function $h(\cdot)$ to all users. $h(\cdot)$ accepts a variable-length input string of bits to produce a fixed-length output string of bits and $h(m) < \min(p', q')$, where m denotes the input string and $\min(p', q')$ denotes the minimal values of p' and q'.

When a user U_i, whose identity is d_i, wants to join the system, U_i randomly chooses a secret key x_i and computes

$$y_i = g^{x_i} \bmod n.$$

Then, U_i sends d_i and y_i to the SA. The SA computes and publishes

$$p_i = (y_i - d_i)^{h(d_i)^{-1}} \bmod n$$

as U_i's public key. Finally, U_i checks whether

$$p_i^{h(d_i)} + d_i = g^{x_i} \bmod n$$

so as to determine whether p_i is a valid public key.

2.2   Signature Generation Phase

When U_i wants to sign message M to a specified receiver U_j, the generation procedure of the signature is performed as follows:

U_i chooses a random number k and computes r_1, r_2 and s as follows:

$$r_1 = M \cdot (p_j^{h(d_j)} + d_j)^{-k} \bmod n,$$
$$r_2 = M \cdot (p_j^{h(d_j)} + d_j)^{-k \cdot r_1} \bmod n,$$
$$s = r_1 \cdot k - x_i \cdot h(r_2).$$

Then, U_i sends the signature (r_1, r_2, s) to the verifier U_j.

2.3   Message Recovery Phase

After receiving the signature (r_1, r_2, s), the verifier U_j uses d_i, p_i and x_j to recover the signed message M by computing

$$M = r_2 \cdot (g^s \cdot (p_i^{h(d_i)} + d_i)^{h(r_2)})^{x_j} \bmod n.$$

Finally, in order to verify the recovered message M, the verifier U_j checks whether

$$(r_1 \cdot M^{-1})^{r_1} \bmod n = r_2 \cdot M^{-1} \bmod n$$

holds.

3   Known Plaintext-Ciphertext Attack on Chang et al.'s CCH-AEDSMR Scheme

In this section, we will show that Chang et al.'s CCH-AEDSMR scheme cannot withstand the known plaintext-ciphertext attack. That is, an attacker E can recover all messages from the signature that are sent between the signer and the specified receiver. Suppose that E obtains two signature messages, (r_1, r_2, s, M) and (r_1', r_2', s', M'), such that $h(r_2)$ and $h(r_2')$ are relatively prime. Then, E can perform the known plaintext-ciphertext attack as follows:

Shared information: n. g. $h(\cdot)$. p_i. d_i. p_j. d_j.
Information held by Signer: secret key x_i.
Information held by Verifier: secret key x_j.

Signer U_i   **Verifier U_j**

Signature generation phase:
Choose $k \in GF(q)$
$r_1 = M \cdot (p_j^{h(d_j)} + d_j)^{-k} \bmod n$
$r_2 = M \cdot (p_j^{h(d_j)} + d_j)^{-k \cdot r_1} \bmod n$
$s = r_1 \cdot k - x_i \cdot h(r_2)$

$$\xrightarrow{\quad (r_1, r_2, s) \quad}$$

Message recovery phase:
Recover $M = r_2 \cdot (g^s \cdot (p_i^{h(d_i)} + d_i)^{h(r_2)})^{x_j} \bmod n$
Verify $(r_1 \cdot M^{-1})^{r_1} \bmod n = r_2 \cdot M^{-1} \bmod n$

Fig. 1. Chang et al.'s CCH-AEDSMR Scheme

(1*) Since the two signature messages (r_1, r_2, s) and (r'_1, r'_2, s') satisfy equations (1) and (2);

$$
\begin{aligned}
M &= r_2 \cdot (g^s \cdot (p_i^{h(d_i)} + d_i)^{h(r_2)})^{x_j} \\
&= r_2 \cdot (g^{s \cdot x_j} \cdot (p_i^{x_j})^{h(r_2)}) \\
&= r_2 \cdot p_j^s \cdot (p_i^{x_j})^{h(r_2)} \bmod n
\end{aligned}
\tag{1}
$$

$$
\begin{aligned}
M' &= r'_2 \cdot (g^{s'} \cdot (p_i^{h(d_i)} + d_i)^{h(r'_2)})^{x_j} \\
&= r'_2 \cdot (g^{s' \cdot x_j} \cdot (p_i^{x_j})^{h(r'_2)}) \\
&= r'_2 \cdot p_j^{s'} \cdot (p_i^{x_j})^{h(r'_2)} \bmod n
\end{aligned}
\tag{2}
$$

if E acquires the unknown secret common key

$$p_i^{x_j} = g^{x_i \cdot x_j} \bmod n,$$

then, E can easily recover any messages by signed U_i or U_j.

(2*) Since $h(r_2)$ and $h(r'_2)$ are relatively prime, it is easy to find coefficients a and b, such that $a \cdot h(r_2) + b \cdot h(r'_2) = 1$, by using the Extended Euclidean algorithm [4], [9].

(3*) From Equations (1) and (2), it can be seen that

$$M \cdot (r_2 \cdot p_j^s)^{-1} = (p_i^{x_j})^{h(r_2)} \bmod n \tag{3}$$

$$M' \cdot (r'_2 \cdot p_j^{s'})^{-1} = (p_i^{x_j})^{h(r'_2)} \bmod n \tag{4}$$

By using coefficients a and b, E can obtain the secret common key

$$p_i^{x_j} = g^{x_i \cdot x_j} \bmod n$$

between the users U_i and U_j with the following computation:

$$(M \cdot (r_2 \cdot p_j^s)^{-1})^a \cdot (M' \cdot (r_2' \cdot p_j^{s'})^{-1})^b$$
$$\equiv ((p_i^{x_j})^{h(r_2)})^a \cdot ((p_i^{x_j})^{h(r_2')})^b$$
$$\equiv (p_i^{x_j})^{h(r_2) \cdot a} \cdot (p_i^{x_j})^{h(r_2') \cdot b}$$
$$\equiv (p_i^{x_j})^{h(r_2) \cdot a + h(r_2') \cdot b}$$
$$\equiv p_i^{x_j} \bmod n$$

(4*) By using this secret common key $p_i^{x_j}$, E can easily recover any message M'' from the signature (r_1'', r_2'', s''), that is sent between U_i and U_j due to

$$M'' = r_2'' \cdot p_j^{s''} \cdot (p_i^{x_j})^{h(r''_2)} \bmod n.$$

Therefore, Chang et al.'s CCH-AEDSMR scheme cannot satisfy their claim regarding security requirements nor dose it provide confidentiality.

4   Proposed Scheme

In this section, we present an improvement of Chang et al.'s CCH-AEDSMR scheme. In order to remove the above-mentioned attack, the secret common item $p_i^{x_j} \bmod n$ should be protected. The system initialization phase is the same as the one presented in Section 2. In the following, we only describe the other two phases.

4.1   Signature Generation Phase

When U_i wants to sign a message M to a specified receiver U_j, the generation procedure of the signature is performed as follows:

U_i chooses a random number k and computes r_1, r_2 and s:

$$r_1 = M \cdot (p_j^{h(d_j)} + d_j)^k \bmod n,$$
$$r_2 = M \cdot h((p_j^{h(d_j)} + d_j)^{k \cdot r_1} \bmod n),$$
$$s = r_1 \cdot k - x_i \cdot h(r_2).$$

then, U_i sends the signature (r_1, r_2, s) to the verifier U_j.

4.2   Message Recovery Phase

After receiving the signature (r_1, r_2, s), the verifier U_j uses d_i, p_i and x_j to recover the signed message M by computing

$$M = r_2 \cdot h(g^s \cdot (p_i^{h(d_i)} + d_i)^{h(r_2)})^{x_j} \bmod n)^{-1}.$$

Shared information: n. g. $h(\cdot)$. p_i. d_i. p_j. d_j.
Information held by Signer: secret key x_i.
Information held by Verifier: secret key x_j.

Signer U_i **Verifier** U_j

Signature generation phase:
Choose $k \in GF(q)$
$r_1 = M \cdot (p_j^{h(d_j)} + d_j)^k \bmod n$
$r_2 = M \cdot h((p_j^{h(d_j)} + d_j)^{k \cdot r_1} \bmod n)$
$s = r_1 \cdot k - x_i \cdot h(r_2)$

$$\xrightarrow{\quad (r_1, r_2, s) \quad}$$

Message recovery phase:

Recover $M = r_2 \cdot h(g^s \cdot (p_i^{h(d_i)} + d_i)^{h(r_2)})^{x_j} \bmod n)^{-1}$
Verify $h((r_1 \cdot M^{-1})^{r_1} \bmod n) = r_2 \cdot M^{-1} \bmod n$

Fig. 2. Proposed Scheme

Finally, to verify the recovered message M, the verifier U_j checks whether

$$h((r_1 \cdot M^{-1})^{r_1} \bmod n) = r_2 \cdot M^{-1} \bmod n$$

holds.

5   Security Analysis

In this section, we shall only discuss the enhanced security features. The rest are the same as Chang et al.'s CCH-AEDSMR scheme, previously described in literature [8]. Readers are referred to [8] for complete references. First, we define the security terms [4] needed in order to provide the security for the proposed scheme:

Definition 1. *A secure one-way hash function* $y = f(x)$ *is one in which given* x *to compute* y *is easy and given* y *to compute* x *is hard.*

Definition 2. *The discrete logarithm problem (DLP) is the following: Given a number* $n = p \cdot q$, *a generator* g *of* Z_n^*, *and an element* $\alpha \in Z_n^*$, *find the integer* α, $o \leq \alpha \leq n - 2$, *such that* $g^\alpha \equiv \beta \bmod n$.

In light of the above definitions, we analyze the security of the proposed scheme as follows:

Theorem 1. *In the proposed scheme, only the specified verifier can recover the signed message* M *and verify the signer's public key* p_i.

Proof: Since $s = r_1 \cdot k - x_i \cdot h(r_2)$, the verifier can use the signer's public key p_i to compute

$$g^{r_1 \cdot k} = g^s \cdot (p_i^{h(d_i)} + d_i)^{h(r_2)} \bmod n.$$

Due to the fact that only the specified verifier U_j knows the corresponding secret key x_j, only U_j can compute

$$g^{r_1 \cdot k \cdot x_j} = (g^s \cdot (p_i^{h(d_i)} + d_i)^{h(r_2)})^{x_j} \bmod n.$$

Since $r_2 = M \cdot h((p_j^{h(d_j)} + d_j)^{k \cdot r_1} \bmod n)$, U_j can retrieve the signed message M by computing $M = r_2 \cdot h(g^{r_1 \cdot k \cdot x_j})^{-1}$. U_j can easily check whether the message M retrieved from the signature is correct by determining whether $h((r_1 \cdot M^{-1})^{r_1} \bmod n) = r_2 \cdot M^{-1} \bmod n$.

Moreover, $g^{x_i} \bmod n = p_i^{h(d_i)} + d_i \bmod n = y_i$ is implied in the first step while the verifier recovers the signed message. It is known that only the SA knows the order of g, hence only SA has the ability to calculate $p_i = (y_i - d_i)^{h(d_i)^{-1}}$. If the verifier can retrieve the correct y_i, according to the public p_i, to complete the message recovery procedure, the signer's public key p_i is verified indirectly. As mentioned above, only U_j knows the corresponding secret key x_j, hence only U_j can recover and verify the message. As a result, Theorem 1 is confirmed.

Theorem 2. *The proposed scheme can resist the above-mentioned known plaintext-ciphertext attack.*

Proof: Due to Definitions 1 and 2, now the common item $p_i^{x_j} \bmod n$ is protected, not only by the one-way hash function but also by the discrete logarithm problem over $GF(n)$. As a result, an attacker E cannot recover any message M'' from the signature (r_1'', r_2'', s'') because he or she cannot get the secret common key $p_i^{x_j} \bmod n$ that is sent between U_i and U_j from Step (3*) in Section 3. Therefore, the proposed scheme can resist the above-mentioned known plaintext-ciphertext attack. Also, it can reduce computational costs by using the one-way hash function $h(\cdot)$ on $h((p_j^{h(d_j)} + d_j)^{k \cdot r_1} \bmod n)$.

6   Conclusion

The current paper demonstrated the vulnerability of Chang et al.'s CCH-AEDSMR scheme whereby an attacker can perform the known plaintext-ciphertext attack and can recover all messages from the signature that are sent between the signer and the specified receiver. Also, we proposed improvements to the scheme in order to overcome such weaknesses.

Acknowledgements. We would like to thank the anonymous reviewers for their helpful comments in improving our manuscript. This research was supported by the MIC(Ministry of Information and Communication), Korea, under the ITRC(Information Technology Research Center) support program supervised by the IITA(Institute of Information Technology Assessment).

References

1. Nyberg, K., and Rueppel, R.A.: Message Recovery for Signature Schemes Based on the Discrete Logarithm. Advances in Cryptology – EUROCRYPT'94, Springer-Verlag. (1994) 175–190
2. Nyberg, K., and Rueppel, R.A.: Message Recovery for Signature Schemes Based on the Discrete Logarithm. Designs, Codes and Cryptography **7** (1996) 61–81
3. Lee, M., Kim, D., and Park, K.: An Authenticated Encryption Scheme with Public Verifiability. Japan-Korea Joint Workshop on Algorithms and Computation (WAAC2000) (2000) 49–56
4. Menezes, A.J., Oorschot, P.C., and Vanstone, S.A.: Handbook of Applied Cryptograph. CRC Press, New York. (1997)
5. Hwang, S.J.: Improvement of Tseng et al.'s Authenticated Encryption Scheme. Applied Mathematics and Computation **165** 1 (2005) 1–4
6. Girault, M.: Self-Certified Public Keys. In: Proceedings of EUROCRYPT_91 (1991) 491–497
7. Tseng, Y.M., Jan, J.K., and Chien, H.Y.: Digital Signature with Message Recovery Using Self-Certified Public Keys and Its Variants. Applied Mathematics and Computation **136** 2-3 (2003) 203–214
8. Chang, Y.F., Chang, C.C., and Huang, H.F.: Digital Signature with Message Recovery Using Self-Certified Public Keys without Trustworthy System Authority. Applied Mathematics and Computation **161** 1 (2005) 211–227
9. Rosen, K.H.: Elementary Number Theory and Its Application. 2nd ed., Addison, Wesley, Reading, MA (1988)

Small Independent Edge Dominating Sets in Graphs of Maximum Degree Three

Grażyna Zwoźniak

Institute of Computer Science, Wrocław University, Poland
grazyna@ii.uni.wroc.pl

Abstract. In this paper we consider the problem of finding minimum independent edge dominating sets in graphs of maximum degree three. The problem is NP-hard. We present an algorithm which finds the dominating set of size at most 4n/9+1/3. Using this bound we achieve an approximation ratio of 40/27 for the minimum independent edge domination set problem in cubic graphs.

1 Introduction

Given a connected undirected graph $G = (V, E)$, the minimum independent edge dominating set problem is to find a minimum set of edges E' which fulfils the following conditions: (a) for every edge $(u, w) \in E(G)$ either $(u, w) \in E'$ or one of $(x, u), (w, y) \in E(G)$ belongs to E' (b) no two edges of E' share a common endpoint. The problem is also referred as minimum maximal matching and it has applications in telephone switching networking. Yannakakis and Gavril [5] showed that this problem is NP-hard, even when restricted to planar or bipartite graphs of maximum degree 3. In their paper they also gave a polynomial time algorithm for trees. Later Horton and Kilakos [3] showed that the problem remains NP-hard for planar bipartite graphs, line graphs, total graphs, perfect claw-free graphs and planar cubic graphs. Chlebík and Chlebíková [1] proved that it is NP-hard to approximate the minimum edge dominating set problem within any factor smaller than 7/6 in general graphs and smaller than 1+1/487 in cubic graphs. It is easy to obtain approximation ratio of 2 for the problem: constructing any maximal matching is sufficient, because no matching in graph G can be more than twice larger than any maximal matching.

Duckworth and Wormald [2] concentrated on cubic graphs. They showed that the size of the minimum independent edge dominating set of an n-vertex cubic graph is at most 9n/20+O(1). It is the first non-trivial result for cubic graphs. Their proof uses a linear programming technique to analyse the performance of some greedy algorithm. In their paper they also showed that there are families of cubic graphs for which the size of the minimum independent edge dominating set is at least 3n/8. The lower bound for any cubic graph equals 3n/10.

In our paper we concentrate on graphs of maximum degree three. This more general class of graphs seems to be more useful in practical applications than the class of cubic graphs. We present an algorithm which finds $EDS(G)$ – independent edge dominating set of a graph G of size at most 4n/9 + 1/3. Note that if

J. Wiedermann et al. (Eds.): SOFSEM 2006, LNCS 3831, pp. 556–564, 2006.

we apply the algorithm to cubic graphs and use the known lower bound for this class of graphs then we will achieve an approximation ratio of 40/27 for the minimum independent edge domination set problem in cubic graphs. The approach to the problem is quite novel. We observed that using the structure of the forest with large number of leaves enables to construct small $EDS(G)$. Hence, in the first step our algorithm constructs the appropriate forest F, then it processes small subtrees of the trees $T \in F$ and adds some edges to $EDS(G)$. Since finding the minimum independent edge dominating set in the graph of maximum degree two is trivial we assume that G has at least one vertex of degree three.

The paper is organized as follows. In Section 2 we introduce some notation. In Section 3 we show how to construct the forest F and give some of its properties. In Section 4 we present the second part of the algorithm – adding edges to $EDS(G)$. The proofs of the facts and the theorem can be found in the full version of the paper.

2 Preliminaries

Let G be a connected undirected graph. We use $V(G)$ to denote the set of vertices in G and $E(G)$ to denote the set of edges in G. For a vertex $v \in V(G)$ let $\Gamma_G(v)$ denote the set of vertices $\{w : (v, w) \in E(G)\}$. The degree of v in G, $deg_G(v)$, is the number of edges incident to v in G. If T is a rooted tree, then we use $LCA_T(u, w)$ to denote the lowest common ancestor of vertices u, w in T, and $h(T)$ to denote the height of the tree T. By $\bar{L}(T)$ we denote the set of leaves of T.

3 Construction of the Forest F

Let G be a connected undirected graph of maximum degree three, where at least one vertex has degree three.

In the first step our algorithm builds successive trees $T_0, \ldots, T_k$ of a forest F for G by using three rules (see Fig. 1). Two of them are applied to the leaves of the current tree T_i. Rule 1 puts to the tree T_i two vertices $u, w \notin V(F)$ adjacent to a leaf $v \in \bar{L}(T_i)$. Rule 2 puts to T_i a vertex $u \notin V(F)$ adjacent to a leaf $v \in \bar{L}(T_i)$ together with both further neighbours w_1, w_2 of u, where $w_1, w_2 \notin V(F)$. We name the two leaves added by Rules 1 and 2 the left and the right son of their father.

Rule 3 initiates a new tree $T_j, j > i$. Let P be a path which starts at $v \in \bar{L}(T_i)$, goes through vertices $u_1, \ldots, u_s \notin V(F)$, $s \geq 1$ and ends at the first vertex $w \notin V(F)$, where $deg_G(w) = 3$, $\Gamma_G(w) = \{u_s, x, y\}$ and $x, y \notin V(F)$. The vertex u_s proceeds w on P. Rule 3 starts to build T_j rooted at u_s and adds u_s, w, x, y to $V(T_j)$ and $(u_s, w), (w, x), (w, y)$ to $E(T_j)$. We refer to T_i as the father of T_j. This relation determines a partial order in F, so we use some other related terms as e.g. ancestor of the tree.

Let $F = \{T_0, \ldots, T_k\}$. In our algorithm and analysis we use the following notions:

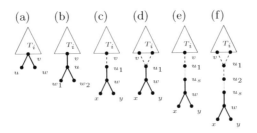

Fig. 1. (a) Rule 1. (b) Rule 2. (c)-(f) Rule 3.

Definition 1. *A vertex $v \in V(G)$ is an* exterior vertex *if $v \notin V(F)$. Let EX denote the set of all exterior vertices in G.*

Definition 2. *Let r_0 be a root of T_0. Let R be the set of roots of the trees $T_1, \ldots, T_k$.*

Construction of the forest F.

1. $F \leftarrow \emptyset$
2. $V(T_0) \leftarrow \{r_0, v_1, v_2, v_3\}$, where r_0 is any degree three vertex of G and $v_1, v_2, v_3 \in \Gamma_G(r_0)$;
   $E(T_0) \leftarrow \{(r_0, v_1), (r_0, v_2), (r_0, v_3)\}$; let r_0 be a root of T_0; $i \leftarrow 0$
3. if it is possible: find the leftmost leaf in T_i that can be expanded by the Rule 1 and expand it; go to the step 3;
   else: go to the step 4;
4. if it is possible: find the leftmost leaf in T_i that can be expanded by the Rule 2 and expand it; go to the step 3
   else: $F \leftarrow F \cup T_i$ and go to the step 5
5. if it is possible: find the leftmost leaf v in T_i such that Rule 3 can be applied to v and apply this rule to v; $i \leftarrow i + 1$;
   let T_i be a new tree created in this step; go to the step 3 with T_i
   else: go to the step 5 with the father of T_i.

The properties of the forest F are described by Fact 1. The possibilities for edges $e \in E(G) \backslash E(F)$ are presented in Fig. 1(c)-(f) and 2.

Fact 1. *Let $v \in V(T_i), T_i \in F$.*

1. *If $deg_{T_i}(v) = 2$ and $w \in \Gamma_{T_i}(v)$ then $deg_{T_i}(w) = 3$.*
2. *If $deg_{T_i}(v) = 2$ and $w \in \Gamma_G(v)$ then $w \in V(T_i)$.*
3. *If v is adjacent to the vertex $w \in EX \cup R$, $u \in \Gamma_G(v)$ and $u \neq w$ then $u \in V(T_i)$.*

The following facts let us dominate the edges $E(F)$ in some order described precisely in the next section.

Fact 2. *Let $deg_T(u) = deg_T(w) = 2$, where $T \in F$, $(u, w) \in E(G) \backslash E(F)$, $a = LCA_T(u, w)$, and let u be on the left of w in T. Then w is the right son of a, and there are no vertices of degree 2 on the path from u to a in T.*

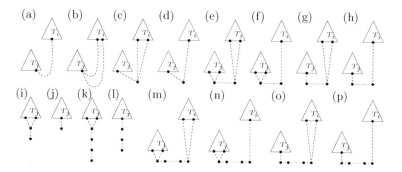

Fig. 2. The edges $(x, y) \in E(G)\backslash E(F)$, $x, y \in EX \cup \bar{L}(F)$ (dashed lines). Either $T_i = T_j$ or T_i is an ancestor of T_j. Dotted lines denote the paths where all vertices have degree two in G.

Fact 3. *Let r be a root of a tree $T \in F$. Let $u \in \bar{L}(T)$ and let w be the first vertex of degree 2 on the path from u to r in T. If there is $v \in V(T)$ such that $deg_F(v) = 2$ and $(u, v) \in E(G)\backslash E(T)$ then w is an ancestor of v in T.*

4   Finding Independent Edge Dominating Set

Let G' denote a current graph, F' a current forest and $EX' = V(G')\backslash V(F')$. At the beginning $G' = G$, $F' = F$ and $EX' = EX$. In our algorithm G' is always a connected graph. Let S'_x denote the subtree of $T' \in F'$ rooted at some vertex $x \in V(T')$. In successive steps of our algorithm we consider small subtrees S'_x, add some edges to $EDS(G)$ and remove these added edges with all edges incident to their endpoints from $E(G')$. We say that removed edges are *dominated*. A vertex u is removed from $V(G')$ when the last edge incident to u is removed from $E(G')$.

The process of adding edges to $EDS(G)$ is realized by the procedures DOMI-NATE$_i()$, $i \in \{1, 2, 3\}$. DOMINATE$_1(S'_x \cup S'_y)$ dominates the edges of the subtrees S'_x, S'_y, where $deg_{T'}(x) = 2$ and $(x, y) \in E(G')\backslash E(F')$, together with edges $e \in E(G')\backslash E(F')$ incident to $V(S'_x) \cup V(S'_y)$. DOMINATE$_2(S'_x)$ dominates the edges of some paths which end at the leaves of S'_x and go through the edges $e \in E(G')\backslash E(F')$. DOMINATE$_3(S'_x)$ dominates $E(S'_x)$ and all the edges incident to $V(S'_x)$. These procedures are constructed in such a way that the following property holds:

Property 1. *The procedure* DOMINATE$_i()$*, $i \in \{1, 2, 3\}$ adds $\bar{m}$ edges to $EDS(G)$ and removes $\bar{n}$ vertices from $V(G')$, where $\bar{m} \leq \frac{4}{9}\bar{n}$. The only exception may be the case when* DOMINATE$_3()$ *is applied to the tree rooted at r_0 or at the son of r_0; then $\bar{m} \leq \frac{4}{9}\bar{n} + \frac{1}{3}$.*

Now we briefly describe the main idea of our algorithm. We consider in post-order small subtrees S'_x of the trees $T' \in F'$, where the edges $e \in E(G')\backslash E(F')$

are not incident to the interior vertices of S'_x. Our goal is to dominate $E(S'_x)$ and all the edges incident to the leaves and the root of S'_x. If x is the endpoint of the edge $(x, y) \in E(G') \backslash E(F')$, we try to apply the procedure DOMINATE$_3(S'_x)$. Then we recursively process the subtree S'_y. If after these steps $deg_{G'}(x)=3$ or $deg_{G'}(y)=3$ we apply the procedure DOMINATE$_1(S'_x \cup S'_y)$. In the case when x is not the endpoint of any edge $(x, y) \in E(G') \backslash E(F')$, we try to apply DOMINATE$_3(S'_x)$, and if it is not possible, S'_x is processed as the subtree of the tree rooted at the father of x.

When we process S'_x, some of the edges $e \in E(G') \backslash E(F')$ incident to the leaves of S'_x are marked as *required* and added to the set $REQUIRED(S'_x)$. If we added them to $EDS(G)$ then all the edges incident to the leaves of S'_x would be dominated. In most of cases it is possible to add all required edges with some edges of S'_x to $EDS(G)$ and keep Property 1. To avoid the situation that after the procedure DOMINATE$_3(S'_x)$ some paths P which go through the edges $e \in E(G') \backslash E(F')$ are not connected to F' and it is not possible to dominate their edges keeping Property 1, we earlier check if there are such paths and apply DOMINATE$_2(S'_x)$ to dominate their edges.

The algorithm starts with the procedure EDS_T(T_0).

EDS_T(T')

1. apply procedure EDS_T() to the sons $T'_i \in F'$ of T' (successively from the leftmost to the rightmost);
2. EDS(T').

EDS(S'_x)

Let $W = \{u \in V(S'_x) : deg_{F'}(u) = 2$ and $deg_{G'}(u) = 3\}$.

1. while $W \neq \emptyset$
   (a) apply in-order search and find the first vertex $u \in W$;
      let w be such a vertex that $(u, w) \in E(G') \backslash E(F')$;
   (b) EDS(S'_u);
   (c) if $w \in V(F')$: EDS(S'_w);
   (d) if $deg_{G'}(u) = 3$ or $deg_{G'}(w) = 3$: MARK_REQUIRED$(S'_u \cup S'_w)$;
      DOMINATE_PATHS$(S'_u \cup S'_w)$; DOMINATE$_1$ $(S'_u \cup S'_w)$;
2. MARK(S'_x).

Let $W = \{w \in V(T) : deg_T(w) = 2$ and $deg_G(w) = 3\}$. We make use of the fact that every tree $T \in F$ is a union of the trees C_u rooted at u, where $u \in \{r_0\} \cup R \cup W$, all leaves of C_u are in the set $W \cup \bar{L}(T)$ and all interior vertices $v \in \{w \in V(T) : deg_T(w) = deg_G(w) \geq 2\}$. Let $C'_u = C_u \cap G'$.

The trees $T' \in F'$ are processed by the procedure EDS(). This procedure finds in post-order the trees C'_u and applies the procedure MARK() which processes small subtrees $S'_x \subseteq C'_u$ and adds appropriate edges to $EDS(G)$. If u is the end-point of an edge $(u, v) \in E(G')\backslash E(F')$ then after processing C'_y we recursively dominate the edges of descendants of C'_v (if they exist) and $E(C'_v)$. At the end if $deg_{G'}(x) = 3$ or $deg_{G'}(y) = 3$ then required edges are marked, the edges of some paths which end at the leaves of C'_u, C'_v are dominated and $\text{DOMINATE}_1(C'_u \cup C'_v)$ is applied. Otherwise the remaining parts of C'_u, C'_v are processed with the father C'_z of C'_u and C'_v. Subtrees C'_u are processed in post-order, and it follows from the Facts 2 and 3 that processing C'_v just after C'_u does not disconnect T'. The parameter S'_x of $\text{EDS}()$ is the subtree of $T' \in F'$ rooted at x. In fact the procedure $\text{MARK}()$ is not applied to C'_x, but to $S'_x = C'_x \cup C'_{w_1} \cup \ldots \cup C'_{w_k}$, where C'_{w_i}, $i \in \{1, \ldots, k\}$ are the children of C'_x which have not been completely removed yet, and the edges $e \in E(G')\backslash E(F')$ are incident solely to x or to the leaves of S'_x.

$\text{MARK\_REQUIRED}(S'_x)$

Let $W = \{(u, w) \in E(G')\backslash E(F') : u \in \bar{L}(S'_x)\}$.

1. $REQUIRED(S'_x) := \emptyset$
2. while there is a vertex $u \in \bar{L}(S'_x)$ and the edges $(u, v), (u, w) \in W$, $v \in \bar{L}(S'_x)$, $w \notin \bar{L}(S'_x)$:
   (a) apply in-order search and find the first vertex u described above;
   (b) add (u, w) to $REQUIRED(S'_x)$;
   (c) remove the edges incident to u, w from W.
3. while there is a vertex $u \in \bar{L}(S'_x)$ and the edge $(u, w) \in W$, $w \in EX \cup R$:
   (a) apply in-order search and find the first vertex u described above;
   (b) add (u, w) to $REQUIRED(S'_x)$;
   (c) remove the edges incident to u, w from W.
4. while there is a vertex $u \in \bar{L}(S'_x)$ and the edge $(u, w) \in W$:
   (a) apply in-order search and find the first vertex u described above;
   (b) add (u, w) to $REQUIRED(S'_x)$;
   (c) remove the edges incident to u, w from W.

$\text{DOMINATE\_PATHS}(S'_x)$

1. if $TAILS_1(S'_x) \neq \emptyset$ or $EARS_1(S'_x) \neq \emptyset$: $\text{DOMINATE}_2(S'_x)$;
2. $\text{MARK\_REQUIRED}(S'_x)$;
3. if $TAILS_2(S'_x) \neq \emptyset$ or $EARS_2(S'_x) \neq \emptyset$ or $EARS_3(S'_x) \neq \emptyset$: $\text{DOMINATE}_2(S'_x)$; goto 2.

The procedure $\text{MARK\_REQUIRED}(S'_x)$, constructs the set $REQUIRED(S'_x)$. To reduce the number of possible cases we introduced some order of adding the edges to the set $REQUIRED(S'_x)$. The procedure works also for the sum of the trees.

The procedure DOMINATE_PATHS(S_x') applies the procedure DOMINATE2(S_x') to the paths P which end at some leaves of S_x'. The edges $e \in P$ incident to $\bar{L}(S_x')$ are in the set $REQUIRED(S_x')$ and if $(u, v) \in P$ is not incident to e then $u, v \in EX'$. There are five types of paths P which we keep in the sets $TAILS_i(S_x')$, $EARS_j(S_x')$, $i = 1, 2$, $j = 1, 2, 3$. Since some of required edges can be dominated, the new set $REQUIRED(S_x')$ is constructed, and the new paths are checked. The procedure works also for the sum of the trees.

The procedure MARK(S_x') is applied to a subtree S_x' of $T' \in F'$, where the edges $e \in E(G')\backslash E(F')$ are incident solely to the root x or leaves of S_x'. If $h(S_x') > 2$ then the procedure is recursively applied to the trees rooted at the sons of x. Then required edges are marked and the edges of some paths which end at some leaves of S_x' are dominated. After these steps $h(S_x')$ could decrease by one, if some of the edges incident to $\bar{L}(S_x')$ were added to $EDS(G)$. Then we try to apply the procedure DOMINATE3(S_x'). The function DOMINATION_POSSIBLE3(S_x') returns false if $h(S_x') = 0$ and $V(F') > 1$, or $h(S_x') = 1$ and $x \notin \{r_0\} \cup R$, or $h(S_x') = 2$ and S_x' looks like in Fig. 3; otherwise it returns true. If MARK(S_x') returns without dominating $E(S_x')$ then S_x' will be processed as the subtree of the tree rooted at the father of x, or dominated by the procedure DOMINATE1() in EDS() (if x is the endpoint of the edge $(x, y) \in E(G')\backslash E(F')$).

If $x = r_0$, $deg_{F'}(r_0) = 3$ and $h(S_{r_0}') > 1$ then we split S_{r_0}' into trees $\bar{S}_{r_0}'$ and S_{u_3}' as follows. Let $E(\bar{S}_{r_0}') = E(S_{u_1}') \cup E(S_{u_2}') \cup (r_0, u_1) \cup (r_0, u_2)$, where u_1, u_2 are the sons of r_0, $h(\bar{S}_{r_0}') = h(S_{r_0}')$ and if it is possible $\bar{S}_{r_0}'$ with required edges does not look like in Fig. 3(f). Let S_{u_3}' be the subtree of S_{r_0}' rooted at the third son u_3 of r_0.

When we dominate successively subtrees S_u', S_v' of S_x' we set $REQUIRED(S_u')$ as $\{(z_1, z_2) : (z_1, z_2) \in REQUIRED(S_x')$ and $(z_1 \in \bar{L}(S_u')$ or $z_2 \in \bar{L}(S_u')\}$. $REQUIRED(S_v') = REQUIRED(S_v')\backslash REQUIRED(S_u')$, or is constructed for S_v' if $x = r_0$ and $v = u_3$.

MARK(S_x')

1. if $h(S_x') > 2$: apply procedure MARK() to the trees rooted at the sons of x (successively from the leftmost to the rightmost);
2. MARK_REQUIRED(S_x');
3. DOMINATE_PATHS(S_x');
4. if x has at most two sons u_i, $1 \leq i \leq 2$:
   (a) while DOMINATION_POSSIBLE(S_{u_i}'): DOMINATE3(S_{u_i}');
   (b) if DOMINATION_POSSIBLE(S_x'): DOMINATE3(S_x'); else: return;
5. if x has three sons u_i, $1 \leq i \leq 3$ (in this case $x = r_0$):
   (a) while DOMINATION_POSSIBLE(S_{u_i}'): DOMINATE3(S_{u_i}');
   (b) if $h(S_{r_0}') > 1$ and $deg_{G'}(r_0) = 3$: let $u_3 \notin \bar{S}_{r_0}'$;
      i. DOMINATE3($\bar{S}_{r_0}'$);
      ii. if $u_3 \in V(G')$: MARK_REQUIRED(S_{u_3}'); DOMINATE3(S_{u_3}');
   (c) else if $r_0 \in V(G')$: DOMINATE3(S_{r_0}').

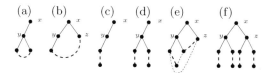

Fig. 3. The trees $S_x^{'}$, where $h(S_x^{'}) = 2$ which may be returned by the procedure MARK($S_x^{'}$). The edges $e \in REQUIRED(S_x^{'})$ are dashed and bold. In the case (e) also some other edges from the set $E(G^{'})\backslash E(F^{'})$ are presented (dashed and thin).

DOMINATE$_1(S_u^{'} \cup S_w^{'})$ adds to $EDS(G)$ the edge $(u, w) \in E(G^{'})\backslash E(F^{'})$, $deg_F(u) = 2$ and the edges from the set $REQUIRED(S_u^{'} \cup S_w^{'})$, which are not incident to (u, w).

DOMINATE$_3(S_x^{'})$ is applied to the subtree $S_x^{'}$ of $T^{'} \in F$. Let S_x^* be $S_x^{'}$ without the edges incident to $e \in REQUIRED(S_x^{'})$. Let $BASIC(S_x^*) = \{(x, y)\}$ if $h(S_x^*) = 1$ and y is a son of x or if $h(S_x^*) = 2$ and x has only one son y; $\{(x, y_1), (y_2, z)\}$ if $h(S_x^*) = 2$ and x has two sons y_1, y_2, where y_1 has at least as many sons as y_2 and z is a son of y_2.

If DOMINATION_POSSIBLE$_3(S_x^{'})$ returns true then the edges $REQUIRED(S_x^{'})$ $\cup BASIC(S_x^*)$ are added to $EDS(G)$ in the following cases:

1. if $h(S_x^{'}) = 2$, $|REQUIRED(S_x^{'})| < 4$ and $|E(S_x^*)| > 1$;
2. if $h(S_x^{'}) \leq 2$, $S_x^{'}$ is the last processed tree and it is not the case 2 described below;
3. if $h(S_x^{'}) = 3$ and $|REQUIRED(S_x^{'})| < 3$ or $V(S_x^*) \neq \{x, y_1, y_2, z_1, z_2\}$, where y_1, y_2 are sons of x, z_1 is a son of y_1 and z_2 is a son of y_2.

If the conditions given above are not true:

1. if $h(S_x^{'}) \in \{1, 2\}$ and $x \in R$ then the edges $REQUIRED(S_x^{'}) \cup (x, w)$ are added to $EDS(G)$, where $(x, w) \in E(G^{'})\backslash E(F^{'})$ (if there are two edges (x, w) we choose the leftmost one);
2. if $h(S_x^{'}) = 2$:
   (a) if y_1, y_2 are sons of x, z_1 is a son of y_1 and $REQUIRED(S_x^{'}) = \{(z_1, w_1), (y_2, w_2)\}$, $w_2 \notin V(S_x^{'})$ then the edges $(x, y_2), (z_1, w_1)$ are added to $EDS(G)$;
   (b) else if x has two sons y_1, y_2 and y_1 has two sons z_1, z_2:
      i. if $|REQUIRED(S_x^{'})| = 3$, $(y_2, w) \in REQUIRED(S_x^{'})$ then the edges $(x, y_2) \cup (REQUIRED(S_x^{'})\backslash(y_2, w))$ are added to $EDS(G)$;
      ii. if $REQUIRED(S_x^{'}) = \{(y_2, z_2), (z_1, w)\}$, $w \notin V(S_x^{'})$, $deg_{G^{'}}(y_2) = 2$ or $deg_{G^{'}}(z_2) = 2$, then the edges $(x, y_2), (y_1, z_1)$ are added to $EDS(G)$;
3. if $h(S_x^{'}) = 3$:
   (a) if there is an edge $(z, w) \in REQUIRED(S_x^{'})$, where z is a son of y_2, $w \notin V(S_x^{'})$ then the edges $(REQUIRED(S_x^{'})\backslash(z, w)) \cup (y_2, z) \cup (x, y_1)$ are added to $EDS(G)$;

(b) otherwise the edges $(REQUIRED(S'_x)\backslash(u, v)) \cup (z_1, u) \cup (x, y_2))$ are added to $EDS(G)$, where $(u, v) \in REQUIRED(S'_x)$, $v \notin V(S'_x)$, u is a son of z_1 and a grandson of y_1.

The main contribution of this paper is the following theorem.

Theorem 1. *Let G be a graph of maximum degree three, where $|V(G)| = n$. Our algorithm constructs for G an independent edge dominating set $EDS(G)$ of size at most $4n/9 + 1/3$ in linear time.*

References

1. Chlebík, M., and Chlebíková, J.: Approximation Hardness of Minimum Edge Dominating Set and Minimum Maximal Matching. Algorithms and Computations, 14th International Symposium, LNCS **2906** (2003) 415–424
2. Duckworth, and W., Wormald, N.C.: Linear Programming and the Worst-Case Analysis of Greedy Algorithms on Cubic Graphs, unpublished.
3. Horton, J.D., and Kilakos, K.: Minimum Edge Dominating Sets. SIAM Journal on Discrete Mathematics, **6** 3 (1993) 375–387
4. Loryś, K., and Zwoźniak, G.: Approximation Algorithm for the Maximum Leaf Spanning Tree Problem for Cubic Graphs. Proceedings of the 10th Annual European Symposium on Algorithms, LNCS **2461** (2002) 686–697
5. Yannakakis, M., and Gavril, F.: Edge Dominating Sets in Cubic Graphs. SIAM Journal on Applied Mathematics **38** 3 (1980) 364–372

Level-of-Detail in Behaviour of Virtual Humans*

Ondřej Šerý, Tomáš Poch, Pavel Šafrata, and Cyril Brom

Charles University, Faculty of Mathematics and Physics,
Malostranské nám. 2/25, Prague, Czech Republic
{ondrej.sery, pavel.safrata}@seznam.cz, tom.poch@post.cz,
brom@ksvi.mff.cuni.cz

Abstract. An application featuring virtual humans is a program that simulates an artificial world inhabited by virtual people. Recently, only either small artificial worlds inhabited by a few complex virtual humans, or larger worlds with tens of humans, but performing only walking and crowding, are simulated. This is not surprising: a large world inhabited by complex virtual humans requires unreasonable amount of computational and memory resources. In this paper, we report on the project IVE, a common simulation framework for huge artificial worlds, pointing out the level-of-detail technique used at the behavioural level. The technique addresses the issue on reducing simulation demands by gradually decreasing simulation quality on unimportant places, while keeping the simulation plausible, with minimum scenic inconsistencies.

1 Introduction

Virtual humans are becoming increasingly popular both in the academic and industrial domains. Applications featuring virtual humans include computer games, virtual storytelling, movie industry, entertainment, military simulations, and behavioural modelling. An overview of domains of virtual humans is given for example in [11].

From the technical point of view, typically, each virtual human is viewed as an autonomous intelligent agent in the sense of Wooldridge [12]; such an agent that carries out a diverse set of goals in a highly dynamic, unpredictable environment with the objective to simulate behaviour of a human.

The research on virtual humans (v-humans in the following) is mostly focused around graphical embodiment and action selection mechanism. Generally, the former means a graphical visualization of a v-human's body, and the latter means deciding of what action to perform next in the virtual world. The main problem with the visualization is that v-humans must look believably. For example, it has been shown (*e.g.*, [9]) that emotional modelling plays a significant role in a posture and face visualization. The main problem with the action selection is that the environment is dynamic and unpredictable. A v-human must respond in a timely fashion to environmental changes that are beyond the v-human's control.

In this paper, we address a different issue. During our previous work on a toolkit ENTs for prototyping v-humans [1], we discovered that it was not a problem to

---

* This work was partially supported by the Czech Academy of Sciences project 1ET400300504.

J. Wiedermann et al. (Eds.): SOFSEM 2006, LNCS 3831, pp. 565–574, 2006.

develop a single v-human with meaningful and believable behaviour. The problem was to populate a large artificial world with tens of v-humans running on a single PC, because of the limited computational and memory resources. Most of the current v-humans either "live" in a small artificial world (*e.g.*, in a room, not in a village), or do exhibit only a small portion of human-like behaviour (*e.g.*, only object-grasping, walking, or a few tasks, not weekly human activities). An application or a technique that would challenge large simulations is missing. Such a technique would be extremely useful in the fields of computer games, and virtual storytelling.

At the time, we are working on a project IVE (*an intelligent virtual environment*) [2], [7], which is focused on v-humans in large and extensible simulations. One of the goals of the project is to explore and implement the *level-of-detail technique* (LOD). This technique is widely used in computer graphics for reducing computational cost. Our aim is to use it at the behavioural level; it means to transfer it to the domain of artificial intelligence.

The LOD technique for behaviour of v-humans is based on the simple idea: there often exist only few places in the artificial world important at a given simulation time and the unimportant places do not need to be simulated precisely. If the artificial world is simulated only partially, the demands of the simulation can be reduced significantly. However, there are three problems coming out with the implementation: 1) how to identify the important places, 2) how to simplify the simulation in the unimportant places, 3) how to gradually simplify the simulation between an important and an unimportant place?

In this paper, we present our approach to LOD technique at the behavioural level. We are motivated by the growing need of large simulations with v-humans in the domains of computer games, and virtual storytelling. The goal is to address the three aforementioned problems. The algorithms presented here are already implemented in the on-going project IVE.

The rest of the paper proceeds as follows: First, we describe related work on the LOD technique in artificial simulations. Second, we briefly present our framework and its view of the artificial world. Then, in Section 4, we present main concepts of the simulation LOD followed by a brief description of our implementation, in Section 5. Finally, we conclude in Section 6.

2 Related Work

The LOD technique is widely used in computer graphics, but not often in behavioural simulations. The idea behind is simple: compute only such details that are important at a given simulation time. At the behavioural level, that means places observed by the user, and other places important for the overall course of the simulation.

Sometimes, this idea is exploited in computer games, but only to a limited degree. Behaviour of the creatures out of the sight of the user is not simulated at all typically. This often causes a storyline inconsistency - the simulation is not believable. Instead of "non-simulation", there is a need for a gradual simulation simplifying.

More robust idea how to use the LOD at the behavioural level using hierarchical finite state machines is presented in [3], but it is only a sketch not further explored.

Sullivan *et al.* utilised the LOD for conversational behaviour by means of rules and roles filtering [10]. In a simplified fashion, the rules and roles can be viewed as pieces of a code layered upon a basic v-human. If the v-human is not seen, the role is not passed to it, and consequently only the basic behaviour is performed. Contrary to our approach, they simplify only the behaviour of v-humans, not the overall simulation.

A robust approach to (non-pre-emptive) scheduling of processor time to individual v-humans is presented in [13]. However, as the not-scheduled behavioural scripts are not run, this approach seems to fit into the realm of "yes/no simulation".

3 Project IVE

Let us first describe our framework and our view of the artificial world. In our framework we distinguish between *objects*, *actors* and *processes*. All physical objects in the artificial world are objects. Special objects that can manipulate with other objects are called actors. The only way how to affect objects is to perform a process.

In our framework, the world consists of *locations* on which objects can be located. Locations are organised in a hierarchical structure related to the LOD technique. The structure is always a tree and levels of the tree correspond to the LOD levels. *LOD value* of an object is defined as a corresponding LOD level of the location on which the object is situated.

Objects presented in our framework are *smart* (in the sense of [8]), which helps with world's extensibility. They contain necessary graphical information and description of low-level actions (*e.g.,* grasping the object). However, they do not contain the artificial intelligence itself. Our objects also provide *affordances* [5] - each object is able to give a list of processes it is designed to participate on.

In our framework, processes can be also labelled as smart. Each process has a number of sources on which it operates. When executing a process, objects are substituted as these sources. Some of the sources have a special actor position. From the view of the process, the position of actors differs from the other sources especially in the connection to the LOD, as we shall see later. Our processes have also an ability of *suitabilities* - they can say how much are the given objects suitable for being substituted to the process. In other words, each process can say, if it is a "good idea" to be executed with some particular objects as sources or not.

Processes in our framework are organised in a hierarchical structure tightly connected with the LOD technique, as well. Each process can be performed atomically, or expanded to subprocesses. The structure is not as strict as in the case of the locations—process can be atomic at more LOD levels. Each executed process can stay in one of these states:

- *Not-existing* – the LOD value is too low, a super process is running. This process does really not exist in the world. If the process is running and the LOD value goes too low, it is stopped, partially evaluated and discarded.
- *Atomic* – the process is running atomically. It waits till its finish time and then changes the world's state.
- *Expanded* – the process is expanded to subprocesses. Such process performs no action, it only waits for it's subprocesses to do all the work. However, it can become atomic as a consequence of the LOD changes.

To define the process' state, we need for each process two border LOD levels - *minimum* level (border between not-existing and atomic process) and *maximum* level (border between the atomic and the expanded process). The state of the particular process is then determined by the LOD values of its actors in relation to the border levels. That means, the process is atomic (the only process' state in which the world's state is influenced) if the actor's LOD is between the process' minimum and maximum levels, similarly for the other states. The process can have any number of actors, but their LOD values must not require different states of the process (they all must have the LOD value at the same side of the border levels). It is up to the framework to adjust LOD values in the corresponding locations.

Hierarchical if-then rules are used to describe the processes. However, the subprocesses of an expanding process are not hardwired. The action selection is driven by a goal concept [4, 12]. The actor has a goal (an intention to reach some objective) and can try various processes to satisfy the goal. Processes also do not expand directly to subprocesses, but rather to the subgoals (see Fig. 1). In this concept, the actor obtains the list of goals needed to satisfy the parent process and its task is to find and perform appropriate processes.

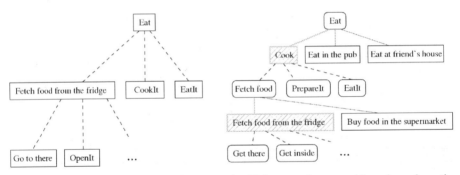

Fig. 1. Left – process hierarchy without goals. Right – goal-process hierarchy, where the process acts as an implementation of a goal.

The actual artificial intelligence is not encapsulated in the actor's object. This is the purpose of a presence of entities called *geniuses*. Genius is the one who chooses the processes, looks for the suitable sources and asks the framework to perform the chosen processes. An actor can have its own genius, which is actually his brain. But in addition to that, dedicated geniuses are present in our framework. These geniuses are specialized to particular activities and are able to control actors passed by another geniuses. This concept allows for example creation of dummy actors, which are driven by geniuses of locations as they travel within the world, or geniuses with ability to perform some non-trivial interaction among more actors. For example playing cards in a pub could be easily driven by a single specialized genius, while controlling such an action from more individual geniuses would be a tremendous task.

4   Simulation LOD

In the previous section we have introduced our view of the artificial world and both the location and process hierarchy. Now let us take a closer look at the simulation LOD. In this section, we shall introduce few rules that control location hierarchy expansion and then, in the next section, we shall describe implementation of the component that enforces their abidance.

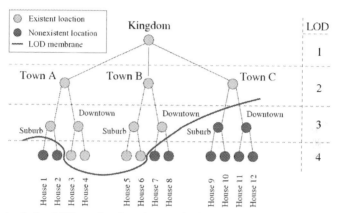

Fig. 2. The simulation LOD can be viewed as an elastic membrane cutting thought the location hierarchy. If no other force exists, the membrane presses LOD to low values (fewer details).

The best way to imagine the simulation LOD is an elastic membrane cutting through the location hierarchy (see Fig. 2). Only the locations above this membrane do currently exist and so only these locations are simulated. Objects are located only in leaves of the clipped hierarchy tree and their LOD values are equal to the LOD value of these leaf locations, as described in the previous section.

The base framework aims to keep details low (the membrane presses upward) in order to simplify (and thus speed-up) the simulation. On the contrary, simulated objects press the membrane down to ensure enough details necessary for their own simulation.

Each object has two values: the *existence* level and the *view* level. The existence level marks the border LOD value below which the object is not simulated. The view level is a LOD value which is enforced by the object if current LOD value is greater or equal to existence level (see Fig. 3). Situation, in which the actual LOD would be between the view and existence level, is considered invalid and our framework either expands or shrinks all such locations to adjust LOD value out of this interval.

All objects in given location and their existence and view levels define possible LOD values that would not result in the invalid state (invalid states forms invalid areas on the Fig. 3). This is the basic rule that our framework must obey and that can be violated whenever an object changes its location.

Typical use for an important object (such as the user's avatar) is low existence level and high view level which enforces high LOD values in the location where the object stays. On the other hand, unimportant objects would have the existence level close to the view level and both quite high. This does not enforce nearly any changes in LOD (corresponding invalid area is small) but rather only specifies whether such an object exists or not.

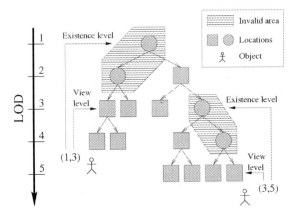

Fig. 3. Valid and invalid LOD values based on the existence and view levels of more objects

Unfortunately, this is not enough to ensure fluent simulation. Problem occurs when an important object frequently moves between two locations from different branches of the location hierarchy. This could cause many expansions and shrinks constantly which is definitely not acceptable. We would prefer a LOD membrane to create a 'crater' rather than a narrow 'hole' around the important objects. This would make neighbouring locations to prepare for a visit of the VIP object before it reaches their borders by gradually increasing their LOD value (expanding to sublocations).

This idea is handled by adding *LOD influence* between locations. It is a relation which marks nearby locations by a certain number. This number defines how much can the LOD values differ between these two locations.

These rules, when enforced, answer the three basic questions from Section 1. Important places are identified as places containing objects with low existence level and high view level. Even more, these levels can also say how much important the objects are. Answer to the second and the third question is inherent in the fact that the whole world is hierarchical with each hierarchy to some extend corresponding to the LOD levels. So we can easily simulate on different levels. Gradual LOD changes are assured by the use of LOD influence between neighbouring locations.

5   Implementation

In this section, we describe a component called LOD Manager which enforces abidance of the rules mentioned in the previous section.

LOD Manager aims to expand and shrink locations to achieve valid LOD values with regard to objects' view and existence levels and LOD influence. On the other hand, it keeps LOD value as low as possible to assure a fast simulation.

Another requirement, that LOD manager must comply, is to avoid ineffective expands and shrinks when an object constantly moves around the border between two locations. Such situation would happen with a naïve solution that would shrink locations as soon as their existence was not strictly enforced. Such an object could cause unnecessary load on the system. We could solve this requirement by defining a second LOD crater with the same centre and greater radius. The inner crater would affect expansions and the outer one shrinking. This approach would need additional information describing outer crater in the world description, so we decided to implement another solution. It resembles the garbage collection technique known from programming environments.

LOD manager is gathering information about objects' position and movement from the framework by a simple interface containing methods addObject(object, location), removeObject(object, location) and moveObject(object, oldlocation, newlocation). Beside these methods, LOD Manager can be asked to remove locations that are not needed—to push the LOD membrane upwards. It is up to the framework to decide when to invoke cleanup()—time by time or when the simulation goes too slow.

LOD manager changes the state of the location tree by invoking expand() and shrink() methods on particular locations. During execution of expand() method, the location generates a net of its sublocations and objects specific for this location (e.g., flowers in the garden). All objects fall down to the new sublocations. Also an option of object's expansion to subobjects is plausible but we have not implemented it yet. Method shrink() makes the target location atomic. Its location subtree is forgotten. Objects form the subtree are either placed on the shrunk location (if their existence level is lower than its LOD value) or cease to exist (these are typically specific for the given location and can be generated again during the expand() call).

We say that the location holds the *basic condition* if there is no object placed in its subtree such that LOD value of the location would be between the object's existence (included) and view (excluded) level. Such a location could easily be atomic without causing an invalid state (see Section 3) and so the shrink() method can be called on it. However, we could still violate influences between locations and lose the 'crater' optimalization. Fig. 3 shows 11 locations that hold the basic condition as squares and 4 that do not as circles.

During the simulation, LOD Manager is accepting notifications about objects' movement (via methods mentioned above). It keeps notion about locations that hold the basic condition and also controls LOD influence. Thus it can dynamically detect an invalid state or violated influence. In both cases, it reacts by calling expand() on offending locations.

This way, locations can get only expanded. The shrink() method is not called dynamically but only during the cleanup() method execution. In this method, LOD Manager finds a cut through the location hierarchy that is closest to the root while still acceptable with respect to the basic condition and LOD influence.

For this purpose, we use the depth first search (DFS) algorithm. If a location is intended to be shrunk it is marked. In the instant moment, if the location is marked, no of its descendants or ancestors can be marked. We can see three types of edges in the graph of currently existing locations:

- *Disabled* – heads from the location that holds the basic condition to each its child. This edge cannot be used during the traversal (unless shortcut by an influence edge).
- *Enabled* – other edges that head from the parent to its child. These can be freely used during the traversal.
- *Influence edge* – edges that correspond to the LOD influence. These are used too, but it could happen that an ancestor of influence target is already marked. In such a case the ancestor is unmarked and all its children are traversed.

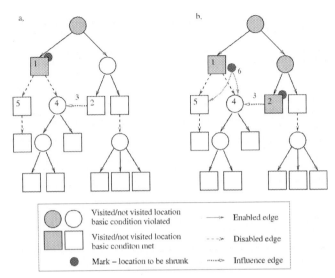

Fig. 4. On the picture a, DFS algorithm have visited location 1 and have found no enabled edge to continue. So location 1 is marked and DFS continues by traversing the second child of the root location. This is shown on the picture b. On this picture DFS have found the influence edge 3 at location 2. Because there is no enabled edge going from location 2, it is marked. DFS then continues by traversing the influence edge to location 4. In this case there is a marked ancestor of influence target. So we must remove its mark 6 and traverse all its children (location 4 and 5). In this case the influence value is zero - general case is slightly different.

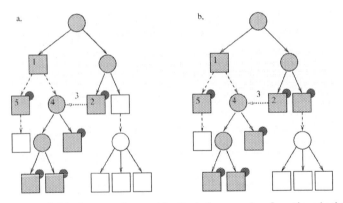

Fig. 5. a, DFS have finished traversal caused by the influence edge. Locations in the subtree of location 1 are marked properly. Picture b, shows state of the location tree after whole DFS traversal. All marked locations will become atomic.

Location is marked if there is no usable edge heading to any of its children. After completion of the DFS traversal, method shrink() is called on every marked location. This makes all marked locations atomic. See Algorithm 1, 2 and Fig 4, 5 for further details.

Algorithm 1: `Cleanup`

```
markRecursive(rootLocation);
foreach (loc : marked locations)
    loc.shrink();
```

Algorithm 2: `MarkRecursive(loc)`

```
if (location loc was already traversed)
    return;
if (no enabled edge from the location loc)
    mark(loc);
else
    foreach (target : targets of enabled edges)
        markRecursive(target);
foreach (edge : influence edges from location loc) {
    target = edge.target;
    while (loc.LODvalue - target.LODvalue < edge.value)
        target = target.parent;
    while (there is a marked ancestor of target) {
        ancestor = the marked ancestor of target;
        unmark(ancestor);
        foreach (child : children of ancestor)
            markRecursive(child);
    }
}
```

6 Conclusion

Simulation of large artificial worlds with tens of v-humans with complex behaviour is a task requiring a special technique that can cope with limited computational and memory resources. In this paper, we have presented our approach to this issue. The approach is based on level-of-detail technique (LOD) that decreases simulation quality at unimportant places. Contrary to the common use of LOD in computer graphics, we have used it in the domain of artificial intelligence. Contrary to a few exploitations of LOD in the domain of computer games [3], [10], [13], our approach is robust. That means it simplifies the quality of simulation gradually, and it simplifies not only behaviour of v-humans, but also an underlying topology of the artificial world. The contribution is obvious: owing to the smoothness, we achieve better believability while preserving reasonable computational and memory demands.

The technique is used in project IVE [2], [7]. The project itself is still in progress.

References

1. Bojar, O., Brom, C., Hladík, M., and Toman, V.: The Project ENTs: Towards Modelling Human-like Artificial Agents. In SOFSEM 2005 Communications, Liptovský Ján, Slovak Republic (2005) 111-122
2. Brom, C.: Virtual Humans: How to Represent Their Knowledge. In: Proceedings of ITAT 2005, Slovak Republic (to appear) (in Czech)

3. Champandard, A.J.: AI Game Development: Synthetic Creatures with Learning and Reactive Behaviors. New Riders, USA (2003)
4. Georgeff, M., and Lansky A.L.: Reactive Reasoning and Planning. In: Proceedings of the 6th National Conference on Artificial Intelligence, Seattle, Washington (1987) 677-682
5. Gibson, J.J.: The Ecological Approach to Visual Perception. Boston: Houghton Muffin, (1979)
6. Huber, M.J.: JAM: A BDI-Theoretic Mobile Agent Architecture. In: Proceedings of the 3rd International Conference on Autonomous Agents (Agents'99). Seatle (1999) 236-243
7. IVE, the project homepage: http://mff.modry.cz/ive/
8. Kallmann, M., and Thalmann, D.: Modelling Objects for Interaction Tasks. In: Proceedings of EGCAS 98 (1998) 73-86
9. Mateas, M.: Interactive Drama, Art and Artificial Intelligence. Ph.D. Dissertation. Department of Computer Science, Carnegie Mellon University (2002)
10. O'Sullivan, C., Cassell, J., Vilhjálmsson, H., Dingliana, J., Dobbyn, S., McNamee, B., Peters, C., and Giang, T.: Level of Detail for Crowds and Groups. In: Computer Graphics Forum 21 4 (2002) 733-742
11. Prendinger, H., Ishizuka, M.: Introducing the Cast for Social Computing: Life-Like Characters. In: Predigner, H., Ishizuka, M. (eds.): Life-like Characters. Tools, Affective Functions and Applications, Cognitive Technologies Series, Springer, Berlin (2004) 3-16
12. Wooldridge, M.: An Introduction to MultiAgent Systems. John Wiley & Sons (2002)
13. Wright, I., and Marschall, J.: More AI in Less Processor Time: 'Egocentric' AI. In: Gamasutra on-line (2000) http://www.gamasutra.com/features/20000619/wright_01.htm

Author Index

Lecture Notes in Computer Science

For information about Vols. 1–3754

please contact your bookseller or Springer